The Cambridge Handbook of Organizational Community Engagement and Outreach

This is an ideal reference for those looking to understand, study, and practice community engagement and outreach. It discusses the different ways individuals – including faculty, administrators, and management in organizations – engage in their communities.

It supplies case studies, best practices, and theoretical approaches to the study of community engagement. Scholars active in this field can use this book as an integration of the current knowledge concerning community engagement and as an inspiration for future research agendas.

While directing how to implement effective community engagement practices, it also facilitates the application of organizational theory to community engagement. This will appeal to academics who are interested in the theoretical background of community engagement.

JOSEPH A. ALLEN, PHD, is an associate professor of Industrial/Organizational (I/O) Psychology at the University of Nebraska Omaha (UNO). His research focuses on three major areas of inquiry, including the study of workplace meetings, organizational community engagement, and emotional labor in various service-related contexts. He directs the Center for Applied Psychological Services as well as the Volunteer Program Assessment at the University of Nebraska at Omaha (VPA-UNO).

RONI REITER-PALMON is the Varner Professor of Industrial/Organizational (I/O) Psychology and the Director of the I/O Psychology Graduate Program at University of Nebraska Omaha (UNO). She also directs the Center for Collaboration Science. Her research focuses on innovation in the workplace and the development and assessment of creativity, teamwork, and leadership skills. She has received UNO's College of Arts and Science Excellence in Research Award and the UNO Award for Distinguished Research and Creative Activity.

The Cambridge Handbook of Organizational Community Engagement and Outreach

Edited by

Joseph A. Allen
University of Nebraska Omaha

Roni Reiter-Palmon
University of Nebraska Omaha

CAMBRIDGE
UNIVERSITY PRESS

CAMBRIDGE
UNIVERSITY PRESS

University Printing House, Cambridge CB2 8BS, United Kingdom

One Liberty Plaza, 20th Floor, New York, NY 10006, USA

477 Williamstown Road, Port Melbourne, VIC 3207, Australia

314–321, 3rd Floor, Plot 3, Splendor Forum, Jasola District Centre,
New Delhi – 110025, India

79 Anson Road, #06-04/06, Singapore 079906

Cambridge University Press is part of the University of Cambridge.

It furthers the University's mission by disseminating knowledge in the pursuit of
education, learning, and research at the highest international levels of excellence.

www.cambridge.org
Information on this title: www.cambridge.org/9781108417464
DOI: 10.1017/9781108277693

First published 2019

Printed in the United States of America by Sheridan Books, Inc.

A catalogue record for this publication is available from the British Library.

Library of Congress Cataloging-in-Publication Data
Names: Allen, Joseph A., 1981– editor.
Title: The Cambridge handbook of organizational community engagement and outreach /
edited by Joseph A. Allen, University of Nebraska at Omaha, Roni Reiter-Palmon,
University of Nebraska at Omaha.
Description: New York : Cambridge University Press, 2018.
Identifiers: LCCN 2018024269 | ISBN 9781108417464
Subjects: LCSH: Community organization. | Community power. | Social advocacy.
Classification: LCC HM776 .C35 2018 | DDC 361.8–dc23
LC record available at https://lccn.loc.gov/2018024269

ISBN 978-1-108-41746-4 Hardback
ISBN 978-1-108-40525-6 Paperback

Joe: To Joy, Karen, Rachel, Alice, and Julia.
Roni: To Ophir, Shir, and Tomer.

Contents

Figures

Tables

Contributors

JOSEPH A. ALLEN

ALEXANDER ALONSO

THOMAS ARCARO

RACHAEL A. ARENS

JULIE DIERBERGER

KERISTIENA S. DODGE

ALEXANDRA M. DUNN

JENNIFER EARLY

SAMANTHA ELLIOTT

ANNIE EPPERSON

ORENTHEIAN EVERETT

SCOTT T. FITZGERALD

TRACEY GENDRON

ELIZABETH GILBERT

MEGHAN GOUGH

JENNA GREENE

MICHAEL B. HEIN

ANGIE HODGE

BARBARA A. HOLLAND

VALERIE HOLTON

MATHEW JOHNSON

RACHAEL JOHNSON-MURRAY

DIANN OLSZOWY JONES

JOSEPH JONES

SIMONE KAUFFELD

RENAE S. KEHRBERG

FABIAN KLAUKE

SHAWN D. LONG

CHRISTINE MARSTON

ROBERT MARTIN

ANNIKA L. MEINECKE

RICHARD G. MOFFETT III

JOSEPH E. MROZ

LENA C. MÜLLER-FROMMEYER

MICHAEL D. MUMFORD

APRIL POST

KELLY A. PRANGE

JANICE RECH

RONI REITER-PALMON

DOUG REYNOLDS

STEVEN G. ROGELBERG

DEBORAH ROMERO

RICHARD RONAY

ENRICA N. RUGGS

EDUARDO SALAS

JOHN SALTMARSH

LORILEE R. SANDMANN

DEBORAH SMITH-HOWELL

SABRINA L. SPEIGHTS

ANTHONY STARKE

OSCAR J. STEWART

VALERIE STREETS

E. MICHELLE TODD

SHERIDAN B. TRENT

DIAN VAN HUIJSTEE

LISA SLATTERY WALKER

SHONNA D. WATERS

RASHEDA L. WEAVER

CHELSEA R. WILLNESS

SARA WOODS

MICHAEL YOERGER

CINDY S. YORK

STEPHEN J. ZACCARO

See Appendix A: Contributor Biographies for full contributor details.

Acknowledgments

A special thank you goes out to our editorial board members for their diligence and helpful feedback in crafting this volume: Nale Lehmann-Willenbrock (University of Hamburg), Steven Rogelberg (University of North Carolina at Charlotte), Mike Mumford (University of Oklahoma), Mike Hein (Middle Tennessee State University), Eduardo Salas (Rice University), Steve Zaccaro (George Mason University), Valerie Holton (Virginia Commonwealth University), Alexandra Dunn (University of Mary Washington), Julie Dierberger (University of Nebraska Omaha), and Alexander Alonso (Society for Human Resource Management). We are extremely grateful for the tireless efforts of our assistant editor, Kelly Prange, as well as for the assistance provided by Sheridan Trent in assembling the final volume. We appreciate our university's support, the University of Nebraska Omaha.

PART I

Introduction: Organizational Community Engagement over Time

1 The Cambridge Handbook of Organizational Community Engagement and Outreach

Introduction, Statement of Need, and Overview of the Volume

Joseph A. Allen, Roni Reiter-Palmon, & Kelly A. Prange

Community engagement is the collaboration between organizations/institutions, often of higher education, and their larger community (local, regional/state, national, global) for the mutually beneficial exchange of knowledge and resources in a context of partnership and reciprocity (McCormick & Zhao, 2005). Considerable momentum regarding organizations working toward community-engaged projects, partnerships, and collaborations has been gained in recent years (Holland, 2016). The work of the Carnegie Foundation to initiate the "Community-Engagement Classification" for institutions of higher education created some of this momentum, while the overt benefits that corporations gain by working with their community has also furthered these efforts (Sandy & Holland, 2006). Essentially, there are members of higher education (faculty and administration) leaders in organizations at all levels and community members/leaders who are collectively reaching out to one another in an effort to mutually benefit from the exchange of knowledge and resources. For example, having students from a university volunteer to help a nonprofit to carry out events (e.g., Suzan Komen Foundation Race for the Cure) provides great relief to the nonprofit organization in terms of time and resources, as well as opportunities for students to develop a lifelong desire to give back to their community. The body of research and practice surrounding community engagement continues to grow, and yet no definitive volume exists that defines, synthesizes, and provides best practices for organizational community engagement and outreach. As such, the purpose of this book is to provide the current "state of the field" in terms of the study and practice of community engagement in its many forms (e.g., university–community partnerships, disciplinary/interdisciplinary outreach, corporate social responsibility, and so forth). This edited volume includes both science- and practice-oriented contributions so as to assist both the academic seeking to engage in science-based outreach and the practitioner seeking to initiate a more socially responsible effort in their firm.

The book is structured around different ways individuals in organizations, including faculty, administrators, and management, engage in their communities. Specifically, contributors who have expertise in community engagement address best practices for impacting communities through partnerships and collaboration. Domains of community engaged efforts include overt university–community partnerships, disciplinary/interdisciplinary outreach, and leading community-engaged efforts in both institutes for higher education and for-profit organizations. This handbook provides a definitive reference for people looking to understand, study, and practice community engagement. Scholars active in this field can use this book as an integration of the current knowledge concerning community engagement and as an inspiration for future research agendas.

Because community engagement takes many forms and is topically considered across disciplines, areas of academia, and corporate life, a wide range of scholars and practitioners may have interest in the book. For example, community engagement scholars would be interested in this book because community engagement efforts are often complex, challenging, and difficult to carry forward. The authors of the chapters in this handbook discuss success stories of community engagement efforts and outline best practices that are of value to all who engage in such efforts. Each chapter of the handbook endeavors to include sections discussing applied implications as well as best practices from the content presented, where applicable. Because community engagement is interdisciplinary, the scholars who contributed to this handbook include industrial/organizational psychologists, communication scholars, management scholars, social work scholars, public policy and public administration scholars, and higher education and leadership scholars. Because of its broad representation of perspectives and disciplines, the handbook serves as a state of the field of the work related to organizational community engagement.

Organizational Community Engagement and Outreach: An Overview of This Volume

The balance of this introduction is devoted to providing a summary and overview of the volume. We proceed by providing a note on each section, including brief summaries of each chapter, why it is included in the volume, and, in some cases, who may find the chapter of particular interest. The hope is that the following summary will aid readers in identifying the sections most applicable to their current need, as well as providing them with ideas for future efforts falling in the other sections.

Part I Introduction: Organizational Community Engagement over Time

This introduction chapter and Chapter 2 are meant to introduce the book and the topics that will be covered. In particular, this first section of the book highlights the components of community engagement and outreach and the issues that lie within both the research and practice of engagement.

Chapter 2: Sustaining Community Engagement in Times of Leadership Transition. Olszowy Jones and Sandmann raise and explore a core issue: the sustainability of community outreach and engagement efforts over time. Specifically, they discuss the competing purposes of and philosophies that exist within the realm of higher education and the role of leaders in shaping an institution's community-based mission. We decided to include this chapter before all other contributions in order to shed light on the core issues facing the key stakeholders in community engagement and outreach efforts.

To illustrate the vulnerability of community engagement efforts in leadership transitions, the authors describe a university case study within a theoretical framework centered on universities. They developed key insights for organizational stakeholders who wish to improve the sustainability of their partnerships and programs. Their work highlights the importance of informal and formal leaders and their ability to change systems and procedures that will help fulfill an integrated mission of community engagement.

Part II University–Community Partnerships

The chapters in this section describe ways in which universities and their students and faculty can engage with their communities in meaningful and sustainable ways. Many of the chapters in this section discuss service learning and provide case studies of successful and lasting service-learning partnerships that have transformed students, faculty, and communities. Much of the focus of this section is applied and practical in nature.

Chapter 3: Volunteer Program Assessment: A University–Community Partnership. Trent, Prange, and Allen describe a university-based outreach program that provides free assessment services to volunteer programs. The contributors describe how the chapter at the University of Nebraska at Omaha serves its clients in a reciprocal manner, sustains itself over time, and maintains a high-quality relationship with university stakeholders. Readers of this chapter will find a discussion of the following: (a) place-based institutions; (b) a review of current issues in volunteerism and volunteer management in the United States; (c) a full description of the Volunteer Program Assessment and its services; and (d) a list of best practices for those who wish to improve or develop a new university partnership. Anyone interested in program evaluation, student programs, volunteers, or anchor-based institutions should read this chapter. The contributors also include many figures and replicable suggestions in order to appeal to a practical audience.

Chapter 4: Introducing Engaged Civic Learning: An Emerging Approach to University–Community Partnerships. Weaver's chapter is the first academic work that describes the pedagogical technique of engaged civic learning. She introduces the concept both theoretically and practically by exploring a case study in which two interdisciplinary university classes and a nonprofit organization collaborated to provoke policy change in a community. Readers of this chapter will find a review of the history and core concepts of experiential learning, a full description of the case and its benefits to all participants, as well as research and the practical implications of the case study's outcomes. The author calls for rigorous research methods for empirical study of the construct and provides valuable "lessons learned" from her own experience. Appealing to a broad audience, university educators and administrators, students, nonprofit members, and government workers all would benefit from reading this chapter.

Chapter 5: Service-Learning Partnerships in Secondary Education. Arens, a high school science educator, describes multiple service-learning courses in which she partnered with college classes from the University of Nebraska at Omaha. By participating in multiple science-based service-learning programs, she helped to transform her department and developed an outdoor classroom curriculum. The contributor's practical perspective will give readers key takeaways for developing their own service-learning curricula, networking with community organizations, and evaluating their service-learning efforts. Practitioners and faculty interested in helping students develop skills for twenty-first-century applications and applied knowledge should read this chapter.

Chapter 6: Integrating Foreigners into Local Communities for Mutual Benefit: Chances, Challenges, and Best Practice. Klauke, Meinecke, Müller-Frommeyer, and Kauffeld are German authors who wrote a chapter about the importance of helping international and refugee students develop a sense of community by involving them in service learning. In their chapter, they describe the research-based structure of the two programs they use as case studies, the students, organizations, and communities impacted by the programs, and the ways that all actors benefit from the programs. Readers should expect to learn about migration and its impact on learning institutions, a detailed description of the programs at Technische Universität Braunschweig in Germany, a list of best practices that helped successfully integrate foreign students into the community, as well as some challenges that the authors experienced. This chapter in particular addresses how globalization impacts universities and communities.

Chapter 7: A Case Study on Community and Identity in a Study Abroad Program. Whereas many service learning courses and programs serve the community in which their school resides, Slattery Walker and Fitzgerald describe the implementation of a study abroad service-learning course in which they take students from North Carolina to the United Kingdom. The program has been operational for nine years, and the authors describe the motivations behind the creative program and how community organizations are chosen at the international site. A convenient list of best practices will be useful for any faculty looking to implement or develop a similar program.

Part III Disciplinary Outreach

The chapters in this section describe various community engagement and outreach strategies used to accomplish goals within a single academic discipline or content area. Results of case studies are used to illuminate the challenges of this kind of work, yet many of the recommendations that contributors offer are transferrable to any content area.

Chapter 8: Faculty and Students Consulting in the Community: The Center for Applied Psychological Services. Mroz, Yoerger, Allen, and Reiter-Palmon describe a campus organization for graduate students seeking applied experience within their field of study – industrial/organizational psychology. The faculty-managed consulting group serves many organizations in need of affordable organizational development and human resources services. A few of the group's projects are described, illustrating the wide range of skills that students can hone as members of the group. The authors posit that these types of campus organizations could be replicated across departments in any institution to the mutual benefit of students, the university, and the community. This chapter contains detailed information about outreach efforts and consulting strategies that may be of interest to faculty, administrators, and practitioners.

Chapter 9: Discipline-Specific Outreach: Client Projects through Graduate Classes and University-Based Consulting Centers. In Chapter 9, Hein and Moffett compare two ways in which faculty and graduate students could implement disciplinary outreach and engagement efforts with community organizations: service-learning courses or a campus-based consulting group, as discussed in Chapter 8. The contributors offer detailed best practices for each method, specifically regarding how to initiate and build relationships with community organizations. Points of tension when conducting the projects are also discussed. Readers wishing to know the benefits and intricacies of university-based disciplinary programs would benefit from reading this chapter.

Chapter 10: Driving Workforce Readiness: The Case for Community-Based HR Initiatives. Jones, Johnson-Murray, Streets, Alonso, and Waters address the social issue of workplace preparedness in their discussion about how human resources professionals and businesses can instigate change in their communities that is beneficial for both the labor force and organizations alike. Community-based human resources can be conducted by current or past human resources professionals, as well as one or more organizations through corporate social responsibility programs or professional organizations like the Society of Human Resource Management. Business practitioners and students in the human resources and related fields would be most interested in this chapter.

Chapter 11: University Educators and Disciplinary Specialists Working Together to Enhance Community Outreach and Deepen K–12 Teacher Content Knowledge. The last chapter in the section on disciplinary outreach was written by faculty from three separate universities. Together, Hodge, York, and Rech recommend best practices to increase communication across department silos in university settings. The case study in this chapter illustrates a program that promoted regular meetings among education subject matter experts, content specialists, and K–12 educators. The chapter reports the results of the program's evaluation. The success of the program is attributed to strong interorganizational partnerships, strong planning of events, and feedback from participants. The authors provide useful information for anyone who may be interested in encouraging more frequent communication between community members around a single content area.

Part IV Interdisciplinary Outreach

Whereas Part III contained chapters that offered guidance on community engagement and outreach within a single content area, the chapters in Part IV describe best practices and challenges in work that crosses multiple content areas.

Chapter 12: The Organizational Science Summer Institute: Community Outreach to Diversify the Graduate Education Pipeline. Speights, Stewart, Ruggs, Rogelberg, Reynolds, and Long describe key success factors for their interdisciplinary program, called the Organizational Science Summer Institute. The Institute is designed to help racial minority students gain access to graduate school programs. Based on their experience, they emphasize the importance of aligning the values of multiple organizations when creating a new partnership. They also offer a step-by-step guide to building such a program on any college campus. This chapter would be particularly useful for readers interested in diversity, education inequity, and university programs.

Chapter 13: Periclean Scholars: An Interdisciplinary Model of Civic Engagement on College Campuses. In Chapter 13, Dunn, Arcaro, and Post shed light on a three-year program that leverages interdisciplinary work, service learning, and community service to get students involved in their communities and enhance their education. A primary component of the Periclean Scholars program is to help students become leaders who are prepared to take action in their communities. The contributors provide an in-depth review of service learning, a description of the program and its outcomes, and a reader-friendly process to help people wanting to implement similar programs at their institutions. The authors hope that their writing will inspire readers to conduct more service-learning courses for the benefit of the community, as well as faculty and students.

Chapter 14: University, School District, and Service-Learning Community Partnerships That Work. Dierberger, Everett, Kehrberg, and Greene collaborated to illustrate the multidimensionality of P–16 service-learning projects, which are service-learning courses with at least three partners: (a) a P–12 class; (b) a college-level class; and (c) a community organization. Because of the complexity of such projects, the authors identified that successful partnerships rely on mutually beneficial goals and goal progress, systematic communication, and trusting interpersonal relationships. The chapter contains a formal study that answers the following research question: What are the key ingredients to a successful P–16 service-learning partnership? To learn about P–16 service learning, interorganizational theory, and boundary-spanning partnerships, take a look at this chapter.

Part V Leading Community Engagement Efforts

The chapters in this section of the handbook explore how and why community, organizational, and leadership factors play a part in the community outreach and engagement efforts of institutions. According to the authors in this section, leadership is both an antecedent to successful partnerships and an outcome of such partnerships.

Chapter 15: Leading Social Innovation and Community Engagement: Strategies for Picking the Right Actions. To kick off the topic of leadership, a group of leadership researchers, Mumford, Martin, Elliott, and Todd, argue that social innovation is essential for successful community engagement efforts. In addition, they claim that leaders play an essential role in setting the stage for sustained community engagement practices. To find out what seven leadership skills are essential for successful community engagement in an organization and how leadership can change the course of community engagement efforts, flip the page to Chapter 15 for a theoretical review of leadership concepts in relation to organizational community engagement.

Chapter 16: Community-Based Partnerships for Capacity Building: Stakeholder Engagement through Governance and Leadership. Willness provides an overview of an undergraduate experiential learning program at the University of Saskatchewan within a framework of stakeholder engagement and organizational governance. The author claims that such strategies can and should be used to achieve reciprocity, trust, and voice among organizational partners. A business professor, Willness applies management principles in order to appeal to a broad audience. A description of the Governance and Leadership Development Practicum, lessons learned, and best practices can be found in this chapter, and it will be of particular interest to administrators, curriculum specialists, and faculty.

Chapter 17: "Make the World a Better Place": Local Leadership as a Vehicle for Personal and Community Development. Chapter 17 takes a different perspective on leadership from the other chapters in this section. Rather than writing about organizational leadership as a factor in community engagement success, van Huijstee and Ronay discuss how community engagement and outreach (e.g., experiential learning) improves leadership skills in the individuals who participate in such initiatives. To illustrate, the authors describe a number of projects that they have implemented within a master's-level graduate class to achieve improved leadership ability and personal growth. The contributors hope to challenge faculty to be creative and thoughtful in their curriculum development to ensure they are meeting the needs of students and community partners.

Part VI Putting It All Together

The chapters in this section of the handbook address discrepancies in the field and offer directions for future research and practice of community engagement and outreach. Topics such as assessment, culture, institution-wide strategy, anchor institutions, and the state of research will be addressed.

Chapter 18: Assessing and Classifying the Institutionalization of Community Engagement. Johnson and Saltmarsh describe two instruments to assess community engagement as an institutionalized practice for campuses in the United States. Specifically, the National Assessment of Service and Community Engagement and the Carnegie Foundation Elective Community Engagement Classification are discussed. The chapter provides background information on the development and evolution of each of the measures and how they have been used. Both measures are designed to create accountability and for quality improvement and support organizational innovation and change. In addition, the authors suggest that using these measures can provide an alternative to traditional rankings by providing information that is typically not considered in those rankings.

Chapter 19: Fostering an Integrated Culture of Community Engagement. In this chapter, Dodge, Starke, Smith-Howell, and Woods discuss how universities can create a culture that values community engagement. They suggest that creating and sustaining such a culture requires cultural change for most universities. As such, they start their chapter with a discussion of the complexities and difficulties associated with implementing change. The authors then provide ten strategies that encourage cultural change and the institutionalization of community engagement in higher education. They conclude the chapter by providing a case study of the University of Nebraska at Omaha and show how these ten strategies have been used together to strengthen each other, resulting in a cultural shift toward inclusion of community engagement in the institutional culture.

Chapter 20: After Institutionalization: Enacting University–Community Engagement as a Process of Change. Romero, Epperson, Gilbert, and Marston focus on an illustrative case study of how the landscape of community engagement evolved and changed on their campus. Specifically, they discuss the institutionalization of community and civic engagement and how the earning of the Carnegie Engaged Campus classification assisted with defining the institution and its many collaborations as truly community engaged. The chapter provides a unique perspective that could be emulated by others as desired. For other institutions seeking to grow into the community engagement domain, this chapter provides a blueprint for success, or at least some best practices to enact and pitfalls to avoid.

Chapter 21: Building a University Climate to Support Community-Engaged Research. In this chapter, Holton, Early, Gough, and Gendron discuss the compelling need for institutions of higher education to lay the groundwork for community-engaged research. Their goal is to provide a comprehensive approach to changing the organizational culture/climate associated with community-engaged research, thereby launching the organization into the future that demands collaboration with community. They elaborate on the structures, competence, incentives, and barriers to community-engaged research, while emphasizing a need to also measure and evaluate the effectiveness of such efforts. Those seeking a framework from which to launch their own community-engaged research platform at their institution or organization may find this chapter particularly useful and compelling.

Chapter 22: Putting It All Together: An Interview with Barbara Holland and Final Thoughts. The final chapter in this handbook is uniquely structured because it contains an in-person interview with Barbara Holland, an internationally renowned community engagement expert. She offers her perspective on the state of the field and how organizations can achieve their goals regarding community engagement and outreach. The editors offer concluding thoughts that reflect on Holland's interview.

Closing Remarks

The chapters in this volume capture research, practice, and cases of great success in the area of organizational community engagement and outreach. Further, the section on leadership in community engagement efforts provides a unique set of readings that may help individuals preparing to lead on such projects. We conclude the volume by interviewing a known luminary in the field of community engagement, Dr. Barbara Holland, who provides insights into where community engagement has been and where it is going. Hopefully, those who find and read this volume will be well informed and prepared for that future, which holds such promise for organizational community engagement and outreach.

References

Holland, B. A. (2016). Factors influencing faculty engagement – Then, now and future. *Journal of Higher Education Outreach and Engagement, 20*, 73.

McCormick, A. C. & Zhao, C. M. (2005). Rethinking and reframing the Carnegie classification. *Change: The Magazine of Higher Learning, 37*(5), 51–57.

Sandy, M. & Holland, B. A. (2006). Different worlds and common ground: Community partner perspectives on campus–community partnerships. *Michigan Journal of Community Service Learning, 13*(1), 30–43.

2 Sustaining Community Engagement in Times of Leadership Transition

Diann Olszowy Jones & Lorilee R. Sandmann

Consider this scenario: your college or university has been successfully integrating community engagement (CE) into its policies, procedures, programs, and norms. The president has been a critical leader in the efforts to advance CE as core to achieving the institution's mission. Upon her announcement that she is leaving this position, concerns of uncertainty escalate within the university. Although there has been meaningful and noteworthy work that has advanced CE as *a way things are done* within the university, there is still more work to be done in its development. Transitions take time, especially ones involving culture, faculty, long-term community relationships, and leadership. Will CE initiatives continue to thrive, or will the change of leadership lead to a change in priorities? This chapter discusses the actors and actions within higher education that are needed to sustain the momentum for CE and institutionalize it over time.

Setting the Stage: The Problem

A twenty-first-century university president is challenged with managing multiple priorities and responding to a rapidly changing global society. For example, in a 2014 *Chronicle of Higher Education* survey (Selingo, 2014), 350 presidents provided their thoughts about changes in American higher education. They believed that many American institutions would lose their ranking; traditional higher education practices required a faster pace of change; institutions of higher education (IHEs) provided value, even with the current public debate; the dominant topic of lowering costs diminished the needed solutions to change how individuals are taught and how they learn; and faculty played an important role for these changes instead of politicians.

These survey responses add to the ongoing debate about scholarly ethics, relevancy of research, funding, academic freedom, shared governance, tenure, tuition costs, diversity, inclusion and access, undocumented students, on-campus protests, the choice of guest speakers who may bring an opposing view to a campus, and other issues of the day. Moreover, these challenges are exacerbated by the political agendas that often do not align with an IHE's mission (Bok, 2013; Duderstadt, 2000). Kezar (2009) concluded that these challenges and, in many cases, competing goals and initiatives with various stakeholders were "destroying the capacity to implement meaningful change" (p. 19). The president is expected to promote and support the students, faculty, staff, and community, but retain the principles and traditions of the university. However, the quality of education, rankings, and self-funding are mounting issues that rest with the president. Indeed, the role of a twenty-first-century university president is daunting, and the job description is in a state of debate (Bok, 2013; Duderstadt, 2000; Eckel & Kezar, 2011; Kezar, 2009).

Resulting from these challenges and competing expectations, presidential turnover is an issue (Sanaghan, Goldstein, & Gaval, 2008). The most recent 2012 report on the state of higher education predicted 52 percent of presidents would leave their position within the next five years and another 21 percent would leave within six to nine years (Kurre, Ladd, Foster, Monahan, & Romano, 2012). Although there are no current data to confirm these estimates, there is a steady flow of research and publications providing additional support that the president position is churning. For example, the argument that age was the reason for this turnover as baby boomers are retiring was countered by evidence that presidents were leaving for increased salaries by assuming another presidential position (Monks, 2007, 2012). Additionally, Monks (2007) found that presidents from public IHEs were more likely to leave than presidents from private IHEs. Saul (2015) summarized, "Despite pressure on institutions of higher learning to hold down costs, the compensation of private college presidents continues to climb" (p. 1). Further, Bauman, Davis, Myers, and O'Leary (2017) published the individual executive compensations of private and public college presidents, indicating significant increases for both.

One reason that may contribute to these salary increases is the lack of candidates in the pool for presidents. The data generated from a 2009 American Council of Education (ACE) report indicated only 30 percent of provosts – the traditional position from which to search for candidates – were interested in becoming an IHE president. Therefore, the challenge of finding and retaining a president for more than five years (and possibly less) to lead a modern, twenty-first-century university is expected to continue (Bok, 2013).

The Impact on Community Engagement

Vulnerability emerges for CE during these presidential transitions. Its initiatives are in various stages of development (Furco, 2002a; Furco & Holland, 2013; Holland, 2009). Since Boyer's (1996) call to action for America's universities to engage more collaboratively with their communities, momentum has increased on many campuses. IHEs have concentrated their efforts on student-centered curricula, assessment tools to measure their CE activities and level of commitment, and preparing and applying for the Carnegie Foundation for the Advancement of Teaching Elective Community Engagement Classification. Moreover, there is more interest in conducting evidence-based, empirical research studies and in building this knowledge capacity through collaborative partnerships and interdisciplinary practices; however, more work is needed (Checkoway, 2013; Furco & Holland, 2013). These collaborative relationships and levels of commitment require presidents to make them part of their strategic plans, personal agendas, and work to integrate them as part of their institutions' mission. These *engagement champions* (Weerts & Sandmann, 2010) have taken active roles by participating locally, in their state, nationally, and internationally.

Presidential transitions have one specific concern: What is the effect on CE when a committed president leaves? Most of the research about IHE presidential transitions focused on the lack of succession planning or the search process (Martin, Samels, & Associates, 2004; Sanaghan, Goldstein, & Gaval, 2008). Additionally, the current findings in the literature appear to focus on what happens before the transition. Within the field of CE, although there has been research addressing its institutionalization, which identified leadership as a key factor (Billig, 2002; Bringle & Hatcher, 2000; Furco, 2002a, 2002b; Gelmon, Seifer, Kauper-Brown, & Mikkelson, 2005; Holland, 1997, 2009; Sandmann & Plater, 2009; Stanton, 2008; Weerts & Sandmann, 2010), there is a lack of empirical work on what occurs when the leader leaves. Kezar (2009), a well-known IHE scholar, added to this study's interest. She compared the average time of 10–15 years for a change to be embedded in an institution to the average tenure of an IHE president. She concluded that no meaningful change would occur unless the successor adopted the initiative or other factors sustained it. With CE in a development phase in most IHEs and not fully institutionalized and with the gap in the literature, there is a potential risk to sustain these CE efforts when a committed CE president leaves. Therefore, the purpose of this study was to understand how a university presidential transition affects a university's CE initiatives.

Literature Review

The literature inside and outside the field of CE is helpful for understanding the previous research and data we can draw from to assist in identifying effective policies and practices in sustaining CE throughout a presidential transition.

The Carnegie Foundation for the Advancement of Teaching Elective Community Engagement Classification

The Carnegie Foundation's Elective Community Engagement Classification provides a credible national recognition that the IHE has demonstrated a commitment toward institutionalizing CE. The application contains specific sections to address institutional identity, culture, and academic initiatives that extend to community participation and partnerships. A key review item is the IHE's process in collecting and analyzing data to measure their progress (Driscoll, 2009; www.brown.edu /swearer/carnegie). Four questions offer some insight into the president's position:

1. Does the executive leadership of the institution (President, Provost, Chancellor, Trustees, etc.) explicitly promote community engagement as a priority?

2. Is community engagement defined and planned for in the strategic plans of the institution?
3. Does the institution have search/recruitment policies or practices designed specifically to encourage the hiring of faculty with expertise in and commitment to community engagement?
4. Are internal and external budgetary allocations and fundraising directed to community engagement? Does the institution invest its financial resources in the community for purposes of community engagement and community development? (www.brown.edu/swearer/carnegie)

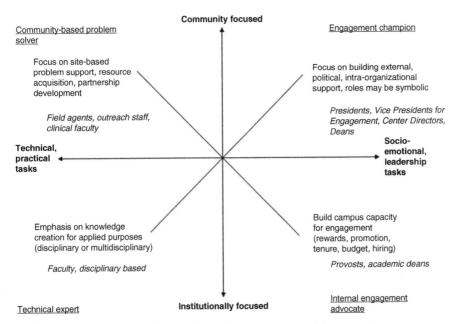

Figure 2.1 *Weerts and Sandmann's boundary-spanning model.*
From Weerts, D., & Sandmann, L. (2010). Community engagement and boundary-spanning roles at research universities. *Journal of Higher Education, 81,* 651. Copyright 2010 by Taylor & Francis. Reprinted with permission

The President's Role and Leadership Theory

According to Weerts and Sandmann's (2010) boundary-spanning model (Figure 2.1), university presidents act as *engagement champions*, a role that is instrumental in advancing the CE mission (Sandmann & Plater, 2009; Weerts & Sandmann, 2008, 2010). As the top administrator within a university responsible for aligning institutional priorities (Beere, Votruba, & Wells, 2011), the president has strategic and symbolic power to communicate the organization's commitment to CE as part of its mission and to act as a bridge between internal and external stakeholders.

While essential, presidents are conduits in creating networks of leaders at various levels to facilitate change (American Association of State Colleges and Universities,

2002). Collaborative leadership involves more than just customary administrators; it includes leaders within a CE center, deans, departments, programs, and community partners working together (Sandmann & Plater, 2009). As leadership is diffused, leaders can act as intermediaries between the campus and communities to develop institutional capacity (Walshok, 1995, 1999).

There is increasing evidence that certain types of adaptive leadership, such as distributed (also referred to as shared or collective) leadership, are effective (Gronn, 2002; Hargreaves & Fink, 2006; Harris, 2008; Liang & Sandmann, 2015; Robken, 2007). This type of leadership is more compatible with modern society's need for interdependency and collaboration to solve problems and increase knowledge. Research on effective CE leadership has found that a core characteristic among many executive leaders is their ability to distribute their leadership by compelling others to lead within their institutions (Hartley, 2009). Other studies have found that distributed leadership strengthened engagement work for those in administrative leadership positions (Kezar, Gallant, & Lester, 2012; Plater, 2011).

Moreover, CE requires organizational change, thus connecting it to the scholarly work conducted in organizational change theory (Burke, 2011; Goleman, 2006; Kouzes & Posner, 2007; Northouse, 2010; Rosenbach & Taylor, 2006; Zaccaro, 2001). If executive leadership is considered one of the critical components driving a major change, then changing the leader during the process risks the change not happening (Burke, 2011; Zaccaro, 2001). We contend that "sustaining the leadership is sustaining the momentum towards institutionalizing community engagement" (Jones, 2016, p. 40).

Presidential Transitions

Martin, Samels, and Associates (2004), in their comprehensive volume, *Presidential Transition in Higher Education: Managing Leadership Change*, stated that IHEs should "treat transition as a strategic moment" (p. 225). An important focus to their work is maintaining institutional advancement while the IHE is disrupted. Their warning is the following: "While presidents ultimately come and go, how they come and go has a profound effect on the institution and largely determines the difference between extended periods of failure and success" (Martin et al., 2004, p. 22). Others had similar concerns with the process of transitioning the president. Basinger (2001) believed that if institutions did not vigilantly manage the transition process, they would jeopardize the welfare of their institutions. Similarly, Padilla (2004) stressed this "passing the baton" activity as a critical function to an IHE. Even with these concerns about the important role of the president and how an institution should manage the transition of his/her departure, there have been minimal empirical studies that have addressed retaining the momentum of initiatives and their mission throughout this transition. Additionally, these studies were not specific to CE.

Sustainability and Institutionalization

A common understanding of how institutionalization is defined is necessary. For this discussion, institutionalization is a process by which an action, idea, or practice becomes an accepted part of the cultural norms and daily practices of an organization (Scott, 2001). Welch (2016) explained: "Implementing institutionalization requires infrastructural platforms from which to provide the necessary support for community engagement" (p. 109). He also maintained that the process for achieving it comprised "a dynamic and complex interplay of cultural and systematic factors" (p. 109). For example, Holland (1997, 2009) developed the *Holland Matrix*, which enabled IHEs to self-assess their levels of commitment to CEs through eight organization factors: (1) mission; (2) leadership; (3) promotion, tenure, and hiring; (4) organization, structure, and funding; (5) student involvement; (6) faculty involvement; (7) community involvement; and (8) external communications and fund-raising. She described institutionalization as CE transitioning from a peripheral activity enclaved within an IHE to an integrated method of practice (Holland, 1997, 2009).

CE scholars have struggled with the term *institutionalization* and its associations with organizational structure (Billig, 2002; Butin, 2006; Cuban & Anderson, 2007). The concern is that once CE is deemed part of the formal organizational structure of a university, most would assume (incorrectly) that it had been officially institutionalized. This interpretation does not capture the dynamic and continual action required to sustain CE, nor does it recognize that sustaining CE does not lead automatically to its institutionalization. Sustainability more clearly emphasizes the ability to maintain momentum, a critical success factor over time. It includes the formal and informal activities of building constituencies, fostering longer-term relationships, and identifying and enhancing resources (Billig, 2002). Thus, the contention is that sustainability and institutionalization are similar in that they relate to CE and depend on each other.

Methodology

Inevitably, university presidents leave their positions. An overarching interest is in how these leave-taking actions affect the sustainability of CE. Jones's (2016) research focused on one specific transition: the resignation of a university president who was considered an exemplar CE leader. Schlossberg (1981, 2003) provides a framework for considering such transitions.

Schlossberg's Transition Theory: Coping with Change

Schlossberg (1981, 2003) argued that all individuals experience transitions, whether through the death of a loved one, retirement, parenthood, rejection, or other work/life changes. She was intrigued not by how these individuals transition through the various stages, but why some individuals transition easier than others. As a result of years of studying various individuals and their specific transitions, Schlossberg (1981, 2003) developed the *4S* model:

• Situation: what was the transition and how was it perceived by the individual (e.g., positively, negatively, or unexpectedly)?

- Self: what were the personal characteristics of the individual?
- Support: what types of resources were available to the individual, such as family units, relationships, and networks?
- Strategies: based on the first three S's, what types of actions and coping strategies did the individual use to manage his/her transition?

Although most of the studies using Schlossberg's transition model predominantly explored individuals in lieu of organizational transitions, Schlossberg (2004) found her model was applicable to any change, including those within organizations. She further explained that it was not "the transition per se that is critical, but how much it changes one's roles, relationships, routines, and assumptions" (Schlossberg, 2004, pp. 3–4). Recognizing that a transition must take place for a change to become a norm is helpful in examining the institutionalization of CE from the individual and organizational levels. Another way to think about this is how individuals and organizations adapt to change and how the complexity of the change can be addressed with adaptive solutions.

Therefore, using Schlossberg's transition model of the 4Ss (Schlossberg, 1981), four questions guided Jones's (2016) single case study:

1. Situation: what was the status of community engagement throughout the presidential transition?
2. Selves: how did community engagement advocates react to the president's departure and throughout the transition?
3. Support: how was community engagement supported throughout the presidential transition?
4. Strategies: how was community engagement managed throughout the presidential transition?

The Case

For this single case study, Jones (2016) identified a public, four-year, graduate-level university that received the elective Carnegie Community Engagement Classification for at least two application years. A presidential transition occurred within the last three years, which allowed Jones to collect and analyze data before, during, and two years after the new president was in his/her position. An important selection criterion was that the departing president exhibited high levels of commitment to CE. The study's leader supported and actively participated in many initiatives to move CE forward within the university and within the field. For example, she began the nascent process of achieving the university's first Carnegie Community Engagement designation, established the campus CE center, participated actively in external CE organizations and initiatives, recognized faculty research focused on CE, became the president of Campus Compact, and recognized publicly students involved in CE activities. Therefore, the university chosen for this study was an institution that demonstrated higher levels of commitment toward institutionalizing CE (Holland, 1997, 2003), starting with an exemplar departing president.

Another important aspect in this case was a community partnership between the university and the city called the University City Initiative (pseudonym), which could be explored. Although there had been evidence of support by the long-term city benefactors, the city was struggling with its identity as it struggled economically, educationally, and culturally. A planning group was formed with representation from the university and the city. At the time of the president's announcement of her departure, a formalized charter, a joint vision statement, a conceptual structure, and success measures had been established; however, nothing had been implemented. Therefore, the study represented an important opportunity to understand the effects of leadership transition on a specific initiative.

Qualitative Research. A goal for this study was to understand specific factors from one case to gain a deeper understanding about how CE was sustained, or not, during a presidential leadership change. Yin's (2014) definition of a case study – "an empirical inquiry that investigates a contemporary phenomenon within its real-life context, especially when the boundaries between phenomenon and context are not clearly evident" (p. 18) – guided the research. Since there was a recognized gap in the literature on presidential transitions and their effect on CE, the argument for a single case study was to gain knowledge from one case to conduct subsequent studies.

The research design included ten semi-structured interviews (most face-to-face): current and former president, provost, director and assistant director of CE, former and current directors of the state Campus Compact, professor and former faculty senate during the transition period, and co-chairs of the University City Initiative. Additionally, documents and field memos were collected. The qualitative data were analyzed using thematic analysis, pattern matching, and explanation building (Yin, 2014). A coding scheme included a preliminary coding stage, code mapping, and second-cycle coding, which led to the surfacing of major themes to answer the research questions (Saldaña, 2013) within the Schlossberg (1981, 2003) conceptual framework.

Findings and Results

In synthesizing the findings, the focus was on the actors, strategies, and actions. Common behaviors, skills, and competencies emerged: (a) the presence of infrastructure processes, strategic planning, internal and external relationships, and scholarly acts were all factors of institutionalization and sustainability within adaptive environments; and (b) CE advocates served in key organizational positions of power and political influence. The findings also suggested the following conclusions: (1) organizational adaptation is essential to sustainable CE; and (2) external forces are critical to infusing new perspectives and people into sustainable CE efforts. Moreover, these findings offered several practical strategies and actions around improving adaptive leadership, increasing the pool of CE leaders, and identifying activities that have higher impact, including supporting engagement infrastructure, hiring advocates, enacting scenario planning, supporting boundary spanners, building CE expertise, and creating open organizational boundaries.

Table 2.1 *Case study findings*

Research question	Findings from data	Sub-category of findings
Situation: what was the status of community engagement (CE) throughout the presidential transition?	High level of commitment to community engagement	• Institutional mission and CE commitment • Leadership continuity • Solid infrastructure • Supporting data • Faculty mattered • Deep network of CE scholars
Selves: how did CE advocates react to the president's departure and throughout the transition?	Highly skilled Personal characteristics	• Process over product skill • High-performing CE director • Balanced humility and professional will • Confident and empowered
Support: how was CE supported throughout the presidential transition?	Infrastructure Scholarly acts Relationships	• Carnegie designation • Location and functionality • Formal agreements • Faculty driven • Internal working relationships • Network of professionals
Strategies: how was CE managed throughout the presidential transition?	Adapted to a hierarchical model of governance Represented in search process Proactive CE activity	• Search process • Adapted to organizational leadership • Ability to influence search criteria • Ability to influence selection • Interim president's influence • Enhanced the CE activities • Coalition building

Therefore, the major findings related to individual and organizational perspectives. At the individual level, utilizing boundary spanners and politically positioned academic leaders helped to advance and sustain CE initiatives. At the organizational level, the importance of strategic planning, processes, and infrastructure was confirmed and provided important insights. Using Schlossberg's (1981, 2003, 2004) four-part transition model as the conceptual framework (situation, self, support, and strategies) characterized accurately the elements that organizational actors attended to in their efforts to achieve and sustain CE institutionalization. Table 2.1 summarizes these findings.

Situation – High Level of Commitment

For this case, there was a high level of CE commitment throughout the transition. What factors assisted it in retaining this level through the university's leadership transition?

Mission statements are often cited as an important factor to declaring an IHE's commitment (Holland, 1997, 2006); however, Sandmann and Weerts (2008) found most mission statements with CE declarations did not actualize into practice. In Jones's (2016) study, not only did the university include CE as a core theme within their mission, but it also overlapped with others' missions externally. For example, it complemented other state universities' missions, shared common themes with Campus Compact, aligned with Carnegie's CE vision, and adapted to connect with the city's mission and the departing and new presidents' personal missions and top agenda items.

This finding is supported by DiMaggio and Powell's (1983) influential institutional theory and their description of isomorphism. Isomorphism is the convergence of multiple parts coming together from an organization's culture, structure, and outcomes to become more uniform. Because of the overlap of missions, the uncertainty caused by an important transition emerging was managed by internal and external individuals who shared common missions and initiatives. This mission alignment remained strong throughout the transition.

There were other situational factors that existed prior to the departure of the president. Many of the university's CE advocates were in traditionally recognized positions of influence. The provost and faculty senate head were in power positions. Moreover, the director of CE held a prominent position as a tenured professor and scholar. All these individuals were on the search committee for the new president based on their positions. Having these individuals as CE champions positioned CE in a power position and thus CE was represented at the planning table in the search for a new president.

The university had an established CE infrastructure. The template used in establishing its organizational structure followed the criteria used in the Carnegie Elective Community Engagement application. Using the application as a framework served multiple functions by: (1) having the plan in place to continue renewing their Carnegie designation; (2) producing data to measure their success; and (3) ensuring their prominence because they were credible and visible. Both presidents (outgoing and incoming) sought the data often to tout the success of the university's accomplishments. CE was good for public relations.

It is important to include the significant role of faculty in this discussion. CE's early development was started by faculty. They sought external CE scholars to help with integrating it with the student curriculum, research, and teaching. It originated from empirically based research rooted in scholarship and new knowledge. For example, the CE center acted as a one-stop shop, which included assisting faculty with syllabus and curriculum development, fellowships, and partnerships. We contend that if the churning at the president level continues, then faculty, with less turnover, become critical in sustaining and advancing CE.

Lastly, the deep network of *external* CE advocates played a significant role during the transition. From the onset, the university used outside CE scholars to understand how to embed critical practices within their institution. They fostered networks with the city, Campus Compact, and other state universities and participated in conferences and workshops. They treated CE as a field of study and a critical component to advance important initiatives in the community (an intentionally broad term) that they were a part of.

Selves

If there is one takeaway in describing the study's participants and their CE work, it is the importance of experience and empowerment. The participants interviewed were not only CE advocates, but also highly skilled with strong backgrounds in academics, managing, facilitating, and fostering relationships. Thus, they got things done.

They also had political savviness in understanding that their work needed to coincide with the university's work and culture. For example, the former president emphasized the need to be patient to get buy-in from the individuals who drive the university, which included the regents:

> So it wasn't just what could be done but how it worked and how you would go about it to fit with the culture. Culture eats strategy for lunch. So, if you do something, even though it's strategic and you think it's really important but you don't figure out how to do it in the appropriate way based on your culture, you have a possibility of failing.

The exemplar. There were many individuals in the case study who contributed essential skills and competencies to affecting change in their institutions and, in this case, a departing president who was a committed CE champion; however, one participant stood out as a CE exemplar for understanding important policies and practices. This academic and practitioner actor was a leader of CE. As a newcomer to the position, she stated, "And let me tell you, if you tell me to build something, I'm going to build it, and it's going to be ready to roll." In addition to having high levels of energy and enthusiasm, she had credentials – that is, she was a researcher and instructor and had followers. Moreover, she was hired at a level (already tenured) that aligned her with other decision makers; thus, she had influence. She also utilized her external relationships to build out her university's mission, expand on the president's initiatives for the university and legacy, and collaborate with community leaders/advocates. When the long-term president and a CE champion resigned, this leader adapted to a different president. After building out the CE center, she was promoted to a higher position within her university (after this study). She is also recognized as a CE scholar within the field. Even without her direct responsibilities of leading the center for CE, the university's CE work flourishes. Although this chapter has emphasized the role of actors and their actions, the goal is to have enough actors and actions that the eventual elimination of an actor will not derail the CE momentum – meaning that enough depth and breadth exist to sustain it.

Support

Much of the support occurred prior to the transition through establishing an infra-structure, internal and external networks, and long-term relationships (situation). Recruiting and fostering new relationships were considered strategic practices by inviting new people to participate. The goal was to create depth and breadth within the university and the community. Further, having a deeply competent group of individuals who were highly skilled added important resources to manage the leadership transition (selves). The findings confirmed Martin et al.'s (2004) conclusion that what occurred *prior* to a presidential transition was where the strategic planning needed to happen and determined success or failure.

Beyond committed individuals, the university had a solid infrastructure and an established formal process to follow. For example, the University City Initiative was in its first phase of development; however, a signed charter was in place between the university and the city. Therefore, it was believed (by committee members) that a lack of support from a new university president or mayor would not jeopardize the initiative simply due to a lack of interest.

Additionally, the CE center was prominently located within the student center. It was visible and continuously used by students, faculty, and partners who dropped in. A question that needs further research is whether the physical location of the CE center affects its development.

Strategies

Although this university exhibited many practices that appeared to have been more progressive than other IHEs, it adhered to the traditional approach of choosing an IHE president. There was no succession planning. This condition adds to Klein and Salk's (2013) findings that succession planning is almost nonexistent in IHEs. Furthermore, 72 percent of the presidents surveyed believed that it went "against the belief and traditions of the academy" (p. 339).

Additionally, it was assumed the new president would come from the outside, the regents led the search, and the search committee members were chosen based on position and department representation. Uniform questions would be established. The new president would be announced and, in this case, the former president disappeared intentionally, even though she left in good standing. The new president, with his own agenda and leadership style, would self-direct his own orientation (Kezar, 2009; Smerek, 2011). This search process adheres to the previous research showing that there is more emphasis on the search and selection process than the actual transition (Lohse, 2008; Martin et al., 2004; Sanaghan et al., 2008).

Following a traditional model of changing presidents did not derail CE. Rather, working within this known model, advocates were members of the search committee, thereby having the ability to influence the process from the "inside." For example, there was a specific CE question crafted for all candidates to address. Candidates were dismissed if they were not aware that the university was a designated Carnegie Community Engagement recipient. The regents were removed from the day-to-day happenings of the university; however, working side-by-side with the regents throughout the arduous search process, the CE advocates were able to foster relationships and educate the regents on the importance and success of their CE initiatives.

While these activities were occurring, the city manager was proactively contacting fifty new individuals within the university to discuss the University City Initiative. The departing president asked individuals how they were planning to orient the new president, encouraging them to be proactive in ensuring their programs and initiatives were sustained. Once the new president took the helm, the CE director adapted to a new leader's management style, which was initially more hierarchical compared to the former president's style. Campus Compact directors (former and current) proactively sought ways to integrate the new president into the organization, which ultimately led to him becoming the president. Although the newly selected president came with an appreciation of CE, he transitioned into a strong advocate because it assisted in achieving his top priorities and agenda, fostering external relationships, and promoting the university.

Putting It All Together: Discussion for Policy and Practice

The case study provided an opportunity to explore what higher education-based CE leaders do to move CE forward. Realizing that the ultimate objective is to integrate CE into the *way things are done*, this work offers a practical handbook on what IHEs can do to advance their CE initiatives, and how they can prevent these initiatives from becoming derailed because of expected or unexpected transitions.

Additionally, this study adds to the ongoing body of CE work focused on understanding what leads to the sustainably of CE. A common theme found was that the most effective initiatives require leadership, advocacy, an emphasis on scholarship and process, political savviness, and fostering internal and external relationships by integrating the IHE with the community. While the construct of mutual benefit is foundational to the principle of CE, in this research, it was shown to be an essential approach to achieving sustainability. This reciprocity was a core strategy to achieving the mutual or common missions and vision for community (of which higher education is a part).

This understanding is not revolutionary, but it does require that CE advocates adapt to changes in their institutions and communities. Effective CE advocates adapt to different leadership styles, find overlap between missions (personally and organizationally), and generally get in the mix of things. Effective individuals who do this type of work have experience and expertise in handling situations. Collins (2001) called it "level 5 leadership" (p. 22), representing that balance between humility and professional will.

Policy and Practice: Considerations for Organizations

The findings led to three conclusions for policy and practice: (1) organizational adaptation is essential to sustainable CE; that is, "treat transition as a strategic moment" (Martin, Samels, & Associates, 2004, p. 225); (2) external forces are critical to infusing their perspectives and people in relation to sustainable CE; and (3) Schlossberg's (1981, 2003) transition model can apply to a CE transition within a presidential transition. There are fundamental policies and practices that support these broad conclusions. Developing an effective infrastructure, involving the right actors, and inserting adaptive scenario planning into strategic planning discussions are important policies to implement. An additional policy is fostering actors as boundary spanners to continually open and connect internal and external boundaries.

Table 2.2 *Adaptive organizational policies and practices for sustaining community engagement*

Policy	Practices
Establish a community engagement (CE) infrastructure	• Strategically create and support centralized CE efforts • Organize CE structure using the components of the Carnegie Community Engagement Classification application process
Hire and recruit CE advocates with multiple boundary-spanning skills	• Expand desired competencies for CE positions to champion change, influence others, foster relationships, and demonstrate adaptability • Add a CE-related question to interview protocol for executive-level positions • Strategically assess the organization's inventory of internal and external CE advocates
Include scenario planning in strategic planning initiatives and activities	• Conduct exercises around how strategic and action plans could change and draft alternative actions in response • Use a modified Schlossberg's transition model to determine the strength of the organization's 4S's (i.e., situation, self, support, and strategies) • Execute formal written plans and agreements

What practices should leaders, academics, and practitioners consider when implementing such policies? Table 2.2 summarizes key policies and practices for enhancing organizational adaptation toward sustainable CE.

Many of the suggested policies and practices in Table 2.2 are refinements of already well-established institutional processes. For example, strategic plans are not a new concept; what is important is infusing CE into existing and ongoing plans, thereby positioning the institution to better integrate CE with high-priority initiatives and to address issues internally and externally to create cohesion between CE and the institution.

CE policies and practices may also be built upon well-established external processes. These may include building a CE center or network using components of the Carnegie application, which is recognized internationally and is attached to a well-known designation, providing a conduit between the internal and external workings of a university. For example, in Jones's (2016) study, the Carnegie designation was viewed favorably by the city manager who was working with the university to expand the city into a college town. He perceived this designation as a component of rebranding the city.

CE, by its nature, centers on the value added by actors and influences outside of the organization; therefore, embracing and then institutionalizing CE requires an organization to learn and grow from external experiences, knowledge, and perspectives. Table 2.3 outlines external policies and practices for sustaining CE.

Lastly, Schlossberg's transition model provides a framework for assessing the strength of an IHE's CE and its ability to adapt to a presidential transition before it happens. Figure 2.2 identifies characteristics and the study's findings in terms of why

Table 2.3 *External policies and practices for sustaining community engagement*

Policy	Practices
Identify and promote internal and external boundary spanners and their activities	• Budget for and promote local, national, and international participation at recognized community engagement (CE) organizations and conferences • Broaden CE's reach by seeking opportunities to integrate its promotion among university and community events • Position the president and other executive-level leaders within recognized CE organizations
Build internal and external CE expertise	• Emphasize and integrate CE as scholarship and a field of study • Seek expertise from individuals outside of the institution • Utilize community expertise to mutually achieve the institution's and outside organizations' missions
Create open boundaries for community access and participation	• Assess external stakeholders' level of ease at navigating the institution • Create easy access to the institution

and how the university was able to transition and, most importantly, retain its momentum and sustainability. Although future studies need to be conducted to confirm that these characteristics are consistent with other institutions' presidential transitions, the activities leading up to how well CE adapted to a presidential leadership change were based on resources, support, personal characteristics, and individual perceptions as they compared pre- and post-transition.

Starting at the top of Figure 2.2, a presidential transition can change assumptions, networks, and perceptions (pro and con) as they relate to CE. These perceptions can be neutral, by which a transition has no perceived effect on CE initiatives. Timing and duration are considerations (left-hand box). Personal attributes and skill levels of the individuals within an institution and community partners (right-hand box) are critical factors to sustain CE. We argue that even if the IHE has an incoming president who may lessen the importance of CE, these advocates will continue to bolster its prominence. Additionally, these individuals have power within the system. To use this schema as a diagnostic tool, readers could list and analyze their CE advocates and leaders: are they politically positioned, respected, skilled, and scholarly? Do you have enough bench strength to withstand the transition?

The list of characteristics of pre- and post-transition environments (middle box) can also be used as a preplanning tool to assess an institution's support. Figure 2.2 lists the findings from Jones's (2016) case study of what was present or not and their effects; however, each institution can use these factors as a guide. Lastly, we contend with Schlossberg (1981, 2003) that how an institution adapts (bottom box) through a transition is due to the balance and synergy between these four factors. We expect there will be some variation by institution; however, not treating transitions as a strategic exercise through preparation will put CE activities at risk.

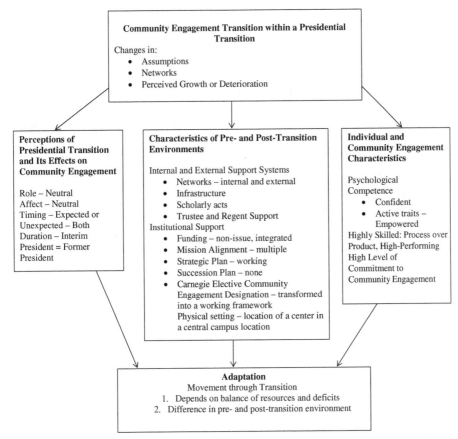

Community Engagement Transition within a Presidential Transition

Changes in:
- Assumptions
- Networks
- Perceived Growth or Deterioration

Perceptions of Presidential Transition and Its Effects on Community Engagement

Role – Neutral
Affect – Neutral
Timing – Expected or Unexpected – Both
Duration – Interim
President = Former President

Characteristics of Pre- and Post-Transition Environments

Internal and External Support Systems
- Networks – internal and external
- Infrastructure
- Scholarly acts
- Trustee and Regent Support

Institutional Support
- Funding – non-issue, integrated
- Mission Alignment – multiple
- Strategic Plan – working
- Succession Plan – none
- Carnegie Elective Community Engagement Designation – transformed into a working framework

Physical setting – location of a center in a central campus location

Individual and Community Engagement Characteristics

Psychological Competence
- Confident
- Active traits – Empowered

Highly Skilled: Process over Product, High-Performing
High Level of Commitment to Community Engagement

Adaptation
Movement through Transition
1. Depends on balance of resources and deficits
2. Difference in pre- and post-transition environment

Figure 2.2 *Jones's community engagement (CE) leadership transition model using Schlossberg's framework*

Conclusion

This chapter focused on the actors and actions of university leaders that contribute most significantly to sustaining CE through a presidential transition. CE at the organizational level can be sustained – even through major transitions – if there are fundamental structures and practices in place, even if CE is not fully embedded. Drawing on research from a single case study, we found that individuals dispersed throughout the institution can take actions at the individual and organizational levels to institutionalize CE and sustain it over time. Although CE needs many advocates, an IHE needs a core group of these advocates to hold credentials and positions of power and to be able to influence decisions and outcomes. They need to be skilled professionals and nimble in their approach in order to adapt. These actions center on infrastructure, recruitment, strategic planning, and investing in boundary spanners and engagement experts to foster open boundaries with the community to achieve mutual benefit and co-created knowledge.

Like other researchers before us, we were struck by the extent to which leaders matter to the institutionalization of CE. We experienced leaders, executive level and lower, formal and informal, who demonstrated initiative and the ability to start moving at whatever stage they were at in their CE work. Some initially acted as loners relying on external CE advocates and scholars; over time, the transformation began, and others joined the group, whereupon the *loners* acquired new relationships and broadened their networks. We know that higher education institutions' and society's systemic problems require systemic solutions. This case study offered compelling evidence and useful lessons of movement toward systemic solutions on both fronts.

This case study provides an approach for future research specifically focused on executive leadership transitions. Although the turnover of an IHE president is expected to continue, whatever the tenure, *presidents matter*. They hold the power and can be effective contributors to CE beyond acting as a titular head. However, CE advocates and leaders need to adapt in order to ensure CE initiatives can accommodate the president's priorities and agenda.

Others also matter to sustaining the momentum. Faculty, acting as the nerve center in any IHE, can highlight CE through scholarly acts, research, and instruction. Thus, making faculty an integral member within CE initiatives will ensure a strong, sustainable foundation. Moreover, as Jones (2016) stated, "It is in the best interests of CE advocates to become more political, in a positive and proactive way, to ensure that CE initiatives are not only acknowledged but also integrated within the mission and vision of their institutions" (p. 194). Leaders that bring individuals together and establish processes and structure can propel and sustain powerful engagement partnerships committed to building civic capacity and addressing today's critical problems – the ultimate achievement.

References

American Association of State Colleges and Universities (2002). *Stepping forward as stewards of place: A guide for leading public engagement at state colleges and universities*. Washington, DC: Author.

Barge, J. K., Lee, M., Maddux, K., Nabring, R., & Townsend, B. (2008). Managing dualities in planned change initiatives. *Journal of Applied Communication Research, 36*(4), 364–390.

Barnett, K. (2011). System members at odds: Managing divergent perspectives in the higher education change process. *Journal of Higher Education Policy and Management, 33*(2), 131–140.

Basinger, J. (2001). When a president quits early, the damage can linger on. *The Chronicle of Higher Education, 49*, A22–A23.

Bauman, D., Davis, T., Myers, B., & O'Leary, B. (2017). Executive compensation at private and public colleges, *Chronicle of Higher Education*. Retrieved from www.chronicle.com /interactives/executive-compensation?cid=FEATUREDNAV#id=table_public_2016.

Beere, C., Votruba, J., & Wells, G. (2011). *Becoming an engaged campus*. San Francisco, CA: Jossey-Bass.

Billig, S. (2002). Adoption, implementation, and sustainability of K-12 service learning. In A. Furco & S. Billig (Eds.), *Service-learning: The essence of the pedagogy* (pp. 245–267). Greenwich, CT: Information Age Publishing.

Bloomfield, V. (2005). Public scholarship: An administrator's view. In S. Peters, N. Jordan, M. Adamek, & T. Alter (Eds.), *Engaging campus and community: The practice of public scholarship in the state and land-grant university system* (pp. 363–392). Dayton, OH: Kettering Foundation.

Bok, D. (2013). *Higher education in America*. Princeton, NJ: Princeton University Press.

Boyer, E. (1996). The scholarship of engagement. *Journal of Public Service and Outreach, 1*, 11–20.

Bringle, R. & Hatcher, J. (2000). Institutionalization of service learning in higher education. *Journal of Higher Education, 71*, 273–290.

Brown University Swearer Center (2017). Retrieved from www.brown.edu/academics/college/swearer.

Burke, W. (2011). *Organization change: Theory and practice*. Thousand Oaks, CA: Sage.

Butin, D. (2006). Disciplining service learning: Institutionalization and the case for community studies. *International Journal of Teaching and Learning in Higher Education, 18*(1), 57–64.

Checkoway, B. (2013). Strengthening the scholarship of engagement in higher education. *Journal of Higher Education Outreach and Engagement, 17*, 69–84.

Collins, J. (2001). *Good to great*. New York, NY: Harper Collins.

Collins, J. & Porras, J. (1994). *Built to last*. New York, NY: Harper Collins.

Cuban S. & Anderson, J. (2007). Where's the justice in service-learning? Institutionalizing service-learning from a social justice perspective at a Jesuit university. *Equity and Excellence in Education, 40*, 144–155.

DiMaggio, P. J. & Powell, W. W. (1983). The iron cage revisited: Institutional isomorphism and collective rationality in organizational fields. *American Sociological Review, 48*(2), 147–160.

Drew, G. (2010). Issues and challenges in higher education leadership: Engaging for change. *Australian Educational Researcher, 37*(3), 57–76.

Driscoll, A. (2009). Carnegie's new Community Engagement classification: Affirming higher education's role in community. *New Directions in Higher Education, 147*, 5–12.

Duderstadt, J. (2000). *A university for the 21st century*. Ann Arbor, MI: University of Michigan Press.

Eckel, P., & Kezar, A. (2011). Presidents leading: The dynamics and complexities of campus leadership. In P. Altbach, P. Gumport, & R. Berdahl (Eds.), *American higher education in the twenty-first century: Social, political, and economic challenges* (pp. 279–311). Baltimore, MD: The Johns Hopkins University Press.

Furco, A. (2002a). Institutionalizing service-learning in higher education. *Journal of Public Affairs, 6*, 39–67.

Furco, A. (2002b). *Self-assessment rubric for the institutionalization of service-learning in higher education*. Berkeley, CA: University of California Press.

Furco, A., & Holland, B. (2013). Improving research on service learning institutionalization through attention to theories of organizational change. In P. Clayton, R. Bringle, & J. Hatcher (Eds.), *Research on service learning* (pp. 505–535). Sterling, VA: Stylus Publishing.

Gelmon, S., Seifer, S., Kauper-Brown, J., & Mikkelsen, M. (2005). *Building capacity for community engagement: Institutional self-assessment*. Seattle, WA: Community-

Campus Partnerships for Health. Retrieved from http://depts.washington.edu/ccph/pdf_files/self-assessment-copyright.pdf.

Goleman, D. (2006). What makes a good leader? In W. Rosenbach & R. Taylor (Eds.), *Contemporary issues in leadership* (pp. 159–173). Boulder, CO: Westview Press.

Gronn, P. (2002). Distributed leadership as a unit of analysis. *Leadership Quarterly, 13*, 423–451.

Hargreaves, A. & Fink, D. (2006). *Sustainable leadership*. San Francisco, CA: Jossey-Bass.

Harris, A. (2008). Distributed leadership: According to the evidence. *Journal of Educational Administration, 46*, 172–188.

Hartley, M. (2009). Leading grassroots change in the academy: Strategic and ideological adaptation in the civic engagement movement. *Journal of Change Management, 9*, 323–338.

Holland, B. (1997). Analyzing institutional commitment to service: A model of key organizational factors. *Michigan Journal of Community Service Learning, 4*, 30–41.

Holland, B. (2006). Levels of commitment to community engagement. Adapted from Holland, B. A. (1998). *Michigan Journal Community Service Learning, 4*, 30–41. Retrieved from https://static1.squarespace.com/static/56942366cbced6cface3bc8b/t/56cc97800442621c56f07df3/1456248704964/HollandMatrix.pdf.

Holland, B. (2009). Will it last? Evidence of institutionalization at Carnegie classified community engagement institutions. *New Direction for Higher Education, 147*, 85–98.

James, K. T. (2011). *Leadership in context: Lessons from new leadership theory and current leadership development practice*. London, UK: The King's Fund.

Jones, D. (2016). *Community engagement: Exploring its effects during a university presidential transition* (Unpublished doctoral dissertation). University of Georgia, Athens, GA.

Kezar, A. (2009). Change in higher education: Not enough or too much? *Change, 41*(6), 18–23.

Kezar, A., Gallant, T., & Lester, J. (2012). Everyday people making a difference on college campuses: The tempered grassroots leadership tactics of faculty and staff. *Studies in Higher Education, 36*(2), 129–151.

Klein, M. F. & Salk, R. J. (2013). Presidential succession planning: A qualitative study in private higher education. *Journal of Leadership & Organizational Studies, 20*, 335–345.

Kouzes, J. & Posner, B. (2007). *The leadership challenge*. San Francisco, CA: Jossey-Bass.

Kurre, F., Ladd, L., Foster, M., Monahan, M., & Romano, D. (2012). The state of higher education in 2012. *Contemporary Issues in Education Research, 5*, 233–256.

Liang, J. & Sandmann, L. (2015). Leadership for community engagement – A distributed leadership perspective. *Journal of Higher Education Outreach and Engagement, 19*(1), 35–63.

Lohse, M. (2008). *The organizational entry of a new college president: Twenty-four months of sensemaking and socialization* (Doctoral dissertation). Retrieved from Dissertation Abstracts International Section A: Humanities and Social Sciences (2008-99190-394).

Martin, J., Samels, J., & Associates (2004). *Presidential transition in higher education: Managing leadership change*. Baltimore, MD: Johns Hopkins University Press.

Meyerson, J. & Johnson, S. (1993). Planning for strategic decision making. In R. Ingram & Associates (Eds.), *Governing public colleges and universities: A handbook for trustees, chief executives, and other campus leaders*. San Francisco, CA: Jossey-Bass.

Monks, J. (2007). Public versus private university presidents pay levels and structure. *Economics of Education Review, 26*, 338–348.

Monks, J. (2012). Job turnover among university presidents in the United States of America. *Journal of Higher Education Policy and Management, 34*, 139–152.

Northouse, P. (2010). *Leadership: Theory and practice*. Thousand Oaks, CA: Sage.

Padilla, A. (2004). Passing the baton: Leadership transitions and the tenure of presidents. In J. Martin, J. Samels, & Associates (Eds.), *Presidential transition in higher education: Managing leadership change* (pp. 37–58). Baltimore, MD: The Johns Hopkins University Press.

Plater, W. M. (2011). Collective leadership for engagement: Reclaiming the public purpose of higher education. In J. Saltmarsh & M. Hartley (Eds.), *"To serve a larger purpose": Engagement for democracy and the transformation of higher education* (pp. 102–129). Philadelphia, PA: Temple University Press.

Purcell, J. W. (2013). *The engaged community college: Supporting the institutionalization of engagement through collaborative action inquiry* (Unpublished doctoral dissertation). University of Georgia, Athens, GA.

Robken, H. (2007). Leadership turnover among university presidents. *Management Revue, 18*, 138–152.

Rogers, E. (1962). *Diffusion of innovations*. New York, NY: Free Press of Glencoe.

Rogers, E. (1971). *Communication of diffusion: A cross-cultural approach*. New York, NY: Free Press.

Rogers, E. (2003). *Diffusion of innovations*. New York, NY: Free Press.

Rosenbach, W. & Taylor, R. (Eds.) (2006). *Contemporary issues in leadership*. Cambridge, MA: Perseus Books Group.

Saldaña, J. (2013). *The coding manual for qualitative researchers*. Thousand Oaks, CA: Sage.

Sanaghan, P., Goldstein, L., & Gaval, K. (2008). *Presidential transitions: It's not just the position, it's the transition*. Westport, CT: Praeger Publishers.

Sandmann, L. & Plater, W. (2009). Research on institutional leadership for service learning. In P. Clayton, R. Bringle, & J. Hatcher (Eds.), *Research on service learning* (pp. 505–535). Sterling, VA: Stylus.

Sandmann, L. & Weerts, D. (2008). Reshaping institutional boundaries to accommodate an engagement agenda. *Innovative Higher Education, 33*, 181–196.

Saul, S. (2015). Salaries of private college presidents continue to rise, Chronicle survey finds. *The New York Times*. Retrieved from www.nytimes.com/2015/12/07/us/salaries-of-private-college-presidents-continue-to-rise-survey-finds.html.

Schlossberg, N. (1981). A model for analyzing human adaptation to transition. *Counseling Psychologist, 9*, 2–18.

Schlossberg, N. (2003). *The transition guide: A new way to think about change*. Potomac, MD: Transition Works.

Schlossberg, N. (2004). Transitions: Theory and application. Paper presented at the IAEVG-NCDA Symposium, San Francisco, CA.

Scott, W. R. (2001). *Institutions and organizations: Ideas, interests, and identities* (2nd edn.). Thousand Oaks, CA: Sage.

Selingo, J. (Ed.) (2014). *The innovative university: What college presidents think about change in American higher education*. Washington, DC: The Chronicle of Higher Education.

Smerek, R. (2011). Sensemaking and sensegiving: An exploratory study of the simultaneous "being and learning" of new college and university presidents. *Journal of Leadership & Organizational Studies, 18,* 80–94.

Stanton, T. (2008). New times demand new scholarship: Opportunities and challenges for civic engagement at research universities. *Education, Citizenship and Social Justice, 3,* 19–42.

Tarde, G. (1903). *The laws of imitation* (trans. by E. Parson). New York, NY: University of Chicago Press.

Walshok, M. (1995). *Knowledge without boundaries.* San Francisco, CA: Jossey-Bass.

Walshok, M. (1999). Strategies for building the infrastructure that supports profession-related public service. *Educational Record, 65,* 18–21.

Weerts, D. & Sandmann, L. (2010). Community engagement and boundary-spanning roles at research universities. *Journal of Higher Education, 81,* 632–657.

Welch, M. (2016). *Engaging higher education.* Sterling, VA: Stylus.

Yin, R. (2014). *Case study research: Design and methods.* Thousand Oaks, CA: Sage.

Zaccaro, S. (2001). *The nature of executive leadership: A conceptual and empirical analysis of success.* Washington, DC: American Psychological Association.

PART II

University–Community Partnerships

3 Volunteer Program Assessment

A University–Community Partnership

Sheridan B. Trent, Kelly A. Prange, & Joseph A. Allen

This chapter is a case study of the Volunteer Program Assessment (VPA), a program composed of six chapters at universities across the United States. The VPA brings together faculty and students from various disciplines to address the key problem of volunteer satisfaction and retention. The rate of volunteerism has been steadily declining since 2002 (Bureau of Labor Statistics, 2016). Beyond these general statistics, most researchers have also identified volunteer turnover to be a key problem for many nonprofit and for-profit organizations. The VPA is a program that seeks to reduce volunteer turnover and increase volunteer program effectiveness by utilizing the expertise of faculty and students from universities to provide organizations with free assessment and consultation services. Specifically, the VPA provides a reliable, psychometrically valid, legally defensible survey that can be distributed to volunteers to gather information regarding their experiences. Students and faculty also meet directly with volunteer managers to discuss the evaluation findings and develop recommendations for addressing issues or leveraging strengths identified through the survey. This information is critical for community agencies, especially today in what has been referred to by many as an era of accountability (e.g., Carman, 2007; Carman, 2013; Murphy, 2009; Wing, 2004).

Such evaluations, however, can be difficult for nonprofits to accomplish without assistance. For example, researchers have reported multiple issues nonprofits face when attempting to evaluate their programs, including a lack of expertise in evaluation and technical know-how, a lack of time to conduct the evaluation itself, a lack of support by leadership, and a general lack of resources (Carman & Fredericks, 2010; Carman & Millesen, 2005). In spite of the difficulty an organization might face in conducting a volunteer program assessment independently, such evaluations can be highly beneficial, helping volunteer leaders with the following: (a) assessing the general state of their volunteer programs; (b) identifying organizational issues that may be contributing to volunteer turnover; and (c) determining aspects of a service that volunteers find the most meaningful. Helping to support program managers, the community–university partnerships fostered throughout the assessment and consultation process of the VPA have proven to be highly beneficial for both community agencies and the students and faculty involved.

Addressing Community Issues: Partnerships and Place-Based Institutions

The role of higher education and the university has changed substantially over the past few hundred years, shifting from the domain of the elite in the earliest institutions, to accessible state universities providing more practical education geared toward addressing societal needs (Roper & Hirth, 2005). Coupled with this shift has been a gradual devolution of the university being perceived as an isolated "ivory tower," to today's universities that are increasingly embedded within their communities. The changing nature of the interaction between universities and surrounding communities highlights opportunities for programs and partnerships that leverage university resources for the good of the community and for community involvement in initiatives to facilitate student learning and civic engagement.

In considering the actors and stakeholders involved in initiating community–university partnerships, one must acknowledge that although the individual faculty, students, and staff within universities play a key role in establishing and maintaining their relationships with the community, their affiliated institutions are involved in the collaboration as well. Due to their ties with the communities in which they reside, many universities are considered "anchor" institutions, or place-based institutions. Anchor institutions have historically been defined as central city institutions "that have a significant infrastructure investment in a specific community and are therefore unlikely to move" (Fulbright-Anderson, Auspos, & Anderson, 2001, p. 1). The specific characteristics of anchor institutions include the following: (a) spatial immobility; (b) corporate status; (c) scale; and (d) a mission of social justice, equity, and democracy. When universities are rooted in their geographical communities and are home to many resources that their communities need (i.e., skilled job candidates), they are uniquely positioned to create and sustain lasting partnerships that target community needs.

As the world becomes more and more globalized, place-based institutions help to "root" or "moor" urban people to their communities, while also keeping up with the changing times. As Birch, Perry, and Moor (2013) note, anchor institutions are not fixed and unchanging, but rather constantly evolving, "grounded in geographic fluidity." Thus, they play a major role in community development (Fulbright-Anderson, Auspos, & Anderson, 2001). Place-based institutions should embrace a modern mind-set of working collaboratively with communities instead of in the community. For example, allowing students to volunteer within a community organization on an annual basis would likely benefit one organization. However, doing so may not fulfill a community need that is larger in scope, but rather one organization's need for a few hours. Working "with" a community would entail addressing a need that is identified by community members and communicating with them to identify a creative solution. When partners keep communication lines open and are willing to adapt to the changing needs of the people who surround their place-based institutions, true change and beneficial outcomes can occur.

Community–university partnerships have been conceptualized in multiple ways, but some critical definitional elements include bringing together partners from both the university and the community, being able to identify a specific starting point, and leveraging the relationship to accomplish a goal (Bringle & Hatcher, 2002; McRae, 2012). It is also important to note that partnerships in and of themselves are a form of community engagement. To address the increasing demand from non-profits for program evaluative skills, some researchers have proposed solutions such as pairing advanced college students working to develop skills in evaluation with nonprofits who seek to utilize such skills (Bakken, Núñez, & Couture, 2014). The benefits students derive from this type of applied consulting experience are well documented and difficult to obtain without some form of hands-on learning (Schneider, Piotrowski, & Kass, 2007). Learning through direct experience, aptly referred to as experiential learning, or service learning when projects are tied to a class, are methods of education that characterize such partnerships, with a dual focus of providing benefits to both the students involved and the partnering organization. The VPA represents one example of a partnership between a university organization and the community, which provides mutual benefits to both parties.

Supporting faculty and student engagement with the community, the universities at which VPA affiliates reside are multiple examples of the anchor institutions that help make collaboration and partnerships possible, and these partnerships demonstrate how university resources can also serve specific community needs (e.g., volunteer retention and engagement problems) and thereby the larger public good.

Universities are uniquely positioned to support the community through community engagement programs, such as service learning, co-curricular service, research, and student-run organizations. We describe one such student-run, faculty-led organization that demonstrates how community engagement programs can be sustainable while also reciprocally benefiting all parties involved. The rest of the present chapter will give a brief review of the state of volunteering in the United States, a thorough overview of the VPA – how it began, what the program does for the community, the student and faculty roles, how it measures its impact, and what lies ahead. The VPA operates within a university, and a VPA program exists in multiple universities. We specify which VPA affiliate, or chapter, we are speaking about by adding the university's acronym. For example, VPA-UNCC is the chapter at the University of North Carolina at Charlotte. Although the present chapter will discuss the entirety of the VPA organization, particular focus will be allocated to VPA-UNO, the affiliate operating from the University of Nebraska at Omaha. The reasons for this are twofold. First, aside from the initial chapter at UNCC, the VPA-UNO chapter is the longest-running chapter. Second, as the primary authors currently direct the VPA-UNO chapter, it is the affiliate about which we have the most information. The practical takeaways from this chapter are a list of best practices and lessons learned.

The Role of Volunteers in the United States

The Size of the US Volunteer Workforce: A Decline in Volunteerism?

Determining the rate of volunteerism (and number of volunteers) in the United States is a challenging pursuit. Although there is some evidence that individuals in the US volunteer quite a bit compared to those in other countries, other surveys show discrepant trends. There are also definitional issues to contend with when attempting to identify the size of the volunteer workforce. For example, are volunteers only individuals serving a particular organization, or does informal helping count? What about individuals who only volunteer one time, as opposed to those who serve long-term?

To gain insight into the current state of the US volunteer workforce, we triangulated the results of two major surveys: the World Giving Index and the Current Population Survey. The Charities Aid Foundation (CAF) World Giving Index is an international survey designed to assess charitable giving in 139 countries. Conducted by Gallup across six continents every year since 2010 as part of its World Poll Initiative, the central goal of the survey, according to the authors of the report, is to "provide insight into the scope and nature of giving around the world" (Charities Aid Foundation, 2017, p. 5). This goal is accomplished by surveying approximately 1,000 individuals each year in each country, and includes individuals who are aged 15 and older (Charities Aid Foundation, 2017). The portion of the survey pertaining to volunteer work asks respondents if they have done any of the following in the past month: (a) helped a stranger or someone you did not know who needed help; (b) donated money to charity; or (c) volunteered your time to an organization. Each country's index is calculated by averaging the responses of participants. Countries are also ranked in terms of the number of their volunteers and the percentage of the population currently volunteering (i.e., extrapolated from the percentage of respondents who affirmed they volunteered in the past month).

When one purely examines the rates of volunteering country to country, the US ranks highly, and is consistently in the top ten countries with the highest percentage of the population volunteering in the past month. The most recent report released in 2017 stated that, on average, 41 percent of individuals in the United States volunteered in 2016, ranking seventh out of 139 countries in terms of the proportion of individuals volunteering, and second overall in terms of the sheer number of volunteers (approximately 106 million individuals). Evaluating the United States data by year (see Figure 3.1), one can note the general increasing trend, which was interrupted in 2016. According to the authors of the CAF report, the decrease from 46 percent to 41 percent demonstrates that "14 million fewer Americans volunteered their time in 2016" (p. 24).

Unfortunately, these numbers are not consistent with those found by other agencies. The Current Population Survey, conducted by the US Census Bureau for the Bureau of Labor Statistics, surveys 60,000 households or approximately 90,000 individuals across the United States each year. The aim of the survey is to obtain "information on employment and unemployment among the nation's civilian

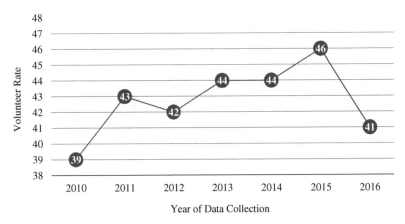

Figure 3.1 *Percentage of individuals who volunteered their time in the United States from 2010 to 2016, according to the Charities Aid Foundation World Giving Index*

noninstitutional population age 16 and over" (Bureau of Labor Statistics, 2016, p. 5). The specific supplement distributed in September of 2015 reported information on the incidence and characteristics of volunteers in the US. Survey respondents were asked if they had conducted any volunteer activities through or for an organization since September 1 of last year, giving the survey a different frame (i.e., the past month vs. the last year) than the CAF World Giving Index.

Out of those surveyed, 24.9 percent reported they had volunteered for an organization at least once between September 2014 and September 2015. The report notes that this translates to about 62.6 million people, a decline of 0.4 percent from the previous year. Further examination of the data from 2002 to the present (see Figure 3.2) suggests that the rate of volunteering has been steadily decreasing each year. Considering the number of volunteers reported by the same survey in 2014 was 62.8 million (Bureau of Labor Statistics, 2015), the current declination suggests that 180,000 fewer individuals volunteered in the US in 2015 compared to 2014.

There are major discrepancies between the findings of both surveys, with the CAF World Giving Index estimating the number of volunteers in the US at 106 million individuals and the Bureau of Labor Statistics estimating the number of volunteers in the US at 62.6 million individuals. The rates of volunteering are similarly discrepant. It is difficult to say which results might be closer to the "true" rate of volunteering in the US. On the one hand, survey data collected by the US Census Bureau represent a much larger sample of the US than the data collected by Gallup (i.e., 90,000 individuals vs. 1,000 individuals), so it could be more representative. Another potential issue is that both surveys do not assess the same individuals year after year, making it problematic to examine comparisons across years. Finally, it should be noted that the surveys provide different reference periods for recalling the volunteer work and collect responses from individuals beginning at different ages

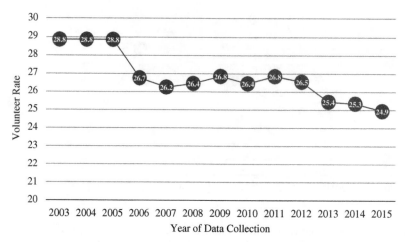

Figure 3.2 *Percentage of individuals who volunteered their time in the United States from 2003 to 2015, according to the Current Population Survey distributed by the US Census Bureau*

(i.e., 15 years vs. 16 years). In terms of the reference period, it is possible that the Gallup survey reports a higher percentage of individuals volunteering because it is easier to recall volunteer activities completed in the last month rather than the last year, which would suggest it might be more representative. An article by Abraham, Helms, and Presser (2009) discussed a potential connection between the likelihood of responding to a survey and the likelihood of volunteering, noting that variability in various estimates of volunteer activity (e.g., the Current Population Survey vs. the American Time Use Survey) could be explained by varying response rates and measurement error. Unfortunately, there is not a solution to this problem.

As of the writing of this article, no report has been released from the Bureau of Labor Statistics reporting on the rate of volunteerism in 2016. If we compare only the rates reported by both surveys for 2015, we see very different patterns. However, given the declination that the Gallup survey reported in 2016, it is not out of the realm of possibility to suggest that the volunteer rate found by the Bureau of Labor Statistics would similarly decline if it had been measured. Moving away from the substantial numeric discrepancies, however, the general finding from the most recent available data presented in both is that the rate of volunteering in the US is declining.

The Importance and Challenges of Managing Volunteers

Volunteers are a key part of thousands of organizations, donating their time to perform a variety of functions that would otherwise need to be done by paid workers, or possibly not done at all. Their contribution effectively enables many nonprofits to achieve their missions. However, beyond these general observations are key questions about precisely how much volunteers contribute to the US economy and where we would be without them. Further, the declining rate of volunteerism highlights the need to understand the effects a loss of volunteer labor might have on the public good.

Volunteers fulfill numerous functions for the organizations they serve. The most recent Bureau of Labor Statistics report released in 2016 identified some of the activities volunteers perform, including: (a) collecting, preparing, distributing, or serving food; (b) tutoring or teaching; (c) fundraising; (d) engaging in general labor; (e) coaching, refereeing, or supervising sports teams; (f) conducting religious functions; (g) providing general office services; (h) providing counseling, medical care, fire/emergency medical services, or protective services; (i) professional or management assistance (e.g., serving on a board or committee); (j) mentoring youth; (k) collecting, making, or distributing clothing, crafts, or goods other than food; or (l) engaging in music performance or other artistic activities. It is clear from these categories that at least some volunteers are completing tasks that can be considered as challenging as paid work. Investigations of this topic have characterized the relationship between paid staff and volunteers as complex. A study by Chum, Mook, Handy, Schugurensky, and Quarter (2013) found a high degree of interchangeability between volunteers and paid staff in 836 nonprofits in Canada, with 80 percent of nonprofits in the sample indicating that some tasks at their organizations were interchangeable between volunteers and paid employees. Other comparisons of volunteers and paid workers have found that volunteer workers tend to show fewer withdrawal behaviors and higher organizational commitment than paid workers in the same organization (Laczo & Hanisch, 1999). Volunteers carrying out similar tasks to employees are also more likely to be satisfied and report lower intentions to leave the organization in contrast to paid employees (Pearce, 1983).

In attempting to evaluate the value of volunteers to nonprofits, many researchers have found various ways of assigning a dollar amount to volunteer service. A popular metric is the "Estimated Value of Volunteer Time" reported by the Independent Sector, which is based on data from the Bureau of Labor Statistics (i.e., yearly earnings plus 12 percent fringe benefits). The most current estimate places the value of an hour of volunteering at $24.14 nationally, though specific values are also available by state. Data from the Bureau of Labor Statistics are also used by the Corporation for National and Community Service, which places the value of volunteer service in 2015 in the US at $193 billion dollars. Others have also explored this issue. Goulbourne and Embuldeniya (2002) proposed eight different ways of assigning economic value to volunteers, including four human resource productivity measures, two program efficiency measures, and two community support measures. King (2010) described the value of skilled volunteers in helping organizations make the best use of financial resources. Hager and Brudney (2005) highlighted net benefits such as cost savings, increased quality of services and products, improved community relations, and access to new skills possessed by volunteers. Similarly, Handy and Brudney (2007) noted how volunteer labor creates certain positive externalities, such as promoting public health, socializing and providing diverse experiences for younger volunteers, and role modeling. Finally, a report published by the Points of Light Institute (Wu, 2011) examining the social impact of volunteerism described several notable findings, including that volunteers help to build social connections between sectors, assist in promoting safe and strong communities, promote civic engagement, and assist in the delivery of services.

Taken together, it is clear that although it is difficult to quantify the precise contribution of volunteerism to society, the value of volunteer work cannot be overstated, providing direct and indirect benefits to nonprofit organizations, society, and the volunteers themselves. Given their importance, how can organizations make the best use of volunteers and what challenges stand in their way?

Research on volunteer turnover has implicated several culprits. First, one study of volunteer management practices found that the adoption of management practices was relatively minor, and the only practice widely adopted by charities was providing regular supervision and communication with volunteers, with 67 percent of organizations indicating that they performed this activity to a large degree (Brudney & Hager, 2004). Some of the practices identified in the study tied to volunteer retention included providing recognition of volunteers, providing training and development opportunities, and devoting more time to properly placing them. In this same vein, after conducting extensive interviews with volunteer managers, Backer, Allen, and Bonilla (2012) noted that although volunteers are unpaid, they are not "free," but rather expect to be compensated by feeling like they are part of an organization's mission, feeling recognized, and being provided with adequate oversight. Overall, oftentimes volunteer programs with high volunteer turnover may have issues related to the identification and implementation of effective volunteer management strategies. It was while working with a nonprofit to conduct the Volunteer Program Assessment Research (VPAR) study that these and other similar issues began to arise, which ultimately led to the creation of the VPA.

The First VPA

Prior to the construction of the VPA program, Dr. Steven Rogelberg built a partnership with the Humane Society of the United States (HSUS) investigating employee well-being-related issues in animal welfare organizations. During that process, Dr. Rogelberg noticed that many animal welfare organizations have two workforces they leverage to accomplish their goals: the paid staff and volunteers. The idea that volunteers might bring the stigma associated with dirty work into the organization was intriguing in that the very people who could bring relief and aid to the situation employees' face actually end up harming them via enacting the stigma. Furthermore, a review of the literature showed just how little work existed on the impact of volunteers on employees and vice versa (Rogelberg et al., 2010).

After these initial investigations, Dr. Rogelberg proposed a partnership with the HSUS aimed at investigating volunteer program effectiveness in animal welfare organizations. In 2007, with a grant from HSUS, the original VPA team was created at UNCC. The project was dubbed the "Volunteer Program Assessment Research" or VPAR. Dr. Rogelberg supervised two doctoral students at the time, Dr. Joseph Allen and Adrian Goh, as they developed the initial survey tools and reached out to animal welfare organizations to get commitments to participate. The study included three surveys, two for the volunteer coordinator and one directed at the volunteers of the organization. Of the 90 organizations contacted, 87 completed the entire process (i.e., two coordinator surveys and one volunteer survey) and received a technical report concerning the perceptions of the volunteers regarding the volunteer program at their organization (Allen, Goh, & Rogelberg, 2008; Goh, Allen, & Rogelberg, 2009).

Based on the enthusiasm from the leaders of these nonprofit organizations and general interest on the part of Dr. Rogelberg and HSUS, the survey directed at the volunteers as part of the VPAR study became the basis for the VPA survey used today. In 2008, Dr. Rogelberg worked with two graduate students, Dr. Allen and Dr. Bonilla, to develop the initial survey, process, and consulting materials. This officially led to the launch of the first VPA chapter at UNCC in 2009 (Olien et al., 2014).

Assessing Volunteer Programs

Rogelberg and Fuller (2004) stressed the importance of pro bono work and how the relationship between psychologists and agencies is more than one profession "giving something away," but rather is a collaborative relationship in which all community agencies, psychologists, and students involved receive substantial benefits from working together. For example, student consultants involved in organizational projects develop real-world problem-solving skills that are hard to teach in the classroom and gain considerable applied experience from such work, professionals are provided research and networking opportunities, and community agencies receive consulting services for a free or reduced cost. In addition to elucidating this viewpoint, Rogelberg and Fuller also discussed several challenges associated with working in a non-university setting, including: (a) identifying a service recipient; (b) engendering psychological commitment; and (c) providing high-quality work. To illustrate this complex process, we will share some concerns that arose as the VPA was being implemented at different institutions. Although the VPA may experience different challenges depending on the institution in which is exists and its surrounding community, the following concerns were central to the development of the VPA process and have been key considerations when working to implement new chapters of the VPA.

Construction of the VPA Survey

The VPA survey utilized by all VPA affiliates is composed of 15 constructs meant to highlight many diverse facets of a volunteer's experience, as well as the attitudes of volunteers. The survey was developed through a year-long process of rigorous evaluation and modifying well-validated and reliable scales typically used in employee evaluation to suit a volunteer workforce. The 15 constructs can be found in Table 3.1 and encompass volunteers' perceptions of the organization, their coworkers, their management, and the work itself. Because the VPA process is flexible

Table 3.1 *Constructs on the VPA survey*

	Construct	Definition	Source
Perceptions of the organization	Organizational commitment	The emotional attachment a volunteer has to their volunteer job	Meyer, Allen, and Smith, 1993
	Recognition by the organization	The degree to which volunteers feel appreciated for their service	Developed for the VPA survey
	Satisfaction with communication	Volunteers' satisfaction with the communication they receive from the organization	Spector, 1985
	Perception of voice	The extent to which volunteers believe that their advocacy is being heard by other organizational members	Van Dyne and LePine, 1998
Perceptions of volunteer work	Competence	The extent to which a volunteer feels they can successfully carry out tasks and meet professional standards	Deci et al., 2001; Spreitzer, 1995
	Role ambiguity	The extent to which volunteers are certain of their duties, how to complete those duties, and the organizations' goals and policies	Rizzo, House, and Lirtzman, 1970
	Satisfaction with volunteer work	Volunteers' overall affective appraisal of their volunteer service for an organization	Spector, 1985
	Engagement	The extent to which a volunteer feels vigor, dedication, and absorption when volunteering or thinking about their volunteer work	Schaufeli, Bakker, and Salanova, 2006
	Satisfaction with volunteer contribution	The extent to which a volunteer feels that what they do for the organization and its clients makes a positive difference for others	Backer, Allen, and Bonilla, 2012
Interpersonal perceptions	Satisfaction with volunteer coordinator	Volunteers' satisfaction regarding their relationship or interactions with their volunteer supervisor/ manager	Spector, 1985
	Satisfaction with volunteer colleagues	Volunteers' satisfaction regarding their relationships or interactions with other volunteers at the organization	Spector, 1985
	Satisfaction with paid staff	Volunteers' satisfaction regarding their relationships or interactions with paid staff at the organization	Spector, 1985

Table 3.1 (*cont.*)

	Construct	Definition	Source
Volunteer management practices	Training	The extent to which volunteers are aware that the organization has provided various types of training to volunteers and those working with them	Hager and Brudney, 2005; Rogelberg et al., 2010; Brudney, 1999
	Support	The extent to which volunteers are aware that the organization has mechanisms in place to provide support to volunteers	
Constraints	Organizational constraints	Aspects of an organization that can interfere with or prevent volunteers from performing their best when completing their assignments	Spector and Jex, 1998
	Burnout	An emotional state some volunteers may experience characterized by emotional exhaustion, depersonalization, and a reduced sense of personal accomplishment	Pines and Aronson, 1988
	Intentions to quit	A volunteer's behavioral decision to stop volunteering for an organization	Horn, Griffeth, and Sellaro, 1984; Jaros, 1997

Notes: All VPA chapters utilize the same base survey with these constructs. The exception are survey items involving training and support in the volunteer management practices section, which are only included on the VPA survey distributed to client organizations by UNO.

and each chapter has the opportunity to adapt their surveys, the VPA chapter at UNO added two additional constructs to assess volunteers' perceptions of the management practices in place at their organization, including training and support questions. All constructs, as well as their definitions and the source of each scale, are provided in Table 3.1.

As one can imagine, a survey asking volunteers this many questions can be long. To preemptively address this problem, many of the initial scales were shortened. Unfortunately, the length of the survey is still a concern, typically taking volunteers anywhere from 15 to 30 minutes to complete. The issue of length still represents two distinct challenges: first, ensuring that volunteers complete as much of the survey as possible; and second, ensuring that volunteers care enough to answer the questions in an effortful manner. These issues have been addressed in multiple ways. Consistent with the recommendations by Podsakoff et al. (2003) and Podsakoff, MacKenzie, and Podsakoff (2012), the survey is always stressed and marketed to volunteers as being completely anonymous. Further, the survey contains instructions in both the survey itself and in the survey recruitment email to let participants know how much the organization appreciates their honest feedback and how their responses will be used. Finally, the survey itself is endorsed by the volunteers' direct manager and is distributed to volunteers in an email from the volunteer manager rather than from an unfamiliar source (e.g., a VPA consultant). Using these methods, VPA consultants can be assured of a better response rate than they would otherwise receive. Utilizing best practice recommendations with regard to survey development also helps to ensure that the VPA is providing high-quality, useful, and evidence-based data to clients.

The Assessment Process

The process by which student consultants conduct the VPA with client organizations is streamlined and largely consistent across affiliates. From start to finish, working with a client organization can take anywhere from five to eight weeks depending on the client and consultant schedule. Typically, each consultant will spend anywhere from one to four hours a week working with their VPA client. Sometimes a consultant will put in four hours and other times less than one depending on the step the consultant is on (see below). For example, if the VPA is in Step 3 (survey program), the survey is open to collect responses from volunteers for two weeks and the consultant is simply monitoring the survey and answering any questions that may come from volunteers. Some of the consultants' work includes attending a weekly meeting and working to mentor new VPA consultants if they are already fully trained themselves, but the bulk of the time spent volunteering consists of conducting the VPA process with each client, which can be broken down into seven steps (see Figure 3.3).

Step 1: Identifying VPA Recipients. Reaching out to client organizations is conducted by consultants via phone or email. Recipients of the VPA are identified in one of five ways. First, potential partners may be identified by student consultants themselves who have a history working at various nonprofits or may know individuals who are interested. Each VPA affiliate also maintains a list of client organizations they have partnered with in the past, and reaching back out to those organizations a year after the previous VPA survey to see if they are interested in a repeat assessment often yields interest. A third option is through referral, and future clients are often identified by current clients who forward the VPA's information to organizations who might find an assessment of their volunteer program useful. For newer chapters, the VPA-UNCC chapter will often distribute clients to help them get started building their client base. Finally, an increasing trend is that of client organizations reaching out to a VPA chapter after hearing about the organization

Figure 3.3 *The seven steps of the VPA process*

online, through social media, from a conference, or through other nonprofits in the community.

Providing outreach can take anywhere from one day to one month, with some organizations requesting additional information about the service and some wanting to get started right away. Although oftentimes the volunteer manager is the direct contact at the agency, some organizations do not have a dedicated individual responsible for managing volunteers. In these cases, additional research is necessary to determine who would be the best employee at the agency. An important part of this step for student consultants lies in clearly communicating VPA services and in determining if the organization is both interested and ready to conduct the assessment.

Step 2: Commit to VPA. Once an organization has verified their interest, consultants, typically one or two per client, will work directly with the volunteer coordinator or manager at each organization. Sometimes a presentation, meeting, or several phone conversations are necessary in order to fully explain what the VPA is and how it works. At this juncture, consultants will send the coordinator a document that serves as an informal contract that the client should sign. The coordinator also needs to complete a questionnaire that will give VPA consultants important information about their job, the volunteer duties, the volunteer program, and the organization as a whole. Volunteer managers fill out the questionnaire, sign the letter of commitment, and send it back to their consultant. The questionnaire is useful in order to gather some preliminary organizational information (e.g., the number of volunteers and types of volunteer roles available), and the letter of commitment outlines the responsibilities of both the student consultant and the volunteer manager. Upon receiving the signed letter of commitment, consultants will review the questionnaire to confirm that the volunteer program is suited for the VPA (e.g., they have enough volunteers to conduct the survey) and begin negotiating a timeline with the coordinator to determine the survey launch date. The timeline may be created according to a particular event the organization is having, a certain time of year, or the volunteer manager's personal preference.

Step 3: Survey Program. When a timeline has been agreed upon, VPA consultants provide the coordinator with a link to the VPA survey and two email templates that contain language explaining the survey to the organization's volunteer base. These templates can be modified according to the coordinator's specifications if desired, but are general enough to make the process simple. Volunteer coordinators need only copy and paste the templates into their email system and click "send" to distribute the survey to the appropriate volunteers.

Once the survey has been sent out by the coordinator, consultants monitor the response rate. After one week, a consultant will contact the coordinator to let them know what the current response rate is, prompt them to send a reminder email to the volunteers, and provide the email templates again for easy access. After two weeks, the consultant will contact the coordinator again with a final response rate. Occasionally, if the response rate is lower than anticipated, the consultant and coordinator will alter the timeline to allow for another week's worth of data collection. Consultants will also provide the coordinator with a list of suggestions for improving the response rate, such as reminding volunteers in person when they come to the organization, allowing volunteers to take volunteer time to complete the survey if the agency has a computer on site, and providing a reward to volunteers if a particular percentage of respondents is reached (e.g., a pizza party for all volunteers). After data collection ends, the consultant will close the survey, send a final response rate to the coordinator, and begin building the reports.

Step 4: Build Report and Analyze Results. The process of generating a report for clients differs between VPA affiliates. Although all volunteers at client organizations answer the same questions utilizing the same response scales, consultants create reports based on how they were trained at their respective institutions. Ultimately, the key element of reports is that they must include all survey items, a full breakdown of volunteer scores, demographic information, and an overview somewhere in the report summarizing scores among the 15 constructs. Those key elements are present for all VPA affiliates; however, each affiliate institution may add to the core VPA process to suit the needs of their consultants and clients. For example, the VPA-UNO chapter works with many repeat clients and thus includes previous years' survey results into the report so that volunteer managers can view side by side scores from one year to the next. The UNO chapter also aggregates volunteer scores into line graphs for client organizations that have been surveyed with the VPA three or more times. Also referred to as a "trend report," an example line graph is provided later in this chapter during the section discussing the development of the trend reports.

Step 5: Pre-Consult. Once consultants have completed the report, they meet with all other consultants who wish to participate in the client consultation to discuss the client's results; we call this meeting a pre-consultation. A typical team consists of two to five consultants, and always at least one individual with a master's degree to provide oversight. The senior consultant will take the role of debriefing the other analysts on the report. Together, the team will then determine what questions they have for the client organization, the client's strengths, and the client's growth areas, and brainstorm some recommendations for improvement. These recommendations are a good start, but the best recommendations emerge organically during the final consult call where the consultant and client work together to fully understand the context of each client's organization. Without such context, it is difficult to know if a recommendation is feasible or likely to be successful. The pre-consultation ends by planning out what each consultant's role will be during the consultation.

Step 6: Consult. After completion of a pre-consultation meeting, two to four student analysts meet with the client to discuss the report's findings. The typical consultation can be conducted via conference call if the client is in a different city or state, but is conducted in person whenever possible, with consultants meeting with the client at their location or at the respective university. Consultations typically takes one hour, with particular emphasis placed upon the discussion of three strengths, three areas for growth, and questions developed during the pre-consultation. The best consultations occur when the meeting itself is more of a dialogue, with the volunteer coordinator talking for approximately 50 percent of the time and the VPA consultants talking for 50 percent of the time. In addition to the main discussion points and dialogue, each consultation ends with the VPA consultants asking if the volunteer coordinator is interested in a repeat assessment. If the client is interested, the consultant will collect information about when might be a good time for that next assessment. Finally, the consultant will ask if the client has any referrals for organizations they think would be interested in working with the VPA.

Step 7: Follow-Up. Following the consultation, consultants are not finished yet. A summary of the consultation is typed up by a senior consultant, who sends it to the rest of the team for review and feedback before sending the summary back to the client. The process of drafting the summary and going back and forth with other consultants typically takes one week, after which the summary is emailed to the volunteer manager, along with a link to the VPA client satisfaction survey. This survey can be filled out at the manager's discretion, is only reviewed by VPA leadership, and asks about the manager's experiences with the VPA, including things that could be improved upon in the future.

The Expansion and Development of VPA over the Past Ten Years

Since its inception in 2009 at UNCC, interest in the VPA has grown. UNCC realized that the VPA model could work at other universities and decided to try and expand the VPA to other service-focused universities interested in student development outside the classroom. UNCC thought this would be a mutually beneficial process since more students and faculty would be exposed to the VPA and more clients could be served as the number of consultants grew. The first affiliate university was started in 2011 by Dr. Joseph Allen at Creighton University with a group of undergraduate student analysts. The program at Creighton flourished and developed a broad base of clients. In 2013, Dr. Allen began teaching graduate students at UNO, and he was able to successfully start a new VPA chapter at UNO. This group quickly grew, utilizing graduate students in the industrial/organizational psychology program as the first UNO analysts, and later expanding to include undergraduates studying psychology, and then undergraduates studying multiple majors across the campus. In 2012, the VPA also expanded to George Mason University (GMU) and Illinois State University. Dr. Eden King spearheaded the chapter at GMU, recruiting graduate students from the industrial/organizational psychology doctoral program. The chapter at Illinois State University is headed by Dr. Kim Schneider. The most recent chapter was developed in 2013, when Dr. Tammy Allen and Dr. Mark Poteet assembled a team of graduate students at the University of South Florida. This expansion has allowed the VPA to offer services to more volunteer programs, as well as to provide a record number of student consultants with professional consulting opportunities (Olien et al., 2014).

Developments and Specializations

The need to streamline organizational processes in an effort to meet demands for service have led to ongoing improvement initiatives for all VPA affiliates. In particular, several issues that have come up during program development have included how to handle repeat clients, how to work with diverse organizations who may not be well represented by what is thought of as a typical volunteer program, how to meet the growing demand for additional data visualization by clients, and how to ensure that the VPA has mechanisms in place to obtain feedback from key stakeholders (i.e., client organizations, student consultants). These recent developments are expanded upon below.

Repeat Clients. The original process of the VPA was designed with client organizations who would have their volunteers take the survey once. Following this process, VPA consultants would collect the data, create a report, conduct a meeting with the volunteer management team from each organization to discuss trends in the data and recommendations to address growth areas, and send the client a summary of the report. However, given the number of organizations interested in conducting the VPA a second, third, or even fourth time, the process has shifted to allow for a more robust client report that includes the results of the previous year's assessment, and the consultation format has been reworked to allow for a discussion of any changes that have occurred within the organization since the previous time point, as well as if the coordinator had the chance to implement any suggestions and how the implementation has worked out to date.

Meeting the Needs of Diverse Client Organizations. Nonprofits are not one size fits all, but differ in a number of respects, including the populations they serve, the manner in which they assist others, and the unique challenges they face. To provide an idea of scope, the Bureau of Labor Statistics (2016) reports separate volunteer information for those serving the following: (a) religious institutions; (b) educational and youth organizations; (c) social and community establishments; (d) civic, political, professional, or international groups; (e) environmental or animal care organizations; (f) hospitals or health organizations; (g) public safety groups; (h) sport, hobby, cultural, or arts undertakings; and (i) undetermined organizations.

Further, within these categories are clear differences with respect to the makeup of volunteers serving within a given group. For example, the largest group of volunteers serving hospitals is composed of those who are between 20 and 24 years of age, while volunteers over the age of 65 are much more likely to serve in religious organizations. With regard to the VPA, the challenge then becomes how to ensure that we are effectively serving a broad range of volunteer programs. Efforts to ensure fit include two formal initiatives and one informal initiative. Formal procedures to address this issue have been the creation of a screening questionnaire that is sent to all potential clients prior to their participation and the development of national norms by category. The screener is a survey for volunteer coordinators or managers to fill out and contains questions about the volunteer workforce, organizational policies, relevant concerns they have about their program, and the number and type of volunteers serving the organization. Utilizing this information, consultants are able to make sure that the client organization has a sufficient number of volunteers to complete the assessment. The screener also collects data regarding the structure of the volunteer program (e.g., number of volunteer coordinators, number of volunteers, types of volunteer duties) and the type of organization, with the following five options: (a) animal welfare; (b) health and human services; (c) police, fire, and rescue; (d) arts and sciences; and (e) youth mentoring and development. Once volunteer managers fill out this survey, consultants note the type of organization and use it later to compare the client's results to their respective organization type. For example, an animal shelter's results would be compared against national norms for other animal welfare organizations, accounting for some of the differences that naturally occur in different types of organizations. Apart from this procedure, which helps to ensure good fit and generalizability of results, consultants spend quite a bit of time explaining and discussing what the VPA is and how it can be used in an organization with volunteer managers before ever implementing any elements of the VPA process.

Client Satisfaction Survey. Introduced in 2015, the client satisfaction survey is a short, eight-question survey distributed to volunteer managers soliciting feedback after their organizations have completed the VPA process in full.

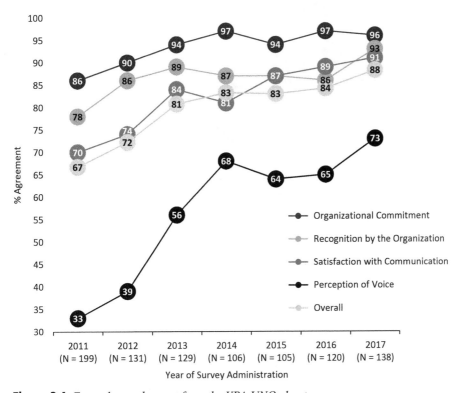

Figure 3.4 *Example trend report from the VPA-UNO chapter*

The survey inquires as to the utility and ease of filling out the screening questionnaire, if the timeline was sufficiently developed, the quality and timeliness of their consultant, and what the VPA as an organization can do to improve its processes. Thus far, it has been an invaluable mechanism for collecting feedback to implement changes.

Trend Report. In the spring of 2016, feedback from volunteer managers who had worked with the VPA more than once began indicating a desire for better visualization and more integration of previous VPA reports with the newest results for their organization. After a feedback session among VPA consultants and leadership, the UNO chapter developed the first trend report, an addendum to the original VPA report that included assessment results from previous years in an easy-to-read line graph, enabling volunteer program leadership to clearly see their individual organization's results over time. After an initial pilot semester, wherein the report was provided to all long-term VPA clients and feedback was gathered, the report was further revised. It is currently in use and available for all organizations who have worked with the UNO chapter at least three times. An example report is presented in Figure 3.4.

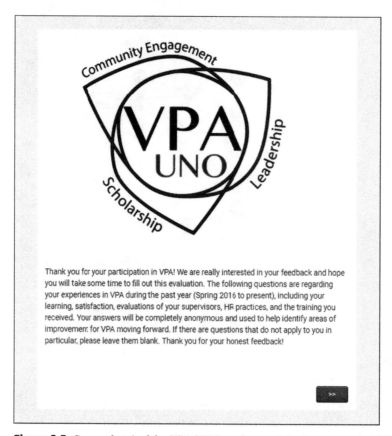

Thank you for your participation in VPA! We are really interested in your feedback and hope you will take some time to fill out this evaluation. The following questions are regarding your experiences in VPA during the past year (Spring 2016 to present), including your learning, satisfaction, evaluations of your supervisors, HR practices, and the training you received. Your answers will be completely anonymous and used to help identify areas of improvement for VPA moving forward. If there are questions that do not apply to you in particular, please leave them blank. Thank you for your honest feedback!

Figure 3.5 *Screenshot 1 of the VPA-UNO student satisfaction survey in 2016*

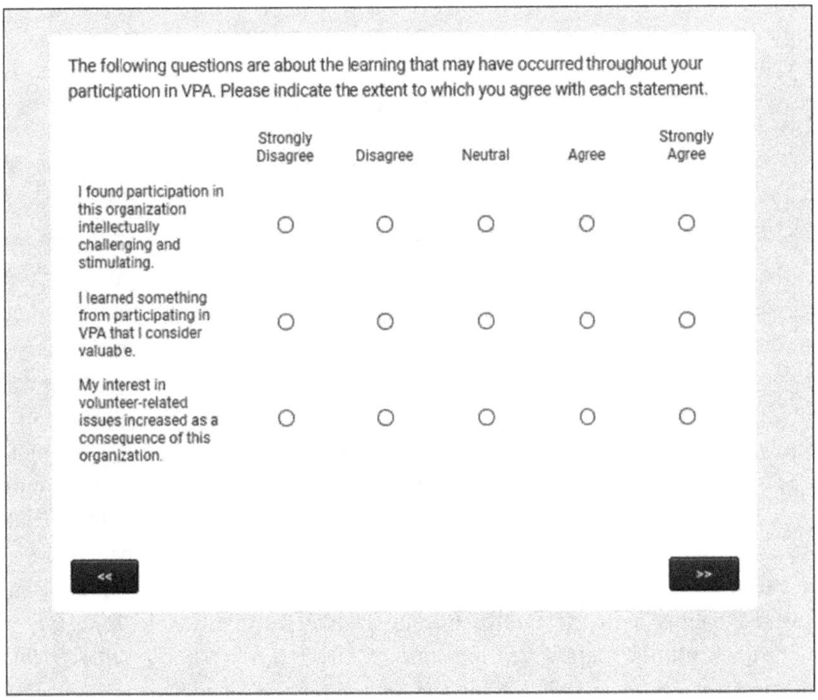

Figure 3.6 *Screenshot 2 of the VPA-UNO student satisfaction survey in 2016*

Student Survey. The spring of 2017 brought a new innovation for the VPA; the creation of a survey for student consultants. The purpose of the survey was to collect feedback from student analysts regarding their experiences with the VPA, with the goal of improving the program. Students at the UNO chapter provided feedback about their supervisors (e.g., faculty director and assistant directors), their quality of learning, the human resources practices of the VPA, their interactions with other consultants and their student mentors, and their training. They were also asked what they liked about the VPA and how the VPA could improve going forward. Five out of ten analysts filled out the survey. This initiative was incredibly useful to the UNO chapter in two ways. First, in keeping with many of the VPA's own recommendations to client organizations, it provided its volunteers with a formal mechanism through which to express voice. Second, the survey feedback identified two areas in which the UNO chapter could improve to make the VPA a more positive experience for its volunteers. Two screenshots of the survey provided to the student consultants of the UNO chapter are presented in Figures 3.5 and 3.6.

Annual Meeting. The growth and rapid learning curve associated with VPA activities necessitated finding ways to enhance affiliate collaboration. Beginning in the spring of 2015, representatives from each VPA-affiliated chapter began meeting at the annual Society for Industrial and Organizational Psychologists conference.

The purpose of this meeting was to allow student consultants from different chapters the chance to interact, discuss best practices and meaningful experiences for the current year, and celebrate successes together. The annual meeting has helped to increase synergy and communication between chapters.

The Organizational Structure of VPA-UNO

The VPA team at UNO consists of 15 individuals as of the writing of this chapter, including one faculty director, Dr. Joseph Allen, two graduate student assistant directors, and 12 graduate and undergraduate consultants. Since the UNO chapter was founded by Dr. Allen in 2013, 49 students from UNO have participated with the VPA as consultants and seven students have served as assistant directors. Historically, the population of consultants at the UNO chapter has been the most diverse of all VPA affiliates, with both graduate and undergraduate students serving the program with a variety of majors, including the following: (a) Industrial/ Organizational Psychology; (b) Psychology; (c) Urban Studies; (d) Business Administration; (e) International Studies; (f) Bioinformatics; (g) Management Information Systems; and (h) Public Administration. In addition to bringing in students from multiple majors, the chapter at UNO has typically utilized two assistant directors per year, one working in an operational capacity and the other working in a research capacity. In contrast to the student assistant directors, student consultants serve as junior or senior consultants with the program.

Although the VPA is a service designed to benefit volunteer programs, it has the additional benefit of helping to train students by providing them with real-world experiences. This is especially relevant given the calls by some researchers for a greater need to align lessons learned in the classroom with particular job functions (Carducci et al., 1987; Smith, 2000). Occasionally referred to as "experiential learning," this method of learning, which must involve specific content, incentives, and interactions between students and the real world (Illeris, 2007; Jordi, 2011), has been found to be highly beneficial to students. Specific competencies developed by students working with the VPA include both job skills and soft skills. For example, during the process of providing initial outreach to client organizations, students practice effective communication (e.g., email, in person, and telephone), teamwork, mentoring or mentorship, and utilization of Microsoft Word and Excel. Beyond general skills acquired from performing client-related work itself, students are able to spend approximately a year getting a feel for consulting, which helps them make decisions later on about the directions of their own careers once they have graduated.

Scope of the Student and Faculty Volunteer Roles

Although each chapter has a different population of consultants and some are uniquely structured, the roles of consultants remain similar at every affiliate, with students learning to perform all steps of the VPA process from the initial outreach phone calls and emails to client organizations, to internally setting up the survey and putting together a timeline, to closing the survey and building reports for each client. Training new consultants is a process that typically takes three to six months, so prospective student consultants are asked for a minimum time commitment to the VPA of a year to allow for training and then to allow students to take a more independent role. Job descriptions of the student role of consultant generally include, at a minimum, the four elements described below.

Purpose. To provide quantitative and qualitative data and feedback to nonprofit organizations from the perspective of their volunteers with the goal of improving volunteer and organizational outcomes.

Duties and Responsibilities

- Attend all weekly meetings during the school year.
- Provide outreach and follow-up to nonprofit organizations regarding their participation in the VPA.
- Work with interested agencies to ensure the completion of relevant paperwork and setting up of timelines for project completion.
- Serve as a point of contact for volunteer managers before, during, and after the VPA process.
- Utilize survey data to build technical reports for client organizations.
- Research clients in advance of consultations and come prepared to all consultations with your notes.
- Interpret technical reports and other sources of data with team members.
- Present information to clients via an in-person or telephone meeting.
- Create meeting summaries and send them to clients following consultations.

Overview of the Training Process. The training process consists of four steps. The first step is referred to as "Pre-Shadow" and includes both readings and orientation. Readings can be found in an electronic folder and are completed as the consultant moves through the training process. Orientation is completed with an assistant director; new consultants are provided with a handbook and an overview of tools used by the chapter and are assigned a senior consultant mentor. The second step is called "Shadowing" and consists of new consultants working directly with their senior consultant mentor as they work with their clients. Using this method, new consultants are able to see how the VPA process works up close, and mentors are instructed to provide the opportunity to assist with client responsibilities as well. Following an initial shadowing process, the next step of training is called the "Mock VPA" and is essentially a simulated VPA process that each consultant completes with the VPA assistant directors. During this step, they portray the role of a fully trained VPA consultant; the assistant directors in turn play a new client. New consultants must successfully complete all steps of the Mock VPA during this simulated exercise, which usually takes two to three hours. Upon completion of the Mock VPA, consultants are provided with a review in which they are given feedback on their performance and afforded the opportunity to ask questions and receive clarification. Finally, assuming successful completion of the Mock VPA, consultants are promoted and soon reach out to their first client.

Community Impact

Measuring Impact

The metrics for assessing impact at the UNO chapter are aggregated on a yearly basis and include the following: (a) informal assessment of program effectiveness for participating organizations year after year during consultation meetings; (b) calculating metrics such as the number of assessments conducted, the number of students who participated, and the number of organizations partnered with; and (c) seeking feedback from partner organizations regarding the utility and impact of the assessment through the client satisfaction survey. Seeking feedback from clients who have worked with VPA-UNO is crucial in order to determine if the VPA is adequately achieving its purpose and addressing the needs of clients. With regard to the two impact indicators that require some calculation (i.e., indicator [b]), results from the VPA-UNO annual report for the year of 2016 are provided in Figure 3.7.

Beyond these basic metrics and informal mechanisms, another common way of assessing impact is through calculating the dollar value of a particular service, as seen in the annual report snapshot. These types of figures can be useful in seeking

17,240
The number of volunteers served by VPA-UNO in 2016.

38
The number of clients served by VPA-UNO in 2016.

40
The number of VPA-UNO surveys distributed to client organizations in 2016.

$585,000
The VPA-UNO in-kind donation provided to community agencies in 2016.

9
The number of new analysts who joined the VPA-UNO team in 2016.

1,114
The number of hours donated by VPA volunteers in 2016.

Figure 3.7 *VPA-UNO annual report metrics*

grant funding and evaluating the utility of the VPA for the community. Finally, the overall impact of the VPA can be assessed more directly by evaluating the client retention rate for the organization year after year. Ultimately, we have taken the feedback received from partnering client organizations as the greatest indicator of utility, as volunteer coordinators themselves, who spend every day working directly with volunteers, are in the best position to know whether the VPA has been useful to their organization. For example, 53 percent of client organizations have chosen to conduct a follow-up assessment with the UNO chapter approximately a year after the initial assessment, which is one indication of usefulness, as we would not expect volunteer coordinators, who often have limited time and resources, to continue conducting an activity they did not feel was valuable to their organization.

Best Practices/Lessons Learned

Developing, Sustaining, and Enhancing Programs at Universities

The development of any program rests with first identifying a real need in the community, as well as putting in the initial groundwork to ensure that the program will fulfill its intended purpose. Identifying such a need may occur organically through a particular project (e.g., the HSUS project) or in a more targeted way through research. Seeking input from local community organizations or conducting a targeted needs assessment may be ways to get started. Sustaining a program is an equally challenging endeavor, and is something that can rarely be done alone. Practical issues with program implementation and sustainability can include funding, finding space to conduct activities, facilitating support from other faculty and administrators, and gaining support from university leadership. The value of being connected to a university already embedded within the community is a critical boon in the development and continued existence of the VPA and other similar programs.

One of the most salient challenges of conducting the VPA within universities is attempting to balance client needs with the reality that volunteer time on the part of faculty and students can only get you so far. Relegating interested organizations to waiting lists to obtain VPA services is unfortunate but necessary to ensure that students do not overextend themselves and are able to provide high-quality consulting services to the organizations they are working with. The growth of the VPA as an organization, both within the universities in which it is already anchored as well as in new universities, is not possible without lines of funding.

Finally, financial constraints aside, program expansion in general can be a challenge. Identifying qualified and interested students to participate in an initiative takes time. The VPA has addressed this issue in two ways. First, attaching the organization to industrial/organizational psychology graduate programs helps to provide a pool of student consultants who will use these program evaluation skills after graduation, though not all will have the time or inclination to participate. The UNO chapter has also utilized various university communication outlets (e.g., news emails that are sent to students each week, fliers in common areas, talking to classes) to recruit students from other majors, and has developed an in-depth selection system to determine the best applicants. Such an infrastructure may become necessary as new programs develop.

Program Goals

Specific lessons that were helpful to the VPA as the organization began to take shape should be kept in mind, especially when creating new VPA affiliates or similar VPA-type programs. General research on community–university partnerships has drawn attention to common issues and even conflicts that can occur when collaborating. For example, Prins (2005) described conflicts as inherent to the types of partnerships that bring together individuals from different backgrounds and work contexts, noting that specific "tensions may arise about partner roles, decision making, grant management, reward structures, diverging agendas, modes of work, mismatched timelines, forms of knowledge, and status differences" (p. 59). Analysis of a conflict between a public university and several nonprofits yielded several practical lessons, including the importance of clarifying the goals of collaborations, discussing expectations of both the university and community partner, and understanding the institutional pressures under which community members may be operating. Other researchers have echoed such concerns, drawing attention to the problematic mindset that "simply creating a partnership magically produces resources that will solve problems, without realistically analyzing the problems, strategizing to address them, and organizing necessary resources" (Baum, 2000, p. 234). Two lessons we will discuss in greater detail include mutuality and continuous improvement.

Mutuality. Collaborations between universities and communities can be highly beneficial, with universities receiving practical experiences for their students and the ability to conduct research, and communities receiving assistance addressing various organizational and community constraints. Even so, there is a real concern within much of the service-learning literature that communities can be forgotten when implementing projects that are meant to be for their benefit (Cruz & Giles, 2000). In terms of the VPA, ensuring the service is beneficial to community partners is something that initially occurred informally through discussions during consultations for client partners, as well as by taking lessons learned from other researchers and articles to develop materials and an evaluative process that clarified expectations (e.g., letter of commitment), provided an agreed-upon time frame for the university and community partner in advance (e.g., survey administration timeline), and worked with clients to identify recommendations that were specified to their organization during consultations (e.g., consultants are advised to develop solutions that are feasible and realistic for the particular organization). However, such informal valuations are not enough, which ultimately prompted the creation of the client satisfaction survey. Analyzing the client responses to this survey has been invaluable in determining their satisfaction with the program and the student consultant with which they worked, as well as whether or not they wished to continue. Additionally, while partners may choose to disclose their name or organization, the survey itself is completely anonymous, and thus more likely to receive authentic reactions (Podsakoff et al., 2012). Having a mechanism to assess the ongoing utility of the service is absolutely crucial in terms of both assessing impact and guiding future program development and decision-making.

Focus on Continuous Improvement. To truly work with the community in a meaningful way, university organizations must focus heavily on continuous improvement. More than simply taking informal feedback into account, it is necessary to build in ways to assess how the organization is doing with respect to both achieving its mission and facilitating student learning. Although the VPA developed in 2009 provided a useful service to participating client organizations and to the students involved, through feedback from clients, students, and faculty, the program has been able to expand its bandwidth, the effectiveness of its services, and the opportunities granted to students. Building feedback mechanisms into a program can be done in multiple ways, such as an anonymous comment box, interviewing individuals involved, conducting focus groups, or implementing a yearly survey. Regardless of how feedback is sought, it is ultimately necessary in order to ensure that any program continues to be useful and relevant.

Conclusion: An Invitation to Join the VPA

Although the VPA and affiliates have collectively served over 300 non-profits across the United States, making a real, lasting impact on both students and the volunteer programs they serve may require more sustained effort and even greater collaboration efforts. One long-term aim is to work with other universities and faculty to produce additional VPA affiliates. Articles and academic pieces such as the current writing represent one method by which such an offer is extended. Interested parties are also invited to check out the website of VPA-UNO, or any other affiliate, for more information.

References

Abraham, K. G., Helms, S., & Presser, S. (2009). How social processes distort measurement: The impact of survey nonresponse on estimates of volunteer work in the United States. *American Journal of Sociology, 114*, 1129–1165.

Allen, J. A., Goh, A., & Rogelberg, S. (2008). *Volunteer program assessment research (VPAR) report for Indianapolis animal care & control*. Indianapolis, IN: Indianapolis Animal Care & Control.

Backer, A. M., Allen, J. A., & Bonilla, D. L. (2012). Identifying and learning from exemplary volunteer resource managers: A look at best practices in managing volunteer resources. *The International Journal of Volunteer Administration, 24*, 65–72.

Bakken, L. L., Núñez, J., & Couture, C. (2014). A course model for building evaluation capacity through a university–community partnership. *American Journal of Evaluation, 35*, 579–593.

Baum, H. S. (2000). Fantasies and realities in university–community partnerships. *Journal of Planning Education and Research, 20,* 234–246.

Birch, E., Perry, D. C., & Taylor Jr, H. L. (2013). Universities as anchor institutions. *Journal of Higher Education Outreach and Engagement, 17,* 7–16.

Bringle, R. G. & Hatcher, J. A. (2002). Campus–community partnerships: The terms of engagement. *Journal of Social Issues, 58,* 503–516.

Brudney, J. L. (1999). The effective use of volunteers: Best practices for the public sector. *Law and Contemporary Problems, 62,* 219–255.

Brudney, J. L. & Hager, M. A. (2004). *Volunteer management practices and retention of volunteers.* Washington, DC: The Urban Institute.

Bureau of Labor Statistics (2016). *Volunteering in the United States – 2015 (BLS Publication No. USDL-14-0314).* Washington, DC: U.S. Government Printing Office.

Carducci, B. J., Deeds, W. C., Jones, J. W. et al. (1987). Preparing undergraduate psychology students for careers in business. *Teaching of Psychology, 14,* 16–20.

Carman, J. G. (2007). Evaluation practice among community-based organizations. *American Journal of Evaluation, 28,* 60–75.

Carman, J. G. (2013). Evaluation in an era of accountability: Unexpected opportunities – A reply to Jill Chouinard. *American Journal of Evaluation, 34,* 261–265.

Carman, J. G. & Fredericks, K. A. (2010). Evaluation capacity and nonprofit organizations: Is the glass half-empty or half-full? *American Journal of Evaluation, 31,* 84–104.

Carman, J. G., & Millesen, J. L. (2005). Nonprofit program evaluation: Organizational challenges and resource needs. *Journal of Volunteer Administration, 23,* 36–43.

Charities Aid Foundation (2017). CAF world giving index 2017: A global view of giving trends. Retrieved from www.cafonline.org/docs/default-source/about-us-publications/cafworldgivingindex2017_2167a_web_040917.pdf.

Chum, A., Mook, L., Handy, F., Schugurensky, D., & Quarter, J. (2013). Degree and direction of paid employee/volunteer interchange in nonprofit organizations. *Nonprofit Management and Leadership, 23,* 409–426.

Cruz, N. I. & Giles, D. E. (2000). Where's the community in service-learning research. *Michigan Journal of Community Service Learning, 7,* 28–34.

Deci, E. L., Ryan, R. M., Gagne, M. et al. (2001). Need satisfaction, motivation, and well-being in the work organizations of a former eastern bloc country: A cross-cultural study of self-determination. *Personality and Social Psychology Bulletin, 27,* 930–942.

Fulbright-Anderson, K., Auspos, P., & Anderson, A. (2001). *Community involvement in partnerships with educational institutions, medical centers, and utility companies.* Baltimore, MD: Annie E. Casey Foundation.

Goulbourne, M. & Embuldeniya, D. (2002). *Assigning economic value to volunteer activity: Eight tools for efficient program management.* Toronto, Ontario: Canadian Centre for Philanthropy.

Hager, M. A. & Brudney, J. L. (2005). Net benefits: Weighing the challenges and benefits of volunteers. *Journal of Volunteer Administration, 23,* 26–31.

Handy, F. & Brudney, J. L. (2007). When to use volunteer labor resources? An organizational analysis for nonprofit management. *Departmental Papers (SPP), 91.* Retrieved from https://repository.upenn.edu/cgi/viewcontent.cgi?article=1092&context=spp_papers.

Horn, P. W, Griffeth, R. W, & Sellaro, L. (1984). The validity of Mobley's (1977) model of employee turnover. *Organizational Behavior and Human Performance, 34,* 141–174.

Illeris, K. (2007). *How we learn: Learning and non-learning in school and beyond*. London: Routledge.

Jaros, S. J. (1997). An assessment of Meyer and Allen's (1991) three-component model of organizational commitment and turnover intentions. *Journal of Vocational Behavior, 51*, 319–337.

Jordi, R. (2011). Reframing the concept of reflection: Consciousness, experiential learning, and reflective learning practices. *Adult Education Quarterly, 61*, 181–197.

King, M. (2010). Skilled volunteers help strapped charities stretch finances. *Chronicle of Philanthropy, 22*, 12.

Laczo, R. M. & Hanisch, K. A. (1999). An examination of behavioral families of organizational withdrawal in volunteer workers and paid employees. *Human Resource Management Review, 9*, 453–477.

McRae, H. (2012). Creating a common space for community engagement. *Canadian Journal of University Continuing Education, 38*, 1–17.

Meyer, J. P., Allen, N. J., & Smith, C. A. (1993). Commitment to organizations and occupations: Extension and test of a three-component conceptualization. *Journal of Applied Psychology, 78*, 538–551.

Murphy, D. M. (2009). Beyond accountability: An empirical study of the factors associated with the use of evaluation for organizational learning in North Carolina's nonprofit sector. *Dissertation Abstracts International, 69*, 5819.

Olien, J. L., Dunn, A. M., Lopina, E. C., & Rogelberg, S. G. (2014). Outreach to nonprofit volunteer programs: Opportunity for impact, improving graduate education, and an invitation to become a part of the volunteer program assessment. *The Industrial Organizational Psychologist, 51*, 51–60.

Pearce, J. L. (1983). Job attitude and motivation differences between volunteers and employees from comparable organizations. *Journal of Applied Psychology, 68*, 646–652.

Pines, A. & Aronson, E. (1988). *Career burnout: Causes and cures*. New York: Free Press.

Podsakoff, P. M., MacKenzie, S. B., Lee, J. Y., & Podsakoff, N. P. (2003). Common method biases in behavioral research: A critical review of the literature and recommended remedies. *Journal of Applied Psychology, 88*, 879.

Podsakoff, P. M., MacKenzie, S. B., & Podsakoff, N. P. (2012). Sources of method bias in social science research and recommendations on how to control it. *Annual Review of Psychology, 63*, 539–569.

Prins, E. (2005). Framing a conflict in a community–university partnership. *Journal of Planning Education and Research, 25*, 57–74.

Rizzo, J. R., House, R. J., & Lirtzman, S. I. (1970). Role conflict and ambiguity in complex organizations. *Administrative Science Quarterly, 15*, 150–163.

Rogelberg, S. G., Allen, J. A., Conway, J. M. et al. (2010). Employee experiences with volunteers. *Nonprofit Management and Leadership, 20*, 423–444.

Rogelberg, S. G. & Fuller, J. A. (2004). Helping those who help others: The necessity, benefits, and challenges associated with pro bono work. *Organization Development Journal, 22*, 61.

Roper, C. D. & Hirth, M. A. (2005). A history of change in the third mission of higher education: The evolution of one-way service to interactive engagement. *Journal of Higher Education Outreach and Engagement, 10*, 3–21.

Schaufeli, W. B., Bakker, A. B., & Salanova, M. (2006). The measurement of work engagement with a short questionnaire: A cross-national study. *Educational and Psychological Measurement, 66*, 701–716.

Schneider, S., Piotrowski, C., & Kass, S. J. (2007). Training masters students through consulting experiences: Benefits and pitfalls. *Organization Development Journal*, *25*, 47–55.

Smith, E. A. (2000). Applying knowledge-enabling methods in the classroom and in the workplace. *Journal of Workplace Learning*, *12*, 236–253.

Spector, P. E. (1985). Measurement of human service staff satisfaction: Development of the job satisfaction survey. *American Journal of Community Psychology*, *13*, 693–713.

Spector, P. E. & Jex, S. M. (1998). Development of four self-report measures of job stressors and strain: Interpersonal conflict at work scale, organizational constraints scale, quantitative workload inventory, and physical symptoms inventory. *Journal of Occupational Health Psychology*, *3*, 356–367.

Spreitzer, G. M. (1995). Psychological empowerment in the workplace: Dimensions, measurement, and validation. *Academy of Management Journal*, *38*, 1442–1465.

Van Dyne, L. & LePine, J. A. (1998). Helping and voice extra-role behaviors: Evidence of construct and predictive validity. *Academy of Management Journal*, *41*, 108–119.

Wing, K. T. (2004). Assessing the effectiveness of capacity-building initiatives: Seven issues for the field. *Nonprofit and Voluntary Sector Quarterly*, *33*, 153–160.

Wu, H. (2011). Social impact of volunteerism. Points of Light Institute. Retrieved from www.pointsoflight.org/sites/default/files/site-content/files/social_impact_of_volunteerism_pdf.pdf.

4 Introducing Engaged Civic Learning

An Emerging Approach to University–Community Partnerships

Rasheda L. Weaver

Engaged civic learning is an emerging pedagogical technique that involves designing courses to meet the dual objectives of advancing student learning *and* community development. While a growing number of universities use experiential education to strengthen student community involvement, educational outcomes, and social responsibility (Hurd, 2006; Ryan, 2017; Saltmarsh, 2005), there is a growing desire to make these experiences more beneficial to the communities these students engage with and learn from (Carpenter & Krist, 2011). Engaged civic learning, however, emphasizes student, faculty, and community outcomes with the aim of benefiting everyone involved (Dahan & Seligsohn, 2013; Watson & D'Italia, 2017). The term was developed by the Office of Civic Engagement at Rutgers University – Camden in Camden, New Jersey, after the office was created in 2010 (Rutgers Today, 2012). Then Chancellor, Wendell Pritchett, PhD, launched the Office of Civic Engagement in order to incorporate service-learning curricula to the mutual benefit of students, faculty, and the community (Rutgers Today, 2012). Contextually, Camden, New Jersey, is one of the most impoverished cities in the United States (Friedman, Haber, & Klothen, 2013). As a self-proclaimed anchor institution (an institution aiming to be a long-term contributor to the community where it operates; Adams, 2003; Weightman, 2013), Rutgers University – Camden uses its Office of Civic Engagement to train scholars to teach engaged civic learning courses that seek to benefit all stakeholders involved.

This chapter is the first academic manuscript of its kind to describe and explore how engaged civic learning is used in practice. To date, other materials on engaged civic learning consist of training workbooks for faculty and students (see Dahan & Seligsohn, 2013 and Watson & D'Italia, 2017 for examples). The chapter examines a case study that involves a university–community partnership pertaining to the restoration of Cooper River Park West, a park in Camden, New Jersey, that has been closed for over 14 years. In the case study, students from two engaged civic learning courses collaborated to develop a survey of community attitudes and desires regarding the restoration of the park. One course revolves around unpacking environmental injustice in urban areas, while the other course teaches students to apply quantitative analysis techniques to examine community-based issues in local organizations. Together, students in both courses work with a local nonprofit organization called Friends of Cooper River Park West to present their survey findings to the Delaware River Port

Authority (DRPA), a government agency that owned the park, but subsequently transferred their ownership to another government agency called the Camden County Municipal Utilities Authority (CCMUA), which promises to open the park in the near future.

This case illustrates that through engaged civic learning, a university and a community organization were able to combine their knowledge and skills to, in a small way, move a community development effort forward. While there are a variety of approaches to experiential education (e.g., service learning, community service, field education) (Carpenter, 2014; Furco, 1996), engaged civic learning differs from these approaches in that it is designed to benefit all stakeholders involved. Specifically, engaged civic learning seeks to enhance students, the communities they serve, the professors guiding them, and the community-based organizations with whom they work. However, aside from the training workbooks mentioned earlier, the academic literature has yet to really explore the concept. This book chapter fills this gap in knowledge by describing a case study that shows how engaged civic learning may be implemented in practice and the impacts it may have on stakeholders.

The first section of this chapter describes the history of engaged civic learning and the training process for faculty. The second section outlines the case study at the center of this book chapter, including the courses involved and the collaborative research project aimed at advancing a local community development effort. The third section describes the benefits the featured case has had on the faculty, students, and community-based organization at the center of it. The final section outlines the conclusions of this chapter and its contributions for research and practice regarding approaches to experiential education.

Engaged Civic Learning

Engaged civic learning was introduced by the Office of Civic Engagement at Rutgers University – Camden, which was developed by the campus's former chancellor, Wendell Pritchett. Rutgers University – Camden is one of three main campuses in the Rutgers University system. It is located in Camden, New Jersey, one of the poorest cities in the United States. Its Office of Civic Engagement received the National Carnegie Foundation Community Engagement Classification in 2015 for its programming that fosters civic values and civic skills, as well as for its work with various community-based, governmental, and educational institutions around the city. Today, their campus strategic plan aims to universalize engaged civic learning courses throughout the entire student curriculum in an effort to foster local and regional community development (Dahan & Seligsohn, 2013; Rutgers University – Camden, 2014).

Over the years, Rutgers University – Camden has used its Office of Civic Engagement as an intentional initiative that aims to foster redevelopment in the once-thriving city. As such, it has joined a growing number of universities and colleges aiming to increase the civic skills and values of students, while also deepening their

Table 4.1 *Common approaches to experiential education*

Common approaches to experiential education	Main benefactors
Engaged civic learning	Service provider
	Faculty member
	Student
	Community
Service learning	Student
	Service provider
Community service	Student
Field education	Service provider
Volunteerism	Student
Internship	Service provider

engagement with community residents and organizations (Saltmarsh, 2005; Welch & Saltmarsh, 2013). However, engaged civic learning is unique to other experiential education approaches because of its strong emphasis on community development (Watson & D'Italia, 2017). Table 4.1 outlines the key characteristics of common approaches to experiential education. The table draws upon the work of Furco (1996) that outlines how these approaches distinguish themselves from one another.

According to Furco (1996), service learning involves service and learning goals of equal weight, and each enhances the learning goals of participants. Service-learning programs are distinguished from other approaches to experiential education by their intention to equally benefit the provider and the recipient of the service, as well as to ensure equal focus on both the service being provided and the learning that is occurring. Community service is the engagement of students in activities that primarily focus on the service being provided, as well as the benefits the service activities have on the recipients (e.g., providing food to the homeless during the holidays). The students receive some benefits by learning more about how their service makes a difference in the lives of the service recipients.

Volunteerism is the engagement of students in activities where the primary emphasis is on the service being provided and the primary intended beneficiary is clearly the service recipient. Field education programs provide students with co-curricular service opportunities that are related to but not fully integrated with their formal academic studies. Students perform the service as a part of a program that is designed primarily to enhance students' understanding of a field of study, while also providing substantial emphasis on the service being provided. Internship programs engage students in service activities primarily for the purpose of providing students with hands-on experiences that enhance their learning or understanding of issues relevant to a particular area of study.

Unlike the other forms of experiential education, engaged civic learning courses take a multidimensional approach to achieving their dual goals of advancing student learning and community development efforts. Watson and D'Italia's (2017) Civic Engagement Faculty Fellows Course Design Workbook shows that characteristics of engaged civic learning courses include:

- Being in a partnership that benefits both the university and community-based organization(s) and communicating about that partnership appropriately;
- A central experiential or community-based component that requires students to participate in its activities;
- The opportunity for students to analyze, interpret, or reflect on course experiences and relate it to its content.

In order to develop and execute engaged civic learning courses, the Office of Civic Engagement hosts periodic training sessions and provides monetary stipends for instructors (referred to as Faculty Fellows) and graduate student teaching assistants (known as Civic Engagement Graduate Fellows). Fellows are provided resources and tools that aid faculty research on engaged scholarship (e.g., a designated librarian for such research). The Office of Civic Engagement also provides faculty with a list of community partners that are local, nonprofit organizations or for-profit, socially conscious businesses and a description of their work. The list enables faculty to identify organizations that are open to collaborating on university initiatives on a short- or long-term basis. The Office of Civic Engagement hosts several networking events throughout the academic year to connect faculty and students to community partners (e.g., Community Leaders Breakfasts). Lastly, since 2017, course instructors must complete and sign a contract that outlines the benefits for all stakeholders prior to the class (shown in Watson & D'Italia, 2017). The contract is for the community organization and faculty member.

While the majority of Faculty Fellows work independently, some are assigned Civic Engagement Graduate Fellows who receive a stipend to coordinate activities, lecture in classes, review/grade some coursework, and/or lead critical reflection sessions. In regard to students taking engaged civic learning courses, students must spend a minimum of 15 hours a semester participating in civic engagement activities (Kopchinski, 2014). These activities vary based on the goals of a course and the community development effort the course seeks to advance.

Case Study

Courses, Collaborative Research Project, and Influence on Local Policy

This case focuses on a collaboration between the two engaged civic learning courses outlined in Table 4.2, that sought to increase student understanding of local community development issues while simultaneously advancing efforts to redevelop a local park. The first course is "Ecology: The Urban Science?" an undergraduate course taught in the Rutgers University – Camden Honors College. The course focuses on exploring and fostering natural ecosystems in urban areas. This particular

Table 4.2 *Engaged civic learning courses for Cooper River Park West*

Course	Academic level	Goals	Main assignments	Expected outcomes
"Ecology: The Urban Science?"	Undergraduate course	The course teaches students about theories related to urban ecology and sustainability while also engaging them in community development efforts	Five assignments (one for each student group) including: 1. Research report on community survey findings 2. Water quality and soil analysis and report 3. Historical literature review 4. Planning a community bird-watching event 5. Developing a social enterprise business plan	– Increase understanding of natural ecosystems – Teach students how to develop an advocacy project and how to use research to inform policy
"Quantitative Analysis II"	Doctoral course	The course aims to train students to conduct research with a local community-based organization as a consultant in order to apply their quantitative analysis skills to a current project related to local community development efforts	Research report on a community-based research study from a local organization. Students must reach out to an organization of choice	– Provide experience conducting community-based research – Increase consulting skills, particularly with community-based organizations

semester, the course was oriented around advancing restoration efforts by local activists aiming to restore Cooper River Park West, a park that was created in the year 2000 when a strip of go-go bars and motels were closed and bulldozed along Admiral Wilson Boulevard to make way for the Republican National Convention in Philadelphia (Riordan, 2015).

Managed by the DRPA, Cooper River Park West, also known as Gateway Park, was developed in its place, but never opened to the public (Kopchinski, 2014; New Jersey Conservation Foundation, 2013). Yet it is one of the largest sources of green space in Camden, one of the poorest cities in the United States (Friedman, Haber, & Klothen, 2013).

Officials reportedly kept the park closed for over 14 years due to a lack of monetary funds needed for its operation; however, Kopchinski (2014) reports that Camden County plans to make a $23 million investment into improving the east side of the park, which borders the predominately white (United States Census Bureau, 2017) township of Pennsauken (Camden County, 2012). Despite investments to the east side of the park, restoration efforts for Cooper River Park West as of 2014 were stagnant (Delaware River Port Authority, 2014). The inconsistency sparked a green space injustice debate as investments were only made to the area of the park bordering the wealthier, whiter township of Pennsauken, despite the great need for green space in the poorer, predominately minority city of Camden (Kopchinski, 2014).

The role of the "Ecology: The Urban Science?" course in regards to restoring the park is to utilize the skills of students to strategically increase public understanding about the value of the park, as well as to gauge resident desire to restore it. Specifically, the course revolves around the following five group projects: (1) a community survey; (2) water quality and soil testing; (3) a historical analysis of the literature regarding the park and green space in Camden; (4) a bird-watching event; and (5) the development of a business plan for a local, aspiring entrepreneur who aimed to establish a canoeing business in the park. The community survey captured information about resident attitudes and utilization of the park. The historical literature review uncovered information about how the park was developed and the role of green space in the region. The water and soil tests aimed to identify the quality of water and soil in the park to determine whether hazardous chemicals are present, which would prevent/delay the park from opening. The bird-watching event was a technique to bring residents and visitors to the park to see how important it is to the community. Lastly, the business plan project sought to help an aspiring entrepreneur start a business in the park once it is restored, while also conveying the potential economic value the park may bring by attracting businesses. Each student group worked with mentors and consultants to guide them in their efforts. While each project conveys the importance of the park as an untapped asset in Camden, this book chapter focuses on the community survey project and its influence on local government decisions to restore the park.

Being that the undergraduate students in the "Ecology: The Urban Science?" course had little experience with survey development and administration, a doctoral student in the engaged civic learning course (now the author of this chapter) entitled "Quantitative Analysis II" was recruited to design the community survey. "Quantitative Analysis II" is a doctoral-level course that is taught in the Department of Public Policy and Administration at Rutgers University – Camden in the Public Affairs – Community Development PhD program. The course trains students to conduct quantitative analyses using the statistical program STATA and requires them to reach out to local community-based organizations that may utilize their data analysis skills for research on their organization that is related to community development.

During the first two weeks of the graduate course, students must select an organization to provide consultations for. Once chosen, the students work with the organization to collect, manage, analyze, and/or interpret data on a project. Students are required to write up their findings in a final research report and to present their work in class and (if applicable) at a meeting with or on behalf of the organization (e.g., a government meeting). The doctoral student from the "Quantitative Analysis II" class advised undergraduate students in the "Ecology: The Urban Science?" course on research-driven survey development. In order to aid in the work of the Friends of Cooper River Park West, the students designed a survey (provided in Appendix 4.1) that examines community attitudes regarding the current and prospective utilization of Cooper River Park West. The undergraduate students disseminated the survey at a bird-watching event at the site of the closed park and at institutions (e.g., schools, universities) throughout the city. The doctoral student analyzed the preliminary results and provided them to the "Ecology: The Urban Science?" students and their professor to present at a pre-scheduled meeting with the DRPA, who knew the students were working on the project with the Friends of Cooper River Park West.

In April 2014, students presented the survey findings at the DRPA board meeting, where park stakeholders and community members also advocated for the park's restoration. The findings revealed the following: (1) the lack of maintenance of the park relates to residents feeling that it is unsafe; (2) residents desired safety features such as lighting, park rangers, and a park curfew because many walk through or near the park during their daily activities and some even use the park's river for fishing; and (3) residents desire amenities such as biking and walking trails, playgrounds, and picnic tables as opposed to concert venues and sports fields. At a meeting that took place several months after the results were revealed, the DRPA announced they would transfer ownership of the park to the CCMUA (Kopchinski, 2014). They mentioned the community survey results while discussing their decision. The transfer of ownership was completed in October 2014 at a CCMUA meeting where the CCMUA announced they would partner with the New Jersey Conservation Foundation to manage and maintain the park (Camden County Municipal Utilities Authority, 2014).

In summary, students in the two engaged civic learning courses successfully helped to transfer ownership of Cooper River Park West to a government entity that aims to restore it. In addition, the Cooper River Gateway West Vision Plan was developed, in part, with the survey results informing the design and amenities of the park in accordance with community needs (Kopchinski, 2014). However, while the transfer of ownership is complete, the soil analysis tests are positive for chemicals. The park is currently undergoing a costly remediation process to remove these chemicals before it may be opened to the public. Friends of Cooper River Park West and other community organizations and residents occasionally hold meetings about the status the park.

Benefits to Stakeholders

Though Cooper River Park West is still in the process of restoration, there are several benefits that have come from using engaged civic learning in this case. These benefits are outlined below.

Benefits to Students. Like other experiential education programs, students in the two classes saw their professional skills advance, as well as their interest in the courses and their community (Ryan, 2017). Students learned how to organize events, recruit participants for research, and utilize research to influence government policy. Seeing the attention brought to the development of the park after many years of closure due to their efforts increased their understanding of the power their education and training provides them. One unforeseen benefit for students in this case is the media attention brought to their work. The doctoral student (now a professor and the author of this chapter) was featured in several local newspapers and elected to the board of trustees of a local, nonprofit organization. One undergraduate student from the community survey group received summer funding to continue research on this project and also received media attention for his role in the project.

Another outcome of this research on students relates to a deepened understanding of the challenges that arise when conducting research pertaining to community development. For instance, while the project took place in 2014, students have seen how issues pertaining to the funding and implementation of soil remediation efforts have left the park unrestored years later. These issues are important for community development scholars to understand because it prepares them for the diversity of issues that influence community development, such as time, funding, policy, and public support. In addition, some students, particularly the doctoral student, were not prepared for the amount of work this project would take after the classes were over. In order to see the true influence of the community survey, the doctoral student attended various meetings over the course of one year and was called on for further quantitative analyses on several occasions. As a result of this and similar instances in other courses at Rutgers University – Camden, the Office of Civic Engagement outlines the expected completion date of each engaged civic learning course collaboration to ensure all stakeholders are discussing the boundaries of the work prior to collaborations.

Benefits to the Community. Another beneficiary in this case is the community, especially Friends of Cooper River Park West, who saw their initiative progress. Results from the community survey motivated the transfer of ownership of the park from the DRPA to the CCMUA and were used to design a vision plan for the park's redevelopment. Though Friends of Cooper River Park West have been advocating to restore the park for years, collaborating with Rutgers University – Camden via engaged civic learning courses helped them spread awareness to the university, the community, and the region through media outlets, promotional events, and courses. The outcome of this collaboration supports existing research on university–community partnerships that suggests such partnerships can be of real benefit to communities over time (Carpenter & Krist, 2011). As such, engaged civic learning courses have the potential to make a substantial impact on the city of Camden. One challenge the community may face, however, is a lack of understanding about why the park has taken years to open to the public. While residents that attend community meetings on the project may understand this, those reading about it in the newspaper may not. Thus, making an effort to communicate with the public is important. Several people involved in the project have been featured in news articles to foster public awareness (Riordan, 2015).

Benefits to Faculty. This case was also beneficial for faculty members, who were able to write research manuscripts and gain public attention for their work. Some faculty members associated with the project were featured in local news stories and saw an increase in their civic and leadership involvement in the city overall. Creating opportunities for scholars to benefit from experiential education initiatives is beneficial to their overall success and desire to do this kind of work. A growing number of scholars seek to engage in experiential education initiatives (Post, Ward, Longo, & Saltmarsh, 2016), but may have difficulty doing so because they often take a good amount of time and are often not considered in tenure and promotional requirements (Lewing & York, 2017). Developing ways to support engaged scholars in their work is essential, especially given that engaged civic learning is one tool Rutgers University – Camden is using to foster redevelopment in Camden. As mentioned above, Rutgers University – Camden now has trained librarians who provide resources and support for their Faculty Fellows in an effort to encourage them to publish research and promote their engaged civic learning efforts as well. These librarians also undergo specialized engaged civic learning training and attend networking workshops and events with faculty and students.

Conclusion

This chapter introduces engaged civic learning to the literature on experiential education. Engaged civic learning is a pedagogical technique that involves designing courses to meet the dual objectives of advancing student learning and community development. It was developed by Rutgers University – Camden in an effort to use university–community partnerships to advance community development in Camden, New Jersey, one of the poorest cities in the United States. In order to illustrate how engaged civic learning courses may benefit various stakeholders, this book chapter examines a case study of two engaged civic learning courses that successfully influenced restoration efforts regarding a closed urban park in Camden. Based on the case study, this chapter argues that engaged civic learning is an approach to experiential education (and university–community partnerships in particular) that strives to benefit all stakeholders involved. Engaged civic learning courses are intentionally designed for students to gain practical and experiential skills, for faculty to strengthen their community networks and publishing opportunities, and for community organizations to enhance the visibility and human capital needed to advance their initiatives.

Research Implications

By introducing the concept of engaged civic learning, this chapter contributes to research that promotes experiential education, as well as community development. Scholars studying experiential education should explore the concept of engaged civic learning further and utilize rigorous research methods to examine its impact on its stakeholders. In addition, studies comparing engaged civic learning to other forms of experiential education (e.g., service learning) should strive to deepen understanding about when and in what geographic contexts using these approaches is most suitable. Another avenue for research is to examine how engaged civic learning may be applied in economically diverse geographic areas, as it has only been applied in a distressed geographic context. Similarly, scholars studying community development may seek to explore its use as a strategy for improving distressed communities over time. In the Rutgers University – Camden strategic plan, engaged civic learning is seen as a community development strategy that may slowly improve socioeconomic conditions in Camden, New Jersey. Examining the efficacy of using this strategy would advance knowledge about its usefulness to communities.

Practical and Pedagogical Implications

This book chapter contributes to practice by serving as an example of *how* engaged civic learning can be used as a pedagogical tool for fostering student learning and community development. Instructors seeking to teach engaged civic learning courses may use this chapter as a guide for teaching students about different approaches to experiential education. It can be used to explain and illustrate the concept of engaged civic learning or to compare it to other community development strategies as shown in Table 4.1. Instructors, as well as university offices that promote experiential education, may also use this chapter to guide them in their development of engaged civic learning courses.

As experiential education becomes an increasingly important tool that universities use to transform students into engaged citizens, this book chapter is valuable for understanding this emerging approach and how it can foster student learning along with community development. Some pedagogical lessons learned from this case include:

- Developing a short guide that outlines community partners for the university or a course that faculty and/or students can use to choose potential collaborations.
  - A major principle of good community partnerships is good communication (Community–Campus Partnerships for Health, 2006). Communicating early and regularly with community partners is essential for successful experiential education initiatives (Carpenter & Krist, 2011). Developing a guide that outlines community partners, their contact information, and a short description of their work or mission may aid in the design of engaged civic learning courses. This was key to kick-starting the "Quantitative Analysis II" course, which required students to choose partners early in the semester. The guide used in this course

was developed by the Office of Civic Engagement and is provided in their Faculty Fellows Training Program and their Civic Engagement Graduate Fellows Training Program.

- Organizing events that connect faculty, community partners, and students.
  - The Rutgers University – Camden Office of Civic Engagement hosts various events throughout the year to connect faculty, community partners, and students. One of their most successful events (in regards to high attendance rates) for developing engaged civic learning courses is their Community Leadership Breakfasts. The breakfasts happen twice a year and consist of faculty, community partners, and students coming to together in a large banquet room in the university campus center to simply eat breakfast and network for about one hour. Prior to the event, participants complete a short survey on the focus area of their work (e.g., poverty, human rights, environment) and are then seated with people who have similar interests at the breakfast. The event is very popular and leads to various engaged civic learning and other academic collaborations each year.
- Designing an engaged civic learning resource guide.
  - As mentioned, the Rutgers University – Camden Office of Civic Engagement now trains librarians to support and develop resources that aid their Faculty Fellows and their Civic Engagement Graduate Fellows with their work. The librarians developed a web-based resource guide of academic journals and books that have work related to experiential education in order to provide examples to faculty regarding where and how they may publish their work.
- Creating a contract for all stakeholders to sign before the project starts.
  - Factors such as clear expectations and having good communication are essential to good university–community partnerships (Carpenter & Krist, 2011; Community–Campus Partnerships for Health, 2006). Having a contract that outlines the benefits of the engaged civic learning course for all stakeholders and expected time boundaries/project duration aids in making expectations clear and establishing good communication in these relationships. While a contract was not used in this particular case, a contract template was developed by the Office of Civic Engagement and is now provided in their training programs because, over time, the office realized it was needed to prevent issues like the one in this case where the doctoral student expected to work on the project for one semester, but ended up working on the project for one year.

Acknowledgments

There were many people and organizations involved with this amazing, community-changing project. As such, there are many people and organizations to thank. I would first like to thank Rutgers University – Camden for creating an academic environment filled with courses that have the dual goals of enhancing student learning and local community development efforts. I would also like to thank the Office of Civic Engagement for developing a curriculum and a host of positive community–university partnerships with various organizations in Camden, New Jersey, so that this kind of engaged scholarship may take place. I would like to thank Tom Knoche, the instructor of the class "Ecology: The Urban Science?" and Dr. Adam Okulicz-Kozaryn, the instructor of the course "Quantitative Analysis II" for developing the courses featured in this chapter. Tom Knoche has also played various roles in this community development effort and has been instrumental in its progress. I am also grateful and honored to have worked with organizations like the Friends of Cooper River Park West, the New Jersey Conservation Foundation, the CCMUA, and the DRPA. I would like to thank the students from the "Ecology: The Urban Science?" class who worked with me on this project, especially Gary Kopchinski, Sara Mignano, and Maggie Bennett. Last but not least, there are many people that showed up to protest and advocate for the restoration of Cooper River Park West – I do not know all of their names, but I thank them for their passion and commitment to restoring this large source of open, green space in the city of Camden, New Jersey.

Appendix 4.1

Cooper River Park West Attitudes and Utilization Survey

Demographic Information

1. Please identify your age group (Circle)
   15 & under, 16–25, 36–45, 46–55, 56–65, 66 or over

2. What is your gender? (Circle)
   Male, Female

3. Are you a resident of Camden?
   a. No
   b. Yes

Current Use

1. Have you ever heard of Cooper River Park West?
   i. No
   ii. Yes

2. Do you currently use the park?
   i. No
   ii. Yes

3. If you answered no, why don't you use the park?

   _____

   _____

4. If you answered yes, please answer the following.
a) What do you currently use the park for?

   _____

   _____

b) What time of day do you use the park? (Circle all that apply)
   i.   Morning
   ii. Afternoon
   iii. Evening

c) How do you get to the park? (Circle all that apply)
   i.   Walk
   ii. Drive
   iii. Bike
   iv. Bus

5. Do you use currently use any other parks in Camden?
   i.   No
   ii. Yes   (Name)_____

Prospective Use

1. What recreational amenities/attractions would you like the park to have? (Answer all that apply)
   a. Community events
   b. Sports fields/courts
   c. Playgrounds
   d. Walking/biking trails
   e. Concession stands
   f. Picnic tables
   g. Vending machines
   h. Canoes/kayaks
   i. Historical attractions/information
   j. Education about wildlife
   k. Other_____

2. What safety features would you like the park to have?
   a. Fences
   b. Lights
   c. Telephones
   d. Park rangers/security personnel
   e. Other:

   _____

   _____

3. Would you prefer an enforced park curfew?
   a. No
   b. Yes

Attitudes

1. How do you currently feel about the maintenance of the park?

   _____

   _____

2. Do you feel safe in the park?
   a. No

      i. Why not?

         _____

         _____

   b. Yes

References

Adams, C. (2003). The meds and eds in urban economic development. *Journal of Urban Affairs*, *25*(5), 571–588.

Camden County (2012). Cooper River Park Vision Plan. Camden County. Retrieved from www.camdencounty.com/sites/default/files/files/1132-cooper%20river%20booklet.pdf.

Camden County Municipal Utilities Authority (2014). October board meeting minutes. Camden County Municipal Utilities Authority. Retrieved from www.ccmua.org/wp-content/uploads/2014/11/201411181506.pdf.

Carpenter, H. L. (2014). A look at experiential education in nonprofit-focused graduate degree programs. *The Journal of Nonprofit Education and Leadership*, *4*(2), 114–138.

Carpenter, H. L. & Krist, P. (2011). Practice makes perfect: Impact and use of nonprofit master students applied projects on nonprofit organizations in the San Diego region. *The Journal of Nonprofit Education and Leadership*, *1*(2), 61–77.

Community-Campus Partnerships for Health (2006). Principles of good community–campus partnerships. Retrieved from www.unf.edu/uploadedFiles/aa/ccbl/Principles%20of%20Good%20Comm_Campus%20Partnerships%20CAP%202_0%20OCT%2030%20Wkshp.pdf.

Dahan, T. & Seligsohn, A. J. (2013). Engaged civic learning course design workbook. Rutgers Camden. Retrieved from https://leap.aacu.org/toolkit/wp-content/uploads/2013/07/Engaged-Civic-Learning-Course-Design-Workbook-2013.pdf.

Delaware River Port Authority (2014). Delaware River Port Authority March 2014 board meeting minutes. Delaware River Port Authority. Retrieved from www.drpa.org/publish/library/3%2019%2014%20DRPA%20Board%20Meeting%20Minutes.pdf.

Friedman, J., Haber, C., & Klothen, E. B. (2013). Educating young people about law in a disadvantaged city: Rutgers University School of Law and the City of Camden, New Jersey. *Denver University Law Review*, *90*(4), 937–957.

Furco, A. (1996). Service-learning: A balanced approach to experiential education. *Service Learning, General*. 128. Retrieved from www.shsu.edu/academics/cce/documents/ Service_Learning_Balanced_Approach_To_Experimental_Education.pdf.

Hurd, C. A. (2006). Is service-learning effective?: A look at current research. Retrieved from www.fresnostate.edu/craig/depts-programs/mktg/documents/Is%20S.L.% 20Effective-.pdf.

Kopchinski, G. (2014). Cooper River Park West: Its time is now. *Unpublished Honors Internship Paper*. Camden, New Jersey: Rutgers, The State University of New Jersey – Camden.

Lewing, J. M., & York, P. E. (2017). Millennial generation faculty: Why they engage in service learning. *Journal of Community Engagement & Higher Education, 9*(3), 35–47.

Post, M. A., Ward, E., Longo, N. V., & Saltmarsh, J. (2016). Introducing next-generation engagement. In M. A. Post, E. Ward, N. V. Longo, & J. Saltmarsh (Eds.), *Next generation engagement and the future of higher education: Publicly engaged scholars* (pp. 1–11). Sterling, VA: Stylus Publishing.

Riordan, K. (2015). 15 years later, park is still closed. Retrieved from http://articles.philly .com/2015–06-10/news/63228322_1_gateway-park-camden-county-cooper- river-park-west.

Rutgers Today (2012). Rutgers presents human dignity awards to six honorees. Retrieved from https://news.rutgers.edu/news-release/rutgers-presents-human-dignity -awards-six-honorees/20120427#.WjPqvtOGOCQ.

Rutgers University – Camden (2014). Shaping our future: Rutgers University – Camden strategic directions for the campus, 2014–19. Retrieved from www.camden.rut gers.edu/pdf/StrategicPlan.pdf.

Rutgers University – Camden (2016). Engaged civic learning. Retrieved from www.cam den.rutgers.edu/civic-engagement/engaged-civic-learning.

Ryan, G. R. (2017). Social and cognitive outcomes of service-learning: Results from a pre- post and control group comparison. *Journal of Community Engagement and Higher Education, 9*(3), 19–34.

Saltmarsh, J. (2005). The civic promise of service learning. *Liberal Education, 91*(2), 50–55.

United States Census Bureau (2018). City quick facts. United States Census Bureau. Retrieved from www.census.gov/quickfacts/fact/table/camdencitynewjersey/ PST045217.

Watson, N., & D'Italia, M. (2017). Civic Engagement Faculty Fellows Course Design Workbook. Retrieved from www.camden.rutgers.edu/civic-engagement/faculty-fel lows-program.

Weightman, J. (2013). Anchor institutions driving redevelopment of Detroit and other cities. Retrieved from https://urbanland.uli.org/planning-design/anchor-institutions-driv ing-redevelopment-of-detroit-other-cities/.

Welch, M. & Saltmarsh, J. (2013). Current practice and infrastructures for campus centers of community engagement. *Journal of Higher Education Outreach and Engagement, 17*(4), 25–55.

5 Service-Learning Partnerships in Secondary Education

Rachael A. Arens

Service learning is a pedagogical practice that allows teachers to immerse students in hands-on projects that solve problems for their community, while still incorporating state standards/content into the experience (Service Learning Academy, n.d.). Students develop civic responsibility, twenty-first century skills (core competencies such as collaboration, digital literacy, critical thinking, and problem-solving that advocates believe schools need to teach to help students thrive in today's world; Rich, 2010), and tools for self-reflection and personal growth. Many universities, such as the University of Nebraska Omaha (UNO), incorporate service learning into their Community Outreach departments with the hopes of connecting the university with local schools and members of a community to emphasize critical thinking and content with real-world experiences (Service Learning Academy, n.d.). According to Furco (1996), service learning is different from other hands-on learning opportunities, such as community service or internships. In typical community service projects, students are not connecting the experience to content standards, and during internships, students are usually participating in the service at his/her own benefit, rather than for the benefit of the community. Service learning distinguishes itself "by the intention to equally benefit the provider and the recipient of the service as well as to ensure equal focus on both the service being provided and the learning that is occurring" (Furco, 1996, p. 12). All parties benefit from the experience, and students learn content, civic duty, twenty-first century skills, reflection, and content standards while actively participating in the project.

To implement service learning, all parties must be aware of the needs of the community and of the classroom learning. Projects must be properly matched to achieve both learning and civic duty. When choosing a community partner, teachers should work with their students to incorporate their interests while still following the curriculum. Allow students to brainstorm community issues they would like to work on so that they can have increased buy-in from the beginning of the project. Student choice also allows students to be involved in inquiry-based learning by allowing them to conduct background research and develop a methodology for their ideas. For example, Rachael Arens' Horticulture students at Omaha Northwest High School, Steve Rodie's Environmental Sustainability students at UNO, and the City of Omaha identified a local problem that needed a solution. According to Clean Solutions for Omaha (n.d.):

> The federal government has identified at least 772 communities nationwide, including Omaha, that must reduce their combined sewer system overflows in order

to improve water quality in the receiving stream. This federal mandate means Omaha must reduce the number of combined sewer system overflows of raw sewage to the Missouri River and Papillion Creek from about 52 per year to under eight per year or achieve 85 percent capture of the wet weather volume. Unlike federal mandated improvements to wastewater treatment facilities in the 1970s and 1980s that provided federal funding to support the projects, the federal mandate to reduce the occurrence of combined sewer overflow (CSO) discharges to the receiving streams is not federally funded; thus, local users of the system are required to pay for the improvements.

To alleviate this local problem, Northwest High School, UNO, and the City of Omaha decided to engineer and build a rain garden on the Northwest High School campus to control storm water runoff and to collect surface pollutants, while also promoting native plant growth for declining pollinator species. The garden collects stormwater runoff from the roof of the greenhouse and provides an outdoor learning environment for Northwest classes.

Both high school and college students gained many benefits from participating in the project. They learned about content standards of biodiversity, chemical analysis, energy cycling, native plants, environmental sustainability, the scientific method and designing a research project, and the engineering principles aligned with the Next Generation Science Standards. Not only did they learn content, but also both the Northwest and UNO students acquired many twenty-first century skills in engineering the project, such as using tools effectively to construct and plant the garden. The students also learned valuable leadership skills and effective communication skills outside of classroom hours with students of varying ages in order to develop an aesthetically pleasing, functional design. These designs were then presented to the community at UNO, to an Omaha Green Tour, and to low-impact development conferences. The rain garden not only serves as an outdoor learning space for many science classes, but also other cross-curricular courses at Northwest High School. For example, the Art class students designed a rain barrel to collect additional runoff from the roof, and the technology students created a website that connects to a QR code on a sign in front of the rain garden. The website introduces the purpose of the garden, and students can learn about the different plant and insect species present in the garden.

The City of Omaha also mutually benefitted from the collaboration by fulfilling the mandate set by the federal government, while also creating awareness and activism among Omaha youth. Because the rain garden proved to be a major development for the city, the students created and submitted an informational video to the Samsung Solve for Tomorrow Contest. This project placed first in the state of Nebraska and earned Northwest High School $20,000 worth of Samsung technology. Students were asked to give interviews for the news media, and the project was displayed in National Geographic's Next Generation Environmental Leaders webpage, a huge accolade for the students.

The rain garden project provided an excellent example of a successful service-learning project in which all parties involved benefitted, student learning occurred, and student civic responsibility increased. Service learning can be achieved across any age group or subject if a willing partner can be appropriately matched.

To appropriately match, teachers must first ask themselves, "What do I want my students to learn?" By answering this question, the teacher can then begin researching local problems that can address his/her standards. A university with a Service Learning department, such as UNO, may also facilitate this research by identifying a local need and then matching the teacher with a researcher or community partner with similar goals. This newfound relationship will not only benefit students' learning, but also foster the teacher's growth by giving him/her a more meaningful approach to teaching and improving engagement in the classroom.

To make the project successful, the school, university, and community partners identified common goals among everyone involved. It was imperative to ensure

Observe: Observe genuine needs and issues within the community.

Research: Gather data, artifacts, and opinions on the community's needs and analyze methods that were already implemented.

Student Ownership: Students make the conscientious decision to take ownership of the local issue and take action.

Collaboration: Identify and network with the university and local partners to establish a team to develop a solution to the local need.

Construct a Plan: Set up meetings to ensure goals are developed, all foreseen materials are purchased, deadlines are established for project completion, and dates of project implementation are solidified. The plan must also include learning objectives that align with content curriculum and include secondary plans in case the original does not work.

Take Action: Students will work with the university and local partners to solve the local issue they identified. During this time, learning and engagement will be monitored by the teacher.

Evaluating Outcomes: Various assessments will be provided for students to determine engagement and learning. Students will self-reflect to determine personal and academic growth and their impact on their environment/community. Overall success of the project will also be evaluated and modifications will be made to ensure project sustainability.

Communicate Results: Share the project's results with the school, public, news, etc., to showcase student learning and commitment to improving their local communities.

Go Deeper: All parties will reflect on the impact of the project and determine future modifications. They will generate further questions, and at this time, they can maintain their current project, modify the project, or add extensions onto the project.

Repeat if Necessary

Figure 5.1 *Service-learning model for project implementation*

everyone benefitted to create a sustainable project and prevent burnout. Choosing partners who were accountable and worked well with youth was also important for the success of the project. All people involved worked out a timeline of project implementation and a list of items needed and worked together to write grants for additional funds needed.

To assess student learning and engagement throughout service-learning projects, teachers can implement a variety of assessments. Teachers can provide pre- and post-surveys to determine student learning of the content. In these surveys, students can also indicate their level of engagement compared to traditional classroom teaching. Teachers can also have students write reflections, keep a learning portfolio, create project posters, present their learning to the class/public, or incorporate project questions into content-related tests/assignments. These assessments differ from other classes without service learning because they include meaningful self-reflections that allow students to go above and beyond just the content. The teacher can also assess student learning and engagement by evaluating the amount of time students stay on task, the amount of time students participate and voice their opinions, and the level of questions the students formulate.

The following case studies in this chapter underwent a series of steps to ensure that all parties benefitted from the experience and that student learning was taking place. Figure 5.1 shows the protocol that was followed in each service-learning project.

Case Example

Rachael Arens' Horticulture and Environmental Science classes also collaborated with Stephanie Lynham's UNO International classes (ILUNO) for the service-learning "Seed to Salad" project to complement the learning opportunities of the rain garden/outdoor classroom space. The Seed to Salad project began in the fall of 2014 with the expectation of allowing students to investigate foreign food, plants, and food crises around the world. By doing this, both Northwest and ILUNO students learn about each other's cultures and get to transgress racial or gender stereotypes and barriers often placed in today's society.

Both the Northwest and ILUNO students began by meeting in each other's classrooms, where students presented on their respective cultures. They prepared cultural dishes for each other, focusing on the plants and foods from the areas of the world where they originate. They also took a field trip to the food bank for the Heartland food pantry to learn about food shortages, and then boxed foods for hungry families. After getting to learn about one another's cultures and foods/plants, the students decided they wanted to create their own community garden to provide healthy produce for the Northwest community. Rachael Arens wrote and received a grant from Big Gardens to install 12 wooden garden beds on Northwest High School's campus. The ILUNO students helped the Northwest Horticulture students and Big Gardens build the boxes and then fill them with topsoil.

Once the boxes were built, the Horticulture and ILUNO students met to discuss the plants that they wanted to be planted into the boxes. They presented on plants from their own cultures, medicinal plants, produce, and native plants to Nebraska. They had to research whether the plants could handle the hardiness zones of Nebraska, how the plants were to be cared for, and spacing requirements for each plant. Once the plant lists were developed, seeds were purchased and the ILUNO and Northwest students met multiple times to start the seeds in Northwest's greenhouse and care for them as they grew large enough to be transplanted outside in late spring. After the last average frost-free date, the ILUNO students assisted the Northwest Horticulture students in transplanting the plants and producing plugs to the garden beds outside. They also practiced directly planting seeds into the garden beds for some of the plants that could not be transplanted, putting up fencing to keep out rabbits, and labeling all the plants to inform community members of the produce. Both Northwest and ILUNO students learned best gardening practices and were able to learn about plants from other cultures in the process. The collaboration of preparing and planting the community garden each spring continues to be a highlight among both student groups as they get to break down cultural and language barriers and come together for the common purpose of feeding others. This is important since Northwest High School is a Title 1 school where 74 percent of families qualify for free/reduced lunches (Nebraska Department of Education, n.d.). The produce from the community garden is used in both Horticulture and Food courses at Northwest, but also for families and students to acquire fresh produce and bond with other community members while gardening. This teaches both the ILUNO and Northwest students not only content skills, but also civic responsibility to help feed the hungry within their community.

After learning how to garden, the Northwest and ILUNO students created a "Bridge to Worlds" painting for the Adams Park Community Center in North Omaha and a "Foods Around the World" painting for the Sienna Francis homeless shelter in downtown Omaha. Both centers needed artwork to beautify their empty walls and to brighten the spirits of each center's members.

Throughout the gardening project, both the Northwest High School and ILUNO students learned about gardening practices, energy cycling, global food shortages, native plants and pollinator species, pest management, and environmental and civic awareness. The ILUNO students were also able to benefit by practicing the English language with the Northwest students. The community also experienced the following benefits: (1) the Northwest community had free access to a community garden with fresh produce; (2) the Sienna Francis House and Adams Park Community Center gained student-made, culture/food-inspired artwork to beautify their walls; and (3) the Sienna Francis House had boxed foods prepared for them. All of these needs were met within the community while students were able to learn about each other's cultures and break down stereotypes often constructed due to lack of understanding.

The Northwest and ILUNO students also built an aquaponics system to support the Seed to Salad project. They partnered with Whispering Roots, a local nonprofit organization, to assist with the design and materials and to find a sustainable way to provide fresh food for the Northwest community. Aquaponics combines aquaculture (raising fish) and hydroponics (growing produce) in one integrated system. The fish waste provides a natural nutrition source for the produce, and the plants, in turn, filter and clean the water for the fish. The students learned about nutrient cycling and species interactions with both biotic and abiotic factors. This allowed them to fully understand how the system worked as they were building it. The students then grew fresh pepper plants, kale, and basil, and raised tilapia fish in their aquaponics system. This produce was given to the Food classes at Northwest, as well as to the families of Northwest students.

Northwest High School and ILUNO students also helped build community gardens in other locations in Omaha after they gained expertise from building the community garden at Northwest High School. They partnered with Nebraskans for Civic Reform to address the food desert problems in North Omaha. They discussed the issues that lead to food deserts and the community gardens' provision of not only nutritious food, but also community involvement. In the spring of 2016, the students started construction of a community garden at the Sherman Center in North Omaha. They constructed boxes, filled the boxes with soil, planted seeds, spread mulch, and mixed compost. They returned the following year to help with planting and ensuring weeds were not spreading into the boxes. The ILUNO students enjoyed seeing multiple sides of Omaha and felt proud that they could help feed others on a different side of the world. From data collected from student pre- and post-surveys, the Northwest students were happy that they could give back to their community and provide their expertise of gardening to others. In this case, they were the teachers providing direction on construction, planting, composing, and pest control.

The Seed to Salad service-learning project also supported the community garden in other ways. For example, many pollinator species are declining due to habitat infringement, pesticides, etc., and these pollinators are crucial for produce production. The Northwest and ILUNO students decided also to focus on this issue and collaborated with the Omaha Henry Doorly Zoo and the Monarch Watch program. Monarch Watch is a nonprofit education, conservation, and research program based at the University of Kansas that focuses on the monarch butterfly, its habitat, and its fall migration (Lovett, 2017). They asked for citizen scientists around the globe to collect data on the monarch butterflies that could not have been collected by one or a small group of researchers alone. The Henry Doorly Zoo trained the students in how to tag monarch butterflies' wings and then upload this information to a national database. The students tracked and monitored the southern migration patterns of the butterflies as well as the population numbers of the species. Throughout the project, students learned about content standards of biodiversity, populations, human impacts, and species interactions. Students also learned science fieldwork techniques and had the opportunity to work with technology and an international research database.

The project also served as an incredibly engaging method for students to obtain content knowledge. Students were actively involved in capturing monarch butterflies in large nets and then carefully placing sticker tags on their delicate wings. They also had to determine the sex of the butterflies, record the size, and identify where each butterfly was found. Students had a lot of fun running around capturing the butterflies and were more engaged than if the teacher had provided direct instruction about the content in a typical classroom setting. Both ILUNO and Northwest students also had time to reflect on how monitoring the monarch butterflies impacted their community and world. To reflect on the experience, students discussed the impacts though a Socratic Seminar discussion. A Socratic Seminar is a pedagogical method that "is a formal discussion, based on a text, in which the leader asks open-ended questions. Within the context of the discussion, students listen closely to the comments of others, thinking critically for themselves, and articulate their own thoughts and their responses to the thoughts of others. They learn to work cooperatively and to question intelligently and civilly" (Israel, 2002, p. 89). Students discussed how human interactions can impact biodiversity and how their own actions can directly or indirectly hurt the monarch or other pollinators' populations. They also discussed what they could do to make a difference, how they could create more awareness, and how they could encourage others to also work toward preserving biodiversity and ecosystems.

The Seed to Salad project also incorporated water quality in its efforts to teach students about healthy gardening practices. Both Northwest High School and ILUNO students collaborated with the UNO Watershed Network to test for atrazine levels in local streams. Atrazine is a common herbicide applied in the United States that has been found to be an endocrine disruptor for many aquatic species, including fish and frogs. This causes a trophic (the feeding habits or food relationships of different organisms in a food chain; Biology Online, n.d.) imbalance in many aquatic ecosystems, so UNO wanted to test for the presence of this pesticide around the state of Nebraska. UNO does not have enough researchers to collect data multiple times through the spring around the state, so they called out to high schools to act as citizen scientists to collect the large amounts of data for them.

Northwest Environmental and Horticulture students as well as the ILUNO students were initially trained by UNO researchers to collect and test water samples. This taught students how to look for microorganisms and how to work with the various technologies needed. The students then collected water samples every week in April and May from the Papio Creek near Northwest High School. They tested for water turbidity, for high phosphate and nitrate levels, and for the presence of atrazine. Students then uploaded this information to an online database that allowed them to also see data from other schools around the state. Students learned about standards of energy cycling, human impacts, and biodiversity, and they were able to work with scientific technology and to collaborate with other citizen scientists around the state and at UNO. Students also reflected on how pesticides impact ecosystems and how integrated pest management and best management practices should be utilized when growing crops. Students weighed the pros and cons of utilizing pesticides and their economic benefits versus organic farming, and the Northwest and ILUNO students discussed the differences between farming practices and exposure to pesticides within their own communities and countries.

Lastly, Northwest High School and ILUNO students focused on another water quality issue in Omaha for their Seed to Salad project. Since Omaha has a combined sewer system, any pollution that enters the storm drains will run into local creeks and eventually major rivers. Consequently, litter and illegal dumping in storm drains pollute our streams/rivers and negatively impact aquatic ecosystems. To alleviate this problem, the Northwest High School and ILUNO students collaborated with Keep Omaha Beautiful to clean and label storm drains around Omaha. Keep Omaha Beautiful is a nonprofit organization in Omaha that "is committed to litter reduction, community beautification, and education on recycling and environmental steward-ship in the Omaha area" (Keep Omaha Beautiful, n.d.). They reach out to community members and schools to help them with their cleanup efforts in order to keep up with the rapid accumulation of pollution in Omaha's streets.

Keep Omaha Beautiful taught the Northwest and ILUNO students about pollution, human impacts on the ecosystem, and the difference they can make in their com-munity. After the initial instruction, maps showing all the streets and storm drains in Northwest Omaha were provided to the students. The students were then taught how to properly clean and label the storm drains, how to let others know that the drains had been cleaned, and also how to create an awareness of pollution prevention. The students then walked around the streets, cleaning and labeling every individual storm drain. Storm drains at the bottom of large watersheds accumulated a lot of pollution and organic matter that the students collected in large trash bags for Keep Omaha Beautiful. They kept a log of how many bags of pollution they had filled and how many storm drains had been labeled. Northwest and ILUNO students clean the storm drains every fall and spring semester to ensure that pollution and organic matter does not accumulate in the drains around their community.

After cleanup, students reflected on the impacts they had made on their commu-nity. The ILUNO students shared how pollution was dealt with in their countries and how working with Omaha students allows them to be part of a global effort. The Northwest students revealed how they can start making more of an effort to keep pollution out of the watershed and streets and how they can be more conscien-tious of what they pour down their drains. Both Northwest and ILUNO students took accountability for their efforts in pollution prevention and wanted to raise more awareness in order to help others become environmental stewards in their commu-nity and world.

The Seed to Salad service-learning project plans on continually growing and remaining flexible regarding the needs of the classroom and student body. As the needs of the community and world change, so too will the direction of the project. Future plans for the project include the continuation of planting and caring for the Northwest community garden, monarch tagging, assisting with storm drain labeling and cleanup with Keep Omaha Beautiful, caring for the aquaponics system with Whispering Roots, and building other community gardens around Omaha with Nebraskans for Civic Reform. The Seed to Salad project, as well as the Rain Garden project with Steve Rodie's UNO class, will be collaborating with more environmental partners throughout the city to strengthen student learning and expand the rain garden and community garden into an outdoor classroom. Advanced Placement Environmental Science students will work with Steve Rodie's UNO Environmental Appreciation class to perform waste inventories of UNO, the Omaha Public School District, and Northwest High School. They will then create an action plan for alleviating the waste accumulation in each location, and subsequently conduct research on the efficacy of the implementation of their plans. The Northwest Horticulture and AP Environmental Science students will also continue to design the outer spaces of the rain garden and community garden and expand them into an outdoor classroom that includes a solar panel, a seating area with a writing board, an orchard, a medicinal/herbal plot, and an additional rain garden. These areas will contribute more produce for the community and will provide more environmental learning opportunities for students.

The Northwest Horticulture and AP Environmental Science students will also collaborate with the ILUNO students and the Henry Doorly Zoo to test for chytrid fungus on frogs at the Safari Park in Nebraska. Chytrid fungus is a highly infectious amphibian disease caused by *Batrachochytrium dendrobatidis*. Thirty percent of amphibian species across the globe have been experiencing declines in populations, and the chytrid fungus disease is thought to be a major contributor to the decline (Stuart et al., 2004). Scientists do not know how to stop the spread or control the disease in wild frog populations, so there is a dire need for further scientific research of the fungus. Both Northwest and ILUNO students plan to assist the Henry Doorly Zoo with their Amphibian Conservation Education Project, conducting an amphibian survey to determine the viability of amphibian habitats and health and to test for the presence of chytrid fungus. Both Northwest and ILUNO students will learn about a global problem that affects amphibians from countries around the world and about the impact the fungus has on biodiversity, populations, and tropic imbalances.

Project Implementation

Service learning is an incredibly worthwhile style of teaching that will beneficially impact the teacher, students, and community. However, it can be time-consuming for teachers to successfully plan and implement the projects in their classes. To make the projects successful, time and financial needs must be considered before a project is started.

Teachers, professors, and community partners work many hours, making it difficult to incorporate extra projects. The UNO Service Learning Academy recognizes this time constraint, so they hire graduate students to assist each service-learning project and to alleviate any potential stress or burdens that would otherwise be placed on the teachers or professors. The graduate students set up meetings between the teachers, UNO professors, and community partners, and they ensure that the projects meet service-learning standards (NYLC, 2008). During these meetings, everyone plans the upcoming events and the desired project outcomes. They also discuss items that need to be ordered, and the graduate student facilitates setting up interactions between the schools, the university, and the community partners. This can be difficult since teaching schedules do not often align with the professor's class schedules. The graduate student may then brainstorm other options, such as Skype communication or after-school meetings. Transportation is also supported by the UNO Service Learning Academy, so the graduate student arranges bus transportation for the students. This alleviates cost responsibilities for the school, making the projects more affordable and achievable. Lastly, the graduate student attends all of the interactions between the school, the university, and the community partners to ensure that everything runs smoothly. Snacks/refreshments are often provided for the students, and any supplies such as crafts, aquaponics systems, seeds, soil, etc., are also purchased through the UNO Service Learning Academy to ensure that all the projects run smoothly and components are procured.

Despite the support from the UNO Service Learning Academy, additional funds were needed for larger expenses and were paid for via other grants. For example, the Northwest High School rain garden was funded by the Nebraska Arboretum Sustainable Schoolyards Project Grant, the Natural Resources District Best Management Practices (BMP) Stormwater Grant, the Natural Resources District Outdoor Classroom Grant, and the Omaha Northwest High School Alumni Foundation. The Northwest High School community garden was funded by the Big Gardens Grant, the Lowes Toolbox for Education Grant, the National Council of Jewish Women's Grant, and multiple individual Northwest family donations. The expansion of the outdoor classroom at Northwest will also have to be funded through state and community grants, which requires a large time commitment from a teacher or administrator at the school. In addition, further meetings may have to be attended to ensure that school facilities are aware of the projects and that construction on the school site does not interfere with any previous structures, such as sprinkler systems, wires, etc.

To make service-learning projects successful, the teacher also must have an innate drive to want to think outside the box and implement experiential teaching strategies in the classroom. The service-learning pedagogy fosters hands-on, immersive projects that allow students to tap into their curiosity, design their own learning experiences, and participate in full-inquiry laboratory experiences. The greatest rewards are seen by teaching in this manner. Students often start the semester apprehensive and scared to explore their abilities, yet finish the semester with a great amount of confidence. In addition, by providing open-ended inquiry projects, teachers and professors obtain the opportunity to learn alongside their students, and the line between teacher and student is blurred. These experiences can be most powerful and rewarding when not only the students grow, but also teachers grow and learn along with them. Many teachers fear relinquishing control in the classroom and stick to cookie-cutter-style experiments that do not allow students to learn beyond the content (Abdi, 2014). Anyone can read and follow a lab manual, so it is difficult to determine if the students learned or if they simply followed directions. This style does not embody true science or learning. This is like someone teaching a student to play the piano but never allowing them to play music. The magic is in the performance. The service-learning style of teaching embraces students to get messy, make mistakes, learn from those mistakes, and reach for a higher understanding by participating in each part of the scientific method to give back to their community. Students need to conduct and be part of real-life science experiments and projects – where the real magic and learning occur. Therefore, teachers must possess the tools of flexibility and patience to make service-learning projects possible. They too must be willing for mistakes to occur and to grow from them. They must be willing to be flexible with their time and scheduling to make projects work, and they must be creative in their approach to student reflection to ensure that learning is occurring.

The impacts and learning achievable through service learning are lost if all partners are not reflecting throughout the project. The teacher must incorporate reflection throughout the experience not only to gauge whether content learning is taking place, but to also gauge the students' understanding of their impacts on their community or world. This allows the students to make meaning of their learning and to understand how they have been personally impacted by the experience. Personal reflection empowers students to take the next steps in the growth of their ideologies and how they want to continue to learn and give back to the world (Ash & Clayton, 2004). Students also learn to ask higher-level questions on the content, which leads to increased in-depth learning. Students also get to ask themselves questions regarding the choices they made and the intention behind those choices. Through these reflections, students can analyze their successes and failures and contemplate options for continued growth and change. Reflections can take the form of student journals, surveys, debates, discussions, essays, etc., and should be provided to the students throughout the experience to monitor growth (Molee et al., 2011).

The graduate student also facilitates an end-of-semester/year reflection among the teacher, professor, and community partner. These reflections are just as imperative as the student reflections since they rely on the teacher, professor, or community partner questioning the aspects of the project that worked well and the parts that need improvement. Any concerns can be addressed, including student behavior, engagement, time management, needed materials, and communication. Teachers and professors can ask themselves whether they felt students truly learned the content and civic responsibility and whether they themselves also learned and benefitted alongside the students. This reflection allows the project to remain fluid enough to change regarding the needs of the community and classroom and the needs of the individuals involved.

To create a sustainable project, it is also important to foster strong communication and bonds between the members in the project. The professor can act as a mentor and provide valuable content knowledge, and the community partner can also provide other networking opportunities with others in the community. The teacher, in turn, can provide expertise on behavior management, student interactions, and teaching strategies. The partnerships naturally become friendships over time, which strengthen the integrity of the project by increasing enjoyment of its implementation and sustainability. In addition, all appropriate school administration staff should be aware of the project and included in meetings to ensure proper communication and that any changes to curriculum or school sites are approved.

Troubleshooting

Since there are many people involved throughout the project, one can assume challenges may arise that may threaten the integrity of the expected outcome. Many challenges can be predicted and hopefully solved during the meetings directed by the graduate student at the beginning of the project, but some issues may arise that cannot be predicted. Based on the author's experience, some of the most common issues that arise during service-learning include the following: (1) the community partner backs out of the project or the teacher struggles to find an appropriate community partner; (2) the university partner backs out or the teacher cannot find an appropriate university partner; (3) communication is poor among partners; (4) students misbehave throughout the project; and (5) administrative support changes.

If the community partner backs out or one simply cannot think of an appropriate community partner, engage with resources such as the UNO Service Learning Academy, which has a great understanding of who could benefit and align with your content and vision. The teacher can also allow students to conduct research and brainstorm potential community partners. This gives the students a voice and choices in their learning outcomes. Lastly, the teacher can also be flexible and slightly change their vision to meet the need of another community partner.

If the university partner does not exist or backs out, a teacher can simply wait it out and hope for another potential partner. Again, they should contact the partners at the university and see if there is another appropriate match that can be made or if there is another angle the project can take to align with another professor. If a professor is simply not available for the year, the teacher can get creative and write mini-grants that will provide transportation and funding for their current vision.

Due to hectic schedules and the number of people involved, poor communication among partners may arise throughout the project. The graduate student should be used as the first line of communication to ensure that all dates and meeting notes are verified by everyone involved. If communication issues persist, the partners should reach out to each other to share their concerns about ineffective communication. It is imperative that personal relationships and mentorships are fostered throughout the project so that lines of communication remain open and that not all interactions are strictly business. Building positive personal relationships allows all members to feel comfortable discussing potential issues and keeps the project sustainable for the future.

Student behavior may be the most unpredictable aspect for all parties involved and can make or break projects if not managed appropriately. The teacher must first remove the student from the situation to prevent escalation and then identify whether the misbehavior is an acute or chronic problem and handle the situation accordingly. The teacher can use this opportunity to empower students to see the implications of their actions on the project and to see how they can further connect to the meaning of the project in order to become more engaged.

Administrative support may change throughout the project. This can cause challenges for addressing content standards in the classroom, transportation, grant funding, school site preparation, or scheduling meetings. To address this issue, the partners need to ensure that administration staff are always aware of the details of the project and to stress the impact that service learning has on student learning, engagement, and civic responsibility and the impacts it has on the community. It also helps to have additional stakeholder buy-in, such as other administrators, cross-curricular involvement, or grant funders, to ensure the project remains sustainable after one person leaves.

One can never can truly anticipate the issues that may arise during a service-learning project, but remaining open-minded and flexible and realizing things will go wrong at times can alleviate any potential stress. One should develop a contingency plan for things that can be predicted (such as weather, scheduling conflicts, etc.) and sustain an open line of communication between partners, administration, and stake-holders. Things that go wrong can also be used as learning experiences and turned into something positive. For example, the Northwest rain garden was supposed to be completed in a semester; however, the benches and signs were not funded by the original grants, some plants died, and obvious gaps were seen in the garden. Teacher Rachael Arens used this time to teach students to design other parts of the garden, recognize sick plants/pest problems, and learn how to write grants to ask for funding for the benches and signs. The students also used the time to develop the website that the sign linked to in order to provide information about the purpose of the rain garden, as well as information on individual plant species. The benches and signs were installed a year and a half later than anticipated, but the experience was transformed into one of positive learning.

Conclusion

This chapter provided readers with real-life classroom examples of current practices of community engagement, implementation practices to make service-learning projects thrive, and means to strengthen student learning projects and twenty-first century skill development. Today's jobs are requiring more than just content knowledge from graduating students. They desire students who possess twenty-first century skills, have experience working with a variety of personalities, are passionate, think outside the box, and have a desire to give back to their community (Waterman, 2014). Service learning provides students with the tools to develop these traits in order to prepare them for college and life outside of school. Teachers should challenge themselves to evolve their pedagogy to include hands-on service learning in their classrooms. Not only will they transform their students' learning and way of thinking, but they will also transform themselves and how they approach the philosophy of teaching. The fruits that service learning provides for everyone invested in its projects are plentiful; it simply takes careful planning, flexibility, an ardent desire for learning and civic engagement, and reflection to create successful projects that can change an individual, a community, and the world.

References

Abdi, A. (2014). The effect of inquiry-based learning method on students' academic achievement in science course. *Universal Journal of Educational Research, 2*(1), 37–41.

Ash, S. L. & Clayton, P. H. (2004). The articulated learning: An approach to guided reflection and assessment. *Innovative Higher Education, 29*(2), 137–154.

Biology Online (n.d.). Trophic level. Retrieved from www.biology-online.org/dictionary/ Trophic.

Clean Solutions for Omaha (n.d.). Our Combined Sewers. Retrieved from http://omahacso .com/program/csocombdsewers/.

Furco, A. (1996). *Service-learning: A balanced approach to experiential education. Service learning, general*, 128. Retrieved from www.shsu.edu/academics/cce/documents/ Service_Learning_Balanced_Approach_To_Experimental_Education.pdf.

Israel, E. (2002). Examining multiple perspectives in literature. In J. Holden & J. S. Schmit (Eds.), *Inquiry and the literary text: Constructing discussions in the English classroom* (pp. 89–103). Urbana, IL: NCTE.

Keep Omaha Beautiful (n.d.). Mission and history. Retrieved from www.keepomahabeautiful .org/who-we-are/mission.html.

Lovett, J. (2017). Monarch Watch. Retrieved from www.monarchwatch.org.

Molee, L. M., Henry, M. E., Sessa, V. I., & McKinney-Prupis, E. R. (2011). Assessing learning in service learning courses through critical reflection. *Journal of Experiential Education, 33*(3), 239–257.

Nebraska Department of Education (2008). K–12 Service-Learning Standards for Quality Practice. St. Paul, MN: National Youth Leadership Council. Omaha Northwest Magnet High School 2011–2012 State of the Schools Report. Retrieved from https://reportcard.education.ne.gov/20112012/Default.aspx?AgencyID=28–0001 -011&AgencyName=OMAHA%20NORTHWEST%20MAGNET%20HIGH% 20SCHOOL.

Rich, E. (2010). How do you define 21st-century learning? In *Education Week Teacher PD Sourcebook*. Retrieved from www.edweek.org/tsb/articles/2010/10/12/01panel.h04 .html.

Stuart, S. N., Chanson, J. S., Cox, N. et al. (2004). Status and trends of amphibian declines and extinctions worldwide. *Science, 306*(5702), 1783–1786.

Service Learning Academy (n.d.). University of Nebraska Omaha. Retrieved from www .unomaha.edu/service-learning-academy/.

Waterman, A. S. (2014). Service-learning: Applications from the research. What is Service Learning? In *UNO Service Learning Academy*. Retrieved from www.unomaha.edu /service-learning-academy/.

6 Integrating Foreigners into Local Communities for Mutual Benefit

Chances, Challenges, and Best Practice

Fabian Klauke, Annika L. Meinecke, Lena C. Müller-Frommeyer, & Simone Kauffeld

Recent years saw a recognizable increase in migration. Increased global mobility and more permeable borders create a growing body of migrants. Particularly in the aging societies of industrialized countries, immigration, especially by highly educated individuals, is thought to have a beneficial influence on a country's long-term welfare. But while immigration brings benefits with regard to labor markets, as well as promoting exchange between cultures, integrating foreigners into communities' everyday lives challenges both natives' and internationals' intercultural competencies.

An important group of migrants are students, who no longer restrict their search for a fitting educational institution to their home country. The number of students studying abroad has doubled from 2005 to 2012, when 4.5 million students were enrolled in a country they did not hold citizenship of, with emerging markets of China and India being the largest countries of origin of foreign students (OECD, 2015). These countries have different norms and cultures from the main receiving regions of Western Europe and the USA (Institute for International Education, 2016).

A second group of migrants are refugees. Unless specified, we use the term "refugee" in its broader sense, including asylum seekers and other individuals who were forcibly displaced and have fled their country of origin (Moore et al., 2016). An increasingly large part of migration classifies as forced migration. Due to violent conflicts, such as the currently ongoing civil wars in the Middle East, as well as extreme economic inequality between Europe and Africa, the number of refugees coming to Europe over the Mediterranean Sea doubled from 2014 to 2015 (Holmes & Castañeda, 2016). This poses major challenges for local communities. On the one hand, there are numerous bureaucratic hurdles to overcome and questions of (re) location to be answered. On the other hand, efforts to integrate refugees into their new local communities should not be postponed in order to prevent social unrest. Additionally, the integration of refugees is particularly difficult because the group itself is very heterogeneous. Thus, there is likely no such thing as a "one-size-fits-all" approach to integration. Instead, tailored programs are needed that can benefit both refugees and the local community.

Community engagement – a process in which a service system establishes an ongoing partnership with a community that is shaped by the community's priorities (Moore et al., 2016) – can be used as a way to facilitate intergroup contact and integration of all kinds of foreigners. Community engagement initiatives can help migrants make a new home, as well as educate and reduce prejudice in members of the majority, thereby helping the community to make use of its growing diversity.

The initiatives we introduce here are a mixture of the following two types of community engagement: community building and service learning. Community building is an enabling process aimed at creating a sense of belonging and continuity as well as a shared set of values and ideas within a local group, such as a neighborhood or city (Brown, 2001; Rappaport, 1984). To achieve these goals, we focus on various strategies derived from Allport's (1954) contact hypothesis, which we explain in the following section. The second component of our programs – service learning – essentially combines academic tuition with service to a community for mutual benefit. Students apply their knowledge in an organized way to advance the community and meet their identified needs, while they gain experience from their community engagement that helps them to further understand their course content. In addition, being able to apply their knowledge to real-world issues helps students develop a broader, more integrated perspective on their discipline and stimulates personal growth with regard to values and responsibility (Bringle & Hatcher, 1995, 2009). To ensure a service-learning initiative's success and discern it from other forms of (qualified) volunteer work, it is crucial to accompany it with guided reflection, systematically linking the experiences to the curriculum's content (e.g., Artz, 2001).

In the following, we first describe the need for community engagement partnerships to help integrate international students as well as refugees, but also to deepen intercultural skills within the native population. Second, we portray two successful community engagement initiatives at a German university. One of those initiatives addresses the concerns of international students, whereas the other one focuses on refugees. Third, we condense our experiences into "how-to" guidelines for implementing community–university partnerships to help international students or refugees integrate, adapt, and succeed in their new environment. Finally, we address challenges of the presented university–community engagement programs and provide future directions.

Foreigners and the Community: Contact Is Key

Migration can offer a range of benefits to the receiving country, such as a rejuvenation of the population in case of an influx of younger migrants (Jaumotte, Koloskova, & Saxena, 2016), as well as "brain gain" and mid- and long-term economic benefits (Letki, 2008). However, increased diversity can also affect a community negatively. Ethnic diversity has a negative (albeit small) effect on social capital (Letki, 2008), and in some more diverse places, higher levels of intergroup antipathy can be observed (e.g., Ayers et al., 2009; Hudson et al., 2007; Stein, Post, & Rinden, 2000). This seems to contradict the classical contact hypothesis, in which it is stated that intergroup contact can reduce prejudice – a hypothesis that has received overwhelming overall empirical support, as a meta-analysis of 515 studies showed (Pettigrew & Tropp, 2006). Taking a closer look, these ostensible contradictions resolve. Whereas sole spatial proximity has been found to have varying (and, when combined with ongoing segregation, even negative) effects on intergroup antipathy (Enos, 2017; for positive effects, see Laurence, 2011; Wagner et al., 2003; Wagner et al., 2006; for negative effects, see Barlow et al., 2012), the effect of intergroup contact depends largely on the valence of this contact. In particular, negative encounters have been found to strongly increase racism, avoidance, and prejudice, whereas positive encounters between groups improve groups' attitudes toward each other (Pettigrew & Tropp, 2006). The better the conditions under which the contact takes place, such as those provided by structured programs, the larger and more likely the reduction in prejudice (Pettigrew & Tropp, 2006).

Specifically, the following four key factors for achieving a prejudice-reducing effect via positive intergroup contact have been proposed by Allport (1954): First, group members should meet on a basis of equal status. Specifically, differences in social rank (e.g., as in teacher–pupil relationships) should be avoided. Second, contact should be cooperative in nature, such that group members work together over group boundaries and not against one another. Third, and related to the idea of cooperation, group members should work toward a common, shared goal. Thus, they should ideally work on a task that requires group members to pool their efforts. Fourth, contact should be based on established norms of acceptance by authorities or customs. This includes that contact should not be left to chance. Instead, relevant authorities (e.g., governments, managers, program coordinators) should show support for interaction. Fostering positive contact also pays off beyond the situation itself: the effect of intergroup contact is usually found to generalize to the entire outgroup (Allport, 1954; Pettigrew & Tropp, 2006).

Benefits of Community Engagement

To avoid conflict between groups (i.e., foreigners and locals), foreigners need a chance for integration and friendship formation, and both groups need opportunities to overcome their prejudices toward each other. There are two major ways in which community engagement can benefit and help foreigners and locals when making contact: first, it can provide the aforementioned optimal setting with regard to the contact hypothesis (Addleman et al., 2014); and second, it can increase the benefits that both parties may directly derive from the situation, besides mere contact and prejudice reduction. Both parties can hone their intercultural competencies, allowing them to bond, mingle, and work with others from diverse cultural backgrounds more easily. Those learning outcomes in intercultural settings have been shown to be particularly likely to occur when backed by structures that help participants to reflect on their experiences (Addleman et al., 2014). "Hands-on" experience of actual intercultural contact can deepen the understanding of otherwise theoretical multicultural knowledge and make it more applicable (Allport, 1954). This feature of intergroup contact connects well to service learning, which, by definition, highlights the aspect of integrating experience into knowledge (Bringle

& Hatcher, 2009). In a qualitative study of an intercultural service-learning initiative, Einfeld and Collins (2008) found that participants challenged stereotypes and developed empathy, patience, attachment, reciprocity, trust, and respect, skills that are useful to intercultural interaction. They also expressed strong other-orientation and interest in further civic engagement and volunteerism for the benefit of the community, making the program effective beyond its duration (see also Giles & Eyler, 1994; Kezar & Rhoads, 2001).

Taken together, a structured program supporting the integration of foreigners can help to reduce prejudice, avoidance, and racism, as well as further intercultural competencies in both migrants and hosts and connect both to the local community. To achieve this, such a program should aim to have participants meet at an equal status, make sure they work cooperatively toward a common goal, and establish mutual acceptance as a norm (Addleman, Brazo et al., 2014). Furthermore, it should help participants reflect on their new experiences to ensure promotion of competencies (Addleman, Brazo et al., 2014).

In our chapter, we introduce two successful university–community engagement initiatives that strive to bring together the local community on the one hand and two very distinct groups on the other hand: international students and refugees. Although the cultural novelty they experience is largely comparable, their situations are quite different, and hence the challenges they are facing are too.

The Case of International Students. International students represent a large – and growing – group of migrants and sojourners. They make up for a considerable percentage of the whole student population (e.g., about 20 percent in Germany; Heublein et al., 2014). However, they are much more likely than native students to drop out of their studies and, if they do graduate, they are likely to leave their host country again after finishing their studies (King & Raghuram, 2013). Taking into account that they are at the same time considered sought-after future young professionals and some countries make huge investments in national as well as international students by providing high-quality, low-cost education, their background and the way they adjust to their host countries' cultures is surprisingly scarcely researched (Sawir et al., 2007). Some potential reasons for their higher dropout rates can be found in the loss of their familiar cultural environment, lack of social support systems, and the cultural novelty of the host country (Hechanova-Alampay et al., 2002), adding to the novelty of the new learning environment that almost every student faces (Zhao, Kuh, & Carini, 2005).

Whereas international students in general seem to be more engaged in activities directly benefitting their education (Bochner, McLeod, & Lin, 1977; Furnham & Alibhai, 1985), the same is not necessarily true for activities that bring them together with locals. International students often have a preference for other international students as friends, although at the same time they benefit greatly from host-national friendships, as they help them to adjust and adapt more easily (Hendrickson, Rosen, & Aune, 2011). International students with relatively more friends from their host country were found to be more satisfied with their situation, more confident, and less homesick (Walton & Cohen, 2007, 2011). Furthermore, getting a sense of belonging, such as via friendship formation with host nationals, can be beneficial. Walton and Cohen (2011) showed that such an increased sense of belonging predicted multiple positive outcomes: it benefited students' academic performance, as well as their self-reported health and actual number of doctoral visits. Additionally, the better integrated international students are, the higher their reported well-being (UNHCR, 2017).

The Case of Refugees. Particularly since the outbreak of the Syrian civil war, the world has seen a dramatic rise in people seeking asylum. As by the end of 2016, more than 22 million people were registered refugees, and another 2.8 million were still seeking asylum, thus applying to be granted official refugee status (Crawford et al., 2015). In 2016, 3.4 million new refugees and asylum seekers were registered, with Germany being the country with the largest amount of new individual applications (722,400 new asylum claims in 2016). The vast majority of those refugees and asylum seekers came from countries with ongoing and mostly long-running conflicts. Therefore, integration of this large group of forcefully displaced people into the host society automatically becomes important. Even if they wish to return to their home country, this might not be a viable option until the distant future due to ongoing (civil) wars or persecution. More specifically, over 80 percent of past refugee crises lasted ten years or more, and about 40 percent lasted even longer than 20 years. Before the Syrian civil war, 50 percent of refugees fled their home country on average more than 22 years ago (UN General Assembly, 1957).

Since refugees did not plan to migrate, but were forced to leave their country, their integration situation is different from other migrants. They are likely to arrive unprepared and completely unfamiliar with the host country's customs, culture, and language. Also, they are more heterogeneous with regard to their socioeconomic status than international students: while the latter are, by definition, highly educated, this is not necessarily true of refugees. Another aspect that sets refugees apart from other migrants or sojourners is Article 34 of the Refugee Convention (Gurin, 1999; Stifterverband für die Deutsche Wissenschaft, 2015; Zhao et al., 2005): "The Contracting States shall as far as possible facilitate the assimilation and naturalization of refugees. They shall in particular make every effort to expedite naturalization proceedings and to reduce as far as possible the charges and costs of such proceedings."

Asylum seekers who have not been granted refugee status yet are another special subcase. They do not (yet) have the rights that registered refugees do, which means that they can also be excluded from public integration programs. However, particularly during humanitarian crises, processing applications for asylum and refugee status determination takes time and their status may be pending for quite a while, so valuable time that could be spent building social support systems and learning about the host country's culture is often wasted.

The Case of the Native Population. While community engagement for the integration of foreigners seems to be an enterprise benefiting foremost the involved foreigners, competency in navigating a diversifying world gains importance for both professional and personal development and is a sought-after, but often lacking, skill in the workforce (Amerson, 2010; Baldwin, Buchanan, & Rudisill, 2007). Studies showed that participation in university–community engagement initiatives is a potential way to train cultural awareness and competency (Kudo & Simkin, 2003; Rivas, 2009; Urberg, Degirmencioglu, & Tolson, 1998). Thus, locals can also greatly benefit from community engagement programs that bring them into contact with both international students and refugees (Bringle & Hatcher, 1995, 2009; Einfeld & Collins, 2008; Giles & Eyler, 1994; Kezar & Rhoads, 2001).

Community Engagement Initiatives

We highlight two successful programs for the integration of foreigners into the local community in this chapter. Both programs currently take place at Technische Universität Braunschweig, Germany (further information on both initiatives is available upon request from the authors). The programs are conceptualized as peer programs in which one native and one international participant – students in one case, refugees or asylum seekers in the other – are matched and work together on certain tasks. As outlined above, both programs share their focus on service learning. Hence, both programs aim to link more traditional knowledge acquisition at the university with hands-on experiences outside the university. An accompanying reflection on the experiences ensures that what has been learned is internalized and embedded in the students' existing knowledge. Table 6.1 provides an overview showing how these three main components – knowledge, experience, and reflection – play out during the two programs.

A Program for International Students

The first program we want to highlight is the "SCOUT – Program to Connect and Support International Students." SCOUT is a cooperation of the Department of Industrial/Organizational and Social Psychology and the University's International Office. The goal of the program is to integrate international students into everyday life at a German university and to connect international students with native students. Equally, native students get the chance to make in-depth contact with foreign cultures and increase intercultural competency. The program is open to all students at the university. Depending on the students' field of study, they can receive extra-curricular credits for participating in the program.

To integrate international students into the local community first and foremost means to help them mingle with the local, native students' community. To do so, dyads of one international and one native student each are formed. Those dyads then spend one semester together to enable participants to build a longer-lasting relationship and ensure a more detailed examination of each other's culture. The program, which is managed by a full-time research associate, is constituted as depicted in Table 6.1.

After recruiting participants, each new semester starts with three days of preparatory training for the native students. They are taught basic intercultural psychology and are prepared for their part in the program (see also Table 6.1). Participants also learn about how to help international students navigate native everyday culture and

Table 6.1 *Implementation of service learning in both programs*

Focus area	Implementation – Initiative I: program for international students	Implementation – Initiative II: program for refugees

Knowledge: acquiring and applying academic knowledge	• Preparatory three-day intercultural training for native students covering the following main topics:
	  • Detailed introduction to the program
	  • Definition and classification of (national) culture
	  • Development and presentation of cultural profiles for specific national cultures
	  • Input and exercises on culture shock
	  • Practical exercises for deepening communication skills, specifically focused on asking open questions and active listening
	  • Simulation of the individual pre-structured dyadic meetings
	  • Exchange of experiences with participants from previous semesters
		• Preparatory two-day intercultural training for native students covering the following main topics:
		  • Detailed introduction to the program
		  • Definition and classification of (national) culture
		  • Input and exercises on critical whiteness and culture shock
		  • Information about the situation of refugees
		  • Development and presentation of cultural profiles, specifically focused on the refugees' countries of origin
		  • Q&A session with a representative of the municipality responsible for the refugees
		• Literature study throughout the semester

Experience: participating in community engagement activities	• Literature study throughout the semester • Participation in five pre-structured dyadic meetings, each of which is focused on one specific content topic; each dyadic meeting lasts for about 1.5–2 hours • Participation in at least four activity meetings (usually carried out as a group activity); each activity meeting lasts for about four hours and aims to connect international students with the local community	• Participation in at least five meetings that aim to connect refugees with the local community • Participants can meet on their own (i.e., dyads of one native students and one refugee) or in groups • Typical meeting lasts for at least two hours

Table 6.1 *(cont.)*

Focus area	Implementation – Initiative I: program for international students	Implementation – Initiative II: program for refugees
Critical reflection: linking students' experiences with course content	• Preparatory training, including reflection components focused on the native students' own culture, their cultural upbringing, and their own role during the program • Participation in at least one 90-minute mixed group reflection meeting (i.e., native students and their international partners) • Participation in at least one 90-minute non-mixed group reflection meeting (i.e., native students only) • A joint closing event in which the experiences and findings are summarized	• Preparatory training, including reflection components focused on the native students' own culture, their cultural upbringing, critical whiteness, their own intercultural awareness, and their role during the program • Reflective journaling throughout the semester (i.e., native students only) • Participation in at least one 90-minute group reflection meeting (i.e., native students only) • Essay that focuses on the experiences collected throughout the program (i.e., native students only) • A joint closing event in which the experiences and findings are summarized

simultaneously not change theirs into a teacher–pupil relationship, but to maintain equal status. The training is further set up to spark curiosity about foreign cultures. It points out learning opportunities and provides native students with a solid base from which to expand their intercultural competencies.

Next, dyads are formed. Information collected during the recruitment process is used to match participants, aiming for matches that facilitate positive contact. We take into account three considerations that facilitate positive contact and have been found to be good predictors of friendship formation: similarities of age, similarities of interests, and similarities of activities, such as mutual hobbies (Elliot, Heesterbeek, Lukensmeyer, & Slocum, 2005). Apart from that, we also respect specific wishes the participants state, such as a preference for same-gender matches and shared language proficiency.

The matching process is followed by the kickoff meeting, where the dyads get to know the group and each other and the goals and structure of the program are laid out once more. It is emphasized that the foremost goal of the program is for them to get to know each other and connect to each other's communities, to work together as a team through the program, and to explore each other's cultural background, thereby practicing their intercultural competency.

During the remainder of the semester, the participants work much more independently. Their main task is to conduct two types of meetings: five pre-structured, dyadic meetings and four activity meetings. For each dyadic meeting, participants receive short manuals. They consist of detailed suggestions for topics to talk about and accompanying worksheets, such as on cultural similarities and differences, to help them reflect on their experiences. A sample guideline for conducting a dyadic meeting focused on the topic of friendship is presented in Table 6.2. The activity meetings' goal is to directly foster contact between the international participants and the local community. They constitute an easy way to get to know the region and local cultural life. Activity meetings are recommended to be carried out in a group, either with other participants or local organizations, such as sports clubs, museums, the volunteer fire brigade, or international student organizations. By partnering with such communal organizations, international students form connections that extend beyond the project's immanent scope and time frame. Contacts with organizations or initiatives outside the university are usually initiated by the local native students themselves in order to promote their independence in the program. The local students usually have a strong social network and can use their existing contacts to build a bridge to the local community.

To promote learning and personal development, the dyads participate in at least one reflection meeting during the semester. The meetings, led and moderated by a faculty member (i.e., the program coordinator) or an experienced graduate student, are structured to achieve the following three aims: (1) have participants get to know each other to facilitate the creation of a trusting environment; (2) intensify contact across and within groups of native and international students and plan further activities; and foremost (3) reflect on participants' experiences and incorporate them into existing knowledge. Topics covered range from the participants' learnings about cultural similarities, differences, and how to approach them, to individual and cross-cultural relationship formation. Further, native participants take part in an additional reflection meeting that focuses on further integrating their experiences into their intercultural competencies, and additionally gives them the opportunity to get help on issues such as integrating very introverted international students. Finally, during the closing event, the concept of reflecting on the intercultural learnings is revisited. Using a world café approach to facilitate structured, on-topic discussions and feedback within a large group (Elliot et al., 2005), participants discuss and reflect on their learnings and intercultural highlights in small groups at different work stations.

The program received positive feedback from both native and international students. In 2016, the program received the "Award for Excellent Support of Foreign Students" by the German Academic Exchange Service (DAAD) and the German Federal Foreign Office, which highlighted its structure and scientific foundation.

Due to its interdisciplinary nature, the SCOUT program is easily transferable to other educational institutions, both as a whole and in part. A conceptual transfer of the program to non-university contexts is feasible as well. Corporations could use an adjusted version to integrate new international employees. The meetings' topics can

Table 6.2 *Sample guideline for conducting a dyadic meeting in the SCOUT program*

	Topic Meeting 3: Friendship			
Name of Scout:				Date/time
Name of International:				

Duration	Topic	Sample question/subject matter	Material	Notes
10 minutes	Welcome	Smalltalk ☺	Question cards	
15 minutes	Follow-up or interim discussion of the diary study	• Did you have an exclusion experience that you would like to discuss? – How did you solve the situation? – What did you wish for in terms of how the situation turned out? – How could you have achieved that? • Who did you meet? • Who did you get to know better?		Also talk about your own experiences here
20 minutes	Social network	• Update your networks (explain how to make the additions) • What has changed?	Network 1, page 1 Network 2, page 2 Guide to completing the network (handout)	
15 minutes	What does friendship mean?	• If possible, use diary study: – How did you meet new people? – What did you do to make friends? • Both of you, take 10 minutes and answer the following question. Write your answers on a set of cards (separately): – What is/what does friendship mean to you?	Presentation cards	

Table 6.2 (*cont.*)

	Topic Meeting 3: Friendship			
Name of Scout:				Date/time
Name of International:				

Duration	Topic	Sample question/subject matter	Material	Notes
20 minutes	Differences and similarities	– What is especially important to you? • Present you cards to each other and explain your ideas • Cluster your cards: – What are the similarities? – What are the biggest differences? – What reasons could there be for these differences? – Which ideas of friendship are under-lying these differences?		
20 minutes	How can I make friends?	• In view of the differ-ences: at which points could there be difficulties? – When meeting new people? – When making friends? – When staying with friends? • How could one over-come these difficul-ties? What could help? • How can you build on the similarities? • Own experiences: what works well?	Optional: sample text "The day after the party"	
10 minutes	Completion and preparatory exercise for the next topic meeting	• Task for Topic Meeting 4 – cultural features • Compare the culture in your home country	Task sheet for Topic Meeting 4	

Table 6.2 (*cont.*)

		Topic Meeting 3: Friendship		Date/time
Name of Scout:				
Name of International:				
Duration	Topic	Sample question/subject matter	Material	Notes
		with the culture in Germany • For orientation, there are a few predefined categories and sample questions • Go through the task together and check if the task is clear		

easily be customized to cover more job-relevant issues. In particular, parts of the training can also be used to prepare a company's workforce for intercultural cooperation or for going abroad.

A Program for Refugees

The second program is aimed at connecting refugees and native students. It is part of a course in the master's degree program in psychology at Technische Universität Braunschweig. Thus, all native students that take part in the program have a background in psychology and receive curricular credit for their participation. The program was first implemented in 2015, after large numbers of refugees arrived in Germany. Contact with the refugees is made through officials from the local municipality and volunteers on site. A close exchange, especially shortly before the program is about to start, is important to reach the refugees and inform them about the program. The refugees who have participated in the program thus far came from Syria, Eritrea, and Sudan.

The overall purpose of the program is to provide refugees with assistance in everyday life and help them to adjust to their new environment. In doing so, the program first and foremost focuses on refugees' social and cultural adjustment to their new surroundings and less on structural support. One principal aim, therefore, is to provide a context where refugees and native students can meet and learn from one another. As a result, the aim is to build a bridge between these different social groups that, at first glance, seem to have little in common apart from their age. Through the program, native students acquire comprehensive knowledge of intercultural skills, and they gain insights into cultures that were previously fairly unknown to them. As such, the native students play a key role in connecting refugees and the larger community.

The program takes place once a year and lasts for the duration of one semester. Similar to the SCOUT program outlined above, all native students participate in a preparatory two days of training (see Table 6.1). Since the program described here is specifically directed at psychology students pursuing their master's degree, students are already familiar with more basic intercultural topics (e.g., the role of prejudice and stereotyping, social perception). The training therefore focuses more strongly on the students' specific role within the program, how they can promote independence on the part of the refugees, and how they can effectively deal with language barriers. Moreover, students reflect on their culture and cultural upbringing, as well as on critical whiteness and their own intercultural awareness, and can engage in a Q&A session with a volunteer from the local municipality who is in close contact with the refugees.

Next is the joint kickoff meeting between native students and refugees, where both groups meet for the first time and get to know each other. The kickoff meeting usually takes place in the evening and is followed by a dinner in a relaxed atmosphere. Due to organizational reasons and language barriers, it is not possible to match the dyads based on common interests prior to the kickoff meeting. Overall, the refugees' language skills vary greatly, with some refuges speaking only very little to no German. This makes in-depth communication difficult, but in return provokes and promotes improvisation. Moreover, for many refugees, this is the first time that they will have participating in a program specifically aimed at helping them with their social and cultural adjustments. Because most refugees have been on language courses, they therefore assume that the focus is on language acquisition instead. Thus, the kickoff meeting is also used to inform the refugees about the aims and scope of the program. Finally, each native student is paired with one refugee and the participants exchange their contact data (usually mobile numbers).

From then on, the program is very flexible. Students are required to meet with their foreign partner at least five times during the semester. The dyads are free to meet on their own or in groups. Depending on the refugees' language proficiency, specific cultural topics can be discussed during these meetings (ranging from the meaning and imperativeness of road signs to cultural values). To facilitate communication, students are equipped with specific worksheets and games, many of which do not require speaking (i.e., they work with pictures). Similar to the SCOUT program, dyads are also encouraged to explore the city and local cultural life. In general, we ask students to give the refugees an insight into their typical student life in Germany (e.g., going to a football game or the Christmas market). At the same time, refugees are also encouraged to report on their own culture, their reasons for coming to Germany, and their life in their home countries. For example, many dyads organize a joint cooking evening at which German and foreign dishes are prepared.

To facilitate reflection on and integration of the new knowledge acquired during the semester, students are asked to keep a brief reflective journal (see also Pink et al., 2016). That is, students are asked to answer a set of questions after each meeting with their foreign partner. Additionally, students are required to participate in at least one reflection meeting during the semester, which is led by a faculty member and covers topics such as intercultural learning, cultural adjustment, and social exclusion.

Table 6.3 *Guideline for reflective journaling used in the program for refugees*

Reflection of the meeting with your tandem partners

The aim of this exercise is to critically reflect on your inner attitude and behavior when meeting with your tandem partner. In addition, this written reflection task should give you the opportunity to express your feelings and thoughts in words. Please answer the respective question directly after each meeting (or on the same day). There are no right or wrong answers. Your individual impression counts.

At the end of the project, please also draw an overall conclusion. To do this, relate your experiences from interacting with your tandem partner to current societal challenges, as well as to the theoretical concepts and findings of intercultural psychology. This conclusion should be around 1,000 words (±200 words) in length.

If you have any questions, please contact your lecturer.

MEETING 1

Your name:	Date/time:

Questions	**Answers**
What was the content of today's meeting? In case of activities, what exactly did you do?	
What went well?	
What did not go so well?	
How did you perceive the mood of your conversation partner?	
How do you feel after the meeting? Why?	☺☺☺☹☹
How would you describe your relationship today?	
What was your main learning from today's meeting?	

Finally, at the end of the semester, students are also asked to prepare an essay reflecting on their experiences throughout the program. The written reflection guide used for the reflective journaling exercise as well as the instructions for handing in the final reflective essay are shown in Table 6.3.

The program ends with a closing event for all students and refugees. Overall, we can see great curiosity on both sides and generally obtain positive evaluations of the program. Students frequently report that they acquired a rich intercultural skill set and gained experiences that they would not want to have missed (sample statements from the student evaluation from form include the following: "It was a great way to get a glimpse into another culture. The general framework was helpful and suppor-tive"; "I do not see a better way to learn about and gain intercultural competency. The direct practical relevance was great. Socially relevant."). The faculty members involved in the program also describe it as very meaningful and enriching. The organizational effort is significantly greater than in a classic seminar. However, the social relevance of the topic and the direct promotion of intercultural competency in dealing with members of other cultures contribute to a large increase in learning.

This program is transferable as well, though additional education of the native participants with regard to coping with vicarious trauma is advisable if they have no background in psychology or similar fields (see also Pink et al., 2016). For both programs, more detailed information is available from the authors. If a complete transfer is not advisable or desired but a dyadic program for the integration of foreigners should be created, we condensed some our most important learnings in the next section.

Best Practices in Implementing Community–University Partnerships

Looking at both programs, we identified several key aspects that make them successful community engagement initiatives for the integration of foreign-ers into the local community. We sum up the experiences we gathered while organizing programs centered around dyads meeting alone as well as in larger groups that aim at fostering positive contact and support acquisition of inter-cultural competencies.

Preparing the Community

Preparing the community means involving all stakeholders early in the planning process of the initiative. Key questions include:

- Who is directly and indirectly affected by the initiative?
- What is the overall aim of the initiative and what sets it apart from other programs?
- Are there similar programs?
- If so, how can efforts be pooled?
- Who has decision-making power?
- Who has access to the target group and can spread information (e.g., a university's institutes or international offices for reaching international students; governmental institutions to gain access to refugee hostels)?

Arranging oneself with other initiatives early can avoid trouble and disappoint-ment by making sure that all relevant information is gathered beforehand. Similarly, recruiting and motivating participants from the local community (in our case, native students) requires thought and preparation. Universities can, for example, incenti-vize engagement by students through recognizing their intercultural learnings as part of coursework and embedding it into lectures.

Preparing for the Program

Several organizational steps have to be taken beforehand in order to run the program effectively. Since it is important for contact to be positive, it is desirable, particularly for dyadic programs, for participants to like each other. If possible, we advise trying to get information about factors such as age, interests, and activities, so that participants can be matched to someone with whom they share similarities (e.g., Rivas, 2009; Urberg et al., 1998). With dyadic programs, it is also important to keep in mind that equal numbers of participants from each group are needed. This requires balanced recruitment and participant commitment to avoid disappointments. From our experience, it is easier to recruit international students and refugees. Their (probable) lack of social support is a more pressing issue than the (probable) lack of intercultural skills and intercultural contact in the native population. As a result, although the topic as well as the experience-based service-learning approach create considerable interest in native students, their interest is still outmatched by the international students' and refugees' enthusiasm. Thus, recruiting an equal number of native participants requires comparably more effort.

Balancing Structure and Flexibility

Giving structure to a program's participants is important, not only to promoting interaction and preventing people from disengaging, but also to fostering learning. This can be achieved by providing worksheets, sample timetables, or regular meetings. Providing structure and joint meetings with all participants also increases commitment, as participants would meet even if their everyday lives get more stressful (e.g., during students' exam periods) or when initial empathy for their partner is low. Thus, structure helps to ensure continuous engagement over the course of the initiative.

On the other hand, most initiatives only thrive if participants get the chance to shape their engagement in the way they like, so it is important to allow for flexibility and adjustability with regard to schedules, the specific content of (dyadic) meetings, or other activities. Specifically, we have had positive experience with giving dyads the opportunity to organize their activity meetings independently. For example, one student has made contact with the local fire brigade, while another student initiated collaboration with a swimming club.

Implementing Dyadic, Cooperative Learning and Teaching

Both individuals of the dyads are the focus of the program as experts of their own cultures. Not only does this notion and mind-set contribute to a more optimal contact situation (Allport, 1954), it is also motivating for participants to experience that their opinion and experience is valued. By mutually teaching and learning, both native and foreign participants can build important intercultural and didactical competencies, which furthers personal development and, in the long run, employability.

Creating a Sense of Community and Establishing Norms

Joint meetings with all participants, such as kickoff events or trainings, are excellent opportunities to stress the importance and value of intercultural contact and cooperation. If there are incentives for the participants to take part in the program, emphasizing the need for cooperation in order to earn them can be advisable. Pre-program trainings can also be used to help participants understand basic cultural psychology, prepare them for cultural differences, and stress the importance of meeting their peers on a basis of equality.

Expecting Ambiguity

The crucial part of the programs presented here takes place during the dyadic interactions: when the participants get along well and contact is positive, prejudice on both sides is more likely to be reduced, social capital can be built, and friendship formation can happen more easily. However, it is also important to prepare participants to deal with ambiguity. Intercultural contact is not automatically easy. In fact, communicating effectively with someone from another culture is almost always more exhausting or stressful than mingling with individuals from one's in-group. Language barriers and sometimes profound cultural differences can make it difficult to interpret and understand the behaviors and actions of one's foreign partner. Especially when working with refugees, who each have their own personal history of displacement and potential escape, terror, and trauma, unforeseen situations might arise. Such uncertainties in interaction should not be ignored, but embedded in the learning experience of the participants.

Creating Space to Learn and Reflect

Following up on the previous point, supporting participants in their reflections on their experiences is of great use to maximizing learnings. This can be achieved by designing topical (dyadic) meetings with questions that make participants reflect on their own and their partner's cultures and their differences and similarities by structuring joint meetings for reflecting purposes or by written reflections.

Reaching Out to the Broader Community

Reaching out further to the community – to communal organizations, friends of participants, families – allows the extension of the program's benefit beyond its immanent scope and time frame. At the same time, former participants will also become representatives of the program and its cause. They pass on their experiences, impressions, and learnings to future participants, and the community as a whole. In addition, they might also act as multipliers by enabling further contact between their newly acquired international contacts and their native peers.

Challenges and Future Directions

As with every initiative, the ones we presented do have some drawbacks that we would like to address. First, the dyadic programs depicted are deliberately designed to pursue an individual, high-quality approach. That makes the initiatives not very cost-efficient and, in combination with the comparably lower number of native applicants, limits their reach to that very number of native participants. Also, the high amount of commitment the initiatives demand from their participants puts some potential applicants off. Feedback we received from participants supports our belief that our structured approach makes a difference with regard to the initiatives' quality, but it does further constrain reach.

In addition, the prejudice-reducing effect of the initiatives is reduced by a self-selection bias: participants applying for a community engagement initiative in which they engage in contact with foreigners are unlikely to be highly prejudiced, while highly prejudiced individuals are suspected to be unlikely to apply, thus bearing the risk of creating an "intercultural bubble." On the other hand, this also facilitates the implementation of the program, as the participants are generally very motivated, open-minded, and interested to learn about different cultures.

Lastly, both initiatives aim for social integration and, to some extent, cultural integration. However, integration is not limited to these facets. Structural integration, such as becoming part of the workforce or becoming part of the educational system, are important parts of integration that need to be addressed outside of the initiatives described. And while these initiatives do provide a conversational partner, they do not directly aim nor claim to improve language proficiency, neither for natives nor foreigners. With regard to potentially traumatized refugees, the initiatives are also limited in their ability to provide support, relying on professionals to help with that.

Conclusion

In light of increasing globalization and numerous global conflicts, migration from foreigners will continue to diversify local communities. This increase in diversity makes our communities more multicultural and colorful, but can also pose a threat to the social cohesion of communities, creating conflicts and leading to prejudices between locals and foreigners. In closing, we would thus like to refer back to Allport (1954), who, when postulating what is referred to as the contact hypothesis, stated that intergroup contact can in fact reduce prejudice – but that under which conditions the contact takes place is also important, and that particular caution is required with regard to preventing negative contact experiences. When combined with a service-learning approach, with the local student population engaging either international students or refugees, programs entail benefits for all stakeholders. Both local students and international participants hone their intercultural competencies, and particularly the local students gain theoretical knowledge, backed by their experiences from their intercultural interaction. Participants grow together with each other, forming a community that interacts with and integrates into the local community. In light of globalization and continuing internationalization, community engagement initiatives like the two programs described are viable means for avoiding having different ethnic groups in proximity but segregated and avoiding tension, but allowing the receiving community to fully reap the benefits of migration.

References

Addleman, R. A., Brazo, C. J., Dixon, K., Cevallos, T., & Wortman, S. (2014). Teacher candidates' perceptions of debriefing circles to facilitate self-reflection during a cultural immersion experience. *The New Educator, 10*, 112–128.

Addleman, R. A., Nava, R. C., Cevallos, T., Brazo, C. J., & Dixon, K. (2014). Preparing teacher candidates to serve students from diverse backgrounds: Triggering transformative learning through short-term cultural immersion. *International Journal of Intercultural Relations, 43*, 189–200.

Allport, G. W. (1954). *The nature of prejudice*. Oxford: Addison-Wesley.

Amerson, R. (2010). The impact of service-learning on cultural competence. *Nursing Education Perspectives, 31*, 18–22.

Artz, L. (2001). Critical ethnography for communication studies: Dialogue and social justice in service-learning. *Southern Communication Journal, 66*, 239–250.

Ayers, J. W., Hofstetter, C. R., Schnakenberg, K., & Kolody, B. (2009). Is immigration a racial issue? Anglo attitudes on immigration policies in a border county. *Social Science Quarterly, 90*, 593–610.

Baldwin, S. C., Buchanan, A. M., & Rudisill, M. E. (2007). What teacher candidates learned about diversity, social justice, and themselves from service-learning experiences. *Journal of Teacher Education, 58*, 315–327.

Barlow, F. K., Paolini, S., Pedersen, A. et al. (2012). The contact caveat: Negative contact predicts increased prejudice more than positive contact predicts reduced prejudice. *Personality and Social Psychology Bulletin, 38*(12), 1629–1643.

Bochner, S., McLeod, B. M., & Lin, A. (1977). Friendship patterns of overseas students: A functional model. *International Journal of Psychology, 12*, 277–294.

Bringle, R. G., & Hatcher, J. A. (1995). A service-learning curriculum for faculty. *Michigan Journal of Community Service Learning, 2*, 112–122.

Bringle, R. G., & Hatcher, J. A. (2009). Innovative practices in service-learning and curricular engagement. *New Directions for Higher Education, 2009*(147), 37–46.

Brown, R. E. (2001). The process of community-building in distance learning classes. *Journal of Asynchronous Learning Networks, 5*, 18–35.

Crawford, N., Cosgrave, J., Haysom, S., & Walicki, N. (2015). Protracted displacement: Uncertain paths to self-reliance in exile. London: ODI. Retrieved from www.odi.org/sites/odi.org.uk/files/odi-assets/publications-opinion-files/9851.pdf.

Einfeld, A., & Collins, D. (2008). The relationships between service-learning, social justice, multicultural competence, and civic engagement. *Journal of College Student Development, 49*, 95–109.

Elliot, J., Heesterbeek, S., Lukensmeyer, C. J., & Slocum, N. (2005). The world café. In S. Steyaert & H. Lisoir (Eds.), *Participatory methods toolkit: A practitioner's manual* (pp. 141–152). Brussels: King Baudouin Foundation, Flemish Institute for Science and Technology Assessment.

Enos, R. D. (2017). *The space between us: Social geography and politics*. Cambridge: Cambridge University Press.

Furnham, A., & Alibhai, N. (1985). The friendship networks of foreign students: A replication and extension of the functional model. *International Journal of Psychology, 20*, 709–722.

Giles, D. E., & Eyler, J. (1994). The impact of a college community service laboratory on students' personal, social, and cognitive outcomes. *Journal of Adolescence, 17*, 327–339.

Gurin, P. (1999). Selections from *The Compelling Need for Diversity in Higher Education*, expert reports in defense of the University of Michigan. *Equity & Excellence in Education, 32*(2), 36–62.

Hechanova-Alampay, R., Beehr, T. A., Christiansen, N. D., & Van Horn, R. K. (2002). Adjustment and strain among domestic and international student sojourners: A longitudinal study. *School Psychology International, 23*, 458–474.

Hendrickson, B., Rosen, D., & Aune, R. K. (2011). An analysis of friendship networks, social connectedness, homesickness, and satisfaction levels of international students. *International Journal of Intercultural Relations, 35*, 281–295.

Heublein, U., Richter, J., Schmelzer, R., & Sommer, D. (2014). *Die Entwicklung der Studienabbruchquoten an den deutschen Hochschulen – Statistische Berechnungen auf der Basis des Absolventenjahrgangs 2012 [The development of student drop-out quotas at German universities – Statistical calculations based on the alumni* year group of 2012]. Hanover: Deutsches Zentrum für Hochschul- und Wissenschaftsforschung.

Holmes, S. M., & Castañeda, H. (2016). Representing the "European refugee crisis" in Germany and beyond: Deservingness and difference, life and death. *American Ethnologist, 43*, 12–24.

Hudson, M., Phillips, J., Ray, K., & Barnes, H. (2007). *Social cohesion in diverse communities*. York: Joseph Rowntree Foundation.

Institute for International Education (2016). *Project Atlas 2016 release*. New York: Institute for International Education.

Jaumotte, F., Koloskova, K., & Saxena, S. C. (2016). *Impact of migration on income levels in advanced economies*. Washington, DC: International Monetary Fund.

Kezar, A., & Rhoads, R. A. (2001). The dynamic tensions of service learning in higher education. *The Journal of Higher Education, 72*, 148–171.

King, R., & Raghuram, P. (2013). International student migration: Mapping the field and new research agendas. *Population, Space and Place, 19*, 127–137.

Kudo, K., & Simkin, K. A. (2003). Intercultural friendship formation: The case of Japanese students at an Australian university. *Journal of Intercultural Studies, 24*, 91–114.

Letki, N. (2008). Does diversity erode social cohesion? Social capital and race in British neighbourhoods. *Political Studies, 56*, 99–126.

Moore, T., McDonald, M., McHugh-Dillon, H., & West, S. (2016). *Community engagement: A key strategy for improving outcomes for Australian families*. Melbourne: Australian Government – Australian Institute of Family Studies. Retrieved from https://aifs.gov.au/cfca/sites/default/files/cfca39-community-engagement.pdf.

OECD (2015). *Education at a* glance *2015*: OECD indicators. Paris: OECD Publishing.

Pettigrew, T. F., & Tropp, L. R. (2006). A meta-analytic test of intergroup contact theory. *Journal of Personality and Social Psychology, 90*, 751–783.

Pink, M. A., Taouk, Y., Guinea, S. et al. (2016). Developing a conceptual framework for student learning during international community engagement. *Journal of University Teaching and Learning Practice, 13,* 21.

Rappaport, J. (1984). Studies in empowerment: Introduction to the issue. In R. E. Hess (Ed.), *Studies in empowerment: Steps toward understanding and action* (pp. 1–8). New York, NY: The Haworth Press.

Rivas, J. (2009). Friendship selection. *International Journal of Game Theory, 38,* 521–538.

Sawir, E., Marginson, S., Deumert, A., Nyland, C., & Ramia, G. (2007). Loneliness and international students: An Australian study. *Journal of Studies in International Education, 12,* 148–180.

Stein, R. M., Post, S. S., & Rinden, A. L. (2000). Reconciling context and contact effects on racial attitudes. *Political Research Quarterly, 53,* 285–303.

Stifterverband für die Deutsche Wissenschaft (2015). *Hochschulbildungsreport 2020 – Jahresbericht 2015 [University education report 2020 – annual report 2015].* Essen: Stifterverband für die Deutsche Wissenschaft.

UN General Assembly (1957). *Convention relating to the status of refugees.* Geneva: UNHCR.

UNHCR (2017). *Global trends: Forced displacement in 2016.* Geneva: UNHCR.

Urberg, K. A., Degirmencioglu, S. M., & Tolson, J. M. (1998). Adolescent friendship selection and termination: The role of similarity. *Journal of Social and Personal Relationships, 15,* 703–710.

Wagner, U., Christ, O., Pettigrew, T. F., Stellmacher, J., & Wolf, C. (2006). Prejudice and minority proportion: Contact instead of threat effects. *Social Psychology Quarterly, 69,* 380–390.

Wagner, U., van Dick, R., Pettigrew, T. F., & Christ, O. (2003). Ethnic prejudice in East and West Germany: The explanatory power of intergroup contact. *Group Processes & Intergroup Relations, 6*(1), 22–36.

Walton, G. M., & Cohen, G. L. (2007). A question of belonging: Race, social fit, and achievement. *Journal of Personality and Social Psychology, 92,* 82–96.

Walton, G. M., & Cohen, G. L. (2011). A brief social-belonging intervention improves academic and health outcomes of minority students. *Science, 331,* 1447–1451.

Zhao, C.-M., Kuh, G. D., & Carini, R. M. (2005). A comparison of international student and American student engagement in effective educational practices. *The Journal of Higher Education, 76*(2), 209–231.

7 A Case Study on Community and Identity in a Study Abroad Program

Lisa Slattery Walker & Scott T. Fitzgerald

In this chapter, we present a case study of a successful, faculty-led, study abroad program that incorporates service learning with the aim of improving student understanding of the dynamics of community and identity while also being of use to the community in which the students are living and volunteering. In 2018, this program ran for the tenth time. Every summer since 2009, 5–12 students from the University of North Carolina at Charlotte have accompanied one of the authors to Manchester, UK. While there, they learn about the city, study urban sociology, and participate in volunteer activities with several local organizations, most notably Victoria Baths, Birchfields Park Forest Garden, and Swinton Grove Park.

Programs that focus on developing relationships between universities and communities through service learning can and often do provide benefits both to students and community partners. At the same time, while the sheer variety and number of study abroad options have grown substantially in recent years, there is comparatively little known about service learning in international contexts (Crabtree, 2008). Our chapter highlights how building community partnerships to provide service-learning opportunities for students enrolled in short-term study abroad programs can provide potential benefits to students, communities, and civil society.

We describe our experience with the design, initial implementation, and ongoing conduct of this faculty-led study abroad program. The program utilizes experiential learning to explore the following question: How do people find, build, and sustain communities in a diverse and changing metropolitan area? In this five-week program, our students: (1) learn key theories and concepts in community and urban sociology; (2) apply this knowledge to the study of historical and contemporary Manchester; and (3) participate in service-learning opportunities with organizations in Manchester. To this end, the program involves ongoing work with several local partners in Manchester with whom we have built ongoing, collaborative relationships. This chapter concludes with lessons learned and best practices developed during this program.

We created our community-focused study abroad program to pursue both the private and public goals of higher education. To do so, we focus on cultivating individual experiences and learning opportunities for our students while providing needed labor power to multiple community organizations in Manchester, UK.

Background and Motivation

Recent national and international developments have highlighted both the promise and perils of increased globalization. A college degree no longer serves as a ticket to long-term, stable employment in most professions, and the demands of a competitive international labor market means that today's students need to gain a variety of skills beyond simply earning a degree. These developments, coupled with increased costs and student debt, have focused attention on maximizing the private benefits of higher education. However, as the Association of American Colleges and Universities has reaffirmed in two reports on college learning, *Greater Expectations* (2002) and *College Learning for the New Global Century* (2007), a preoccupation with the private benefits of higher education has obscured the public benefits and civic value of producing broadly educated citizens. As Schneider (2011) observes, the guiding rationale for higher education that developed in the aftermath of World War II was premised on the notion that democracy, and by extension global peace, required citizens to develop "a rich understanding of the larger context in which they live, work and contribute" (p. 1). The need for civic-mindedness and broad concern for developing adaptable, global citizens still ring true today, but have been eclipsed by individualistic language and material pursuits. There are at least three broad goals of higher education consistent with both public and private interests: (1) substantive knowledge formation; (2) professional skill development; and (3) civic engagement. Study abroad programs that incorporate experiential learning and community partnerships can serve an important role in realizing each of these goals.

To be competitive in the labor market and to develop as a thoughtful and engaged citizen, today's students require not only discipline-based knowledge, but also communication and critical-thinking skills (Lo, 2010; National Leadership Council for Liberal Education and America's Promise, 2008; Pillay & Elliot, 2001). The scholarship of teaching and learning has identified the importance of student engagement, inquiry, and active learning in producing a wide array of desired outcomes (Crone, 1997; Justice et al., 2007; Lee, 2011; McCarthy & Anderson, 2000; McKinney et al., 2004; Pitt & Packard, 2010).

Faculty and administrators are continuously in search of "high-impact educational practices" (Kuh, 2008). We have found that an experiential learning model that utilizes service learning with ongoing community partners provides a framework for intellectual exploration that often proceeds in a non-linear fashion. Non-linear learning can be very challenging for students accustomed to PowerPoint lectures that proceed in bullet-point fashion to convey information in a clearly defined and step-by-step manner. As Caulfield and Caroline (2006) note, "Trained throughout their educational careers to sit back and maybe take notes, many students actively resist having to take an active and engaged role in their education" (p. 49). Additionally, cultural and institutional differences experienced while studying abroad add an additional layer of challenges for students.

Mooney and Edwards (2001) provide a typology of community-based learning that distinguishes different approaches based on types of activities, level of

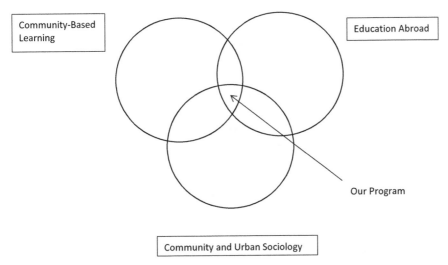

Community-Based Learning

Education Abroad

Our Program

Community and Urban Sociology

Figure 7.1 *Conceptualizing the course*

engagement, and links to course content. Consistent with other definitions (e.g., Duncan & Kopperud, 2008; Marullo, 1998; Mobley, 2007), this model defines service learning as including a service provided in the community where students apply/develop skills, engage in structured reflection, and receive curricular credit. The 1990 Community Service Act defines service learning as a method of learning in which students render needed services in their communities for academic credit, using and enhancing existing skills with time to "reflect on the service activity in such a way as to gain further understanding of the course content, a broader appreciation of the discipline, and an enhanced sense of civic responsibility" (Bringle & Hatcher, 1996). Service learning seeks to enhance student learning by combining course content with community service experiences (Duncan & Kopperud, 2008; Everett, 1998; Rashotte, 2002) and is consistent with an experiential learning model that builds on "learning by doing" (Everett, 1998; Kolb, 1984). Much the same way as learning communities can be used to create integrative learning environments (Mahoney & Schamber, 2011), working with community partners in an international context provides opportunities for sustained, collaborative explorations of ideas from multiple perspectives. We designed our course to be located at the intersection of community-based learning, education abroad experiences, and community and urban sociology (see Figure 7.1).

Community and Identity in Manchester

Flora et al. (1992) posit that in order for community development to occur, the people in a community must first believe that working together can make a difference and then must organize to address their shared needs. We concur with this view and thus attempt to instill in our students a feeling of belonging in their local Mancunian community, as well as equipping them with the tools they need to organize. Similarly, Christenson et al. (1989) define community development as a group of people in a community reaching a decision to initiate a social action process to change their economic, social, cultural, and environmental situation. Issues of social justice, local action, and social change are all prominent in our program as well.

A primary focus of our program is the relationship between community and identity. We see this recursive relationship (community affects individuals' identities that in turn have an effect on the community) as essential to understanding both places and people. Many scholars of community development see this focus on the individual's role as essential. Indeed, the United Nations sees community development as the interaction of individuals in a community with governmental authorities to improve the economic, social, and cultural conditions of communities (Biggs, 1999).

Another focus of our program is change over time. Manchester is a rapidly changing place (see background details below), and we see the interplay among a changing group of individuals as important to understanding the city itself. Shaffer (1989) calls this "vitality," and says that community vitality is the capacity of the local socioeconomic system to survive and persist in generating employment, income, and wealth and to maintain if not improve its relative economic position. We also see the preservation of a community's history as an important part of community vitality.

Sanders' (1958) definition of community development included the notion of a movement sweeping people up in emotion and belief. For us, this is also important. We try to connect our students with Manchester and the local neighborhood not just intellectually, but emotionally as well.

Manchester is a city with a long history and a rapid pace of change and growth, particularly in the past 150 years or so. Since one of the foci of our program is urban sociology, we tend to highlight the more recent history of the city. We here offer a brief outline of Manchester since the Industrial Revolution to make the case for why it is an ideal place to study both urbanity and community. Much of the historical detail below comes from Peck and Ward (2002). Manchester is often described as the first industrial city. Early in each of our trips, we conduct a walking tour that includes the site of the world's first true factory (which is today a parking lot). Wool, silk, and cotton were manufactured during the nineteenth century, and large numbers of working people worked 12-hour days in the mills. Much of the cotton being processed there came from the Carolinas, where many of our students reside. As Peck and Ward (2002) note, the twentieth century brought many changes and challenges to Manchester. Having been the first industrial city, Manchester was also among the first to face deindustrialization – a process that led to a dramatic increase in unemployment and abandonment of factories and buildings across the area. This is important for our program because industry had not only meant jobs for the city, but also "cultural identity for a city that had long prided itself on the tradition of no-nonsense graft and money-making" (Peck & Ward, 2002, p. 1). During the latter half of the twentieth century, manufacturing went from providing over half of the jobs in the city to less than 20 percent of them. While recent additions to the economic landscape, notably in media/broadcasting and tourism, have meant new jobs, the sense of coherent community previously enjoyed city-wide has been fractured.

The demographics of the city have changed as well. During the twentieth century, many people moved out of the city center to live in the suburbs. The population of the city center dropped dramatically, although in recent years a boomerang effect has been seen in Manchester, as in many other urban areas. Today, the population of Manchester proper is around half a million, with a metropolitan area of 2.5 million, making it the second largest metropolitan area in the UK.

Two notable aspects of Manchester's history are especially relevant for our program. First, in 1996, an Irish Republican Army (IRA) bomb devastated much of the downtown area. Holden (2002) notes that 1,200 buildings were damaged in some way over an area of more than a million square meters and that 674 businesses were displaced. The traumatic effect on the area and the opportunity for redevelopment that it presented have shaped the look and feel of modern downtown Manchester. Holden cites that the media were quick to discuss the "resilient spirit of the city and its people" when discussing the aftermath of the bombing (p. 134).

Second, the demographics of the city are in constant flux. Early immigration of European Jews and of Chinese people have had their effects on the city. More recent immigrants have come from everywhere from Africa to Wales, including large groups of Eastern Europeans, Kosovan refugees, and South Asian people (Bullen, 2015). Of the 541,300 people living in Manchester, 67 percent are white, 13 percent are black or mixed race, and 19 percent are Asian, Chinese, or Arab (Manchester City Council, 2017a).

The area in which our students live and work is a heavily immigrant area, and understanding the dynamics of immigration in a community is part of what our students learn, both through course readings (see Appendix 7.1), but also – more importantly – through talking to the neighbors. In addition, there are a number of notable museums in Manchester, including the Museum of Science and Industry, the People's History Museum, and the Imperial War Museum, all of which help to tell the story of Manchester to visitors.

Community Partnerships

While in Manchester, we work with a number community partners to give our students an opportunity to gain firsthand experience with community organizations and issues of community development. While we try to stay open to different opportunities that might arise, there are three main partners with whom we have developed ongoing relationships: Victoria Baths, Birchfields Park Forest Garden, and Swinton Grove Park. We will briefly describe each in turn and identify the types of activities that we engage in with each group.

Victoria Baths. Victoria Baths was designed as a public baths facility in 1902 by the city architect, Henry Price. It was opened in 1906 by the then Lord Mayor, J. Herbert Thewlis, who described it as a "water palace of which every citizen of Manchester is proud." It was designed to be a showpiece, the grandest of all of the public bath facilities in Manchester at the time. No expense was spared, and the total building cost was £59,000. Its facade was constructed in red brick and terracotta, and much of the interior is covered in glazed tiles, including some of the staircases. Most of the windows had decorative stained glass, including the famous Angel of Purity, which resides in the front, central window of the building.

Until 1992, Victoria Baths provided both hygiene and leisure facilities. At the time of opening, few of the homes in Manchester had running water or even indoor bathrooms, so its 64 "slipper baths" or bathtubs were an essential hygiene aid. In addition, there were three Olympic-sized swimming pools originally designated for segregated use by First-Class Males, Second-Class Males, and Females. Water was moved from one pool to the next, with only the First-Class Males pool receiving fresh water. Mixed-gender bathing was first introduced in 1914, and by the 1920s, mixed bathing sessions were held every weekend for families.

In the early 1990s, Manchester City Council decided to close Victoria Baths due to the high cost of maintenance and repairs along with decreased demand. The decision prompted community protests, including an effort to occupy the building. Despite this, the Baths were closed in March of 1993. Soon after, the Victoria Baths Trust was formed to begin to investigate the possibility of running the Victoria Baths

Figure 7.2 *Inside the men's first-class pool at the Victoria Baths, 2015*

independently. The Trust was eventually registered as a charity and, in 2001, was granted a license to restore, develop, and use the Baths.

In 2003, Victoria Baths won the BBC's landmark competition series "Restoration." As a result of this win, the Heritage Lottery Fund donated £3 million and the BBC's Restoration Fund raised another £500,000 for the restoration of Victoria Baths. English Heritage has also subsequently supported the restoration with a grant of £450,000 (BBC, 2014).

Today, the Baths operate in several ways. First, for one day during each of the summer months, the Baths are open to the public for tours. These open days often include other activities like choral concerts, tea dances, sports days, or vintage sales. Over 50,000 people have visited the Baths since they reopened in 2003. Second, Victoria Baths is now a highly sought-after site for special events such as weddings, parties, and the filming of various period movies and television programs. Finally, the building is used for various community activities including stained glass classes taught by local artisans. At this time, the Baths are not regularly used for swimming, although plans are in the works for greater use of the gala pool and for restoration and operation of the Turkish bath.

Over the years, our actual tasks at the Baths have varied considerably. In the early years, much of the work entailed cleaning and repairing a building that had been abandoned for many years in order to make it possible for the building to meet safety and health standards and to be used at all. We have cleaned and scraped walls and painted indoors and outdoors.

More recently, our work at the Baths consists of supporting the activities described above, including the open days and special events, as well as working on the continuing restoration of the building. The open days are held once a month during the summer months and provide the public with an opportunity to come tour the Baths, learn more about their history, and spend the afternoon eating, drinking, and relaxing. Along with our students, we help clean and prepare the building for the visit during our stay and help collect tickets, serve food, and clean up throughout the day. One particularly meaningful special event that we provide volunteer assistance for is the annual Ward 84 Party hosted for children and families from a children's cancer ward located a few streets away.

Our students get to know the staff and volunteers at the Baths, many of whom live in the local area. They learn about the history of the building, the neighborhood, and its residents. While in Manchester, the students live just a couple of streets from the Baths and begin to form attachments to the building and community.

Birchfields Park Forest Garden. Near to Victoria Baths is Birchfields Park. Here, we work with a local group of volunteers who operate a forest garden using the principles of permaculture. The land that became Birchfields Park was acquired by Manchester City Council in 1887 from local landowner, Sir William Anson. It was opened officially as a public park by Prince Albert in 1888.

The group with which we work, the Friends of Birchfields Park, has developed a small forest garden in the corner of Birchfields Park. The Friends are an all-volunteer group. A forest garden is a form of permaculture gardening that attempts to replicate the natural flora of an area – here, as a natural forest. It is also hoped that it will produce a wide variety of edible fruit and vegetables with a minimal amount of work. Use of chemicals is kept to an absolute minimum.

The garden itself is a circle of about 50 meters in diameter. It is divided into four arched sections arranged in a ring, and a different volunteer is charged with the weeding and maintenance of each of the four sections. Plants currently in the garden include apple, damson, plum, and pear trees; currant, blackberry, and walnut bushes; and many varieties of herbs, including oregano, mint, valerian, balms, and nettles.

Our work here consists primarily of weeding, replanting stray plants, putting down mulch, and picking up trash. While the students do value the outdoor activity and the time in the park, the real benefit is the time we spend with the volunteers. As with the Baths, most of the volunteers live in the local area – many within a short walk of the park – and the perspective they provide on the community is invaluable. Conversations take place while working side by side, as well as when we break for a shared lunch.

Swinton Grove Park. Another nearby park is Swinton Grove Park. This park was originally formed on the grounds of the family home of the author, Elizabeth Gaskill. Her home still stands nearby as a museum of sorts and is also an occasional community partner. While this was a fairly rural area at the time Elizabeth Gaskill was in residence in the 1850s, it is now very much in the center of Manchester proper (Friends of Swinton Grove Park, n.d.). At times during its history, the Park has contained playgrounds, bowling lawns, flower gardens, and sports fields. Today, it is primarily grassland and wooded areas. Black mulberry trees and other mature trees provide a green and shady place in which local residents can relax (Manchester City Council, 2017b).

Our partnership is with the Friends of Swinton Grove Park, a group of local volunteer residents who have taken on the mission of maintaining the park and providing programming for the local neighborhood. Our work with them primarily takes the form of supporting their annual festival day. The festival brings together the residents of the neighborhood for games, music, and performances. In addition, local service providers are able to share information with the local community. Our students serve lunch, put up and take down tents/awnings, and pick up trash. They also get to meet lots of neighbors and sometimes even the Lord Mayor of Manchester, who often puts in an appearance. In 2015, the organizers changed the date of this annual event in order to ensure that the "group from America" would be able to be there to help. As discussed below, the organizers of this event value the labor power that we can provide.

Student Learning and Organizational Outcomes

We center this course on the service work we do with our community partners and the experiences students have with community members, local volunteers, and staff. Additionally, it also includes museum visits, walking tours of various parts of the city, visits to nearby cities and towns for the purpose of comparison, and students' own individual experiences in Manchester. The required reading and writing assignments are designed to augment these experiences in a nonlinear learning process consistent with Kolb's (1984) experiential learning model.

Students earn a total of six credit hours for participation in the five-week program and are in residence in Manchester, UK, during the entirety of the program. There is one major project for each of two three-credit courses: Urban Sociology and Community and Identity. Participation in all contact hours is required (this would be like attendance in any other course). Weekly writing assignments are also conducted for Urban Sociology and a journal is kept for Community and Identity.

For Urban Sociology, the major writing project combines individual observations with academic sources. Students must research the history of Manchester from the 1800s through to the current day. They are instructed to focus on issues of economics, demographics, space, and place. Then each choose one section of the city as their special geographical focus area. They are asked to consider the history of the area, including descriptions of the physical area over time, key industries, peoples/populations, and issues that the area has faced. Then, for their chosen area, students do participant observations and keep field journals. They are required to make these observations on different days of the week and at different times of the day. (For safety reasons, they must do their observations with at least one other student.) These observations include noticing the physical area and how it is used, who the people in the area are, how people move around the area, and how and by whom the spaces are defined. This is all written up in a final product that integrates their observations with the required readings and our class discussions.

For the Community and Identity course, the final project is a reflective personal essay. It augments their service-learning journal entries (see below) with additional reflections on the city and on travels in the UK, as well as additional reflections on questions of community and identity that we discuss throughout the program as a class and with the neighbors. These papers force the students to take a critical and thoughtful look at what it means to be a community and how identity and community are related. The service-learning journals are an essential part of the students' experiential learning experience. By having students think about what they are doing and what they are learning from the experience, reflective writing can increase the amount of learning that takes places (Cooper, 1998). It can also make them aware of what they do not know, which can and should lead to new questions worthy of future exploration and study. In our program, students are required to produce a journal entry for each visit with a community partner (see Figure 7.3).

Do a journal entry each time you work at the community site. Take a few minutes before you leave the site to make your entry or do it within a few hours of your experience to facilitate making an accurate entry. Each journal entry should include all of the following elements. Please clearly divide each entry into the following categories: Journal entries:

1. Date and hours worked
2. Objective description of your experience

- *What happened? Write a factual account of the behaviors you observed that does NOT include your opinion. Write at least 100 words.*

3. *Personal opinions/feelings and learning*

- *Thoughts/opinions. Interpret what you saw and heard today. What does it mean to you?*
- *Feelings. Use emotion words (e.g., happy, surprised, frustrated) to describe your feelings.*
- *What knowledge and/or skills did you acquire today?*

4. *Interpretation/explanation*

- *Now try and understand the behaviors and experiences you described above. Use principles and concepts from previous coursework to reflect on what underlying sociological, psychological, and/or political processes are involved.*

Figure 7.3 *Excerpt of a service-learning journal writing prompt*

Students differ in their preparation and openness to community engagement, and this can limit the effectiveness of community partnerships and experiences for both students and community members (Crabtree, 2008; Palmer & Savoie, 2002). While we do not have formal pre- and post-participation assessment data, our extensive interaction with students throughout all of the service-learning and other program activities, as well as our reading of both their reflective and analytic writing assignments, allows us to identify some patterns in student experiences and learning. Additionally, we routinely interact with organization members throughout the program and have coordinated our activities with these contacts each year for the past ten years (Victoria Baths and Birchfields Forest Gardens) and five years (Swinton Grove Park), which provides multiple opportunities to discuss the outcomes of our program for these organizations and communities.

Benefits for Students

In this chapter, we have identified our program as contributing to both the private and public benefits of higher education. It is designed to do so by producing substantive knowledge formation, professional skill development, and civic engagement.

The primary academic focus of this program is the sociological study of urban areas, community, and identity. Using an experiential learning model, the course assignments integrate academic writing and theorizing with student experiences in the city and working with community partners. This approach has proven to be beneficial for our students – both those who are sociology majors and those who are new to the discipline. The evidence of this learning is gleaned from their written assignments and our group conversations. It has been interesting to see how this model has supported different types of learning. For example, we have witnessed some "academically" focused students gain a greater appreciation of the relevance and importance of the theories they have read about once they see them at work in the

Table 7.1 *Organizations, service-learning activities, and outcomes*

Organization	Organization type	Student activities	Interaction with members of organization	Interaction with community members	Primary skills developed
Victoria Baths	Formal	Building repair; cleaning; special events	Extensive	Moderate	Teamwork; oral communication; cross-cultural awareness
Birchfields Park Forest Garden	Informal	Gardening	Moderate	Minimal	Teamwork; cross-cultural awareness
Swinton Grove	Informal	Special Event	Moderate	Moderate	Teamwork; oral communication; cross-cultural awareness

real world. Gentrification, dislocation, segregation, community empowerment – these terms begin to take on additional levels of meaning once they become linked to particular people the students have met and particular places in which they have spent time. Conversely, we have also witnessed "experience"-focused students who at first are only interested in their own study abroad experiences begin to seek out further information. The combination of self-reflective and analytic assignments encourages them to draw from the body of sociological knowledge to make sense of what they are witnessing and feeling and to apply theoretical insights.

The particular structure of our program and tasks performed limit the amount of direct professional skill development opportunities for our students. We can imagine programs designed for social work or counseling students that might involve working directly with at-risk populations in the community, or a marketing course collaborating with a community group to develop a new marketing campaign. However, our program is not limited to sociology students and does not require any prior training or experience in order to participate. As a result, we are not able to develop collaborations with our community partners that require more specialized or professional skills. What students can and do develop are teamwork and communication skills (see Table 7.1). Learning to successfully work together as a group and also alongside local community members requires students to pay attention to group dynamics, differing norms of behavior, and various cultural expectations. Given the diverse communities that we work with, even learning how to ask for help or provide assistance for participants at an event requires students to develop and expand their communication skills and cultural awareness.

The program also provides an opportunity to participate in various civic engagement activities. As discussed above, students participate in numerous activities designed to bring people together and build a sense of community for area residents.

They witness firsthand the smiles and laughter of families dealing with childhood cancer who, for one day at least, can relax at the Ward 84 Party. At the Forest Garden, they gain greater appreciation for the constant work that is needed to maintain a community park in the face of declining city budgets and a demographically changing neighborhood. They are awed when they meet one of the elderly neighborhood women who, in an act of civil disobedience, prevented the Victoria Baths from being demolished in the 1990s. They are surprised to learn that these women did not think of themselves as activist or leaders, but simply as mothers who remembered generations of families growing up swimming in the pools at the Victoria Baths and recognized the importance of this building to the local community and local history. This act of defiance inspired others to get involved and contribute to the preservation and renovation of this landmark. Our students have written about how thankful they felt to meet these community members and to be a part of something bigger then themselves, and also how it has motived them to seek out further volunteer opportunities and ways to engage in their own communities upon returning to the United States.

Benefits for Community Organizations

The primary benefit for our community partners is the labor power provided by our group each summer. Since 2009, we have provided over 6,000 person-hours of free labor to these organizations. Approximately 70 percent of these hours have been spent at our primary community partner, Victoria Baths. The majority of our hours at Victoria Baths have involved manual labor, completing tasks that otherwise would not be completed or would require local volunteers to complete. By assisting with these tasks, we allow local volunteers and staff to focus their attention on other needed tasks, such as fundraising and educational outreach.

Multiple local volunteers and staff have shared with us how much they enjoy talking with the students each year. Many of the local volunteers and staff have little or no travel experience in the United States, so it is an eye-opening experience for them to talk with American students and for both groups to learn about each other (and challenge the generalizations and stereotypes we have about each other based primarily on media and pop culture depictions). For example, on multiple occasions we have heard the surprise when a local volunteer learns that not everyone in America has a gun – and the surprise of our American students that other people would assume they did!

A final benefit for our partners that we have observed is the opportunity to talk with us about the challenges they face in attempting to organize and work in the community. For example, in a recent conversation, the organizers of the Swinton Grove Park festival shared their frustration at two situations that have emerged. The first is the small number of local residents who volunteer at the event. While the organizers appreciate the fact that the American group can provide this support – and thus allow the festival to continue – they ultimately would like more local residents to be actively involved. The second and related issue was in reference to two different confrontations that took place during the event in 2017. In both situations, local residents who were at the event verbally accosted the organizers, complaining about how long it took to get food and participate in some of the activities. (Everything at the festival is provided free of charge and all of the workers are volunteers, so lines tend to get fairly long at times.) What was particularly disheartening to the organizers was the "sense of entitlement" that they felt was demonstrated by these confrontations – that these particular residents had become accustomed to "getting handouts" and had no interest in helping. One organizer asked, "Don't they realize this is all done through donations and volunteers?" In the following conversation, we were able to provide an outside perspective and suggest that they probably do not realize that it was all done through donations and volunteers. We then brainstormed together different strategies that could be used to encourage greater local resident participation, community ownership of the event, awareness about the nature of the event, and culturally sensitive ways to encourage volunteerism within the community. Afterwards, the organizers thanked us for "sharing our expertise" and helping them view the situation from a different perspective.

Lessons Learned

Our experiences over the past decade of developing, implementing, and refining this study abroad program provide the basis for a series of recommendations designed for others interested in pursuing this form of community engagement. We focus on the university–community partnerships that are at the heart of our service and experiential learning program.

Building Trust. There are multiple relationships between the university and community partners that develop during this type of program: faculty and community/organization leaders; faculty and community/organization members; students and community/organization leaders; and students and community/organization members. Building trust across each set of relationships is essential for a successful collaboration and program.

Anticipate the Concerns of Community Partners. This is particularly important during the development stage of the program. When we first began developing this program, the second author traveled to Manchester and set up a series of introductory meetings with community organizations. Our initial email exchanges with potential community partners explained our goals for a five-week program and that we were seeking opportunities to volunteer with community organizations to incorporate into our service-learning course design. Our first and primary contact was with Victoria Baths. The working director of Victoria Baths was gracious and willing to discuss matters further, but was also a bit reluctant to fully commit to working with us that first year. Fortunately, we were able to anticipate some of her concerns and proactively address them. In particular, we recognized that although having the labor power of a group of

American university students could be beneficial, it would also require considerable time and energy of the staff at Victoria Baths to accommodate us. By clearly discussing this early on with our potential partner, we were able to overcome some initial reservations and received an invitation to work with them.

Be "Of Service." In the initial conversations and first year of the program, we discovered that it was also unclear what exactly *we* expected of these community organizations. To address these concerns, we very intentionally positioned our group as wanting to be of service to the organizations. We were willing to do whatever tasks were needed – no matter how dirty or menial – that could free up staff and other volunteer resources to more directly address their mission. We did not require "fun" or "high-profile" activities, nor did we expect the organizations to connect the tasks to our course. We simply wanted to be of service to the organization and learn more about what, why, and how they do what they do. By following through on this promise, we built trust.

Be Flexible. A final component of our working relationships with our community partners is a commitment to being flexible. Each year, we reach out to our various partners at least six to eight months prior to our arrival and provide the specific dates we will be in the country. This begins a process of building schedules for the various events and work days. By the time we arrive, most of the schedule has been confirmed; however, we always remain flexible and routinely shift days and activities around to benefit the organizations that we work with. This flexibility also extends to other activities that we participate in while in Manchester to take advantage of the multitude of events and performances that take place sporadically throughout the city.

Conclusion

We believe we have successfully created a community-based study abroad program that achieves both the public and private goals of higher education. The students and the community partners both benefit from their participation in the program, though obviously in very different ways (as do the faculty facilitators). Students learn substantive knowledge about theories of urban life, community development, social psychology, and social history. They develop their skills in the areas of communication (speaking and writing) and critical thinking as they navigate the many and varied stories of the people they encounter in Manchester. And the students certainly engage in the community, both through the intentional channels of the program and through other, more informal means that arise while living abroad. The experiential nature of the program and the ongoing community partnerships facilitate this deep and rich development of our students while providing benefit to the local organizations and the community as a whole.

Appendix 7.1

Reading List for Student Participants

Duncan, D., & Kopperud, J. (2007). *Service-learning companion*. Boston, MA: Wadsworth.

Engels, F. (1993). The great towns. In F. Engel (Ed.), *The conditions of the working class in England* (pp. 36–86). Oxford: Oxford University Press.

Haslam, D. (1999). Immigrants, merchants, anarchists: the birth of the city. In D. Haslam (Ed.), *Manchester, England: The story of the pop cult city* (pp. 3–28). Manchester: Fourth Estate.

Haslam, D. (1999). Manchester: Past imperfect, present tense, future uncertain. In D. Haslam (Ed.), *Manchester, England: The story of the pop cult city* (pp. vii–xxxi). Manchester: Fourth Estate.

Holden, A. (2002). Bomb sites: the politics of opportunity. In J. Peck & K. Ward (Eds.), *City of revolution: Restructuring Manchester* (pp. 132–154). Manchester: Manchester University Press.

Mellor, R. (2002). Hypocritical city: Cycles of urban exclusion. In J. Peck & K. Ward (Eds.), *City of revolution: Restructuring Manchester* (pp. 213–235). Manchester: Manchester University Press.

Peck, J., & Ward, K. (2002). Placing Manchester. In J. Peck & K. Ward (Eds.), *City of revolution: Restructuring Manchester* (pp. 1–17). Manchester: Manchester University Press.

Simmel, G. (1903). The metropolis and mental life. In G. Bridge & S. Watson (Ed.), *The Blackwell city reader* (pp. 103–110). Oxford and Malden, MA: Wiley-Blackwell.

Somerville, P. (2011). Making sense of community development. In P. Somerville (Ed.), *Understanding community: Politics, policy, and practice* (pp. 33–66). Bristol: Policy Press.

Ward, K. (2002). Capital and class. In T. Hall, P. Hubbard, & J. R. Short (Eds.), *The Sage companion to the city* (pp. 109–122). Thousand Oaks, CA: Sage Publications.

Wilson, D. (2002). Segregation and division. In T. Hall, P. Hubbard, & J. R. Short (Eds.), *The Sage companion to the city* (pp. 210–230). Thousand Oaks, CA: Sage Publications.

References

BBC (2014). Victoria Baths: A brief history. Retrieved from www.bbc.co.uk/manchester/content/articles/2008/09/17/victoria_baths_history_feature.shtml.

Biggs, S. (1999). Community capacity building in Queensland: The Queensland Government service delivery project. Unpublished paper. Brisbane: Office of Rural Communities.

Bringle, R. G., & Hatcher, J. A. (1996). Implementing service learning in higher education. *The Journal of Higher Education, 67*(2), 221–239.

Bullen, E. (2015). *Manchester migration: A profile of Manchester's migration patterns*. Manchester: Manchester City Council.

Caulfield, S. L., & Caroline, H. P. (2006). Teaching social science reasoning and quantitative literacy: The role of collaborative groups. *Teaching Sociology, 34*(1), 39–53.

Christenson, J. A., & Robinson, J. W. (1989). *Community development in perspective*. Ames, IA: Iowa State University Press.

Cooper, D. D. (1998). Reading, writing, and reflection. *New Directions for Teaching and Learning, 1998*(73), 47–56.

Crabtree, R. D. (2008). Theoretical foundations for international service-learning. *Michigan Journal of Community Service Learning, 15*(1), 18–36.

Crone, J. A. (1997). Using panel debates to increase student involvement in the introductory sociology class. *Teaching Sociology, 25*(3), 214–218.

Duncan, D., & Kopperud, J. W. (2008). *Service-learning companion*. Boston, MA: Houghton Mifflin.

Everett, K. D. (1998). Understanding social inequality through service learning. *Teaching Sociology, 26*(4), 299–309.

Flora, C. B., & Flora, J. L. (1993). Entrepreneurial social infrastructure: A necessary ingredient. *The Annals of the American Academy of Political and Social Sciences, 539*(1), 48–58.

Flora, J. L., Green, G. P., Gale, E. A., Schmidt, F. E., & Flora, C. B. (1992). Self-development: A viable rural development option? *The Policy Studies Journal, 20*(2), 276–288.

Friends of Swinton Grove Park (n.d.). History of Swinton Grove Park. Retrieved from www.fosgp.org.uk/history-of-the-park.html.

Green III, C. S., & Klug, H. G. (1990). Teaching critical thinking and writing through debates: An experimental evaluation. *Teaching Sociology, 18*(4), 462–471.

Holden, A. (2002). Bomb sites: the politics of opportunity. In J. Peck & K. Ward (Eds.), *City of revolution: Restructuring Manchester* (pp. 132–154). Manchester: Manchester University Press.

Justice, C., Rice, J., Warry, W. et al. (2007). Inquiry in higher education: Reflections and directions on course design and teaching methods. *Innovative Higher Education, 31*(4), 201–214.

Kolb, D. (1984). *Experiential learning: Experience as the source of learning and development*. Englewood Cliffs, NJ: Prentice Hall.

Kuh, G. D. (2008). *Excerpt from high-impact educational practices: What they are, who has access to them, and why they matter*. Washington, DC: American Association of Colleges and Universities.

Lee, V. S. (2011). The power of inquiry as a way of learning. *Innovative Higher Education 36*(3), 149–160.

Lo, C. C. (2010). Student learning and student satisfaction in an interactive classroom. *The Journal of General Education, 59*(4), 238–263.

Manchester City Council (2017a). *Annual population survey*. Manchester: Chief Executive's Department (Performance and Intelligence, PRI).

Manchester City Council (2017b). Swinton Grove Park. Retrieved from www.manchester.gov.uk/directory_record/89314/swinton_grove_park/category/304/play_areas.

Mahoney, S., & Schamber, J. (2011). Integrative and deep learning through a learning community: A process view of self. *The Journal of General Education, 60*(4), 234–247.

Marullo, S. (1998). Bringing home diversity: A service-learning approach to teaching race and ethnic relations. *Teaching Sociology, 26*(4), 259–275.

McCarthy, J. P., & Anderson, L. (2000). Active learning techniques versus traditional teaching styles: Two experiments from history and political science. *Innovative Higher Education, 24*(4), 279–294.

McKinney, K., Howery, C. B., Strand, K. J., Kain, E. L., & Berheide, C. W. (2004). *Liberal learning and the sociology major updated.* Washington, DC: American Sociological Association.

Mobley, C. (2007). Breaking ground: Engaging undergraduates in social change through service learning. *Teaching Sociology, 35*(2), 125–137.

Mooney, L. A., & Edwards, B. (2001). Experiential learning in sociology: Service learning and other community-based learning initiatives. *Teaching Sociology, 29*(2), 181–194.

National Leadership Council for Liberal Education and America's Promise (2008). College learning for the new global century. Retrieved from www.aacu.org/leap/documents/GlobalCentury_final.pdf.

Palmer, C. E., & Savoie, E. J. (2002). Challenges to connecting sociology and service learning. *Sociological Practice: A Journal of Clinical and Applied Sociology, 4*(1), 89–97.

Peck, J., & Ward, K. (Eds.) (2002). *City of revolution: Restructuring.* Manchester: Manchester University Press.

Pillay, H., & Elliott, B. (2001). Emerging attributes of pedagogy and curriculum for the "New World Order." *Innovative Higher Education, 26*(1), 7–22.

Pitt, R. N., & Packard, J. R. (2010). Stakeholder meetings as a means of engaging student learning of complex social problems. *Teaching Sociology, 38*(3), 215–225.

Rashotte, L. S. (2002). Service learning in a small groups course. *Sociological Practice, 4*(1), 79–87.

Sanders, I. T. (1958). Theories of community development. *Rural Sociology, 23*(1), 1–12.

Schneider, C. G. (2011). President's message: Civic learning in college: Our best investment in the future of our democracy. *Liberal Education, 97*(2). Retrieved from www.aacu.org/publications-research/periodicals/presidents-message-civic-learning-college-our-best-investment.

Shaffer, R. (1989). *Community economics. Economic structure and change in smaller communities.* Hoboken, NJ: Wiley-Blackwell.

Williams, P. (2004). *Victoria Baths: Manchester's water palace.* Salisbury: Spire Books.

PART III

Disciplinary Outreach

8 Faculty and Students Consulting in the Community

The Center for Applied Psychological Services

Joseph E. Mroz, Michael Yoerger, Joseph A. Allen, & Roni Reiter-Palmon

Across the nation, there are numerous examples of academic institutions that have created programs designed to offer students hands-on, applied learning while simultaneously providing high-quality services to local communities. At the University of Nebraska Omaha, the Center for Applied Psychological Services (CAPS) is a faculty-managed consulting group wherein graduate students partner with organizations in the community to provide affordable consulting solutions. The current vision of CAPS aims to develop future psychologists by providing training and field experience, while providing high-quality, research-based, legally defensible, and scientifically sound consulting services to local, public, and private organizations.

In each project, CAPS partners with an organization in the community to assess their needs and design a consulting plan that will most effectively bring about desired changes. CAPS associates specialize in conducting interviews and focus groups, designing organizational surveys, and engaging in observation of work processes to collect the necessary evaluation data for an organization. In every case, CAPS associates take confidentiality seriously, including signing nondisclosure agreements as needed to ensure the protection of the client, their employees, and the CAPS associates. The university must approve any legal agreements with clients, and agreements must sometimes be altered to comply with university guidelines. A key part of the process is effectively balancing the needs of clients with the needs of the university and ensuring that contractual agreements do not become economically cumbersome to clients. Some of the ways CAPS can assist organizations are by developing recommendations for enhancing employee engagement, job satisfaction, employee performance, meeting effectiveness, leader development, and customer satisfaction, just to name a few areas. In the past, CAPS has provided area organizations with job analyses, workflow analyses, program evaluations, and promotional exam development, as well as a variety of other projects that make use of CAPS associates' extensive array of skills. Additionally, CAPS works on projects in the fields of school psychology and social psychology, which helps increase collaboration among psychology department faculty from different domain areas.

Faculty-directed, student-involved consulting organizations based within universities can be mutually beneficial endeavors for students, faculty, clients, universities, and the broader community. From a student perspective, CAPS provides students with paid field experience in which they can develop skills (e.g., interpersonal, problem solving, critical thinking, teamwork, etc.), gain valuable experience writing project proposals and contracts, and build confidence in using the knowledge they have learned through their courses. Faculty benefit from supervising these projects by receiving salary support and occasional support for their research, although the demands of consulting projects can contribute to issues related to time management as faculty work to strike a balance between competing demands to fulfill research, teaching, and service requirements. Fortunately, there have also been a variety of research outcomes that have come from CAPS consulting projects, such as posters presented at the Engagement scholarship conference and a published manuscript in an academic journal. Additionally, the training received by the students via the faculty supervision results in students being capable of meaningfully contributing to a consulting firm or organization once they graduate. Doing so builds an alumni network that is capable of supporting both new student jobs and CAPS projects for years to come. Similarly, as universities face increasing competition, limited funding, and, in some cases, declining enrollment, one way that administrators can boost a university's reputation is to enhance ties with community and business (Korn, 2017). Thus, in all of these ways, the collaborative efforts of CAPS are aligned with our program's strategic priorities and allow consulting programs, like CAPS, to boost the reputation of a university as a whole.

Clients benefit from high-quality consulting services that can enhance organizational processes and outcomes at rates much lower than traditional consulting firms offer. As a nonprofit organization based at a public university, CAPS projects need only cover operating expenses, materials, and time spent by consultants and faculty. Furthermore, based on how CAPS is embedded within the university, clients do not experience any high-pressure sales tactics, and they know that whatever materials or services CAPS provides are based in scientific research and are not subject to any conflicts of interest that may arise if CAPS were to sell specific, premade tests or surveys.

CAPS-like programs exist in many industrial/organizational (I/O) psychology graduate programs in the United States. For example, Bowling Green State University's I/O psychology program operates the Institute for Psychological Research and Application (Bowling Green State University, 2018), the University of Akron has the Center for Organizational Research (University of Akron, 2018), Wayne State University has the Applied Psychology and Organizational Research Group (Wayne State University, 2018), AROS (Applied Research for Organizational Solutions) Consulting is at Louisiana Tech (AROS, 2018), Middle Tennessee State University has the Center for Organizational and Human Resource Effectiveness (Middle Tennessee State University, 2018), and the Organizational Effectiveness Research Group is based at Minnesota State University, Mankato (Minnesota State University, 2018). Whether a graduate program offers master's or doctoral degrees, faculty and students realize the benefits of conducting in-house consulting projects. Each of these programs has a similar structure and mission. I/O psychology faculty supervise projects, manage administrative tasks, and oversee the graduate students who complete much of the work. For many graduate programs, the consulting organizations serve as the primary opportunity for students to apply their knowledge and skills fostered in the classroom to real organizational problems, and some students ultimately find internship opportunities or employment with client organizations.

The theoretical contribution of this chapter is the extension of empowerment theory to apply to collaborative relationships between academia and organizations within a community. Empowerment theory helps explain how individuals or groups can demonstrate a value orientation by developing an understanding of the processes that can be used to exert a positive influence within other individuals, organizations, or the larger community (Perkins & Zimmerman, 1995; Zimmerman & Warschausky, 1998). Although there are a variety of different ways that empowerment may be conceptualized, Mechanic (1991) describes empowerment as a process in which people are encouraged to strengthen their awareness of how recommended efforts relate to goals or outcomes. Instead of providing a one-time service for organizations, members of CAPS focus on working with organizations to develop goals and strategies for positive change. The reason for this approach is so that clients can develop a deep understanding of the factors necessitating efforts for improvement or change and are able to use that contextual information to better guide and inform the implementation of any recommendations made by CAPS.

In this chapter, we review several CAPS projects – ranging from a workflow analysis in a county government to an evaluation of a leadership development program – with a focus on how each project allowed students to learn and apply unique skill sets. Then, we highlight the benefits to students, faculty, the university, the client, and the wider community that exist because of the unique service learning structure of CAPS. In addition, we conclude with helpful tips and strategies for how to start, sustain, and grow similar programs at other universities. We hope that this chapter demonstrates the importance and power of hands-on learning opportunities.

Project: Workflow Analysis in a County Government

Outreach

One of the key takeaway points from our consulting experience is that the first step of interacting with a potential client should be focused on relationship building. A critical determinant of whether a client will enlist the assistance of an external vendor is the degree to which the client feels a sense of trust has been fostered between the two parties. In the case of one of CAPS's first major consulting projects – a workflow analysis for a local Iowa county government – the conversation between client and consultant began with an informal conversation between a CAPS associate and a leader in the county. Once trust had been established, subsequent discussion was able to be simultaneously focused on diagnosing the needs of the client and maintaining and growing the relationship.

Once a formal meeting had been planned between county decision makers and the CAPS leadership team, a variety of informal meetings took place to understand the concerns of various department heads and the Board of Supervisors. Such conversations were incredibly helpful in fostering a sense of trust necessary for us to have strong, open communication regarding the issues faced by the county. When it came time for the first official meeting to discuss a partnership between our organization and the county government, many of the board members had already decided to support the project.

Overview of the Project

Part of the impetus for this workflow analysis was due to issues related to physical space; in order to develop an understanding of how to optimally locate county departments, there first needed to be an understanding of the degree to which each department interacted with each other. However, the county also had a strong interest in working with the CAPS team to create a comprehensive list of known issues hindering county work processes and identify previously unknown issues, as well as build a prioritized list of recommendations to utilize in addressing roadblocks to interdepartmental interactions. It is always optimal for a client to not only be willing to share their understanding of the issues in their organization, but also to be open to accepting that there may be a variety of issues that were largely unknown prior to the consultant's arrival. Fortunately, the county government indicated a willingness to consider opportunities for optimizing organizational functioning in areas in which the leadership had not initially focused before the conversation with CAPS began.

Following the initial meetings regarding the clients' needs, the CAPS team drafted a proposal to send to county government leadership. This proposal provided an overview of CAPS's plan to conduct a workflow analysis study in order to achieve a comprehensive understanding of the county's civic leadership structure from both an intra- and inter-departmental perspective. We informed the county that the information collected in the work analysis process would provide the foundation for the development of both department-specific and organization-level recommendations.

Who Was Involved

For this project, the number of departments involved included the departments under the Board of Supervisors, with the exception of the Emergency Management Agency, and the Assessor, Auditor, Treasurer, Recorder, and Attorney departments. Although we sought participation from additional entities within the county, the Board of Supervisors was only able to provide approval for the participation of the departments under their control. Additionally, acquiring formal participation from the Board was only part of the preparation to collect departmental data; in many instances, members of the CAPS team had to engage in discussion with departmental leaders and other employees to foster a sense of understanding and shared purpose between the CAPS team and employees.

Project Coordination and Scheduling

A necessary step in workflow analysis and design was to examine current work processes without interference or disruption to these preexisting work procedures. Considerable time was spent on coordinating schedules to find times for collecting data that presented minimal disruption to county work. For example, any department whose employees were involved in assisting with elections was not scheduled for interviews or focus groups in October or November. Such advanced preparation did much to ease planning throughout the course of the project, yet there were numerous unanticipated roadblocks that led to much more time being devoted to scheduling than had been planned. For example, county elections occurred during the project, so it was sometimes difficult to find times to meet with elected department heads. Further, because one member of the CAPS team was in charge of planning and coordinating with everyone in the country government, the amount of time spent coordinating detracted from available time to make degree progress or to work on other aspects of the project. The entire timeline for department interviews and focus groups was developed very early on in the process, with plenty of flexibility included in case of unforeseen events that could change employee availabilities.

In order to become familiar with the organization, the county provided CAPS with a wide variety of documents, including organizational hierarchy charts and job descriptions. These documents, in addition to extensive conversations and in-person tours with county leaders, provided contextual information that proved to be very helpful in shaping our understanding of the county's functioning, as well as its basic processes and procedures. We were also notified about the nature and goals of the unions, which was important to keep in mind as we collected data.

Data Collection

CAPS analysts, who were provided with extensive training and experience collecting and synthesizing information from multiple sources, collected the initial data concerning the workflow within the county civic government. Aside from informal conversations and one-on-one meetings with department heads, as well as some degree of observations, the primary form of data collection for each department took the form of semi-structured interviews and focus group meetings. Subsequently, the information from these meetings and the observations of CAPS associates helped provide guidance for the organizational survey.

Focus Groups and Interviews

The basic script for the focus group and interview meetings was developed and modified depending on whether the participants were regular employees, department heads, or a member of the Board of Supervisors. Due to many employees not having been informed about the workflow analysis or its purpose, we began each of these meetings by introducing ourselves, the CAPS department lead, and the CAPS designated note taker (who could occasionally ask questions for clarification as well). While attempting to convey a somewhat casual tone, we explained the general purpose of CAPS and the specific purpose of the workflow analysis, which we described as an evaluation to provide an in-depth study of the processes at their organization to help determine where strengths and weaknesses lay and address them accordingly. We told them that they could expect the meeting to take approximately an hour and stated that their responses were very important because, as a participant in this analysis, their experience and expertise would allow us to gain a thorough understanding of work processes and to generate high-quality recommendations. Yet, we also made efforts to preserve the confidentiality of their responses. We told them that we would combine their answers with other interview data, survey data, and observation data to develop an understanding of county work processes. Finally, we gave them an opportunity to ask any questions they had prior to the start of the interview questions. Although CAPS's designated note taker attempted to write down notes of employees' responses, CAPS requested employees' consent to being audio-recorded, just to make sure we had a complete record to refer to in case we would later need it or if the physical notes were lost. Participants were assured that the recording would not be shared with anyone beyond the CAPS evaluation team.

In general, the first part of the focus groups (approximately 30 minutes) focused on within-department information. For example, we asked employees to describe the major activates or tasks that they perform within their department. Beforehand, CAPS associates reviewed job descriptions from HR and compared the information being communicated by the employee with the official job description. In some instances, there were considerable differences between the two that needed to be discussed. Regarding their work tasks, we also asked how they are accomplished, how much time each takes, which are most critical, what materials, equipment, or types of information were needed to complete each, and what types of knowledge or skills were needed to complete key tasks and processes. Given the importance of physical space needs within the county's buildings, we placed a special emphasis on the physical space needs of the employees and asked for their thoughts on how the physical space might be changed or adapted to improve work processes. We tried to get a sense of which other employees within their department they worked with most to complete tasks, find out information needed to complete their work, fix technical issues, or resolve interpersonal problems/conflicts.

The second portion of the focus groups placed more of an emphasis on their interaction with other departments, including the frequency and extent of collaboration with each of the other departments whose employees they work with. Participants were asked to describe the nature of their interactions and the types of materials or type of communication needed between them and the other department employees that they encounter. In the final portion of the focus groups, we provided employees with the opportunity to make suggestions for processes or tasks that are in need of improvement, to identify issues or challenges that had an especially negative impact on their work, and to share with us anything else on their mind that they wanted an opportunity to communicate.

The focus group development and utilization process throughout this project highlighted some valuable lessons that could be applied to future focus groups. First, regardless of whether facilitators ensured employees that everything said in the focus group would be anonymized and could not be connected to individual participants, some employees still demonstrated considerable hesitation. One factor contributing to the hesitation, but also to the quality of the focus groups, was the presence of an audio recorder. Most participants did not mind being recorded, but, especially in departments going through difficult periods of management, participants were unwilling to open up fully when the recorder was present. As such, going forward, we recommend that focus group facilitators have a clear understanding of the preexisting contextual factors – the relationship between department managers and unionized workers, in this case – that could influence how willing people are to provide open and honest feedback to outside evaluators.

For the senior leaders, such as department heads and elected officials, their interviews were a bit less structured. While there were considerable similarities in how CAPS associates began the interviews, these leaders were more familiar with the project as a whole and the associates involved. As in the focus groups, these leaders were assured that the responses they gave in these meetings would be kept confidential. A key distinction between the interviews with leaders and the focus groups with lower-level employees is that the leaders were able to provide a broader picture of how the responsibilities of their subordinates fitted together to accomplish the goals of their department and the county as a whole.

Organizational Survey

Upon completion of the programed interviews and focus groups within the county government, the CAPS team identified and synthesized the organizational-level issues and challenges that had become apparent during the process of collecting information. After a list of issues and challenges were developed, the CAPS team sought out questions that had been used and validated within research to probe issues affecting the workflow. These measures were combined into a survey that assessed information sharing, employee interaction, performance feedback, and clarity of goals, among other areas. This survey was presented to the HR Manager as well as to the Board of Supervisors and revised based on the feedback that was received. The finalized organizational survey was primarily delivered to county employees via Qualtrics, an online survey management software. Additionally, a paper form of the survey was also developed and distributed to county employees who did not have an active county email address. In total, CAPS had a 65 percent response rate. Survey results were analyzed using SPSS statistical software. Following data analysis, the CAPS team met to interpret the results and integrate the findings into a tentative list of organizational recommendations.

After all the organizational-level data had been synthesized, the CAPS team developed an organizational report that outlined a picture of the workflow analysis based on the data and recommendations provided, focusing on highlighting organizational efficiencies, location pressures of interdepartmental handoffs, duplication of effort, and possible rearrangement to improve efficiencies. Similar to the process used in generating the departmental reports, the organizational report was reviewed and revised by numerous members of the CAPS team prior to being sent to the Board of Supervisors for feedback. Based on feedback from the board, the report was finalized and presented publicly at a county board meeting.

Benefits to Students

The opportunity to work on the workflow analysis project was rewarding to students in many ways. It was a unique opportunity that allowed them to apply what they had learned in textbooks and articles to real life. Specifically, students had the opportunity to develop or improve upon the following skills:

- Collecting observational data
- Interview protocol development
- Conducting interviews/focus groups
- Data analysis
- Communication skills – oral and written

Working with some employees who misunderstood the nature and/or purpose of the project could be frustrating for them, but it helped them realize the importance of reacting to such misunderstanding in a calm and constructive manner and ensuring that communication with staff is as clear as possible. This project served as a positive influence in forcing them to maintain effective time management practices and to work well under pressure. Not only did they develop a much greater understanding of formal processes within county government, but they also gained insight into the nature of work interactions on a more informal level, beyond what can be communicated by reading official policies and procedures. Students' experience with developing data collection materials was invaluable. First, they learned a great deal more about qualitative data collection, including the need for the structure of interviews and focus groups to be somewhat limited. This experience also helped them expand their knowledge of the features of both Qualtrics and SPSS, as well as data analyses. They have also learned that being able to communicate to others the value in and results of employee surveys can be of paramount importance. Finally, the workflow analysis project benefited students by connecting them to professionals in the local community that they may be able to benefit from in their search for employment.

Benefits to Faculty and the University

Applied projects like this one provide development opportunities for faculty and benefits for the university. Specifically, faculty gain additional experience in managing students on applied projects and provide important, real-world experience for students who need hands-on work opportunities. Additionally, faculty may gain insights they can share in their classrooms. In terms of the university, and related to the faculty benefits, the incredible amount of data collected in this project creates the real possibility that the project's findings could be developed into research outcomes, such as journal publications, for faculty members and the universities they represent.

Benefits to the Client

Ultimately, the project was successful to the extent that the client received the outcomes they paid for and in a way that allows for immediate application and action. It was clear that the project was successful, as some county employees communicated to us that the experience was very positive and thanked us for the perspective that we provided. Numerous employees indicated that they appreciated the data-driven recommendations and have begun incorporating some of the recommendations we suggested. Following the project, some employees have voiced that the changes they have since implemented have made their work more efficient and have saved time, as well as made the work experience more enjoyable.

Benefits to the Community

Ultimately, many of the recommendations we made will likely prove beneficial to residents of the county. For example, in some departments, we were able to recommend the use of self-service kiosks in which information may be entered by a resident and then reviewed by a county employee, instead of having the resident complete a form that must then be entered into a computer by an employee. Such streamlining of processes simultaneously helps reduce service time costs for employees and residents, enhances the customer experience, and increases the cost-effectiveness for tax payers. In summary, the consideration of the recommendations that CAPS proposed may enable the county to better serve its residents.

Project: Developing a Police Department Sergeant Exam

Outreach

For a long time, CAPS's primary (and almost exclusive) client was a local police department. In recent years, our outreach process has started with reaching out to a police department captain to assess interest in once again working together to develop a promotional exam. This discussion includes determining if the existing materials, such as job analysis information and job descriptions, are up to date or if they are in need of revision.

Overview of the Project

The primary project that CAPS completed for a police department was to develop a promotional exam that tested the knowledge and the effective application of knowledge of applicants for the position of police sergeant. The first portion of the sergeant exam consists of 100 multiple-choice questions, and these questions have traditionally been generated by the CAPS team along with a panel of subject matter experts (SMEs). CAPS associates used a wide variety of source materials, including a General Orders Manual, a Police Officer's Association handbook, training updates, and union agreements. The second portion of the exam consists of ten situational essay questions, for which individuals taking the exam must answer how they would respond in particular scenarios. Similar to the development of the multiple-choice section of the exam, SMEs also assisted CAPS associates in generating scenarios for the situational essay questions.

Development of the 100 Multiple-Choice Questions

Members of the police department have suggested best practices for CAPS to use in item construction. These best practices and expectations for question structure were communicated to item writers through a brief training session. Following CAPS associates' review of necessary tasks for police sergeants, as well as the dimensions that relate to these tasks, the associates divided up the different content areas. There were four members of the CAPS team who participated in item writing, and each member created 50 multiple-choice items, resulting in a list of 200 questions. SMEs from the police department reviewed these questions and indicated which questions should be removed, revised, or kept in their current form. Common reasons for revision or removal were due to questions being considered too simple or too confusing. Additionally, each of the police SMEs prepared ten multiple-choice questions for CAPS personnel to review in case that they might be needed as replacement questions.

Development of the Ten Situational Essay Questions

The first step in constructing the situational essay component of the exam was to meet with the police SMEs to generate critical incidents that are applicable to the responsibilities of a police sergeant and use those incidents to draft essay questions and multiple benchmarks for these questions. Based on their ideas, the CAPS team generated 20 situational essays, which were sent to the police captain in charge of the process. The CAPS team then met with the captain and the other SMEs to review and revise these questions, as well as the benchmarks for each. At this meeting, we also discussed the scoring process that we decided to use and made an argument for why our process would be simpler than in the past, while still preserving the variability in scores. After completing the revisions, a total of ten essay questions were selected. The relevant tasks and dimensions were linked to each essay. Each of the essay's combined benchmarks were made to be worth five points so that each of the essays was given equal weight.

Scoring

The scoring process for the multiple-choice test was fairly straightforward; examinees marked their responses on Scantron sheets that were easily scored by machine. However, two multiple-choice questions were removed; one question had more than one correct answer and the other referenced information that was not made available to all examinees. In order to grade the situational essays, nine students from the graduate student team were recruited to serve as graders. Two raters graded each essay; the partners for each question met to ensure a common understanding of the question prior to grading. Students initially graded the essays independently and then later met with their grading partners to resolve any discrepancies. Following grading, a final report was compiled and sent to the police captain, the original files were placed in a secure location, and the extra copies of the exam answers were destroyed.

Test Development and Scoring Challenges

Developing and administering selection or promotional tests for public safety positions can be high stakes and more litigious than other industries (Barret, Doverspike, & Young, 2010). Creating such tests often requires the developers to respond to political concerns, layers, unions, and tight budgets. In the past, CAPS has encountered several challenges in the developing and scoring process of this assessment, but we implanted several recent changes that helped to minimize those challenges. First, as demonstrated in the above sections, we used an iterative process to develop test questions by frequently soliciting feedback from panels of SMEs to review test content. This helped to prevent the inclusion of especially difficult items, unclear items, and items that did not represent full understanding of the content, each of which could result in biased, inaccurate test scores or such perceptions that may lead to litigation. Second, two raters scored each essay question, and we implemented a process for rescoring essays if needed. For instance, candidates could request that their essays be rescored if they were unsatisfied with the results. Rescoring a few exams helped to prevent such issues from developing into litigation.

Benefits to Students

One of the key benefits to participating in this project was that it gave students the opportunity to gain firsthand experience in quickly achieving a basic understanding of source materials, understanding the relationship between tasks and task-related dimensions relevant to the position of a police sergeant, and constructing new multiple-choice questions and situational essay questions based on this knowledge, as well as the grading process used. This experience may be very helpful to students considering developing exams as part of their career. In fact, one CAPS alumni even went on to work in developing police exams after serving as a lead for this project. In general, this project provided students with an opportunity to develop or improve upon the following skills:

– Facilitation of discussion groups
– Promotional exam development
– Providing advice for promotion and succession planning

Benefits to Faculty and the University

As in many of the other projects discussed in this chapter, one of the ways in which faculty may benefit from collaboration on this project is that it provides an opportunity to engage in networking and build a reputation that increases the likelihood of partnering with other organizations in the future. It is likely that part of the reason CAPS has been so successful in acquiring new contracts to work with clients is because it has earned a solid reputation from its past clients. Specific to this project, the relationships that developed provided CAPS with stronger credibility in approaching other, similar types of organizations. Furthermore, the university benefits from this type of project, as the work has even greater meaning when taking place in an applied setting and building a stronger relationship with the local community as a partner that has an interest in not only providing learning opportunities for students, but also taking action that promotes the long-term well-being of the community.

Benefits to the Community

Ultimately, by assisting a local police department in its promotional exam, CAPS is helping ensure that only the best, most qualified individuals are being placed in higher positions of authority. We believe it is likely that the long-term impact of these types of projects is that police will tend to be even more effective at implementing law enforcement. Thus, it is our hope that these efforts will result in a more safe and secure community. Additionally, this work raises the opportunity for even greater collaboration on future projects.

Project: Program Evaluation of a Nonprofit Technology Library

Another large CAPS project that provided learning experiences to students in several domains was a two-year program evaluation of a new, innovative nonprofit organization called Do Space®. Embracing the fundamental principles of a traditional public library, Do Space provides anyone in the community with free access to computers, the Internet, basic and advanced software, 3-D printing, and classes and events focused on technology. Four key principles guide Do Space:

- We're a technology equalizer, giving people from all walks of life access to software, computing and emerging technology.
- We're a technology enabler, empowering everyone with the tools and guidance needed to learn, create, explore and invent with technology.
- We're a technology educator, creating a new path for technology literacy and understanding its potential while providing opportunities for advanced learning.
- We're a technology innovator, changing the shape of technology education and actively playing a role in technology advancement and creation. (Do Space, 2018)

As an organization with a completely unique purpose and mission, when Do Space first opened in November 2015, Do Space leadership and its entirely private, philanthropic funders needed to be able to quickly determine what aspects of Do Space were successful, what needed improvement, and how to make appropriate changes. Do Space learned about CAPS through the university's website, and in the summer of 2015, Do Space contacted the director of CAPS to see how and if CAPS could help them achieve a data-informed approach to reviewing organizational effectiveness.

Through discussions with the client, CAPS proposed a two-phase program evaluation that defined the meaning of success from a variety of organizational stakeholders, and then developed metrics and a reporting mechanism for tracking success. Phase 1, the eight-week pre-design project, was conducted to answer the following question: What would a successful digital library look like? To collect the data, CAPS conducted interviews and a focus group and distributed a survey to the wider community.

Do Space leadership identified key stakeholders in Do Space's success, including philanthropic organizations, educational institutions, school district leaders, and public library staff. CAPS then created and conducted customized, structured interviews designed to elicit responses on a variety of success factors for the new organization. Additionally, CAPS conducted a focus group with community members that focused on how Do Space could impact the community if it were successful. CAPS also collected data through the distribution of a survey to the community to gain further insight into how Do Space could impact the community. CAPS then identified the following five success themes: technological access, educational opportunities, community empowerment, affiliated organizational partnership, and marketing. CAPS worked with Do Space leadership to rank order these themes, which informed Phase 2 of the project.

Phase 2, a two-year program evaluation, built on the findings from the pre-design in that CAPS created measurement tools and developed other metrics to assess Do Space's standing within each success theme. The evaluative tools consisted of surveys, analyses of internal data systems, and qualitative methods including focus groups and interviews.

Key Project Tasks

Surveys. We developed four surveys, each designed for a different target population. The largest survey was a satisfaction survey that was administered three times over two years to all Do Space members. It included custom and preexisting measures of constructs such as engagement, satisfaction, and commitment. The second survey was intended for affiliated organizations, and the purpose was to assess the health of organizational collaborations and partnerships. Third was the community survey, which was intended to assess the average citizen's awareness of Do Space and their general thoughts. Finally, in order to evaluate programs, courses, and workshops, we created a short survey to be completed by anyone who participated in an event such as a class or special technology workshop.

Internal Data. As a completely technology-focused environment, Do Space had a unique opportunity to set up technology systems that would generate a large amount of data concerning what, how, and when people interacted with its services. For example, CAPS developed processes by which data could be extracted from the systems that informed Do Space about the number of patrons who entered the building, the popularity of specific technology items or events, the demographic characteristics of members and users, the busiest time of day for computer use, and specific characteristics of frequent users.

Qualitative Data. To supplement the surveys and analyses of internal data, we created four types of focus groups and two types of interviews. Similar to the surveys being targeted to specific populations, the focus groups were likewise geared toward collecting data from different Do Space stakeholders. For instance, we planned focus groups for Do Space users and members, which centered on their experiences with using Do Space. Other focus group types targeted affiliated and collaborating organizations, community members not necessarily associated with or users of Do Space, and high-volume users. In addition to the focus groups, we also included interviews of users who used Do Space for innovative or long-term projects, and finally interviews of funding organizations.

Reporting. The main deliverable products throughout the evaluation were quarterly, semiannual, and annual reports that summarized the survey, internal data, and qualitative data that CAPS collected in the months preceding the report. Reports included numerous charts, graphs, infographics, and brief narratives of key findings from each evaluative tool. Do Space used the reports to find areas of improvement, adjust programming and staffing levels, and provide updates to the nonprofit's board of directors.

Challenges with the Development and Execution of the Evaluation

Although starting the evaluation before Do Space opened was a great opportunity and allowed the organization to track its success from inception, there were also some unique challenges related to beginning the evaluation so early. The largest challenge was working with the various technology systems and providers to determine the following: (a) what information each system captured and in what format; and (b) how to extract desired information. We had to collaborate with many service provides to overcome issues with data, and, because we developed the evaluation plan prior to the grand opening, plans had to be altered after opening to conform to available data. Indeed, the evaluation plan was quite dynamic because Do Space was committed to using all available data to improve their services – great from an organizational perspective, but challenging from an evaluation perspective because a great deal of flexibility and responsiveness was required.

Benefits to Students

This wide-ranging project offered numerous opportunities for students to apply classroom experiences to a real-world situation, and the project provided a chance to begin developing consulting skills that cannot be taught in typical classrooms. Benefits included:

- Developing surveys, focus groups, interviews, and assessment methods
- Accessing, managing, and integrating large databases
- Writing engaging, easy-to-read reports
- Data visualization

As part of the project, students developed a variety of surveys, focus groups, and interviews, thereby giving the students experience in producing high-quality data collection tools amenable to a client in an applied setting. In addition, the firsthand experience managing the logistics involved with scheduling, conducting, and attracting participants to focus groups and interviews was something students could not receive in a traditional classroom setting. Next, writing comprehensive yet easily digested reports for the client was an important learning opportunity, because most students are used to writing long, formal research reports filled with statistical notations, pages of citations, and regimented figures and tables. However, many clients are not necessarily familiar with scientific jargon, and it is more important to focus on presenting the key findings in a visually appealing way than putting a lot of emphasis on the method that produced those findings. Overall, the project allowed students to learn about developing surveys, interviews, and focus groups for non-research settings, analyzing qualitative data, preparing reports for client consumption, and managing the logistics associated with a long program evaluation with many components.

Benefits to Faculty and the University

Do Space was the first large client for CAPS, so it allowed faculty to demonstrate their acumen and the expertise of the organization in managing and successfully conducting a large project, which can help expand the number of clients willing to work with CAPS. Additionally, by forming partnerships and good relationships with many organizations and funding organizations, the university builds its reputation and, through word of mouth, business leaders and committee organizations may look more favorably on the university as a resource, rather than simply a source of potential new employees.

Benefits to the Client and the Community

The client really appreciated and recognized the value of beginning a program evaluation of the organization from the opening day because it allowed them to use multiple data sources to assess their progress and to make changes as necessary. Many nonprofit organizations do not have surplus funding available to pay a consulting firm for a scientific program evaluation from day one. Fortunately, Do Space had some funding available, and CAPS provides services at a much-reduced rate because of its learning-based nature and association with the university.

One of the overarching purposes of this program evaluation was to make sure that Do Space leadership took the community and users' technology needs and wants into account as the organization planned services, events, and classes. Therefore, all the surveys, focus groups, and interviews with community members can really help benefit the community because Do Space used that information – lists of technology resources people needed access to, for instance – to make informed decisions when planning services and programs.

Project: Assessing the Effectiveness of a Leadership Development Program

Outreach and Overview

The client for this project, a legal and insurance services firm, had developed a three-month personal leadership program to be delivered to employees. The goals of the program were to encourage organizational leaders to cultivate self-awareness, embrace new choices and possibilities, deepen confidence in leadership, strengthen concentration around intention, and increase the personal capacity for growth. Despite having developed the program, the client was unsure of the best way to evaluate its effectiveness. After reading some publications that CAPS-affiliated faculty had written on leadership, the client reached out to see if CAPS could help them evaluate their leadership training program.

Key Project Tasks

The project was broken into four broad modules. The first module entailed analysis of preexisting quantitative data collection to evaluate the outcomes of the personal leadership program. The client had already collected some data, so CAPS was able to conduct a pre- and post-training evaluation using this client-generated information. A pre–post evaluative method allows for evaluators to examine the effectiveness of the training intervention over time.

The second module included identification of additional quantitative and qualitative measures that could be added to the personal leadership program to offer a more holistic view of the training program. CAPS members examined the goals of the leadership development program, examined the academic literature on the topic, and worked in concert with client leaders to select assessments to best evaluate the leadership program. Eventually, CAPS developed a pre- and post-program survey that contained nine key dimensions such as leadership self-efficacy and resilience to change. Next, as part of the second module, CAPS created a structured interview protocol that would be administered to every program participant. One goal of the interview component was to develop a rich body of data in order to provide a thorough evaluation of the program's effectiveness.

The third module contained the data collection of qualitative measures identified in the second module. Using skills gained on other projects, CAPS student consultants conducted over 30 interviews with program participants and a number of interviews with managers of the participants. In most cases, interviews were conducted in person at the client's nearest office. However, some participants were unavailable, so several interviews were held over the phone. During each interview, one CAPS member took detailed field notes while the other CAPS member interacted with the program participant. Each interview was audio-recorded. When the interview was complete, the audio was sent to a third-party organization for transcription. The transcriptions and field notes were then analyzed in the final module.

In the final module, the CAPS team analyzed the outcomes of the interviews and focus groups for themes emerging from the personal leadership program. The thematic analysis of all interviews identified broad themes among interviewee responses about how the program impacted their approach to work and leadership. Each module built on the one before it. At the end of the project, CAPS delivered a report along with a presentation to the CEO and executive team that detailed the evaluation, methodologies employed, results of data analysis, and recommendations for future steps.

Benefits to Students

This assessment project gave students the chance to learn how training evaluations are conducted in real-world settings. This represented a challenge for this project. In consulting work, it is often necessary to find the right balance between scientific rigor and practicality, and this project was a great example of how to reach an acceptable balance, which is a necessary skill for any student wishing to consult or work in an applied setting. The most rigorous approach to this evaluation would have been a two-group experimental design with a control group, wherein participants would be randomly assigned to receive or not receive the training, and then, at the conclusion of the training, the two groups would be compared on outcomes of interest relevant to the training. Although very rigorous, this method is not always practical, especially if the pool of available trainees is small or if other evidence suggests that the training is at least minimally effective (Noe, 2010). In this project, we balanced practicality with rigor by using a pre–post design wherein all participants received the training, but we were able to compare their post-training performance to their pre-training performance. Additionally, CAPS used a formalized, qualitative coding method to analyze interviews. Much of the data collection and analysis techniques that I/O psychology graduate students learn in school are focused on quantitative data, so learning this thematic analysis approach in CAPS supplemented their coursework.

Benefits to Faculty and the University

As with any successfully completed project, associated faculty and the university benefit by increasing the number of successful partnerships between the university and outside organizations. Furthermore, as more CAPS projects develop, faculty are able to hone their skills and training of students on how to be successful consultants.

These experiences also provide an opportunity for less experienced faculty to observe how students work and where students typically need training or additional support.

Benefits to the Client and the Community

This project was incredibly beneficial to the client because it provided them with objective, evidence-based, qualitative and quantitative data that supported the efficacy of their leadership development program. Previously, the client did not have any data to support that the training program changed participant behavior or that participants learned anything in the program. Now, the client has such evidence, which can help secure additional resources to conduct the training. Additionally, through the data analysis, CAPS found that the leadership program had a positive impact on most individuals who participated. Now that there are data to support the client's claims, it is possible that the program can reach a wider audience and benefit more employees and managers in the community.

Conclusion

CAPS at the University of Nebraska Omaha is a consulting organization based largely in the I/O psychology graduate program. Faculty oversee master's and PhD students who conduct the work in order to gain valuable experience in applying I/O psychology practices to organizations for fair compensation. We provide a conceptual, theoretical explanation of our efforts through the lens of empowerment theory. As an organization embedded within a university, university staff handle many administrative burdens (e.g., billing, payments, tax withholdings, contracts, legal services, etc.), which allows students and faculty to focus less on the overheads and mechanics of running an organization and more on the work itself. In this chapter, we have provided a series of example consulting projects and how each project helped benefit students, faculty, the client, and the wider university. Please see Table 8.1 for a list of some of these benefits.

In addition to providing students with hands-on learning opportunities, CAPS projects, exemplified by the projects discussed above, benefit faculty, the university, the client, and, in some cases, the community at large. Despite the difficulties or challenges that can arise, such as pressures due to time demands or the uphill battle to raise community awareness of a new consulting service (and convince them of its merits), projects allow faculty to build their professional networks, improve the quality of training provided to students, secure research and salary support, increase opportunities for collaborative research, and develop their own consulting skills. Increasing the number of university–community partnerships is beneficial to the university because it increases its reputation and changes the perception of the university among business leaders from only a source of job applicants to an organization with valuable resources that can help their businesses. Additionally, CAPS projects allow I/O psychology graduate students to demonstrate their skills

Table 8.1 *Summary of benefits and challenges to students, clients, faculty, and the university*

Role/level	Benefits	Challenges
Students	• Provides opportunities for development • Offers important real-world experience to students who need hands-on work opportunities to develop specific competencies/skills	• Excessive involvement may hinder academic performance and degree progress
Clients	• Receive the outcomes they paid for in a way that allows for immediate application and action • Potentially enhances the experience of clients/customers/residents/users	• May not have work completed by individuals with as extensive experience as would be found in an established private organization
Faculty	• Provides opportunities for development • Offers experience managing students on applied projects • Allows faculty to build experience that they can share in their classrooms • Provides faculty with more opportunities to publish research	• Requires extensive time commitments, as faculty must oversee all deliverables being shared with the client
University	• Provides a rich source of data that university faculty may use to generate research outcomes and build the name of the university • Offers an opportunity to engage in networking and build a reputation that makes it more likely the client will work with the university in the future	• Any time that work is performed in the community by students of the university (in this type of project), the university may be placing itself at some level of legal risk

and abilities developed through the graduate training program, which can help improve the employability of program graduates throughout the community. Because of CAPS's main purpose as a learning experience without a profit motive, clients gain access to high-quality, evidence-based consulting services at a much lower costs than traditional consulting organizations require.

References

AROS (2018). Applied research for organizational solutions. Retrieved from www .arosconsulting.org/.

Barret, G. V., Doverspike, D., & Young, C. M. (2010). The special case of public sector police and fire selection. In J. C. Scott & D. H. Reynolds (Eds.), *Handbook of workplace assessment: Evidence-based practices for selection and developing organizational talent* (pp. 437–462). San Francisco, CA: Jossey-Bass.

Bowling Green State University (2018). Institute for psychological research and application. Retrieved from www.bgsu.edu/arts-and-sciences/psychology/institute-for-psychological-research-and-application.html.

Do Space (2018). What is Do Space? Retrieved from www.dospace.org/about.

Korn, M. (2017). Emory University looks to be incorporated into city of Atlanta. *The Wall Street Journal*. Retrieved from www.wsj.com/.

Mechanic, D. (1991). *Adolescents at risk: New directions*. Paper presented at the Seventh Annual Conference on Health Policy, Cornell University Medical College.

Middle Tennessee State University (2018). Center for organizational and human resource effectiveness. Retrieved from www.mtsu.edu/cohre/.

Minnesota State University (2018). Organizational effectiveness research group. Retrieved from www.mnsu.edu/oerg/.

Noe, R. A. (2010). *Employee training and development* (5th edn.). New York: McGraw Hill.

Perkins, D., & Zimmerman, M. (1995). Empowerment theory, research, and application. *American Journal of Community Psychology, 23*, 569–579.

University of Akron (2018). Center for organizational research. Retrieved from www.uakron.edu/cor/.

Wayne State University (2018). Applied psychological and organizational research group. Retrieved from www.clas.wayne.edu/io/Applied-Research-Opportunities.

Zimmerman, M. A. (1995). Empowerment theory, research, and application. *American Journal of Community Psychology, 23*, 569.

Zimmerman, M. A., & Warschausky, S. (1998). Empowerment theory for rehabilitation research: Conceptual and methodological issues. *Rehabilitation Psychology, 43*, 3–16.

9 Discipline-Specific Outreach

Client Projects through Graduate Classes and University-Based Consulting Centers

Michael B. Hein & Richard G. Moffett III

There has been a long history in the United States of universities and colleges providing services to their communities. In 1862, the Morrill Act was passed that established land-grant institutions to assist communities "through widespread education in agricultural and practical arts" (Roper & Hirth, 2005, p. 4). This was later followed by the establishment of agricultural experiments stations, cooperative extension service organizations, etc. (Association of Public and Land Grant Universities, n.d.). These efforts were designed to extend the research and expertise of college and university disciplines to the community. Roper and Hirth (2005) contend that outreach has evolved from this one-way service to a more interactive relationship between universities and their communities (i.e., community engagement). Community engagement reflects a reciprocal partnership in which members of the university and their community collaborate for mutual benefit (New England Resource Center for High Education, n.d.). These partnerships can take various forms, one being disciplinary outreach.

From our perspective, disciplinary outreach is community engagement that centers on building a campus–community partnership through a specific academic discipline rather than interdisciplinary or campus-wide initiatives. These partnerships can involve scholarship, research, and creative activity; education and learning; and public service projects to assist organizations and the people in them. Disciplinary outreach can benefit student education and faculty development by providing opportunities to apply the theory and research of their discipline to problems or projects in community organizations, which at the same time can enhance the effectiveness of organizations and the people who work in them. While there is room for original research in disciplinary outreach, our experience is that the primary goal needs to be meeting the needs of the client. Consequently, the primary focus on this chapter will be on the lessons learned from the application of theory and research. We will use the discipline of industrial/organizational (I/O) psychology as the lens through which we will discuss disciplinary outreach.

From the perspective of I/O psychology, campus–community partnerships are related to the scientist–practitioner model (i.e., the importance of both theory and application). Engagement in these partnerships can contribute to the development and/or refinement of theory using Kurt Lewin's action research model (Lewin, 1946). Additionally, the *Guidelines for education and training in industrial–organizational psychology* (Society for Industrial and Organizational Psychology, 2016) contains areas of competence that have been identified and that should be developed in an

I/O psychology program (both doctoral level and master's level). According to the guidelines, knowledge about core content areas such as job/task/work analysis, training and development, performance appraisal/performance management, and personnel recruitment, selection, placement, and classification is expected to be developed through formal coursework. It is also expected that such knowledge will be learned through supervised field experience. In addition, six areas of general knowledge and skills identified in the guidelines are deemed appropriate for educating and training I/O psychologists and practitioners. One of these skill areas is professional skills, which include effective communication, business/research proposal development, consulting, and project management skills. These professional skills are expected to be learned in formal coursework and supervised field experience. We contend that one way this knowledge and these skills can be developed is by disciplinary outreach activities conducted in partnership with community organizations. To illustrate how disciplinary outreach could meet these education and training requirements, we provide examples from our experiences in conducting applied class projects and leading a university-based I/O psychology consulting center.

Applied Class Projects

We use a cohort model of training so most students in a class have a common background of knowledge. We have one course per semester of the two-year sequence that is most likely to have a client-based project. The courses in order are performance appraisal and job analysis (first fall), advanced training and development (first spring), internship (summer), organizational survey (second fall), and organizational change and development (second spring). Generally, these classes increase in complexity and build on each other. For example, job analysis skills often underlie training needs analysis and training programs often support organizational change efforts. Class projects have been conducted with many different external clients including government entities, nonprofit organizations and for-profit companies. Some examples of class projects are updating job descriptions, conducting a training needs analysis, analyzing training evaluation data, developing and delivering training, and surveying the members of a professional organization.

After they are taught the declarative knowledge, students gain the procedural knowledge through application. This is essentially experiential learning (Simmering, Napper, & Sheets, 2012). These projects are a combination of teaching and service to the community because while the students are learning from conducting the project, they are also indirectly, and to a certain extent directly, providing faculty expertise to the client while providing their own expertise and ultimately finished products. Faculty members generally write the proposals for these projects and then act as a resource for the students as they conduct the project. While there is no charge to the client for these projects, we do include a dollar value in the proposal based on what the cost would be if it were a project run through our university-based consulting center. For-profit organizations are asked to contribute ($3,000–$5,000) to a graduate student support fund and they generally do so. Projects generally have an estimated value of between \$10,000 and \$30,000 for the client organization.

There are many advantages to incorporating client projects into graduate classes. In addition to applying what they have been taught, students learn about proposal writing, budgeting, communication, client management, teamwork, and project management. Students finish with products they can show potential employers, contacts within a specific company, and a client project to put on their resume. Students also have an opportunity to cross-train each other on specific skills. Students often enter the program with different backgrounds, providing them with different strengths. One may have extensive experience in customer relations, while another may have strong software skills. Rather than compartmentalizing and each student just doing what they already are good at, they use class projects as an opportunity to cross-train each other. Students also take turns taking on leadership positions in different class projects so that it is not always the same students getting leadership experience. Both cross-training and rotating leadership were student-initiated developments. Based on this experience, we now encourage students to evaluate both their skill sets and their developmental needs as they form and execute project teams. We encourage students to pair strong skill sets with developmental needs. Ultimately, organizations in the community get expert help in an I/O psychology-related area and at the same time learn about our program and our discipline.

There are significant challenges to having client-based projects in a graduate course. Some of the challenges that have arisen include scope creep, micromanagement by the client, level of autonomy to give the students, project resistance by members of the organization, and the restricted timeline of doing a project in six to seven weeks. Scope creep occurs when clients attempt to expand the deliverables of the project beyond the original agreement. Scope creep occurs in paid consulting projects as well as class projects. It is not always a calculated attempt to get more for less; often, clients are just excited about the potential for the project, and once they start working with the students and realize their capabilities, they see that they are capable of doing some great work. On the other hand, some clients are not willing to let go of control and do not want to allow the students to have any real input into the project. We have had to call projects off because clients were not willing to let the students do graduate-level work. Determining the level of autonomy to give the students is the classic delegation issue. We want the project to be successful for the client, but we also want to maximize the learning experience for the students. One of the biggest challenges to conducting class-based projects is defining the scope as something that can be accomplished within a semester or primarily in the second half of a semester, depending on the structure of the course. This is especially true if the class is breaking up into groups to conduct different projects. Generally, we estimate the hours it would take to conduct the work as if it were a consulting project. We then determine the number of students for each group based on the number of hours needed using a rule of thumb of 12 hours a week for the number of hours a week a graduate student could be expected to spend on a three-credit hour graduate class. Class size is typically around 12 students and they have seven weeks, so that is around 1000 hours to be allocated for project work.

One of the keys to a successful project is a written proposal that is signed by the client (see Appendix 9.1). A professional-looking proposal starts the project off on the right foot. The proposal includes a timeline and deliverables and specifies the support needed from the client for successful completion of the project. A written proposal is a strong mechanism for handling scope creep and ensuring the project can be done in the allotted time. It also helps to ensure that students will be engaged in graduate-level work.

Other best practices include vetting the clients ahead of time, establishing communication protocols, kickoff meetings, and requiring final presentations as well as written reports. Finding the right clients can be a challenge. It is best to start looking for potential projects/clients well in advance in order to be sure you will have something that will work. Shoenfelt (2003) has provided good lists of the desirable characteristics of a client and potential sources for clients.

I. Host organization characteristics

✓Understanding of I/O psychology
✓Understanding of the scope of the project
✓Understanding of student capabilities
✓Understanding of student time constraints
✓Previous experience with student projects
✓Willingness to provide on-site support
✓Willingness to provide resources (p. 111)

II. Sources for host organizations

✓Graduates of our program
✓Organizations who have hosted an intern
✓Organizations with history with us
✓Organizations requesting free consulting
✓Word of mouth
✓Faculty interaction (p. 111)

Alumni make ideal clients because they bring with them an understanding of the process and realistic expectations about what can be accomplished within the time frame. A strong champion can be extremely valuable in helping overcome project resistance by other members of the organization.

University-Based Consulting Centers

University-based consulting centers related to the discipline of I/O psychology provide disciplinary outreach with organizations in their community. This disciplinary outreach can include activities such as applied research, statistical consultation, and I/O psychology practice. Most I/O psychology-related consulting centers are associated with PhD programs. Some examples include the Institute for Psychological Research and Application (Bowling Green State University), the Center for Organizational Research (University of Akron), the Center for Applied

Psychological Services (University of Nebraska Omaha), the Applied Psychology, Organizational Research Group (Wayne State University), and the Center for Research and Service (Illinois Institute of Technology). Some I/O psychology-related consulting centers are associated with master's programs such as the Center for Applied Psychology (University of West Florida) and the Center for Organizational and Human Resource Effectiveness (Middle Tennessee State University). Our experience in leading the Center for Organizational and Human Resource Effectiveness (COHRE) will serve as the basis for our discussion of how our discipline-specific, university-based consulting center is used to develop disciplinary outreach partnerships between our I/O psychology master's program and our community.

COHRE was established in 2003 with the purposes of providing applied education and training opportunities for our I/O psychology students, creating mutually beneficial partnerships with organizations in our community, and providing financial support for our students through paid applied consulting projects. Start-up funds were provided by our university president with the understanding that the center would become self-funding (which it has achieved). COHRE is currently led by two faculty members of the I/O psychology program who have a course release each semester to serve as director and associate director. The I/O psychology program faculty members (n = 7) serve as senior consultants on the projects and are paid an hourly rate for their work as consultants. In addition, they supervise the I/O psychology students who work on the projects as project associates (i.e., student consultants). COHRE provides funding for four ten-hour per week graduate assistants (GAs); two are second-year graduate students who served as GAs in their first year and two are first-year graduate students. The GAs also work additional hours on projects and are paid a competitive hourly rate. We hire additional graduate students to staff the consulting projects on an as-needed basis.

The consulting work COHRE does includes a variety of I/O psychology-related practice areas and includes a variety of types of clients. For example, COHRE has engaged in projects such as conducting job analysis for a state human resources department and an engineering firm; developing and delivering leadership training for a background-screening corporation and multiple government organizations; developing selection and promotional systems for law enforcement; and developing and conducting organizational surveys for an energy corporation, a church, and multiple higher education entities. Projects can range in scope from a half-day leadership development workshop to a yearlong organizational assessment and strategic planning process.

A key aspect of the consulting projects is that they align with the educational goals of the I/O psychology program. The consulting projects provide students with an opportunity to apply the theory and research they have learned in the class to applied settings under the supervision of PhD faculty from our I/O psychology program. In addition, the students learn relevant professional skills by observing the senior consultants and actual practice. The skills include writing technical reports, giving presentations to clients, delivering training, managing client relationships, developing project proposals, and managing projects.

The consulting projects also provide resources and benefits to our community partners. Our partners receive high-quality consultations from PhD I/O psychologists and supervised graduate students in the form of evidenced-based solutions tailored to their specific needs. This can be accomplished at a reasonable cost as students are used as part of the consulting project team. Beyond the benefits derived from the project itself, these organizations can also benefit from the partnership in the future, such as through hosting possible class projects and hiring our students as interns (current students) or employees (graduating students).

Partnerships between organizations in the community and COHRE are not without challenges. There is always a balance to be struck between meeting the needs of the client and ensuring the students working on the consulting projects are receiving opportunities for professional development. For example, a client may need to have an organizational assessment conducted that is of a highly sensitive nature. In such a case, it may be inappropriate to have students work on the project, and it may require that only senior consultants (PhDs) be involved. Another challenge we have experienced is how to balance the students' and faculty members' academic responsibilities with the client's need to have a project completed in a certain time frame. Balancing these concerns can also create tension between work and nonwork roles for students and faculty members. This challenge also relates to the challenge of the difference between a business world (i.e., partner) time frame and an academic campus time frame. For example, a client may like to start a project immediately, but the university contracting process may take a while. This can result in stress for all parties: clients, faculty consultants, and students who will be working on the project.

Another challenge we have faced with our center is our ability to staff projects. Even though a client has an important need that would be an interesting and highly desirable project, our faculty consultants and/or our students may not have the time available to take on the project. Sometimes we have to let a potential client know we are unable to meet their needs at this time, but could do so later. This can be disappointing to a potential client, especially one with whom we have a history of collaborating on past projects. Of course, if they choose to conduct the project with another consulting group, it can be disappointing to the students and faculty consultants.

We have found some best practices that seem to help ensure that our consulting projects with our community partners are successful for them, our students, our faculty, and our center. Many of the best practices discussed in the section on class projects apply to consulting projects and will not be repeated in this section. Some best practices unique to our consulting center include best practices regarding operations within COHRE and best practices regarding our relationship with our community partners.

At COHRE, we found that creating a shared mission, vision, and values among the faculty at the beginning is critical to being successful (see Appendix 9.2). This shared mental model guides our decisions about what projects we pursue, how we involve students, and our operational procedures for running the center. This shared mental model helps COHRE meet the challenge of balancing client needs with the professional development needs of students. Our preference is for projects that provide meaningful educational experiences for our students rather than those that just provide income for COHRE and its consultants. This, and the fact that the Senior Consultants are faculty members, sensitizes COHRE to try to balance the academic responsibilities of students and faculty members. For example, we try to coordinate class assignments and client project work to avoid overloading both students and faculty, especially during times when their academic workload is heavy (mid-terms, finals).

Another best practice for COHRE is that you must obtain top-level support from the university administration. The president of our university invited faculty members of the campus to submit ideas for innovative projects that he would consider supporting. The faculty of the I/O psychology program created a business plan and got support for the concept from our department chair, our dean, and the provost. The faculty presented our business plan to the president and his senior vice president (SVP). We included a budget that requested initial start-up funds over five years with the goal to become self-supporting. The president funded the business plan for our center at that meeting. He has also supported us throughout the years by highlighting our work to various audiences. This support from the top level of our university greatly facilitated our visibility and financial viability. One of the ways the SVP supported COHRE was by creating a streamlined contracting process for the center. This ability to process contracts with our community partners in a timely manner helps us meet the challenge of aligning the academic time frame of processing contracts with the time frame expectations of the business world.

Some of the other best practices regarding our internal operations at COHRE revolve around the students. First, we believe it is important to use rigorous selection and onboarding of our GAs and the other graduate students we hire on consulting projects. Selecting GAs for COHRE involves an application that includes a résumé and a cover letter explaining why they are interested in working as a GA for COHRE, in addition to the materials submitted for acceptance into the program. The director and associate director conduct a joint, behaviorally based interview. Once selected, the GAs go through an onboarding process with the director and associate director in which job expectations and the culture and values of the center are discussed. Then they go through an onboarding/training process conducted by the second-year GAs, which includes familiarizing the incoming GAs with extensive job aids developed for the center. The job aids support a structured, on-the-job training process where all the tasks that need to be performed are covered in a systematic fashion.

Another best practice is the policy that students are paid first. Sometimes senior consultants may underestimate the budget for a consulting project. This policy ensures that students are not harmed financially and are paid for their work on the consulting project. Students also receive developmental feedback on the projects on which they work. This comes as informal, immediate feedback and more extensive after-project reviews. Finally, we developed a practice of providing vicarious learning for students who are not yet employed by COHRE. We invite students to "ride along" on consulting projects in which they can observe client meetings, delivery of training, etc. Senior consultants debrief the students after the experience about their observations and what they learned and answer any questions.

We have also established some best practices regarding developing and maintaining our relationships with our community partners. Part of our vision at COHRE is to be valued by clients and the communities where we work and live; one of our core values we have at COHRE is collaboration. Consequently, we view our consulting projects as a two-way relationship with our clients in which we embrace the reciprocal nature of community engagement that benefits both parties. This view is exemplified in the ways we interact with our clients throughout our projects – from our very first meeting through to the end of the project. In developing our proposals for our consulting projects, for example, we tell our potential clients that the proposal is not a "take it or leave it" document. We let them know that we view the proposal as a means to continue our joint conversation about their needs and to see how COHRE can collaborate with them to help meet their needs. The emphasis on collaboration even applies to those projects that COHRE may be unable to undertake because we cannot staff the engagement. If the potential client is unable to delay the project, COHRE will work to try to identify and refer them to consultants we believe meet their needs. This helps the client with their project and helps COHRE to be seen as a value to others in the community, even when not providing direct services.

Another one of our core values is learning. While this certainly applies to the education and training or our students, it also applies to our relationship with our community partners. We embrace a continuous learning process, seeking to continue improving our work with our clients by requesting feedback on the work we perform and the relationships we have with them. In addition, we see our clients as equal and valued partners in a relationship that may extend beyond the project. For example, members of two different community organizations were part of a discussion panel one of our faculty members organized for a recent professional meeting.

Conclusions and Recommendations

Synergies and Tensions

Our program has the following three major ways of interacting with the community around us: a required internship that is usually completed in the summer between students' first and second years; class-based consulting projects; and our consulting center. Typically, the internship is 40 hours per week across a minimum of 10 weeks. This experience deepens their knowledge of core content areas and professional skills through their application in a work environment. Class projects are closely supervised applications of very specific content areas. In consulting projects, students work closely with faculty on a wide range of projects and are able to develop consulting skills through observational learning of the faculty serving as consultants. All three of these activities are closely tied to the following two major strategic goals of the university: student-centered learning and establishing community partnerships. Performing these three activities together creates both synergies and tensions.

Synergistically, potential clients have a multitude of ways to learn about our program and our students. Once they have experienced the quality of work the students are capable of, they often want more. Thus, a class project could lead to a summer internship and even an eventual job offer. That may result in eventually being contacted for a larger-scale consulting project. These relationships are largely all reciprocal, meaning that a connection through any one venue could lead to any of the others.

The main tensions can arise from the pricing structure and course scheduling. Generally, class projects are conducted for entities that cannot afford to pay an intern or interns to do the project or pay for a consulting project through our consulting center. However, there is no clear line demarking who is eligible for a class project in lieu of more expensive alternatives. There are natural limits on the scope of a class project due to personnel and time constraints, so certain projects simply do not fit into the scope of a class project.

In order to allow for blocks of time for student project groups to meet with clients, meet with each other, and generally do the work of the project, everyone's schedule must be calibrated. In an environment where senior faculty generally teach the classes they want to teach when they want to teach them, class projects introduce unfamiliar constraints on faculty scheduling.

Another potential tension could exist between applied projects and faculty needs and desires to conduct research. We have addressed this in our program by having a clear priority for accomplishing the consulting goals first and only trying to do research based on project work as a secondary priority. We were able to do this for several reasons. First, our focus was on having an applied educational program, so consulting involving students was viewed as an instructional activity by our peers and administration. Second, at the time of the creation of the consulting center, all of our I/O faculty were tenured.

A final tension exists between internships and staffing consulting projects. We generally have a lot of flexibility in staffing projects, as there is a pool of graduate students available and interested in working on projects and a number of faculty available to act as senior consultants. Consulting is a fluctuating endeavor, and there can be periods of little work interleaved with multiple large-scale, concurrent projects. Every year as we approach summer, students are looking to be placed in summer internships, which are typically 40-hour-a-week commitments. While it is possible for them to do their internship through COHRE, we do not always know how much work will be available in the summer at the time when students are making decisions about their summer internships. If a consulting project comes in after the majority of students have committed to internships elsewhere, we may find ourselves short-staffed.

As a discipline, I/O psychology is a natural fit for disciplinary outreach. Our field's scientist–practitioner model and, in particular, our I/O program's emphasis on training students to enter into the workforce align well with our internships, applied class projects, and consulting projects. While there are many challenges and multiple priorities that have to be managed to make everything work, the resulting benefits for the faculty, students, and community partners have been highly satisfying.

Appendix 9.1

Purpose

This proposal outlines the parameters for developing a study skills workshop for the MTSU Veterans and Family Center and a plan for Onboarding Veterans to the Center. While it is beyond the scope of this project to implement a general onboarding plan for veterans to the university itself, the group may make recommendations along those lines.

Approach and Timeline

Conduct background research on study skills, veterans transitioning to college, and onboarding prior to the week of March 14.

- Review information provided by Drs. Hein, Holt, and Miller.
- Review the literature.

Interview/discussion with veterans and family center leadership sometime during the week of March 14.

- Meet with the Dr. Hilary Miller to understand the goals of the project and obtain an overview of the Veterans and Family Center and veterans at MTSU.

Interview veterans and Veterans and Family Center staff to determine training needs by April 1.

- Meet individually (60 minutes) or in focus groups with veteran students to determine training needs and onboarding issues to include, but not limited to, optimal ways to deliver the training.

Develop training objectives based on the above by April 8.
Develop workshop and onboarding plan by April 22.
Develop evaluation plan and instruments for the workshop and onboarding process by April 22.
If possible, conduct a pilot workshop with veteran students and collect evaluation data. (This may make more sense to do at the beginning of next semester rather than the end of this semester.)

Total Cost Estimate

(This is actually a class project and costs figures are included for pedagogical purposes only.)
The total cost for the above work would be capped at $22,000. Any costs exceeding the total cost cap would not be charged. Initial payment of $11,000

would be due upon approval of the contract by both parties. A final payment of $11,000 would be due at the completion of the full project.

Veterans and Family Center Responsibilities

Veterans and Family Center will provide:

- Timely access to people and information as agreed upon
- Relevant supporting documents
- A primary point of contact and logistical support for coordinating activities with the Veterans' Center
- Extension of schedule if delays occur by Veterans and Family Center due to unanticipated factors
- Appropriate space for interviews with participants

COHRE Responsibilities

COHRE will provide:

- Drs. Michael Hein and Aimee Holt as a resource for the team
- Use of Adobe Acrobat
- Project associates to conduct the project
- A final copy of all training and onboarding materials in electronic and/or paper form
- A final report detailing the processes used to conduct the analysis and the results
- Office space, phone and computer access, office supplies, incidental copying, a laptop, and an LCD projector

Accepts Contents of Proposal

MTSU Veterans and Military Family Center

_____   _____
          Signature   **Date**

Appendix 9.2

Center for Organizational and Human Resource Effectiveness

Our Vision

We will be the most valued organization to clients, colleagues, business partners, governments, educational institutions, and the communities where we work and live.

Our Mission

To enhance the quality of the MTSU's I/O Psychology program, serve its students, represent the university with pride, contribute to the community, and impact organizations and the people in them with integrity.

Our Values

Integrity
People
Learning
Excellence
Collaboration

References

Association of Public and Land Grant Universities (n.d.). History of APLU. Association of Public and Land Grant Universities. Retrieved from www.aplu.org/about-us/history-of-aplu/.

New England Resource Center for Higher Education (n.d.). Carnegie Community Engagement Classification: How is "community engagement" defined? New England Resource Center for Higher Education. Retrieved from http://nerche.org/index.php?option=com_content&view=article&id=341&Itemid=618#CEdef.

Lewin, K. (1946). Action research and minority problems. *Journal of Social Issues*, 2(4), 34–46.

Roper, C. D., & Hirth, M. A. (2005). A history of change in the third mission of higher education: The evolution of one-way service to interactive engagement. *Journal of Higher Education Outreach and Engagement*, 10(3), 3–21.

Shoenfelt, E. L. (2003). Utilizing applied projects in I-O graduate training: A checklist to help ensure successful experiences. *TIP: The Industrial–Organizational Psychologist*, 41, 109–115.

Simmering, L., Napper, C., & Sheets, T. (2012). Experience based training for I–O graduate students. *TIP: The Industrial–Organizational Psychologist*, 49(4), 56–61.

Society for Industrial and Organizational Psychology (2016). *Guidelines for education and training in industrial/organizational psychology*. Bowling Green, OH: Author.

10 Driving Workforce Readiness

The Case for Community-Based HR Initiatives

Joseph Jones, Rachael Johnson-Murray, Valerie Streets, Alexander Alonso, & Shonna D. Waters

Today's knowledge economy – and the employers and employees that support it – has a major problem. High-demand positions, such as those that are key to an organization's success and those that are more stable and financially rewarding to employees, are not being filled by skilled workers ready and able to contribute. Some debate exists as to whether the problem lies with a lack in the supply of available skills in the labor market or elsewhere, such as with poor recruiting or internal training practices. It is not a new challenge – for decades the business and political worlds have raised concerns about the inability to fill important positions for business success. However, many factors both in the workforce and internal to organizations can be credited for leading to this issue. And despite the many years of discussing and seeking solutions to this issue, the problem only seems to be growing.

Given this challenge, employers now often find themselves relying on nontraditional methods for sourcing the talent needed to be successful (e.g., crowdsourcing, talent platforms, interactive postings). These organizations go beyond the traditional approach of defining the job, posting the job requirements, recruiting and screening for the job, and making a hiring decision. Many are developing a more systemic approach that considers careers from a lifelong perspective and organizations as part of an economic ecosystem in which each component of the ecosystem is interdependent (e.g., the environment is dependent on business, business is dependent on education, education is dependent on government).

To build connections within this ecosystem, organizations launch or engage in a variety of initiatives that bridge internal communities (i.e., the community of employees within an organization) with external ones (e.g., other organizations, educational communities, minority or disadvantaged communities, veterans' groups, the general public), such as that shown in Figure 10.1.

Among these methods are grassroots, community-based initiatives in which employers and educators partner with local talent to "manufacture" a workforce. These efforts focus on reaching the micro levels (i.e., the level of individual members of the workforce) to resolve workforce readiness issues with potential workers who appear to lack the motivation to work, the planning skills necessary to find work, the skills necessary to apply and interview for positions effectively, and both the skills and the ability to develop the competencies to perform the work (Conway & Giloth, 2014; Spaulding & Martin-Caughey, 2015). Essentially, these groups are preparing potential workers to enter or become more competitive in the job market, improving

Community/Workforce
Community-Based Change
Workforce Readiness and Employability

| **Government/Chambers of Commerce**
Funding
Business Interventions for Sourcing | **Business**
Corporate Social Responsibility
Skilled Position Placement | **Education/Colleges and Universities**
Business Connections
Learning and Development |

Human Resources
Workforce Planning and Recruiting
Community-Based HR Initiatives

Figure 10.1 *Community-based change network*

the individuals' workforce readiness. These efforts seek to prepare workers in general for the world of work, whether through focusing on a specific career path (e.g., career readiness), secondary educational training (e.g., college readiness), or basic skills in gaining employment (i.e., employability skills). Strengthening the workforce also means strengthening the community (Hesselbein et al., 1998). While meeting business needs is paramount to sustainable organizational success, these initiatives also have the advantages of serving the broader society, driving development among aging professionals and marginalized members of society, and building ties between several civic organizations.

These efforts to improve the skills gaps of workers ultimately fall into the domain of human resources (or *human capital*). In other words, human beings as *resources* are viewed not exclusively as parts of organizations – they are viewed as parts of the system of resources (along with financial, information, physical resources, etc.) that exist in various economies and in the world in general. Because human resource management (HRM or simply HR) serves as the facilitator of effective *human* resources for organizations, it is ideally suited to help with the issues of skills gaps and workforce readiness outside the organization. For example, organizations often call upon HR to lead workforce analysis efforts across the entire enterprise or within specific departments. HR professionals, therefore, must understand how to estimate the gap between the existing knowledge, skills, and abilities (KSAs) and the KSAs the organization needs, and then determine whether the organization can train its employees or, if not, whether the KSAs exist in the relevant labor market. Although many individuals in organizations have a responsibility to find, optimize, and retain human talent, most organizations today view HR as the central regulator and driver of this key organizational function and expect those in HR to have the knowledge and behavioral competencies to ensure that it is successful.

It is important to mention that when we write of HR here and throughout this chapter, we are looking at the profession broadly, noting that some of the more specialized roles within HR (such as human resource information systems [HRIS], management, and talent acquisition) may have less external reach in general to support the workforce because they are more focused on an organization's specific needs (e.g., security and control or filling specific roles). Despite the unique and ideal function that HR can serve in community-based organizational initiatives, HR has played a limited role in the past, whether leading or supporting these efforts (Chartered Institute for Personnel and Development, 2013). While some professions have been more engaged in leading community-based efforts in the past, HR is only recently becoming involved in these efforts. HR's delay may be due to the less strategic role it has historically played in business operations (Francis & Keegen, 2006).

This lack of partnership with the community must change, and things have started moving in that direction. Recent efforts by HR to lead and support community-based initiatives have been challenging due to the traditionally limited role of HR; there has also been a lack of research examining the extent to which HR has led or supported community-based efforts, and even less research showing what approaches are most effective and provide the greatest return on investment (ROI) for organizations while simultaneously helping the communities in which they are engaged.

In this chapter, we provide additional clarity and guidance on identifying and addressing the challenge in filling jobs that are critical for business success by strengthening the role that HR plays in community-based efforts. In addition, we provide a taxonomy of community-based HR initiatives with tangible examples. We also include a framework for ensuring the success of these types of initiatives. We finish with guidance for ensuring that evidence-based practice sits at the heart of organizational community engagement.

The Workforce Challenge: A Lack of Skills in High-Demand Positions

Many organizations face an issue that continues to keep their leaders up at night: high-demand positions requiring skills that help drive organizational goals remain vacant or are filled by unskilled workers. In other words, leaders have the challenge of filling vacancies with qualified talent whom they can retain for extended periods. This challenge has an even bigger impact on the organization's success when vacancies occur in high-demand roles that are closely or directly aligned with key business objectives.

A frequently cited study by the Manpower Group (2016) reported that at least four out of ten business leaders indicate that difficulty filling critical positions remains one of the most pressing business challenges they face today. Recent studies by the Centre for Economics and Business Research (CEBR) on behalf of online job search and recruiting platform Indeed estimated in 2014 that US organizations lose approximately $160 billion annually in revenue because of unfilled positions (Indeed, 2014). In addition, research indicates that 68 percent of HR professionals find it difficult to hire for full-time positions (Society for Human Resource Management [SHRM], 2016). In particular, respondents struggle to find qualified candidates in fields that require a strong educational or vocational foundation, such as medicine, science, mathematics, engineering, architecture, and other skilled trades (e.g., electrician, plumber, mechanic).

The impact of the skills gap on organizations is substantial. In addition to the time and other resources dedicated to finding and acquiring skilled staff for open positions, additional costs are incurred due to reduced productivity resulting from unfilled positions, or underperforming positions filled with under-skilled or unskilled labor. These suboptimal staffing conditions can lead to expensive and time-consuming investments in training. Additional research by the careers site CareerBuilder in 2017 indicates that the annual cost of unfilled positions in organizations on average approaches $1 million (CareerBuilder, 2017).

Why High-Demand Positions Are Not Being Filled

Many reasons have been proposed regarding why positions are not being filled in the USA and other economies (Cappelli, 1995; Cappelli, 2015). Probably the most cited reason is what is often referred to as the "skills gap." The skills gap can be defined as a lack of skills (usually technical) available in the relevant workforce for in-demand roles in organizations (usually critical or key roles). The argument goes that organizations cannot find and cannot attract technically skilled workers. The reasons cited for the skills gap are varied, including lack of adequate education and more lucrative opportunities in other roles. For instance, in PricewaterhouseCooper's (PwC) 19th Annual Global CEO Survey, 72 percent of CEOs reported the availability of key skills as a top threat to the organization and more specifically cited interpersonal skills and adaptability skills as the most critical concerns (PwC, 2016). However, as some have noted, a lack of skills in the workforce (a) may not be as extensive as has been reported and (b) may not be the only reason for unfilled positions (Hurrell, 2016; Rosenberg, Heimler, & Morote, 2012).

The reasons for unfilled positions are many, including the skills gap, and can be split between workplace issues (i.e., employer issues) and workforce issues (i.e.,

Workplace Issues	Workforce Issues
• Poor or noncompetitive recruiting and succession management practices • Poor or noncompetitive workforce planning • Poor or noncompetitive training and performance management • Poor or noncompetitive total rewards • Poor or noncompetitive career management support	• Lack of technical skills • Lack of "soft skills" • Lack of career management skills • Contextual limitations (e.g., geographic, family, cultural restraints) • Socioeconomic barriers (e.g., age and gender biases, low investment in continued development, disproportionate focus on college prep)

Figure 10.2 *Sources of unfilled positions*

issues relevant to both employees and potential employees). Figure 10.2 shows some of the issues that fall within these two categories.

Workplace issues that contribute to the lack of skilled positions center on failure to:

• Clearly assess and define jobs and attract and select candidates for those jobs
• Adequately onboard and upskill employees
• Keep employees engaged
• Provide employees with the support and resources they need so that they want to remain employed (Cappelli, 2015; Hurrell, 2016; Romo, 2013)

Workforce issues include the aforementioned technical skills gap, as well as gaps in "soft skills" (e.g., interpersonal skills, leadership, decision-making) and a lack of career management skills that allow members of the workforce to seek out, select among, position themselves for, obtain, and stay employed in desirable positions. Workforce issues are not limited to a lack of skills, however, as members of the workforce who are skilled may not be able to seek or accept some open positions because of other constraints (e.g., having children in school, working spouses, elder care responsibilities, or other financial or social obligations).

As noted earlier, the challenge of filling high-demand, skilled positions is not a new issue (Cappelli, 1995; Casner-Lotto & Barrington, 2006). However, with so much discussion on the issue and suggestions about how to address it, the questions of why various approaches have not worked and what more can be done to resolve the challenge remain. Addressing these issues requires community-based partnerships between government, educational institutions, and business. For such partnerships to be successful, it is critical that they be led and supported by people whose competencies and expertise relate directly to the challenge – in other words, individuals who understand the importance of having a skilled workforce to business success; grasp where businesses stand with regard to skills gaps; are effective at finding and developing skills in both the internal and external labor pools; know how to maintain skills over time; and are experienced in building and navigating internal and external stakeholder relationships. As the organizational function that strategically performs this role and scopes the organization-wide landscape of employee work to meet business needs, HR professionals are key to successfully driving community-based partnerships.

HR's Role in Organizations

Noe, Hollenbeck, Gerhart, and Wright (2017) defined HRM as "the policies, practices, and systems that influence employees' behavior, attitudes, and performance" (p. 4). In organizations, HR professionals serve in a variety of roles to drive the process of designing systems to manage human talent. These roles require having a systems perspective of the organization as a whole, the individual employees, the external environment in which both organizations and employees exist, and the interactions between all three of these.

As such, HR professionals must be experts who possess competencies in a variety of areas focused specifically on optimizing human capital (Strobel et al., 2015). From an organizational perspective, HR professionals must have business acumen and an ability to navigate both inside and outside the organization while building strong relationships. They must also have an understanding of the tools, systems, technology, laws, and policies that are at play in the organization to make the work of the human capital function seamless and effective. HR professionals also play a key role in understanding the different jobs across an organization, how to define those jobs, and how to acquire and train the talent needed to fill those jobs.

From an individual perspective, HR professionals must have a clear understanding of what makes individuals want to work for an organization, qualified to work for an organization, succeed within the organization, develop when they are not succeeding, and want to stay with the organization. Thus, HR requires professionals who can critically evaluate the human capital needs in an organization, the positioning of internal and external talent to fill those needs now and in the future, and relevant causes of recruiting difficulty and skills shortages and their solutions.

HR professionals must also understand the external environment that the organization exists within. This means not only knowing what the labor market looks like for filling positions, but also having a keen sense of the social, cultural, and ethical environments in which the organization functions. HR professionals must be familiar with the various institutions, such as schools, governments, and other businesses, that affect the organization and can serve as possible resources to support both the company and the current and potential employees who live within that ecosystem. For years, HR departments have worked as an operational partner within the organization, but there has been a growing trend to take a business partner approach to HR that is more holistic, strategic, and aware of the implications of business processes, HR activities, and organizational outcomes (Francis & Keegen, 2006).

Unlike other functions inside and outside of organizations, due to knowledge and skills in a variety of areas directed at workforce, talent, and human capital issues, HR can help address the workforce readiness issue in a number of ways (SHRM, 2015). With a well-defined need, HR can drive sourcing by specifying what educational institutions (e.g., high schools, career and technical education programs, vocational schools, trade apprenticeship programs, colleges, universities) should emphasize for their students. With this specification, educational institutions can design programs to meet business needs directly. HR can then draw a community-oriented pipeline from educational institutions to employers. Leveraging organizations like local SHRM chapters and chambers of commerce, HR professionals can multiply their impact on the community. The only way HR succeeds at this endeavor is by taking a broader view of the community and its role (Cohen et al., 2010), perhaps one that matches the role as defined by SHRM in its competency model (Strobel et al., 2015).

Organizational Attempts to Address Skills Gaps through an HR Perspective

To address these issues, employers have taken different approaches in the past. For workplace issues that contribute to difficulty in filling positions, many organizations have launched internal efforts to improve their human capital and talent management systems and processes. Employers have begun to use nontraditional sourcing methods (e.g., crowdsourcing, talent platforms, interactive postings) to attract and hire the talent they need to be successful. These organizations go beyond the traditional approach of defining the job, posting the job requirements, recruiting and screening for the job, and making a hiring decision. Employers have also increased the use of a variety of job-skilling techniques beyond traditional training, including certifications, online training, and apprenticeships (Carter, 2005; McNamara, 2009).

In addition, there has been an increased emphasis in recent years on building more effective career management resources for employees. This trend coincides with increased expectations for employees to continuously improve so that their skills remain relevant. Career ladders and paths have become blurred; organizations and employees have begun to share greater responsibility for anticipating and preparing for skills demands, and research suggests that this approach has positive effects on organizational performance (De Vos & Cambré, 2017).

For workforce issues, the majority of efforts tend to fall under the category of workforce readiness. Workforce readiness (or similarly *career readiness* or *employability*) looks systemically and comprehensively at the current lack of skills in the workforce. However, this broader lack of skills is different from the concept of a "skills gap" because it extends beyond *just* job-related skills (which is typically the focus of the "skills gap"). It additionally reflects whether individuals are prepared to seek, find, prepare for, obtain, start, and remain in a job. Workforce readiness initiatives therefore seek to understand the underlying causes of and factors contributing to a lack of readiness for work. These initiatives seek remedies that prepare individuals for entry (or reentry) into the workforce. Such remedies may include learning how to search for and find jobs, as well as how to match abilities with job requirements and how to increase soft skills (Hurrell, 2016).

A clear and widely agreed-on definition of workforce readiness is lacking. Defining this concept has proven challenging because candidates' experiences and employers' needs vary across industries and occupations. While numerous public and private sector stakeholders have crafted their own definitions, several common themes have emerged regarding workforce readiness. Across professional organizations, educators, researchers, and other stakeholders, workforce readiness is discussed with regard to three overarching areas (ACT, 2016; Bradbard, Armstrong, & Maury, 2016; Torpey, 2015):

- Possession of technical and soft skills and the motivation to further develop those skills
- Ability to navigate the job market and identify realistic opportunities
- Ability to translate one's experiences and demonstrate the skills necessary to perform a given job

For the purposes of this chapter and from our perspective, workforce readiness thus encompasses not only potentially having the prerequisite skills necessary for a job, but also being ready to obtain those skills (if they do not exist), developing the right mind-set to become and stay employed, and building effective skills for seeking and obtaining employment.

The first area is what we most often think of when we think of workforce readiness – developing the skills (both hard and soft) needed by employers; in other words, the skills gap referenced above. Nearly every industry and sector has raised concerns about the lack of skills available in the workforce to meet their needs. Some of the areas most commonly cited include science, technology, engineering, math and analytics, leadership, interpersonal skills, basic time management and organizational skills, and general manual labor skills (O'Neil Jr. et al., 1992; Robinson, 2000; Rosenberg et al., 2012; SHRM, 2015).

Much of the concern about the skills gap issue points to increased globalization (Williams, Moser, Youngblood II, & Singer, 2015), generational differences (Rosenberg et al., 2012), and inadequate educational systems (Rosenberg et al., 2012) as key sources of the existing gap. Globalization is seen as a cause in the following two ways: (a) more global opportunities exist that allow skilled workers to find more lucrative opportunities outside of their home country (i.e., "the brain drain"); and (b) global competition and innovation have increased the need for skills in a way that has outpaced educational systems and corporate training. Generational differences have been suggested as a cause as well, suggesting that younger generations are less interested in a variety of career paths that are less rewarding, less aligned with their values, and more manual (or less technology-based). Educational systems are possibly the most frequently proposed cause of the skills gap; high school and secondary education is seen as having curricula that are outdated, too focused on test scores, or simply out of touch with business needs (Rosenberg et al., 2012). In addition, current or potential members of the workforce may be at a disadvantage in school because they lack academic competencies (e.g., the competencies necessary to be successful and proficient in a learning environment) (Bishop, 1992).

The second area of workforce readiness involves being capable of and motivated to seek work. Many individuals, whether entering the labor market through more formal educational paths or with limited education, have not developed effective skills in searching for and finding work for which they will be a good fit. They face challenges such as knowing where to find job opportunities, how to build networks, what information is necessary to create a résumé, how to complete an application, how to submit a résumé or an application, and how to time job searches and applications. These actions require significant skills in planning, organizing, attention to detail, communication, and strategy. These skills are difficult for many individuals to obtain before entering the workforce, especially for younger workers, workers from low socioeconomic backgrounds, immigrants, and older workers who have been removed from the workforce for significant periods of time.

Unfortunately, most of the workforce acquires proficiency in these areas from the experience of going through the job search process. For example, when individuals decide to seek employment, they must first decide what types of jobs they would be most interested in or qualified to perform. They would then need to find out what the requirements and details of a certain job include and whether they are, in fact, qualified. Then, to be considered for the job, they would need to find out when applications are due, when or if an interview is required, and whether there are other steps in the process. They would also need to review the details of their résumé, fill out the application, prepare for an interview and/or test, and have transportation to and from hiring events.

Multiply this process across many job openings and it requires significant time management and organizational skills that, without practice, many job applicants may lack. The good news is that the skills needed to search for and find meaningful work are trainable. Programs that help unemployed workers develop these job-hunting skills (e.g., time management, résumé preparation, application submission, interviewing) should therefore be included in any workforce readiness program to ensure it addresses skills gap challenges comprehensively and effectively.

In addition to simply having the skills to search for and obtain work, two major barriers to many workers are those of motivation and confidence (Cappelli, 2015). Many potential employees – both skilled and unskilled – struggle when searching for and applying to jobs because they are overwhelmed by the amount of effort that a job search may entail, they are not confident that they can interview for and obtain the work they desire, and/or they are fearful of the change that may occur as a result of finding and starting work. They may also have a cultural, ethical, political, or geographical aversion to working for various businesses.

The third area of workforce readiness entails workers positioning themselves to receive job offers and gaining employment, and this can be a major barrier to many job seekers. Obtaining an offer for a job is often not just about having the right skills for the job, but also about convincing others to see that the candidate has the right skills and to believe that the individual will be a good fit for the organization and well-qualified for the role. To do that, a job seeker must be an effective communicator and understand how to convey an image that aligns with the culture, values, and expectations of the organization.

A candidate's ability to manage his or her image is important during a job interview, and for some employers, a potential new hire's social media image may be just as influential in the decision-making process (Sameen & Cornelius, 2015; Smith & Kidder, 2010). Not every job requires an interview, but many organizations use interviews as one of or the only screening tool (other than the application and background check) when making decisions about job candidates (Judge, Cable, & Higgins, 2000). Being able to communicate well in an interview, answer questions effectively, and present oneself in the best light possible will often make or break the candidate's chance of getting the job. Some highly skilled workers may not be considered for certain positions because they failed to clearly explain their qualifications, used poor nonverbal behaviors during the interview, or dressed in a manner that indicated they did not understand the work environment and may not be a good fit.

Today's recruiting and selection process has been expanded to include the use of social media to gauge whether there is consistency between how candidates present themselves in the application and interview process and how they present themselves to a broader audience (SHRM, 2016). Recruiters use social media to determine whether candidates have indicated their past experience truthfully and consistently through platforms such as LinkedIn, whether candidates have expressed views that could pose a risk to the organization on platforms like Twitter, or whether they have displayed a lack of professionalism via platforms such as Facebook. Regardless of whether such an approach by organizations is appropriate or even legal, job candidates must have a better understanding of how their image on social media may affect their ability to obtain and keep highly desired positions.

A job candidate's ability to manage his or her image on social media or during an interview essentially boils down to an understanding of the level of professionalism that is expected in a potential employer's work environment – coming across as laid back and casual may be appropriate in some organizations, but in others (and probably most) a certain level of professionalism is expected. In today's era of social media, job seekers need to know this in advance of even applying for a job to ensure that the job and cultural expectations align with what potential employers see online and in the interview setting. Yet this lack of advanced preparation and foresight may actually be a reason some skilled employees are not considered for open positions.

Other areas important to workforce readiness – readiness to start work and remaining employed – appear to be larger issues than most organizations realize, given that they are not consistently included in workforce readiness definitions. However, a 2016 SHRM study of 919 HR professionals across a wide range of industries indicated an average first-year separation rate of 34 percent (SHRM, 2016). There are multiple causes of turnover within the first year (e.g., poor fit to the culture, inconsistencies between the advertised and actual role); however, better preparation of the workforce in organization, interpersonal skills, adaptability, resilience, and other competencies necessary to prepare for and remain employed may improve the likelihood that newly hired workers remain in roles for at least the first year (Cappelli, 2015; Royalty, 1996).

Over the last few decades, academic institutions, businesses, nonprofits, and the government have attempted a variety of efforts to improve workforce readiness.

These programs represent community-based efforts to build a stronger and more employable workforce. Several examples of these initiatives are listed below:

1. Business–education partnerships (including assistance in curriculum development)
2. Apprenticeship and internship programs.
3. Employees volunteering in community outreach programs that improve the workforce readiness of others
4. Nongovernmental organizations (NGOs) dedicated to skill enhancement of unskilled workers
5. Career and technical education programs
6. Joint union–management training programs
7. Thought leadership and other online tools and resources to advance workforce readiness

Efforts such as the Partnership for Twenty-First Century Learning, Career Readiness Partnership Council, Goodwill Industries, and The Alliance for Employee Growth and Development, Inc., all represent efforts to increase workforce readiness, employability, and skills through partnerships across businesses, NGOs, educational institutions, and government. These initiatives provide various skill development opportunities through classroom, online, and on-the-job learning, as well as coaching and counseling from experienced professionals in a variety of skilled professions.

Despite the efforts underway for decades both within organizations and in the broader workforce to address the issue of filling positions, it seems little progress has been made to fully address this talent dilemma. One reason may be the limited evidence available supporting the efficacy of these programs in resolving the problem at hand. A solution to this problem is to build evidence-based practice into the planning and decision-making regarding proposed solutions.

Evidence-Based Practice

To ensure that programs are targeting the relevant skills for development and the proper methods to motivate while also accurately assessing the readiness of and hurdles facing participants, HR community-based efforts need to use evidence to guide decisions. Barends, Rousseau, and Briner (2014) define *evidence-based practice* as "making decisions through the conscientious, explicit and judicious use of the best available evidence from multiple sources" (p. 4). Evidence-based practice emerged from the field of medicine, in which concerns over erroneous medical decisions led to a desire to make decisions based not simply on practitioner knowledge and training, but on all the available evidence, including research findings (Briner, Denyer, & Rousseau, 2009; McKibbon, 1998). The concept of using evidence to make critical decisions migrated to other fields such as architecture, education, finance and HR, in which mistakes in decision-making could have significant legal, financial, physical, or other consequences. Evidence-based practice can help decision-makers create better plans for implementing internal and external initiatives and programs to improve the staffing of difficult-to-fill positions.

HR has begun to embrace the use of evidence-based practice as part of its human capital strategy and decision-making in organizations. The organization ScienceforWork (see https://scienceforwork.com) has emerged to try to sift through the plethora of business research and other evidence that exists (or to uncover where evidence is lacking) and provide guidance regarding specific HR practices and assumptions so that leaders can make more informed and valid decisions going forward. As evidence-based practice continues to grow, decisions made internally and externally regarding talent and human capital will become better situated for success. Applying the principles of evidence-based practice to the establishment of community-based HR initiatives can help ensure that workforce readiness efforts are successful. Before providing a framework for applying evidence-based practice to community-based HR initiatives, we next describe such initiatives and how they support workplace readiness.

How Community-Based HR Initiatives Help

As HR continues to become a more strategic part and facilitator of organizational success, organizations place more value on its potential impact in other areas such as community-based initiatives. Community-based HR takes advantage of HR's unique position as an expert in human capital and in understanding the needs of the organization – specifically expertise in identifying, assessing, motivating, developing, and retaining skilled professionals – to support the broader community. Through such efforts, HR can build better ties between workers and organizations even before those workers are hired. These areas are of critical importance to HR professionals because workforce readiness helps improve efficiencies and recruiting while bringing in more skilled and possibly more committed workers.

A reason organizations continue to struggle with filling needed positions may be that they are not looking at the problem from a holistic, systemic perspective. In other words, the issue is not just the technical skills gap, the soft skills gap, poor recruiting, or poor total reward policies, but all of these. The issue of unfilled key positions is one for which sources reside both within the workplace community and within the workforce community, as well as in the interaction between the two communities.

For example, fixing the soft skills gap in the workforce will do nothing if an organization still has poor recruiting practices. Yet resolving both of these independently may also not be fully successful unless an organization focuses on fixing how the two causes interact. In other words, an organization could increase the quality of its interviewing process so that it is more structured, but if it still focuses on hiring only for technical skills, then improving the soft skills of the workforce will have little impact. To solve the business challenge of filling skilled positions requires a more systemic, holistic approach that involves the connection between and development of communities (Hesselbein et al., 1998).

Fortunately, the HR profession of today is ideally situated to take the systems perspective needed to identify and address both the internal and external challenges driving unfilled positions in organizations. As the primary implementer of organizational human capital practices, HR professionals must have the competencies necessary to work both within and outside the organizational system to ensure the optimal use of talent. Following this lead, we propose that the HR profession takes on an even greater role in what we refer to as community-based HR initiatives.

Community-based HR initiatives reflect efforts – coordinated through corporate HR or HR professional associations – for organizations, employees, or independent HR practitioners to connect with and support local communities or society more broadly. Like other community-based initiatives, community-based HR initiatives may focus on a range of social issues or challenges such as veterans' issues, support for people with disabilities, environmental sustainability, and workforce readiness. Community-based HR initiatives are part of the broader concept of HR involvement in corporate social responsibility (CSR) efforts proposed elsewhere (e.g., Cohen, Taylor, & Muller-Carmen, 2010; Inyang, Awa, & Enuoh, 2011). CSR reflects responsible efforts by an organization to balance profit with accountability toward internal stakeholders (i.e., employees) and external stakeholders and resources (e.g., suppliers, educational institutions, local and national communities, the environment) (Johnson, 1971).

The type and level of support for these efforts vary depending on factors such as:

- Needs of the organizations donating their HR professionals' time
- Availability of HR professionals
- Nature and extent of skills gaps or readiness issues existing in relevant labor markets
- Availability and types of institutions located near the workforce
- Extent, type, and historical success of existing readiness programs
- Resources available to address the issue

Unlike traditional HR, community-based HR is not confined to an organization. HR professionals or retired HR professionals volunteering independently or through professional associations can also serve as valuable resources. They can implement and facilitate community outreach initiatives and communications that will help assess and address the skills gap and workforce readiness issues. For example, members of SHRM's Ethics/Corporate Social Responsibility and Sustainability Special Expertise Panel discuss issues such as the skills gap and workforce readiness, generate ideas, and identify ways that HR can play a more effective and strategic role both within and outside the organization. We outline three other examples of community-based HR initiatives below.

SHRM and the SHRM Foundation. SHRM has been working to address the issues of workforce readiness and the skills gap for years (Casner-Lotto & Barrington, 2006; SHRM, 2015; SHRM, 2016) through research, advocacy, thought leadership and community connections. SHRM's website lists resources and tools for HR professionals and others to learn about and address workforce readiness issues (www.shrm.org/resourcesandtools/hr-topics/talent-acquisition/pages/work force-readiness-resource-page.aspx). Further, SHRM drives workforce readiness by making it a core leadership area of focus for all of its chapters. SHRM's 575 chapters are required to engage in initiatives at the local level to combat the workforce readiness issues within their communities.

At the profession-wide level, the SHRM Foundation is an example of community-based HR in which current and retired HR professionals support the broader society through donations and Foundation-run research and initiatives. The SHRM Foundation, now in its 51st year, recently shifted its strategy to be even more focused on specific social concerns. Similar to the larger driving force of SHRM, the Foundation's mission is to champion workforce and workplace transformation through the provision of research-based HR solutions to inclusion issues, scholarships to support HR professionals seeking to make change, and opportunities for HR professionals to make an impact in their local communities.

This mission relates directly to the three benefits of community-based HR initiatives noted earlier: (a) connecting HR professionals with communities; (b) improving workforce readiness; and (c) supporting broader CSR efforts. Through outreach, academic scholarships, community volunteering, and thought leadership efforts, the Foundation focuses on helping veterans transition into the workforce, addressing the needs of aging workers, and creating more inclusive work cultures. In the future, the Foundation seeks to address other issues important to the broader community.

Employer Support of the Guard and Reserve. The link between members of the National Guard and Reserve and their civilian employers led to the creation of the Employer Support of the Guard and Reserve (ESGR). A Department of Defense program, the ESGR assists Reserve Component service members and their civilian employers, providing information, resources, and assistance for resolving issues. Paramount to the ESGR's mission is encouraging employment of Guardsmen and Reservists who bring integrity, global perspective, and proven leadership to the civilian workforce. Established in 1972, the ESGR operates via a network of thousands of volunteers and support staff within all 50 US states, Guam–Commonwealth of the Northern Mariana Islands (CNMI), Puerto Rico, the US Virgin Islands, and the District of Columbia.

The ESGR informs and educates service members and their civilian employers regarding their rights and responsibilities governed by the Uniformed Services Employment and Reemployment Rights Act (USERRA). The ESGR does not enforce USERRA, but serves as a neutral, free resource for employers and service members. The ESGR's trained ombudsmen provide mediation for issues relating to compliance with USERRA. The law applies to all public and private employers in the United States, including federal, state, territory, and local governments, regardless of size. Provided that a service member meets all criteria, employers must provide the following: prompt job reinstatement; accumulation of seniority, including pension plan benefits; reinstatement of health insurance; training/retraining of job skills (including accommodations for employees with disabilities); and protection against discrimination. Many HR professionals have volunteered their time to the ESGR as part of or independent of their employers' efforts to support the ESGR's work.

National Fund for Workforce Solutions. The National Fund for Workforce Solutions was founded in 2007 to improve "the education and workforce systems responsible for providing opportunities for low income or disadvantaged individuals to gain skills and obtain careers paying family-supporting wages and benefits, while simultaneously addressing business needs" (Soricone, 2015, p. vii). The National Fund partners with a variety of communities and for-profit and nonprofit organizations to identify, develop, and promote employer-led workforce initiatives designed to assist in the employment of low-wage job seekers. Additional benefits of these programs are the strengthening of talent supply chains and the local economies in which they exist.

HR professionals can assist by identifying opportunities in their organizations to build and promote workforce development efforts aligned with National Fund initiatives. For example, the Youth/Industry Partnership Initiative (YIPI) focuses specifically on programs to help find opportunities for the employment and development of disadvantaged youth. HR professionals in organizations interested in or currently engaged with such programs can help by working to connect their employer with YIPI resources and seek ways to better advance and gain attention to their efforts.

To better define the potential space for community-based HR initiatives focused on workforce readiness issues, we have provided the taxonomy shown in Figure 10.3. This taxonomy shows the types of programs that exist or could exist

Workforce Readiness Issues and Community-Based HR Initiative Solutions					
Areas for Readiness Improvement	Technical and Knowledge Competencies	Academic Competencies	Job Searching Skills	Candidate Positioning Skills	Work Attitude, Organizational and Interpersonal Skills
Initiative Owner	**Initiative Examples**				
Company-based programs	•Apprenticeships •Internships •Scholarships			•Job fairs with feedback	•Apprenticeships •Internships
Nonprofit programs	•Assessments •Seminars •Coaching •Competitions	•Seminars	•Thought leadership •Seminars •Coaching	•Thought leadership •Seminars •Coaching	•Thought leadership •Seminars •Coaching
Business–education partnerships	•Curriculum support	•Mentoring programs	•Mentoring programs	•Mentoring programs	•Mentoring programs
Business–union partnerships	•Joint apprenticeships •Training programs		•Joint apprenticeships •Training programs	•Joint apprenticeships •Training programs	•Joint apprenticeships •Training programs
Government-based programs	•Scholarships	•Mentoring programs •Training programs	•Mentoring programs •Training programs	•Mentoring programs •Training programs	•Mentoring programs •Training programs

Figure 10.3 *Taxonomy of community-based HR initiatives*

based on initiative type and the specific readiness issue that the program can be designed to address.

Examples of this taxonomy in action include:

- Providing speakers for local community groups on topics such as careers, leadership, the value of organizations to the local area, and the organization's history and future plans
- Allowing schools and other community-based organizations to participate in work experience programs or conduct site visits
- Offering scholarships for talented locals to support their career development goals
- Advertising job vacancies in the local community initially and establishing a local job board with schools, educational institutions, and community groups in the area
- Promoting/hosting community events
- Providing mentors to build capability within the community

Although this taxonomy can provide a general foundation for what types of programs do or could exist to address specific workforce readiness and skills gaps issues, it does not address whether these programs are actually effective in decreasing the issue. To know whether a program is effective or ineffective requires evidence. We therefore propose that any initiative of these types undertaken by HR must be evidence-based.

Using Evidence to Drive Community-Based HR Initiatives: A Framework

"Evidence-based" in the context of community-based HR reflects building community support systems that are backed by research and expert judgments of what works and does not work. Research is essentially a process for gathering evidence through a professionally recognized, systematic, and standardized methodology to make a confident prediction about answers to questions or hypotheses. Questions and hypotheses, in turn, are steps toward decisions. By having an answer one way or another, individuals and groups can choose between different options for change (or, in some cases, for no change).

In the realm of community-based HR, or HR and CSR in general, evidence based on research is currently limited (Morgeson et al., 2013). Further, our review of the literature uncovered no research studying the benefits or costs of community-based programs, led or supported by HR departments or individual HR practitioners, to the organization, HR professional, or consumer of the program. Thus, additional research is needed in this area. Part of the reason for this lack of research may be the limited focus on the broader CSR efforts until recently, thus making study in this area either unnecessary or an afterthought for HR researchers and community-based researchers alike. On a related note, when CSR efforts are undertaken, it may sometimes be unclear what part of the organization is responsible for leading such efforts or what, if any, role HR should play (Morgeson et al., 2013; Schoemaker, Nijhof, & Jonker, 2006).

Another reason for the lack of research may be the lack of clarity about the research questions or hypotheses to consider. Should research focus on the effectiveness of specific community-based programs supported or led by HR? Should they focus on the ROI of such efforts? Or should research focus on other areas, such as how community-based efforts led by HR affect employee engagement, recruiting, or other variables important to HR and to organizational success? There is substantial potential for impactful research in this arena. If increasing the quality and quantity of HR-driven, community-based programs is the goal, then we need to start decreasing the ambiguity concerning research questions.

It is one thing to know that using evidence to drive the strategy and execution of a community-based HR initiative leads to greater success; implementing an evidence-based approach in practice within an organization to help attract, retain, and foster the growth of key talent is a different story. To do so effectively, having a framework for success helps. We propose the following steps to implementing an effective evidence-driven, community-based HR initiative focused on addressing the issue of unfilled, skilled positions within an organization (see Figure 10.4).

To successfully build and conduct a community-based HR initiative within an organization, it is important not to perform this work in isolation. The first step, therefore, is to establish a team that is led and/or supported by HR to address the issue of unfilled positions. The more diverse the group of HR professionals engaged in the effort, the more likely it is that the team will uncover and find solutions to the range of causes affecting an organization's ability to fill positions effectively.

The second step in the process is for the team to gather data to identify the underlying cause of unfilled positions. As mentioned previously, the potential causes of unfilled positions in an organization can go beyond technical skills alone and may include issues both internal and external to an organization. Uncovering these causes

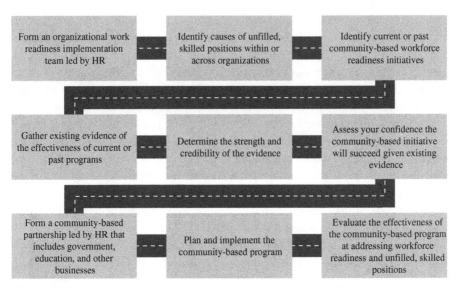

Figure 10.4 *A framework for evidence-driven, community-based HR initiatives*

allows the team to determine what areas to focus on and how a community-based initiative could best address those issues.

Once the HR team has identified an area of focus, it should explore options for developing a solution. This process involves addressing the underlying cause by researching both current and past initiatives, those driven internally by the organization, and those implemented externally or by other similar organizations. For example, using the taxonomy presented earlier, the initiative team could examine whether similar local businesses had established mentoring programs for disadvantaged youth in the nearby community to address a lack of soft skills in the local workforce.

The fourth step is to determine if any existing evidence indicates whether current or past initiatives have been effective in addressing the issue. Evidence can take several forms, from objective performance data to subjective feedback from other HR professionals who were involved in the effort. The gathering of evidence should be robust but efficient. Gathering evidence from sources that are widely outside the scope of the effort, that only somewhat reflect a similar approach, or that only minimally reflect an organization's context may not be worth the time and effort as evidence in support of the proposed initiatives.

The next step in the framework is to take an even closer look into the strength and credibility of the evidence gathered and assign weight to the evidence according to how solid it appears. This step involves diving into the details of the evidence and looking at the following: (a) the strength of the methodology used; (b) the objectivity of the approach; (c) the recency of the evidence; (d) the magnitude of the findings (i.e., effect size); and (e) the credibility of the source. Although these factors should not in themselves rule out a piece of evidence, they should help in determining whether to give more or less weight to the information as part of the HR team's decision-making process.

Before moving forward with a decision to launch a community-based HR initiative, the HR team should consider two other important steps. The first is to go back and check the assumptions that the team made along the way: Was its assumption of the underlying issue correct? Are its assumptions about the sources of evidence correct? Is the assumption that an initiative is related to the team's situation accurate? If any of these assumptions are questionable, the team may need to go back and retrace some steps.

The other important step before making a decision is to examine the confidence level regarding whether the team is ready to make a decision. The outcome of this step does not mean that the team should forgo one or more initiatives. However, it may give the team members enough pause to determine that the cost of launching or becoming involved in an initiative that could end unsuccessfully may not be worth the investment. It may also give them a chance to consider whether making modifications to an initiative would provide greater confidence in its feasibility.

Once the team has followed all of these steps, to a greater or lesser degree, it will be prepared to decide on the correct approach going forward. Of course, this decision will not be based on evidence alone, and other issues such as resources, availability, and stakeholder support will also affect the decision. But the success of the team's decision to proceed in one direction or another can be greatly enhanced by this evidence-based framework.

But there is one last step. It would be ironic for the outline of an evidence-based approach launching a community-based HR initiative to miss this key step: gathering additional evidence for evaluating how the initiative worked. To be most useful, such evaluation would include both developmental (i.e., how the process worked) and summative (i.e., what were the impacts and outcomes from the initiative) elements. This information is useful as evidence not only for determining whether to continue the initiative, but also for identifying where the HR team should make adjustments to increase success and to help support others who may consider using a similar initiative in their organization.

Summary

The fundamental idea of community-based HR rests in the concept that HR programs in organizations must consider themselves as parts of a larger ecosystem of society and work. Rather than existing as discrete entities (i.e., the HR department) within discrete entities (i.e., the organization), HR fits within a broader sociocultural and economic system and network. The more involved HR is in that network, the stronger the network becomes both within and outside the organization.

For example, as described in this chapter, efforts led by HR to help transitioning veterans return to the workforce (such as the ESGR's veterans transition program) increase social bonds for veterans and veteran families, enhance armed forces recruiting and retention, and provide the organization with both an additional pool of talent and enhanced brand recognition and satisfaction. In addition, SHRM's chapter-based efforts to increase HR community engagement seek to address issues more broadly in the economy and society. Community-based HR has grown over the years as organizations have increased CSR efforts in combination with recognition of HR's unique role and skill in supporting such efforts.

As indicated in this chapter, HR is ideally positioned inside and outside organizations to drive evidence-based change by leading people, leading business, and leading communities. One area in which HR's unique role and skill set are particularly useful is in the critical issue of reducing the difficulty and costs of filling key positions. As the frontline within organizations, HR professionals attract, onboard, and retain skilled workers; this function is therefore well positioned to lead workforce readiness efforts. Additionally, as a function of overseeing strategic talent acquisition and employer branding efforts, HR must be involved in these efforts.

To help with this effort, our taxonomy of community-based HR programs can serve as a guide for organizations seeking ways to expand such initiatives. In addition, we have provided a framework for implementing such initiatives using the principles of evidence-based practice. Through evidence-based design of community-based initiatives driven by a view of the entire human capital ecosystem, HR can lead the charge in helping both businesses and workers reap the benefits in building a stronger and more rewarding world of work.

References

ACT (2016). The condition of college & career readiness 2016. Retrieved from www.act.org /content/dam/act/unsecured/documents/CCCR_National_2016.pdf.

Barends, E., Rousseau, D. M., & Briner, R. B. (2014). *Evidence-based management: The basic principles*. Amsterdam: Center for Evidence-based Management.

Bishop, J. (1992). The impact of academic competencies on wages, unemployment, and job performance. *Carnegie–Rochester Conference Series on Public Policy, 37*, 127–194.

Bradbard, D. A., Armstrong, N. J., & Maury, R. (2016). Work after service: Developing workforce readiness and veteran talent for the future. Retrieved from https://ivmf .syracuse.edu/wp-content/uploads/2016/05/USAA_Report_Jan27FINAL.pdf.

Briner, R. B., Denyer, D., & Rousseau, D. M. (2009). Evidence-based management: Concept cleanup time? *Academy of Management Perspectives, 23*(4), 19–32.

Cappelli, P. (1995). Is the "skills gap" really about attitudes? *California Management Review, 37*(4), 108–124.

Cappelli, P. H. (2015). Skill gaps, skill shortages, and skill mismatches: Evidence and arguments for the United States. *ILR Review, 68*(2), 251–290.

CareerBuilder (2017). The skills gap is costing companies nearly 1 million annually according to new CareerBuilder survey [press release]. Retrieved from http://press .careerbuilder.com/2017-04-13-The-Skills-Gap-is-Costing-Companies-Nearly -1-Million-Annually-According-to-New-CareerBuilder-Survey.

Carter, S. D. (2005). The growth of supply and demand of occupational-based training and certification in the United States, 1990–2003. *Human Resource Development Quarterly, 16*(1), 33–54.

Casner-Lotto, J., & Barrington, L. (2006). *Are they really ready to work? Employers' perspectives on the basic knowledge and applied skills of new entrants to the 21st century US workforce*. Washington, DC: Partnership for 21st Century Skills.

Chartered Institute for Personnel and Development (2013). The role of HR in corporate responsibility stewardship. Retrieved from www.cipd.co.uk/knowledge/strategy/ corporate-responsibility/hr-role-report.

Cohen, E., Taylor, S., & Muller-Carmen, M. (2010). HR's role in corporate social responsibility and sustainability. Retrieved from www.shrm.org/foundation/ourwork/initia tives/building-an-inclusive-culture/Documents/HR's Role in Corporate Social Responsibility.pdf.

Conway, M., & Giloth, R. P. (Eds.) (2014). *Connecting people to work: Workforce intermediaries and sector strategies*. New York, NY: Aspen Institute.

De Vos, A., & Cambré, B. (2017). Career management in high-performing organizations: A set-theoretic approach. *Human Resource Management, 56*(3), 501–518.

Francis, H., & Keegan, A. (2006). The changing face of HRM: In search of balance. *Human Resource Management Journal, 16*(3), 231–249.

Hesselbein, F., Goldsmith, M., Beckhard, R., & Schubert, R. F. (Eds.) (1998). *The Drucker Foundation: The community of the future*. New York, NY: The Peter Drucker Foundation for Nonprofit Management.

Hurrell, S. A. (2016). Rethinking the soft skills deficit blame game: Employers, skills withdrawal and the reporting of soft skills gaps. *Human Relations, 69*(3), 605–628.

Indeed (2014). Unfilled jobs cost employers $160 billion annually. Retrieved from http://blog .indeed.com/2014/11/18/unfilled-jobs-cost-employers-160-billion-annually/.

Inyang, B. J., Awa, H. O., & Enuoh, R. O. (2011). CSR-HRM nexus: Defining the role engagement of the human resources professionals. *International Journal of Business and Social Science, 2*(5), 118–126.

Johnson, H. L. (1971). *Business in contemporary society: Framework and issues.* Belmont, CA: Wadsworth.

Judge, T. A., Cable, D. M., & Higgins, C. A. (2000). The employment interview: A review of recent research and recommendations for future research. *Human Resource Management Review, 10*(4), 383–406.

The Manpower Group (2016). 2016–2017 talent shortage survey. Retrieved from www .manpowergroup.com/talent-shortage-2016.

McKibbon, K. A. (1998). Evidence-based practice. *Bulletin of the Medical Library Association, 86*(3), 396–401.

McNamara, B. R. (2009). The skill gap: Will the future workplace become an abyss. *Techniques: Connecting Education and Careers, 84*(5), 24–27.

Morgeson, F. P., Aguinis, H., Waldman, D. A., & Siegel, D. S. (2013). Extending corporate social responsibility research to the human resource management and organizational behavior domains: A look to the future. *Personnel Psychology, 66*(4), 805–824.

Noe, R. A., Hollenbeck, J. R., Gerhart, B., & Wright, P. M. (2017). *Human resource management: Gaining a competitive advantage* (10th edn.). Boston, MA: McGraw-Hill.

O'Neil, H. F. (Ed.) (2014). *Workforce readiness: Competencies and assessment.* Mahwah, NJ: Psychology Press.

O'Neil Jr., H. F., Allred, K., & Baker, E. L. (1992). *Measurement of workforce readiness: Review of theoretical frameworks* (CSE Technical Report 343). Los Angeles, CA: National Center for Research on Evaluation, Standards, and Student Testing.

PricewaterhouseCooper (PwC) (2016). Redefining business success in a changing world CEO survey. Retrieved from www.pwc.com/gx/en/ceo-survey/2016/landing-page/pwc -19th-annual-global-ceo-survey.pdf.

Robinson, J. P. (2000). What are employability skills? *The Workplace, 1*(3), 1–3.

Romo, G. M. (2013). Improving human performance: Industry factors influencing the ability to perform. *Knowledge Management & E-Learning: An International Journal, 5*(1), 66–83.

Rosenberg, S., Heimler, R., & Morote, E. (2012). Basic employability skills: A triangular design approach. *Education + Training, 54*(1), 7–20.

Royalty, A. B. (1996). The effects of job turnover on the training of men and women. *Industrial & Labor Relations Review, 49*(3), 506–521.

Sameen, S., & Cornelius, S. (2015). Social networking sites and hiring: How social media profiles influence hiring decisions. *Journal of Business Studies Quarterly, 7*(1), 27–35.

Schoemaker, M., Nijhof, A., & Jonker, J. (2006). Human value management. The influence of the contemporary developments of corporate social responsibility and social capital on HRM. *Management Revue, 17*(4), 448–465.

Smith, W. P., & Kidder, D. L. (2010). You've been tagged! (Then again, maybe not): Employers and Facebook. *Business Horizons, 53*(5), 491–499.

Society for Human Resource Management (SHRM) (2015). SHRM research: Workforce readiness and skills shortages. Retrieved from www.shrm.org/hr-today/trends-and -forecasting/labor-market-and-economic-data/Documents/Workforce%20 Readiness%20and%20Skills%20Shortages.pdf.

Society for Human Resource Management (SHRM) (2016). The new talent landscape: Recruiting difficulty and skills shortages. Retrieved from www.shrm.org/hr-today /trends-and-forecasting/research-and-surveys/pages/talent-landscape.aspx.

Soricone, L. (2015). Systems change in the National Fund for Workforce Solutions. National Fund for Workforce Solutions. Retrieved from https://nationalfund.org/wp-content /uploads/2016/09/Systems-Change-in-the-National-Fund-120415.pdf.

Spaulding, S., & Martin-Caughey, A. (2015). *The goals and dimensions of employer engagement in workforce development programs*. Washington, DC: Urban Institute.

Strobel, K. R., Kurtessis, J. N., Cohen, D. J., & Alonso, A. (2015). *Defining HR success: Nine critical competencies for HR professionals*. Alexandria, VA: Society for Human Resource Management.

Torpey, E. (2015). Career planning for high schoolers. Retrieved from www.bls.gov/careerout look/2015/article/career-planning-for-high-schoolers.htm.

Williams, M., Moser T., Youngblood II, J., & Singer, M. (2015). Competency-based learning: Proof of professionalism. *Academy of Business Journal*, *2*, 50–61.

11 University Educators and Disciplinary Specialists Working Together to Enhance Community Outreach and Deepen K–12 Teacher Content Knowledge

Angie Hodge, Cindy S. York, & Janice Rech

University–community partnerships are not a new idea. Partnerships can be based on a number of different concepts, such as service learning, community-based applied research, community-based training programs, authentic learning experiences for university students, as well as others. Community can also be defined in different ways, such as local organizations, institutions, agencies, neighborhoods, individuals, social groups, and so on. Our chapter is about partnerships between university content specialists, university education specialists (discipline-based education researchers), and K–12 teachers. First, we discuss the benefits of university–community partnerships, having a shared vision, discipline-based education and science, technology, engineering, and mathematics (STEM) reform, and how these all tie together. Then we discuss our university–community partnership via the Omaha Area Math Teachers' Circle. This chapter will also connect it all with a discussion on what made our partnership a success, as well as some challenges encountered and how we overcame them. Ideas for future research and ways for other institutions to start similar partnerships in any content area will conclude this chapter.

Benefits of Partnerships

Studies have shown that there are a number of benefits to having effective, meaningful, and significant university–community partnerships (Bouwma-Gearhart et al., 2014; Soska & Butterfield, 2013). Identifying those benefits for everyone involved in the partnership helps to clarify expectations, partnership roles, and intended outcomes. University–community partnerships can enhance university research, teaching, and learning and community recognition and status (Buys & Bursnall, 2007, p. 82). Buys and Bursnall (2007, p. 82) described some of the university–community partnership benefits as:

> . . . additional sources of funding, international research collaboration opportunities, increased publication output, development of "cutting-edge" research projects,

enhanced research skills and opportunities to inform practice through applied research. Teaching and learning outcomes include enhanced quality and relevance of teaching curriculum, increased student placements, student access to applied projects, increased student enrolments and increased job opportunities for students. These research and teaching outcomes, in turn, enhance university profile and status through national and international recognition and mass media exposure, and raised profile of faculties, schools and research centres.

Specifically, in our case, some benefits for our university partners have been gaining greater knowledge of K–12 teaching and learning, making connections with practicing teachers, informing the university teacher education program, and learning new subject matter. Benefits to K–12 teachers include gaining enhanced content knowledge, making connections with other teachers, making connections with the university, learning new ways to teach, and learning about "new" subject matter and innovative ways to teach this subject matter. Ultimately, well-established models of effective partnerships can "build relationships with the immediate community, improve [university] image and support, and increase funding or recruitment or retention of students" (Holland & Gelmon, 1998, p. 105). This is something we have aimed to do with our Omaha Area Math Teachers' Circle.

Shared Vision

No matter the approach to or benefits from university–community partnerships, a shared vision or goal should be delineated (Pharo et al., 2013). This could include community change, authentic learning experiences for university students, professional learning experiences for community members, building a reciprocal learning relationship, and so on. We aligned our shared goal with the national Math Teachers' Circle Network, which states that, "The mission of the Math Teachers' Circle Network is to support teachers as mathematicians, to connect mathematics professors with K–12 education, and to build a K–20 community of mathematics professionals" (MTCN, 2017). In our case, the shared goal is one that is specific to mathematics; however, this goal could be modified to the needs of any discipline. For example, if history was your subject area focus, you could replace mathematics with history and mathematicians with historians. Essentially, we are connecting university discipline specialists, discipline-based education researchers, and K–12 educators in a way that strengthens each group involved.

Stronger Together

In order to fully understand the value of the players involved in this university–community partnership, it is helpful to understand what discipline-based education research is and the value of including such people in this type of university–community partnership. In the STEM fields, there has been a term coined for researchers who specialize in discipline-based education research, namely

DBER. Due to calls for improving undergraduate STEM education (Ferrini-Mundy & Güçler, 2009), a focus on how students best learn content knowledge at the university level has arisen. Specialists in DBER have gained widespread recognition for their work in all arenas from special journals on undergraduate education to job searches specifically seeking such researchers. These researchers inherently come with a focus on wanting to understand how people best learn content-specific knowledge. Having such people in a university–community partnership helps bridge the gap between K–12 education and university education, as well as puts groups together with a shared vested interest in teaching content knowledge. These specialized university faculty bring a focus on research-based content learning to the partnership, while K–12 teachers bring practical knowledge to the table from being in a K–12 classroom on a regular basis. Together, when learning new content and/or sharing ideas, they can learn from each other. Talanquer (2014) agreed and stated that DBER faculty would benefit from collaborations with others in order to determine how their work fits into the bigger picture and to have their work be impactful on a broader scale. Hence, we stress the value of having these different players interact in university–community partnerships that are similar to our Omaha Area Math Teachers' Circle.

Although the mission of the national Math Teachers' Circle Network is to focus on mathematicians, the Omaha Area Math Teachers' Circle has extended a welcome to other disciplinary specialists in order to enhance the quality of the circle. For example, we have had faculty in instructional technology provide sessions on technology integration in mathematics utilizing free web tools. We also had a session on Bricklayer coding and how it seamlessly integrates with mathematics. Prior to the solar eclipse, we also hosted sessions where specialists in astronomy taught both safety about the eclipse to the audience and STEM lessons related to this unique event. The possibilities are endless for any discipline to make their circles interdisciplinary and open to a wider group of partners. By becoming interdisciplinary, broader applications of education can become more authentic learning experiences for everyone involved.

Disciplinary Outreach Program

Math teachers' circles are one example of interdisciplinary outreach in the STEM fields that can engage a wide audience, including university professors, pre-service teachers, and K–12 STEM teachers. We use mathematics/STEM as our content area focus, but such content circles could be created in any discipline. In fact, later in this chapter, we will discuss how a calculus teachers' circle evolved out of our math teachers' circle model. Similar specialization to any content area could occur following this model. This section should be read with an open mind regarding how one could create either a disciplinary circle or an interdisciplinary circle in other fields.

Currently, once a month during the academic year, faculty at the University of Nebraska Omaha (UNO) arrange a Math Teachers' Circle meeting, and although faculty from the mathematics department lead the event, the individual session leaders have been from various STEM disciplines, including computer science and science education. Some may call this event a problem-solving night or a math club for teachers. The purpose of the events is that everyone who attends can participate in mathematical thinking and mathematical problem-solving at some level. Although the mathematical content is essentially geared toward middle school teachers, the events regularly get attendees from across the gamut of K–12 schools. In fact, many university professors and pre-service teachers also attend the events. We will discuss ways in which this partnership between departments and the community allows for such a diverse audience to interact together at the same events (and for all to get something out of the circle).

Omaha Math Teachers' Circle

In order to more completely provide the reader with the results we have learned over the past eight years, we must describe our own Omaha Math Teachers' Circle context. As you read this chapter, please note that although mathematics is the content area discussed, these circles could be implemented in any content area. These content circles, of which ours is described in detail in the following section, have been successful across the country. However, not all of them have sustained attendance from content specialists, education specialists, and K–12 teachers for years like ours has.

What has made our particular circle so successful and allowed it to withstand the test of time? How have even more groups become engaged over time? Who are these new groups being engaged in the content circle? How has engagement played a role in the success of this circle? In order to help answer these questions, the long-standing success of our content circle in mathematics has been analyzed and outcomes will be shared.

The initial Math Teachers' Circle session held in the area was a result of a partnership with the University of Nebraska – Lincoln (UNL), and specifically through NebraskaMATH. NebraskaMATH is a "statewide partnership that works to educate and support Nebraska's K–12 students and teachers at critical junctures, with an overall goal of improving achievement in mathematics for all students and narrowing gaps of at-risk populations" (UNL, 2017). We used a modified version of a national model called "Math Teachers' Circles" (Donaldson et al., 2014). Faculty from both campuses (UNL and UNO) worked together to bring public school teachers together in an interactive night exploring ropes and knots with UNL mathematics faculty. The fire was lit! From that initial meeting, relationships formed between UNO faculty, UNL faculty, and, most importantly, the public school teachers. The K–12 teachers were eager to continue meeting and being engaged in higher-level mathematics. The mathematics was presented at a very accessible level, and middle school teachers left with the feeling that they could really "do" higher mathematics – more than just being able to memorize formulas and do rote work. The faculty from UNL had successfully launched Math Teachers' Circles in the

Lincoln area. With their assistance, the Omaha Math Teachers' Circles were off to a great beginning. The reins were handed over to the UNO faculty, who further refined the circles and made them truly "their own."

UNO faculty from both teacher education and mathematics were involved in the program's success, but the mathematics faculty were the leaders in terms of organization in this effort. The need to connect with the public school teachers and administrators appeared to be a logical next step. Developmental planning took place, with the mathematics faculty leading the efforts and school personnel providing necessary input. The greater Omaha area simultaneously engages the following three major groups of people: (a) mathematicians, (b) mathematics educators (discipline-based education researchers), and (c) K–12 teachers on a regular basis. The first meetings were held at a local public school, in close proximity to the university. However, numbers quickly dropped (among all three groups of attendees), and we had to problem solve to find a way to bring back that initial excitement for the university–community partnership members.

In the next year, UNO hired a community chair whose job description included outreach to the community, in particular outreach to K–12 teachers. She was involved in Math Teachers' Circles at her former institution and believed strongly in the value of this university–community partnership for everyone involved. However, she heard about the declining attendance at the Omaha Area Math Teachers' Circles and wanted to find out why numbers were dropping. To discuss the future of the Math Teachers' Circles, the new community chair set up a meeting with the mathematics curriculum coordinator, the DBER faculty, and the education faculty who specialized in mathematics at the university to discuss best options for the group.

The attendees of the meeting were able to brainstorm ideas to try to revive the circles. It was determined that the facilities at the university would better meet the needs of the groups. They also decided that having regular meeting times (such as the first Tuesday of each month) would help teachers plan better, as they would know when the meetings were going to be held and save the date. In addition, the possibilities of utilizing local expertise and also national leaders in mathematics education at the circles were discussed. A combination of both resources surfaced as the best option for the future of the group. Local experts were important, as they often provided an immediate connection for teachers throughout the area, and they promoted a level of confidence in the community of teachers. The combination of local and national experts was an excellent choice for the circles. The Math Teachers' Circles clearly represented a coming together of like-minded people who were interested in bettering themselves as mathematicians in order to better serve their students.

There were many details to consider when making final arrangements for the Math Teachers' Circles. Things that had worked well for the circles in Lincoln were not always considered the best option for the Omaha teachers. For example, we abandoned the idea of serving a light dinner to participants, as was standard practice in Lincoln (and many other circles across the country). After consulting with local teachers, we found that the desire was to wrap up the Math Teachers' Circles in time to be home for dinner with families. Teachers would be more receptive to invitations to participate if there was a demonstrated respect for their time and energy. The Math Teachers' Circles were not only to be well worth their time based on what we did at the events, but the time of day in which we met was also to be best suited for teachers with families at home as well. This is not always the case across the United States, so we recommend surveying your audience members to determine if a meal or light refreshments is best. Most circles meet at around dinnertime and provide a social break mid-meeting or at the beginning of the meeting. This provides time for networking among the groups of attendees. The Omaha area has heavy traffic, and the area is very family focused, so for our attendees, this modification suited their needs best.

With all items under consideration, the time was set for meetings, right after school, yet before family dinner. The location was to be the Alumni House of the university. Excellent facilities were available (rooms with tables and ample space for collaboration), with easy access to the middle of the city and ample parking. Additionally, catering service was available to provide snacks for all participants. The physical setting was excellent (you will have to define what "excellent" means for your particular content group, but we suggest spaces that encourage collaborative learning) and provided a welcoming environment for teachers. The location met the needs of the group and provided a backdrop that was upscale. If teachers were to dedicate time outside of their workday to another learning opportunity, we thought they should be treated exceptionally well.

To provide quality presenters in a first-rate locale required financial support. For years 2 and 3 of the program, we had a small grant from the American Institute of Mathematics to purchase refreshments and supplies, as well as to provide stipends for speakers. After that support was used, we found funding through the Dual Enrollment program with local schools. High school students in local schools that have a Dual Enrollment arrangement with UNO may receive university credit in calculus in the Advanced Placement Calculus course. The university directs a portion of all funds generated directly to the mathematics department. The mathematics department works closely with local schools to discern the best options for fund dispersal, with the ultimate goal of providing assistance to teachers and students. This assistance has taken on many forms, including teacher scholarships and student mathematics competitions. It was a logical extension of the Dual Enrollment program to use funds generated by the schools to benefit more mathematics teachers in those schools. In order to fill the calculus pipeline with highly qualified students, good mathematics teachers were needed at each level that leads up to calculus. Funding Math Teachers' Circles that serve K–12 teachers (often middle school teachers) is an excellent strategy to ensure motivated mathematics students are entering the local high schools.

The Math Teachers' Circles began with dialogues and discussions with local public school teachers and administrators. It was soon obvious that there was a large population of teachers who were not represented in these discussions. The city of Omaha has over 25 Catholic K–8 schools that serve thousands of children throughout the metropolitan area. Efforts were initiated to reach out to the elementary school principals. The students in the Catholic schools and the teachers are often not invited to participate and attend professional development offerings. The Math

Teachers' Circles provide a great opportunity to include these dedicated teachers and bring them together as part of a broader community of mathematics teachers throughout the area.

Over the past eight years, the Math Teachers' Circles have continued to exist, but have experienced growing pains along the way. Attendance has fluctuated, and the university faculty members have at times struggled to attract large numbers to the circles. Tapping into local expertise, particularly teachers who were already well known and well respected within the city, has been a strategy that has piqued interest and brought several new teachers to the circles. Joint planning efforts with the public school administrators has also been helpful in this regard. Attendance was at times counted toward professional development hours for teachers.

The development of the STEM programs within the teacher education department has also provided new directions for the Math Teachers' Circles. Teachers came together to learn about the upcoming solar eclipse and be better prepared to share the experience with students. New programs to help students learn to code and expand their mathematical thinking was introduced to teachers through a Math Teachers' Circle as well. Mathematics has so many connections with the STEM fields that the branching out to these areas became a natural extension.

There were clear benefits being realized by the teachers who participated in the Math Teachers' Circles, but calculus teachers did not always benefit from the circle events. Hence, the structure was copied and utilized in the development of Calculus Teachers' Circles. In many schools, there is only one calculus teacher. That person often works in isolation, with no other teacher to discuss ideas and compare notes with. The Calculus Teachers' Circle was created to address that need. Nationally known experts in the teaching of high school calculus were brought to campus. They shared teaching strategies and concept development with local high school teachers. Teachers were provided opportunities to actually "dig into" the calculus material and have lively discussions about content and the deep conceptual understandings that underlie the calculus course.

The Empirical Study

To kick off the program, we had a teacher quality grant that let us do two one-week workshops for teachers in the summer (one per summer for two years). For one week, these participants engaged in Math Teachers' Circle activities daily. After each week-long program, the survey in Table 11.1 was administered. The survey was given to each participant in pencil/paper form, and the researchers typed up and analyzed the responses as part of a report for the Teacher Quality grant.

From this initial survey, we learned about our area teachers and the needs of theirs that we could attend to in monthly Math Teachers' Circles. The monthly Math Teachers' Circles were extensions of the summer programs, but all were encouraged to attend the circle events. They were also encouraged to bring a friend, and sometimes there were door prizes that they could enter to win if they brought another teacher to the event.

Table 11.1 *Survey provided to Math Teachers' Circle participants*

1. Teaching experience	(a) Student
	(b) First-year teacher
	(c) Teacher of 6–10 years
	(d) Student teacher
	(e) Second-year teacher
	(f) Teacher of 11–20 years
	(g) Para-professional
	(h) Teacher of 3–5 years
	(i) Teacher of over 20 years
	(j) Administrator
2. Gender	(a) Female
	(b) Male
3. Race/ethnicity	(a) White, non-Hispanic
	(b) Black, non-Hispanic
	(c) Native American
	(d) Hispanic
	(e) Asian/Pacific Islander
	(f) Other
4. Grade/s taught (or planning to teach)	(a) Elementary
	(b) Middle/junior high
	(c) High school
	(d) Other
5. Subject/s	(a) Math
	(b) Science
	(c) English/Language Arts
	(d) Geography/History/Social Studies
	(e) Fine Arts
	(f) Foreign Language
	(g) Self-contained class
	(h) Other
6. Approximate percentages of students who are	(a) White, non-Hispanic
	(b) Black, non-Hispanic
	(c) Native American
	(d) Hispanic
	(e) Asian/Pacific Islander
	(f) Other
7. Approximate percentages of students who qualify for free/reduced lunch	(a) 0–24%
	(b) 25–49%
	(c) 50–74%
	(d) 75–100%
	(e) Don't know
8. School location is	(a) Rural
	(b) Town/city
9. School is	(a) Public
	(b) Private

Table 11.1 (*cont.*)

10. School size (number of students)	(a) 1–25
	(b) 26–50
	(c) 51–100
	(d) 101–200
	(e) 201–500
	(f) 501–1,000
	(g) Over 1,000
11. Average number of students taught each year	
	1 = lowest/least often
12. Understanding of core content in my discipline	1 2 3 4 5
13. Effectiveness as a teacher	1 2 3 4 5
14. Enthusiasm about teaching in my subject area	1 2 3 4 5
15. Students work in groups cooperatively	1 2 3 4 5
16. Students learn concepts and processes through hands-on approaches	1 2 3 4 5
17. Material is presented through teacher-led lectures	1 2 3 4 5
18. Student progress is assessed using conventional methods (e.g., paper and pencil exams)	1 2 3 4 5
19. Instructional technology is used in the classroom	1 2 3 4 5
20. Appropriate instructional techniques were used for reaching the objectives	1 2 3 4 5
21. Sufficient time was provided to achieve the objectives	1 2 3 4 5
22. Adequate follow-up was provided	1 2 3 4 5
23. Useful methods were suggested for transferring new knowledge and skills to the classroom	1 2 3 4 5
24. As a result of the Math Teachers' Circle (MTC) activity, I am better prepared to teach	1 2 3 4 5
25. As a result of the MTC activity, the quality of student work and achievement has improved	1 2 3 4 5
26a. Please specify why you do or do not feel better prepared to teach	
26b. Please give any examples of improvements in student learning in your classroom	

Additional surveys were administered at several of the Math Teachers' Circle events to gain a sense of participant satisfaction, both in terms of logistics (e.g., location, time of day, parking, food) and content (e.g., mathematical topics). See Table 11.2 for survey details.

We customized each survey to match up with the activity that was held at that particular Math Teachers' Circle meeting. The one provided here was given during the last ten minutes of the Math Teachers' Circle session on the mathematics behind the game of SET (a card game that has a variety of mathematics in it). This is a card game that can be played solely to practice thinking and pattern-building skills with young kids all the way up to thinking about high-level probability and geometry with university students. Our intent with the surveys was to learn about a the following items: (a) what the teachers liked/disliked about the circle; (b) how they found out

Table 11.2 *Participant satisfaction survey*

Q1: What did you think about today's mathematical activity?	o I really liked the game o It was fun o Terrific o Engaging o Fits in with teaching requirements o Will share with eighth graders/students o Never played o Loved it o Liked it o Great information on how to use it in class o Challenging/critical thinking
Q2: What did you find most enjoyable about the session?	o Playing the game o Learning how to relate it to teaching o Working on the questions with others o Learning the math behind the game o The presentation was engaging o How it could be used to teach math to students
Q3: How do you think we could improve our future presentations and events?	o Nothing o Local teacher who has used the product being present o Put people at the same table who have played the game already to make it more challenging o More people o More time o Can purchase game on site
Q4: What mathematical practices or problem-solving behaviors did you observe?	o Statistics o Critical thinking o Grouping o Elimination o Justifying your answer o Working together o Unwillingness to be wrong
Q5: This presentation was	(a) Very interesting (b) Somewhat interesting (c) Not that interesting
Q6: I found this presentation	(a) Very informative (b) Somewhat informative (c) Not that informative
Q7: I found this presentation	(a) Very fun (b) Somewhat fun (c) Not that fun
Q8: How did you hear about this event?	(a) Email (b) Newsletter from Lincoln (c) Omaha Public School Math Supervisor

Table 11.3 *Email survey example questions*

1. What keeps you coming back to the Omaha Area Math Teachers' Circles?
2. What keeps your colleagues who do not attend the circle events from attending?
3. What has been your favorite circle event and why did you like this event so much?
4. Please comment on the logistics of the events that you have attended (timing, parking, location, food). What can we do to improve upon the logistics of the circles?
5. Did you find the events useful for your classroom teaching? Why/why not?

about the circle; and (c) what we could do to make the circle better for them. We often added an open-ended question or two at the end of the surveys so that they could comment on the circle. We would read, type up, and analyze the results immediately following each event. In this way, we could respond to the teachers' needs as quickly as possible, if meeting these needs was feasible.

In addition, informal surveys (see Table 11.3) and emails were frequently sent to K–12 administrators to continually meet the growing needs of the community in the Omaha area. This community included both public and private schools, as the Omaha area has a large number of private Catholic schools that we determined were not always included in university–community partnerships.

The results of all of these surveys, as well as informal discussions with administrators, informed our decisions about future Math Teachers' Circle topics and logistics. Often, these informal surveys were discussed with the leaders of the Math Teachers' Circle before the next one was planned. We wanted to be as attentive as possible to the needs of our local teachers so they would continue to enjoy the events and gain valuable skills from our circle events.

Outcomes and Successes

One might wonder how a program with so many partners can be sustainable. What is it that made this program one that is still highly attended eight years after its formation? Here, we discuss the main components that can help you create your own successful and sustainable content circle.

The first success is related to the interdisciplinary university–community partnership that UNO has formed with the Omaha area schools. As described above, this partnership was founded on a statewide partnership entitled NebraskaMATH. Beginning on a solid foundation with dedicated team members in the university–community partnership has helped this program last many years.

The second success is related to the planning and the logistics of the Math Teachers' Circle events. This success is also coupled with some lessons learned along the way and being attentive to the constituents of the circle. Being aware that the needs of the constituents may change over time and being willing to try new things along the way has helped with the sustainability of the circle. For example, the circle has seen ebbs and flows over the course of its eight years. Our attendance at circle meetings has been as high as over 50 people and as low as five people. Any time we noticed a drop in attendance for more than two meetings in a row (or when we could not explain the low attendance due to something like the weather), we examined the reasons for the lows. We had a contact person in the schools (in this case, it was the mathematics curriculum supervisor, but anyone leading professional development is also a good contact person). We would ask this person if there had been a meeting we had missed that teachers were required to attend or if there had been something else going on that we should have been aware of when planning our circles. Some of the items we learned to check for conflicts with on a regular basis were the following: (a) professional development meetings; (b) parent–teacher conferences; (c) state testing times; (d) timely content topics; (e) logistical issues in getting to campus; and (f) teacher suggestions. These suggestions allowed us usually to avoid time conflicts that would prevent large numbers of teachers from attending and have sessions that were meaningful to our local teachers. Thus, communication between vested groups is essential for a successful content circle.

In addition, we regularly surveyed our teachers to determine sessions that they would find engaging. Through these survey data, we learned that teachers really liked the sessions when there was something they could take back with them to their classrooms. They also appreciated it when a K–12 teacher helped with the planning of the events. This helped the community partners (the teachers) to gain buy-in to the circle. This last item recently helped us bring our numbers back up. The teachers felt that when a classroom teacher helped lead the sessions, there were always ideas that they could bring back to also engage their students differently in mathematics.

In summary, we suggest when starting a content circle, have a contact person in the schools who can help you with logistics and also encourage teachers to attend the events. Sometimes, they can even be given professional development credit for their attendance. We also recommend checking in with your audience on a regular basis, as their needs may change over time (both in terms of the time of day to meet up that works for them and topics that are most relevant for them in their classrooms).

Last, what happened at the Math Teachers' Circle events has contributed to the success of the partnership. The following section describes the components of the program that were the most valued and other parts that were modified to improve attendance and satisfaction with the events.

Corollary Successes

Teaching Engagement in Disciplinary Education

Aside from the relationship building that naturally occurs in this environment, perhaps the most valued part of the Math Teachers' Circles for all of the constituents was engagement with the content. Engaging any learner in the topic being taught is a necessary component; this includes K–12 teachers during professional development. We believed that for the success of the program, all of the partners needed to be engaged in the content. For this to occur, engagement with the content in mathematics means *doing mathematics.* This means being actively engaged with the materials – solving problems, discussing problems, experimenting, and thinking. This high amount of engagement, we believe, has contributed greatly to the sustainability of our circle. Engagement being a critical piece of the success of the partnership is supported by Buys and Bursnall (2007), who agreed that there can be social engagement as well as content engagement during these partnership events. The feedback from surveys made it clear that all partners involved (especially the teachers) enjoyed sessions when they engaged with both mathematics and with the other attendees of the session. If a session leader, for example, lectured most of the time, there was often a lower attendance for the next circle meeting (sometimes we even noticed the next two circle meetings had lower attendance).

To help ensure active, engaging sessions, we would make the following suggestions: (a) invite the session leaders to attend a session prior to giving one themselves; (b) call these events sessions and not talks; (c) have the session leaders write in his/ her abstract how they will engage the audience; and (d) invite people to lead sessions who you have seen engage an audience in the past.

Teaching Technology

Integrating technology into education and educational community outreach is not domain specific. In fact, it has been shown that if more methods teachers (university professors who teach pre-service teachers how to teach their content) integrated technology on a regular basis, the teacher education students would be more apt to do this when they get into the classroom (Inan & Lowther, 2010). Thus, by utilizing technology in the Math Teachers' Circle, more teachers should become comfortable with the ideas and thus effectively integrate technology into their own classrooms. With twenty-first century skills denoting the use of technology, we hope that our circles will entice K–12 teachers to try out more technologies and use them in their classrooms to meet the needs of their students.

The teachers viewed learning about new technology or ways to use technology in a fundamentally different way (often to engage students) as a positive aspect of our Math Teachers' Circles. Over the years, our teachers have learned how to use coding software and mathematics to design art, how to use mathematical computer games to engage students in the classroom, and how to use calculators to teach conceptual understandings of mathematics. These are just some of the examples of ways in which technology can be integrated into a content circle to promote technology-enhanced STEM education, a concept that Wu and Anderson (2015) have said is valuable in today's STEM classrooms.

Moving Forward

The Omaha Area Math Teachers' Circle has not only kept itself going, but has also branched off to form a new community partnership. Two of the faculty partners in the Omaha Area Math Teachers' Circle leadership group decided to start an additional circle based on specific mathematical content, namely calculus. This partnership is called the Omaha Area Calculus Teachers' Circle. Each semester, UNO now hosts circles focusing specifically on the teaching of calculus at the high school level. Speakers have engaged the teachers in activities to provide them with opportunities to explore calculus further and to expand on their knowledge of calculus content. This "branching out" has created connections and communities that are different from those formed through the original Math Teachers' Circles. This shows how one partnership can lead to other partnerships. In the future, we hope to see other similar partnerships formed in other disciplinary (or interdisciplinary) fields – both in the Omaha area and from our readers of this book chapter.

Starting Your Own Circle

To help you all get started on forming a circle, here is a checklist of items that are helpful when starting your own engaging content circle.

☐ Choose a content area.
☐ Find a core team.

- o Include content specialists.
- o Include discipline-based education research specialists.
- o Include K–12 partners (e.g., teachers and administrators).
- o Determine the best way to communicate among team members (phone, email, video conference, in-person).
- o Clarify the vision, goals, and/or objectives of the circle.
- o Clarity the benefits to each party involved in the partnership.

☐ Meet regularly.

- o Find a convenient location (consider drive time, school finishing times, and parking).
- o Find a good space (tables are usually welcoming for collaboration).
- o Find a good time of the day to meet.

☐ Implement your circle.

- o Find engaging, high-quality session leaders.
- o Include K–12 teachers in leading the sessions.
- o Find a way to fund refreshments (or meals).
- o Find a way to obtain (or purchase) supplies.
- o Survey your partners regularly to gauge satisfaction.
- o Revisit your vision, goals, and/or objectives of the circle.

Possibilities for Collaborative Research Endeavors

In addition to creating a circle, research for university faculty can come about from the formation and study of such circles. It can be advantageous to invite the partners to also become involved in the research aspect, as it helps with partner buy-in, and they can see the results of the research being put into action. Cheruvelil et al. (2014) would argue that collaborative research is the best way for scientific work to be conducted. They stated that the best research teams include partners with a common vision – similar to those in university–community partnerships (Cheruvelil et al., 2014). Collaborative research allows for different perspectives to be brought to the table when thinking through a research plan, conducting research, and analyzing data. The next step in our circle's growth is to begin such collaborative research projects.

Conclusion

Ultimately, we hope this chapter has helped you to envision how you can start forming your own university–community partnership in your area, no matter your discipline. We close our chapter by reiterating the following four key issues that led to our program's success: (a) constituent convenience; (b) open resource distribution; (c) linkage to practical payoffs (professional development hours); and (d) progressive outreach to other relevant communities. A summary of the key issues and suggestions for resolving them can be found in Table 11.4.

Table 11.4 *Key issues*

Issue	Meaning	How to implement	Notes
(a) Constituent convenience	Find a location/time that fits the needs of your constituents	Survey constituents and talk to them to find out what these needs are	You cannot make everyone happy, but try to meet the needs of your target audience
(b) Open resource distribution	Make the program free and open to anyone who wants to attend	Advertise with flyers, emails, and through a curriculum supervisor	If the event gets too big, then implement a first come, first served sign up for the event, such as with Eventbright
(c) Linkage to practical payoffs (professional development hours)	Find a way to reward people for attending the event	Connect with a supervisor to determine what the practical payoff is for your constituents	If funds are low, this could be achieved via door prizes donated by local vendors
(d) Progressive outreach to other relevant communities	Make others aware of what you are doing	Invite colleagues and others to your events	You never know what other events could springboard off of your disciplinary circle from others attending your outreach program

We have provided our own experiences with the Omaha Math Teachers' Circle as an example of ways to form interdisciplinary university–community partnerships, along with some suggestions you can "take back" and implement immediately, just as our teachers enjoy taking back new mathematics ideas into their classrooms. Please do not hesitate to email any of the authors with questions if you wish to start your own disciplinary circle. We also offer workshops for a nominal fee for those wishing to get assistance in starting her/his own outreach program that will impact their local community.

References

Appleton, E., Farina, S., Holzer, T., Kotelawala, U., & Trushkowsky, M. (2017). Problem posing and problem solving in a math teacher's circle. *Journal of Research and Practice for Adult Literacy, Secondary, and Basic Education*, *6*(1), 33.

Baum, H. S. (2000). Fantasies and realities in university–community partnerships. *Journal of Planning Education and Research*, *20*(2), 234–246.

Bouwma-Gearhart, J., Perry, K. H., & Presley, J. B. (2014). Improving postsecondary STEM education: Strategies for successful interdisciplinary collaborations and brokering engagement with education research and theory. *Journal of College Science Teaching*, *44*(1), 40–47.

Buys, N., & Bursnall, S. (2007). Establishing university–community partnerships: Processes and benefits. *Journal of Higher Education Policy and Management*, *29*(1), 73–86.

Cheruvelil, K. S., Soranno, P. A., Weathers, K. C. et al. (2014). Creating and maintaining high-performing collaborative research teams: The importance of diversity and interpersonal skills. *Frontiers in Ecology and the Environment*, *12*(1), 31–38.

Cooper, J. G., Kotval-K, Z., Kotval, Z., & Mullin, J. (2014). University community partnerships. *Humanities*, *3*(1), 88–101.

Donaldson, B., Nakamaye, M., Umland, K., & White, D. (2014). Math teachers' circles: Partnerships between mathematicians and teachers. *Notices of the AMS*, *61*(11), 1335–1341.

Ferrini-Mundy, J., & Güçler, B. (2009). Discipline-based efforts to enhance undergraduate STEM education. *New Directions for Teaching & Learning*, *2009*(117), 55–67.

Holland, B. A., & Gelmon, S. B. (1998). The state of the "engaged campus": What have we learned about building and sustaining university–community partnerships. *AAHE Bulletin*, *51*(2), 105–108.

Inan, F. A., & Lowther, D.A. (2010). Factors affecting technology integration into the K12 classroom: A path model. *Educational Technology Research and Development*, *58*(2), 137–154.

Math Teachers' Circle Network (MTCN) (2017). *Mission*. American Institute of Mathematics. Retrieved from www.mathteacherscircle.org/about/missionandvision.

Pharo, E., Davison, A., McGregor, H., Warr, K., & Brown, P. (2014). Using communities of practice to enhance interdisciplinary teaching: Lessons from four Australian institutions. *Higher Education Research & Development*, *33*(2), 341–354.

Soska, T., & Butterfield, A. K. J. (2013). *University–community partnerships: Universities in civic engagement*. Abingdon: Routledge.

Talanquer, V. (2014). DBER and STEM education reform: Are we up to the challenge? *Journal of Research in Science Teaching*, *51*(6), 809–819.

University of Nebraska – Lincoln (UNL) (2017). NebraskaMATH. Retrieved from http://scimath.unl.edu/nebraskamath.

Wu, Y. T., & Anderson, O. R. (2015). Technology-enhanced STEM (science, technology, engineering, and mathematics) education. *Journal of Computers in Education 2*(3), 245–249.

PART IV

Interdisciplinary Outreach

12 The Organizational Science Summer Institute

Community Outreach to Diversify the Graduate Education Pipeline

Sabrina L. Speights, Oscar J. Stewart, Enrica N. Ruggs,
Steven G. Rogelberg, Doug Reynolds, & Shawn D. Long

Universities and community organizations benefit from partnering to address social issues. Resource and access inequities within higher education are social issues that are best addressed through university–community partnerships. Universities and broader communities within society play an integral role in helping to rectify the underrepresentation of minority students in graduate programs, as individuals within these institutions have the power to influence recruitment, selection, promotion, and advancement. Given the systematic discrimination and disadvantages faced by black, Latinx, and Native American individuals, leaders within universities must put forth a conscious effort to bring in and retain underrepresented minority students and faculty. Such efforts require motivated people, resources (e.g., time, money), and a concerted commitment from those in positions of power and influence.

Partnerships in which community organizations aid in rectifying social inequities within higher education institutions are less common examples of university–community engagement. However, given the mutual goal of universities and the broader community to solve societal problems, the development of partnerships between the two is ideal for increasing the number of underrepresented students who apply, enter, and successfully complete graduate school.

In this chapter, we discuss the importance of establishing *value-aligned partnerships* in which the independent values of university and community organizations are brought together to support a diversity-focused initiative. We demonstrate how programs and departments within universities can work together with community partners to develop successful, long-lasting programs designed to improve the pipeline to advanced degrees for minority students.

Specifically, we provide a case analysis of the Organizational Science Summer Institute (OSSI) initiative at the University of North Carolina at Charlotte (UNC Charlotte) in which community partners engage with a doctoral program to address the problem of disproportionately low rates of underrepresented minority students in graduate programs within fields related to organizational science (OS), namely communication, management, psychology, and sociology. We begin by discussing the unique nature of this form of university–community relationship and how value-aligned partnerships provide the foundation to sustain an initiative to increase diversity in graduate education. Next, we describe how OSSI maps onto the value-aligned partnership model and outline the challenges and successes of this program. To conclude, we provide an instructional guide that can be used by other institutions to develop similar programs. Throughout the chapter, community organizations refer to all entities outside of the university who work to support the diversity initiative.

Higher Education Inequities: The Benefit of Community Partners

Traditional university–community partnerships involve university members and community organizations entering the community. These partnerships often develop through service-learning courses and may be directed toward issues such as homelessness, limited educational opportunities, or child hunger. Many community engagement scholars examine the efficacy of these relationships and assess resource and knowledge exchanges and how to avoid institutional and communication barriers (Clifford & Petrescu, 2012). However, universities working with community partners to address social problems *within* higher education are not the norm (Bruning, McGrew, & Cooper, 2006). Few examples directly address university–community partnerships designed to address problems within the institution of higher education itself.

One important social issue within higher education involves racial inequities to access and completion of academic degrees. Academic institutions are embedded with structures that restrict access to resources and advancement for marginalized groups of people. The demographics in the United States continue to change, making historically underrepresented racial minorities comprise an increasingly significant portion of the US population (Colby & Ortman, 2015). It is impossible to overlook the systematic historical and contemporary forms of discrimination that result in disproportionate underrepresentation of racial minorities in graduate education.

Traditionally underrepresented racial and ethnic minorities (specifically black, Latinx, and Native American populations) enroll in and complete graduate programs at a lower rate than white individuals (Posselt, 2016). Racial and ethnic discrimination exists in various realms of higher education, including undergraduate and graduate admissions (Karabel, 2006; Posselt, 2016), faculty hiring (Turner, González, & Wood, 2008), and faculty tenure and promotion (Gutiérrez y Muhs et al., 2012). How can we address these inequities? One way is to connect with community partners.

University–community partnerships may be ideal in helping to increase enrollment of underrepresented students in graduate programs because community organizations are able to offer valuable resources to students seeking advanced degrees. Community partners have intimate knowledge of what their organizations look for in graduates and can provide mentorship, expertise, and advice for students preparing for graduate programs in hopes of obtaining a job within an industry (e.g., Axtell, Avery, & Westra, 2010). Further, community partners can provide more tangible resources such as financial sponsorships needed to develop and run successful programs designed to help develop students from underrepresented backgrounds (e.g., the PhD Project; see Milano, 2005). Further, given their investment in the program, community partners help to keep the academic institution accountable to the long-term goal as well.

Fostering community partnerships to address inequities in higher education differs slightly from traditional university–community partnerships. One key difference is the long-term commitment of the community partner to the university. Graduate education takes anywhere from two to ten years to complete after receiving an undergraduate degree. Thus, to see tangible results (e.g., successful graduation, hiring of minority graduates), community partners need to be committed long-term and must be comfortable with going years without visible or tangible results.

To foster this type of long-term commitment, we propose the concept of *value-aligned partnerships*, defined as long-term university–community relationships focused on initiatives that support the independent values of both the community organization and the university. In the next section, we discuss the components of a value-aligned partnership in the context of diversity-focused initiatives.

Creating Value-Aligned Partnerships

Value-aligned partnerships have the following three key components: (1) independent value for both community organizations and the university; (2) alignment between those values; and (3) affirmation of partners.

Independent Values

Developing community partnerships requires a clear mission, clear goals, and clear roles of the initiative because, with a clear direction, community partners are more likely to engage (Suarez-Balcazar, Harper, & Lewis, 2004). To foster the long-term commitment needed to establish a value-aligned partnership, all partners and stakeholders must have a long-term commitment to diversity that exists separate from the collaborative initiative. These independent values are necessary because they motivate each partner to invest in the initiative over time, despite the lack of immediate or direct returns.

These independent values are maintained through the organizational cultures of both the community organization and the university. Organizational culture is composed of underlying assumptions, values, and visible practices and processes (Schein, 1996). At the core, community organizations and university partners must have a basic assumption that diversity is a good thing. Diversity is good for problem solving and creativity (DiTomaso, Post, & Parks-Yancy, 2007) and is aligned with social justice beliefs (Adams et al., 2016). From underlying assumptions come values that shape the missions, goals, and philosophies of each organization independently. When developing initiatives related to increasing diversity in higher education, university members must value the long-term goal of more diverse graduate programs and department faculty, and community-level organizations must value recruiting and selecting a more diverse pool of applicants.

Based on these values, each organization must engage in independent practices to promote diversity within their respective organizations. Thus, when these organizational cultures exist separately, the partnership initiative becomes an additional visible practice that reinforces an already-established culture. The independent values of each partner garner the long-term commitment needed in order to be patient enough to see the visible and tangible results of student success.

Value Alignment

Compatibility between university and community partners in terms of interests and goals is required to initiate a university–community partnership (Bringle & Hatcher, 2002). To establish a value-aligned partnership, compatibility goes beyond simple agreement about the mission and goals of the specific initiative. University partners and community organizations must have aligned cultural values.

Using the example above, the university partner must be committed to the long-term outcome of increasing diversity in graduate programs and of faculty. The community organization must be committed to increasing workforce diversity. Both commitments are accomplished through increasing the diversity of those with graduate degrees. Thus, the initiative represents a way that both the university partner and the community organization address their independent values. Conversely, if university partners and community organizations are only committed to the initiative (perhaps because engagement makes the organization look "charitable"), but that commitment is not anchored in organizational values, the partnership is at greater risk of ending because of pitfalls such as budget cuts, changing leadership, and time demands (Suarez-Balcazar et al., 2004). Each partner must have an independent value that is supported by the initiative to ensure a long-lasting, successful relationship.

Affirmation of Partners

Community partners bring a wide array of knowledge, experiences, and resources (Suarez-Balcazar et al., 2004), and these attributes should be acknowledged and praised as frequently as possible. Affirming the importance and knowledge of community partners is a critical yet underappreciated aspect of creating value-aligned partnerships. Consistent affirmation is not only nice, but also functions to sustain long-term commitment and helps to maintain the relationship (Bringle & Hatcher, 2002). Affirmation is particularly important when university members seek community organizations to address social inequities within higher education. Initiatives that require long-term commitments to see results need small celebrations along the way.

These acknowledgments serve to remind partners that their engagement with the initiative is worthwhile and aligned with their individual values as an organization. Affirmations should be in the form of communicating appreciation, but also in more public displays. Public displays may take on different forms. For instance, if the initiative has a web presence, acknowledge community partners on this platform. University partners should also allow community partners to advertise their organization to initiative participants, leaders, and other stakeholders. University partners should also engage community partners in active ways, such as inviting representatives to be involved in initiative programming by hosting presentations or workshops, inviting community partner representatives to initiative milestone celebration events (e.g., anniversary celebrations), and inviting community partner representatives to meet with other university departments to foster additional relationships.

Taken together, value-aligned partnerships are unique university–community relationships that are well suited for initiatives that require long-term commitments before tangible results are realized. Although value-aligned partnerships may function well across a variety of community partnerships, they are particularly important when universities seek out community organizations to aid in addressing problems within the institution of higher education. Community partners are well suited to addressing these issues; however, these types of relationships may be uncommon for most community organizations. Thus, to build and maintain relationships with community partners that are lasting, value-aligned partnerships are key. Independent values, an alignment of those values between university partners and community organizations, and continued acknowledgments set a strong foundation that will sustain the partnership and the initiative over several years.

In the following sections, we present a case study as an example of how university members can work with community organizations to address the social inequities within higher education. We discuss how the impetus for the initiative began with one faculty member and how organizational culture, values, and value-aligned partnerships have supported and sustained the initiative over time. We also outline the challenges of developing such partnerships and steps to ensure success.

The Organizational Science Summer Institute: A Case Study of Diversity-Focused Community Outreach

Initiative History

The OSSI is a week-long graduate school preparatory program that began in 2009. The program is run through the OS doctoral program at UNC Charlotte. The original idea came from an OS faculty member, who sought to create a program to help improve the pipeline and recruiting efforts for racial minority students within OS and related fields. The concept for the OSSI initiative was immediately supported in the OS program, because the program is built on the values of diversity and inclusion.

In building the case for the need for OSSI, the social problem of racial inequity in higher education, and specifically within OS, needed to be specified: inequality persists. As of 2015, collectively black, Latinx, and Native American students across communication, psychology, and sociology made up 19.2, 22, and 20 percent of graduate students, respectively. These numbers include postgraduate, master's, and doctoral students. In 2015, across communication, psychology, sociology, and management, only 8, 7.5, and 0.3 percent of doctoral recipients were black, Latinx, or Native American, respectively.

The vision and intention for OSSI was centered on two primary barriers to entry for underrepresented students: standardized testing scores and research experience. On average, black, Latinx, and Native American students score lower than white test takers (Miller & Stassun, 2014). These systematically lower standardized test scores are extremely detrimental because graduate school admissions committees generally place a disproportionate amount of weight on these scores to cut down applicant pools to the final list of potential admitted applicants (Jaschik, 2016). Thus, providing preparation for these entrance exams (at no cost to the student) helps to better prepare students who complete OSSI to earn competitive exam scores.

The second barrier identified was the potential lack of research experience. Research experience, such as working in a faculty research lab or conducting an independent study research project, is another important criterion (particularly for doctoral programs) for graduate admissions. The lack of underrepresented minority faculty in higher education may leave black, Latinx, and Native American students feeling less comfortable seeking out mentors and advocates who can provide them with the meaningful research experiences needed to be a competitive applicant. Further, underrepresented racial/ethnic minority students are more likely than white students to enroll in historically black colleges/universities or Hispanic-serving institutions. Many of these institutions may not be viewed as prestigious relative to some predominately white institutions. The prestige of undergraduate institutions, however, is also often an important (and often implicit) criterion for graduate admissions committees (Posselt, 2016).

Addressing the barriers of standardized testing and research experience became the primary foundation upon which the program was built. Thus, although other aspects of the institute have changed over the years, the fundamental services related to directly addressing these gaps in standardized tests scores and research experience remain constant. Commitment to these specific barriers has helped to maintain the program over the years as faculty and students change. It also provides a clear vision and scope of the institute for external community partners.

With these central tenets in mind, the faculty member worked with the director of the OS program to identify partners within the institution and within the broader community who would be willing to help financially support the program through sponsorship. High-level sponsorship within the university was important to help get the program off the ground and show the commitment of the university to outside community partners. University-level sponsorship came from various levels, including both the college (college of business and college of liberal arts and sciences) and the university level (through support from a diversity initiative sponsored by the chancellor).

To build a sustainable program, the leaders of this initiative narrowed the list of potential community partners to organizations related to the organizational sciences. From this list, organizations with aligned values were selected because these partners would bring a practical knowledge of recruitment and selection barriers and act as external advocates who could later benefit from the partnership through access to a pool of diverse candidates who are bright, engaged, and motivated. Identifying organizations with which value alignment could occur was essential for establishing a truly collaborative relationship (Weerts & Sandmann, 2010). Representatives from potential partner organizations were contacted and provided information about the initiative. Those who decided to partner were then invited to play an active role in contributing ideas for initiative programming.

General Process of OSSI

Rising junior and senior undergraduate students are eligible to apply for the OSSI program. Students submit a formal application and supplemental essays demonstrating their interest in graduate education and the study of organizations. The faculty and graduate student directors manage this application process. These materials are evaluated by a committee of faculty and graduate students, who select each year's cohort – called OSSI fellows. In the early stages of the program, only a few students applied each year. However, through the growth of the program and the use of extended professional networks, the applicant pool has grown and includes students from colleges and universities of all types from across the country. The program can support a total of ten students each cycle.

Once the selection process is complete, each fellow is matched with a graduate student and faculty mentor. This pairing usually happens about two months before OSSI begins and is made based roughly on the research interests described by the fellow in their application. During those two months, accepted fellows book their travel and complete reimbursement forms, faculty and graduate student mentors coordinate datasets and potential readings for their OSSI mentee, and the faculty and graduate student directors finalize catering (this is best done once allergies and dietary restrictions of the accepted fellows are known) and program logistics.

During the week of OSSI, the fellows and their mentors meet each day to work on a small research project that is presented at the end of the week. Additionally, fellows receive ten hours of in-class graduate record examinations (GRE) training and additional resources for eight months after they leave. Fellows also participate in professional development and preparation workshops and presentations on a wide range of topics, such as writing personal statements, communicating research, and the various jobs available with a graduate degree in the organizational sciences. Experts on various topics from UNC Charlotte and from across the region and country are brought in to engage with and teach each year's fellows.

Faculty members across disciplines (specifically organizational psychology, communication, sociology, and management) participate in OSSI. This interdisciplinary participation provides several benefits. First, broader professional networks are used in recruiting efforts. Second, faculty participation across disciplines expands the scope of research topics fellows can investigate. Thus, fellows are exposed to data collected using different methods (e.g., quantitative and qualitative data; survey and experimental). Third, interdisciplinary faculty participation exposes fellows to disciplines they may otherwise be unfamiliar with and provides new perspectives on avenues to pursue after they complete their undergraduate education. Fourth, faculty members often serve as panelists and workshop leaders and can provide diverse perspectives on topics such as graduate school admissions, personal statements, research requirements, and expectations. Thus, although others have discussed the difficulty of working across disciplines (Clifford & Petrescu, 2012), the interdisciplinary nature of OSSI is beneficial to the program's success.

During each OSSI, we ask fellows to provide feedback on their experience. Overall, we see that fellows have positive experiences with the program and receive continued support from mentors after OSSI ends. It is also important to evaluate and measure our long-term goals (Holland, 2005). Thus, to evaluate the success of the OSSI, we disseminated a survey to all the OSSI alumni in 2015 (fellows who had already completed OSSI), seven years after the first cohort was accepted into the program. This allowed enough time for some students to fully matriculate through doctoral programs, if applicable, thus providing us with metrics related to the long-term goals of the program.

The results indicated that all students who applied to graduate programs were accepted into either a master's or doctoral program. The OSSI alumni were accepted to programs in schools all over the country. Further, alumni reported that their experience with OSSI helped them feel prepared to take the GRE, feel confident about their applications, and prepared to enter graduate school overall. These placements and feedback from alumni demonstrate the success of OSSI.

Benefits for Stakeholders

Fellows. The primary stakeholder whom we want to benefit from OSSI is the fellows – the underrepresented students. The institute provides instrumental support through GRE training and research experience that students can leverage when applying to graduate programs to craft more competitive application packets. In addition to the instrumental support, OSSI provides students with social support beyond the institute, as mentors continue to help students through the search and application process. In this way, fellows expand their network of people within the field(s) in which they are interested in pursuing a career. As students begin graduate programs, these mentor relationships help students navigate the graduate school process so they successfully graduate.

Graduate Students and Faculty. Students and faculty benefit from OSSI because it allows them the opportunity to give back in a way that aligns with their professional responsibilities. The structure of the program (one week for both faculty and student mentors) allows graduate students and faculty to work together to craft a project and share in mentor responsibilities. The shared mentoring and the intense, one-week program allow both graduate students and faculty to participate in a meaningful initiative without the competing demands of research and other academic requirements that often impede the creation of university–community partnerships (Clifford & Petrescu, 2012). Both faculty and graduate students report receiving intrinsic motivation from their participation. In addition, although the time is brief, graduate students gain mentoring experience that may not otherwise be available to them in graduate programs.

Graduate Program. The broader OS program benefits from OSSI because it provides clear evidence of the values of the graduate program that are communicated when recruiting new students. New and current students know that diversity and inclusion are core values of the program. OSSI provides students and faculty with a way to live that value that continuously fortifies the commitment from the entire graduate program. Additionally, OSSI provides the OS program with access to a more diverse pool of applicants. Although promoting the OS program is not a part of OSSI and no faculty, students, nor community or institutional partners actively recruit fellows, some OSSI alumni do apply to the graduate program.

Community and Institutional Partners. The institute is also beneficial for our partners. From our community partners' perspective, the primary reason for their engagement is to have an influence on the field. The organizational sciences will benefit from drawing in professionals from a wide range of backgrounds. Aiding in such a program also helps community partners build diverse recruiting pipelines. Although the benefits are for the long-term, our partners see the value in helping develop potential talent for the future, and they recognize the long-term benefits of helping address this university-level issue. In addition, OSSI provides opportunities in the short-term for representatives of these organizations to present directly to the fellows, which has built engagement with more individuals who are interested in helping develop the OSSI program. In sum, there are several benefits to a community engagement initiative such as OSSI. There are still, however, challenges to creating and maintaining this sort of initiative. In the next section, we outline some of these challenges.

Challenges to Overcome

The efficacy of OSSI is grounded in value-aligned partnerships. Sustaining success within value-aligned partnerships, however, requires navigating potential barriers. Most notably, although the goals related to diversity and inclusion are similar, each partner may view the paths to success differently. Thus, the need for independent values also contributes to the biggest challenge because the OS program, institutional partners, and broader community partners have distinct interests in diversity and inclusion. Attempting to appease all parties in every way possible, however, can exhaust resources and end the initiative.

For instance, some students and faculty in the OS program have suggested we expand the selection criteria to include those from lower socioeconomic backgrounds and/or first-generation students. Similarly, each year, white women and other minority students (e.g., Asian) request entry into the program. Addressing the needs of these groups is certainly warranted; however, within the scope of our available resources (e.g., financial, personnel), accommodating all of these groups is not feasible. Maintaining commitment to the goal of diversifying the graduate education pipeline with underrepresented racial minorities provides the anchor and focus that is paramount for success. Moreover, this commitment from all stakeholders must be for the long-term. Partners who seek only short-term gains are likely not right for this initiative.

Similarly, it is important to clearly articulate the target population of the initiative. OSSI is intended to diversify the pipeline to graduate education. As such, we generally identify the following two types of fellows: (1) students who may not otherwise receive the resources and tacit information needed to successfully navigate graduate admissions; and (2) students who may be at institutions where they are receiving experiences needed for graduate admissions, but whose placement at OSSI may help boost them over the top.

The former often translates into students being accepted who do not have the highest grade point averages (GPAs) and who do not attend elite colleges and universities. The latter translates into finding students who may benefit from specific portions of the program (e.g., broadening their understanding of types of research and fields that fit their interests) more than other portions. It is important for all mentors and community partners to understand these goals and to be able to meet students where they are and not assume they come with a wealth of knowledge of conducting research in the organizational sciences or that they are well versed in the graduate admissions process.

Another challenge is sustained resources. As with many community engagement initiatives, resources – personal and financial – are a real concern (Holland, 2005). Over the years, we have encountered fluctuating participation from faculty and student mentors, which strains others who volunteer to participate. We have also experienced fluctuating university support and, most recently, one of our community partners has been evaluating its continued support and participation. With rising costs of logistical needs, such as catering, hotel accommodations, and travel, and increasing demands of students and faculty, maintaining the resources needed to sustain OSSI is a challenge. To combat these challenges, we have experimented with group mentor models in which one faculty mentor is paired with two fellows and two graduate students, continued to seek out additional external partners and donors, connected with local OSSI alumni to conduct workshops, and begun to consider alternative housing options for the fellows that are more cost-effective.

An additional challenge we face is one of the scope of the program. The OSSI and OS program director often grapple with questions related to how many fellows should be accepted each year and whether the program can and/or should be expanded. Improved recruiting efforts and developing the program's reputation in recent years have resulted in increased student applications. Expanding the program would perhaps broaden the reach of the initiative; however, this expansion may dampen the relationships that are built during OSSI and are a cornerstone to student success. There are many diversity initiatives that bring in large groups of students, but the one-on-one graduate student and faculty interactions with fellows that occur during OSSI and well beyond are the real keys to fellows' success and satisfaction with the program. Keeping the importance of building and maintaining relationships at the forefront is key to not overextending resources, providing fellows with a quality experience, and relaying success stories to our community partners.

Despite the challenges, OSSI has persisted for almost ten years. We believe two unique features have helped with the current (and expected future) success of OSSI. The first is continuous improvement. The structure and planning of OSSI is always evolving based on participant feedback. Fellows complete surveys at the end of each day to provide feedback on the day's workshops and presentations. Additionally, we seek and incorporate feedback from doctoral student mentors, faculty mentors, faculty and staff presenters, and community partners.

We use this feedback to help plan subsequent years of OSSI. Based on this feedback we have improved fellow–faculty mentoring relationships, increased opportunities for relationship building, included additional workshops, added time for students to practice writing, and altered the structure of our evening programming. Being flexible and implementing changes caters the program to students' needs and constantly improves the program for the subsequent cohorts. At the same time, we can remain within the program's scope and use our resources wisely.

A second feature key to the success of OSSI is celebrating OSSI fellow achievements with our partners. To do so, we must stay connected with fellows. Thus, when the fellows complete OSSI, the communication does not end there. Mentors and fellows continue to communicate as students navigate the graduate school application process. When students do enter and graduate from a graduate program, their success is shared widely. OSSI alumni success is a symbol of the program's success and information is shared among faculty, students, and community partners. One key element of a value-aligned partnership is to affirm the community partner. It is important to communicate success metrics to current community partners and potential future sponsors because it allows them to see the benefits of their investment. Never take partners for granted. Highlight and celebrate their contributions and always keep them in the communication loop about student success and major changes to the program.

Steps for Implementing a Diversity Initiative at Your Home Institution

Throughout this chapter, we have discussed diversity-focused community engagement and the importance of value-aligned partnerships. In this section, we discuss the key steps to successfully launch an initiative focused on increasing racial and ethnic diversity, and we provide examples of how this process is implemented in OSSI. As shown in Figure 12.1, this type of program requires program leadership, local support, and support from the institution and broader community. The underlying connection between all of these levels is the aligned value of commitment to diversity and inclusion.

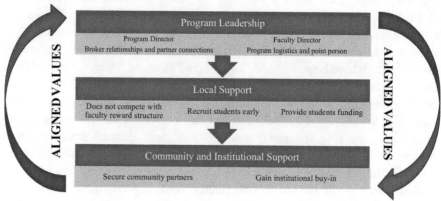

Figure 1. Diversity Initiative Implementation Steps

Figure 12.1 *Diversity initiative implementation steps.*

Program Leadership

The first step to the successful implementation of a value-aligned partnership is strong leadership and support at the program or unit level. Initiatives such as OSSI must be overseen by a program or department within the university (e.g., an academic department or college). The program level represents the unit where individuals within the university are housed who will be responsible for ensuring that the initiative is actually implemented. At this level, there must be leaders in place who will work on developing value-aligned partnerships to ensure that there are resources necessary for the initiative to take place, and also leaders who organize and oversee the logistics of the initiative to ensure that all tasks within the initiative are completed. Although one leader may be able to navigate both responsibilities, through OSSI, we have found that having a tiered leadership system within the program level is most beneficial to guaranteeing that both community partner relationship building and daily functioning of the initiative are successful.

In the case of OSSI, this initiative is housed in the OS PhD program at UNC Charlotte. As such, the director of the graduate program brokers the relationships between the graduate program, the initiative, and community partners. The OS program director functions as an *engagement champion* (Weerts & Sandmann, 2010), who is instrumental in facilitating fundraising efforts and creating community relationships that are fruitful and long-lasting. This type of leadership is critical (Holland, 2005). A committed leader is needed to identify and maintain relationships with partners whose values align with the initiative (Weerts & Sandmann, 2008).

OSSI also needs leadership from within the academic program to handle the logistics of the initiative. For OSSI, this is accomplished through a faculty director and a graduate student assistant. Having a dedicated faculty director with a student assistant maintains consistency and continuity from year to year, which allows OSSI to grow from a strong, established foundation. Faculty directors also provide an avenue for meaningful changes to the initiative because they can learn from past mistakes and incorporate fellow feedback into subsequent year planning. The faculty director functions in a capacity that is most closely aligned with what Weerts and Sandmann (2010) refer to as an *internal engagement advocate*, in that they ensure that the infrastructure is in place to allow the program to function effectively. Without a committed faculty director in charge of logistics, the initiative would likely flounder. A clear initiative leader is needed to follow through on the relationships established by the *engagement champion*. Clearly defining the roles between the leadership of the program, faculty, and graduate student directors of the initiative is a process that will unfold over time. Clarity in these roles, however, is an important component to spreading out the workload so that no one is overtaxed, maintaining future faculty and student buy-in.

Local Support

The second tier of Figure 12.1 articulates the need for local support. This refers to people within the program who will be responsible for working in the initiative. These individuals may serve in various roles in the initiative and actually implement the tasks within the initiative. In OSSI, the faculty and students who serve as mentors and work with the fellows every day throughout the week have the most hands-on experiences with the fellows. This two-tiered mentoring creates a "triangle of success" between graduate students, faculty, and OSSI fellows. This mentoring structure works well because fellows can feel comfortable working with a student, and the graduate student always has the faculty mentor who can provide support and answer questions. With ten participants accepted each year, nearly half of the students and faculty in the OS program serve in a mentoring capacity during OSSI.

There are several ways to garner local support, but we focus on a few aspects we have found the most important to the sustained success of OSSI. For faculty support, the most important aspect is that the program does not compete with the faculty reward structure. It is well known that although faculty are expected to participate in service, those activities often go unrewarded at best and are chastised at worst (Boyer, 1996; Holland, 2005). OSSI, however, is a one-week commitment with a few additional scheduled meetings with graduate student mentors before the institute begins. Compared to other forms of service work (e.g., committee obligations), participating in OSSI is far less time-consuming. Moreover, it is often more gratifying because faculty can mentor students on topics of interest. Thus, mentoring aligns with faculty values of research and teaching (Clifford & Petrescu, 2012).

For those faculty members who cannot mentor, many serve as speakers for the workshops that occur during the week. In addition to mentoring and speaking during the week of OSSI, we rely on our graduate students and faculty to help with recruiting applicants for OSSI using their professional networks. Given the interdisciplinary nature of the program, the OS program can successfully recruit students across several majors from colleges and universities across the country.

The most effective ways to garner student support are through early recruitment and modest summer stipends. The OSSI initiative is advertised during our annual recruitment day for potential new students. OSSI is a core way of demonstrating that the doctoral program is committed to diversity and inclusion. As such, potential new students are exposed to OSSI before they even accept an offer of admittance. Being vocal about the OSSI initiative in this way also reminds newer students that they can have an opportunity to mentor an undergraduate student. Many students are very interested in the opportunity to mentor and help eager students through a process they are still navigating themselves.

In addition to catering to graduate students' affinity to mentor, we recommend providing modest stipends, if possible. These stipends serve a few different purposes. First, the stipends very practically help students, particularly in programs where summer funding is not guaranteed. Thus, OSSI provides students with some income in exchange for their mentor efforts. This can help reduce stress induced by financial concerns and can ultimately help graduate students be productive both within OSSI and on other academic projects needed to help them progress in the program. Second, the stipend garners commitment from graduate students. By offering payment, students are more inclined to do their best regarding mentoring because they are being paid for their services. Students likely will not participate in the initiative solely for the modest stipend, but providing some type of incentive helps to fortify students' commitment to the process and helps to retain graduate students to mentor year after year.

Community and Institutional Support

Once the internal leadership and support are established, securing community and institutional financial support is a vital final step to being able to launch a higher education diversity and inclusion initiative (Figure 12.1). Intuitional support is critical to gaining legitimacy for the initiative. This legitimacy will help with gaining community partners and buy-in from faculty and students. Beyond institutional support, securing a committed community partner is vital for the initial launch and for maintaining success. Additionally, engaging community partners in the initiative beyond financial sponsorship can help to foster the partnership and deepen the commitment to the value-aligned goals.

The institutional and community partners (e.g., the university graduate school, corporate partners, individual donors) for OSSI are not simply donors; they are part of the initiative. Each year, representatives from our community partners provide key workshops focused on job opportunities and graduate entrance materials. To deepen this relationship with our community partners, we have begun to ask recent OSSI alumni if they are interested in job information from one of our corporate donors. This is done in the hopes of diversifying the applicant pool and extending job opportunities to OSSI alumni.

Aligned Values

Enveloping each tier of support is the key component to launching and sustaining a diversity initiative like OSSI – aligned values (Figure 12.1). At each level, buy-in and support rests largely on individuals at each level feeling committed to diversity and inclusion in higher education. Establishing value-aligned partnerships with community organizations is essential. Without aligned values existing independently within each organization that diversifying higher education is good and necessary, the university–community partnership will fizzle out because the fruits of the labor are only seen in the long-term. To keep a program funded year after year, aligned values sustain the energy and connection between partners.

At the program support level, deep values and commitment are required to broker partnerships and to have continuity in the faculty leading the initiative. Finding faculty who are willing to coordinate the logistics of an initiative like OSSI requires more than just a sense of service to the graduate program or the feeling of professional obligation. An aligned value for diversity and inclusion keeps faculty committed to leading each year. This continued leadership is critical to both streamlining and making changes to the overall initiative program.

The faculty and students who are involved in the day-to-day execution of the initiative recognize that they are members of a community with an organizational culture that values diversity and inclusion. As such, being good organizational citizens involves some degree of support for this core value. At this level, individual commitment or belief in diversity and inclusion may be less likely because the broader cultural norms and expectations are often enough to gain buy-in from students and faculty to serve as mentors and presenters.

Conclusion

Community engagement through university–campus partnerships provides a unique opportunity to address social issues. Through understanding the mutual relationship between universities and the broader community, we suggest that community partners can play a key role in addressing issues within higher education. We believe that this type of relationship, however, requires a different commitment from community organizations because completing graduate education is a long process. To maintain the sustained commitment of all stakeholders, we discussed a model for value-aligned partnerships. Within these partnerships, the independent values of each organization are brought together and result in an initiative that becomes a visible representation of those underlying, independent values. Having the initiative connected to the independent values of each participating organization helps to ensure the long-term commitment needed to sustain the initiative and to avoid pitfalls such as budget cuts and changes in leadership. These independent values also produce the greatest challenge to value-aligned partnerships because each stakeholder may have a different idea of how to structure the program. We believe that maintaining a clear focus on the core components of the initiative while staying flexible and the evolution of the program over time are key to navigating the challenge of multiple viewpoints.

As an example, we outlined the OSSI initiative run through the OS program at UNC Charlotte. This case study demonstrates how an interdisciplinary program can successfully establish a diversity and inclusion initiative through creating and sustaining value-aligned partnerships. We attest that not only will underrepresented students benefit from more racially diverse graduate students, but the general student body will benefit, as interactions with peers and professors from diverse backgrounds are pivotal in the development of the competencies necessary to interact with dissimilar others at work (Avery & Thomas, 2004; Bell, Connerley, & Cocchiara, 2009; Pettigrew & Tropp, 2000).

We hope that the insights provided in this chapter will begin a conversation about the ways in which community partnerships can be used to improve deficits within the institutions of higher education and how working across disciplinary boundaries can function as a key to success as opposed to an institutional barrier. OSSI can serve as a road map in developing similar types of university–community engagement initiatives. We recognize that other marginalized identities (e.g., gender, sexual orientation, disability, social class) also present additional challenges in graduate degree attainment. To focus on a clear mission and target population, OSSI currently only addresses issues for black, Latinx, and Native American undergraduate students. However, we believe the tenants of the value-aligned partnership will prove successful for any initiative that requires long-term commitment before visible results are realized.

References

Adams, M., Bell, L. A., Goodman, D. J., & Joshi, K. Y. (Eds.) (2016). *Teaching for diversity and social justice*, 3rd edn. New York: Routledge.

Avery, D., & Thomas, K. (2004). Blending content and contact: The roles of diversity curriculum and campus heterogeneity in fostering diversity management competency. *Academy of Management Learning & Education*, *3*, 380–396.

Axtell, S. A., Avery, M., & Westra, B. (2010). Incorporating cultural competence content into graduate nursing curricula through community–university collaboration. *Journal of Transcultural Nursing*, *21*, 183–191.

Bell, M. P., Connerley, M. L., & Cocchiara, F. K. (2009). The case for mandatory diversity education. *Academy of Management Learning & Education*, *8*, 597–609.

Boyer, E. L. (1996). The scholarship of engagement. *Bulletin of the American Academy of Arts and Sciences*, *49*, 18–33.

Bringle, R. G. & Hatcher, J. A. (2002). Campus–community partnerships: The terms of engagement. *Journal of Social Issues*, *58*, 503–516.

Bruning, S. D., McGrew, S., & Cooper, M. (2006). Town–gown relationships: Exploring university–community engagement from the perspective of community members. *Public Relations Review*, *32*, 125–130.

Clifford, D., & Petrescu, C. (2012). The keys to university–community engagement sustainability. *Nonprofit Management & Leadership*, *23*(1), 77–91.

Colby, S. L., & Ortman, J. M. (2015). Projections of the size and composition of the US population: 2014 to 2060. *US Census Bureau*. Retrieved from www.census .gov/content/dam/Census/library/publications/2015/demo/p25-1143.pdf.

DiTomaso, N., Post, C., & Parks-Yancy, R. (2007). Workforce diversity and inequality: Power, status, and numbers. *Annual Review of Sociology*, *33*, 473–501.

Gutiérrez y Muhs, G., Niemann, Y. F., González, C., & Harris, A. (2012). *Presumed incompetent: The intersections of race and class for women in academia*. Boulder, CO: University of Colorado Press.

Holland, B. A. (2005). Reflections on community–campus partnerships: What has been learned? What are the next challenges? In P. A. Pasque, R. E. Smerek, B. Dwyer, N. Bowman, & B. L. Mallory (Eds.), *Higher education collaboratives for community engagement and improvement* (pp. 10–17). Ann Arbor, MI: National Forum on Higher Education for the Public Good.

Jaschik, S. (2016). An Unlikely Campaign to Move beyond GRE Scores. *Inside Higher Education*. Retrieved from www.insidehighered.com/news/2016/06/06/ets-plans -encourage-graduate-departments-de-emphasize-gre.

Karabel, J. (2006). *The chosen: The hidden history of admission and exclusion at Harvard, Yale, and Princeton*. New York: Houghton Mifflin.

Milano, B. J. (2005). The PhD project: Filling the academic pipeline with minority professors. *The Diversity Factor, 13*, 30–33.

Miller, C., & Stassun, K. (2014). A test that fails. *Nature, 510*, 303–304.

Pettigrew, T. F., & Tropp, L. R. (2000). Does intergroup contact reduce prejudices? Recent meta-analytic findings. In S. Oskamp (Ed.), *Reducing prejudice and discrimination* (pp. 93–114). Mahwah, NJ: Erlbaum.

Posselt, J. R. (2016). *Inside graduate admissions: Merit, diversity, and faculty gatekeeping*. Cambridge, MA: Harvard University Press.

Schein, E. H. (1996). Culture: The missing concept in organization studies. *Administrative Science Quarterly, 41*, 229–240.

Suarez-Balcazar, Y., Davis, M. I., Ferrari, J. et al. (2004). University–community partnerships: A framework and an exemplar. In L. A. Jason, C. B. Keys, Y. Suarez-Balcazar, R. R. Taylor, & M.I. Davis (Eds.), *Participatory community research: Theories and methods in action* (pp. 105–120). Washington, DC: American Psychological Association.

Turner, C. S. V., González, J. C., & Wood, J. L. (2008). Faculty of color in academe: What 20 years of literature tells us. *Journal of Diversity in Higher Education, 1*, 139.

Weerts, D. J., & Sandmann, L. (2008). Building a two-way street: Challenges and opportunities for community engagement at research universities. *The Review of Higher Education, 32*, 73–106.

Weerts, D., & Sandmann, L. (2010). Community engagement and boundary-spanning roles at research universities. *The Journal of Higher Education, 81*, 702–727.

13 Periclean Scholars

An Interdisciplinary Model of Civic Engagement on College Campuses

Alexandra M. Dunn, Thomas Arcaro, & April Post

Service learning helps students become good citizens by getting them out of the traditional classroom setting and allowing them to ask and realistically implement the answer to the question, "What should I do?" While service learning has a variety of meanings, it can be defined as a process of reflective education in which students learn civic and social responsibility through scholarship, community engagement, and the idea of reciprocity (Caspersz, Olaru, & Smith, 2012). By working in groups, discussing ideas, and creating networks, service learning helps students go beyond the passive question of "What should be done?" and understand the answer to the question "What should I do?" For example, a professor could ask a class, "What should be done about global issues like poverty, civil wars, and global warming?" and students can provide a list of answers to these questions, but their responses are likely still to be passive (e.g., "Carbon should be taxed"). If we want students to know what they should do, professors have to be creating activities that give students the power to solve problems (e.g., turning off lights or driving less). That is what service learning allows students the opportunity to do. It gives students the chance to combine academic inquiry with hands-on action, deliberation, experimentation, and reflection to better answer the question "What should I do?"

This chapter explores the idea of service learning on college campuses. It provides an overview of service learning and information about what universities are currently doing to initiate service-learning classes and programs on their campuses. We then introduce one specific model of service learning: the Periclean Scholars program at Elon University. The Periclean Scholars program is a cohort-based, three-year, interdisciplinary program in which undergraduate students take a series of academic classes under one mentor. The program is dedicated to increasing civic engagement and social responsibility on campus and in local and global communities. Students embark on a journey of promoting awareness about a particular issue in a selected country of focus and develop and sustain meaningful partnerships in order to put their ideas into action. After describing the program in more detail, we highlight program accomplishments both locally and globally. We conclude with detailed advice about how others can start thinking about creating a program at their home institutions and what to do once the vision becomes a reality. Our hope is that this chapter inspires others to think big and think creatively about how their institution can help students actively answer the question, "What should I do?"

What Is Service Learning?

Civic engagement involves actions designed to identify and address issues of public concern and encompasses a range of activities (e.g., working in a soup kitchen or at a local YMCA). One form of civic engagement – academic service learning – has become a growing interest on college campuses (Billig & Welch, 2004; Welch & Saltmarsh, 2013). Academic service learning integrates academic rigor with real-world projects that students complete with the community and organizations, while reciprocally offering the community a service that they need (Mayhew & Welch, 2001). Service learning encompasses enhanced academic learning, purposeful civic engagement, and relevant and meaningful service to the community (Saltmarsh, 2010). Service learning is different from other forms of learning at universities because it is reciprocal; it aims to benefit both the student and the community, not just the student (e.g., internships). This idea of reciprocity also makes service learning different from volunteerism because volunteerism is focused on helping the recipient of the voluntary action and ignores structured learning (Deeley, 2010).

Service learning, often referred to as a "pedagogy for citizenship" (Mendel-Reyes, 1998), adds a "reality element" to the traditional academic classroom by applying what students are learning in class, what they may already know from previous classes or experiences, and what they can learn from the community into a unique, gratifying, and more memorable learning experience. Service learning focuses on both learning and service and is based on the assumption that experience is the foundation for learning and that community service can provide that experience (Mayhew & Welch, 2001). The in-class teaching, discussions, and instruction allow students to grapple with what issues certain communities are facing and what skills are needed to help address those community issues (Caspersz & Olaru, 2017). The service component then allows students to learn how to address the issues they identified in the classroom and helps develop students into critical thinkers and activists (Mayhew & Welch, 2001).

With service learning, it is essential that the service is connected directly to the course and that students then make direct connections back to the course through critical reflections (Deeley, 2010). Service learning involves the following four phases: investigation, planning, action, and reflection. First, students investigate, identify, and research community issues. Second, students and faculty work together to identify community partners, evaluate the partners, and figure out how to address issues facing the community (Mayhew & Welch, 2001). After the group plans, the students then put those plans into action. This is the step where service-learning classes diverge from more traditional classes. Instead of stopping with discussions, students implement the plans they made in class by engaging with the community of focus and doing activities that help address the issues they have identified. A final step in the process is that students come back to the classroom, reflect, and evaluate in a structured environment what they have done. That is, students and faculty reflect on what they have learned about the community, their actions, their influence, and what worked and did not work (Mayhew & Welch, 2001). This step is potentially the most important one as it helps cement student learning and hopefully encourages them to continue being engaged, civic individuals after the class and after graduation.

Who Does Service Learning Benefit?

Service learning has potential benefits for multiple parties, including students, faculty, and the community. Students can benefit academically, professionally, and personally. The main academic benefit is that service learning can increase technical knowledge and one's understanding of a topic (Eyler & Giles, 1989). It can also help students explore and act on their values and beliefs while developing critical-thinking and problem-solving skills. Service learning tends to help students have a better understanding of diverse cultures and communities, learn more about social issues and their root causes, and satisfy their goal of public service and civic engagement (Ngai, 2006; Toncar et al., 2006). Service learning can help develop students' skills such as handling ambiguity and change, being flexible, increasing communication, collaboration, and leadership (Caspersz & Olaru, 2017).

From a student perspective, service learning can help students connect with professionals and community members, grow their networks, and realize potential career paths. Students perceive service learning as providing them with the opportunity to develop their employability skills, and it can potentially give them a competitive advantage (Caspersz & Olaru, 2017). When developing these skills and growing their networks, students also have a moment of realization where they start to believe that they can make a difference and that the opportunity to engage in service learning provides them with an experience of personal growth (Caspersz & Olaru, 2017). Overall, this leads to students understanding what it takes to create social change and how to create that social change.

Faculty can benefit both personally and professionally as well. Service learning allows faculty to use more interactive teaching methods that can add new insights to class discussions, develop student leadership skills, and lead to new areas for research and publication. Service-learning courses can also increase course enrollment and attract highly motivated and engaged students, creating a more positive classroom environment overall. It also provides a classroom design that acknowledges various student learning styles and cognitive preferences, which can help students understand the course objectives more easily (Saltmarsh, 2010). By providing students with multiple modes of learning, the professor is no longer privileging one type of learning (e.g., reading/lecturing), and students are likely not only to learn more, but also to enjoy the class more (Saltmarsh, 2010).

Not only does service learning have positive benefits for teaching, but it can also help faculty develop professionally by providing networking opportunities with other engaged faculty in multiple disciplines, create relationships between the local community and the institution, and help faculty learn more about local and global issues. This will be most successful if the university integrates service learning into their core institutional values. Teaching a service-learning class can be beneficial for teaching and networking, but we know that research culture dominates faculty tenure procedures in higher education (Saltmarsh et al., 2009). In order to get faculty buy-in to the extent that the university needs in order to make service learning part of the core curriculum, universities need to consider integrating community engagement into the criteria for scholarly work (Weerts & Sandmann, 2008). If not, faculty are not as likely to integrate service learning into their individual goals until later in their careers because it may be viewed as distracting and unrewarding (Saltmarsh et al., 2009).

Of course, there are obvious benefits of service learning to the community, both locally and globally. The communities in need can gain more social capital, which may be necessary to achieving their goals. It can also increase public awareness of key issues, educate the community on these key issues, and build important relationships between the community, individuals (e.g., students and faculty), and the institution. One important thing to remember about service learning and community service is that they are not just about monetary donations to a community in need. It is important that these service-learning classes are not just about giving, but more about partnering (Periclean Scholars, 2016). While giving tends to be faster, easier, and helpful, partnering seems to have sustainable, long-term benefits for the community, develops a meaningful connection with the community, and tends to be more culturally sensitive. Service learning should concentrate on creating these partnerships and sustaining them for as long as the community needs them, until the community can be self-sustaining in this area.

Ultimately, service learning appears to be mutually beneficial to all parties involved. Service learning is important because of the influence it can have on current students' and faculty members' lives and on the lives of the people at whom the service is directed. Service learning can help clarify, change, or catapult student career trajectories. It clearly also helps individuals in need both locally and globally. In all cases, there seem to be major and lasting impacts. We use the rest of this chapter to demonstrate one successful service-learning program at Elon University. The program, Periclean Scholars, has moved a step beyond a one-semester, service-learning class toward a multi-year model of interdisciplinary civic engagement, service learning, and ongoing reflection and evaluation. We describe how the program was created, what the program looks like from a student perspective, and the accomplishments of the classes thus far, and we provide some advice and guidance for those who are interested in instituting a similar program at their college or university.

What Is Periclean Scholars?

The Periclean Scholars program was started at Elon University in 2002. The program emerged from Elon's dedication to making service learning a central part of their academic mission. The idea for Periclean Scholars was sparked by a call for proposals from Project Pericles, sponsored by the Eugene Lang Foundation. Project Pericles started in 1999 as a not-for-profit organization aimed at addressing the national problem of civic disengagement among young adults. The founder, Eugene M. Lang, knew that universities were responding to this concern, but thought that most programs were only peripheral to the main curricula, having little lasting impact on the civic engagement of students. Project Pericles provides a framework to help universities commit to educating students for civic and social responsibilities. The initiative started with ten universities, and to date, there are 31 other universities who have taken on the Project Pericles challenge (Project Pericles, 2017).

Because Elon University was ready to incorporate service and innovative student learning into their academic mission, a three-person team was put together to write a grant through Project Pericles aimed at expanding civic engagement initiatives. Driven by the mission of Project Pericles, the three professors were challenged to promote civic engagement in the classroom, on campus, and in the community. Together, Drs. Tom Arcaro, Jim Bissett, and Nancy Midgette received the grant, and the Periclean Scholars program was born. While these 31 universities have responded to the Project Pericles call in various ways, Elon University is the only one to develop a Periclean Scholars program.

The mission of Periclean Scholars is to promote awareness of global issues and foster meaningful partnerships that provide solutions to problems that accompany these issues in culturally sensitive and sustainable ways. Periclean Scholars is grounded in cohort-based learning and student leadership. Program directors, class mentors, and students work together and cross disciplinary boundaries to learn about a particular issue (e.g., AIDS/HIV, environmental sustainability, civil wars, human trafficking) in a chosen country of focus (e.g., Namibia, Mexico, Sri Lanka, Haiti). See Table 13.1 for a complete list of each class's country of focus and the main issue

Table 13.1 *Class countries of focus, global issues, and faculty members' home disciplines by graduation year*

Class year	Country of focus	Global issue	Faculty member home discipline
2006	Namibia	HIV/AIDS awareness and education	Sociology and anthropology
2007	Honduras	Pediatric malnutrition	History and geography
2008	Mexico	Poverty and education	Communications
2009	Zambia	Rural development	English
2010	Ghana	Socioeconomic development	History and geography
2011	Sri Lanka	Environment and education	Mathematics
2012	India	Empowering adolescent girls	Physics
2013	Mexico	Poverty and health issues	Business
2014	Appalachia (USA)	Poverty and the environment	Art
2015	Haiti	Restavek and human trafficking	Human services studies
2016	Honduras	Youth and community development	Foreign languages and cultures
2017	Namibia	Sustainable agriculture	Health and human performance
2018	Zambia	TBA	English
2019	Sri Lanka	TBA	Psychology

they focused on. The knowledge gained as a class is then put into action as students work to create long-term, sustainable partnerships in their country of focus. Through these partnerships, students embark on a multi-year journey to create solutions *with* their partners on the ground in their country of focus. To be a Periclean means that a student does the following: commits to learning about general global social issues; promises to not only think about the *what* but also the *why* in the hope of coming up with solutions to root causes; continues to educate themselves on breaking news and research related to their issue and country of focus; stays informed about other organizations already working on similar issues in the country of focus; and is aware of the intended and unintended consequences of the actions that are decided upon.

One of the unique features of the Periclean Scholar program is that it is, by definition, an academic program. In their second semester of the freshman year at Elon, students apply for the Periclean Scholars program. Approximately 30 students are selected to start the three-year, cohort-based, on-campus journey. Once selected, students commit to take seven classes, approved by the University Curriculum Committee and reviewed regularly by outside accreditation entities, over the course of their sophomore, junior, and senior years. Except for the initial semester as a Periclean, the courses award two credits to ensure that the students can fit them into their regularly scheduled major and minor class requirements. The courses, which are facilitated by the faculty mentor for that class, integrate academic reading, research, and writing with service and experiential learning activities.

Because students have a variety of majors and the faculty mentor is not necessarily an expert on the class's issue or country of focus, the classes operate as interdisciplinary seminars. The seminar-style class places heavy ownership on students and sets up a space where students must take leadership roles and prepare for in-class discussions and activities outside of class. During these classes, students learn to communicate with non-experts (e.g., other students in their class, their mentor, their partners) about what theoretical and methodological knowledge they can offer to the class goals. Therefore, there is constant integration of what students are learning in their majors to their Periclean seminar classes, and students are constantly learning about new tools from their peers to add to their own toolsets. While there are projects that all class members must contribute to, there are also opportunities for students to branch off and work on individual or smaller group projects that are directly related to their own interests or areas of expertise. This gives students the opportunity to bridge majors, integrate multiple perspectives, and present to a wide audience.

What Does Periclean Scholars Look Like from a Student Perspective?

Being accepted onto the Periclean Scholars program is viewed as both a privilege and an honor. Students take their role very seriously and understand that to do anything less would be socially irresponsible. While it is a demanding role, the multi-year commitment makes the program unique, rewarding, challenging, and

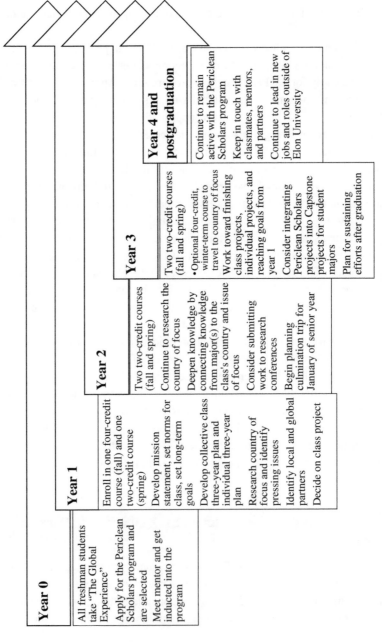

Figure 13.1 *Periclean Scholars program outline from starting at Elon University until postgraduation*

thought-provoking. Many students come to care deeply about their country of focus and continue to dedicate time and resources to their cause after graduation. To provide a better picture of what it means to be in the program, we briefly describe what each year as a Scholar looks like. Of course, these descriptions may vary from student to student (e.g., not all students will visit their country of focus), but for the most part, experiences are universal and cumulative, such that what happens in year 1 should still be happening in year 3. See Figure 13.1 for a description of the four-year Periclean Scholars process.

As an overview, the program consists of students committing to taking four to five courses under the direction of one mentor, which focus on a cohort-identified issue in their target country or region. The classes are designed as seminars that start in the fall of a student's sophomore year. As a cohort, the students select an issue of focus in their sophomore year and then spend the next two years engaged in activities that integrate reading, research, and writing with service and experiential learning activities. Students not only focus on and travel to their country of focus, but also choose to have a local outreach component to their efforts. This challenges students to creatively integrate their global and local efforts into a "glocal" perspective.

Year 0 (First Year at Elon). During a student's first year at Elon, while not yet a Periclean Scholar, they take a required class called "The Global Experience." After completing that required course, students have the opportunity to apply for the Periclean Scholars program. The Global Experience begins to expose students to a survey of global issues, which sets them up nicely to make an educated choice on their issue and country of focus in year 1. Students go through a rigorous application process, including a written application and an in-person interview with their mentor. At the end of the academic year, selected students meet their mentor and Periclean classmates and get inducted into the program. Over the summer, students are expected to keep in touch with their class, network to find students with similar interests, and get to know each other. This ensures that their first semester class in year 1 starts smoothly.

Year 1 (Sophomore Year). Students enroll in a four-credit course with the rest of their Periclean class in the fall semester and a two-credit course in the spring semester. In the fall, the class develops a mission statement, researches topics related to their mission, decides how they will make decisions, and develops individual and group short- and long-term goals. To be successful, students must research topics and issues outside of class and learn as much as they can about their country of focus. To make the most out of the program, students develop a collective class three-year plan as well as an individual three-year plan. The individual three-year plan should outline the contributions a student can make on their own based on their major, their areas of interest, and their expertise. With their plans in mind, students begin to identify and communicate with potential local and global partners in their country of focus. In the spring, students continue to brainstorm about potential projects and partners and emphasize setting realistic goals for the future. Since the spring class is only two credits and meets once a week, it is expected that group and individual work and making connections occur outside of class.

Year 2 (Junior Year). During the second year, students can enroll in a two-credit course in both the fall and spring semesters. In terms of class cohesiveness, this is a challenging year because many students study abroad for a semester. These absences teach students how to deal with changing group dynamics and leadership, as well as how to ensure that progress is made despite such changes. Under the guidance of the class mentor, students continue to learn, research, explore, and understand the issue and country of focus from multiple perspectives. Students not only focus on broadening their knowledge, but also work on deepening their knowledge by applying what they are learning from their majors to their class mission. Students are encouraged to submit what they have been working on to research conferences (both on and off campus) and plan various Periclean events. Finally, the class begins to plan its culmination trip to its country of focus, which normally takes place during their senior year winter term. While it is not a requirement, visiting the country of focus brings the issue the class has been studying to life, allows students to meet with some of their global partners, and again allows students to put their knowledge into action.

Year 3 (Senior Year). Like the second year, in their third and final year of the program, students can enroll in two-credit courses in the fall and spring semesters. If students decide to travel to their country of focus, they have the option to also enroll in a four-credit, January-term (i.e., winter-term) class. These courses are viewed as the capstone of the program; students fully integrate what they have learned from their Periclean classes and majors finish their class projects and individual projects and reach their goals. In the fall class, students finish up planning and logistics and get any work done that needs to be done before traveling to their country of focus. Students are also encouraged to incorporate Periclean Scholars into their major capstone classes. For example, communications majors may work on a film project highlighting their class accomplishments, or psychology or environmental studies majors may write a final research paper on issues in their country of focus. The class continues to fundraise and plan events for graduation. After their trip to their country of focus, the class focuses on how to sustain their efforts after graduation and begins to explore what it means to become part of the Periclean Foundation (i.e., the Periclean alumni group).

Year 4 and Beyond (Postgraduation). It is the program's hope that students continue to engage with the Periclean Scholars program after graduation. It is encouraged that Periclean alumni stay up to date on their country of focus, keep in touch with partners that they have made, and continue to have a passion for serving and helping others, while being culturally aware.

Ultimately, the Periclean Scholars program is designed to foster the passion that students have for helping others and to develop that passion into real aid. The Periclean Scholars program gives students the time and physical space to work on interdisciplinary teams, apply leadership skills to initiate and execute specific initiatives, and become experts in a specific topic area. Students are constantly learning from other students, their mentor, and their partners. Students learn that partnering is not the same as giving, as well as the importance of being culturally sensitive when providing aid. During this time, the Periclean Scholars program facilitates the growth and transformation of students into the leaders of the twenty-first century. In fact, since 2010, the names of graduating Periclean Scholars have been listed in the graduation program and recognized on graduation weekends during the "Leaders of the 21st Century" celebration alongside other major fellows programs, including Honors Fellows and Leadership Fellows.

Periclean Scholars' Accomplishments

Successes in the Periclean Scholars program are broadly defined. A success one week may be reaching an important decision as a class so that they can move forward, while a success in another week may be raising a certain amount of money for the class's country of focus. Pericleans quickly learn that working to better understand interdisciplinary, complex issues takes time and that donating money is not always the best way to help those in need. Once students realize this, they also quickly understand that success is not always measured by a dollar sign or a number, but instead by the sustainable products created through hard work, dedication, and team efforts. Pericleans learn that the best-laid plans do not always go the way the group hopes, but learning this in real time with other passionate students teaches Pericleans real-world lessons about flexibility, perseverance, and commitment. Below, we discuss a variety of class accomplishments. While impressive, we want to note that these accomplishments are not all-encompassing (for a more comprehensive list, please visit the Periclean Scholars website: www.elon.edu/u/academics/project-pericles/periclean-scholars-program/) and would not have been possible without the many hours of research and critical thinking that yielded a larger pool of ideas and partnerships that did not always come to fruition.

Grants and Monetary Support. The Periclean Scholars program has been fortunate enough to secure a variety of grants and awards. Early in the program's tenure, one organization called the Redwoods Group, an insurance company based in Cary, North Carolina, saw and believed in the Periclean Scholars' vision. In 2008, the Redwoods Group committed to a $125,000 gift to endow the Periclean Scholars Alumni Association, ensuring that partnerships can and will be materially supported in perpetuity. The class of 2006 was also successful in securing external funding. The cohort received two external grants of $25,000 and $12,500 for their work in Namibia, which were used to help create and produce four documentaries.

Periclean-in-Residences. The Periclean-in-Residence program was started as a way to bring experts to Elon's campus. The resident is chosen by the class because they are an expert on the issue the class is focusing on or have personal experience with the issue. The class organizes the one- to two-week visit and arranges various speaking activities (e.g., panel discussions, speeches, question-and-answer sessions) for the resident. These activities are open to various classes at Elon and the broader Elon community. The class also meets with the resident multiple times to get a more in-depth understanding of the severity of the issue at hand and to learn new information from a different perspective. Periclean-in-Residences raise awareness about the issue on Elon's campus and promote the mission and vision of both the Periclean Scholar program and of the university being a global community.

In the past, Periclean-in-Residences have traveled from HIV/AIDS organizations in Namibia, the University of Cape Coast in Ghana, the Restavek Freedom Foundation in Haiti, and the Comprehensive Rural Health Project in India. The Periclean Scholars program has also hosted the founders of Hope for Honduran Children, Schools for Chiapas, and Tesseract Consulting in India, among others. Other types of experts include activists (e.g., HIV/AIDS, anti-mountaintop removal), authors, students from universities in the country of focus, and Habitat for Humanity volunteers. Most recently, a former Periclean Scholar, who is currently serving as the Deputy Chief of Programming and Evaluation for the Peace Corps in Washington, DC, has helped scholars perform community mapping and information gathering and set up project planning and assessment strategies. As you can imagine, these visits from experts are mutually beneficial: students and the Elon community learn more about the issues in a particular country and the Periclean-in-Residence is able to connect with a potentially untapped community that could be a valuable partner in future endeavors.

Documentaries and Other Forms of Media. Because a major goal of the Periclean Scholars program is to raise global awareness, many classes have created documentaries focusing on their planning, travel, global service, and current issues in the country of focus. For example, the class of 2006 produced four documentaries. The sale of the rights to these documentaries raised over $16,000, and that money went directly back to the Namibian nongovernmental organizations with which the class had established relationships. The class of 2017 "recycled" the country of Namibia, and because of the efforts from both classes, there have been eight documentaries produced about the country, two narrative films, several short videos available on YouTube, and two music CDs.

With the help of a Park Foundation grant, the class of 2007 also produced a documentary about poverty and malnutrition in Honduras that has been used in a variety of classes at Elon University. Another example is from the class of 2008, who created a documentary entitled "Painting without Permission," which focused on the Zapatista movement and the struggle of the indigenous people in Chiapas, Mexico. The documentary was subtitled in both English and Spanish and screened by the International Step by Step Association (ISSA) in Budapest, Hungary.

Scholars also focused on sharing information internally. Since the class of 2011, the program has been able to establish a quarterly newsletter that is circulated within the Periclean Scholar community of current students and alumni. In the newsletter, each current class provides highlights and updates, the director provides a program update, and general highlights of on-campus events are provided. The newsletter has proved useful for keeping students who may be abroad and alumni engaged.

Global Partnerships. It is each class's goal to make research-based and careful selection decisions on who to have as global partners and how to establish these partners. To date, all classes have decided to make connections with individuals or organizations on the ground in their countries of focus. One example of a successful partnership is from the class of 2010. The cohort raised over $100,000 during their time as Scholars and built a clinic, nurse's quarters, a drug store, and kindergarten in rural Ghana in partnership with community members and the Government of Ghana. The area where these establishments were built serves a community of approximately 10,000 people.

Local Partnerships. Even though the primary focus of the Periclean Scholars program is to work with global partners in the country of focus, working with local partners has become a Periclean Scholar tradition as well. Some classes have decided to focus more on their global partnerships and remain modest in their local efforts, while others have gone further to integrate the local community with the global community. For example, the class of 2006 decided to give a donation of the proceeds from the screening of their narrative film to a local organization. However, other classes, like the class of 2011 and the class of 2012, went one step further. The class of 2011 set up an email pen pal system between students at a local middle school in Alamance County, NC, and a middle school in rural Sri Lanka. The class of 2012 also linked their local and global communities by connecting the Dream Girls program in Alamance Country, NC, with adolescent girls in rural India. Similarly, the class of 2013 formed a community support group focused on women in Alamance Country, NC. The support group, called Hogares Sanos, had ties with Chiapas, Mexico, and conducted weekly health sessions for women on Elon's campus. The class arranged for transportation, food, and childcare for the participants and offered classes on topics related to food sanitation.

Summits, Forums, and Conferences. On top of the monetary resources raised, the media created, and the partnerships formed, classes have also organized summits, forums, or conferences in the countries of focus. For example, the class of 2006 hosted the "Future Leaders Summit on HIV/AIDS" in Windhoek, Namibia, which was opened by the Prime Minister of Namibia and covered by CNN International. The class of 2011 organized a conference in Colombo, Sri Lanka, called the Leaders in Environmental Advocacy Forum (LEAF), which focused on discussing environmental issues in the country and how to implement ongoing efforts that will improve the environmental conditions in the country.

On a local level, the class of 2015 held an event on Elon's campus called "Stand Up for Freedom: Restavek and Human Trafficking Education Week." "Restavek" is defined as a form of modern-day child slavery in which a child is given to another person or extended family member who treats the child as property and exploits them for labor (e.g., cooking, cleaning, working around the house). In Haiti, 1 in 15 children are living as restavek children (about 300,000 total) (Restavek Freedom, n.d.). The weeklong event was focused on educating the Elon community on the elusive yet widespread prevalence of the issue and empowering the Elon community to end restavek and human trafficking. There were panel discussions, a benefit concert, student undergraduate research presentations, and speeches from the director of the Restavek Freedom Foundation, who traveled from Haiti to the event.

How Can I Start a Similar Program at My University?

If you are interested in learning more about starting a Periclean Scholars program or something similar at your university, we hope this gives you some food for thought. While the program at Elon University works well for us, we encourage you to think big, be creative, and adapt what has been done at our institution to fit your university and vision. We also want to note that starting a program like this is no small undertaking. It may be best to start small and have an active, strategic plan that is revisited often to help the program grow. Starting a program like this will require learning from mistakes, flexibility, and a willingness to be open to new ideas and ways of doing things. We realize that there are sometimes significant barriers that you, as a faculty or staff member, will have to consider when designing your own program. Below, we provide some suggestions and recommendations for starting a similar interdisciplinary service-learning program of your own. We break these suggestions down into the following two parts: (1) understanding, evaluating, and selling how a program would best fit your university; and (2) the plan forward and tasks after the evaluation.

Part 1: Understanding, Evaluating, and Selling How a Program Would Best Fit Your University

See Figure 13.2 for a pictorial representation of the steps in Part 1.

1. *Continue reading about the Periclean Scholars program.* There have been guides and books written about the program. These resources, which are listed in the Appendix 13.1, further discuss the program, success stories, lessons learned from students, and more details on knowledge transfer.
2. *Evaluate the culture of your university.* You will need to evaluate, analyze, and decide if the program would fit with your culture. Starting a program like Periclean Scholars is a large undertaking and will not happen overnight. Is your university open to making an addition like this? Do you think they would be receptive to the idea? Are you prepared with ideas for how the program could be implemented?
3. *Identify a "champion" and other interested human capital (i.e., faculty and staff members).* The program needs a "champion," and that champion needs to be prepared to dedicate time to overseeing all of the moving parts of the model. The champion could be an administrator or a faculty member or perhaps a small team with a mixture of administrators and faculty members. Once you have your champion, you will need a good team. Periclean Scholars was developed by a team of professors from various disciplines. It has been successful because they were open to innovative ideas, but shared the same mission and vision to create a program that embodied service learning.
4. *Evaluate and realistically understand student interest.* The leadership team will be extremely important to sustaining the program, but you will also need students to fill the seats. As you are planning, it would be beneficial to understand whether

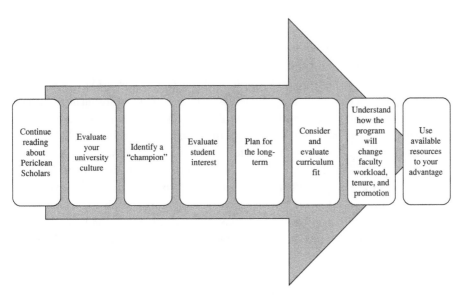

Figure 13.2 *Understanding, evaluating, and selling how a program would best fit your university*

students are interested in a program like this, and to what degree. Will they have time to dedicate to such a program? Are there any aspects that they are most interested in (e.g., local or global partnerships)? Are they prepared to take ownership? To gather this information, you could consider conducting focus groups, interviews, or surveys.

5. *Plan for the long-term.* Part of the reason why the Periclean Scholars program has been so successful at Elon is because the institution gave the program priority. You need to have transparent conversations with your university about why the program matters and how it would be initiated. How do you plan to acquire financial resources? How will the program be sustained? What is the timeline for the "trial" period and assessment? The program can be run with minimal resources beyond faculty reassignment of duties. Despite knowing this, adding a new program can sound expensive, especially in tough economic times where budget cuts are increasingly common. Be prepared to defend the need for the program and how the program leaders and students could begin to offset some of the costs (e.g., by applying for external grants).

6. *Consider how the program would fit into the curriculum.* The Periclean Scholars model involves making curriculum additions at the host institution. This is not always an easy process and often involves time and scrutiny. Adding to the curriculum in the way that is necessary to duplicate the Periclean Scholars program would accurately be seen as a cultural shift in the institution. Explore and understand how adding courses to your curriculum works. Most institutions have a mechanism by which courses can be added on an experimental basis to be reviewed after two to three years. Be open to ongoing discussions with curriculum committees about how the new credits would fit into a student's transcript and

how many credits each class would be worth. Elon University operates on a four-hour system where most classes equate to four credit hours. Other institutions operate on a three-hour system, which may make fitting the classes into the curriculum a bit more difficult.

7. *Think about how the program would fit into a faculty's workload, tenure, and promotion procedures.* There will inevitably be questions regarding how this new undertaking will affect faculty. You will need to think about questions such as: Where does teaching these new courses fit into a faculty's course load? Will (and how will) faculty get compensated for the extra work in designing and running these unique offers? How will departments deal with the loss (for a percentage of time) of a key faculty member? How can you put a positive spin on the extra work for faculty members? One type of pushback you could receive is that it is just easier not to have the program, but if you believe in the cause and the long-term benefits to both students and communities, then it is well worth grappling with these questions.

8. *Use resources that are already available.* Starting the program at Elon University was challenging, but rewarding. As the program continues to grow, faculty, scholars, and alumni continue to personally grow and develop while helping many people and communities. One way to reduce the challenges of starting a program is to use the available resources and to not try to completely reinvent the wheel. The good news is that a template now exists (the Elon University Periclean Scholars program) and there is technical consulting support from Elon administration, faculty, students, and alumni. As institutions start to develop their own programs, our hope is that we can create a network of learning and knowledge that can help to address unforeseen challenges.

Part 2: The Plan Forward and Tasks after Evaluation

See Figure 13.3 for a pictorial representation of the steps in Part 2.

1. *Choosing a name.* Elon University chose to name the program "Periclean Scholars." The "champion," director, and mentors would need to discuss what name would best fit at their institution. Periclean Scholars fit at Elon because they are a founding Periclean institution and the program was created as a direct result of a challenge from Mr. Lang in 2001. The new program could consider the following two potential naming options: (1) a potential funding agency may want the program to be called "XYZ Scholars"; or (2) the institution can simply decide on its own name for the program. Getting the name via a funding source could help create a coherent brand, while the institution choosing its own name could allow the institution to put its own unique, distinctive spin on the program.

2. *Creating goals and assessing outcomes.* To show the value of the program to the leaders of the institution, the curriculum committees, and to potential members (i.e., students), the program leaders will need to agree on goals and outcomes and assess those goals and outcomes. Some things to consider when gathering

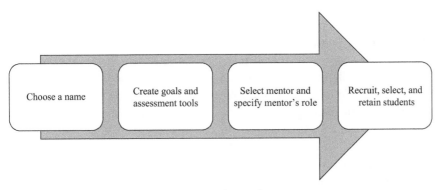

Figure 13.3 *The plan forward and tasks after evaluation*

assessment data include the following: (1) the impact on participating students; (2) the impact on the entire campus; (3) the impact on the partner institutions; and (4) the impact of the people and partners in the country of focus. For students, the program leaders should examine if students become more engaged global citizens over time and, once they graduate, if they stay involved in their cohort (and who does this) and if they stand out when compared to non-scholars at the same institution. For the campus, the program leaders should consider if there is more awareness of global issues on campus due to the program and perhaps if there has been any cultural shift toward a deeper sense of commitment to global issues.

3. *Choosing mentors and the mentor's role.* One of the keys to success for each class and the program overall is choosing committed, passionate, and dedicated mentors. At Elon University, the goal has always been to choose mentors from many different schools and departments on campus, ultimately adding a "silo-busting" element to the interdisciplinary program. Because of the multi-year commitment to the program, it is important that the mentor discusses the opportunity with their department chair and dean before agreeing to be a mentor. The faculty member should typically plan on being on campus for the years that they will be a mentor and should work with their home department to ensure that their reassigned Periclean class duties can work with the department's needs. At Elon University, a modest compensation for the extra preparation time is provided to each new mentor the summer before their Periclean class meets for the first time. The mentor should also be aware that traveling to the country of focus is typical, although not a requirement.

Before starting with students, it is the mentor's responsibility to choose the country of focus. This is done in close consultation with the director. In the past, mentors have decided to either choose an area where they already have deep expertise and contacts or have decided to embrace the same learning journey that students will soon be embarking on. As the Periclean Scholars program has grown, some mentors have chosen to "recycle" their country of focus from previous years (e.g., Chiapas, Mexico, or Sri Lanka). By "recycling," the new class has the opportunity to continue partnerships that have already been established. Clearly, the "recycling" route has many advantages, but the mentor has the ultimate decision about which route to take.

Once a country is selected, the mentor will take a large role in the selection process. The mentor will meet and interview the potential Scholar candidates and make decisions about who will make up their 30-person class. When class starts, the central role of the mentor is to facilitate learning. The mentor should encourage each student to bring the set of skills they have from their own majors to the class and challenge the students to figure out how they can use their skills to help their country of focus. The mentor should run the class as a seminar, focusing on as much student involvement as possible within a rigorous academic setting. The mentor should also explore if his/her research interests can dovetail as much as possible with the direction of his/her class. We recommend that, during the selection process, the mentor considers selecting students with whom research collaborations could be developed.

The mentor will also need to track and play a role in obtaining monetary resources. An obvious way to do this is to write grants. We recommend that each class sets a goal to submit at least one internal and external proposal per year. The mentor needs to empower students and encourage them to find funding opportunities and actively contribute to the grant writing process. Another way to raise money is through fundraising. The mentor will need to oversee fundraising efforts and act as the senior accountant for his/her class. The mentor must make sure that the funds raised are channeled to the proper accounts and that there are overall good accounting practices for the class.

Being a Periclean Scholar mentor is a job with many dimensions. The mentor must establish good relationships with the director, other mentors, and their class. The mentor will meet with the director individually and periodically throughout the year. The mentor should also expect to attend meetings with the director and other mentors to share ideas, coordinate efforts, and pass on the wisdom from one mentor to another. It is the hope that all the mentors communicate and work with one another to maximize the effectiveness of the overall program. The more seasoned mentors should also be available to the new mentor to answer questions, provide support, and give advice. Finally, it is critical that the mentor establishes a good rapport and relationship with the class. A mentor will get to know their students very closely, and vice versa, over the three-year journey. Class dynamics are critical because much of what the class will achieve will be based on how well they can work as a team or in small groups within the larger team. The mentor should be open and have good communication skills and mutual respect with the students.

4. *Recruiting and retaining interested, engaged, and committed students.* It is important to cast a wide net, but then also to select the most interested and well-qualified students. To start the recruitment process, the mentor should consider attending the new student organizational fair as a first attempt to reach out to potential cohort members. The mentor is also responsible for creating handouts about the program and some posters to raise interest. At Elon, each new student is enrolled in a General Studies course, similar to a freshman seminar at other

institutions. The mentor makes short presentations for these General Studies classes in the fall and spring semesters and discusses the mission, vision, and goals of Periclean Scholars as a whole, as well as for their individual class. The mentor should also consider asking the instructors of these classes if they think any of their students are particularly interested. That is actually how the first author got involved – her General Studies professor discussed the program one-on-one with her and she decided to apply.

After these recruiting events, students can go online to apply for the program. Students respond to a prompt, designed by the mentor, and write a short essay. In the past, the essay usually involved doing some research about the country of focus, identifying an issue the country was facing, and the student presenting an argument for why the class should focus on that issue. The student must also ask his/her General Studies professor to write a letter of recommendation for the program. Finally, the mentor will conduct face-to-face interviews. During the interview, the mentor will further educate the applicant about the nature of the program and will collect information that will help them make an informed decision about which students to select.

Once selected, the program has several ceremonies and rituals that help foster a sense of community and create a social environment rather than just an academic environment. For example, during the first week of classes in their sophomore year, there is a formal induction ceremony for the new class of Periclean Scholars. This event is organized and hosted by the second-year students and typically includes charges from class representatives, the director, the new mentor, and potentially a senior administrator. In some years, mentors also hand out a material artifact representing their country of focus. Once a year, there is also a "Celebrating Periclean Scholars" event. This pan-Periclean event is organized by the junior class and highlights the activities and accomplishments of each class. There is also an annual Periclean Scholar of the Year Award that is presented to a rising senior along with a $500 scholarship from the Eugene M. Lang Foundation.

During graduation time, the seniors will organize an end-of-year celebration of the three years of accomplishments for the class and their parents and friends. Graduating seniors also attend the university-wide "Leaders of the 21st Century" celebration and are recognized in front of their family and friends the Friday before graduation. Pericleans have also chosen to have some physical representation of their class displayed on their graduation gowns (e.g., stoles created in their country of focus).

Conclusion

Service learning has become a high-priority interest among institutions across the United States (Caspersz & Olaru, 2017). Institutions are realizing the benefits that service learning offers not only to the local and global communities, but also to students and faculty on campus and beyond (Caspersz & Olaru, 2017; Toncar et al., 2006). It is important that institutions continue to explore service-learning options for their students. We believe that these institutions can learn from each other and should be talking with each other about how to best implement service-learning classes and projects on their campus. One example of a successful service-learning project is the Periclean Scholars program at Elon University. The Periclean Scholars program has exponentially grown and had many successes since its inception in 2002. These successes would not have been possible without the support of the administration and leadership, faculty champions, and engaged and dedicated students. In this chapter, we discussed the Periclean Scholars program and provided information and guidance for faculty, administrators, or students who may be interested in starting a similar program at their institutions. Our hope is that service learning continues to grow and flourish and that the Periclean Scholars model can be a model for how long-term, interdisciplinary student engagement can be beneficial well beyond the walls of the institution the students are attending and well beyond the four years during which the students are on campus.

Appendix 13.1

Books

Arcaro, T., Lane, K., Lubliner, S., & Luther, E. (2016). *Mapping our success: Elon University's Periclean Scholars*. Düsseldorf: Carpe Viam Press.

Periclean Scholars (2016). *Our Periclean journey: Discovering the world of humanitarian aid*. Düsseldorf: Carpe Viam Press.

Note: both books are available on Amazon.

Websites

www.elon.edu/u/academics/project-pericles/
www.elon.edu/u/academics/project-pericles/periclean-scholars-program/

References

Billig, S. H., & Welch, M. (2004). Service-learning as civically engaged scholarship. In M. Welch & S. H. Billig (Eds.), *New perspectives in service learning* (pp. 221–241). Greenwich, CT: Information Age.

Caspersz, D., & Olaru, D. (2017). The value of service-learning: The student perspective. *Studies in Higher Education, 42*(4), 685–700.

Caspersz, D., Olaru, D., & Smith, L. (2012). Striving for definitional clarity: What is service learning? In creating an inclusive learning environment: Engagement, equity, and retention. Presented at: *21st Annual Teaching Learning Forum*. Perth: Murdoch University.

Deeley, S. J. (2010). Service-learning: Thinking outside the box. *Active Learning in Higher Education, 11*(1), 43–53.

Restavek Freedom (n.d.). Ending Child Slavery in Haiti. Retrieved from https://restavekfreedom.org/?gclid=EAIaIQobChMI7vqGtKni1wIVwSWBCh3OFgtGEAAYASAAEgITJ_D_BwE.

Eyler, J., & Giles, D. (1989). The impact of service learning program characteristics on student outcomes. Presented at: *National Society for Experiential Education Conference*. Salt Lake City, UT: Snowbird.

Mayhew, J., & Welch, M. (2001). A call to service: Service learning as a pedagogy in special education programs. *Teacher Education and Special Education, 24*(3), 208–219.

Mendel-Reyes, M. (1998). A pedagogy for citizenship: Service learning and democratic education. *New Directions for Teaching and Learning, 73*, 8–31.

Ngai, S. (2006). Service-learning, personal development and social commitment: A case study of university students in Hong Kong. *Adolescence, 41*(161), 165–177.

Periclean Scholars (2016). *Our Periclean journey: Discovering the world of humanitarian aid*. Düsseldorf: Carpe Viam Press.

Project Pericles (2017). Project Pericles History. Retrieved from www.projectpericles.org/projectpericles/about/history/.

Saltmarsh, J. (2010). Changing pedagogies. In H. E. Fitzgerald, C. Burack, & S. D. Seifer (Eds.), *Handbook of engaged scholarship: Contemporary landscapes, future directions* (Vol. 1, pp. 331–352). East Lansing, MI: Michigan State University Press.

Saltmarsh, J., Giles, D. E., Ward, E., & Buglione, S. M. (2009). Rewarding community-engaged scholarship. *New Directions for Higher Education, 147*, 25–35.

Toncar, M. F., Reid, J. S., Burns, D. J., Anderson, C. E., & Nguyen, H. P. (2006). Uniform assessment of the benefits of service-learning: The development, evaluation, and implementation of the SELEB scale. *The Journal of Marketing Theory and Practice, 14*(3), 223–238.

Weerts, D. J., & Sandmann, L. R. (2008). Building a two-way street: Challenges and opportunities for community engagement at research universities. *The Review of Higher Education, 32*(1), 73–106.

Welch, M., & Saltmarsh, J. (2013). Current practice and infrastructures for campus centers of community engagement. *Journal of Higher Education Outreach and Engagement, 17*(4), 25–56.

14 University, School District, and Service-Learning Community Partnerships That Work

Julie Dierberger, Orentheian Everett,
ReNae S. Kehrberg, & Jenna Greene

Two-thirds of the US population call urban and metropolitan centers home. Metropolitan areas are geographic areas that include at least one urbanized cluster area and a population of at least 50,000 (United States Census Bureau, 2015). These communities approach collaboration and resource allocation in unique ways due to the variety of needs that exist to support the dense population (Klieman, 2015). Educational institutions anchor metropolitan communities and provide support through employment, research, scholarship, problem-solving and collaboration. Service learning is an asset-based approach to sharing resources from educational institutions and community organizations while collectively addressing social justice concerns (Garoutte & McCarthy-Gilmore, 2014).

Jacoby (1996) defined service learning as "a form of experiential education in which students engage in activities that address human and community needs together" (p. 5). In service-learning courses, student learning is connected to service experiences through reflection activities facilitated before, during, and after their experiences. Service learning provides an opportunity for learning and community development by partnering with community organizations to teach course content while sharing assets to develop communities. As a result, students not only better understand their course content in a real-world context, but also contribute to the capacity of the organization and community at no cost. Communities are learning with and from the students and are also helping to identify concerns, educating students and collectively focusing resources to eradicate the identified issue. This chapter will examine how one metropolitan community utilized service learning across educational and community boundaries to share assets and create strong interorganizational partnerships.

Background and Literature Review

In 1994, Ernest Boyer described the concept of a "New American College" as one that "must respond to the challenges that confront our children, our schools, and our cities" (p. A48). Boyer implored higher education institutions that "connected theory to practice" and encouraged creativity for faculty and students to "apply knowledge to real-life problems" (1994, p. A48). He saw this as not only critical to learning, but also essential to the "pressing social, economic, and civic problems" facing the world (Boyer, 1994, p. A48). This call was heard around the nation and inspired a resurgence of both pre-kindergarten through grade 12 (P–12) schools and higher education institutions to engage in forms of experiential teaching and learning, of which service learning was extremely popular (Titlebaum et al., 2004). Zlotkowski (1998) described service learning as an intersection between the following two educational purposes: (1) giving students the opportunity to discover and test truths in real contexts instead of a world of case studies and hypotheticals; and (2) to apply this learning within a context that promotes civic responsibility and community engagement (pp. 3–4).

Metropolitan institutions of higher education have long dedicated campus resources to the health of their urban environments. Metropolitan institutions take on an intentional responsibility to shape how these spaces and the higher education institutions within them can collaboratively innovate, govern, and educate. The Coalition of Urban and Metropolitan Universities (CUMU) issued the following declaration to this point: "We, the leaders of urban and metropolitan universities, declare that our future as knowledge organizations will continue to be forged by sustained, reciprocal engagement with our cities" (Diner & Holland, 2010). Welch and Saltmarsh (2013) surveyed campus engagement center leadership from Carnegie-classified institutions whose 147 respondents indicated almost 91 percent had a central community engagement reporting structure. Nearly 84 percent of respondents indicated community engagement as a strategic priority at their institutions (p. 35). While not all respondents were metropolitan institutions, these results clearly indicate the priority higher education institutions put on community engagement.

Education has a long history of service-learning instruction at all levels. P–12 schools and higher education have similar goals: to educate citizens to lead and contribute to their communities. Reaching across the educational aisle to identify solutions to community development is not easy, but provides a collaborative method of developing civic-minded young people while looking critically at course content in real-world situations. Educational systems are made up of not only policies and procedures, but also people who have the opportunity to build significant relationships in this work. In order to accomplish the goal of engaging students to lead and contribute to their community, partnerships across the P–16 (pre-kindergarten through higher education) spectrum are formed.

As educational institutions – with a special emphasis on metropolitan institutions – work to enhance their students' educational experiences and their community engagement efforts, service learning stands out as a research-based experiential learning tool that can help achieve those goals. In other words, Boyer was correct – educational institutions could teach and learn by bringing creativity and curiosity from the classroom to the community, including through service learning.

Benefits of Service Learning

Research on college students has shown that service-learning instruction increases achievement, civic engagement, and intentions to serve the community in the future (Astin et al., 2000). Similarly, research analysis reported from Lopez and Kiesa (2009) indicated higher education students were more civically engaged than in previous years, and those enrolled in a four-year college or university course were more civically engaged than those attending two-year institutions. Seemingly, students are interested in being engaged in their community, and service learning is a meaningful way to support this generational trend. A study by Astin et al. (2000) collected data from over 22,000 college undergraduates to evaluate the impact of service learning and community service on 11 measures, including academic outcomes and engagement with service after college. The study found academics and service to be reciprocally influencing, and that students engaged in service learning were more likely to be engaged in their community later in life. That is, the study validated what educators long thought to be true: service learning as a method of instruction is a valuable way to teach students while also increasing achievement, civic engagement skills, and short- and long-term intentions to serve in the community.

Research examining P–12 service learning has found the method of instruction to be valuable at this education level as well. Research indicated positive performance outcomes in subject matter exams and assessments (Furco & Root, 2010) as well as increased school engagement (Melchior, 1998) when service-learning instruction was utilized in P–12 schools. Scales et al. (2000) conducted an assessment before and after a service-learning project, which showed significant changes in student motivation for learning, school engagement, and academic achievement in service-learning courses. Kahne and Sporte's (2008) research concluded that service learning was a strong predictor of future student civic participation.

Best Practices in Partnerships in Service Learning

Partnerships are necessary to quality service-learning instruction and have a significant impact on project success (Rue, 1996). Typically, community partnerships represent nonprofit or governmental organizations that partner with educational institutions and participate in engaged teaching and learning (Martin & Crossland, 2017). As a best practice, the service-learning partnership should benefit all partners mutually through a reciprocal approach to meeting goals together, instead of "for" one partner (Jacoby, 2003). Like any relationship, service-learning partnerships vary in depth. Jacoby (2003) identified high-quality partnerships that included shared vision, open communication, and collaboration. Enos and Morton (2003) described campus–community partnerships in a dualistic relationship from "transactional" to "transformational," which deepen with greater time, depth, and complexity in the partnership (p. 27).

The National Youth Leadership Council (2008) developed eight quality standards for effective service-learning practice. The standards were developed from service-learning research and applicable data from evidence on quality practice in service learning (Billig, 2007). The eight standards include meaningful service, link to curriculum, reflection, diversity, youth voice, partnerships, and progress monitoring. These standards are important to consider in implementation to ensure that positive outcomes and high-quality learning occur (Billig, 2007).

The research conducted and compiled by the National Youth Leadership Council (2008) indicated partnerships (one of the standards) that are "collaborative, mutually beneficial, and address community needs" are most successful. Further, research has found that the most successful partnerships involve a variety of youth, educators, and community members, have regular communication, collaborate toward a shared vision and goals, develop action plans to meet goals, and view each other as assets as shown through sharing knowledge (RMC Research, 2008).

P–16 Service-Learning Initiatives

All levels of educational institutions have a long history of service-learning instruction, but collaboration across the educational spectrum is becoming increasingly common. Traditionally, service learning between P–12 and higher education was compulsory and required college students to learn their course content by serving P–12 students. Pickeral (2003) described the following myriad reasons for which P–12 and higher education have often partnered over the years: to prepare students for college; to support student transition by reflecting college admissions requirements in secondary education; to give higher education students the opportunity to apply learning in real time; and to increase access to college through intentional and student-friendly pathways. This type of relationship lacks the deep, collaborative nature of co-instructing in a community setting and establishes an immediate power imbalance between the P–12 and higher education students. Pickeral further suggested that if colleges and universities want to remain competitive and attract civically engaged students to their campuses, highly developed service-learning programs are necessary (Pickeral, 2003).

P–16 service-learning is a new approach to service-learning partnerships in which a P–12 teacher, higher education faculty member, and community partner create a team through which learning and service goals are addressed (Dierberger, 2015). Service-learning partnerships typically include higher education students serving a community partner, which might be a P–12 school or students. P–16 service-learning partnerships include both a P–12 and higher education partner with a community organization serving as border crossers across educational and/or power systems. Through this P–16 service-learning model, both the higher education and P–12 students partner to apply their course content to meeting the community-identified need, with the community partner also acting as a co-teacher (Dierberger, 2015). In this model, all partners are meeting their learning goals while addressing a community-identified need or increasing organizational capacity with

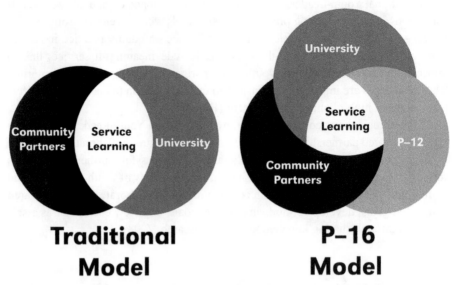

Figure 14.1 *P–16 service-learning and traditional service-learning models*

a community partner. Figure 14.1 provides a visual articulation of the P–16 service-learning and traditional service-learning models.

Relationships guide service-learning instruction, yet can remain difficult to maintain and implement, especially in education where instruction rarely takes a team approach across institutional boundaries. This type of creative collaboration may take more time and require creative problem-solving from committed, enthusiastic partners, but the relationships developed along the way provide a template for innovative resource-sharing in metropolitan communities. Identifying the key ingredients to successful partnerships in this complex P–16 service-learning schema provides valuable information for communities around the globe.

Challenges with P–16 Service-Learning Initiatives

A 2011 report indicated urban and metropolitan areas have a "challenge to develop systemic approaches to collaboration and coordination" of P–12 schools and higher education and that 85 percent of respondents to a recent assessment of CUMU institutions were engaged in P–16 initiatives (Coalition of Urban and Metropolitan Universities, 2011, p. 11). These represent primarily college preparation/readiness and collaborative classroom projects, but do not specifically indicate if P–16 service learning – where all partners share power – is occurring. A 1999 Educational Commission of the States report stated that shared partnerships between P–12 and higher education systems can be thin and challenging, explaining that "[i]t is extremely difficult to develop and implement a *thick* partnership between these two entities, in which students from both institutions serve, learn and enhance their skill" (Harwood & Underhill, 1999, p. 1, emphasis in original). While communities are exploring best practices around P–16 integration, there is no specific focus on service learning or community engagement as they relate to instruction (Mostaghimi, 2015). This chapter explores the ingredients for that "thick" partnership within a P–16 service-learning context in a metropolitan area where collaborating organizations share equal power.

Interorganizational Theory Model of Partnership Formation

Janke's (2013) research connecting management theory and service-learning partnership theory frames a new way to articulate complex service-learning partnerships, not at the individual level, but at the interorganizational level, and provides a lens for the P–16 service-learning partnership assessment. Her review of the literature and phased approach to interorganizational partnerships suggest further research is necessary to examine how inter-organizational partnerships are forged and sustained. She wrote, "[...] examples drawn from extant research may offer a compelling reason to examine closely this and other literature to adopt, adapt, and build on foundations that have already been laid in this area of scholarship and practice" (p. 580). The phased approach to interorganizational partnerships begins with the following pre-partnering characteristics necessary to future collaboration: necessity (voluntary vs. mandatory partnering), asymmetry (resources are available), reciprocity (mutually beneficial), efficiency (input and output are appropriate), stability (factors are predictable), and legitimacy (norms and expectations are appropriate). The next phase examines the processes of organizational learning, trust, and power-sharing necessary to interorganizational partnerships. Finally, the outcomes phase determines the extent to which the partnership accomplished what it set out to do (Janke, 2013, pp. 580–584). Additionally, Enos and Morton's (2003) framework for campus–community partnerships broadens our understanding of the depth and complexity of service-learning partnerships that are created when time is introduced. This model starts with one-time events, and as project and partnership depth and complexity increase, partnerships develop toward the transformation and joint creation of knowledge and work (Enos & Morton, 2003).

Research Gap

This research is unique in that it investigates P–16 partnerships that include a P–12 teacher, higher education faculty member, and community partner – an approach that is currently missing from the literature. These partnerships are indicated in the literature as partnerships between P–12 and higher education for which standard alignment and curricular transition are facilitated in the effort to prepare students to be college and career ready (Chamberlin & Plucker, 2008). Collaborating through service-learning instruction across the P–16 continuum provides an opportunity for the disconnected educational silos to create a more seamless learning experience for students while achieving the aforementioned positive service-learning impacts (Dierberger, 2015).

Process

In order to understand the key ingredients for successful P–16 service-learning partnerships, a group of long-term partners in a metropolitan environment was assembled. The partners in this project included a senior administrator from a large public school district in an urban, metropolitan area, the director of a Parks and Recreation center, and an administrator at a metropolitan higher education institution. These partners had been serving in different capacities in which they supported P–16 service learning in their respective organizations. For example, the school district administrator had also served as a principal at a school at which service-learning collaboration with the higher education institution had occurred. Each partner had been participating in some capacity as a frontline partner or administrative partner in P–16 service learning for at least seven years. The group met initially to learn more about the project and discuss methods, forge a collaborative research team, and discuss the main question this chapter would answer. The group identified the following overarching question to answer through the research: What are the key ingredients to a successful P–16 service-learning partnership?

After the group identified the overarching question, the partners brainstormed sub-questions that were necessary to answer the overarching question. During several meetings, the team identified an exhaustive list of potential questions that were pared down to the priority questions that guided data collection. The team then established a timeline for all partners to reflect on their perspectives on each question and provide detailed responses to those questions. These questions included the following:

1. What are the essential components to effective P–16 service-learning partnerships?
2. Do you think P–16 service learning is institutionalized in your organization? What leads you to that conclusion?
3. Are there tangible impacts you can directly point to that indicate P–16 service learning has been successful or unsuccessful in your organization?

The data were collected by one of the partners, loaded into NVIVO 10, and coded topically by using patterns that were codified and categorized, and then recategorized, cycling the coding to summarize similarities (Saldaña, 2016). Themes emerged when at least two partners indicated similar answers to questions. Initial results were validated through discussions at follow-up meetings. This validation was essential to reframe and confirm data intent.

Results

Components of Effective P–16 Partnerships

In response to the first question, "What are the essential components to effective P–16 service-learning partnerships?" the research team identified three themes and sub-themes related to goals, communication, and relationships. Each theme included two sub-themes as indicated in Table 14.1.

Goals. Establishing set goals at the beginning of the collaboration is essential to P–16 service-learning partnerships. These complicated relationships require a clear articulation and understanding of the project and its immediate impact on the community. While understanding the overall goal of the P–16 service-learning project is important, the partners must also be clear about how the activities they are doing together are contributing to the overall goal.

Data also indicated that the goal development must be mutually beneficial to all partners. There cannot be one partner that feels as though their organizational capacity needs are not being considered in the collaboration. An example of designing joint goals that are mutually beneficial occurred during a service-learning project with middle school students in a web design course supported by higher education technology students that developed a website for a new nonprofit agency to meet their external communication goals. Dr. ReNae Kehrberg, Omaha Public Schools, Assistant Superintendent and former Magnet Middle School principal, indicated the following:

> Even at the initial meeting our focus was on what we could do together that would authentically enhance both our institutions students' skills while supporting the community. Developing a goal to help a community nonprofit create a website matched the course outcomes for the middle school students, matched the course learning goals for the college students, and provided the nonprofit with an interactive, functional website to further their efforts. It was a perfect example of a shared, mutually beneficial goal for all partners.

Interestingly, the partners also included frequent progress monitoring as being essential to the goal-setting process. They indicated that checking in throughout the project about the status of the pre-identified goals was important to the process in order to maintain reciprocity for all partners. Flexibility was also indicated in the data

Table 14.1 *Essential components of P–16 partnerships*

Themes	Sub-themes
Goals	Mutually beneficial
	Progress monitoring
Communication	Intra-partnership communication
	Institutional communication
Relationships	Transactional approaches
	Philosophical approaches

as important in service-learning collaborations, but partners were careful to caution that too much flexibility could derail the project from its agreed-upon goals.

Communication. The researchers approached the concept of communication with an inclusive lens to all that are touched by the P–16 service-learning partnership. They identified the importance of having equal voices in communication and the creation of a culture in which communication is promoted to all partners, participants, contributors, and recipients. For example, the higher education administrator indicated, "Partners must be conscious not to limit communication only to the program managers but to service population as well." She went on to say communication with the organization's clients will "validate" voices. These voices must be heard and validated from the beginning of the process and are essential to success.

From the P–12 school perspective, the systemic communication about P–16 service learning to all partners – staff, students, administration, and families – is essential to maintaining a clear message about service learning. Kehrberg indicated, "Communication, communication, and communication have been key to supporting P–16 service learning in Omaha Public Schools where over 40 schools participate in University of Nebraska Omaha-facilitated service-learning activities with the community." She further explained, "Staff are more likely to implement and use a delivery method for learning that they are familiar with and one that is supported [by administration]. Service learning is a high-yield teaching strategy, in addition to being a tremendous community connection for service. To make this happen, communication about service learning must be done systematically." The school district, in partnership with the local university, used communication tools such as service-learning brochures, literature, presentations to building principals, School Board presentations, one-on-one meetings with administrators, and emails. These communications were all essential to delivering this cohesive message to all who were touched by this teaching strategy.

Relationships. The relationships node of essential components of P–16 service learning included transactional and logistical components, as well as the philosophical approaches the partners took toward relationships. For example, the partners described how essential establishing trust with all partners was to the project success. Trust was developed through transactional means such as completing tasks, being consistent with communication, and meeting goals as established. As partnerships deepened, the researchers indicated flexibility and change could occur. However, it is important to have the initial, transactional components of the P–16 service-learning project occur in order to increase trust and flexibility.

The partners also approached relationships in a philosophical way. They identified that P–16 service-learning relationships must also include a belief in the power and benefits of service learning for students in P–12 and higher education and the community. Orentheian Everett, City of Omaha Parks and Recreation director, stated, "Positive relationship building is key in the process of creating awareness and the implementation of data gathering." He emphasized the importance of networking with program partners and program liaisons "at all levels to foster a positive working relationship." This perspective was indicated as essential to beginning the partnership altogether, and without a strong sense of these beliefs from all partners, the relationship cannot develop authentically, even to achieve the transactional components of the P–16 service-learning experience.

Institutionalization of P–16 Service Learning

The results from the second question, "Do you think P–16 service learning is institutionalized in your organization?" received resounding affirmative responses from all partners. They gave different individual examples of how they reached that conclusion. The results are shown in Table 14.2.

This institutionalization was reflected in the internal and external ways in which P–16 service learning is supported at each partner site and included resources to support the staff to implement P–16 service-learning projects such as personnel time, space to administer meetings and project implementation, time for partners to attend professional development together, and prioritizing P–16 service learning in strategic plans. Institutionalization was also reflected in promotional materials and online communications, and supported through internal communication from administration (e.g., campus speeches, School Board presentations, strategic planning sessions, etc.).

The partners also indicated institutionalization would not have been as successful if the partners would have required formal documentation of the collaboration through documents such as a memorandum of understanding or formal contract. Rather, these types of documents would have triggered a need to get School Board, City Administration, or Board of Regents approval, and would have limited the ability for the partners to develop trust by completing the transactional components of the relationship outside of the confines of a contract. Additionally, the partners indicated contracts would have "killed" the creativity that developed through trusting and sustainable relationships.

Table 14.2 *Institutionalization of P–16 service-learning*

Authentic and relational-based institutionalization	Internal resources for support	Personnel time Physical spaces Time for partnership Development Prioritization of P–16 service learning in strategic plans
	Reflection in communication	External Internal

Impacts of P–16 Service Learning

The final question referred to how the partners identified the success and impacts of the P–16 service-learning partnerships: "Are there tangible impacts you can directly point to that indicate P–16 service learning has been successful or unsuccessful?" The results were specific to each of the organizations and are reflected in Table 14.3.

The community partner indicated that successful P–16 programs have provided the opportunity for the organization to deepen its partnerships with other community engagement activities. For example, the P–16 service-learning partnerships provided increased community awareness and developed into other partnerships such as practicum experiences, internship programs, and career exploration collaborations with P–12 and higher education schools. The public school saw increases in student motivation for learning, preparation for work, district-wide support from the community (for bond issues, etc.), increased perceived value of all partners, and increased rigor and authentic application of the curriculum. The higher education partner saw success in increased support for the innovative work across all areas. For example, teachers and administrators across the P–16 spectrum were more interested in learning how to engage in service-learning work and attended professional development more frequently.

Additionally, partnerships were deepening between collaborators, and as a result, capacity was growing. The issue for which the partnership was initially working collectively to address deepened, and the partners started examining the root cause of the issue, which was a lack of affordable, healthy food for the older adults. For example, the issue of providing a weekly meal for a group of seniors grew into identifying a holistic approach to health for older adults. Partners advocated for increased full-time employees for a position supporting recreation and socialization for older adults, which was successful. This changed the landscape of the need in the area and provided an opportunity for the partners to explore other ways to build capacity in the future. This example showcases the truly transformational impacts a P–16 service-learning partnership can have.

Table 14.3 *Impacts of P–16 service-learning partnerships*

All partners: capacity building for supporting community		
Community partner	P–12 school	University
Increased community awareness	Increased student motivation for learning and preparation	Increased engagement of faculty and administrators in service learning
Development of new partnerships	Increased reciprocal support of community and school district Increased rigor and application of curriculum	

Discussion

The data collected from these partners followed Janke's (2013) interorganizational partnerships theory, which is rooted in Oliver's (1990) conditions for interorganization relationships. This helps to construct a new way of thinking about P–16 service-learning partnerships across boundaries. The data returned indicate that the pre-partnering characteristics are consistent with how the P–16 service-learning partnerships were developed in this metropolitan community. The partners identified that the service-learning collaboration was voluntary instead of mandatory and stressed the importance of this concept when they shared that formalizing the relationship would have limited opportunities, or eliminated a desire to collaborate in the first place. They indicated formal, required partnerships would have stopped the collaboration before it started because of the significant red tape and bureaucracy that would have needed to be overcome by each organization. Next, each organization provided resources, both human and financial, to the partnership. These took the form of actual project supplies, administrative support, and promotional materials. All partners indicated that reciprocity was important to the collaboration – each partner benefitted from the collaboration and communicated mutual goals before moving forward with the collaboration. They identified the legitimacy of the collaboration by clarifying norms and expectations before the collaboration took place and agreed to terms from each partner.

The only two components of the pre-partnering phase not stated in this research included efficiency and stability factors. Efficiency factors included conversations about input and output that are appropriate (Janke, 2003; Oliver, 1990). In this case, the partners did not indicate that they were going into the relationship with the goal of increasing resources or return on investment. Oliver (1990) described "stability" in interorganizational partnerships as being predictable. This suggests that the partners were aware of the lack of predictability in the service-learning collaboration, given that, in service-learning instruction, stability factors are extremely difficult to maintain due to the high level of flexibility that can be required, especially in a P–16 service-learning partnership where things such as snow days or testing can affect planning. The partnership is further complicated due to different schedules and norms across P–16 educational systems, and can be impacted by school or departmental culture.

The partners also identified organizational learning components, which the data suggested were where the P–16 service-learning partnership that was examined fell in the model. This phase requires trust and power-sharing (Janke, 2013). In the data collected for this research, trust was built upon goodwill developed through relationships created and nurtured between the partners. Over time, the relationships were further established through the consistent, reciprocal partnerships that developed between the P–16 partners. Power-sharing occurred in this model through all collaborators and reached all audiences, including the following: students, clients served, teachers, faculty members, administrators, and governing bodies. It was important to the partners to establish trust with all those connected to the P–16 service-learning collaboration from the beginning of the project and to ensure they had a voice in the process. For example, one of the partners indicated trust must be established from the beginning of the relationship, otherwise the clients served would not have buy-in and so would not participate. This was especially important because the clientele in the community represented a population of African-American older adults that has a history of disenfranchisement. Engaging them as partners in the process at the beginning and maintaining consistency were identified as important to this partner.

Finally, the data from this project indicated that the outcomes articulated by these partners did not align. The data collected communicated the internal outcomes the partners perceived from their own served populations, such as increased student learning outcomes or increased program attendance. However, the data failed to represent a holistic, community-based approach. The partners did indicate the opportunities to collaborate on mutual outcomes at a deeper level and in diverse ways. However, these outcomes failed to address the eradication of the root issues in the metropolitan area or provide a true social justice lens to service-learning work in a metropolitan community. Despite the partners indicating disparate outcomes, those listed were positive for the individual partner organizations.

Further research about interorganizational relationships and service learning is necessary in order to better understand complicated and boundary-spanning partnerships and their impacts on communities. The data presented in this chapter were gathered from partners across the P–16 educational spectrum, representing P–12 schools and higher education and their seven-year service-learning partnership with a community partner. Future research using a case study methodology would better assist metropolitan communities in understanding how to forge P–16 service-learning partnerships with careful attention to pre-planning, trust, power-sharing, and outcomes. A case study model would provide a strong opportunity to offer generalizability to other metropolitan communities attempting to collaborate interorganizationally.

References

Astin, A. W., Vogelgesang, L. J., Ikeda, E. K., & Lee, J. A. (2000). *How service learning affects students*. Los Angeles, CA: Higher Education Research Institute.

Billig, S. H. (2007). Unpacking what works in service-learning: Promising research-based practices to improve student outcomes. In *Growing to greatness 2007: The state of service-learning* (pp. 18–22). St Paul, MN: National Youth Leadership Council Report.

Boyer, E. L. (1994). Creating the new American college. *Chronicle of Higher Education, 40* (27), A48.

Chamberlin, M., & Plucker, J. (2008). P–16 education: Where are we going? Where have we been? *Phi Delta Kappan, 89*(7), 472–479.

Coalition of Urban and Metropolitan Universities (2011). *The impact of institutions of higher education on urban and metropolitan areas: Assessment of the Coalition of Urban and Metropolitan Universities*. Chicago, IL: The Great Cities Institute.

Dierberger, J. (2015). P–16 service-learning partnerships: A model for success. In O. Delano-Oriaran, M. W. Penick-Parks, & S. Fondrie (Eds.), *The SAGE sourcebook of service-*

learning and civic engagement (pp. 171–178). Thousand Oaks, CA: SAGE Publications, Inc.

Diner, S., & Holland, B. (2010). 21st Century Declaration from the Coalition of Urban and Metropolitan Universities. In *Coalition of Urban and Metropolitan Universities*. Retrieved from www.cumuonline.org/declaration/.

Enos, S., & Morton, K. (2003). Developing a theory and practice of campus–community partnerships. In B. Jacoby & Associates (Eds.), *Building partnerships for service-learning* (pp. 20–41). San Francisco, CA: Jossey-Bass.

Furco, A., & Root, S. (2010). Research demonstrates the value of service-learning. *Phi Delta Kappan 91*(5), 16–20.

Garoutte, L., & McCarthy-Gilmore, K. (2014). Preparing students for community-based learning using an asset-based approach. *Journal of the Scholarship of Teaching and Learning, 14*(5), 48–61.

Groves, R. (2011). *Federal register: Urban area criteria for the 2010 census*. Washington, DC: Department of Commerce Census Bureau.

Harwood, A., & Underhill, C. (1999). *Promising practice for K–16 Project Connect: School–university collaboration for service-learning. Education Commission of the States report*. Denver, CO: Education Commission of the States.

Jacoby, B. (2003). Fundamentals of service-learning partnerships. In B. Jacoby & Associates (Eds.), *Building partnerships for service-learning* (pp. 1–19). San Francisco, CA: Jossey-Bass.

Jacoby, B. (1996). Service-Learning in today's higher education. In B. Jacoby & Associates (Eds.), *Service-learning in higher education: Concepts and practices* (pp. 3–25). San Francisco, CA: Jossey-Bass.

Janke, E. M. (2013). Organizational partnerships in service-learning: Advancing theory-based research. In P. H. Clayton, R. G. Bringle, & J. A. Hatcher (Eds.), *Research on service-learning: Conceptual frameworks and assessment, Volume 2B: Communities, institutions, and partnerships* (pp. 573–598). Sterling, VA: Stylus Publishing.

Kayne, J. E., & Sporte, S. E. (2008). Developing citizens: The impact of civic learning opportunities on students' commitment to civic participation. *American Educational Research Journal, 45*(3), 738–766.

Klieman, N. (2015). Here's how cities and anchor institutions can work together to drive growth. *Vanguard Australia*. Retrieved from https://nextcity.org/daily/entry/anchor-institutions-cities-national-resouorce-network.

Lopez, M. H., & Kiesa, A. (2009). What we know about civic engagement from college students. In B. Jacoby & Associates (Eds.), *Civic engagement in higher education: Concepts and practices* (pp. 31–48). San Francisco, CA: Jossey-Bass.

Martin, L., & Crossland, S. (2017). High-quality community-campus partnerships: Approaches and competencies. In L. D. Dostilio (Ed.), *The community engagement professional in higher education: A competency model for an emerging field* (pp. 161–178). Boston, MA: Campus Compact.

Melchior, A. (1998). *National evaluation of Learn and Serve America school and community-based program*. Waltham, MA: Center for Human Resources, Brandeis University.

Mostaghimi, B. (2015). *Building your P–16: A how to guide for establishing P–16 community engagement councils*. Washington, DC: Center for Education Innovations.

National Youth Leadership Council (2008). *K-12 service-learning standards for quality practice*. St Paul, MN: National Youth Leadership Council.

Oliver, C. (1990). Determinants of inter-organizational relationships: Integration and future directions. *Academy of Management Review, 15*, 241–265.

Pickeral, T. (2003). Partnerships with elementary and secondary education. In B. Jacoby & Associates (Eds.), *Building partnerships for service-learning* (pp. 174–191). San Francisco, CA: Jossey-Bass.

Rue, P. (1996). Administering successful service-learning programs. In B. Jacoby & Associates (Eds.), *Service-learning in higher education: Concepts and practices* (pp. 246–275). San Francisco, CA: Jossey-Bass.

RMC Research (2008). Standards and indicators for effective service-learning practice. Retrieved from http://portal.kidscarecenter.com/sites/ServiceLearning/Document%20Library1/1/K-12%20SL%20Standards%20for%20Quality%20Practice.pdf.

Saldaña, J. (2016). *The coding manual for qualitative researchers*, 3rd edn. Thousand Oaks, CA: SAGE Publications.

Titlebaum, P., Williamson, G., Daparano, C., Baer, J., & Brahler, J. (2004). *Annotated history of service-learning*. Dayton, OH: University of Dayton.

Scales, P., Blyth, D., Berkas, T., & Kielsmeier, J. (2000). The effects of service learning on middle school students' social responsibility and academic success. *Journal of Early Adolescence*, 20(3), 332–358.

United States Census Bureau (2015). Population trends in incorporated places: 2000–2013. Retrieved from www.census.gov/content/dam/Census/library/publications/2015/demo/p25-1142.pdf.

Welsch, M., & Saltmarsh, J. (2013). Current practices and infrastructures for campus centers of community engagement. *Journal of Higher Education Outreach and Engagement, 17*(4), 25–55.

Zlotkowski, E. (1998). A new model of excellence. In E. Zlotkowski (Ed.) *Successful service-learning programs: New models of excellence in higher education* (pp. 1–14). Bolton, MA: Anker Publishing Company, Inc.

PART V

Leading Community Engagement Efforts

15 Leading Social Innovation and Community Engagement

Strategies for Picking the Right Actions

Michael D. Mumford, Robert Martin, Samantha Elliott, & E. Michelle Todd

Organizations, firms, universities, and nonprofits initiate community engagement programs for many reasons (Driscoll, 2008). Firms might initiate community engagement programs as a mechanism for improving employee morale (Cartwright & Holmes, 2006). Firms might initiate community engagement as a mechanism for branding products (Lee, Kim, & Kim, 2011). Firms might initiate community engagement programs as a vehicle for establishing a pro-social firm identity (Algesheimer, Dholakia, & Herrmann, 2005). Firms might initiate community engagement programs as a vehicle for establishing positive relationships with key stakeholders – customers, suppliers, and regulators (Aslin & Brown, 2004).

Although these and other reasons for initiating community engagement programs have value for both firms and the broader community (Redell & Woolcock, 2004), community engagement initiatives often do not work out (Schultz, 2006). For example, many firms in community engagement seek to build stakeholder support for firms' intended actions; however, community engagement seems to enhance firm legitimacy rather than build support for specific actions (Bowen, Newemham-Kahindi, & Herremans, 2010). Firms may hope to inspire employees, but community engagement programs may be seen as "just one more thing to do" (Cartwright & Holmes, 2006). At times, the community may not see the initiative at hand as especially engaging (Head, 2007).

The inconsistent success of community engagement programs poses a fundamental question for those who seek to encourage community engagement: How should community engagement initiatives be managed (Watson, 2007)? Of course, management of any initiative is a complex, multifaceted process (Noe, Hollenbeck, Gerhart, & Wright, 2006). Ultimately, however, effective management of any initiative depends on effective leadership (Yukl, 2011). Leadership has been understood through many lenses – top management teams (Finkelstein & Hambrick, 1990), leader behavior (Fleishman & Harris, 1962; Hu & Liden, 2011), leader–follower exchange (Graen & Uhl-Bein, 1995), and leader abilities (Lord, De Vader, & Alliger, 1986). In accounting for leader performance, however, the skills-based model seems to hold the most promise. Mumford, Todd, Higgs, and McIntosh (2017), in a review of prior studies, found that the skills possessed by leaders were among the most effective predictors of their success in leading various initiatives. Indeed, Zaccaro et al. (2015) found that measures of leadership skills were highly effective ($r \approx 0.40$) predictors of leadership performance over a 20-year period. Given these findings, our intent in the present effort is to identify the key skills leaders must possess to lead community engagement initiatives.

Oftentimes, leaders of successful community engagement efforts are seen as passionate, committed people. Based on these criteria, firms may ask an ill-prepared leader to address complex social innovation problems and lead community engagement efforts. The intent of the present effort is to highlight the set of skills leaders must possess to address social innovation problems inherent to community engagement efforts, and the importance of these skills, Moreover, these recommendations can help firms identify steps to develop leaders and equip them to solve these complex problems and lead successful community engagement projects.

Leadership Skills and Social Innovation

The term "skill" refers to the procedures people apply in acquiring and working with domain-specific knowledge to solve problems arising in a certain domain (Ericsson, 2009). People are assumed to acquire skills as a function of experience and feedback on performance as they work on problems arising in a certain domain (Ackerman, 1992). The growth of these skills is held to depend on more basic abilities as well as the strategies people employ, such as deliberative practice (Ericsson, Krampe, & Tesch-Römer, 1993) and self-reflection (Strange & Mumford, 2005), as they work on problems in this domain. As a result, people may acquire and apply numerous skills depending on the domain in which they are working. Thus, scholars speak of bench skills when describing scientific performance (Hodson, 2014) and expressive interpretation skills when describing musical performance (Hopyan, Dennis, Weksberg, & Cytrynbaum, 2001).

The impact of skills on performance in leadership roles was investigated by Mumford and his colleagues (Connelly, Gilbert, Zaccaro, Threlfall, Marks, & Mumford, 2000; Mumford, Marks, Connelly, Zaccaro, & Reiter-Palmon, 2000; Mumford, Zaccaro, Harding, Jacobs, & Fleishman, 2000). Broadly speaking, they argued that military officers and military leaders confront novel, dynamic, ill-defined problems, and as a result, creative thinking skills should prove especially critical to officer performance. Officer creative thinking skills were assessed through a modified "think aloud" protocol where officers read a problem scenario and were asked to respond to a set of probe questions intended to elicit application of creative thinking skills, such as problem definition, conceptual combination, and idea generation. Judges rated the effectiveness of skill application in response to these probes in a sample of 1,818 army officers ranging in grade from second lieutenant to full colonel. It was found that these skills were strongly ($r \approx 0.45$) related to measures of leader critical incident performance as well as citations awarded. Other research has shown that these skills develop as a function of both abilities (Vincent, Decker, & Mumford, 2002) and experience (Mumford, Marks et al., 2000). Moreover, these skills were found to predict performance, as reflected in being allowed to stay in an "up or out" system, over a 20-year period (Zaccaro et al., 2015), with prediction again proving powerful ($r \approx 0.40$).

These findings indicate that skills are an important determinant of performance in leadership roles (Bray, Campbell, & Grant, 1974). Leaders, however, fill many different roles, and because different types of problems are presented in these roles, different types of skills will be required. This point is of some importance because it, in turn, broaches a question that is fundamental to the present effort: What are the types of skills required by those asked to lead community engagement projects?

To answer this question, one must begin by first considering the nature of the problems presented to those asked to lead community engagement efforts. Perhaps the most obvious fact here is that the problems presented to those asked to lead community engagement efforts are inherently social in nature. Put differently, inter-actions of the firm – and multiple subsystems operating within the firm – with multiple stakeholders, who often do not have a direct investment in firm success, will be entailed in any problem presented (Friedman & Miles, 2006). Thus, the problems presented to leaders of community engagement efforts are inherently social.

Leaders of community engagement efforts, moreover, are typically embedded in the firm – although stakeholders may at times assume a leadership role in interaction with the firm. What should be recognized here, however, is that firms focus primarily on a socio-technical production or transformation process intended to produce a set of products or services for a certain market and market niche (Miles & Snow, 1986). As a result, community engagement initiatives will be outside the scope of routine operations. Put somewhat differently, the problems being presented to the leaders of a community engagement initiative will typically be novel.

Not only will these problems be novel, but multiple stakeholders and stake-holder groups with different needs and objectives will also be involved in any community engagement effort (Aslin & Brown, 2004; Weerts & Sandmann, 2010). The diversity of stakeholder concerns and interests, however, implies that the problems presented to the leaders of community engagement efforts will not only be novel, but will also be highly complex and inherently ill-defined or poorly structured. What should be recognized here, however, is complex, novel, ill-defined social problems – the type of problems presented to leaders of community engagement efforts – are inherently problems that call for social innovation (Marcy & Mumford, 2007; Mumford, 2002).

Some support for the notion that community engagement initiatives require leaders to solve or resolve social innovation problems has been provided by Mumford (2002). In this study, a qualitative analysis of ten significant social innovations formulated by Benjamin Franklin in colonial Philadelphia were exam-ined. Many, in fact most of these innovations – such as establishing volunteer fire departments, establishing the University of Pennsylvania, and establishing the free library – required involvement of multiple stakeholders in the community. What is clear is that Franklin's success in leading those community engagement initiatives was based on his ability to solve social innovation problems. Thus, in establishing the first non-sectarian university – the University of Pennsylvania – he ensured that all local religious groups sat on the university's founding board of directors.

Moreover, Franklin's ability to solve community engagement problems (problems requiring social innovation) seemed to be based on a complex set of skills. Not only did Franklin establish a broad, deep set of contacts in the community, but also he carefully analyzed both the causes of a manifest social problem and the constraints imposed on potential problem solutions. Additionally, he forecasted the effects of various actions that might be taken to resolve a problem – anticipating of both critical actions and critical needs. Furthermore, he sold his proposals through clever demonstration projects – projects that served as low-cost solutions to pressing needs of various constituencies. Put differently, Franklin's success in solving these social innovation problems with solutions all requiring community engagement appears to have been based on the following seven key skills: (1) networking skills; (2) causal analysis skills; (3) constraint analysis skills; (4) forecasting skill; (5) wisdom; (6) integrative skill; and (7) sales skill. In the following sections, we will examine in greater detail how each of these skills contributes to a leader's ability to solve the social innovation problems brought to the fore in any community engagement effort.

Figure 15.1 illustrates how these seven skills may relate to each other when solving social innovation problems. Networking skills allow the leader to establish followers and gather information to define the problem. Once the leader establishes followers and defines the problem, the leader must analyze key causes and constraints on the problem. A leader must then forecast the potential downstream consequences of these causes and constraints. It is then critical for the leader to manage differing interests of stakeholders involved in the community engagement initiative through wisdom. Using wisdom and integrative thinking skills, the leader must then utilize cases that are similar in causes and constraints to the social innovation problem in order to address the issue. Finally, the leader must have

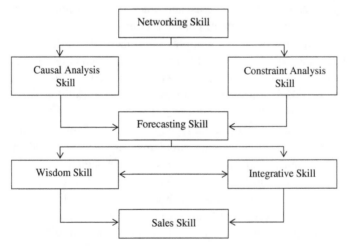

Figure 15.1 *Hypothesized relationships of the seven skills necessary for solving social innovation problems*

sales skills to gain support from key stakeholders, as implementing this community engagement project will require time and resources, often financial resources.

Networking Skills

A key skill likely to underlie leader performance in virtually all community engagement initiatives may be found in networking skill. Networking skill refers to the leader's capacity to establish a broad and deep set of contacts with a number of key stakeholder groups. The value of networking skills is nicely illustrated in the career of Jane Jacobs (Kanigel, 2016). Jacobs, well known for her work on city planning, also led a community engagement initiative intended to stop redevelopment of New York's west village. As Kanigel (2016) describes Jacob's activities during this period: "Jane's days and those of her friends grew thick with calls to make, letters to solicit, or write, hearings to attend, presentations to prepare, petitions to draw up, rallies to organize [. . .] The fight became so frantic we just disconnected the doorbell and left the door open at night so we could work and people could come and go" (p. 232).

Clearly, networking skills are critical to the leadership of community engagement efforts, in part because they help the leader establish a cadre of followers. These followers are necessary because leaders will not always have formal authority over each individual involved in the community, yet will need to lead them through the community engagement effort. With establishment of a cadre of followers, the leader not only builds support for the initiative at hand, but also acquires a group of people willing to invest time and effort in the community engagement initiative. Accordingly, one would expect that many of the behaviors commonly found to be critical to leadership performance in other domains – articulating a positive, emotionally engaging vision (Partlow, Mederios, & Mumford, 2015), effective planning and structuring of followers activities vis-à-vis this vision (Marta, Leritz, & Mumford, 2005), and positive interpersonal exchange with followers (Liden, Wayne, & Sparrowe, 2000) – would contribute to leadership of community engagement efforts.

With regard to leader network skills, however, it is important to recognize that networking serves a number of other functions for those leading community engagement initiatives. Perhaps the most important of these functions is that networking provides leaders with information – information bearing on the problem and information bearing on stakeholders. This need for active gathering of information in solving social innovation problems – problems of the sort confronting the leaders of community engagement initiatives – has been demonstrated in a study by Mumford, Baughman, Supinski, and Maher (1996).

In the Mumford et al. (1996) study, participants were asked to solve a set of social innovation problems – one set of problems involving public policy and the other set involving business leadership. Problem solutions were appraised by judges for quality and originality. Prior to preparing their problem solutions, however, participants were asked to work on another task. In this task, participants were presented with a set of six cards providing information bearing on another problem. These cards presented key facts, anomalies, diverse information, irrelevant information, etc. The time spent reading each card was recorded. It was found that those producing the highest-quality and most original solutions to these social innovation problems spent less time on irrelevant information and more time on key facts and anomalies that presented information inconsistent with these facts. Thus, leaders of community engagement efforts must not only seek key facts bearing on the problem and stakeholders to solve these social innovation problems, but also search for information that does not fit with the "known" facts.

Although it is important for leaders of community engagement initiatives to use networks and networking skills to gather information, information per se is of limited value. For people to act on information, the information obtained from networks must be understood. Understanding requires organizing obtained information with respect to relevant concepts or principles. Typically, these concepts are themselves organized in such a way as to articulate the key relationships among different concepts. Put differently, conceptual organizing structures reflect mental models used in understanding complex socio-technical systems (Day, Gronn, & Salas, 2004; Goldvard & Johnson-Laird, 2001; Rouse & Morris, 1986).

The impact of mental models on solving social innovation problems has been examined in a study by Mumford et al. (2012). In this study, participants were asked to formulate a plan for leading an experimental secondary school taking into account the needs of students, parents, and teachers. The plans provided were appraised by judges for quality, originality, and elegance. Prior to preparing these plans, however, participants were asked to complete a self-paced training program. This training program taught participants how to illustrate their mental models in terms of structural equations models. Participants were then asked to illustrate their mental model of the educational problem prior to preparing their problem solutions. Judges then evaluated attributes of the mental models provided, and these model attributes were correlated with appraisals of the quality, originality, and elegance of solutions to the social innovation problem. It was found that those producing the highest-quality, the most original, and the most elegant solutions had well-organized mental models that identified critical concepts and linkages of these critical concepts to key outcomes.

Of course, it takes time and experience to acquire key concepts and organize these concepts with respect to their impacts on multiple relevant outcomes (Connelly et al., 2000). Thus, as was the case for Jane Jacobs (Kanigel, 2016), one would expect to see a long-standing involvement with the kinds of social innovation problems calling for community engagement. As such, Jacobs had worked for many years on city planning and architectural issues in her role as a journalist. This real-world experience, moreover, will serve to provide leaders with the access to key stakeholder groups, and the leaders of these groups, needed to ensure the success of community engagement initiatives.

Causal Analysis

Communities represent complex, multifaceted social entities where any action taken may or may not have the intended effects. Indeed, the wrong action and the wrong time may make community engagement impossible. As a result, it seems plausible to argue that the leaders of community engagement efforts must carefully and thoroughly analyze key causes of the problem(s) at hand. This point is nicely illustrated in Mumford's (2002) analysis of Benjamin Franklin's establishment of volunteer fire departments – a clear case of community engagement. Franklin, as a newspaper publisher, had for some time been reporting on fire in colonial Philadelphia. Prior to establishing volunteer fire departments, however, he wrote an article on the causes of fires, noting many causes, including building construction (wood), chimney construction, lighting (candles), and zoning (house placement). Many of these causes could not be directly addressed. However, one key cause could be addressed: the lack of an organized response to fires. This observation, in turn, led him to establish volunteer fire companies, which downstream would provide a means for addressing many of the other causes of fires.

Some support for the impact of leaders' causal analysis skills in solving the kind of social innovation problems underlying community engagement has been provided in a series of studies by Mumford and his colleagues (Hester et al., 2012; Marcy & Mumford, 2007, 2010). In a study by Marcy and Mumford (2007), participants were asked to solve six social innovation problems – three drawn from the educational domain and three drawn from the business domain. Judges appraised the quality and originality of solutions to these social innovation problems, often problems (e.g., unionization) requiring community engagement. Prior to preparing these problem solutions, participants were asked to work through a set of self-paced instructional modules. These modules, seven in all, provided participants with strategies that would result in more effective causal analysis – think about changes that have large effects, think about causes that have direct effects, think about causes that work synergistically, and think about causes you can control. It was found that training these strategies resulted in the production of higher-quality and more original solutions to these social innovation problems. Thus, causal analysis skill does appear to contribute to the solution of the social innovation problems underlying community engagement. Moreover, it was found that casual analysis skills were especially valuable when participants approached the problems at hand in a more objective or more distant fashion. Thus, leaders of social engagement initiatives may need to be somewhat less affectively involved and more analytical than followers as they work on relevant problems.

In another study along these lines, Marcy and Mumford (2010) asked participants to work on a leadership simulation exercise. Here, they were to assume the role of a university president whose objective was to improve educational quality across the campus. Again, participants were asked to complete the self-paced instructional modules intended to improve leaders' causal analysis skills. Performance was assessed using the outcomes provided by this simulation exercise. It was found that training in causal analysis skills resulted in better game performance on this simulation exercise. In another study by Hester et al. (2012), participants were again trained in causal analysis skills. They were asked to prepare a plan for leading an experimental secondary school that would serve the needs of students, parents, and teachers. These plans were appraised by judges for quality, originality, and elegance.

Notably, however, participants were asked to illustrate their mental models prior to starting work on the problem. It was found that stronger effects of causal skills training on solution quality, originality, and elegance occurred when participants had available, and presumably employed, stronger mental models for understanding the problem at hand.

Apparently, causal analysis skills – skills employed with respect to viable mental models – contribute to a leader's ability to solve the kind of social innovation problems underlying community engagement. In this regard, however, it is important to recognize that leaders of community engagement efforts must actively seek to develop effective causal analysis skills. One way this might occur is by getting leaders to think about or reflect on their own personal experience as they work on these problems. Thus, Strange and Mumford (2005) found leaders' casual analysis skills become of greater value in solving social innovation problems when leaders actively reflect on their own past experience. Similarly, Mumford, Schultz, and Osburn (2002) have argued that when using cases – past experience – in causal analysis, it is of as much value for leaders to consider cases that failed as cases that proved successful.

Constraint Analysis

One of the most notable cases of community engagement in the twentieth century may be found in the civil rights movement (Hall, 2005). This movement required the engagement of multiple churches, universities, and students at these universities, as well as at least tacit support from the judiciary. Although few would dispute that community engagement was crucial to the success of the civil rights movement, its success was not assured. In part, the potential for failure may be traced to the extreme violence associated with race relations in the southern United States. The potential for violence imposed a significant, noteworthy constraint on the likely success of this movement, and it was a constraint Martin Luther King and his leadership cadre dealt with by expressly calling for non-violence among those participating in the civil rights movement. This policy is noteworthy in part because it helped manage a key constraint impinging on the success of this movement – potential violence by some whites – and it points to the possibility that constraints analysis skills may also be beneficial to those leading community engagement initiatives.

In fact, the available evidence indicates that constraint analysis skills contribute to peoples' ability to solve social innovation problems – problems of the sort confronting leaders of community engagement efforts. In one study along these lines, Medeiros, Partlow, and Mumford (2014) asked participants to formulate marketing campaigns for a new product – a high-energy root beer. Participants' marketing campaigns were appraised for quality, originality, and elegance. As participants worked on these campaigns, they received emails from their putative supervisor. These emails imposed constraints with respect to marketing fundamentals, themes, target environment, and/or objectives. It was found that induction of a balanced set of constraints resulted in the production of higher-quality, more original, and more elegant solutions, especially when participants were motivated. Thus, analysis of constraints may contribute to solving the kind of social innovation problems underlying community engagement initiatives.

Some support for this proposition has been provided in a more recent study by Medeiros, Steele, Watts, and Mumford (2017). The authors asked participants to formulate plans for a new, engaging restaurant chain. Constraints were induced at various points as participants worked on their plans, with the resulting plans being appraised for quality, originality, and elegance. The findings obtained indicated that constraint analysis was particularly important in initial definition of the problem. In another study, Peterson et al. (2013) asked participants to formulate a plan for leading an experimental secondary school that would serve the needs of students, parents, and teachers. The plans provided by participants were appraised for quality, originality, and elegance. Prior to preparing these plans, however, participants were provided with training in the management of resource constraints, system capability constraints, user skill constraints, and goal constraints. It was found that providing people with more effective strategies for constraint management resulted in the production of higher-quality, more original, and more elegant plans for leading this experimental secondary school.

The Peterson et al. (2013) study, of course, provides rather direct evidence indicating that constraint analysis skills contribute to solving the kind of social innovation problems underlying successful community engagement initiatives. As Onarheim and Biskjaer (2015) have pointed out, however, the relationship between constraints and social innovation may be rather complex – an observation supported by the findings of Medeiros, Partlow, and Mumford (2014). More specifically, imposition of certain constraints or too many constraints may inhibit problem-solving. On the other hand, defining problems with respect to a limited number of key critical constraints seems beneficial. Indeed, Martin Luther King's imposition on the civil rights movement of a non-violence constraint served not only to minimize risk to participants, but also to increase social support for the civil rights movement among the population in general and among other relevant constituencies, such as the federal judiciary.

Forecasting Skills

Of course, our foregoing observations imply leaders of community engagement projects must be able to forecast or anticipate the downstream implications of imposing constraints. Bearing in mind the point that a key to success in the entertainment industry is community or audience engagement. Gabler (2006), in describing Walt Disney's work in developing Disney World, nicely illustrates the importance of forecasting in work intended to engage others, noting, "The dream's wide open. There's nothing cut or dried about it. We would write our ideas out on squares of paper [. . .] comparing the planning of the park to the planning of the features, 'put them up on a board, and he'd come down in the afternoon and sit there and look at them and juggle them around.' These sessions would last anywhere from four hours to six hours to the entire day" (p. 495).

The need for extensive forecasting when others are involved in a project has been confirmed in studies of forecasting skill conducted by Byrne, Shipman, and Mumford (2010) and Shipman, Byrne, and Mumford (2010). In the Byrne, Shipman, and Mumford (2010) study, participants were asked to formulate a plan for marketing a new product, while in the Shipman, Byrne, and Mumford (2010) study, participants were asked to formulate a plan for leading an experimental secondary school that would serve the needs of students, parents, and teachers. In both studies, the resulting leadership plans were appraised for quality, originality, and elegance. As participants worked on these tasks, they received emails from a consulting firm "hired" to help them prepare the educational plan (in the Byrne, Shipman, and Mumford [2010] study) or from their supervisor, the vice president of sales, asking them to forecast the downstream implications of their plan (in the Shipman, Byrne, and Mumford [2010] study). These written forecasts were appraised by judges for 27 attributes (e.g., number of positive outcomes, number of negative outcomes, considering obstacles, considering resources). Subsequent factoring of these ratings yielded the following four dimensions: (1) extensiveness of forecasts; (2) time frame of forecasts; (3) forecasting resources; and (4) forecasting negative outcomes. When scores on these dimensions were correlated with appraisals of plan quality, originality, and elegance, it was found that forecasting extensiveness ($r \approx 0.40$) and forecasting over a longer time frame ($r \approx 0.20$) were strongly related to the quality, originality, and elegance of the plans produced. Thus, forecasting skill appears to contribute strongly to solving the kind of social innovation problems leaders must address when seeking community engagement.

In another study along these lines, Martin et al. (2011) asked business students to assume the role of manager of a retail store. After reading through background material, participants were asked to provide solutions to four problems arising in leading this store, all of which were social innovation problems, where forecasting or anticipating downstream consequences was assessed. Prior to starting work on these problems, however, participants were instructed to think about past cases that were successes or failures and to think about processes, outcomes, or both in these cases. It was found that thinking about past case successes with respect to processes or outcomes resulted in the best performance. Thus, forecasting appears to depend on successful experience, which allows leaders to project processes and outcomes. Put differently, leaders of community engagement efforts need a track record of success.

Not only do leaders need a track record of success to forecast effectively, they also need to stay objective. This point is illustrated in a study by Caughron and colleagues (2011). In this study, participants were asked to assume the role of a manager of a pharmaceutical company and provide solutions to four problems – again, all of which were social innovation problems. And again, forecasting or anticipating downstream consequences in problem solutions was assessed. Here, the scenarios were manipulated to induce a personal or organizational framing of the problems at hand, as well as feelings of personal control versus situational control. It was found that forecasting was most effective when people framed problems to the institution as opposed to personally. In fact, in a series of supplemental analyses, it was found that when forecasting was depersonalized, more critical issues and better issue organization resulted from forecasting. Apparently, those who lead community engagement initiatives must lead the organizations involved, putting aside their personal values and concerns.

Wisdom

Those who lead community engagement initiatives are confronted with many stakeholders with different interests, and leaders must navigate between these competing concerns. One implication of this statement is that those who lead community engagement initiatives must be able to balance competing interests. An illustration may be found in Theodore Hesburgh, president of the University of Notre Dame, during the student "revolts" of the 1960s (Padilla, 2005). "During this period, Notre Dame seemed to be consumed in controversy, here and everywhere students were trying to take over. And the toll was heavy [...] In typical Hesburgh style, he decided to write a statement setting forth clean principles of behavior alongside a cogent overview of the larger moral and ethical issues surrounding the controversy. His guiding principle he said was civility. But he wrote it carefully canvassing the university family – faculty, students, trustees, and alumni – about when exactly to draw that line" (Padilla, 2005, p. 154).

In fact, other scholars, such as McKenna, Rooney, and Boal (2009) and Sternberg (2001), have argued that those who hold leadership positions, including leadership positions in community engagement initiatives, must possess wisdom. Some rather compelling support for this proposition and the impact of wisdom on solving the sort of social innovation problems presented to leaders of community engagement initiatives has been provided in a series of studies by Connelly et al. (2000) and Mumford, Marks, Connelly, Zaccaro, and Reiter-Palmon (2000).

In these studies, 1,818 army officers ranging in grade from second lieutenant to full colonel were presented with a series of business social management problems drawn from Shorris (1981). In all of these problem scenarios, significant, emotionally evocative failure occurred. Participants were asked to provide a critical description of what they saw as the central mistake made by the protagonist in this situation and what they would have done in the situation. A panel of judges then appraised the responses to these questions with respect to key dimensions held to underlie wisdom in solving social innovation problems, including the following: (1) self-reflection; (2) self-objectivity; (3) judgment under uncertainty; (4) systems perception or systems awareness; (5) systems commitment; and (6) appraisal of the fit of solutions to the situation at hand.

In the Connelly et al. (2000) study, these appraisals of attributes of wise problem-solving were correlated with various indices of officer performance (e.g., medals won), but also with their performance in solving a set of social innovation problems of the sort presented to military leaders. It was found that leader wisdom was positively related not only to incidents of officer performance ($r \approx 0.25$), but also to performance in solving social innovation problems ($r \approx 0.40$). Moreover, in the Mumford, Marks et al. (2000) study, it was found that these attributes of wisdom grew as officers acquired both age and experience. Specifically, it was found that as officers moved into more senior positions as opposed to more junior positions, the strongest growth was observed in self-reflection, self-objectivity, judgment under uncertainty, and appraisal of the fit of solutions to the context at hand.

Frequently, we do not think of the leaders of community engagement initiatives as especially wise. However, the findings obtained in the Connelly et al. (2000) and Mumford, Marks et al. (2000) studies indicate that wisdom may, in fact, be crucial for solving the kind of social innovation problems presented to those leading community engagement initiatives. The Mumford, Marks et al. (2000) study reminds us, however, that experience obtained in working on relevant community engagement problems may be crucial in providing leaders with the objectivity, judgment, and appraisal skills needed to effectively solve social innovation problems. Moreover, growth of these skills with experience is likely to be prompted by reflection on one's own experience and the experiences of others in working on community engagement efforts. Put somewhat differently, the leaders of community engagement efforts must all be a bit of a historian.

Integrative Skills

For community engagement initiatives, leaders' wisdom may, in part, prove necessary due to the conflicting interests of different stakeholders – and leaders need to navigate these conflicts. Wisdom, however, may also be of some value because it contributes to a leader's ability to integrate the perspectives of different stakeholders in community engagement efforts. What should be recognized here is that integrative thinking skills on the part of leaders may be of some importance in their own right. In fact, Clark Kerr, in leading the University of California, provides an apt illustration of the need for integrative skills. "Clark Kerr's global approach to problems, perhaps as a result of his education as an institutional economist, enabled him to see connections among seemingly unrelated parts of the educational enterprise [...] unlike more sequential leaders, who tend to be convergent in their thinking, Kerr's ability to synthesize complex problems and to understand in a comprehensive way the 'big picture' explains to a notable degree the success of the University of California" (Padilla, 2005, p. 93).

In studies of innovation, this integrative skill is referred to as conceptual combination and reorganization, and the available evidence indicates that combination and reorganization skills in fact contribute to solving the kinds of social innovation problems presented to leaders of community engagement initiatives. Scott, Lonergan, and Mumford (2005) asked participants to assume the role of leader in a new, experimental secondary school, and they needed to formulate a plan for leading the school that would serve the needs of students, parents, and teaches. Judges appraised these plans for quality, originality, and elegance. Prior to working on these plans, participants were presented with cases drawn from the literature describing cooperative learning techniques or, alternatively, the concepts involved in these cases through reports produced by an advisory board. In addition to working with this material, participants were provided with worksheets that would encourage integrative thinking – for concepts, identify critical concepts, list similarities and differences among concepts, combine important concepts, and list new emergent features; for cases, identify critical case attributes, list case strengths and weaknesses, combine strengths, forecast outcomes, and adapt approaches. It was found that effective execution of these conceptual integration strategies, as apprised by judges, was positively related to the production ($r \approx 0.40$) of higher-quality, more original, and more elegant educational plans, with combinatory activities producing especially ($r \approx 0.50$) strong relationships. Other work by Mumford, Baughman, Maher, Costanza, and Supinski (1997) has also shown that these conceptual combination, or intellectual integration skills, contribute to solving social innovation problems.

The Scott, Lonergan, and Mumford (2005) study, however, has another noteworthy implication for those leading community engagement efforts. The number of cases and the number of concepts presented were manipulated in the Scott et al. (2005) study. It was found that when working with cases, higher-quality, more original, and more elegant solutions emerged when people worked with fewer, not more, cases in formulating their plans due to the complexity of case-based knowledge (Hammond, 1990). This finding is noteworthy because it suggests that leaders of community engagement efforts must spend time and resources in investigating and selecting the specific cases they will work with in leading community engagement efforts. What is of note here, however, is that these causes need not be superficially similar to the problem at hand. Rather, as noted by Mumford, Mecca, and Watts (2015), the cases used to provide a basis for integrative thinking should be those that show "deep-structure" similarity to the problem at hand – cases similar with respect to causes and constraints.

Sales Skills

Successful community engagement efforts, of course, require the support of key stakeholders. However, support is not simply a matter of saying the project is a good thing. Instead, time and resources – often tangible financial resources – will be needed from key stakeholders. These sales skills are nicely illustrated in Benjamin Franklin's role in founding the Philadelphia Hospital. The idea for the hospital came from a doctor, Thomas Bond. Franklin's involvement was primarily in building support for the institution. Although Franklin lent his reputation, connections, and publicity apparatus, the newspaper, the *Pennsylvania Gazette*, to the effort, his most significant contribution was primarily financial in nature. "Franklin persuaded the commonwealth's legislature, of which he was a member, to make available matching funds if local citizens provided subscriptions of a certain value within a given period. He used the goal of 'meeting the match' to stimulate subscriptions to the new hospital" (Mumford, 2002, p. 260). In fact, Franklin took particular personal pride in the innovative strategy of selling projects in such a way as to acquire the requisite financial support.

Of course, community engagement projects might be sold on many bases. For example, Mumford and Moertl (2003) have shown that many successful sales efforts are based on the execution and dissemination of successful pilot projects. Alternatively, leaders of successful community engagement efforts might seek to embed their efforts in the context of extant social norms, given people's tendency to embrace norm-consistent initiatives (Rodgers & Adhikarya, 1979). Still another technique that might be used to sell community engagement initiatives is to link the initiative to progress and a better future for specific stakeholder groups and/or the community as a whole, given the value people typically place on progress (Lasch, 1991).

Clearly, many techniques exist that the leaders of community engagement efforts must use to sell their initiatives. However, what our foregoing observations about Franklin remind us of is that leaders must think about who to sell initiatives to and how to sell these initiatives. Thus, interpersonal, persuasive skills are likely to play an important roles in community engagement initiatives. Much has been written of interpersonal persuasion (e.g., Center, Shomer, & Rodrigues, 1970; Fogg, 2008), which indicates the importance of attributes such as engagement, extraversion, empathy, concern, etc.

However, effective sales in community engagement initiatives require sales to sophisticated, thoughtful, and perhaps somewhat cynical stakeholder groups, and often the leaders of these stakeholder groups. Howell and Boies (2004) conducted a study of what allows people to "champion" or "not champion" innovative efforts in firms. Their findings indicate that successful sales of innovative efforts were based on understanding the firm's strategy and the contributions of the effort to the success of the firm in executing this strategy. Moreover, those who were able to "champion" new initiatives could "package" the idea in such a way that its value to the firm was evident. If one replaces the word "firm" with "stakeholders," the same conclusion seems to apply to those asked to lead community engagement efforts. What should be recognized here, however, is that effective sales to stakeholder strategy and effective packaging of ideas for stakeholders implies that leaders of community engagement initiatives must cultivate deep ties with relevant stakeholder groups to acquire the knowledge needed to sell ideas to strategy and package ideas in a way stakeholder groups are likely to find engaging.

Conclusions

Before turning to the broader conclusions flowing from the present effort, certain limitations should be noted. To begin, we have focused on how leaders of community engagement efforts solve the kinds of social innovation problems that provide a basis for successful community engagement initiatives. Here, it should be recognized that leaders do not act alone in solving these problems. Often, collectives (Friedrich, Vessey, Schuelke, Ruark, & Mumford, 2009) – different stakeholders operating together at different levels – are involved. Leaders, moreover, must enact problem solutions through followers. Thus, appropriate and effective leader behavior, such as transformational leadership (Bass & Avolio, 1990), positive leader–follower exchange (Graen & Uhl-Bien, 1995) and charisma (Shamir, House, & Arthur, 1993), may all contribute to successful leadership of community engagement initiatives.

Nonetheless, the qualitative, historic, and experimental evidence examined in the present effort does suggest that those asked to lead community engagement initiatives need certain skills – skills contributing to effective resolution of the social innovation problems presented to those leading community engagement initiatives. In the present effort, we have provided evidence that seven key skills are likely to be involved in leaders' solving of social innovation problems and thus effective leadership of community engagement initiatives. More specifically, we have argued leaders must possess the following: (1) networking skills; (2) causal analysis skills; (3) constraint analysis skills; (4) forecasting skills; (5) wisdom; (6) integrative skills; and (7) sales skills. At this juncture, however, this list of skills must be viewed as tentative. Future research may identify additional skills leaders need to address the kinds of social innovation problems presented in community engagement initiatives.

In addition, in the present effort, no evidence has been provided indicating which particular skills are more or less important in accounting for leader performance. Although prior research indicates leader skills have a critical influence on performance (Zaccaro et al., 2015), we do not at this juncture know exactly which skills are the most important. Moreover, it should be kept in mind that some skills are more important for some types of problems or work in certain areas or domains of community engagement than others (Mumford, Antes, Caughron, Connelly, & Beeler, 2010).

Finally, skills – procedural knowledge – are applied with respect to factual or declarative knowledge (Ericsson, 2009). In the present effort, little has been said about what type, amount, and nature of declarative knowledge leaders must acquire to allow for skilled performance in leading community engagement efforts. Future work intended to address this issue may be of some real importance given prior work (Scott, Lonergan, & Mumford, 2005) indicating that when and how these skills are applied depends on the nature of the knowledge being worked with.

Of course, all of these limitations point to some significant directions for future research. With this said, we believe the present effort provides a basis for future research along these lines. The qualitative, historic evidence obtained in studies examining the leaders of community engagement efforts – leaders such as Benjamin Franklin, Jane Jacobs, and Martin Luther King – along with the evidence garnered in various studies examining how people go about solving social innovation problems indicate that the following seven key skills will be needed by those asked to lead community engagement efforts: (1) networking skills; (2) causal analysis skills; (3) constraint analysis skills; (4) forecasting skills; (5) wisdom; (6) integrative skills; and (7) sales skills.

We repeat ourselves here quite intentionally because this list of skills is somewhat unique. On the one hand, we have complex, distinctly social skills – networking skills, sales skills, and wisdom – apparently contributing to effective leadership of community engagement initiatives. On the other hand, we have distinctly cognitive skills – causal analysis skills, constraint analysis skills, forecasting skills, and integrative skills – that also appear to contribute to effective leadership of community engagement initiatives. It is a rare individual who can acquire and synthesize such a complex skill set – a skill set needed to solve the kinds of social innovation problems presented to leaders of community engagement efforts.

Not only is this skill set complex, it is not consistent with our stereotype of those who lead community engagement initiatives. We see leaders of community engagement initiative as passionate, committed people perhaps. More centrally, however, is that those who lead community engagement initiatives must be thoughtful, analytical people who can think through the many complex issues that arise as firms seek community engagement. The problem here, however, is that due to stereotypes, firms may ask the "wrong" people to lead community engagement initiatives. The resulting lack of requisite leadership skills may, in part, account for the failure of many of those efforts.

Just as important, however, is that firms seeking effective community engagement efforts must see leadership as a serious issue and systematically seek to develop in leaders the skills they will need. These skills – networking skills, causal analysis skills, and forecasting skills – are all complex skills, and the development of such skills requires experience – both "real-world" experience and effective training. Identification of key skills needed by leaders provides the context needed to begin formulating the kind of systematic, multi-stage development programs firms must use to prepare people to lead community engagement initiatives.

In other words, it is critical for firms to pay attention to the developmental needs of their leaders with respect to the context of the problems they are asked to solve. Development of each of these seven key skills – networking skills, causal analysis skills, constraint analysis skills, forecasting skills, wisdom, integrative skills, and sales skills – in leaders addressing social innovation problems is necessary for a community engagement effort to be successful. Through real-world experience and training programs, firms can develop these skills and provide leaders with case-based knowledge for achieving a successful community engagement initiative. We hope the present effort provides an impetus and structure for future work along these lines.

Acknowledgments

We would like to thank Judy Van Doorn, Rich Marcy, Amanda Shipman, Cristina Byrne, and Kelsey Medeiros for their contributions to the present effort.

References

Ackerman, P. L. (1992). Predicting individual differences in complex skill acquisition: Dynamics of ability determinants. *Journal of Applied Psychology, 77*, 598–614.

Algesheimer, R., Dholakia, U. M., & Herrmann, A. (2005). The social influence of brand community: Evidence from European car clubs. *Journal of Marketing, 69*, 19–34.

Aslin, H. & Brown, V. (2004). *Towards whole of community engagement: A practical toolkit.* Canberra: Murray-Darling Basin Commission.

Bass, B. M., & Avolio, B. J. (1990). The implications of transactional and transformational leadership for individual, team, and organizational development. *Research in Organizational Change and Development, 4*, 231–272.

Bowen, F., Newenham-Kahindi, A., & Herremans, I. (2010). When suits meet roots: The antecedents and consequences of community engagement strategy. *Journal of Business Ethics, 95*, 297–318.

Bray, D. W., Campbell, R. J., & Grant, D. L. (1974). *Formative years in business: A long-term AT&T study of managerial lives.* New York: Wiley.

Byrne, C. L., Shipman, A. S., & Mumford, M. D. (2010). The effects of forecasting on creative problem-solving: An experimental study. *Creativity Research Journal, 22*, 119–138.

Cartwright, S., & Holmes, N. (2006). The meaning of work: The challenge of regaining employee engagement and reducing cynicism. *Human Resource Management Review, 16*, 199–208.

Caughron, J. J., Antes, A. L., Stenmark, C. K. et al. (2011). Sensemaking strategies for ethical decision making. *Ethics & Behavior, 21*, 351–366.

Centers, R., Shomer, R. W., & Rodrigues, A. (1970). A field experiment in interpersonal persuasion using authoritative influence. *Journal of Personality, 38*, 392–403.

Connelly, M. S., Gilbert, J. A., Zaccaro, S. J. et al. (2000). Exploring the relationship of leadership skills and knowledge to leader performance. *The Leadership Quarterly, 11*, 65–86.

Day, D. V., Gronn, P., & Salas, E. (2004). Leadership capacity in teams. *The Leadership Quarterly, 15*, 857–880.

Driscoll, A. (2008). Carnegie's community-engagement classification: Intentions and insights. *Change: The Magazine of Higher Learning, 40*, 38–41.

Ericsson, K. A. (2009). *Development of professional expertise: Toward measurement of expert performance and design of optimal learning environments.* Cambridge: Cambridge University Press.

Ericsson, K. A., Krampe, R. T., & Tesch-Römer, C. (1993). The role of deliberate practice in the acquisition of expert performance. *Psychological Review, 100*, 363–406.

Finkelstein, S., & Hambrick, D. C. (1990). Top-management-team tenure and organizational outcomes: The moderating role of managerial discretion. *Administrative Science Quarterly, 35*, 484–503.

Fleishman, E. A., & Harris, E. F. (1962). Patterns of leadership behavior related to employee grievances and turnover. *Personnel Psychology, 15*, 43–56.

Fogg, B. J. (2008). Mass interpersonal persuasion: An early view of a new phenomenon. In H. Oinas-Kukkonen, P. Hasle, M. Harjumaa, K. Segerståhl, & P. Øhrstrøm (Eds.), *Persuasive technology* (pp. 23–34). Berlin: Springer.

Friedman, A. L., & Miles, S. (2006). *Stakeholders: Theory and practice.* Oxford: Oxford University Press.

Friedrich, T. L., Vessey, W. B., Schuelke, M. J., Ruark, G. A., & Mumford, M. D. (2009). A framework for understanding collective leadership: The selective utilization of leader and team expertise within networks. *The Leadership Quarterly, 20*, 933–958.

Gabler, N. (2006) *Walt Disney: The triumph of the American imagination*. New York: Knopf.

Goldvarg, E., & Johnson-Laird, P. N. (2001). Naive causality: A mental model theory of causal meaning and reasoning. *Cognitive Science, 25*, 565–610.

Graen, G. B., & Uhl-Bien, M. (1995). Relationship-based approach to leadership: Development of leader–member exchange (LMX) theory of leadership over 25 years: Applying a multi-level multi-domain perspective. *The Leadership Quarterly, 6*, 219–247.

Hall, J. D. (2005). The long civil rights movement and the political uses of the past. *The Journal of American History, 91*, 1233–1263.

Hammond, K. J. (1990). Case-based planning: A framework for planning from experience. *Cognitive Science, 14*, 385–443.

Head, B. W. (2007). Community engagement: Participation on whose terms? *Australian Journal of Political Science, 42*, 441–454.

Hester, K. S., Robledo, I. C., Barrett, J. D. et al. (2012). Causal analysis to enhance creative problem-solving: Performance and effects on mental models. *Creativity Research Journal, 24*, 115–133.

Hodson, R. (2014). *Workers' earnings and corporate economic structure*. New York: Academic Press.

Hopyan, T., Dennis, M., Weksberg, R., & Cytrynbaum, C. (2001). Music skills and the expressive interpretation of music in children with Williams–Beuren syndrome: Pitch, rhythm, melodic imagery, phrasing, and musical affect. *Child Neuropsychology, 7*, 42–53.

Howell, J. M., & Boies, K. (2004). Champions of technological innovation: The influence of contextual knowledge, role orientation, idea generation, and idea promotion on champion emergence. *The Leadership Quarterly, 15*, 123–143.

Hu, J., & Liden, R. C. (2011). Antecedents of team potency and team effectiveness: An examination of goal and process clarity and servant leadership. *Journal of Applied Psychology, 96*, 851–862.

Kanigel, R. (2016). *Eyes on the street: The life of Jane Jacobs*. New York: Knopf.

Lasch, C. (1991). *The true and only heaven: Progress and its critics*. New York: Norton & Company.

Lee, D., Kim, H. S., & Kim, J. K. (2011). The impact of online brand community type on consumer's community engagement behaviors: Consumer-created vs. marketer-created online brand community in online social-networking web sites. *Cyberpsychology, Behavior, and Social Networking, 14*, 59–63.

Liden, R. C., Wayne, S. J., & Sparrowe, R. T. (2000). An examination of the mediating role of psychological empowerment on the relations between the job, interpersonal relationships, and work outcomes. *Journal of Applied Psychology, 85*, 407–416.

Lord, R. G., De Vader, C. L., & Alliger, G. M. (1986). A meta-analysis of the relation between personality traits and leadership perceptions: An application of validity generalization procedures. *Journal of Applied Psychology, 71*, 402–410.

Marcy, R. T., & Mumford, M. D. (2007). Social innovation: Enhancing creative performance through causal analysis. *Creativity Research Journal, 19*, 123–140.

Marcy, R. T., & Mumford, M. D. (2010). Leader cognition: Improving leader performance through causal analysis. *The Leadership Quarterly, 21*, 1–19.

Marta, S., Leritz, L. E., & Mumford, M. D. (2005). Leadership skills and the group performance: Situational demands, behavioral requirements, and planning. *The Leadership Quarterly, 16*, 97–120.

Martin, L. E., Stenmark, C. K., Thiel, C. E. et al. (2011). The influence of temporal orientation and affective frame on use of ethical decision-making strategies. *Ethics & Behavior, 21*, 127–146.

McKenna, B., Rooney, D., & Boal, K. B. (2009). Wisdom principles as a meta-theoretical basis for evaluating leadership. *The Leadership Quarterly, 20*, 177–190.

Medeiros, K. E., Partlow, P. J., & Mumford, M. D. (2014). Not too much, not too little: The influence of constraints on creative problem solving. *Psychology of Aesthetics, Creativity, and the Arts, 8*, 198–210.

Medeiros, K. E., Steele, L. M., Watts, L. L., & Mumford, M. D. (2017). Timing is everything: Examining the role of constraints throughout the creative process. *Psychology of Aesthetics, Creativity, and the Arts*. Epub ahead of print. DOI: 10.1037/aca0000148.

Miles, R. E., & Snow, C. C. (1986). Organizations: New concepts for new forms. *California Management Review, 28*, 62–73.

Mumford, M. D. (2002) Social innovation: Ten cases from Benjamin Franklin. *Creativity Research Journal, 14*, 253–266.

Mumford, M. D., Antes, A. L., Caughron, J. J., Connelly, S., & Beeler, C. (2010). Cross-field differences in creative problem-solving skills: A comparison of health, biological, and social sciences. *Creativity Research Journal, 22*, 14–26.

Mumford, M. D., Baughman, W. A., Maher, M. A., Costanza, D. P., & Supinski, E. P. (1997). Process-based measures of creative problem-solving skills: IV. Category combination. *Creativity Research Journal, 10*, 59–71.

Mumford, M. D., Baughman, W. A., Supinski, E. P., & Maher, M. A. (1996). Process-based measures of creative problem-solving skills: II. Information encoding. *Creativity Research Journal, 9*, 77–88.

Mumford, M. D., Hester, K. S., Robledo, I. C. et al. (2012). Mental models and creative problem-solving: The relationship of objective and subjective model attributes. *Creativity Research Journal, 24*, 311–330.

Mumford, M. D., Marks, M. A., Connelly, M. S., Zaccaro, S. J., & Reiter-Palmon, R. (2000). Development of leadership skills: Experience and timing. *The Leadership Quarterly, 11*, 87–114.

Mumford, M. D., Mecca, J. T., & Watts, L. L. (2015). Planning processes: Relevant cognitive operations. In M. D. Mumford & M. Frese (Eds.), *Organizational planning: The psychology of performance* (pp. 9–30). New York: Routledge, Taylor & Francis.

Mumford, M. D., & Moertl, P. (2003) Cases of social innovation: Lessons from two innovations in the 20th century. *Creativity Research Journal, 15*, 261–266.

Mumford, M. D., Schultz, R. A., & Osburn, H. K. (2002). Planning in organizations: Performance as a multi-level phenomenon. In F. J. Yammarino & F. Dansereau (Eds.), *Research in multi-level issues: The many faces of multi-level issues* (pp. 3–36). Oxford: Elsevier.

Mumford, M. D., Todd, E. M., Higgs, C., & McIntosh, T. (2017). Cognitive skills and leadership performance: The nine critical skills. *The Leadership Quarterly, 28*, 24–39.

Mumford, M. D., Zaccaro, S. J., Harding, F. D., Jacobs, T. O., & Fleishman, E. A. (2000). Leadership skills for a changing world: Solving complex social problems. *The Leadership Quarterly, 11*, 11–35.

Noe, R. A., Hollenbeck, J. R., Gerhart, B., & Wright, P. M. (2006). *Human resource management: Gaining a competitive advantage*. New York: McGraw Hill Education.

Onarheim, B., & Biskjaer, M. M. (2015). Balancing constraints and the sweet spot as coming topics for creativity research. In L. J. Ball (Ed.), *Creativity in design: Understanding, capturing, supporting* (pp. 1–19). Copenhagen: DTU.

Padilla, A. (2005). *Portraits in leadership: Six extraordinary university presidents*. Westport, CT: Praeger Press and the American Council on Education.

Partlow, P. J., Medeiros, K. E., & Mumford, M. D. (2015). Leader cognition in vision formation: Simplicity and negativity. *The Leadership Quarterly, 26*, 448–469.

Peterson, D. R., Barrett, J. D., Hester, K. S. et al. (2013). Teaching people to manage constraints: Effects on creative problem-solving. *Creativity Research Journal, 25*, 335–347.

Redell, T., & Woolcock, G. (2004). From consultation to participatory governance? A critical review of citizen engagement strategies in Queensland. *The Australian Journal of Public Administration, 63*, 75–87.

Rodgers, E. M., & Adhikarya, R. (1979). Diffusion of innovations: Up to date review and commentary. In D. Nimmo (Ed.), *Communications Yearbook 3* (pp. 67–81). New Brunswick, NJ: Transaction.

Rouse, W. B., & Morris, N. M. (1986). On looking into the black box: Prospects and limits in the search for mental models. *Psychological Bulletin, 100*, 349–363.

Schultz, W. (2006). Behavioral theories and the neurophysiology of reward. *Annual Review Psychology, 57*, 87–115.

Scott, G. M., Lonergan, D. C., & Mumford, M. D. (2005). Conceptual combination: Alternative knowledge structures, alternative heuristics. *Creativity Research Journal, 17*, 79–98.

Shamir, B., House, R. S., & Arthur, M. B. (1993). The motivating effects of charismatic leadership: A self-concept based theory. *Organizational Science, 4*, 577–594.

Shipman, A. S., Byrne, C. L., & Mumford, M. D. (2010). Leader vision formation and forecasting: The effects of forecasting extent, resources, and timeframe. *The Leadership Quarterly, 21*, 439–456.

Shorris, E. (1981). *The oppressed middle: politics of middle management: Scenes from corporate life*. New York: Anchor Press/Doubleday.

Sternberg, R. J. (2001). What is the common thread of creativity? Its dialectical relation to intelligence and wisdom. *American Psychologist, 56*, 360–362.

Strange, J. M., & Mumford, M. D. (2005). The origins of vision: Effects of reflection, models, and analysis. *The Leadership Quarterly, 16*, 121–148.

Vincent, A. S., Decker, B. P., & Mumford, M. D. (2002). Divergent thinking, intelligence, and expertise: A test of alternative models. *Creativity Research Journal, 14*, 163–178.

Watson, D. (2007). *Managing civic and community engagement*. New York: McGraw-Hill Education.

Weerts, D. J., & Sandmann, L. R. (2010). Community engagement and boundary-spanning roles at research universities. *The Journal of Higher Education, 81*, 632–657.

Yukl, G. (2011). *Leadership in organizations*. Saddle River, NJ: Prentice-Hall.

Zaccaro, S. J., Connelly, S., Repchick, K. M. et al. (2015). The influence of higher order cognitive capacities on leader organizational continuance and retention: The mediating role of developmental experiences. *The Leadership Quarterly, 26*, 342–358.

16 Community-Based Partnerships for Capacity Building

Stakeholder Engagement through Governance and Leadership

Chelsea R. Willness

> [...] becoming more responsible and better attuned to public interests is not some-
> thing that can be imposed effectively from the outside. It is a process that hinges on
> the willingness and ability of leadership and faculty to effect such change – and
> overcome the lines of resistance that may be encountered in the process
>
> (Murillo & Vallentin, 2016, p. 744).

Recently, there has been increasing interest in renewing and strengthening civic capacity. Education for citizenship was once seen as essential for developing a well-informed and critically thinking society (e.g., Lynton, 1991), and while that idea may have faded over time, it is now reemerging (Morse, 1989). The increasing societal pressure for educational institutions to be more accountable, responsible, and responsive to their stakeholders has strengthened this call for a reevaluation of the role of higher education in fostering engagement and citizenship. Scholars have called for business schools in particular to be more responsive to the communities in which they operate (e.g., Godfrey, Illes, & Berry, 2005; Rubin & Dierdorff, 2009) and have questioned their contribution to society (Bennis & O'Toole, 2005; Murillo & Vallentin, 2016; Pfeffer & Fong, 2002). More broadly, the higher education system overall is often viewed as a mechanism through which students should develop concerns for citizenship (DiPadova-Stocks, 2005) and social justice (Westheimer & Kahne, 2004). Thus, colleges and universities have devoted time to reevaluating their civic functions (Ehrlich, 2000). As part of this movement, there has also been a growing emphasis on community-engaged learning as one way to address the pressures for educational institutions to engage their stakeholders while simultaneously benefiting students.

This chapter focuses on a model of community-engaged learning that is grounded in the literature on stakeholder engagement and principles of organizational governance. The overarching goal is to create a learning infrastructure that safeguards reciprocity, trust, and voice in mutually beneficial partnerships. As a case study, I describe the Governance and Leadership Development Practicum, a senior undergraduate course that substantiates these values. This type of model is one attempt to answer the recent call to "tear down the walls between our academic institutions and the world around us" (Brown, 2014, p. 507).

Faculty members or instructors can use this chapter to inform or inspire the development of applied courses focused on governance and/or leadership development, as well as community-based experiential courses on any number of topics. Administrators and curriculum development specialists can use it as a basis for adopting a stakeholder engagement approach to course or program development, to design community-engaged learning opportunities, and to inform institutional policy and governance practices regarding curriculum development. Although this chapter cites in particular the literature on business and management education, the contributions are not restricted to this context; rather, the course development process and stakeholder engagement principles described herein could be leveraged in many other disciplines.

Community-Engaged Learning

Definition and Description

> Teaching methods that involve students in active learning, such as undergraduate research, service learning, and workplace internships should be viewed as among the most powerful of teaching procedures, if the teaching goal is lasting learning that can be used to shape students' lives and the world
>
> (Kellogg Commission on the Future of State and Land-Grant Universities, 1999, p. 19).

Community-engaged learning is a method of teaching and learning that is designed to engage students with community partners in mutually beneficial curricular experiences (GMCTL, 2017), subsumed within which are approaches such as service learning and community internships. These approaches are intended to create opportunities for students to meaningfully contribute to the broader community while applying the knowledge and skills they acquire during their academic programs. Ideally, in pedagogies like service learning, a fundamental principle is reciprocity (e.g., Dostillo et al., 2012; Elson, Johns, & Petrie, 2007), whereby all participants (i.e., institutions, students, and communities) are at the same time learners, providers, and recipients – "we should all both teach and learn" (Lowery et al., 2006, p. 53). While sharing some characteristics with other forms of applied or experiential learning, such as internships or cooperative education programs, community-engaged learning is distinct in its core principles of reflection (Godfrey & Grasso, 2009) and, ideally, reciprocity (Dostillo et al., 2012; Godfrey, 2009).

Community-engaged learning is considered a high-impact practice. Past research has cited the benefits to students of community-engaged learning, such as personal and community learning outcomes (Bartel, Saavedra, & Van Dyne, 2001), positive impacts on their communication, teamwork, problem-solving, and professional skills (Madsen & Turnbull, 2006), empathy (Wilson, 2011), moral development (Boss, 1994; Gorman, 1994), sense of social responsibility (Kendrick, 1996), and tolerance for diversity (Dumas, 2002). Students also acquire applied experience in their chosen field (e.g., McLaughlin, 2010), develop interpersonal and other practical skills (Caspersz & Olaru, 2017), and are better able to transform theory into practice, which increases their confidence in their professional and personal skills (McClam et al., 2008). Students who participate in service-learning programs have reported increased intention to seek careers focused on underserved populations (Evans et al.,

2017) and indicated that they highly valued the opportunity to experience personal growth and enhance their leadership skills, among many other benefits (Caspersz & Olaru, 2017).

Although the literature on community benefits is comparatively limited (Castaneda et al., 2017; Srinivas, Meenan, Drogin, & DePrince, 2015), some studies have demonstrated benefits to the community as a result of approaches like service learning. For instance, positive outcomes include improvements to students' energy and new ideas (Brisbin & Hunter, 2003), community participants' perceptions of social support (Castaneda et al., 2017), and stronger university connections (Gray et al., 1998). Additionally, research has observed increases in students' civic engagement (making a difference and being motivated to make a difference in communities; Muturi & Mwangi, 2013), which should positively impact community and society over time.

Although community-based approaches can offer substantive benefits, there have also been challenges in implementing this type of teaching and learning (Clifford & Petrescu, 2012). For instance, it can be both difficult and resource intensive for faculty who implement courses that involve external stakeholders like community partners, particularly in terms of planning, risk, and relationship management (Lenton et al., 2014). Perhaps most relevant to the current chapter, scholars have also pointed out the lack of attention paid to community outcomes and the lack of community voice in the process of engaged teaching and learning (e.g., Stoecker & Tryon, 2009). In other words, the design and implementation of community-engaged learning often takes into account student and/or university needs and objectives more so than those of the community partners.

How Governance Informs Stakeholder Engagement and Stakeholder Engagement Informs Governance

Stakeholder Engagement and Organizations

Stakeholder theory is broadly based on the principle that all organizations affect and are affected by various constituents, and that relationships with these stakeholders can impact both processes and outcomes for all involved (Jones & Wicks, 1999). Adopting a long-range viewpoint and recognizing and incorporating additional or different perspectives (i.e., those of stakeholders) can contribute to the longevity of the organization (Foster & Jonker, 2005). Scholars have asserted that the stakeholder engagement practices that have been successfully applied in organizations – such as ensuring meaningful two-way communication (e.g., Foster & Jonker, 2005) and an inclusive approach to identifying stakeholders (e.g., Cummings & Doh, 2000) – can also be applied in a management education context (Willness & Bruni-Bossio, 2015). Indeed, Samuelson (2009) advocates for applying a stakeholder theory lens to business education in order to place organizational success within the context of "all affected parties – the community, workers and managers, suppliers, the environment, and shareholders" (p. 14). A stakeholder theory approach might then mitigate the criticism and scrutiny leveled at business schools (noted earlier) for their role in perpetuating "bottom line" thinking and other ills, and increase the likelihood that business outcomes are situated within the broader social and environmental context.

That said, management education (like other educational fields) presents unique conditions that are arguably different from typical organizational or business environments, such as a priority to provide a supportive environment for learning, exploration, and the exchange of ideas. The mission of educational institutions is therefore primarily directed at increasing and/or creating knowledge (research) and transferring this knowledge to others (teaching). The result is often a narrow or biased focus on internal stakeholders such as students and faculty, while other stakeholders, like potential employers and the broader community, are not equally considered. Thus, in a conventional educational environment, the input, perspectives, and voices of important stakeholders or stakeholder groups may be excluded (Willness & Bruni-Bossio, 2017).

Curriculum or program development approaches that adopt an incomplete consideration of the stakeholder landscape may constrain the potential for creativity, innovation, and sustainability (Willness & Bruni-Bossio, 2015) – much like inadequate stakeholder engagement limits value creation and competitive advantage in organizations (e.g., Cummings & Doh, 2000). Particularly in the context of community-engaged learning, insufficient stakeholder engagement also increases the risk of unintended (or even negative) consequences for community partners, such as time and resource burdens and unfulfilled or unclear objectives (Eyler & Giles, 1999). Some scholars have debated whether approaches like service learning actually "serve" communities at all (Stoecker & Tryon, 2009). Without adequate consultation and involvement of partners throughout the process, their goals, needs, and boundaries may not be sufficiently understood or met (Willness & Bruni-Bossio, 2017). Conversely, involvement of stakeholders in the process of curriculum development and implementation should better inform and assist the instructor in ensuring successful outcomes while enhancing responsiveness to those stakeholders (including students, businesses, and the broader community). Although there are important differences between educational institutions versus corporations and other types of organizations, they are compelled by a common principle: stakeholders matter in the success of any strategy (Willness & Bruni-Bossio, 2015).

Stakeholder Engagement in Education and Curriculum

Curriculum development (i.e., courses or programs) is typically the realm of a "lone" faculty member serving as a subject-matter expert, who then decides which elements of knowledge or content are important, the means through which the knowledge should be delivered to students, and how student learning outcomes should be evaluated. Owens and Stupans (2007, p. 2) assert that "curriculum design and implementation is often seen as the domain of academics ... who may consult with students or the profession ... but without further involvement in determining decisions about future directions." There is generally little to no stakeholder involvement in this process, with the possible exception of requiring some form of collegial approval for the final course syllabus.

Indeed, there are few, if any, examples in the published literature of broad stakeholder engagement models in business (or other) education. Nonetheless, there is precedent to suggest that implementing some form of stakeholder engagement is beneficial. For instance, scholars have described positive outcomes as a result of consulting industry professionals in directing the curriculum of an information technology program (Kamal & Henson, 2010) or incorporating industry experts to oversee students' applied team projects (Gilbreath et al., 2001). Both of these examples demonstrate the value of engaging another stakeholder perspective in addition to that of the course instructor. Owens and Stupans (2007) describe stakeholder consultation in the curriculum process as follows: involvement in research dissemination about pharmacy students' experiential placements, which primarily involved a feedback loop with some of the groups affected by the program. These groups could provide input on a report, and the authors concluded that stakeholders were indeed able to influence or improve aspects of the students' placements.

While they are positive and creative examples of consultation and involvement, these (and other) cases do not provide a holistic model of stakeholder engagement (i.e., multiple stakeholders), defined in this context as "those who affect or are affected by a particular course or program" (Willness & Bruni-Bossio, 2017, p. 150). Rather, stakeholder inclusion is typically incomplete, and there is a risk of unrealized value creation and inadequate consideration of voice.

There have been provocative arguments for the involvement of practitioners and business leaders in management education, perhaps in large part due to critiques leveled at business schools for not providing students with the skills required by potential employers (Bennis & O'Toole, 2005). Such arguments are provocative – and even controversial – partly because fundamental challenges regarding a fulsome stakeholder engagement approach are *who gets to decide what* and what is the distribution of power and decision-making authority. In an educational context, this could be interpreted as relinquishing control (or at least the perception thereof) by instructors or faculty members.

Stakeholder Governance

To address some of these issues (aspiring for broader stakeholder engagement while recognizing the tensions around who has ultimate decision authority, etc.), I will describe an inclusive and broadly applicable model first proposed by Willness and Bruni-Bossio (2015), which is grounded in the theory, research, and practice of stakeholder engagement and principles of organizational governance. This "stakeholder governance model" draws upon a stakeholder paradigm (e.g., Gilbreath et al., 2001; Heinfeldt & Wolf, 1998; Payne, Whitfield, & Flynn, 2002) and stakeholder engagement literature (e.g., Swanson, 2013), whereby curriculum development and assessment strategies incorporate the perspectives, expertise, and needs of various stakeholders to maximize benefits for all parties. Further, the "typical" stakeholder paradigm is expanded insofar as the proposed process is not limited to considerations of external stakeholders alone; instead, the engagement of internal stakeholders is also integral to building a foundation that is supported by – and responsive to – the operational systems, political climate, and culture of the institution. The integration of organizational governance principles ensures that the instructor (or curriculum developer, administrator, etc.) can manage the issue of "who gets to decide what."

Integrating Principles of Governance. Organizational governance provides a structure through which to balance control and engagement and offers a foundation for achieving greater stakeholder involvement while mitigating power and decision concerns. In traditional governance models, a board of directors is elected by members or shareholders to provide oversight and to guide strategy and the performance appraisal of the executive director (Finkelstein & Mooney, 2003; Hendry & Kiel, 2004). Our model addresses these core governance functions (i.e., oversight, strategy, and monitoring), but it flips the "power" dynamic somewhat in that the instructor appoints a stakeholder board with an advisory function – not a governing function per se – to provide strategy and oversight from multiple perspectives. An advisory board (versus a fiduciary board) does not involve the relinquishment of control, but rather leverages these multiple perspectives to create stronger strategies, provide mentorship, and gain access to additional skills and knowledge (Shaw, 2014).

In articulating our model, we drew upon constituent or representative forms of board governance. Constituent or representative governance emphasizes the relationships between the board of directors and the constituents that it represents, with a focus on active engagement of a wide-ranging set of stakeholders for the purpose of decision-making (e.g., Bradshaw, Hayday, & Armstrong, 2007). In a constituent board, directors are representing their constituencies (i.e., stakeholder groups), and our model retains this focus. Where it differs, again, is that the decision authority rests with the instructor, like an advisory board. The instructor is the critical linchpin (and arguably the only one ultimately held accountable for student learning outcomes) and is empowered in the process of creation, innovation, structure, and engagement. The model does parallel classic governance configurations, however, such that the instructor occupies a role that mirrors an executive director of a nonprofit organization – a role that typically deals with the external environment including funders, regulators, project management, stakeholder relations, and implementing strategy (Miller-Milleson, 2003).

A Stakeholder-Governance Model. Integrating all of the principles described above, the stakeholder-governance model (Willness & Bruni-Bossio, 2015) was manifested in the creation of a stakeholder advisory council for a community-based experiential course in nonprofit governance. The advisory council included individuals representing multiple *internal and external* stakeholders, including community organizations, faculty peers (particularly those who held expertise in fields that were relevant to the focus of the course, such as governance and strategy), and current and former students. The inclusion of former students at once ensures ongoing engagement of alumni while leveraging the firsthand experience of students who have taken the particular course. Although the professor maintains the ultimate decision-making role, the advisory council provides ongoing insights and feedback about curriculum and course structure ideas, offers networking and advocacy supports, ensures voices for their representative memberships, and other functions.

During the initial development phases of the course, the advisory council was particularly active and was consulted regularly for their input and to ensure that each of the structural and content elements were meeting stakeholder needs and objectives in order to ensure mutual benefit and that unintended consequences could be mitigated. As in Purdy and Lawless (2012), advisory council members also served as champions of the course, sharing the information among their networks and providing advocacy beyond the efforts of the core course instructor/developer. This exhibited another benefit of an inclusive stakeholder strategy, such that community, students, faculty, and administrators had voice in the process, and buy-in and support were strong. Accountability to the stakeholders via the advisory council was provided in the form of regular reporting, as well as a fairly comprehensive annual report (see "Best Practices" section for further discussion of annual reports).

Stakeholder Engagement in Implementation. There are numerous benefits to the instructor, students, and other stakeholders as a result of adopting a stakeholder governance model, such as an advisory council. However, these individuals are not generally involved in the day-to-day implementation of curriculum, community or organizational placements, or students' project work. Another element of deep stakeholder engagement in service learning or community-engaged learning where placements, internships, or extensive projects are involved would be the integration of a community mentorship component. Whereas the stakeholder governance model is perhaps more broadly generalizable, incorporating an ongoing mentorship component offers additional engagement, learning and development, and opportunities for beneficial, co-created outcomes. While not the focus of this chapter per se, the close involvement of community and organizational leaders (typically board members, board chairs, or executive directors) as mentors is a distinguishing feature of the case study, as discussed next.

Case Example: The Governance and Leadership Development Practicum

As an illustration of the model and principles described above, this section will describe a case example of a course called the Governance and Leadership Development Practicum (GLDP), for which the author is the developer and core professor (but, as I emphasize in the description to follow, I view this course and its outcomes as a "team effort" involving purposeful and meaningful stakeholder engagement and partnership). Following the description of the course itself, I provide recommendations in the form of my key takeaways after multiple successful cohort completions, and I suggest best practices for developing and implementing stakeholder engagement – both in terms of advisory functions and course participation.

GLDP Overview

The GLDP is a senior undergraduate course administered in our business school that pairs students with community-based nonprofit boards of directors for an eight-month (i.e., an academic year) placement. Each student has a designated mentor who is a member of the board. The students acquire relevant knowledge and training through a series of interactive seminars on topics including the fundamentals of governance, risk management, strategy, leadership, and board composition, so that they can contribute as participating (but non-voting) members of the board, rather than passive observers. The seminar series engages a team of expert faculty and community partners as co-facilitators with the core professor, or as guest lecturers. In order to facilitate a more meaningful relationship between students and their mentor/organization and to allow students to participate in as many board meetings, events, and activities as possible (which benefits both the students and the boards), the GLDP is a three-credit course fulfilled across two semesters, or about eight months.

Course Development and Rationale

Rationale. There were several value propositions that the course offered to its multiple stakeholders, and each of these was a consideration in the design and implementation. In terms of students, the goal was to provide them with an exceptional community-engaged learning opportunity and mentored exposure to elements of organizational structures and leadership and – equally important – to contribute to leadership sustainability and capacity building in the broader community. The impetus for focusing on governance came about at least partly because having an understanding of the principles of governance is particularly relevant for graduates of business and management education programs. Governance is essential knowledge for individuals in nearly all organizational contexts, regardless of whether those organizations are considered for-profit or nonprofit, and regardless of industry or sector. In spite of this, dedicated governance courses are not commonly included in the formal curricula of many business schools, and undergraduate nonprofit governance courses are featured at only "a handful of universities" (Purdy & Lawless, 2012, p. 12). Even where governance training is available, another challenge exists: most undergraduate business students have little to no "real-world" experience with governance and therefore have little upon which to anchor any theoretical or conceptual knowledge they might gain from classroom-based learning. Governance, like leadership (and, in many ways, as a form of leadership), is difficult to learn without practice or application (Bruni-Bossio & Willness, 2015). In addition to these learning outcomes, the focus of the GLDP course on nonprofit governance in particular also fosters greater understanding among students with respect to different sectors in the economy and different business models (including nonprofits and cooperatives) and a stronger connection to community.

Beyond the benefits for student training, offering a practicum course in nonprofit governance was motivated by a desire to build governance and leadership capacity in the nonprofit sector. Speaking from experience, there are many strong, well-run organizations in our community and region, as would likely be the case elsewhere, and there are some smaller, newer, or less experienced boards whose members lack formal governance training or knowledge or who are under-resourced in many respects. Across the spectrum of specific governance functioning, most organizations express their desire to engage younger generations and new and energetic volunteers and leaders, and to refresh their directors' professional development and knowledge of best practices. In some cases, boards are functioning largely at an operational level without strong governance structures, procedures, or capabilities. Participation in the course as a partner board can offer guidance and support as the board moves toward greater governance functioning.

In terms of the university and the business school within which the course is offered, the GLDP complements the strategic goals and directly aligns with the institutional priorities of community engagement, experiential learning, and student leadership. The course demonstrates acting on the institution's espoused values. As stated above, one of the expressed goals of the GLDP is to provide mutually beneficial outcomes for both students and community-based and nonprofit organizations. Thus, the value proposition to both student and community stakeholders is building capacity. Community-based organizations not only have the opportunity to acquire energetic new board members who have been exposed to the fundamental principles of governance, strategy, leadership, etc.; they also gain a contributor with a basis of relevant business knowledge, skills, and abilities that will enable them to actively participate and contribute to the board and its mandate. For students, as soon-to-be business school graduates, they can apply the suite of the knowledge, skills, and abilities they have learned throughout their degree in the "real-world" context of organizational complexity, while also having the opportunity to contribute to the communities in which they live and work.

Development Process. Several initial conversations were held with key stakeholders and interested parties to evaluate whether the idea resonated and there was a perceived need for such a course. During this process, individuals were identified who were ideally suited for and motivated to be involved in the advisory council that would provide stakeholder input, oversight, and feedback for the design and implementation of the course. Members of the founding advisory council included the following: two faculty peers from other departments who also had extensive subject-matter expertise in governance and community engagement; a senior manager/director of the United Way for the municipal area; one current student from the business school and one current student from another academic unit; one former student, who was also involved in nonprofit organizations and social entrepreneurship; and a graduate student with an interest and expertise in community engagement and pedagogy. In subsequent years, two GLDP alumni were added to the advisory council.

Course Structure

A complete description of the course mechanics is beyond the scope and focus of this chapter. However, some of the most relevant elements are described here.

Participants and Partners. The course is designed for fourth-year undergraduate business students. There are no set prerequisites, other than having completed a minimum number of credits toward their degree – roughly equivalent to fourth-year standing – so that students have acquired enough discipline-specific knowledge and skills, as well as maturity and competence, to benefit from this type of course. This approach also increases the likelihood that the students will be comfortable in this type of self-directed and community-based platform, and it increases their potential for meaningful contribution to their partner organization (e.g., through discipline-specific knowledge and skills, such as accounting or human resources). Elements of the rationale for focusing on business students are: (1) governance is an essential but often overlooked component of business and organizations; (2) business students typically have desirable skills and knowledge for nonprofit boards, such as finance or human resources; and (3) the course is administered within our business school and has very restricted enrollment in terms of size, so accommodating students from other colleges would be challenging. However, at the time of writing, there is a student in the course from a science-based degree program who is passionate about business and entrepreneurship, so we are exploring the inclusion of students from other academic backgrounds. Among the many benefits would be a diversity of perspectives within the classroom component, such as seminars and discussions.

Students must apply for permission to register, which includes submitting a statement of interest, résumé, and transcript to the course professor (and see below for a discussion of selection best practices). Criteria include some evidence of community involvement (past experience such as volunteering or intended interest) and a minimum 70 percent overall average grade, which indicates an adequate basis in business skills and knowledge as well as work ethic and maturity. These characteristics are also assessed in a face-to-face interview by the course professor. Lastly, all applications are vetted by a panel of three reviewers – the course professor and two members of the advisory council. In the inaugural year of the course, there were 17 applications and 12 accepted students (with one subsequently withdrawing from school due to health issues, for a total of 11 registered students). In the second year, there were 15 applications and 10 accepted students. Now in its fourth year, the ratio continues to be similar.

The partner boards are also required to apply in order to ensure an appropriate fit for both parties. In order to be eligible to participate, the board and executive director (ED) of the organization must all be aware and in favor of participation and must commit to providing a designated mentor from the board to pair with the student. A representative of the board, typically the board chair or ED, submits a brief application form to the course professor, which is evaluated in terms of fit for the course context and whether there is an appropriate student match. Board applications are likewise vetted by a panel of two to three reviewers – the professor and up to two members of the advisory council. Each year, the partner boards are associated with nonprofit organizations of various sizes and mandates, ranging from large, well-established organizations to small, community-based organizations.

Course Deliverables. The course culminates in several outcomes, including individual reflection assignments and an applied deliverable (like a project) that will contribute to the organization and its governance. All students' deliverables are defined in cooperation with their mentor and board; in other words, the focus, process, and outcomes are co-created between all stakeholders (with ongoing assistance from the professor regarding issues such as scope, quality control, and risk). The deliverable is designed to be something of real value to the board in addition to fostering the student's learning process. To date, the outcomes have been quite successful and many high-quality, useful deliverables have been produced for the partner boards, such as:

> *Deliverable example 1.* Several students have created board orientation manuals, which are fairly extensive documents that include information about the organization and its mission, the board and its members, key activities and goals for the coming year(s), and cross-referencing with policies and bylaws. The students' work often features engaging visuals and electronic formats that enable easier use by the board members, as well as easier updating over time. The boards indicated that these documents could be used immediately.

> *Deliverable example 2.* One student created an approachable and well-researched guidebook to assist the board as it moved from primarily an operational function to a governance function. The guidebook was organized as a "Top 5," and included numerous supplemental resources, web links, templates, and timelines. The student also outlined the main committees that should be created to ensure effective functioning of this board, including step-by-step instructions for setting up and implementing the committee structures. The board implemented or applied all of these resources in the following year.

> *Deliverable example 3.* Another student developed a customized board skills matrix. She researched best practices in the governance and human resources literatures in order to develop a working prototype. She then interviewed key individuals to ensure that the needed attributes were represented. She created an online interface for the board members to complete the matrix and made adjustments so that the tool could be used by the board for multiple purposes including recruiting, development, and engagement. The board skills matrix was well received and the local chapter indicated that they would be presenting it to the national board for potential implementation at that level.

Implementation. Because the course is three credit units but runs across two four-month semesters (our courses are usually three credits for one semester), and in recognition of the time that students will spend attending board meetings or with their mentor off campus, the class does not meet every week. The seminar series occupies six three-hour class blocks, five of which occur in the fall semester so that students acquire as much knowledge and training as possible early on. Class discussions (with no curriculum or assigned content, only open-ended discussion between the student cohort and the professor) occur roughly every third week. In between, the professor holds office hours during the usual class time so that students can "check in" briefly to ask questions or provide confirmation that the placement is going well. The delivery of seminars often involves guest experts such as faculty colleagues, business professionals (e.g., a lawyer or accountant who practices in nonprofit and/or corporate governance issues), and others, which is well-received by students and adds richness and a variety of perspectives to the content delivery.

Further to the descriptions above, I am happy to share materials such as the course syllabus, and I encourage interested readers to contact me with requests or questions. Readers are also referred to Purdy and Lawless (2012) for another model of course design that is described in some detail, which appears to have developed in parallel with but independent of the GLDP described herein. There are several notable differences that comprise some of the unique contributions and innovations of the GLDP, and there is little duplication in terms of the insights provided in this chapter. A few examples include: the duration of the GLDP course is a full academic year; the students' assignments and deliverables are quite different (both in terms of what is required and how they are created/defined with the board partners); and the GLDP follows a different selection process and criteria for boards and for students. Perhaps most importantly, while Purdy and Lawless (2012) engage a steering committee to assist with networking and board recruitment, they do not adopt a full stakeholder engagement or stakeholder governance approach as described in this chapter. However, I would recommend that readers consult Purdy and Lawless (2012), who provide an excellent account of one experiential course model that is complementary and distinct in several ways from the GLDP.

Lessons Learned

Resource Intensity

As noted above, there are about 15 applications per year so far, with 10–11 students accepted. The manageable size range, in terms of pedagogy and implementation logistics, is likely 10–15 students, thus the 10–11 registrations to date have been ideal. However, in terms of resources and time invested, the course is quite intensive for such a small group. Recruitment and planning begins in March for the subsequent September launch each year in order to promote the course to students before the second semester is completed and many students depart for the summer. Board recruitment occurs throughout the summer months and is significantly facilitated by having extensive contacts and networks in the business and nonprofit community – it would likely be even more time-consuming for a new instructor or an instructor who is new to a particular community. Beyond the individual instructor, it may be a difficult case to make for administrators in terms of the implications of having a very small seminar course in the curriculum – for instance, it affects teaching allocations (e.g., there are approximately 10–12 students in this section instead of the usual 40–50), budget considerations (i.e., tuition and registration numbers), and scheduling (i.e., the course operates across two semesters but only "counts" as three credits).

Student Recruitment

Students are recruited through a few different channels, including promotions in the weekly e-newsletter sent to all students in the college, posters, a Facebook page, and, perhaps most importantly, word of mouth from students who have taken (or are taking) the course. These means have been generally successful, yielding adequate application numbers. However, there have been a few challenges to student recruitment that have been identified. First, the course is necessarily two semesters given the pedagogical model, but students (and the professor) receive three credits, which is more typical of a one-semester course (our school does not have six-credit courses). To compensate for this, we do not meet as a class every week, and seminar days are distributed across a longer period of time. However, this may still be a deterrent to some students, and it can also be complicated for students who participate in the cooperative education (i.e., work-term) option at our college, which runs from January to August. Second, whereas in-depth experiential learning courses – those in which students partner with "real" organizations and businesses – were once a novelty, there are now several such courses in our school. This is a success in terms of the exceptional applied learning opportunities that are available to our students, but it is likely that only so many of these courses can be taken by any one student at any one time. Third, "governance" is a relatively unfamiliar term and idea to most undergraduates – when explained as being on a board, etc., many students indicate that this is desirable and attractive, but if just looking at a course listing, they may not really understand what the course is about. Lastly, the course is still relatively new (compared to most other program offerings) and therefore awareness building and promotion is ongoing.

Best Practices

Stakeholder Engagement

Advisory Council. The advisory council is described elsewhere in this chapter, but I emphasize here that it has been a "best practice" for stakeholder engagement with significant success. The advisory council provided extensive insights from a wide variety of perspectives, advocated for and championed the course in its early development and implementation phases, and provided legitimacy in building initial community partnerships. Following the principles of stakeholder governance, the council ensured that affected constituents (i.e., students, faculty, community organizations, etc.) had voice and could facilitate mutual benefit and reciprocity in the model. Importantly, the advisory council has an *advisory* function, not a fiduciary or governing function, and therefore the decision-making authority (along with the accountability) ultimately remains with the instructor.

The advisory council should remain in place for the duration of the academic year and, ideally, across multiple years. This provides continuity, retention of institutional memory/knowledge, and ongoing assistance from informed, experienced advisors.

Terms might be rotated, as would happen in an organization's board or advisory group, where some portion of the council changes over in a given year, but these positions alternate so that there are always some experienced members. The exact composition of such an advisory council (which individuals representing which stakeholder groups) would depend on one's own resource needs, as well as the particular academic and political context.

I recognize that members of the advisory council dedicate (volunteer) time and effort to this process, again for a relatively small number of students each year; nonetheless, my perception is that they do so willingly because they believe in the vision and purpose of this course and its benefits for both students and the community (I would assert the same of the guest lecturers and other partners, who have participated enthusiastically even over multiple years).

Annual Reports. As alluded to above, the role of the advisory council is partly one of oversight and also accountability to stakeholders. As part of this, annual reports have been offered as a way of reporting on the outcomes of the course each year. Topics include aggregate demographic statistics of the student cohort (e.g., academic major, gender, year of study), listing the partner boards and mentors, challenges that were experienced (e.g., in the first year, there were some difficulties with understanding the expectations of the deliverable/project), planned changes for the upcoming year, etc. In addition to offering an accountability structure to the advisory council and other stakeholders, these reports have also proven useful for promotion and information purposes, such as providing them to incoming groups of students and mentors.

Recognition. The board partners, and especially the mentors, should be recognized for their contributions – the mentor role is critical to the success of the course and ensuring students have a positive experience. In our case, the guest faculty and professionals also volunteer their time to contribute to the success of the course and should be recognized. Ways that we have accomplished this include having a year-end event (e.g., a wine and cheese celebration) to showcase some of our community-engaged learning courses and highlight the clients, partners, and students' accomplishments; formal letters of thanks; and recognition in the annual reports.

Selection Processes

Screening Both Students and Board Placements. Not everyone is a fit for this type of course, whether it be students or boards. Well-defined criteria and careful selection are recommended, and these practices have been essential for risk mitigation. For instance, in order to be successful in the course, students need to have good judgment and maturity. Boards need to provide an environment of safety and openness and commit to being responsive in their communication (particularly the mentor, who is the key conduit for the student and professor). This type of course is high stakes in terms of reputation, quality control, and risk. Ask the tough questions in advance. Additionally, the use of diffused decision-making (i.e., using a panel to evaluate applications) in the selection process helps with perceptions of fairness and objectivity, as well as providing additional due diligence and protection for the professor.

Matching. The first priority for matching students with boards has been to capitalize on students' individual interests and passions within the nonprofit sector, which was derived from insights provided by student members of the original advisory council. Although the overarching philosophy is to achieve balanced, mutual benefit through the partnerships in this course, matching the student with a board based on the student's preferences and areas of interest has been a driver of success. This leverages their passion and intrinsic motivation, as well as their willingness to invest time and effort even at times when the placement might be challenging or time-consuming. It also increases the likelihood that the student will remain engaged with the organization and/or the board in the future (although this is not a required outcome of the course, it is certainly desirable) and generally have a positive experience. From there, I match based on particular skills that the board might be seeking, such as finance or human resources (although most senior business students have a well-rounded basis in all areas and need not be majors/specialists in most cases). Sometimes there are also specific requirements that the board might have – for instance, an organization that operates a women's shelter might require a female practicum student.

In order to recruit the appropriate board partners, I first recruit the incoming class of students – this means starting to prepare for the course in March for the forthcoming September start date in order to access the students prior to the summer break. Once the student recruitment is complete, I circulate a short survey that asks them to rank eight different areas of the nonprofit sector (e.g., animal services, community development, public health, arts and culture, etc.) and to list the names of any specific organizations they are passionate about. I am clear, however, that their preferences are not always possible to accommodate and that I use the survey information as a guide to the extent possible. Generally, even when organizations/ boards are approached without prior contact or knowledge of the program, they are eager to learn more and most are enthusiastic about participating unless circumstances (e.g., extensive board turnover or upheaval) prevent them from doing so in a given year. As noted above, the boards must also apply to participate, which allows a chance to vet the placement further, even if there is a match in principle based on student interests.

Format and Delivery

As the core course professor, I strive to create an environment of "supported autonomy," wherein students can develop confidence, self-efficacy, and self-leadership. They manage their board and mentor relationships almost completely independently (the context and parameters of which are defined and discussed with all parties at the outset), but to do so they need to establish a good knowledge foundation fairly quickly and they need a supportive guide and community within which to grow. The materials and format are designed to create these conditions.

Applied, Evidence-Based Materials. There is no textbook for this course. Rather, there is a custom readings list composed of current applied content from well-regarded, publicly available sources such as Imagine Canada, BoardSource, and others. There are also some academic articles (i.e., published research in peer-reviewed journals), but even these are not typically "theory-heavy" choices. The focus is on practical, evidence-based content that students can readily apply to their practicum experience and use immediately for knowledge and skill building. This also puts them in a position to engage in the language of the board more quickly and to have in-depth discussions in class and with their mentors.

Seminars, Not Lectures. The seminar series (typically five seminars in the first semester and one in the second semester) are carried out using mixed methods. Most seminars involve the presentation of material to the students by experts in the respective fields (e.g., faculty, community leaders, lawyers, and auditors), including governance, strategy, risk, and board composition and diversity. This is either followed by or interspersed with in-depth discussion, applied exercises and active practice, or simulations (for an example designed specifically for this course, see Bruni-Bossio & Willness, 2015).

Class Discussion. On meeting days that alternate with the seminars, the class meets as a group with the professor for a discussion session, as noted earlier. These sessions have increased in number since the first iteration of the course, following student feedback that they desired more time together and found these discussion sessions extremely valuable. What has emerged each year is an organic, authentic learning community among the students where they learn from each other's experiences (particularly given their own fairly diverse backgrounds), share in their successes and challenges, and provide mentorship and support. We observe strict confidentiality rules (in addition to the confidentiality commitments to the partner boards, which are respected) and treat our classroom as a place of safety and trust.

Setting Expectations. Related to this, we observe good governance ourselves by enacting intellectual property and confidentiality agreements, codes of conduct (classroom and board contexts), and ethics. In all ways, we endeavor to "practice what we preach" in providing experiential learning in governance and stakeholder engagement. Additional expectations include responsiveness and availability – for instance, in interactions with the mentors (by both parties) and attendance at board and committee meetings. The professor, too, commits to these principles and does not restrict interactions to "usual" office or business hours. Related to the previous description of safety and trust, another important expectation is utmost respect for others.

Conclusions

This chapter highlights an effort to meaningfully engage stakeholders in a community-engaged learning course. The approach is grounded in a stakeholder paradigm in which curriculum development and implementation strategies incorporate the perspectives, expertise, and needs of various stakeholders to maximize benefits for all parties. The "typical" stakeholder frame is expanded beyond external constituents to also encompass the importance of involving internal stakeholders, such as students and faculty peers or administrators. Principles of organizational governance are integrated in a "stakeholder governance" model that can mitigate the tensions between stakeholder input, voice, and oversight against the relinquishment of decision-making authority. A case study of the GLDP course illustrated how these elements were manifested in the creation of a stakeholder advisory council, as well as an integrated mentorship model that substantively involved community partners throughout the duration of the course.

There are several considerations for this type of model. First, and most apparent, is that a stakeholder governance model (or the mentorship component) will not be practical or even necessary for many types of courses – the most appropriate context is intended to be community-engaged learning, or other courses that involve business or organizational partners, extensive applied project work, or internships. Second, the application of representative or constituent governance structures has its advantages in offering broad stakeholder involvement and diverse perspectives and insights. However, one limitation of a representative model is the extent to which any one representative can be assumed to "speak for" his/her members. For instance, does one student share the perspective of – and therefore represent – *all* students? Practically speaking, it would not be feasible to have numerous representatives from each stakeholder group included on a single advisory council (as one example), which would be unwieldy and, in all likelihood, counterproductive. If representativeness is a concern, perhaps conducting focus groups is an alternative approach for gathering a more in-depth account of a stakeholder group's needs, goals, and input.

References

Bartel, C. A., Saavedra, R., & Van Dyne, L. (2001). Design conditions for learning in community service contexts. *Journal of Organizational Behavior, 22*, 367–385.

Bennis, W. G., & O'Toole, J. (2005). How business schools lost their way. *Harvard Business Review, 2005*, 96–104.

Boss, J. A. (1994). The effect of community service on the moral development of college ethics students. *Journal of Moral Development, 23*, 183–198.

Bradshaw, P., Hayday, B., & Armstrong, R. (2007). Non-profit governance models: Problems and prospects. *The Innovation Journal: The Public Sector Innovation Journal, 12*, 5.

Brisbin, R. A., & Hunter, S. (2003). Community leaders' perceptions of university and college efforts to encourage civic engagement. *The Review of Higher Education, 26*, 467–486.

Brown, K. G. (2014). From the editors: Themes, thanks, and thoughts on the future. *Academy of Management Learning & Education, 13*, 505–509.

Bruni-Bossio, V., & Willness, C.R. (2016). The "Kobayashi-Maru" meeting: High fidelity experiential learning. *Journal of Management Education, 40*, 619–647.

Caspersz, D., & Olaru, D. (2017). The value of service-learning: The student perspective. *Studies in Higher Education, 42,* 685–700.

Castaneda, G., Islam, S., Stetten, N., Black, E., & Blue, A. (2017). What's in it for me? Perspectives from community participants in an interprofessional service learning program. *Journal of Interprofessional Education & Practice, 6,* 15–21.

Clifford, D., & Petrescu, C. (2012). The keys to university–community engagement sustainability. *Nonprofit Management & Leadership, 23,* 77–91.

Cummings, J. L., & Doh, J. P. (2000). Identifying who matters: Mapping key players in multiple environments. *California Management Review, 42,* 83–104.

DiPadova-Stocks, L. N. (2005). Two major concerns about service-learning: What if we don't do it? And what if we do? *Academy of Management Learning & Education, 4,* 345–353.

Dostillo, L. D., Brackmann, S. M., Edwards, K. E., Harrison, B., Kliewer, B. W., & Clayton, P. H. (2012). Reciprocity: Saying what we mean and meaning what we say. *Michigan Journal of Community Service Learning, 19,* 17–32.

Dumas, C. (2002). Community-based service learning: Does it have a role in management education? *International Journal of Value Based Management, 15,* 249–264.

Ehrlich, T. (2000). *Civic responsibility and higher education.* Westport, CT: Oryx Press.

Elson, D., Johns, L., & Petrie, J. T. (2007). Jumpstart's service-learning initiative: Enhanced outcomes for at-risk children. In S. Billig & S. Gelmon (Eds.), *From passion to objectivity: International and cross-disciplinary perspectives on service-learning research* (pp. 65–87). Charlotte, NC: Information Age.

Eyler, J., & Giles, D. E., Jr. (1999). *Where's the learning in service-learning?* San Francisco, CA: Jossey-Bass.

Evans, D. V., Krasin, B., Brown, K., Dobie, S., & Kost, A. (2017). Student perceptions about benefits from an extracurricular curriculum: A qualitative study of the underserved pathway. *Peer-Reviewed Reports in Medical Education Research, 1,* 13.

Finkelstein, S., & Mooney, A. C. (2003). Not the usual suspects: How to use board process to make boards better. *Academy of Management Executive, 17,* 101–113.

Foster, D., & Jonker, J. (2005). Stakeholder relationships: The dialogue of engagement. *Corporate Governance, 5,* 51–57.

Gilbreath, B, Manning, M. R., Burchett, O., Wieters, C. D., Wright, C. R., & Powers, T. L. (2001). Using management advisory boards in the classroom. *Journal of Management Education, 25,* 32–53.

GMCTL (2017). *Community-engaged learning.* Gwenna Moss Centre for Teaching & Learning, University of Saskatchewan. Retrieved from https://teaching.usask.ca/articles/community-engaged-learning.php.

Godfrey, P. C. (2009). A moral argument for service-learning in management education. In P. C. Godfrey & E. T. Grasso (Eds.), *Working for the common good: Concepts and models for service-learning in management* (pp. 21–42). Sterling, VA: Stylus.

Godfrey, P. C., & Grasso, E. T. (2009). Introduction. In P. C. Godfrey & E. T. Grasso (Eds.), *Working for the common good: Concepts and models for service-learning in management* (pp. 1–10). Sterling, VA: Stylus.

Godfrey, P. C., Illes, L. M., & Berry, F. C. (2005). Creating breadth in business education through service learning. *Academy of Management Learning & Education, 4,* 309–323.

Gorman, M. (1994). Service experience and the moral development of college students. *Religious Education, 89,* 422–431.

Gray, M. J., Ondaatje, E. H., Fricker, R., Campbell, N., Rosenblatt, K., Geschwind, S., ... Klein, S. P. (1998). *Coupling service and learning in higher education. The Final Report of the Evaluation of the Learn and Serve America, Higher Education Program*. Washington, DC: Corporation for National and Community Service.

Heinfeldt, J., & Wolf, F. (1998). Re-engineering the business curriculum: A stakeholder paradigm. *Journal of Education for Business, 73*, 198–201.

Hendry, K., & Kiel, G. C. (2004). The role of the board in firm strategy: Integrating agency and organizational control perspectives. *Corporate Governance, 12*, 500–520.

Jones, T. M., & Wicks, A. C. (1999). Convergent stakeholder theory. *Academy of Management Review, 24*, 206–221.

Kamal, M., & Henson, K. (2010). The role of advisory board in developing market sustainable IT curriculum. *The Journal of American Academy of Business, 15*, 168–173.

Kellogg Commission on the Future of State and Land-Grant Universities (1999). *Returning to our roots: The engaged institution*. Washington, DC: National Association of State Universities and Land-Grant Colleges.

Kendrick, J. R. (1996). Outcomes of service-learning in an introduction to sociology course. *Michigan Journal of Community Service Learning, 2*, 72–81.

Lenton, R., Sidhu, R., Kaur, S., Conrad, M., Kennedy, B., Munro, Y., & Smith, R. (2014). *Community service learning and community-based learning as approaches to enhancing University service learning*. Toronto: Higher Education Quality Council of Ontario.

Lowery, D., May, D. L., Duchane, K. A., Coulter-Kern, R., Bryant, D., Morris, P. V., & Bellner, M. (2006). A logic model for service-learning: Tensions and issues for further consideration. *Michigan Journal of Community Service Learning, 12*(2), 47–60.

Lynton, E. A. (1991). New concepts of professional expertise: Liberal learning as part of career-oriented education. *The Journal of General Education, 40*, 11–23.

Madsen, S. R., & Turnbull, O. (2006). Academic service learning experiences of compensation and benefits course students. *Journal of Management Education, 30*, 724–742.

McClam, T., Diambra, J. F., Burton, B., Fuss, A., & Fudge, D. L. (2008). An analysis of a service-learning project: Students' expectations, concerns, and reflections. *Journal of Experiential Education, 30*, 236–249.

McLaughlin, E. (2010). The "real-world" experience: Students' perspectives on service-learning projects. *American Journal of Business Education, 3*, 109–117.

Miller-Milleson, J. (2003). Understanding the behavior of nonprofit boards of directors: A theory-based approach. *Nonprofit and Voluntary Sector Quarterly, 32*, 521–44.

Morse, S. W. (1989). *Renewing civic capacity: Preparing college students for service and citizenship. ASHE–ERIC higher education report*. Washington, DC: Office of Educational Research & Improvement.

Murillo, D., & Vallentin, S. (2016). The business school's right to operate: Responsibilization and resistance. *Journal of Business Ethics, 136*, 743–757.

Muturi, N., & Mwangi, S. (2013). Students' expectations and motivation for service-learning in public relations. *Journalism & Mass Communication Educator, 68*, 387–408.

Owen, S., & Stupans, I. (2007). Experiential placements: Dissemination and stakeholder engagement for curriculum planning action to prepare future pharmacy professionals. *Journal of Learning Design, 3*, 1–10.

Payne, S. L., Whitfield, J. M., & Flynn, J. A. (2002). Assessing the business capstone course through a method based on the SOTL and the stakeholder process. *Journal of Education for Business, 78*, 69–74.

Pfeffer, J., & Fong, C. T. (2002). The end of business schools? Less success than meets the eye. *Academy of Management Learning & Education, 1,* 78–95.

Purdy, J. M., & Lawless, J. (2012). Learning about governance through nonprofit board service. *Journal of Management Education, 36,* 33–65.

Rubin, R. S., & Dierdorff, E. C. (2009). How relevant is the MBA? Assessing the alignment of required curricula and required managerial competencies. *Academy of Management Learning and Education, 8,* 208–223.

Samuelson, J. (2009). Business education for the 21st century. In P. C. Godfrey & E. T. Grasso (Eds.), *Working for the common good: Concepts and models for service-learning in management* (pp. 11–20). Sterling, VA: Stylus.

Shaw, D. (2014). The use and value of advisory boards. *Private Company Director.* Retrieved from www.privatecompanydirector.com/index.php?/features/the-use-and-value-of-advisory-boards.

Srinivas, T., Meenan, C. E., Drogin, E., & DePrince, A. P. (2015). Development of the community impact scale measuring community organization perceptions of partnership benefits and costs. *Michigan Journal of Community Service Learning, 21,* 5–21.

Stoecker, R., & Tryon, E. A. (2009). *The unheard voices: Community organizations and service learning.* Philadelphia, PA: Temple University Press.

Swanson, L. (2013). A strategic engagement framework for nonprofits. *Nonprofit Management & Leadership, 23,* 303–323.

Westheimer, J., & Kahne, J. (2004). What kind of citizen? The politics of educating for democracy. *American Educational Research Journal, 41,* 237–269.

Willness, C. R., & Bruni-Bossio, V. (2015). A stakeholder governance framework for curriculum development. In C.R. Willness and K. Brown (Chairs), *Implementation of community-based experiential learning: Challenges, opportunities, and insights.* 75th Annual Meeting of the Academy of Management, Vancouver, BC.

Willness, C. R., & Bruni-Bossio, V. (2017). The curriculum innovation canvas: A design thinking framework for the engaged educational entrepreneur. *Journal of Higher Education Outreach & Engagement, 21,* 134–164.

Wilson, J. C. (2011). Service-learning and the development of empathy in US college students. *Education + Training, 53,* 207–217.

17 "Make the World a Better Place"

Local Leadership as a Vehicle for Personal and Community Development

Dian van Huijstee & Richard Ronay

Community engagement, defined as the collaboration "between higher education institutions and their larger communities (local, regional/state, national, or global) for the mutually beneficial exchange of knowledge and resources in a context of partnership and reciprocity" (Carnegie, 2006), has been positively associated with physical and psychological health, self-confidence, self-esteem, and the development of personal relationships (Attree et al., 2011). In this chapter, we discuss one means of fostering such university–community partnerships and their ancillary benefits within the context of a master's-level course in leadership.

University–Community Partnerships and Engagement

Collaborations between universities and communities can take a variety of forms, with the different roles assumed resulting in varying levels of involvement and engagement for their members (i.e., members of the community, students, university employees, etc.). For example, students might provide service work within a community, community members might participate in evening classes at the university, or the university might act in an advising role toward the community. Moreover, the meaning of the collaboration can differ for different members. For some people, collaboration might be a means to fulfill financial, educational, or professional goals, while for others, the willingness to collaborate might be motivated by more social aspirations, such as effectively living together in a large, extended community. Given these different perspectives, university–community partnerships can be best described as, "the coming together of diverse interests and people to achieve a common purpose via interactions, information sharing, and coordination activities" (Buys & Bursnall, 2007; Jassawalla & Sashittal, 1998, p. 239).

The willingness of a university to actively participate in community projects depends on an array of factors, including but not limited to financial resources, attractiveness of incentives, and extant connections with the community (Ahmed, Beck, Maurana, & Newton, 2004; Buys & Bursnall, 2007). The willingness of universities to collaborate with local communities is also influenced by the nature of the surrounding communities. When the community is located within the same municipality as the university, the motivation to collaborate and the ensuing benefits are greater. For instance, when off-campus facilities such as student housing and recreational offerings need to be established, universities have more to gain from active engagement with their neighboring communities. The demographic profile of community constituents also shapes the kinds of collaborative opportunities that are available. For example, partnerships between universities and communities consisting of members with a similar background or ethnicity might be easier to establish than when the members do not relate to each other at all on these components. Nonetheless, partnerships consisting of individuals with different backgrounds can also benefit as diverse members bring diverse skills, knowledge, experiences, and perspectives to the partnership (Galinsky et al., 2015; Suarez-Balcazar et al., 2004).

University–community partnerships can also lead to higher levels of university–community engagement. In cases of purely service work-oriented alliances, the university might deliver knowledge and services to a community, and the community might play no more than a recipient role. However, *engagement* is more likely to follow from partnerships that involve a bidirectional exchange of knowledge and services, wherein universities and communities cooperate to apply and transfer the knowledge held by the university to the community for the purpose of generating collaborative solutions to local societal problems (Weerts & Sandmann, 2010). Therefore, when students actively participate in the community, levels of engagement are higher for both the students and the community members than when the university only has an advising role toward the community, in which case the students of the university as well as the members of the community are not as involved and hence feel less engaged in the partnership. Just as in other relationships, it is important that partners have mutual goals and that all parties effectively communicate with each other in shaping and executing these goals. In general, engagement leads to increased performance (e.g., Bakker & Bal, 2010; Schaufeli & Bakker, 2004), and so partnerships consisting of engaged parties will in general be more successful than those consisting of parties who are not especially engaged. Moreover, when both parties are equally dependent on each other, the partnership will be healthier (Bringle & Hatcher, 2002).

Benefits of University–Community Engagement

In the following paragraphs, we explicate the benefits of university–community engagement for the different relationship parties, namely the educational benefits for students (and the community members), the benefits that flow to the personal development of the students, the benefits that flow to the communities the students engage with, and the relationships between these different outcomes. Figure 17.1 represents the causal model of university–community engagement and its corresponding benefits.

Educational Benefits. One of the benefits of university–community engagement for students is increased learning. When the community project is part of a course, students learn to combine theory and practice by consolidating theoretical principles

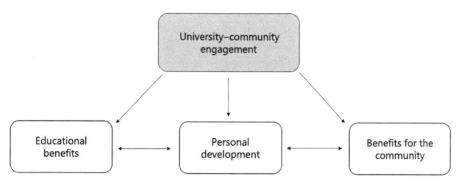

Figure 17.1 *Causal model of university–community engagement and its benefits*

with practical application and interpersonal development. Such experiential learning provides students with an opportunity to reflect on concrete experiences, which can lead to the consolidation of abstract concepts, inspiring new conceptual connections and new ideas for action and implementation (Dewey, 1938; Kolb, 1984; Kolb, Boyatzis, & Mainemelis, 2001; Kolb & Kolb, 2005). Designing and implementing a community project moves students through each of these stages. By applying theory to local problems (*experiencing*) and observing the reaction of the community (*reflecting*), students can gather new insights (*thinking*) for the application of theory, which can be immediately implemented (*acting*).

In addition to teaching how to apply theories to societal issues in the real world, service learning has also been positively linked to more quantitative educational outcomes. For instance, a longitudinal study by Astin, Vogelgesang, Ikeda, and Yee (2000) shows that the grades of participating students (i.e., students who participated in community service work as part of a course or who chose to do so independently) increased, as did their critical-thinking and writing skills, compared to students who did not participate in any community service work. The meta-analysis of Celio, Durlak, and Dymnicki (2011), based on 62 studies containing 11,837 student in total, also supports the large, beneficial effect of service learning on academic performance (effect size = 0.43) compared to control students who did not participate in any service learning. Moreover, their attitudes toward school and learning also improved significantly (effect size = 0.28) compared to the control students.

Astin et al.'s (2000) meta-analysis also revealed that community service work has a positive effect on students' levels of self-efficacy. Self-efficacy – trust in one's ability to reach intended goals (Bandura, 1977) – is in turn linked to increased potential for social learning, as efficacy enhances individuals' confidence to experiment with and incorporate (or not) new behaviors into their own repertoires following the observation of others' behaviors and associated outcomes (Bandura, 1977, 1982). In the case of university–community partnerships, many people from different backgrounds and with different levels and areas of expertise are involved, creating a wealth of opportunities for the principles of social learning to play out.

A further possible educational benefit is the positive link between service work and leadership (Astin et al., 2000). Community work generally increases the amount of leadership activities students have an opportunity to engage in, resulting in heightened perceptions of their own leadership and interpersonal skills. Examples of these leadership activities can be leading the group toward a common goal, delegating and sharing in the completion of tasks necessary to reach the superordinate goal, taking responsibility for one's role in achieving shared goals, and motivating other members of the group to do the same. Improved leadership skills can be seen as an educational benefit when they are developed in the context of a (leadership) course, but this can also be seen as a personal benefit for the students who carry their developed leadership skills and abilities forward into their professional lives. Thus, the benefits of university–community partnerships can be closely intertwined. Of course, this depends on what kind of community service work is performed, but most activities will demand leadership skills in order to realize goals. Nonetheless, social dynamics often result in some people emerging as leaders and others as followers when coordination is needed (e.g., King, Johnson, & Van Vugt, 2009). Therefore, improvement of leadership qualities does not always have to occur after doing community service work, but members of the group do learn about leader–follower dynamics regardless of their role in the group.

Personal Growth. One of the greatest benefits of community engagement is that students are empowered by opportunities to discover and develop attitudes and talents that help them to become "social change agents." By deciding which community they want to help, students are given ownership over the project, increasing their intrinsic motivation (Deci & Ryan, 1985). By experiencing real-world problems and collaboratively seeking solutions, students learn to develop, implement, and share their knowledge with other people (Wilson, Woolger, & Dodd, 2017). This is empowering, as students gain opportunities to use their leadership abilities to change society for the greater good (Astin & Astin, 2000).

To explore the potential benefits of public engagement, Wilson, Woolger, and Dodd (2017) gathered self-report data from students at ten British universities that had participated in several public engagement projects based on volunteering. The authors invited students to complete a short survey assessing their own skill sets pre-project and again post-project. This revealed that student participants felt more confident, that their communication skills increased, and that they experienced opportunities to test previously learned theories via analysis of data collected during the project. This report corroborates other findings by Astin et al. (2000), who also describe how students learn practical skills that accompany and extend what they learn in class and are imbued with a greater sense of civic responsibility following their project involvement. Furthermore, community projects in which students get some organizational freedom provide them with the experience of acting as local leaders (Bonsall, Harris, & Marczak, 2002).

In their extensive meta-analysis, Celio, Durlak, and Dymnicki (2011) also found support for improved attitudes toward the self (effect size = 0.28) and (self-rated) improved social skills (effect size = 0.30). These benefits may be intertwined as well, since feelings of improved social skills might result in improved feelings about the self, or vice versa. In sum, participating in university–community partnerships can have several benefits for the students involved at both an educational and personal level.

Community Benefits. Benefits for the community can be broad – access to resources, the establishing of desirable connections with the students/university, and opportunities to resolve long-standing problems or to identify a problem or shortcoming the community was unaware of. Social capital also increases; the networks, norms, and social trust between students and faculty and the broader community increase, with potential for ongoing and mutually beneficial coordination and cooperation (Putnam, 1995). For instance, Bruning, McGrew, and Cooper (2006) report that community members who attended a campus event had significantly more positive feelings toward the university than non-attending community members. By not only focusing on sending students into the community, but also inviting the community to the campus, community members experienced the intellectual, cultural, and artistic benefits of having a university in the community, leading them to rate the university as a more positive asset in the community.

Moreover, the meta-analysis of Attree et al. (2011), in which they investigated the effect of community engagement programs focusing on health improvement, revealed that community members report higher levels of satisfaction when they were actively involved and given the opportunity to take initiatives. This relationship was in turn linked to enhanced physical and psychological benefits for the participants. Finally, community members also reported that they felt more useful to others, more in control, better able to communicate their ideas, and more aware of individual rights (Attree et al., 2011). The meta-analysis of Celio, Durlak, and Dymnicki (2011) also found that involved students felt higher civic engagement (effect size = 0.27). These results indicate that engagement can not only empower the students involved, but also empower community members.

University–Community Partnerships as Part of the Curriculum

Some universities add service learning to their curricula as an extra course that offers students the opportunity to obtain additional course credit, others expect their students to participate voluntarily (extracurricular), and some universities add service learning to their curricula by conceptualizing it as part of a course. Holland and Gelmon (1998) report that students mention that they learn more about the community and that they can link this obtained information to theoretical perspectives explored in class when the community service is part of a course as opposed to when they do this as a voluntary, extracurricular activity.

Faculty might fear that creating university–community partnerships will impose an additional non-academic burden, potentially decreasing their time for research (Holland & Gelmon, 1998). However, if the partnership is incorporated into their current teaching schedule, this can reduce the burden and increase the benefits to both students and faculty. Nonetheless, there are potential pitfalls related to university–community partnerships that faculty should be aware of before integrating such a service-learning module into their curricula.

Possible Pitfalls

According to Maurrasse (2013), who described eight core characteristics of partnerships, accurately estimating the time needed to make a partnership work is difficult, with underestimations being the common pitfall. Moreover, time estimates cannot always account for unexpected problems that arise along the way, such as unexpected costs or the need to redefine the goals and values of the mutual enterprise. Partnerships can be and often are messy affairs (Cooper, Kotval-K, Kotval, & Mullin, 2014; Maurrasse, 2013). Differences in backgrounds, cultures, values, and the goals of communities and universities can lead to hindrances. However, the versatile nature of the partnership also means that goals and the means of accomplishing them can be negotiated on the basis of common interests. It is relatively easy to skirt conflict under such conditions. Engaging third parties in the shared endeavor can help preserve objectiveness and balance perspectives, attenuating the potential for messy partnerships (Cooper et al., 2014).

Furthermore, power dynamics might create problems within partnerships (Cooper et al., 2014; Maurrasse, 2013) when one side fails to treat the other party as an equal partner. Partnerships that fail to sufficiently attend to the community's interests or those that sacrifice those interests to the potential benefits for the university are neither in the spirit of the enterprise, nor likely to meet with great success. However, this problem may be moderated by the prestige and status of the university, where students and employees might, by way of social identification, assume higher rank and greater entitlement (e.g., Magee & Galinsky, 2008; Winston, 1999). For smaller universities, this problem may well be mitigated. Culture might also mitigate the potential problems of power dynamics. In the United States, relative to the Netherlands and other European countries, differences in power and status between universities are large. In most European countries, attending university is made more accessible due to subsidies and favorable student loans. Moreover, all Dutch (public) university students pay the same tuition fee, regardless of the university's reputation and rank. Problems created by power dynamics can be reduced when parties treat each other as equals, both on an individual level and a group level. This would contribute to a more easily emerging partnership and smooth collaboration.

Community engagement, depending on the level and demands, might also impose some stress on the individuals involved. Either as a result of the time and energy demands or from the tweaking of one's empathic concern. In the case of a course-based project such as ours (which will be described in a following subsection), such possibilities need to be guarded against by staying in contact with the project groups throughout the various stages of their enterprise. Another cause of stress might be the possibility of freeloaders in a group. A possible solution to this is to let project members create a contract before they start the project in which they predefine some rules and divide the workload. By doing this, would-be freeloaders do not get the chance to neglect their responsibilities and the other team members will not be disadvantaged.

Examples of Projects and Partnerships

In the Netherlands, community engagement has been integrated into several learning programs, with ongoing efforts increasing exponentially. For example, the Vrije Universiteit Amsterdam aims to introduce a community service-learning program into every study program within every faculty in 2017. (For more information, see the Vrije Universiteit Amsterdam website: www.vu.nl/en/about-vu-amsterdam/mis sion-and-profile/csl/index.aspx.) Students are encouraged to assist communities in various ways, such as conducting research or completing an internship within a community. For instance, physics students are liaising with local high schools and acting as teaching assistants within the classroom to help attenuate the shortage of teachers in the natural sciences. Health Sciences students have investigated the health of people living in Amsterdam and used the information they gathered to write a health promotion and sickness prevention proposal. Students of the faculty of Economics and Business Administration have worked together with local shopping centers to explore innovations that might foster greater entrepreneurial endeavors. All these examples are described (unfortunately currently only in Dutch) at https://vu .nl/nl/bedrijf-en-samenleving/communityservice/goodpractices/index.aspx. There are numerous possibilities to create service-learning projects on a small scale, providing students with experiential learning opportunities by interacting with members from external communities.

Community Leadership Project

Each year, the Vrije Universiteit Amsterdam offers a graduate course in leadership and organizations. The course takes an applied approach to the topic of leadership, and one key assignment requires students to work together in small teams for the purpose of assisting local and regional communities to address problems or short-comings met by members of their community. Students participating in this course are randomly assigned to groups of three to five students and given the short instruction that they need to work together to plan and implement a community or campus-based service activity. The assessment for this project includes the evaluation of a ten-minute presentation that summarizes the process of designing and implementing the intervention and relating those experiences to the leadership theories discussed in class.

The educational goal of this community leadership project is to provide students with an opportunity to put into practice their developing skills in leadership, colla-boration, negotiation, planning, and project implementation. In addition to core aspects of leadership theory, the course provides a practical focus on applied leader-ship skills, covering issues related to leader–follower dynamics, coalitions and networking, decision processes and implementation, negotiation and conflict resolu-tion, and persuasion and influence. Classes typically involve a practical case or exercise and a subsequent discussion and debrief that highlights the theoretical underpinnings and extensions of the case. The group project provides individuals with an opportunity to implement these skills both at an intragroup level (within their team) and during their interactions with the identified community and relevant third parties. Assessment comes in the form of a presentation and short paper that describe the project goals and processes, and students are encouraged (via specified assessment criteria) to connect their project experience with theoretical perspectives discussed in class.

This hands-on approach to leadership development is complemented by ancillary benefits, both for students' personal development and for the communities with whom the students engage. As discussed, these interrelated benefits follow from heightened engagement (e.g., Attree et al., 2011; Driscoll, 2009), improved educational motivation and outcomes (e.g., Astin et al., 2000; Celio, Durlak, & Dymnicki, 2011; Kolb, 1984), and increased opportunities for self-actualization (e.g., Astin and Astin, 2000; Deci & Ryan, 1985; Wilson, Woolger, & Dodd, 2017).

Examples of Possible Benefits as a Result of the Leadership and Organizations Projects

The following paragraphs include descriptions of projects that were implemented during the Leadership and Organizations course at Vrije Universiteit Amsterdam, together with the potential benefits they might have created for the students involved.

Educational Benefits. In our own Leadership and Organizations course at Vrije Universiteit Amsterdam, students are challenged to show and develop leadership skills by taking the initiative to engage with an external community and offer assistance. Of course, some projects ask more of their leaders than others, but regardless, by managing themselves through their community projects, the leadership skills of the students are tested and developed. In one case, students offered an information evening to refugees seeking to understand the intricacies of the Dutch job market. During this information evening, refugees learned how to compose a Dutch curriculum vitae, what is expected during a job interview, norms of culturally appropriate behavior, and what to expect procedurally during a job search. Planning this workshop required stimulating interest within the refugee community, locating and gaining access to a location, and identifying, inviting, and coordinating with various expert third parties who contributed to the workshop. Accomplishing all of this within the short time frame of a seven-week course is no easy feat. Nonetheless, as students engage and identify with their community's goals, the project provides opportunities for students to realize their own capabilities while in the service of others. However, the extent to which individual students capitalize on this opportunity varies, since the workload division during these projects is something that they need to take care of themselves.

Community Benefits and Personal Benefits. One salient community that captured the interest of several student groups in our leadership course at Vrije Universiteit Amsterdam was that of the refugee communities recently arrived in Western Europe. The refugee crisis has been a matter of great importance in the past years, and it was highly relevant during the times of the community projects. As mentioned, one group organized workshops for those seeking employment opportunities. Another group organized game nights for students and refugees who live together in a building, with the goal of fostering enduring social connections. Yet another group arranged a Dutch night for refugees to introduce them to some of the peculiarities of Dutch culture, celebrating a typical Dutch "Sinterklaas" party. Organizing activities such as these potentially helped the community of refugees in the following ways: they received information that they could use to increase their potential on the Dutch job market; they learned some more about Dutch society; they enjoyed time together; and, perhaps most important, they were given the opportunity to distract their thoughts for a minute from the circumstances that had led to their departure and their ongoing struggles with establishing a new life in the Netherlands. Although several of the student–community partnerships continued when the course concluded, most focused on discrete goals, isolating the project within a specific temporal framework.

Organizing these activities brings the students into contact with people from wildly different backgrounds, providing opportunities for cross-cultural understanding and social connections. Heightened empathy and a strengthened belief in one's own capacity to affect change are the foundations of local leadership, fostering students' sense of civic responsibility and willingness to extend help to other local communities (Astin et al., 2000; Bonsall, Harris, & Marczak, 2002).

Projects can also provide opportunities for professional development. For instance, one student from our leadership course received a job offer from a local hospital on the basis of the community project with which she was involved. The project involved creating menu cards in different languages for the sizable number of patients who do not speak Dutch or English. The menu cards included pictures of the foods labeled in both Spanish and Arabic. This proved to be a very efficient innovation as the nutrition assistants in the hospital no longer needed to be called to explain each meal. This student accepted the offer, working at the hospital on weekends while completing her master's studies.

Vrije Universiteit Community Leadership Project – How To

Context. We have implemented this community leadership project with classes ranging in size from 70 to 120 students. On each occasion, the projects have been developed and implemented within the seven-week period of the course. Longer courses, perhaps extending to 12 weeks, would potentially be preferable, but we offer suggestions based on a seven-week time frame.

1. Prior to the first class, randomly assign students to groups of four to five members. Fewer students imposes a greater workload, while more students can lead to diffusion of responsibility within the group. Create a slide displaying team numbers and the names of the students that make up each team. Provide ten minutes at the end of class for students to meet and exchange contact information.

2. During the first class, encourage students to spend one week identifying and discussing potential local communities with whom to work, as well as the problems those communities might benefit from assistance with. It can be helpful to provide some examples from previous years' teams. We list some examples below as illustrations of possible projects. Consider providing time in class for whole-class discussion of potential projects. This can help to avoid overlap between projects and can help build early strategies.

3. In the second week, discuss the importance of shared responsibility within the groups and the value of coming to a clear, shared agreement about such responsibilities early on. Provide students with an example of a team contract and provide 30 minutes in class for them to develop their own team contracts. These might be submitted electronically within 24 hours. This 30-minute discussion time might also be used to finalize agreements regarding the teams' proposals for the larger project.

4. In week 3, prior to class, proposals should be submitted electronically for review. The level of detail asked for regarding the proposals might vary depending on the timing of the course. With a seven-week course, the main goal is to ensure that students have a target group and goal. In any case, the requested level of detail should be sufficient for the teacher to assess the feasibility of the proposed project before the next class. During class in week 3, groups should be given 30–60 minutes to discuss and develop their project. During this time, the teacher(s) should circulate between the groups and briefly discuss each project's feasibility. Allow sufficient time to visit each group.

5. By the fourth week of class, student groups should have a clear goal and be liaising with the community for the purpose of moving toward implementation of the project. At this time, it can be helpful to provide students with the opportunity to highlight potential problems within the group. To this end, we provide students with the opportunity to identify potential sources of conflict – equity in terms of workload, conflicting work schedules, conflicting goals, and expectations. This anonymous, individual-level feedback is then aggregated and fed back to the group for the purpose of discussion and possibly modification of their team contracts.

6. By week 5, students should be in the process of preparing their ten-minute presentations and accompanying one-page summary. At this stage, it can be helpful to highlight that the project provides various opportunities to connect with theoretical aspects of the course. These connections might arise from interaction with the community group and with internal group processes, or from personal introspection regarding one's own role in the project.

7. In the final week of class (week 7 in our case), student groups present their projects to the rest of the class. These ten-minute presentations, which might need to be scheduled in two separate sessions, are intended to explain how the community and associated project goal was identified, how the project was developed and implemented, and what intra-team and inter-group processes emerged and had to be addressed during the project. Students should be encouraged to make connections with theoretical aspects from class.

8. Many of the student groups report motivation to continue engaging with their community group for the purpose of further developing or extending the project. In such cases, it can be beneficial for the course administrator to provide links with other members of the university whose role it is to foster ongoing university–community partnerships and who might then be able to offer additional services/support.

Some Further Examples of the Projects. In the years we have been implementing this project at Vrije Universiteit Amsterdam, we have seen a rich cross-section of projects emerge. For instance, one group worked with local bike shops in downtown Amsterdam to develop information flyers for the purpose of helping tourists safely navigate the hectic cycleways of Amsterdam. This example implies benefits for several parties. Firstly, the students involved developed interpersonal and leadership skills by creating these partnerships with the local bike shops. Secondly, the tourists will present less of a hazard to themselves and others (there are more than enough other hazards for the Amsterdam tourist to contend with). Thirdly, the bike shops might benefit from the flyers by renting and/or selling more bikes and by receiving fewer damaged rentals as returns.

With the waves of refugees that have entered the Netherlands, a number of groups have targeted this broad community by offering craft and cultural workshops for children or by providing information regarding employment opportunities and application procedures. One project team worked with a local church group to transform a disused church hall into temporary housing for refugee families. These examples show the civic responsibility felt by the students involved. Indeed, many group members continued to work alongside their chosen community after the class project was finalized. Community engagement projects can benefit all involved parties, and these benefits can stretch to unexpected lengths.

Another group provided social media workshops for the elderly for the purpose of helping them connect more regularly with family and friends. This led the students to learn to interact with people outside of their in-group, such as by having more patience when teaching something computer related to someone with more life experience. For the elderly, this workshop probably reduced their feelings of loneliness, not only on the training day, but also by opening up new lines of communication with family and friends. Finally, the most beautiful friendships can emerge between the elderly and younger people, benefitting both the elderly community and the student community.

Conclusion

There are dozens of examples from the hundreds of students who have participated in these projects at Vrije Universiteit Amsterdam. Our observation over the years is that students respond exceptionally well to the challenges of serving others. It is a challenge that they readily meet, and one that empowers them with a sense of both agency and communion. The communities themselves have always been demonstrably appreciative of the interest and support offered to them. We strongly believe that the projects have helped strengthen the social ties between the university and its neighboring communities. By providing the framework for how such community projects can be adapted, we hope to inspire faculty members to take up the challenge of implementing such community projects into their curricula. Remember, if you want to make the world a better place, you have to start with yourself (by helping a community).

References

Ahmed, S. M., Beck, B., Maurana, A., & Newton, G. (2004). Overcoming barriers to effective community-based participatory research in US medical schools. *Education for Health, 17*(2), 141–151.

Astin, A. W., & Astin, H. S. (2000). *Leadership reconsidered: Engaging education in social change.* Battle Creek, MI: W. K. Kellogg Foundation.

Astin, A. W., Vogelgesang, L. J., Ikeda, E. K., & Yee, J. A. (2000). How service learning affects students. *Higher Education: Service Learning. Paper 144.* Retrieved from http://digitalcommons.unomaha.edu/slcehighered/144.

Attree, P., French, B., Milton, B., Povall, S., Whitehead, M., & Popay, J. (2011). The experience of community engagement for individuals: A rapid review of evidence. *Health & Social Care in the Community, 19*(3), 250–260.

Bakker, A. B., & Bal, M. P. (2010). Weekly work engagement and performance: A study among starting teachers. *Journal of Occupational and Organizational Psychology, 83*(1), 189–206.

Bandura, A. (1977). *Social learning theory.* Oxford: Prentice-Hall.

Bandura, A. (1982). Self-efficacy mechanism in human agency. *American Psychologist, 37* (2), 122–147.

Bonsall, D. L., Harris, R. A., & Marczak, J. N. (2002). The community as a classroom. *New Directions for Student Services, 2002*(100), 85–96.

Bringle, R. G., & Hatcher, J. A. (2002). Campus–community partnerships: The terms of engagement. *Journal of Social Issues, 58*(3), 503–516.

Bruning, S. D., McGrew, S., & Cooper, M. (2006). Town–gown relationships: Exploring university–community engagement from the perspective of community members. *Public Relations Review, 32*(2), 125–130.

Buys, N., & Bursnall, S. (2007). Establishing university–community partnerships: Processes and benefits. *Journal of Higher Education Policy and Management, 29*(1), 73–86.

Carnegie Foundation for the Advancement of Teaching (2006). *The Carnegie Classification of Institutions of Higher Education*. 2005 edition. Menlo Park, CA: Author.

Celio, C. I., Durlak, J., & Dymnicki, A. (2011). A meta-analysis of the impact of service-learning on students. *Journal of Experiential Education*, *34*(2), 164–181.

Cooper, J. G., Kotval-K, Z., Kotval, Z., & Mullin, J. (2014). University community partnerships. *Humanities*, *3*(1), 88–101.

Deci, E. L., & Ryan, R. M. (1985). *Intrinsic motivation and self-determination in human behavior*. New York: Plenum.

Dewey, J. (1938). *Education and experience*. New York: Simon and Schuster.

Driscoll, A. (2009). Carnegie's new community engagement classification: Affirming higher education's role in community. *New Directions for Higher Education*, *2009*(147), 5–12.

Galinsky, A. D., Todd, A. R., Homan, A. C. et al. (2015). Maximizing the gains and minimizing the pains of diversity. *Perspectives on Psychological Science*, *10*(6), 742–748.

Holland, B. A., & Gelmon, S. B. (1998). The state of the "engaged campus": What have we learned about building and sustaining university–community partnerships. *American Association of Higher Education Bulletin*, *51*, 3–6.

Jassawalla, A. R., & Sashittal, H. C. (1998). An examination of collaboration in high-technology new product development processes. *Journal of Product Innovation Management*, *15*(3), 237–254.

King, A. J., Johnson, D. D., & Van Vugt, M. (2009). The origins and evolution of leadership. *Current Biology*, *19*(19), R911–R916.

Kolb, D. A. (1984). *Experiential learning: Experience as the source of learning and development*. Upper Saddle River, NJ: Prentice-Hall.

Kolb, D. A., Boyatzis, R. E., & Mainemelis, C. (2001). Experiential learning theory: Previous research and new directions. In R. J. Sternberg & L. F. Zhang (Eds.), *Perspectives on cognitive, learning, and thinking style* (pp. 227–247), Mahwah, NJ: Lawrence Erlbaum.

Kolb, A. Y., & Kolb, D. A. (2005). Learning styles and learning spaces: Enhancing experiential learning in higher education. *Academy of Management Learning & Education*, *4*(2), 193–212.

Magee, J. C., & Galinsky, A. D. (2008). Social hierarchy: The self-reinforcing nature of power and status. *Academy of Management Annals*, *2*(1), 351–398.

Maurrasse, D. J. (2013). *Strategic public private partnerships*. Cheltenham: Edward Elgar.

Putnam, R. D. (1995). Bowling alone: America's declining social capital. *Journal of Democracy*, *6*(1), 65–78.

Schaufeli, W. B., & Bakker, A. B. (2004). Job demands, job resources, and their relationship with burnout and engagement: A multi-sample study. *Journal of Organizational Behavior*, *25*(3), 293–315.

Suarez-Balcazar, Y., Davis, M. I., Ferrari, J. et al. (2004). University–community partnerships: A framework and an exemplar. In L. Jason, C. Keys, Y. Suarez-Balcazar, R. R. Taylor, M. Davis, J. Durlak, & D. Isenberg (Eds.), *Participatory community research: Theory and methods in action* (pp. 105–120). Washington, DC: American Psychological Association.

Weerts, D. J., & Sandmann, L. R. (2010). Community engagement and boundary-spanning roles at research universities. *The Journal of Higher Education*, *81*(6), 632–657.

Wilson, P., Woolger, A., & Dodd, M. (2017). Students: Experience, engagement and communities (report to HEFCE by York Consulting, Leeds; York Consulting LLP). Retrieved from www.hefce.ac.uk/media/HEFCE,2014/Content/Pubs/Independentresearch/2017/Students,Experience,engagement,and,communities/studentseec.pdf.

Winston, G. C. (1999). Subsidies, hierarchy and peers: The awkward economics of higher education. *The Journal of Economic Perspectives, 13*(1), 13–36.

PART VI

Putting It All Together

18 Assessing and Classifying the Institutionalization of Community Engagement

Mathew Johnson & John Saltmarsh

The pervasiveness of institutional ranking systems for higher education reflects not only the prestige culture of higher education, but also policy debates about performance and productivity and the demands for metrics and assessments to determine accountability. There are also, notes Hazelkorn, "a growing range of alternatives to rankings, broadly categorized under the rubric of accountability and transparency instruments" (2015, p. xvi). Among the policy choices and tradeoffs that come with accountability measures is the tension between "rewarding traditional academic outputs" versus "valuing civic and social responsibility." This chapter describes two instruments developed to account for higher education's civic purposes through assessing community engagement as an institutionalized practice of campuses in the United States. Both are designed for accountability and quality improvement, both recognize and encourage organizational innovation and change, and both allow for recognition and acclaim without replicating a traditional rankings hierarchy.

Additionally, within the context of the neoliberal political economy driving higher education to be more market-driven and highly privatized, both the instruments described here are not only alternatives to traditional rankings, but also represent alternatives to rankings and measures that do not account for and are not grounded in the public purposes of higher education. The central goal of neoliberalism is "to transfer numerous public functions, assets, and roles to the private sector [...] [it] seeks to eliminate any notion of the broader public good, including institutions such as schools and public universities" (Rhoads & Szelényi, 2011, p. 13). "For critics of the neoliberal model," note Jones and Shefner, "universities became places of civic engagement," with the result that "one answer to the abuses of neoliberalism became the engaged university, and one strategy was service learning" (2014, p. 11). Thus, the instruments designed to assess community engagement described in this chapter inherently function as public good accountability measures.

The two instruments are the following: (1) the National Assessment of Service and Community Engagement (NASCE); and (2) the Carnegie Foundation Elective Community Engagement Classification. At the most basic level, NASCE seeks to determine the extent to which students at institutions of higher education are engaged in their communities. The NASCE uses student-reported experience to quantitatively measure community engagement among individual students and the institutions in which they are nested. The Carnegie Community Engagement Classification assesses the extent of institutional commitment to supporting and advancing community engagement across the campus. Evidence provided in applying for the classification comes from many sources across the institution. The data gathered through the two instruments show that they complement one another and have similar goals, but they focus on different aspects of campus community engagement.

Creating an Institutional Culture of Community Engagement

For many if not all campuses, committing to community engagement means undertaking a new set of practices, creating new structures, and revising policies – it is coincident with organizational change. Both the NASCE and the Carnegie Community Engagement Classification are premised upon institutionalization through change in institutional culture.

In 1998, Eckel, Hill, and Green conducted a national study examining institutional change, and in particular change that could be considered "transformational." Campuses that were demonstrating transformational change exhibited change that: "(1) alters the culture of the institution by changing select underlying assumptions and institutional behaviors, processes, and products; (2) is deep and pervasive, affecting the whole institution; (3) is intentional; and (4) occurs over time" (Eckel, Hill, & Green, 1998, p. 3). Changes that "alter the culture of the institution" are those that require "major shifts in an institution's culture – the common set of beliefs and values that creates a shared interpretation and understanding of events and actions" (Eckel, Hill, & Green, 1998, p. 3). Their attention to deep and pervasive change focuses on "institution-wide patterns of perceiving, thinking, and feeling; shared understandings; collective assumptions; and common interpretive frameworks are the ingredients of this 'invisible glue' called institutional culture."

Eckel, Hill, and Green (1998) concluded that efforts being made in higher education around "connecting institutions to their communities" offered the potential for transformational change. "This could occur," they write, "because [...] these connections can contribute to the reshaping of institutional practices and purposes [...] they may cause researchers to rethink the types of grants they seek, the ways they disseminate their findings, and the range and types of audiences for their findings [...] They may reconsider the types of service rewarded through merit pay and promotion and tenure policies, and they may adopt wider definitions of scholarship that include application and integration (Boyer, 1990) [...] Faculty may incorporate service and outreach in their classes and curricula, and students may participate in co-curricular activities (such as internships or service learning) that place them in the community where they can apply their learning to solving real-world problems" (Eckel, Hill, & Green, 1998, p. 7).

Transformational change occurs when shifts in the institution's culture have developed to the point where they are both pervasive across the institution and deeply embedded in practices throughout the institution (Eckel, Hill, & Green, 1998, p. 5) (see Figure 18.1).

		Depth	
		Low	**High**
Pervasiveness	**Low**	Adjustment (1)	Isolated Change (2)
	High	Far-Reaching Change (3)	Transformational Change (4)

Figure 18.1 *Institutional transformation. Adapted from Eckel et al. (1998)*

The construct of "deep and pervasive" is a useful lens through which to view the institutionalization of community engagement. According to the Eckel, Hill, and Green model, depth is a key element of transformation, but it is not enough. As they point out, "A deep change is not necessarily broad [...] it is possible for deep changes to occur within specific units or academic departments without being widespread throughout the institution" (1998, p. 4). Pervasiveness, according to Eckel, Hill, and Green, "refers to the extent to which the change is far-reaching within the institution. The more pervasive the change, the more it crosses unit boundaries and touches different parts of the institution" (1998, p. 4).

Institutionalization of community engagement is associated with change in the institutional culture of colleges and universities, or what Cuban identifies as "second-order changes" that "seek to alter the fundamental ways in which organizations are put together. These changes reflect major dissatisfaction with present arrangements. Second-order changes introduce new goals, structures, and roles that transform familiar ways of doing things into new ways of solving persistent problems" (Cuban, 1988, p. 342). Second-order changes are associated with Eckel, Hill, and Green's transformational change (1998). If community engagement is not embedded in the institutional culture, it tends to remain a marginalized activity, and its sustainability is questionable.

The National Assessment of Service and Community Engagement

The NASCE was developed in 2007 to quantify the volume (breadth), frequency, or depth of community engagement activities on individual campuses and among significant numbers of college students. Today, NASCE has launched its fourth iteration with modules to measure student, staff, and faculty engagement across campuses. Aligned with the Elective Carnegie Community Engagement Classification, NASCE measures the community engagement of students at institutions of higher education by using student-reported experience to score overall institutional performance. Now administered more than 100 times at colleges and universities of varying sizes, missions, Carnegie types, and locations, its results provide key insights about what propels community engagement to higher levels on college campuses. Some campuses, like those in the Bonner Foundation and Campus Compact network, have integrated its lessons into long-range planning for community engagement. For further information, see Bonner Foundation (www.bonner.org) or Campus Compact (https://compact.org).

The NASCE provides to participating institutions a measurement of how many students are engaged and to what extent across nine areas of service. The NASCE gives institutions an invaluable strategic planning tool through its use of advanced data collection in the unique Percent of the Possible or POP score system and the foundational "units of service" or Capacity Contribution graphs.

Casting a Wide Net

NASCE is designed to capture the widest potential reporting of engagement both before and after enrollment in college. Students are first presented with a battery of questions related to the year prior to matriculation, followed by the same battery encouraging them to reflect on their time since matriculation. Built on Putnam's concept of social capital, NASCE utilizes a conception of community engagement as the extent to which college/university students contribute time and effort to meet unmet human needs (i.e., housing, healthcare, nutrition, etc.) (1995). NASCE asks students about their participation in "any activity, including internships, work study, and coursework, in which you participate with the goal of providing, generating, and/ or sustaining help for individuals and groups who have unmet human needs in areas like shelter, health, nutrition, education, and opportunity" (see Johnson, Levy, Cichetti, & Zinkiewicz, 2013). Students can report activity in the following areas of engagement:

- Civic participation/promoting public awareness (e.g., voter awareness, human rights, refugees and immigration, public safety)
- Economic opportunity, access, and development (e.g., tax assistance, job training, fair trade)
- Environmental (e.g., local clean-up, environmental advocacy)
- Working to promote health or fitness (e.g., donating blood, visiting the sick, raising money to combat a disease)
- Youth (e.g., tutoring, coaching, working on a toy drive)
- Addressing homelessness or housing (e.g., Habitat for Humanity, affordable housing)
- Elder care (e.g., adopt a grandparent, nursing home)
- Addressing hunger or nutrition issues (e.g., soup kitchen, food drive)
- Religious or spiritual service (e.g., teaching a Sunday school class, mission work)

Across the national NASCE data set, colleges and universities range in size from 800 to 32,000 students and span 26 states in the USA. The institutions differ in characteristics such as religious affiliation, public or private nature, and size. Of these, 50 institutions are private and 31 are public; 14 are religiously affiliated and 67 are secular; 11 are large schools with 10,000 or more students, 15 are medium-sized schools with between 5,000 and 10,000 students, 29 are small schools with between 2,000 and 4,999 students, and 26 are very small schools with fewer than 2,000 students. Of the 64,955 students, 32 percent of the respondents are male and 68 percent are female; 72 percent are Caucasian, 8 percent are African American, 8 percent are Asian, 6 percent are Hispanic or Latino, and 4 percent are multiracial. The average age of respondents is 22 years and their average college Grade Point Average (GPA) is 3.29. All of the colleges and universities in this data set are four-year institutions, and the breakdown of class years is: 28 percent are seniors, 25 percent are juniors, 22 percent are sophomores, and 25 percent are freshman. While sample distribution by "year in school" and a variety of other demographic categories has been representative, we find that women are more likely than men to respond to the survey. The average campus response rate is 18 percent (most response rates fall within 12–25 percent). Additionally, qualitative, supplementary research shows that the NASCE tends to slightly overstate service; engaged students are more likely to complete the instrument.

Breadth, Frequency, and Depth

In these issue area follow-up questions and others, students are encouraged to tally as much as possible by asking students throughout the survey to "keep all the types of community engagement and service in which you engage in mind as you answer the following questions." For each chosen area, students are asked a six-point, Likert-scaled question about their frequency of involvement, with answer choices ranging from "once or twice a year" (1) to "more than once a week" (6). Finally, students are asked about their depth of involvement in each area, with a Likert-scale ranging from "one-shot service" (1) to "deep and committed service" (3). In addition, students are asked a series of questions designed to assess their perception of institutional promotion of engagement, how they participate in engagement (e.g., through a club/organization, as part of a course, as an individual), and how they view engagement opportunities. The survey includes a customizable question that asks students to indicate where they have heard about engagement opportunities by choosing from a given list of campus structures and programs. Students are asked to identify whether they strongly agree, agree, disagree, or strongly disagree with a provided list of 11 reasons that students have given for engaging, including, "I believe I can help people who are in need," "It is the right thing to do," and "I have been required to." A similar question is asked to all students about engagement obstacles, with nine options, including, "I am not interested," "I have to work at my job," and "I do not have transportation." At the end of the survey, students are asked a series of questions that assess their perceptions of institutional engagement promotion and facilitation by the institution itself, including "Overall, I would say that XYZ promotes community engagement and service among the student body," and "Overall, I am satisfied with my personal level of involvement in community engagement and service here at XYZ." Basic demographic questions including gender, class, living status, and family income are asked for analytic purposes. The quantitative analytic method NASCE employs to measure each student's rate, frequency, and depth of engagement is computed as the POP score, which uses the multiplier effect to differentiate surface-level involvement from deep and meaningful involvement across nine areas of need.

POP: Percent of the Possible

While many institutions track how many service hours their students perform each year, the POP variable allows institutions to understand this involvement in more depth. It is meaningful to gauge an institution's total capacity contribution by examining not only how many students serve and in what areas, but at what levels of frequency and commitment, beyond simply tracking hours. By building the POP score (see Table 18.1) based upon measuring the percentage of students that engage, how often, and at what level of depth across nine distinct areas of engagement, the NASCE casts a wide and dense net across a community of students (see Johnson, Levy, Cichetti, & Zinkiewicz, 2013).

Each respondent's values for engagement, frequency, and depth are measured and multiplied to arrive at a raw score in each of the nine areas, and then summed across those areas to find that respondent's total raw score. Individual student scores are then aggregated to generate an overall institutional POP score, as well as POP scores in each of the issue areas both prior to and after matriculation. Institutions are then able to see their POP scores in comparison to the national data set, as well as similar school types.

Table 18.1 *Total capacity contribution: NASCE*

Score	Interpretation
41+ Pervasive	Service and culture are synonymous. Most students are engaged in service at meaningful levels of depth and frequency across the nine need areas. Service is ingrained in the student experience
31–40 Integrated	Service is a focal point of your institution's culture. Students serve frequently and deeply across several areas of need and maintain substantive connections with service programs campus-wide
21–30 Established	Service is a significant component of your culture, but potential for greater contribution exists. Full integration of community engagement requires campus-wide reflection and a greater commitment to deep service
11–20 Evolving	Service is prevalent but uneven. Variations in student participation, frequency, and depth between the nine areas present opportunities for improvement. Data and the POP scores identify areas of opportunity
1–10 Emerging	Service is not a main component of your culture, only taking place intermittently. Service is performed at low levels, primarily taking the form of "one-shot" activities. To enhance service contribution, data point the way

Capacity Contribution and Structured Pathways

Colleges possess and can mobilize a significant capacity to serve their community; many would argue that it is their duty to do so. NASCE presents the data in a variety of ways in addition to the POP score index. Institutions receive a capacity contribution table (CCT) for overall institutional engagement as well as engagement for each issue area. CCTs map the impact of the breadth and depth of engagement against an "ideal" curve representing a campus where all students are engaged, a third are engaged occasionally, a third are engaged regularly, and a third are engaged deeply. Some colleges assert that as many as 95 percent of students perform meaningful community service that has a dramatic, positive effect on the local community. The NASCE shows that just over 50 percent of students in general (more at some institutions, less at others) do any service. Using POP, NASCE shows that, in many areas, little service is done and few students are deeply engaged. This suggests that, rather than being at a ceiling, community engagement in college still has enormous potential to increase. In this way, colleges can see a mapped, visual expression of their active capacity compared to their total potential capacity.

Data about the structured pathways students use to move into engagement are also presented. Pie charts map percentages of students reporting engagement in and through courses, student groups, and organizations, or through individual initiative. Finally, in addition to the presentation of data in each campus report, campuses receive a standard set of cross-tabs, all frequencies, and the raw data file.

Using NASCE to Increase Breadth, Frequency, and Depth of Engagement

The NASCE provides to participating institutions a measurement of how many students are engaged and to what extent across nine areas of service. The NASCE gives institutions an invaluable strategic planning tool through its use of advanced data collection in the unique POP score system and the CCTs. NASCE creates a mechanism for institutions to be continuously collecting and assessing institutional attempts to be an "engaged campus" in line with the Carnegie Community Engagement Voluntary Classification.

The NASCE moves from one measure that offers no specificity and no intensity – aggregate hours – to a rank order of service by area, measures of intensity and depth for each student, descriptions of the avenues of engagement students use and the communications they utilize to find opportunities, students' assessment of college support for engagement, demographic segmentation for all data, and changes between pre- and post-matriculation engagement. Schools can use the NASCE to more strategically target specific need areas for improvement by gaining awareness about where and to what extent they are of service to their community. Schools can study the areas with high POP scores to understand the institutional practices that might be generalized elsewhere. Schools now can say with a far higher degree of reliability what percentage of students are involved in engagement and how involved they are.

The POP score, a composite built out of measures of breadth, frequency, and depth of engagement by students of a college, allows for the development of strategies to increase engagement along all three dimensions. Likewise, CCTs encourage this three-dimensional, strategic thinking about increasing engagement. Schools can use this tool to understand how service expression is measured, how great their expression of capacity is, and to plan strategies to enhance their capacity contribution.

For many institutions, the strategy of increasing overall student participation, even through large-scale, one-time, short-term, or occasional activities such as service clubs, is viable. Many campuses have built an infrastructure for this type of engagement, which, when done well, can lead to sustained engagement. Knowing that the CCT and the curve that represents it are boosted both by increasing the frequency at which participating students engage in any of the nine areas as well as by their depth of engagement, institutions can put strategies in place to do both. They may seek to encourage or to support structures that facilitate students who currently participate sporadically or only at one-shot events to become involved more frequently via community-engaged coursework, long-term projects, community-based research, and structured, long-term engagement. Second, they may similarly identify those students who are involved more regularly and pave the way for their service to deepen through institutional support or the development of meaningful community partnerships. This is a strategy that many campuses with multi-year community engagement initiatives, such as a Bonner Program or a civic engagement minor, choose to augment. Reorganizing service efforts to promote deeper and longer-term engagement, such as through the adoption of site-based teams or clusters, is a viable strategy.

Institutions can use the individual area CCTs to first see the relative contribution in each area and then to target specific areas that they want to focus on for enhancement. In the best cases, these strategies are adopted in tandem with an analysis of the local community context. When a campus finds that its engagement is failing to address a key need (i.e., dropout prevention) or demographic (i.e., growing elderly population or immigrant group), the campus programs can make important shifts.

The strategic permutations an institution can implement are endless. Analysis of the NASCE helps institutions focus their efforts by providing them with concrete measures. With the help of the NASCE, schools can have informed discussions and generate meaningful goals aimed at enhancing community engagement and its institution's capacity contribution. Decisions such as whether or not service should be required of all students or whether or not structures that support service should be funded can be pursued, informed by quantitative evidence as opposed to theoretical ideals. In conclusion, the POP values suggest potential strategies for how to mobilize broader and deeper community engagement. Similar to other measures that institutions use to assess their progress and success, the NASCE can be used to strategically inform the direction, programs, and initiatives for moving community engagement forward. Finally, the NASCE can also be completed periodically as a benchmark to gauge an institution's contribution over time.

NASCE 4.0

Beginning in 2018, NASCE will become a suite of modules. The pre-matriculation battery is now a stand-alone module (NASCE PreMat) for institutions to assess the engagement background of incoming student cohorts. Because institutions typically recruit relatively consistent student cohort types, we recommend this module be administered once every four years. The core battery (NASCE Core) of post-matriculation questions is also now a stand-alone module that is recommended for every two years to track institutional changes and inform strategic planning and program implementation. To these, and built on the NASCE framework aligned with Carnegie, new modules have been added to capture a more robust institutional picture. The NASCE FSA module allows the institution to measure the engagement of faculty, staff, and administrators. The recommended schedule for this module is once every four years.

To assess the alignment of institutional and community perceptions about community needs and assets, the NASCE Community module measures the perceptions of institutional actors (students, faculty, staff, and administrators) and the perceptions of community members in order to develop a gap analysis. To assess the impacts of community engagement on students' values and behaviors associated with global citizenship, the NASCE engaged global citizen (EGC) module has been developed. This module allows institutions to score students across values and behaviors associated with diversity, critical thought, social justice, and political action and allows the institution to measure the gap between values and behaviors in each area while comparing these scores and gaps in engaged and non-engaged student populations, for example. Recommended administration for the NASCE EGC is a four-year schedule.

Finally, the postgraduate (NASCE PostG) module allows institutions to assess the longer-term impact of community engagement on life choices beyond graduation. Figure 18.2 provides a recommended schedule for administration of the modular NASCE across a four-year time span in between application periods for the Carnegie Classifications.

Together, these modules create a manageable yet robust approach to assessment of community engagement at the institutional level.

YEAR 1	YEAR 2	YEAR 3	YEAR 4
NASCE Core	NASCE FSA	NASCE Core	NASCE Community
NASCE PreMat		NASCE EGC	NASCE PostG

Figure 18.2 *Recommended schedule for administration of NASCE*

The Carnegie Elective Community Engagement Classification

Background and Purpose

The Carnegie Foundation has been classifying institutions of higher education since the early 1970s. In the early 2000s, the Foundation sought to design a new "elective" classification for community engagement (Saltmarsh & Johnson, 2018). With this elective classification depending on voluntary participation by institutions, the Foundation created a "special-purpose classification" that would "open the possibility for involving only those institutions with special commitments in the area of community engagement" (McCormick & Zhao, 2005, p. 56).

As a classification of institutional (not program or unit) engagement, the classification's framework focuses on the following three major areas: (1) foundational indicators such as institutional commitment and institutional identity and culture; (2) curricular engagement; and (3) outreach and partnerships. Following the pilot, the first cycle of classification occurred in 2006, followed by a second round in 2008, and a third in 2010. Following the 2010 cycle, the classification shifted to a five-year cycle for classification and reclassification, with campuses receiving the classification retaining it for ten years. An overview of classified campuses between the 2006 and the 2015 cycles can be found in Table 18.2. The classification was designed to respect the diversity of institutions and their approaches to community engagement, encourage institutions to undertake a process of inquiry, reflection, and self-assessment, and honor an institution's achievements while promoting ongoing development of their programs (Driscoll, 2008). The classification is not designed as a ranking tool, but is evaluative in that campuses are either classified or not. There is no hierarchy, nor are there levels of classification. While successful campuses are announced publicly by the Foundation, the results of the process are not released for campuses that are not successful in acquiring the classification. As an "elective" classification, the Foundation is careful not to create a disincentive for seeking the classification and not achieving it.

Defining Engagement

The way in which the Carnegie Foundation defines community engagement has two parts: the first focuses on the processes of engagement and the second on the purposes.

> *Community engagement describes the collaboration between institutions of higher education and their larger communities (local, regional/state, national, global) for the mutually beneficial exchange of knowledge and resources in a context of partnership and reciprocity.*

> *The purpose of community engagement is the partnership of college and university knowledge and resources with those of the public and private sectors to enrich scholarship, research, and creative activity; enhance curriculum, teaching, and learning; prepare educated, engaged citizens; strengthen democratic values and civic responsibility; address critical societal issues; and contribute to the public good.* (Swearer Center for Public Service, Brown University, 2018a)

Central to the standards of the classification is that the partnership relationships between the campus and the community are characterized by collaboration, reciprocity, and mutuality. Community engagement, as defined in the classification, "requires going beyond the expert model that often gets in the way of constructive university–community collaboration [...] calls on faculty to move beyond 'outreach' [...] asks scholars to go beyond 'service,' with its overtones of noblesse oblige. What it emphasizes is genuine *collaboration*: that the learning and teaching be multidirectional and the expertise shared. It represents a basic reconceptualization of [...] community-based work" (O'Meara & Rice, 2005, p. 28).

Framed in this way, community engagement is not an umbrella concept meant to capture any activity associated with civic education, experiential education, or involvement of campuses with local, regional, national, or global communities. These are valuable educational activities, some of which, depending on how they are designed, could be community engaged. Nor is community engagement intended as institutional commitments ranging from investments to procurements, employment, outreach, and economic development. All of these are important activities that can raise the campus's engagement profile, but are not substitutes for, nor are they synonymous with, academic and scholarly engagement. Further, non-scholarly forms of engagement require little in terms of organizational change and have little impact on the educational experiences of students or the core academic and scholarly work of faculty.

The Carnegie Foundation is classifying community engagement, not applied research, public scholarship, internships, economic development, or student volunteerism. It is classifying institutional commitment to activities across the campus that embody the characteristics of engagement and that directly impact the educational experiences of students and the scholarly work of faculty and/or align with and reinforce both.

The Documentation Framework

The application is constructed as a documentation framework for providing evidence of community engagement. It consists of the following three parts:

1. Foundational Indicators
2. Curricular Engagement
3. Outreach and Partnerships

The foundational indicators are divided into the following two sections: "Institutional Commitment" and "Institutional Identity and Culture." The evidence requested in these sections is, as the heading suggests, "foundational" to institutional community engagement. Under the topic of institutional identity and culture, the questions pertain to mission and vision, recognition, assessment and data, marketing materials, and community engagement as a leadership priority. In the area of institutional commitment, the questions focus on infrastructure, budget and fundraising, tracking and documentation, assessment and data, professional development, community voice, faculty recruitment and promotion, student leadership, and the significance of community engagement in the strategic plan of the campus. At the

Table 18.2 *Classification totals by year*

Classification year	Campuses classified
2006	76
2008	121
2010	115
2015	83 first-time
	157 reclassification
	240 total

end of the Foundational Indicators section, the applicants are instructed "to review the responses to Foundational Indicators [. . .] and determine whether Community Engagement is 'institutionalized'" – that is, "whether all or most of the Foundational Indicators have been documented with specificity. If so, applicants are encouraged to continue with the application. If not, applicants are encouraged to withdraw from the process and apply in the next round" of the classification (Swearer Center for Public Service, Brown University, 2018b). The purpose of applying this kind of filter to the process is because the Foundational Indicators are, by definition, "foundational" to the institutionalization of curricular engagement and outreach and partnership activity.

Following the Foundational Indicators is the section on "Curricular Engagement," which is defined in the framework as "the teaching, learning, and scholarship that engages faculty, students, and community in mutually beneficial and respectful collaboration. Their interactions address community identified needs, deepen students' civic and academic learning, enhance community well-being, and enrich the scholarship of the institution" (Swearer Center for Public Service, Brown University, 2018b). The focus in this section is on the extent to which community engagement is part of the central academic experience of the campus, and questions are aimed at the number of students impacted, the number of courses offered, the curriculum, learning outcomes, and community engagement outcomes assessment.

The final section is "Outreach and Partnerships," described as "two different but related approaches to community engagement. The first focuses on the application and provision of institutional resources for community use. The latter focuses on collaborative interactions with community and related scholarship for the mutually beneficial exchange, exploration, and application of knowledge, information, and resources (research, capacity building, economic development, etc.). The distinction between these two centers on the concepts of reciprocity and mutual benefit which are explicitly explored and addressed in partnership activities" (Swearer Center for Public Service, Brown University, 2018b). Outreach questions focus on the programs and institutional resources provided for the community, which are not engagement, but are important complements to engagement activities, and partnership questions focus on evidence of mutuality and reciprocity in partnership relations, and ask for examples of partnerships provided in what is referred to as "the partnership grid," which is intended to capture a sense of the institution's depth and breadth of interactive partnerships that demonstrate reciprocity and mutual benefit. Campuses are asked to provide partnership examples that are representative of the range of forms and topical foci of partnerships across a sampling of disciplines and units.

Motivations for Classification

Campuses seek the Carnegie Classification for a number of reasons, and often for multiple reasons. The most prevalent is to undergo a structured process of institutional self-assessment and self-study. Putting together an application, gathering evidence and reflecting on it, and understanding the areas of strengths and weaknesses of institutional engagement are ways of improving practice and advancing community engagement on campus. The application process is way to bring the disparate parts of the campus together to advance a unified agenda. At the same time, it allows for the identification of promising practices that can be shared across the institution.

Campuses also seek the classification as a way of legitimizing community engagement work that may not have received public recognition and visibility. Additionally, the classification is used as a way to demonstrate accountability that the institution is fulfilling its mission to serve the public good. The classification process can also serve as a catalyst for change, fostering institutional alignment for community-based teaching, learning, and scholarship. The application can foster all of these, and it is further used to crystalize an institutional identity around community engagement. A campus may be a research university or a community college or a liberal arts college, but it also may be community engaged, creating distinction for the campus.

Common Challenges

When campuses are notified of their successful classification, they receive a letter of congratulations from the Carnegie Foundation and some feedback as they continue to advance community engagement on campus. The 2015 letter noted that "even among the most effective applications, there are areas of practice in need of continued development. As a way of improving your institutional practices and to position your campus for successful re-classification in the future," classified campuses were encouraged "to attend to the areas of (1) assessment, (2) reciprocal partnerships, (3) faculty rewards, and (4) integration and alignment with other institutional initiatives" (Swearer Center for Public Service, Brown University, 2018c). These four areas represent common challenges campuses face as they work to institutionalize community engagement.

Assessment. Applications should demonstrate systematic assessment of community engagement that meets a broad range of purposes. Assessment is essential for understanding impact and for continuous improvement, and it is built into the framework through the following: assessing community perceptions of institutional engagement; tracking and recording of institution-wide engagement data; assessment of the impact of community engagement on students, faculty, community, and the institution; identification and assessment of student learning outcomes in curricular engagement; and ongoing feedback mechanisms for partnerships.

Reciprocity. Partnerships require a high level of understanding of and intentional practices specifically directed to reciprocity and mutuality. Campuses are encouraged to attend to processes of initiating and nurturing collaborative, two-way partnerships and to develop strategies for systematic communication. Maintaining authentically collaborative, mutually beneficial partnerships takes ongoing commitment and attention to this critical aspect of community engagement.

Faculty Rewards. With regard to faculty rewards for roles in community engagement, it is difficult to create a campus culture of community engagement when there are no clearly articulated incentives for faculty to prioritize this work. Campuses should provide evidence of clear policies for recognizing community engagement in teaching and learning and in research and creative activity, along with criteria that validate appropriate methodologies and scholarly artifacts. Campuses are encouraged to initiate study, dialogue, and reflection to promote and reward the scholarship of engagement more fully.

Integration with Other Priorities. Finally, campuses that are institutionalizing community engagement should consider how community engagement can be integrated with other institutional initiatives. Community engagement offers often-untapped possibilities for alignment with other campus priorities and initiatives to achieve greater impact, such as the following: first-year programs that include community engagement; learning communities in which community engagement is integrated into the design; or diversity initiatives that explicitly link active and collaborative community-based teaching and learning with the academic success of underrepresented students.

What the Carnegie Community Engagement Classification process has revealed are specific areas that, for many campuses, need greater attention in order to fully realize engagement. Depending on the unique culture and context of the campus, certain areas of change may be more challenging than others. As campuses move forward with advancing their engagement agendas, the classification provides a blueprint for institutionalizing community engagement and the kinds of organizational and cultural changes that will need to be attended to.

Moving Forward

This is a unique and tumultuous time for higher education across the globe. Located squarely between the neoliberal, market-driven, highly privatized university and the need for universities to more effectively address social issues and improve the human condition are the issues of community engagement, publically engaged scholarship, and university–community partnerships. This is the crux of the "crucible moment" identified by the National Task Force on Civic Learning and Democratic Engagement of the Association of American Colleges and Universities (2012) and the "Copernican moment" named by Scobey (2012).

Higher education as a system is deeply entrenched, struggles to define its public good mission, and has functioned as an engine of social and economic stratification instead of an engine of equality and opportunity. "Commercialization and commodification," the "fragmentation of disciples, overspecialization, and divisions among the arts and sciences and the professions" manifest in universities' "unintegrated, fragmented, internally conflicted structure and organization," and all create obstacles that "impede understanding and developing solutions to complex human and societal problems" (Benson, 2017, pp. 145–146). The civic engagement movement has come a long way in higher education, but it has a long way to go. Assessment and classification can assist with advancing community engagement.

Increasingly, campuses are addressing the deep, pervasive, and integrated changes needed in order to enact the implications of the collaborative aspect of teaching and learning, research, scholarship, creative activity, and outreach and service. Often this means focusing on the core culture of the campus and the essential artifacts of culture as identified in the NASCE and by the Carnegie Community Engagement Classification.

As more and more campuses across the USA and internationally are seeking to improve the core academic functions of teaching, learning, and research, are working to improve student engagement in learning and student learning outcomes, and are focusing more intentionally on demonstrating mission-oriented practices that fulfill a public good mission, assessing and advancing community engagement emerges more clearly as an institutional priority. Instruments like the NASCE and the Carnegie Community Engagement Classification are tools that campuses can use to move their engagement agenda forward.

References

Benson, L. (2017). *Knowledge for social change: Bacon, Dewey, and the revolutionary transformation of research universities in the twenty-first century*. Philadelphia, PA: Temple University Press.

Boyer, E. L. (1990). *Scholarship reconsidered: Priorities of the professoriate*. Princeton, NJ: Princeton University Press.

Cuban, L. (1988). A fundamental puzzle of school reform. *Phi Delta Kappan, 69*(5), 341–344.

Driscoll, A. (2008). Carnegie's community-engagement classification: Intentions and insights. *Change: The Magazine of Higher Learning, 40*(1), 38–41.

Eckel, P., Hill, B., & Green, M. (1998). *On change: En route to transformation. An occasional paper series*. Washington, DC: American Council on Education.

Hazelkorn, E. (2015). *Rankings and the reshaping of higher education: The battle for world-class excellence*. Berlin: Springer.

Johnson, M., Levy, D., Cichetti, P., & Zinkiewicz, C. (2013). An untapped reservoir for student community engagement: What we are learning from the NASCE. In *Deepening community engagement in higher education* (pp. 65–79). New York: Palgrave Macmillan US.

Jones, E. J., & Shefner, J. (2014). Introduction: Globalization and the university – A path to social justice. In *Social justice and the university: Globalization, human rights and the future of democracy* (pp. 11–17). New York: Palgrave Macmillan.

McCormick, A. C., & Zhao, C. M. (2005). Rethinking and reframing the Carnegie classification. *Change: The Magazine of Higher Learning, 37*(5), 51–57.

National Task Force on Civic Learning and Democratic Engagement (2012). *A crucible moment: College learning and democracy's future.* Washington, DC: Association of American Colleges and Universities.

O'Meara, K., & Rice, R. E. (2005). Principles of good practice: Encouraging multiple forms of scholarship in policy and practice. In *Faculty priorities reconsidered: Rewarding multiple forms of scholarship* (pp. 290–302). San Francisco, CA: Jossey-Bass.

Putnam, R. D. (1995). Bowling alone: America's declining social capital. *Journal of Democracy, 6*(1), 65–78.

Rhoads, R. A., & Szelényi, K. (2011). *Global citizenship and the university: Advancing social life and relations in an interdependent world.* Palo Alto, CA: Stanford University Press.

Saltmarsh, J., & Johnson, M. B. (Eds.) (2018). *The Elective Carnegie Community Engagement Classification: Constructing a successful application for first-time and re-classification applicants.* Sterling, VA: Stylus Publishing, LLC.

Scobey, D. (2012). A Copernican moment: On the revolutions in higher education. In *Transforming undergraduate education: Theory that compels and practices that succeed* (pp. 37–49). Lanham, MD: Rowman & Littlefield.

Swearer Center for Public Service, Brown University (2018a). Carnegie Community Engagement Classification. Retrieved from www.brown.edu/swearer/carnegie/about.

Swearer Center for Public Service, Brown University (2018b). Classification application information. Retrieved from www.brown.edu/swearer/carnegie/2020-classification-application-information.

Swearer Center for Public Service, Brown University (2018c). Previous classifications. Retrieved from www.brown.edu/swearer/previous-classifications.

19 Fostering an Integrated Culture of Community Engagement

Keristiena S. Dodge, Anthony Starke, Deborah Smith-Howell, & Sara Woods

Throughout the USA, universities and colleges reaffirmed their commitment to civic engagement by recognizing their pivotal role in educating engaged and responsible citizens (Campus Compact, 2012). Black (2013) argues that higher education institutions have an ethical obligation to educate students who are aware of the realities of their community. He asserts that community engagement, service learning, and the scholarship of engagement are mechanisms that connect students to their communities.

Despite this commitment, higher education institutions struggle with the question of how to create a culture that values community engagement as a core feature of university life. In light of these struggles, initiatives such as the Carnegie Foundation Community Engagement Classification, the American Association of State Colleges and Universities, and the Coalition of Urban and Metropolitan Universities gained prominence by exploring how a culture shift away from traditional higher education toward a community-engaged focus could be achieved (American Association of State colleges and Universities, 2002; Hathaway, Mulhollan & White, 1990; New England Resource Center for Higher Education, 2017).

Drawing from the experiences of high-level administrators at the University of Nebraska Omaha (UNO), this chapter will cover the importance of the strategic alliance between academia and the community. UNO leadership created a framework that supports engagement and has resulted in an integrated culture of engagement. This integrated culture is evident in numerous artifacts, including reward structures, daily community presence on campus, high levels of participation in service learning, funding for engaged research, and bottom-up buy-in, which manifests itself in engagement practices occurring across the campus in a variety of forms. The authors will provide guidance on how to establish such an integrated culture by connecting all facets of higher education to engagement.

This chapter will begin with a discussion of the complexities of implementing change in higher education, as institutionalizing community engagement requires change in organizational behaviors. Next, the chapter will unpack key strategies to create an integrated culture of engagement. Proven to be successful strategies at UNO, the authors will explain how different types of institutions can adapt these strategies to fit their needs. An analysis will assert that the strategies can be categorized into the following three groups: identity, infrastructure, and behavior.

The authors will argue that when employing the three categories simultaneously, they reinforce each other and result in an integrated culture of engagement.

The creation of this framework was not without its challenges and missteps. In discussing these challenges, the authors will focus on how to leverage institution-wide structures and policies to foster engagement across a decentralized campus. The authors will also reflect on the responsibilities associated with an institution-wide commitment to engagement, which at UNO has led to a renewed focus on the measurement of community engagement outcomes and impacts.

Sustaining Organizational Change in Higher Education

There are many definitions of organizational change. The term generally refers to alterations in current organizational behaviors, policies, and practices (Rainey, 2014). Implementing and sustaining change are not easy tasks. Change within institutions of higher education can be influenced by many aspects, such as institution size and organizational and governance structures. For example, institutional governance involves faculty, academic staff, administrators, and the governing board working collaboratively to make decisions about the organization, with each group having decision-making authority in specific areas (e.g., curriculum, budget, etc.).

Change in higher education settings may be the result of internal factors, such as new leadership, strategic planning efforts (e.g., modifications to the mission and/or vision), and/or changes in faculty, staff, and student demographics. Sometimes change is the result of exogenous factors, such as demographic changes, technological advancements, financial pressures, and changes in the economy (Keza & Eckel, 2002). Environmental changes force institutions of higher education to both protect their legitimacy and redefine their role within society. Macro-trends have shifted the legitimacy of higher education away from functioning as social institutions and toward functioning as an industry (Gumport, 2000). On the other hand, societies are calling upon institutions of higher education to help address complex problems such as poverty and crime (Bardo, 1990; Diner, 2013). This prominence of an external rather than internal focus is widely discussed as the "town and gown" relationship (Rodin, 2007). It means reconsidering the ways in which higher education institutions function within and contribute to a greater endeavor. Other societal changes may also influence and drive change in higher education institutions. Depending on the role and function of these institutions and their relation to the state, change may occur following changes in political leadership, be evolutionary, mimic change in the power of interest groups and alliances, or depend on the market environment (Gornitzka, 1999). For example, concerns relating to the affordability of higher education for low-income students have been voiced by both government branches and philanthropists. As a response to this concern, the Nebraska Legislature created the Goodrich Scholarship Program in 1972 (University of Nebraska Omaha, 2017c) and the Susan T. Buffett Foundation created the William H. Thompson Scholars Learning Community, which offers scholarships to low-income Nebraska students (Susan Thompson Buffett Foundation, 2017). This example illustrates that the pluralist nature of higher education, with its many stakeholders and competing initiatives, creates an environment where change can occur based on factors outside of the institution's control (Kezar, 2009). With regard to change in higher education, Boyce (2003) writes, "the challenge of successful change is less planning and implementing and more developing and sustaining new ways of seeing, deciding, and acting" (p. 133). Accordingly, successful change in higher education is a form of praxis, the integration of new knowledge into organizational practices and behaviors.

Strategies for Fostering a Culture of Engagement

This section will discuss ten change strategies and describe the origins and implementation of each of the strategies at UNO within the context of community engagement. These strategies are as follows: leveraging the institution's mission; embracing the evolutionary approach; ensuring leadership commitment; creating bottom-up buy-in; engaging boundary-spanning coalitions; employing an inclusive strategic planning process; regularly assessing and refocusing; rewarding engagement; breaking down partnership development barriers; and nourishing relationships with the philanthropic community. While some strategies allowed UNO to elevate the importance of community engagement to the institution, others allowed UNO to sustain these organizational changes by integrating them into organizational structures, practices, and behaviors, making them more resilient.

Strategy 1: Leverage the Institution's Mission

The institution's mission is a key characteristic that can function as a tool for advancing community engagement on campus (Andes, 2006; Bailey, Muse, Todd, & Wilson, 2013; Bardo, 1990; Brownell, 1993; Eckardt & Eisman, 2006; Franz, Childers, & Sanderlin, 2012; Gelmon, Holland, Driscoll, Spring, & Kerrigan, 2001; Pearl, 2014; Weerts & Sandmann, 2008; Zlotkowski & Meeropol, 2006). The metropolitan mission is at the core of UNO's identity. Adopted in 1998, UNO's mission reads: "The University of Nebraska at Omaha is Nebraska's metropolitan university – a university with strong academic values and *significant relationships with our local, regional, national, and international communities that transforms and improves life*" (University of Nebraska Omaha, 2017a, emphasis added). Here, the commitment to community engagement is inherently intertwined with the metropolitan mission – the two cannot be separated from each other. Driving UNO's community engagement are values of reciprocity, collaboration, dialogue, diversity, and continuous improvements (University of Nebraska Omaha, 2017b).

Metropolitan universities were created as a response to the problems facing urban areas, including severe poverty, racial tensions, and crime (Bardo, 1990; Brownell, 1993; Diner, 2013). Bardo (1990) writes: "A metropolitan university is not merely a university *in* a city, it is *of* the city. Its focus is on the total educational needs of its area and the interlinkages of those needs with the changing and shifting conditions in the world at large" (p. 42, emphasis in original). Holland (2002) writes: "For urban or metropolitan institutions, public and private, that engagement agenda and civic relationship is a core characteristic that deeply shapes the entire academic culture of the institution" (p. 20). For example, when in 2005 UNO faced a budget reduction, leadership decided to increase funding to the Service Learning Academy. Leadership's decision to support community engagement in times of fiscal distress was strategic and reaffirmed UNO's commitment to engagement to all its stakeholders. The ability to justify such a decision is directly tied to the metropolitan mission in which the importance of community engagement is not negotiable.

Engagement is also a core component of land-grant universities (Bailey et al., 2013; Diner, 2013; Franz, Childers, & Sanderlin, 2012; Pearl, 2014; Weerts & Sandmann, 2008). In fact, the 1862 Morrill Act, which provided funding for land-grant state universities, embraced land grants as "the beginning of a new era in the life of universities, developing in them a consciousness of their duty to the public." Breaking down the "ivory tower," land-grant universities made higher education accessible to agricultural workers and continue to serve rural areas (Diner, 2013, p. 61). Diner's historical analysis demonstrates that metropolitan universities were actually modeled on land-grant institutions. The University of Omaha entered the University of Nebraska system as the municipal campus, while the University of Nebraska – Lincoln (UNL) was the system's land-grant institution.

To successfully institutionalize community engagement, institutions need to draw on their missions (Andes, 2006; Eckardt & Eisman, 2006). Doing this will allow leadership to inherently connect community engagement with the institution's identity and create the perception that engagement is synonymous with its purpose and existence. Whereas UNO is able to do this by emphasizing its metropolitan mission, other types of institutions can achieve similar results by relying on their identities. Faith-based institutions, for instance, could reaffirm their charitable practices as a core component of their missions. Regardless of the institutional identity – whether it is metropolitan, land grant, or faith based – drawing on an institution's mission can be a powerful justification for establishing, sustaining, and legitimizing engaged practices.

Strategy 2: Embrace the Evolutionary Approach

Administrators argued that adopting the "metropolitan" mission was not a revolutionary step, but rather an evolutionary one. Integrating UNO's culture of engagement into its policies, procedures, and practices was the result of gradual development, each expansion building on the last. Drawing on threads in the institution's history and existing practices, the argument was that adoption of the metropolitan mission would simply solidify an identity that existed since its inception and build on the momentum of engagement.

For example, one of the challenges UNO addressed in the late 1990s was how to adopt its metropolitan mission and create a strategic plan that valued community engagement. This was of interest because UNO had no clear identity and adoption of the metropolitan mission was considered to be a way to solidify UNO's institutional identity. This process led to the creation of an inclusive and comprehensive strategic planning process (more on this later). UNO formally adopted its metropolitan mission in 1998 and the strategic plan that identified community engagement as one of its strategic goals in 2000 (Woods, Reed, & Smith-Howell, 2016). When engaging in the strategic planning process in 1997, UNO administrators argued that the adoption of the metropolitan mission was an appropriate next step in advancing UNO's institutional identity, primarily by leveraging the institution's history and engagement practices.

Administrators argued that when UNO was founded in 1908 as the University of Omaha, it was founded with the primary goal of advancing civic responsibility. To support this claim, they referenced the institution's founding document, specifically Article II, which stated: "The object of this Corporation [the University of Omaha] shall be to establish, endow, conduct, and maintain a University for the promotion of sound learning and *citizenship*" (quoted in Owen, 2016, emphasis added). In 1970, two years after the University of Omaha became part of the University of Nebraska system and was renamed the University of Nebraska Omaha, the Board of Regents published the *Report of the Regents' Commission on the Urban University of the 70's*. Here, the Board of Regents interpreted the role of the urban university to be "a university responsive to the needs of its socio-economic surroundings that draws upon all pertinent resources" and "an institution aware of its role in the societal mission of achieving a better life for all, it is concerned more with society's welfare than with its own self-preservation" (quoted in Owen, 2016).

Further, administrators argued that faculty across campus were already engaged with their community in teaching, research, and service. As community engagement gained momentum at UNO, administrators and faculty advocated that formally adopting this mission would empower the already existing efforts of faculty and staff. Administrators also pointed at UNO's involvement with the Coalition of Urban and Metropolitan Universities (CUMU) since 1993 and that the institution already considered other community-engaged institutions as its peers. The fact that in the 1970s UNO opened the College of Public Affairs and Community Services as a direct response to civil unrest (Woods, Reed, & Smith-Howell, 2016) only reaffirmed the notion that formal adoption of the metropolitan mission would build on UNO's history and existing practices – and sustain the engagement momentum.

Strategy 3: Ensure Leadership Commitment

Executive and mid-level leadership are critical in facilitating the practice of community engagement. Executive leaders need to create a network of mid-level leaders that support and advocate on behalf of community engagement (Franz, Childers, & Sanderlin, 2012).

For the past 20 years, the UNO Strategic Plan, with its metropolitan mission and its community engagement goals, has been resilient regarding leadership changes. Leaders across campus – including senior and mid-level administrators, the chancellor, vice chancellors, deans, directors, and program chairs – have a long-standing history and commitment to the university, demonstrated by their decades-long service to the institution. These individuals have an intimate understanding of the value of community engagement, deep connections to the community, and knowledge of the institution's past failures and achievements.

UNO leaders embody community engagement professionally through their active participation in community engagement conferences and leadership in professional organizations that promote community engagement. For example, prior to becoming chancellor, Chancellor Emeritus John Christensen worked for 30 years in the education field developing relationships with the community. Further, two former chancellors (including Christensen) held the position of president of the Coalition of Urban and Metropolitan Universities. Leadership consistently demonstrates its value for engagement when speaking to internal and external audiences (University of Nebraska Omaha, 2015). Many university leaders serve on numerous community boards. For example, in the 2013 State of the University address, Chancellor Emeritus John Christensen praised the campus engagement efforts, stating:

> The hallmark of metropolitan universities is community engagement [. . .] At UNO, we actively seek partnerships and stand ready to collaborate with all sectors of the city by utilizing institutional assets to enhance the quality of life in Omaha. In turn, this engagement provides exceptional experiences for students, faculty, and staff as they teach and learn in real-life settings, creating wins for all (2013, pp. 4–5).

Additionally, the strategic recruitment of human capital helps to sustain a framework that builds on engagement. The transparent and public hiring processes allow candidates to learn about the mission and core values of the institution from the perspectives of various stakeholders. When, in 2016, UNO started the search for its new chancellor, campus and community input was solicited. Many stakeholders insisted that the new chancellor had to understand the metropolitan mission and needed the skills to build relationships with the community. At UNO, community engagement is so embedded into the campus identity that it is often non-negotiable at every level, and especially in leadership positions. Job announcements include a paragraph pertaining to UNO's metropolitan mission and all candidates receive packets that include information on community engagement. Hiring committees often choose to have finalists interview with campus engagement leaders, such as Barbara Weitz Community Engagement Center (Weitz CEC) staff, the Director of Service Learning, etc. Consequently, the hiring process is a learning process, where candidates get an understanding that, regardless of what they are hired for, they must serve the UNO metropolitan mission with engagement as its core component.

Strategy 4: Create Bottom-Up Buy-In

While leadership is an important contributor to change, the organizational and governance structures of higher education institutions, such as principles of faculty governance, can thwart coercive, top-down attempts at change. Successful change in higher education institutions requires a confluence of strategies, including employing culturally responsive approaches (Keza & Eckel, 2002). Using a culturally responsive approach entails recognizing and respecting aspects of an institution's culture that may deter change implementation strategies. For example, UNO has a culture of decentralization and self-governance; therefore, creating a culture of bottom-up buy-in is essential in sustaining change. When bottom-up buy-in is achieved, individuals across an institution will practice and advocate engagement, creating a powerful support network.

A year-long self-assessment conducted by the university's Office of Academic Affairs and consisting of semi-structured interviews with 32 key leaders, faculty, and staff across campus demonstrated that UNO has a culture of engagement embedded throughout its decentralized campus (Starke, Shenouda, & Smith-Howell, 2017). The study found that community engagement and service occur in every college, department/school, and unit in some shape or form. For example, in the Athletics department, community engagement takes the form of community services, which is different from the classroom instruction, coupled with community-identified service projects in the Service Learning Academy. This lack of uniformity, which is characteristic of a decentralized institution, illustrates the different ways community engagement manifests in the organization's practices. While engagement is strongly encouraged by UNO administration, UNO fosters a bottom-up approach to community engagement (Woods, Reed, & Smith-Howell, 2016). Here, "bottom-up" refers to collective action at the "local" level characterized by decision-making at lower levels (i.e., departments, schools, colleges). This has resulted in community engagement that is fluid, taking the form of its unit. Engagement has become a practice that takes place across all units of campus, in a variety of forms, often without the explicit knowledge of leadership. Building on the previous example of the UNO Athletics Department, their community engagement has become institutionalized as an annual competition between athletic groups (i.e., coaches and athletes) to accrue the most community service hours, known as the MavCup.

Units' community engagement operations are relatively autonomous because UNO does not have a central Office of Outreach and Engagement that monitors community partnerships and engagement activities. The university has created a framework that gives units the freedom to align themselves with the metropolitan mission in ways that are appropriate and amenable to the units' individual needs, traditions, and practices. Each of UNO's six colleges, for example, was founded at a different time with a different mission, but the common value of engagement is present within the various mission-driven partnerships each has with the community. Each college has incorporated engagement in their reappointment, promotion, and tenure (RPT) guidelines to some extent. At times, faculty members were innovative in making the case for their engaged research to count toward their RPT, arguing that they were able to adhere to discipline standards while engaging the community. Their ability to receive promotion based on their engaged teaching and research strengthened others' ability to make similar claims. Here, the decentralized structure empowered individual faculty members to practice community engagement and be rewarded for such work.

Community engagement is risky business. The university is entering into partnerships with other organizations in order to share knowledge and/or resources. Any time institutions of higher education partner with other organizations, they open themselves up to liability and run the risk of an unsuccessful partnership. Adding to this dilemma is the fact that these partnerships are addressing complex problems. When stakes are high, failure is always a possibility. Research has shown that creating a safe space, also known as a climate of security, for people to try new things without fear of excessive punishment in cases of failure is positively associated with successful change (Allen, 2003). At UNO, the combination of top-down support and bottom-up buy-in has led to innovative community engagement. In the 1960s and 1970s, national changes in higher education policy led to increased enrollment, which corresponded with a demand for more faculty. This influx of faculty encouraged a "let's try it" attitude. At about the same time, UNO joined the University of Nebraska system, which brought about state funding. The convergence of new faculty and a stable funding source created an entrepreneurial spirit that is distinctive to UNO. The organization has a history of taking risks to invest in applied research and other work with and in the community. The entrepreneurial spirit was fostered within a climate of security. Faculty were trying new things at the "local" level and were supported by higher levels. These risks included looking for opportunities to reallocate funding and other resources to support engagement. For example, in the late 1990s, service learning pedagogy started as an initiative out of the UNO Center for Faculty Development (Woods, Reed, & Smith-Howell, 2016). As the university weathered a system-wide budget crisis in the early 2000s, UNO made a financial commitment to continue supporting professional development for faculty doing applied research and integrating it into their classroom structure. Today, this seeding effort has grown into the UNO Service Learning Academy, a nationally recognized unit that supports over 200 courses across all colleges annually.

Strategy 5: Engage in Boundary-Spanning Coalitions

While top-down leadership commitment and units' ability to operationalize engagement autonomously across the decentralized campus are important, networks and coalitions combining the two are invaluable to facilitating change throughout the organization. Building alliances, relationships, and partnerships between units capitalizes on innovative ideas, as representatives from across the university must join forces to implement community engagement initiatives. By cutting across traditional, invisible boundaries (e.g., academic and student affairs, the academic and business enterprise, etc.), coalitions identify campus-wide opportunities for investments and increase successful implementation of innovative ideas. For instance, in 2014, UNO opened the Weitz CEC, a building that houses over 30 university and community organizations. The Weitz CEC also offers a free meeting space for nonprofit organizations to advance the public good. One of the few requirements for occupying the meeting space at no cost is that the nonprofit organization cannot charge its visitors for the event. This has allowed UNO to become a hub of community events. The Weitz CEC has also facilitated the creation of partnerships between community organizations (Woods, Reed, & Smith-Howell, 2016). Such success could not have been operationalized without support from UNO Business and Finance, which oversees parking services, or University Communications, which plays a pivotal role in telling the UNO metropolitan story.

Another structure that has allowed UNO to break silos is the creation of a community chair model that promotes interdisciplinary initiatives. Community chairs are faculty leaders with endowments who work across multiple colleges and departments and in close collaboration with community partners to promote community engagement (Grandgenett et al., 2015). Not only have community chairs been able to work across colleges and departments, they have also been key in deconstructing the view that teaching is confined to the walls of a classroom.

Strategy 6: Employ an Inclusive Strategic Planning Process

Having a shared belief and common goal is essential to cultivating loyalty across divisions and organizational boundaries. "Loyalty causes individuals to stay with a system, to save and improve it rather than to leave to serve their self-interest elsewhere" (Clark, 1972, p. 183). One method of sharing organizational goals and beliefs is through organizational sagas. Organizational sagas – which are characterized as having a strong purpose be introduced by a person or small group with a mission that is fulfilled as the organization's practices and values embody the mission – create the foundations for trust and loyalty. Having faculty and staff who are able to communicate to others how organizational values influence practice and how practice embodies values creates a more informed campus. At UNO, this group is the Strategic Planning Steering Committee. The process of strategic planning is an essential method that needs to be leveraged to foster a culture of community engagement (Soto & Drummond, 2002; Wilhite & Silver, 2004). The Strategic Plan, of which community engagement is goal number 3, is part of UNO's identity. The plan explicates that the organization's mission is used to establish performance metrics and guides organizational decision-making. Since the creation of the Strategic Plan in 2000, UNO has engaged in a comprehensive and inclusive strategic planning process. The Strategic Planning Steering Committee, which leads strategic planning efforts, has broad representation across campus and the community. It includes administrators, college representatives, faculty, staff, students, alumni, and community partners.

Facilitated dialogues called "campus forums" were the essential precursors to the current strategic planning forums that occur biennially. These structured dialogues are pivotal for conceptualizing community engagement at UNO. These strategic planning events solicit feedback from faculty, staff, students, and community members. For example, in 2000, when the UNO underwent academic prioritization, the strategic plan and planning forums were critical to identifying campus priorities. More recently, the strategic planning forum was used to solicit feedback on whether the identified priorities were still relevant or should be abandoned. Soto and Drummond (2002) write that strategic planning as a process is useful to establish partnerships between the university and the community. This has been the experience at UNO. The Steering Committee identifies the issues that need attention, and the broad representation of the Steering Committee provides legitimacy to these issues. Every year, two Strategic Planning Forums are organized. During these Strategic Planning Forums, feedback is solicited from audiences consisting of around 200 participants. The relationship between the university and the community is strengthened because visible changes are made based on dialogues and input from university and community stakeholders.

Strategy 7: Regularly Assess and Refocus

Dialogue is a key component of organizational learning and an essential method to achieve bottom-up buy-in. Organizational learning refers to the ways in which organizations create, retain, and transfer knowledge in service to organizational decision-making and improvement. Argyris and Schön's (1996) work on organizational learning posits that an organization's survival is contingent upon its capacity to identify and correct errors, learn from those errors and their corrections, and embed that knowledge into organizational practices. To sustain change, it is important to (re) examine assumptions, explore alternatives, and to be responsive to feedback (Boyce, 2003). Conducting a self-assessment is a highly recommended practice. In addition to conducting stand-alone self-study, self-assessment can be done through the process of applying for the Carnegie Community Engagement Classification (Pearl, 2014) or through accreditation (Andes, 2006).

UNO engaged in a campus-wide dialogue when it conducted a self-assessment pertaining to the conceptualization of engagement across campus. After conducting over 30 semi-structured interviews with campus leaders and engagement professionals about their understanding of community engagement terminology and their operationalization, the Office of Academic Affairs published and disseminated a report to the campus. Most importantly, in it, the university acknowledged the existence of an engagement continuum, which recognizes and values both service and mutually beneficial engagement (Starke, Shenouda, & Smith-Howell, 2017). UNO's experience shows the importance of disseminating information back to campus stakeholders and acting on feedback in an explicit manner. These types of assessments are regularly discussed and shared during strategic planning forums.

In 2017, UNO revised its strategic plan to ensure it reflected the growth and change that had occurred since the adoption of the plan in 2000. The Strategic Planning Committee presented a revised plan and stakeholders were given several months to provide input on the revised draft plan. The report went through multiple rounds of feedback solicited from stakeholders (e.g., faculty, staff, students, community members, etc.) via forums, emails, and surveys. This is not uncommon, because strategic planning is an iterative process in which the university engages in a consistent dialogue with its internal and external stakeholders. Wilhite and Silver (2004) warn that non-engagement could result from a sense of "pseudo-consultation" in which the campus community believes that although their feedback is solicited, it will not impact decision-making. It is therefore important that when feedback is requested, it is not only reviewed, but also shared with the community, and that any resulting changes are explicitly advertised.

Strategy 8: Reward Engagement

The inclusion of community engagement in faculty RPT guidelines is considered a strong indicator of an institution's commitment to community engagement (Eckardt & Eisman, 2006; Franz, Childers, & Sanderlin, 2012; Weerts & Sandmann, 2008; Zlotkowski & Meeropol, 2006), while its absence is considered a barrier to institutionalizing engagement (Terranova, Martello, & Taylor, 2006). At UNO, every college has incorporated community engagement in RPT guidelines to some extent. The College of Public Affairs and Community Service (CPACS) subscribes to the Boyer Model for the Scholarship of Engagement (Boyer, 1996), which argues that applied research and engaged scholarship are invaluable and should be valued in the same way as traditional scholarship, and requires that all faculty must meet its substantial service expectations to receive tenure.

Other ways the university rewards community engagement is through engagement spotlights. Engagement spotlights are stories that feature students, staff, and faculty and their community engagement activities. The spotlights are widely distributed through the website (www.unomaha.edu/campus-commitment-to-community-engagement/index.php) and social media, and the individuals featured are cele-brated. In addition to rewarding individuals for their engagement, the spotlights also make the meaning of community engagement concrete and show its diverse applications (volunteerism, teaching, research, etc.).

Strategy 9: Break Down Partnership Development Barriers

Community partners often indicate the difficulty in navigating a large and complex institution. Decentralization can be considered a particular barrier for partnership development (Sandmann & Kliewer, 2012). For instance, UNO does not have a central Office of Outreach and Engagement to direct its engagement activities. This gives colleges and departments more freedom to engage the community, but it also means that there is less coordination among units, resulting in overlapping activities and a lack of strategic focus.

With innovations such as the Weitz CEC at UNO, community engagement has remained pluralist in nature while providing multiple points of access to the campus for organizations seeking partnerships. The Weitz CEC is not an authoritative body or clearinghouse for engagement; instead, it acts as a hub that facilitates coordination between the community and UNO departments. When a community organization does not know who to contact or partner with in the university, the visibility of the Weitz CEC with its several anchor organizations, including the Service Learning Academy and the Office of Social and Civic Participation, provides a clear point of access.

Further, it is also important to avoid physical barriers to partnership development. At UNO, this resulted in strategic actions being taken to provide access. Placing the Weitz CEC in the middle of the original Dodge Street campus and providing free parking to its visitors were intentional ways of ensuring community members had access to the campus. Visible structures such as the Weitz CEC lower the threshold for community partners to contact and collaborate with the university, which positively impacts the power relationship between the university and the community. The Weitz CEC is recognized throughout the community as a campus resource for the community (Woods, Reed, & Smith-Howell, 2016).

In addition, many units employ staff members who fulfill a coordinating function. These coordinators, who may be associate deans, community chairs, professors, etc., work in or across units to cultivate and manage partnerships with the external community. What distinguishes this group from others is that their primary focus is not the implementation of a specific project, but rather they identify needs, match community organizations with UNO units, and support partnerships. Within their respective department, these coordinators have a clearly defined domain or target audience (e.g., CEC building partners, the Latin/Latino community, K–12, etc.). Their approach to community engagement is pragmatic, and they ascribe a high level of value to working with partners. They fill the gap and build the bridges that connect the university to the community. The Service Learning Academy, for instance, employs a "community liaison," whose job it is to match learning opportunities on campus with strong relationships in the community. Similarly, the "manager of possibilities" works in the Weitz CEC with the primary task of talking to community partners and exploring partnership and collaboration possibilities. The presence of a person who is dedicated to recognizing community needs and possible assets results in unique partnerships. For instance, the manager of possibilities facilitated a partnership between the Girl Scouts of Nebraska, the Black Police Officers Association, Nebraskans for Civic Reform, and the Nebraska Watershed Network. Together, the four organizations engaged inner-city girls in after-school programming pertaining to sustainability, water quality, and citizen science, while being mentored by off-duty police officers (Woods, Reed, & Smith-Howell, 2016).

Strategy 10: Nourish Relationships with the Philanthropic Community

Community engagement entails the mutual exchange of knowledge and resources. Its activities often require a host of resources that neither the institution nor the community partners have at their disposal. Cultivating a relationship with the philanthropic community is not just about securing funds to support operations and capital investments, such as financing the construction of the $24 million Weitz CEC; it is also a method of engagement. At UNO, Omaha's philanthropic community is a major supporter of community engagement. Philanthropy provides funding that independently supports or augments other revenue sources for engagement initiatives. Managing philanthropy is a function of institutional advancement. Andrea McManus, a professional fundraiser, defines a culture of philanthropy as, "walking hand-in-hand with your donor and changing the way that you approach things around fundraising to fully engage the entire organization, from the board on down" (quoted in Davenport, 2013).

Many donors expect their gifts to have significant impacts on society; therefore, donor, institutional, and social needs and objectives need to be aligned (Riggs, 2010). To fulfill the donor's desire to create impact by supporting an organization within the community, the organization must have personnel with civic reach to lead and manage philanthropic relationship-building processes (Vandeventer, 2011). A leader with civic reach has prestige, knowledge, and connections – personal and professional prestige, local knowledge, and community-wide strategic relationships, respectively. He or she must possess the ability to read the external environment and the knowledge to incorporate strategies that place the organization's "programs and services at the confluence of opportunities to make positive change and secure resources" and "advance and defend the organization's mission; connect with diverse audiences; and, access to power" (Vandeventer, 2011, p. 26).

At UNO, civic reach and community engagement tend to be closely associated. UNO's administrators and leaders have spent much of their academic careers at the university, built strong relationships, and made deep investments in the Omaha community. They serve on nonprofit, local, state, regional, and national boards, committees, and commissions. These administrators are also recognized as leaders in their respective fields, having received numerous awards and recognitions for their scholarly and service contributions to their professions and disciplines. Furthermore, these campus leaders act as brokers between the campus and donors, diligently working to match community needs with UNO's mission and programs and donor values.

Managing philanthropy is a cumbersome task that requires building relationships at all levels. Administrators are supported by the University of Nebraska Foundation, an independent 501(c)(3) nonprofit that serves as the philanthropic arm of the university system. The Foundation oversees back-office fundraising functions and works closely with each of the University of Nebraska campuses. Each campus is responsible for building its own philanthropic relationships. Donors are attracted to the type of work that community engagement involves; however, the institution must make the connection between these investments and impacts on the community, as they are not readily identifiable. Through coordination and ongoing relations between donors, the community, the University of Nebraska Foundation, and the UNO campus, external dollars are used to fulfill donors' desires for societal impact and the campuses' desires to carry out mission-driven engagement activities.

An organization's brand also impacts its fundraising potential (Sargeant & Ford, 2007). Having a clear understanding of the organization's mission and vision and a solid case for support can lead to successful fundraising strategies. When leaders know the mission, vision, and values of the organization, they are able to easily determine good matches between external dollars and organizational activities. UNO's metropolitan mission is its brand. Building upon its metropolitan university brand, UNO has established itself in a way that attracts donors seeking to make an impact (Woods, Reed, & Smith-Howell, 2016). Indeed, philanthropists often approach UNO leaders with ideas for funding opportunities. Their confidence in UNO's ability to make an impact is remarkable, especially considering that many donors are not UNO alumni.

Concluding Remarks

Table 19.1 presents each of the ten strategies, summarizes their underlying rationale, and lists specific action steps taken at UNO to implement each strategy.

There is no one right way to institutionalize community engagement. This chapter presents ten strategies employed by one university. The strategies are not mutually exclusive, and certain aspects of each strategy impact others. For instance, employing an inclusive strategic planning process is important to assess the institution's

Table 19.1 *Strategy summary*

Strategy	Rationale	UNO example
Leverage the institution's mission	An institution's mission is key to its identity. By connecting community engagement to the mission, an institution is able to internalize engagement as part of its identity	• Focus on history of engagement • Focus on CUMU peer institutions
Embrace the evolutionary approach	Recognizing community engagement as a core component should be framed as "the next logical step" rather than a revolutionary action. In this way, change is a series of incremental responses to the environment that build on the institution's tradition, mission, and values	• Focus on metropolitan emphasis and citizenship language in founding documents • Focus on existing outreach and community-engaged scholarship
Ensure leadership commitment	Leadership should support, praise, and preferably embody community engagement. This encourages others in the institution to actively support engagement. Further, leadership commitment is pivotal in allocating resources to support engagement	• Chancellors taking leadership positions in CUMU • Hiring process focuses on engagement
Create bottom-up buy-in	Evidence of an integrated culture of community engagement is that engagement occurs on every level of the institution. It is not only leadership that promotes it; it is actually something individuals throughout the institution live by. Bottom-up buy-in is a prerequisite to community engagement institutionalization	• Provide seed money to fund new initiatives • Allow individuals and units the freedom to align community engagement with their units' priorities • Engage faculty and staff in discussions pertaining to engagement through various methods, including strategic planning
Engage in boundary-spanning coalitions	For community engagement to grow, efforts should go beyond traditional silos. Coalitions between academic and student affairs, business and finance, and transdisciplinary efforts should be created	• Coalition between the UNO Business and Finance office and the Weitz CEC • Creation of the community chair model

Table 19.1 (*cont.*)

Strategy	Rationale	UNO example
Employ an inclusive strategic planning process	Strategic planning is a method that allows an institution to assess its engagement landscape and solicit comprehensive feedback, and thus build university-wide buy-in to engagement	• Broad stakeholder representation in Steering Committee • Regular strategic forums that are open to all interested individuals
Regularly assess and refocus	Regular assessing and refocusing efforts allow for community engagement efforts to evolve in an environment where needs and resources are continuously changing while maintaining a "genuine dialogue" in which stakeholders' feedback is solicited, shared, and acted upon	• 2015 landscape analysis • Strategic planning feedback
Reward engagement	Creation of a reward structure encourages faculty, staff, and students to engage the community. The absence of community engagement in the reappointment, promotion, and tenure guidelines is considered a great obstacle for faculty to engage their community in teaching and research	• Engagement as a component of the reappointment, promotion, and tenure guidelines • Community Engagement Spotlights
Break down partnership development barriers	The unequal power structure between a university and the community can form an obstacle in developing partnerships. Especially in a decentralized institution, it is difficult for a community organization to know who to approach in order to start a partnership. Creating structures and resources that reduce these barriers positively impacts outreach efforts	• Creation of the Weitz CEC • Create positions with the purpose of matching university to community • Providing free and accessible parking
Nourish relationships with the philanthropic community	Philanthropists want to make a difference in their community. When the institution is known to impact the community, the solicitation of private funds to support community engagement efforts is facilitated	• Centennial capital campaign • Aligning engagement efforts with philanthropic interests

engagement landscape, yet it also is an important method that allows an institution to assess and reshape its priorities through feedback solicitation and build bottom-down buy-in. The ten strategies can be distilled into the following three key categories: identity, infrastructure, and behavior. These reinforce and strengthen each other and, when accomplished together, result in an institutionalized and integrated culture of engagement. At UNO, the culture of engagement is evidenced by numerous artifacts, including RPT guidelines, awards and recognitions, service learning occurring in every college, promotion of spotlights, high-level participation in engagement conferences, increased research funding for engaged scholarship, and the daily community presence on campus.

Identity

Institutional identity here refers to the set of cultural principles that guide the institution's priorities. These principles are often more tangibly reflected in the institution's mission, strategic plan, and values, and can often be traced back to the institution's history. The authors introduced two specific strategies that proved successful at UNO in creating an institutional identity that encouraged community engagement. With strategy 1, "leveraging the institution's mission," UNO administrators asserted that community engagement is a core component of its metropolitan identity. Similarly, land-grant institutions and faith-based institutions can leverage their identity to focus on aspects that encourage community engagement. Further, strategy 2, "embracing the evolutionary approach," allowed UNO administrators to formalize UNO's commitment to community engagement by explicitly including it in the mission statement and strategic plan. Administrators were able to do this by emphasizing existing engagement efforts and drawing upon threads in its history that focused on community engagement, arguing that community engagement was already a core facet of the university, even though it might not have been an explicitly articulated one.

Infrastructure

Infrastructure refers to a set of structures, processes, and policies. UNO administrators have been able to translate its identity as an engaged institution into an infrastructure. An infrastructure is an important component of change as it reinforcing an identity in a structural, meaningful way.

This chapter introduced four strategies that assist in creating an infrastructure that encourages community engagement. First is the importance of engaging in an inclusive strategic planning process, which allows UNO to engage a broad spectrum of stakeholders in setting the university agenda. Another strategy employed at UNO is the systematic and consistent process of assessing and refocusing community engagement efforts through genuine dialogue. Further, one of the main identified obstacle to institutionalizing engagement is inclusion of engagement in universities' reward structures. Finally, institutions should remove all partnership barriers to remedy the unequal power structure between an institution of higher education and the community.

Behavior

Behavior refers to how administrators, faculty, and staff conduct themselves. Organizational theorists argue that changes built on existing values and strengths are more likely to be sustained and succeed (Boyce, 2003). Scholars also argue that the

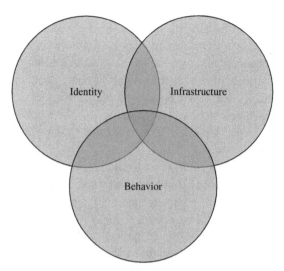

Figure 19.1 *Category integration*

role of leadership should not be underestimated in efforts to institutionalize engagement (Franz, Childers, & Sanderlin, 2012). While top-down leadership is essential to encouraging and sustaining engagement efforts, bottom-up buy-in must be achieved in order to create a framework of engagement. Having top-down support and bottom-up buy-in also facilitates relationship building with the philanthropic community and the creation of networks that span beyond traditional boundaries.

Employing the strategies in these three categories allows an institution to build a framework in which community engagement is institutionalized. As illustrated in Figure 19.1, the categories reinforce and strengthen each other, and when they come together, a culture of engagement can be achieved.

Lessons Learned

Tethering community engagement to UNO's metropolitan mission permanently placed it on the organization's agenda, which allowed UNO to sustain its commitment to engagement. Community engagement became a decision point for UNO's operations and a key component of the organization's strategic planning efforts. Thinking within the context of community engagement and the metropolitan mission became common practice across campus. UNO has always been an institution with a municipal orientation, so adopting a metropolitan mission was not a major change. The notion of "engagement," however, did receive some pushback. While pockets of engaged work (i.e., applied research) were always prevalent across campus, it may not have been defined as such. Developing a common language and understanding of engagement was crucial to its prioritization and integration. Campus forums were the primary mechanisms for engaging stakeholders in discussions about community engagement. Faculty, staff, students, and community members were asked to deliberate on what it means to be a metropolitan institution. The organization's metropolitan mission became the context for every discussion and every decision. Consequently, conversations about what community engagement is and what it might mean for the campus (e.g., "What does research mean for a metropolitan campus?") were inextricably linked to the campus mission. Soon, the dialogue about what "engagement" is led to an awareness of the work itself. Although engaged work (i.e., applied research) was nothing new to the campus, the term "community engagement" was. People started to recognize their work as such and found ways to align it with the campus mission.

Communication, both in terms of bi- or multi-directional dialogue and uni-directional messaging, was an essential component in UNO fostering an integrated culture of community engagement. Once UNO adopted community engagement as a campus priority, messaging involved showcasing community engagement as part of the institution's identity, explaining its relationship to the metropolitan mission, and demonstrating its value by celebrating and highlighting the engaged work of faculty members and staff – a technique that Chip Heath and Dan Heath (2010) call "bright spots." It created the energy and momentum needed to implement organizational change. UNO started creating campus commitment community engagement spotlights featuring students, staff, and faculty and their exemplary engagement activities. The spotlights were broadly disseminated and the individuals featured celebrated. The stories made community engagement, often considered an abstract concept, concrete – and elevated work done by individual faculty members at a unit level to the university level. The spotlights also allowed UNO to expand upon the definition of community engagement and illustrate the full diversity of the engagement spectrum.

As higher education institutions are increasingly pressured to demonstrate their value to the community, the desire to measure community engagement impacts increases. To that end, UNO has established a community engagement measurement and assessment committee charged with creating a framework that allows the institution to systematically document engagement. UNO's ability to demonstrate impact on its student population and community partners will allow it to tell a more powerful story and could promote more outreach.

Regardless of governance and organizational structures, cultural change is most successful when more stakeholders are in favor of the change (Kezar & Eckel, 2002). If faculty favor change and administrators do not, implementing community engagement will lack the necessary organizational resources. If administrators favor change and faculty do not, diffusing community engagement across campus becomes impossible. At UNO, successfully integrating a culture of community engagement required bottom-up buy-in and top-down support. This is not to imply that everyone at both levels supported the change. To appease detractors, community engagement has never been mandated at UNO, although it has been valued. Cultural change should be voluntary, not coerced. Over time, however, community engagement has become UNO's comparative advantage. Onboarding of new faculty and administrators underscores the importance of community engagement and its connection to the metropolitan mission. Emphasizing how these two (community engagement and the metropo-litan mission) are one and the same has made community engagement something faculty and administrators want, instead of something they are told they must do. Avoiding rigid prescriptions of engagement gives individuals the freedom to make it their own, and puts an institution one step closer to institutionalizing community engagement.

References

Allen, D. K. (2003). Organisational climate and strategic change in higher education: Organisational insecurity. *Higher Education, 46*(1), 61–92.

American Association of State Colleges and Universities (2002). Stepping forward as stewards of place: A guide for leading public engagement at state colleges and universities. Retrieved from www.nchems.org/wp-content/uploads/stewardsofplace_02.pdf.

Andes, N. (2006). Negotiating institutional performance and change: Strategies for engaged universities. *Metropolitan Universities, 17*(1), 24–35.

Argyris, C., & Schön, D. (1996). *Organizational learning II: Theory, method and practice.* Reading, MA: Addison-Wesley.

Bailey, G., Muse, W., Todd, L., & Wilson, D. (2013). University presidents see growing role for scholarship of engagement. *Journal of Community Engagement and Scholarship, 6*(1), 88–95.

Bardo, J. W. (1990). University and city: From urban to metropolitan. *Metropolitan Universities, 1*(1), 36–43.

Black, S. (2013). The future of morality: What role should colleges and universities play? *Journal of Community Engagement and Scholarship, 6*(1), 96–101.

Boyce, M. (2003). Organizational learning is essential to achieving and sustaining challenge in higher education. *Innovative Higher Education, 28*(2), 119–136.

Boyer, E. L. (1996). The scholarship of engagement. *Journal of Public Service & Outreach, 1* (1), 11–20.

Brownell, B. A. (1993). Metropolitan universities: Past, present, and future. *Metropolitan Universities, 4*(3), 13–21.

Campus Compact (2012). Presidents' declaration on the civic responsibility of higher educa-tion. Retrieved from https://kdp0l43vw6z2dlw631ififc5-wpengine.netdna-ssl.com /wp-content/uploads/2017/01/Campus-Compact-Action-Statement.pdf.

Christensen, J. (2013). *Why UNO?* [PDF document]. Retrieved from https://digitalcom mons.unomaha.edu/cgi/viewcontent.cgi?article=1002&context=engagementch ancellorsspeeches.

Clark, B. (1972). The organizational saga in higher education. *Administrative Science Quarterly, 17*(2), 178–184.

Davenport, C. (Producer) (2013). 9 signs of a strong philanthropic culture [Video file]. Retrieved from www.moviemondays.com/167-philanthropic-culture/?awt_1=5L gRk&awt_m=J1YNJhRI3WSBtP.

Diner, S. J. (2013). The land-grant analogy and the American urban university: An historical analysis. *Metropolitan Universities, 23*(3), 61–71.

Eckardt, S., & Eisman, G. (2006). If you build it, will they come? Perspectives on institutio-nalizing service-learning in the CSU. *Metropolitan Journal, 17*(1), 10–23.

Franz, N., Childers, J., & Sanderlin, N. (2012). Assessing the culture of engagement on a university campus. *Journal of Community Engagement and Scholarship*, *5*(2), 29–40.

Gelmon, S., Holland, B., Driscoll, A., Spring, A., & Kerrigan, S. (2001). *Assessing service-learning and civic engagement: Principles and techniques*. Providence, RI: Campus Compact.

Grandgenett, N., Boocker, D., Ali, H. et al. (2015). Community chairs as a catalyst for campus collaboration in STEM. *Metropolitan Universities*, *26*(1), 71–96.

Gornitzka, A. (1999). Governmental policies and organisational change in higher education. *Higher Education*, *38*(1), 5–31.

Gumport, P. (2000). Academic restructuring: Organizational change and institutional imperatives. *Higher Education*, *39*(1), 67–91.

Hathaway, C., Mulhollan, P., & White, K. (1990). Metropolitan universities: Models for the twenty-first century. *Metropolitan Universities*, *1*(1), 9–20.

Heath, C., & Heath, D. (2010). *Switch: How to change things when change is hard*. London: Random House Business Books.

Holland, B. A. (2002). Private and public institutional views of civic engagement and the urban mission. *Metropolitan Universities*, *13*(1), 11–21.

Kezar, A. (2009). Change in higher education: Not enough, or too much? *Change: The Magazine of Higher Learning*, *41*(6), 18–23.

Kezar, A., & Eckel, P. D. (2002). The effect of institutional culture on change strategies in higher education: Universal principles or culturally responsive concepts? *The Journal of Higher Education*, *73*(4), 435–460.

New England Resource Center for Higher Education (2017). Carnegie community engagement classification. Retrieved from http://nerche.org/index.php?option=com_content&view=article&id=341&Itemid=618.

Owen, E. (2016). *What does the metropolitan university identity mean at UNO?* Omaha, NE: University of Nebraska Omaha.

Pearl, A. (2014). Predicting community engagement? The Carnegie Foundation's elective classification. *Journal of Community Engagement and Scholarship*, *7*(2), 50–59.

Rainey, H. G. (2014). *Understanding and managing public organizations*. San Francisco, CA: Jossey-Bass.

Riggs, H. E. (2010). The mouths of gift horses. *Stanford Social Innovation Review*, *8*(3), 21–22.

Rodin, J. (2007). *The university & urban revival: Out of the ivory tower and into the streets*. Philadelphia, PA: University of Pennsylvania Press.

Sandmann, L. R., & Kliewer, B.W. (2012). Theoretical and applied perspectives on power: Recognizing processes that undermine effective community–university partnerships. *Journal of Community Engagement and Scholarship*, *5*(2), 20–28.

Sargeant, A., & Ford, J. B. (2007). The power of brands. *Stanford Social Innovation Review*, *5*(1), 41–47.

Susan Thompson Buffett Foundation (2017). The William H. Thompson Scholars Learning Community. Retrieved from https://buffettscholarships.org/learning-community.

Soto, M., & Drummond, M. J. (2002). Establishing a vision and strategic plan incorporating multiple stakeholders' voices: Creating reciprocity and acknowledging community knowledge. *Metropolitan Universities*, *13*(2), 30–44.

Starke, A., Shenouda, K., & Smith-Howell, D. (2017). Conceptualizing community engagement: Starting a campus-wide dialogue. *Metropolitan Universities*, *28*(2), 72–89.

Terranova, M., Martello, J., & Taylor, J. (2006). Reflections on campus engagement: The value of vision, setting, and talent. *Metropolitan Universities*, *17*(1), 84–92.

University of Nebraska Omaha (2015). 2015 Carnegie community engagement classification. Retrieved from https://digitalcommons.unomaha.edu/cgi/viewcontent.cgi?article=1001&context=engagementawardapplications.

University of Nebraska Omaha (2017a). Strategic plan. Retrieved from www.unomaha.edu/strategic-plan/index.php.

University of Nebraska Omaha (2017b). Our values. Retrieved from www.unomaha.edu/community-engagement-center/about-the-weitz-cec/our-values.php.

University of Nebraska Omaha (2017c). Welcome to the Goodrich Scholarship Program. Retrieved from www.unomaha.edu/college-of-public-affairs-and-community-service/goodrich-scholarship-program/about-us/index.php.

Vandeventer, P. (2011). Increasing civic reach. *Stanford Social Innovation Review, 10*(2), 25–26.

Weerts, D. J., & Sandmann, L. R. (2008). Building a two-way street: Challenges and opportunities for community engagement at research universities. *The Review of Higher Education, 32*(1), 73–106.

Wilhite, S., & Silver, P. (2004). Civic engagement and the emergence of a metropolitan identity: The politics of mobilizing an institution to meet metropolitan needs. *Metropolitan Universities, 15*(4), 51–63.

Woods, S., Reed, B. J., & Smith-Howell, D. (2016). Building an engagement center through love of place: The story of the Barbara Weitz Community Engagement Center. *Metropolitan Universities, 27*(3), 84–105.

Zlotkowski, E., & Meeropol, J. (2006). Overview of the Indicators of Engagement Project (IOEP). *Metropolitan Universities, 17*(1), 116–122.

20 After Institutionalization

Enacting University–Community Engagement as a Process of Change

Deborah Romero, Annie Epperson, Elizabeth Gilbert, & Christine Marston

As institutions of higher education strive to redefine their place in society, this work often entails revisiting not only the tripartite mission of teaching, research/scholarship/creative works, and service, but also reconceptualizing the integral relationships between each of these for students, faculty, staff, and communities. This work is complex and messy, and is seldom without challenges. In this chapter, we present an in-depth critical analysis of our university's journey and the professional learning that has resulted from institutionalizing community and civic engagement (CCE) to current work that focused on ascertaining its value as an ongoing process of change.

In 2015, the University of Northern Colorado (UNC) earned the Elective Community Engagement Classification from the Carnegie Foundation for the Advancement of Teaching. While the attainment of such a classification brings with it a degree of prestige and distinction, recognition as an engaged campus is not an end, but rather the means and a process by which universities are redefining their place and commitment to generate knowledge and educate the next generation of socially responsible and civic-minded citizens.

This chapter offers an illustrative case study analysis (Yin, 2012) that examines how we conceptualized, designed, and worked to institutionalize engagement at a mid-sized, four-year public institution. The chapter is divided into five sections. We begin with a brief background that frames how community engagement is unique at UNC. We discuss the importance of recognizing one's institutional history and identity, as well as understanding institutional developments and needs, especially in light of changes in student demographics and funding (Furco, 2010). We examine how CCE is not something that is simply attained, but rather a pedagogical and scholarly approach that defines and permeates much of the teaching, learning, and professional activity that includes research, scholarship, and creative works (RSCW) that happen on campuses and in communities.

In the second section, we examine how this case study draws on the co-authors' insider perspectives and deep knowledge as faculty, researchers, staff, and administrators to examine the theoretical framework of institutionalizing engagement (Beere, Votruba, & Wells, 2011; Moore, 2014). We analyze the institution's evolving roles from its origins as the State Normal School to becoming an anchor institution (Hodges & Dubb, 2012), and more recently to university as place-maker (Herts, 2013; Schneekloth & Shibley, 1995).

Next, we outline the processes we adopted, identify key steps and participants, and describe the methods used to advance engagement from both the top down and the middle out. We provide an in-depth examination of the collective approach we used that led to successes and challenges en route to institutionalizing engagement and receiving Carnegie Classification. We frame this with reference to the history of previous efforts on our campus, share the ways in which we approached cultural change, and describe how we continue to address challenges on the journey.

The fourth section segues from highlights and successes to illustrative examples of the impact. We share how this work occurs in our classrooms and research, as well as in communities prior to and since achieving Carnegie Classification. In addition, we examine lessons learned from the self-assessment process and how this informed subsequent planning, directions, and action steps.

In the final section, we reflect upon current and future goals, especially the design and vision of actions and a framework to sustain and advance engagement. This includes how we plan to address and assess the impact of community-engaged work with students, faculty, and community. We close with considerations and implications for other institutions that are considering or already undertaking this work.

Background and Institutional Context

UNC is located in the city of Greeley, about an hour north of Denver, Colorado. The city has primarily a semi-rural identity; agriculture and food processing, including meatpacking and cheese-manufacturing plants, dominate the local economy. In addition, K–12 and postsecondary education institutions and the health care sector provide significant employment. More recently, the region has experienced a significant growth in oil and gas development (Colorado Department of Labor and Employment, 2017).

UNC has evolved from a teacher preparation school into a doctoral-intensive university, with a distinctive role and place locally and globally. It is a public, mid-sized institution that prides itself as an "exemplary teaching and learning community" (Larson, 1989), UNC remains invested in the notion of transformative education. Classes tend to be small, and there is a strong emphasis on the liberal arts tradition. Census data indicate continued growth in diverse students; 18 percent Latino/a, up from 4 percent in 2006, and 33 percent first generation, and almost the same number are low-income students (UNC Institutional Reporting and Analysis Services, 2016).

UNC's commitment to community extends beyond its founding intentions to prepare teachers for current academic offerings that include a diverse range of programs. In disciplines across campus from all six colleges, faculty members recognize the mutual benefit of community-engaged pedagogies for students and community partners. Recent years have seen increases in the numbers of internships, practica, and field placements offered, as well as an increasing number of faculty offering community-engaged courses and learning experiences.

Several factors have impacted these developments, including national trends over the last decade and the identity crisis experienced in higher education in the face of public concerns about its relevance and efficacy (Beere, Votruba, & Wells, 2011; Furco, 2010). These facts were coupled with rapid declines in state funding of public institutions, which shrank by nearly 70 percent between 1980 and 2011 in Colorado (Mortenson, 2012), and political pressure to limit indicators of success to align with the current job market and graduates' income data. Notwithstanding this predicament, UNC reasserted its purpose and place as a distinctive university that values community engagement. The challenge was to make this explicit and visible throughout the planning and delivery process. To this end, and following the appointment of a new provost who launched a new strategic plan, UNC reaffirmed its commitment to its mission to educate and serve the public good. We did this by centering CCE as a priority among one of nine core plans in the institutional strategic framework. Other plans address internationalization, equity and diversity, and RSCW.

Boundary Spanning and Institutionalizing Engagement

Before we discuss the theoretical framework and the process that shaped our work, we briefly present the authors' insider perspectives and consider the specific knowledge that we each bring. We mention these aspects because when trying to realize any kind of institutional or collective change, we must always consider the individuals involved. Research shows that resistance to proposed change is impacted by several factors, including the following: fear of loss of status, power, or symbols; variable extremes in tension; perceived attacks on current status/ conditions; complexity or uncertainty as to outcomes; perceived value; and lack of time (Lane, 2007, p. 86).

One way to drive change is to enlist individuals who embrace change and who are recognized as leaders or embody what it means to be a "boundary spanner" (Ernst & Chrobot-Mason, 2010). Boundary spanners are people whose roles and responsibilities require and allow them to work across intergroup boundaries within and beyond an organization. Their work crosses levels of power or authority, functions and units, and diverse groups. As the collective profiles below show, we span internal boundaries in that we have held faculty-administrative positions, work across disciplinary units and structures, and all possess an appreciation of the internal university organization. In addition, as engaged scholars, our work bridges external constituents and diverse community partners and organizations.

Furthermore, the authors of this chapter are all tenured faculty with between 10 and 20 years of experience at UNC. Each has held full-time faculty positions and one or more split administrative assignments at UNC, including unit leader, department chair, school director, associate dean, associate director of faculty development, and director of engagement. We each come from different disciplinary backgrounds that represent four of the six colleges, and each has undertaken transdisciplinary teaching and learning, as well as engaged scholarship. The institutional knowledge, coupled with experience across the disciplines of economics, community health, multilingual education, and librarianship, shapes our interest and ability in working to build strong community connections with underrepresented and marginalized populations. In addition, three out of the four of us have experience working at other institutions of higher education in the USA and abroad.

From Anchor Institution to University Place-Making

Central to the strategic planning process was an acknowledgment that community-engaged teaching, learning, and RSCW were already occurring throughout the campus and the region. However, our research process revealed a lack of coordinated institutional recognition and support for this high-impact work (Kuh, 2008).

As our strategic planning update acknowledges, UNC is, by nature, externally focused, and our connection with the community is an integral part of our history (Wacker, 2015). Accordingly, UNC can traditionally be defined as an anchor institution (Hodges & Dubb, 2012), where the types of engagement activities we undertake span different approaches of models, as summarized in Table 20.1. Anchor institutions understand their impact and role in the local community and economy. They deliberately seek out and engage in partnerships with local schools, businesses, and residents and are committed to investing in the general well-being of the community, "so as to better meet the educational and research functions of the institution" (Moore, 2014, p. 30).

Table 20.1 *Types of anchor institution, the approach to community, and UNC examples*

Type	Approach	UNC examples
Facilitator	Tends to place special emphasis on educational opportunity, including a focus on access, academic engagement, and public education and health partnerships, as well as providing in-kind resources for local capacity building across a broad geographic region	Business, Libraries, Nursing, Performing and Visual Arts, and Teaching
Leader	Emphasizes education and health partnerships, but tends to focus on pursuing comprehensive community revitalization, using their business practices for community economic development, often with a specific focus on disinvested neighborhoods that are immediately adjacent to the university	Biz Hub, University District, education partnerships, Community Health, Rocky Mountain Cancer Center, UNC centers and institutes
Convener	Focuses on comprehensive community revitalization, often places greater emphasis on building local capacity and sharing agenda-setting power with other community stakeholders	University District, Social Research Lab, City of Greeley, partnerships with District 6 schools

Note: Excerpt from Office of Engagement, University of North Colorado (2017).

However, the institutional role is ever evolving, and recent efforts are reframing this institutional responsibility to include the notion of place-maker (Herts, 2013). Place-making can be described as follows:

> a holistic approach to planning and development that integrates natural, built, and sociocultural environments through interorganizational collaboration and citizen participation. Urban scholars argue that place competitiveness, place quality, and place attachment are critical in a global-network society in which the fortunes and misfortunes of individuals, organizations, cities, and regions have become tied to the types of places that they are perceived as coming from, currently occupying, and/or moving toward [...] (Herts, 2013, p. 99)

Although this practice has normally been associated with land-grant universities, its central premise includes the idea that an institution that is embedded in a community is also invested in that community, especially through activities that encompass university tourism and city development. We discuss place-making below with reference to the creation of the University District (UD), a collaborative partnership between the city and the institution that was launched at about the same time as last strategic plan was developed.

Institutional Collective Impact

The creation of a UD, in tandem with other institutional planning, illustrates that the approach to institutionalizing engagement was not a linear path, but rather an iterative process. We frame this collaborative process with reference to an ecological perspective, whereby behavior or actions are viewed as being determined by several key factors, including intrapersonal, interpersonal, institutional, community, and political/policies (Brofenbreener, as cited in McLeroy, Bibeau, Steckler, & Glanz, 1988).

The Coordinating Team for the Scholarship of Community Engagement (2010–2011), a group of faculty and administrators, had previously convened to explore the feasibility of applying for Carnegie classification. However, notwithstanding the prevalence of our engagement initiatives, the group quickly realized that there was a lack of institutional oversight and political infrastructure. This rendered a successful application difficult, if not impossible, at the time.

In 2014, and as a result of institutional strategic planning, we had made significant gains, resulting in notable structural differences that yielded a successful self-assessment and application for Carnegie Classification. While space limitations prevent an in-depth account, we highlight key features of the ecological systems approach we adopted. This approach contemplates the interrelatedness between individuals as complex beings and the environmental contexts within which they operate. Accordingly, we framed the work to institutionalize engagement across the following four aspects: (a) leadership and vision; (b) timing and leveraging assets; (c) the right team; and (d) adopting a scholarly and collective approach.

Leadership and Vision

First, we have mentioned a change in senior leadership within academic affairs. With the appointment of a new provost came a new vision. The incoming provost not only brought strong interpersonal campus relationships, but also innovative institutional policies and goals. Already familiar with campus and our culture, and having previously served as an accomplished scholar and faculty, as well as dean of the graduate school, the provost's vision and strategic planning process acknowledged CCE as a priority. This included an understanding that:

> Critical to any institutional or social endeavor is the presence of forward-thinking and acting leadership. Leadership within higher education that sets a tone for how engaged scholarship and other forms of social engagement are valued and aligns with the institution's mission is essential to establishing a culture of engagement on any campus. (Chambers & Gopaul, 2010, p. 65)

Accordingly, the university's strategic plan provided a structural, organizational, and political framework within which to contextualize CCE work, although it did not provide a plan per se.

Timing and Leveraging Assets

Our work to institutionalize engagement was also driven by several simultaneous events that can be viewed from both macro- and more micro-level perspectives. From a macro or top-down approach, these events included university-wide restructuring and the launch of a new strategic plan. At about the same time, and from what we refer to as a middle-out perspective, faculty engagement was also gaining visibility. By middle-out, we seek to acknowledge the position of faculty as leaders or instigators of change. This approach reaches both to administrative mandates and to student-driven interests. Romero coauthored an executive summary report on the 2011 National Outreach Scholarship Conference (NOSC) that emphasized national trends in higher education and the growing prominence of community engagement as a valid pedagogy and the scholarship of engagement as a legitimate field of academic inquiry. In addition, the report accomplished several goals that included leveraging existing assets, reaffirming our historical commitment to community, and acknowledging a lack of institutional infrastructure or recognition for this work. To streamline the commitment across varying levels of the institution and to increase visibility of community-engaged scholarship and teaching, the report recommended the formation of a campus-wide Office of Engagement. Short-term planning included support for an annual on campus community-engaged forum and expanding investment in an Engaged Faculty Institute (EFI) in collaboration with Colorado Campus Compact. Mid-range goals included working with the levels of commitment to community engagement rubric (Holland, 1997). The long-range focus was on alignment and included explicit reference to applying for Carnegie Community Engagement Classification. The report concluded with an extensive bibliography of recommended scholarly resources, stating the following:

> Engagement is not an add-on to the mission of an institution or the workload of faculty. On the contrary, when it is adopted as a strategic priority it enhances the achievement of learning outcomes and students' perceptions of the relevance of their academic experience; enriches pedagogy and scholarship; increases the competitiveness of federal research grant applications; facilitates institutional reaccreditation; and improves university–community relations. (Romero & Kimball, 2011, p. 10)

Not long after this internal report was submitted, the provost convened a task force of core participants that included faculty, administrators, student affairs professionals, and campus leaders to work on the strategic plan to institutionalize engagement.

The Right Team

Having the right team is crucial. The task force for CCE included some of the colleagues who had originally been involved in exploring the Carnegie Classification, and others from across campus who were able to provide experienced-based insights and who could make recommendations to leadership based on scholarly expertise. The progress of the task force for CCE can be attributed to several defining characteristics that further reflect the duality of top-down and middle-out leadership, as well as an internally collective impact approach (Kania & Kramer, 2011). The two faculty authors of the 2011 NOSC report, both with cross-disciplinary academic backgrounds in community-engaged pedagogies and scholarship, cochaired the task force. They shared a recognition and understanding of engaged scholarship and provided valuable input to shape the task force to include recognized institutional boundary spanners with expertise to work across the vertical and horizontal boundaries "to create direction, alignment and commitment across boundaries in service of a higher vision or goal" (Ernst & Chrobot-Mason, 2010, p. 5).

The task force purposefully included faculty, student affairs professionals, and administrators, all of whom can be considered "early adopters" of community engagement and representatives from each of our institution's six colleges: Business, Education and Behavioral Sciences, Humanities and Social Sciences, Libraries, Natural and Health Sciences, and Performing and Visual Arts. In this way, we worked with those who were aware and open to the emerging paradigm shifts in higher education (Buse & Hawkes, 2015; Castillo, 2014; Charney, 2014; Davidson, 2014). The task force composition meant that there were opportunities for interdisciplinary thinking and sharing of expertise that kept present the breadth and scope of engaged work occurring across our institution. Student affairs professionals from Student Life, together with representatives from upper administration, including the dean of the graduate school and the assistant vice president for undergraduate studies, all played key roles on the committee, bringing insights into institutional planning, leadership visions, and engagement endeavors from curricular and co-curricular perspectives.

Adopting a Scholarly and Collective Approach

Collective impact work (Kania & Kramer, 2011) acknowledges the need for the following five interrelated conditions: a common agenda, mutually reinforcing activities, shared measurement, continuous communication, and backbone support. While these elements are often presented in a hierarchical triangle model, we discuss them here more as a series of interrelated steps.

A Common Agenda. The task force, recognizing the potential for resistance to change, agreed very early on that the work they were to undertake should seek to establish a shared agenda. To this end, they researched and stayed theoretically informed about the changing landscape in higher education (Fitzgerald, Burack, & Seifer, 2010; Kezar, Chambers, & Burkhardt, 2005). In turn, they disseminated research about the scholarship of engagement as a legitimate academic pursuit (Boyer, 1996; Glass & Fitzgerald, 2010) across multiple forums and units. Adopting a scholarly approach was deliberate and designed to support the task force and educate the larger campus and community. This is not to say that this work was unfamiliar, but rather, given the diversity of participants on the task force, we lacked a common understanding and, more importantly, a shared discourse to explain how we framed this work within the greater mission of reciprocal benefit and education in the public good. The task force stayed current by sharing academic resources and readings, and the cochairs made a special point to stay abreast of research and developments in the field.

The task force began by affirming our institutional identity as an engaged campus and proposing that our work should be:

> characterized by the authenticity and genuineness with which community engagement is integrated into the research, teaching and service mission of higher education institutions. Authenticity is reflected in the purposes that surround the development and implementation of a campus's community engagement efforts. [...] Genuineness is reflected in the values and norms that undergird the practices within a campus/community partnership. (Furco, 2010, p. 387)

Accordingly, we sought to construct a plan that would provide infrastructure, specific strategies, and action steps to strengthen, coordinate, and systematize community engagement efforts. The comprehensive plan explicitly reflected our institutional traditions and values, and when we launched it in 2013, it was the result of collective research, evaluation, and professional development initiatives spanning more than two years on our campus.

Mutually Reinforcing Activities. As a university-wide effort initiated by the provost and facilitated by the task force, we carefully considered the results of other institutional planning efforts, including our work toward reaccreditation and a self-study report to the Higher Learning Commission, as well as ongoing work on diversity and equity, internationalization, student services, faculty and staff professional development, graduate education, and student success. Our goal was to ensure that a plan to institutionalize community engagement would be infused and integrated into current and future agendas in a mutually beneficial way. Accordingly, we built upon the institutional strategic planning framework that prioritizes engagement in academics and RSCW, and where engagement is embedded across our tripartite mission:

1. Academics – serving students and building exemplary academic programs to fulfill our mission in sustainable ways;
2. RSCW – enhancing our research focus to engage our students and faculty and the public we serve;
3. Community building – creating a respectful and inclusive campus community that connects with the area around UNC and the global community.

Shared Measurement. In order to ensure that our efforts remained aligned with institutional needs, we undertook a variety of formats to gather preexisting and new data and measure indicators from the campus community about engaged teaching and learning and engaged scholarship. This included campus-wide surveys, a listening tour, in-person focus groups and discussion, as well as data requests to institutional research and reporting and careful review of existing sources, such as course listings and faculty publications. The goal was twofold: on the one hand, to document evidence of the scope and diversity of existing engagement work; and on the other hand, to determine the need for additional resources.

Backbone Support and Organization. The provost convened the task force to institutionalize engagement, and also ensured organizational support such as graduate assistants, since all of the individuals involved had other duties and responsibilities. Throughout the process, the cochairs met regularly with the provost to provide updates and allow for leadership input, including that of college deans and unit directors. The cochairs also returned to the NOSC conference to deliver a presentation on initial progress.

The result was that, in just under a year, the task force was able to produce a written plan for the institutionalization of engagement. A first draft was shared with the campus community at large, as well as with executive leadership, for comment and feedback related to the specific sections in the plan (i.e., mission and vision, academic portfolio, engaged research, internationalization, as well as open-ended comments). In addition, we sent the document to critical friends and allies, who are known scholarly leaders in the engagement arena in the USA.

The feedback we received reinforced our plan and reflected how engaged work warranted investment, including the need for an office charged with supporting faculty, student affairs professionals, and community members, who were already undertaking or interested in exploring community-engaged pedagogical and scholarly practices. We revised and updated the plan, incorporated suggestions as relevant, primarily by way of additional examples of current work on campus, and further solidified the need for infrastructure, including an office and a director. The CCE plan was launched late spring 2013, and by the fall, an Office of Engagement was officially in place with a faculty director, hired through an internal search, to lead the work.

Enacting University–Community Engagement

Having an institutional plan to support and develop community-engaged teaching, learning, and research on our campus became a catalyst and a vehicle for augmenting preexisting work and shaping the direction of future efforts. Central to this work was our institutional self-assessment. The director's first actions included meeting with the members from the original CCE task force and inviting them to continue to serve on the leadership committee. Most participants were able to continue, and we broadened representation from other units from across campus, including the Office of Sponsored Programs, UNC Alumni, Development, Housing, and Residential Education, and additional faculty.

In light of the activities and actions planned, the leadership committee formed working subcommittees to address the following three main areas: Carnegie Classification application and process; assessment and evaluation of UNC's engagement initiatives; and organization of a Mountain West Leadership Engagement Academy. These subcommittees met regularly, often collaborating with one another. We also enlisted the support of the Office of Institutional Reporting and Analysis and graduate interns.

As part of the Mountain West Engagement Academy, the director of engagement collaborated with college deans and their leadership teams, as well as with Enrollment Management and Student Affairs, the dean of students, and the UNC Foundation to identify over 45 individuals who could participate in the Engagement Academy. The Academy, facilitated by national engagement leaders Barbara Holland, Judith Ramaley, Lorilee Sandmann, and David Weerts, provided additional campus input and bolstered the collective impact of our engagement efforts. The UNC participants met for an academy workshop and formed seven institutional design teams, grouped around the following areas and institutional priorities:

- Academic portfolio/faculty promotion and tenure (P&T)
- Sustainability partnerships
- Teacher licensure and student engagement
- Global/local engagement: equity and diversity
- Integrated student support services: recruitment and retention
- Integrated student support services: student success
- Student leadership development

The teams produced action plans with concrete proposals for ways to infuse and support academic and co-curricular engagement into each of the above areas. Although each of these are in various stages of implementation, they were all foundational for advancing the next phase of engagement as an ongoing process of change.

Aligning Engagement Efforts

As part of the change process, and through our work with colleagues across campus and in communities, it became ever more apparent that the language and discourse around CCE on our campus reflected a variety of experiences and values that, at times, were confusing. Units and colleges typically referred to engagement activities in different ways, including service learning or field experience. One of the priorities of the Office of Engagement has been to gather these stories and disseminate them to the greater campus community in order to illustrate the diversity of practices and help build a shared language and understanding around this work. Here, we highlight several initiatives that merit mention as distinctive types of community-engaged work.

University District: An Example of Place-Making. In 2011, UNC and the City of Greeley partnered to create the UD, an intentional program to build a connection and improve understanding between the two entities and in the surrounding community. City officials and university executive staff spearheaded the initial work designed to support community engagement and to promote a reinvestment and renewal of this important community area, promoting a "sense of place [. . .] where change is not only envisioned, but lived out" (University of Northern Colorado, 2017), coupled with a sense of place and belonging. While UNC is entirely surrounded by the city of Greeley, it was not "of" the city. The UD sought to lessen the divide and build healthy, new partnerships. Bounded by neighborhoods contiguous with the campus, the UD area includes diverse K–12 schools, athletic fields, medical centers, parks, historic areas, and commercial sites. The UD on its northern boundary touches on the downtown area, recently experiencing revitalization after years of economic decline. Since the formation of the UD, work groups of community members, city representatives, and university stakeholders formed around the following four themes: live, work, play, and learn. Each of these groups achieved some measure of success, building on collaborative efforts.

Some of the successes of the UD initiatives include involving students and community in clean-up activities, a community fest on campus, Chalk Walk (Guinness Book of Records), Study Hall to City Hall bus tours, and student engaged learning projects, including various art murals downtown. Community members welcomed the increase in art, especially in alleys and other somewhat neglected spaces, and city guides now showcase the street art. Other projects have focused on aesthetics, social, and academic endeavors, and infrastructure. Another example is the Biz Hub Collaborative, sponsored by the College of Business and in partnership with the state of Colorado's Small Business Development Center. The Biz Hub provides free consultation and support for the conceptualization and development of business planning, marketing, and other fiscal aspects related to launching or growing a business.

As the UD matures and transitions toward refining the "sense of place" through this collaborative approach to community engagement, adjustment of mission and focus is appropriate in order to include a greater diversity of voices. We acknowledge that caution is required, since place-making can inadvertently "reinforce(s) class, race, and power hegemonies that the university–community engagement movement seeks to address" (Herts, 2013, p. 107). Immigrant and refugee community members have not been equitably represented in the leadership of the UD. As a result, many of their voices have not been heard, and they have received fewer benefits from these redevelopment activities, thus reinforcing current inequalities. The UD has a unique responsibility to reach out to those in nearby neighborhoods. Leaders in these communities are perceived as place-makers and provide access to these important relationships. Accordingly, through planning and some of our own research described below, we are seeking ways to meaningfully engage with the diverse communities that reside within the UD, but are not directly connected to the university, thus strengthening a sense of place, social ties, and civic vitality for short- and long-term residents.

Community-Based Research with Refugee Resettlement. In the College of Humanities and Social Sciences, two faculty members, one from Economics and the other from Sociology, worked with a local nonprofit in Greeley, Colorado, called the Global Refugee Center, to conduct a demographic profile on the secondary migration of local refugees. Community leaders, policy makers, service providers, and social scientists in Greeley hoped to generate a picture of the burgeoning local refugee population so that public and private services could be better tailored in spheres such as employment assistance, education, housing, cultural adjustment, language translation, and navigation of the social services and health care systems. However, generating an accurate count of the Greeley refugee population proved to be a great challenge. Simply stated, data detailing the characteristics and needs of a rapidly growing and changing population composed of newcomers from at least 25 countries, and speaking an even greater number of languages, were extremely hard to come by. After obtaining Institutional Review Board approval for the project, each faculty member trained students in how to conduct migration history interviews with refugees. This allowed the students to have a hands-on learning experience with how social science research is conducted and provided important demographic and descriptive data to the nonprofit. The faculty published their results in several papers, and the Global Refugee Center used this information in their grant applications.

Community-Engaged Partnerships with Native Americans. Another project comes from the Community Health Education program within the College of Natural and Health Sciences in which a partnership was created with a Research 1 institution, the medical campus of a second institution, and a community hospital in a southwest city that is a border town to a Native American reservation. A course was developed that taught students about the demographics and health issues that faced the community. This included information about high rates of diabetes, heart disease, as well as other chronic illnesses that result from a lack of food and physical activity resources and were complicated by high rates of poverty and unemployment. The institutions' Institutional Review Boards and the community partner's Ethics Board approved the research.

At the end of the semester, graduate and undergraduate students from each institution traveled to the border town for a month, during which time teams of students collected data with community members. The community partners identified locations for data collection, which occurred in a snowball fashion. In addition, students spent time exploring the geography and culture of the area and formed relationships with members of the community. When the data collection was completed, the researchers and students conducted an initial analysis. After this, the researchers traveled back to the community to report on initial findings in three separate open forum settings. Input from the forum attendees was received and informed the next phase of analysis. At the end of the project, the community was provided with data and findings for their future work in addressing related health issues in ways they saw to be most effective. In addition, the community partner participated in the development of numerous dissemination opportunities.

Throughout the experience, the students who participated expressed multiple thoughts. They spoke of their discomfort in being immersed in a community so different from anywhere they had previously been. However, the most common theme heard was their excitement at being a part of something that exposed them to a culture, geography, and community that they would have never have experienced had it not been for this project. The response from multiple community agencies and organizations was also positive. Our final meeting with the community was 18 months after the project began. In a meeting with 30 individuals, representing 20 separate agencies, we shared data from focus groups, interviews, and community inventories and engaged in a discussion of next steps for the community.

Community-Engaged Pedagogies for Social Justice. The College of Education and Behavioral Sciences prepares more than half the state's K–12 teachers. While all pre-service teachers are required to complete student teaching and several practica, faculty working in teacher preparation constantly seek additional field-based experiences to equip teacher candidates for an increasingly diverse student body. Although Spanish remains the majority-minority language (83 percent) in Colorado, there are over 200 additional languages, and English learners represent over 14 percent of K–12 students (Colorado Department of Education, 2017).

The Young Authors program is founded on research that community-engaged learning (CEL) constitutes a high-impact practice (Kuh, 2008), benefiting both pre-service teachers and the English language learners with whom they engage. As a partnership program, it supports the interests and needs of teacher preparation programs and those of schools and community partners (Ramaley, 2000). The partnership, which also has Institutional Review Board approval, promotes engaged pedagogies that result in transformative as opposed to transactional relationships (Enos & Morton, 2003). Pre-service teachers mentor and work with high school students to tell their stories in English and other languages. Storytelling is a powerful vehicle that supports education (Dyson & Genishi, 1994; Martínez-Roldán, 2003) and promotes community engagement by teaching about cultural diversity and social justice (Fraizer, 1997; Romero, 2013; Rosaldo, 1986; Solinger, Fox, & Irani, 2008).

For the pre-service teachers, these advocacy experiences with high school students enrich their leadership opportunities. For the English learners, writing and publishing their stories in a book empowers them as authors, sharing their voices. The culmination is students read and present their work on campus at a book launch and celebration. This partnership and the books represent a symbolic catalyst. The stories inspire the next generation of pre-service teachers and students to reimagine how they understand and read the world (Freire, 1987).

Community-Engaged Educational Outreach across Libraries. A final example of collaborative partnership work occurred when three members of the University Libraries faculty worked together with the nearby public library district to implement programming and engaged outreach exploring settlement patterns, economic development, and the impacts of power on diverse populations in the Greeley area. The "Latino-Americans, 500 Years of History" program was funded by a grant from the National Endowment for the Humanities and the American Libraries Association (University of Northern Colorado, 2015). The program featured a series of screenings of a PBS television series by the same name, with each screening accompanied by a discussion. A panel of scholars led a discussion of the central theme of each episode. Response from campus regarding the series was strong enough to warrant additional screenings of related films addressing the history of Latino Americans.

The purpose of the project was to bring scholarship on Latino American histories and cultures to new audiences, to engage people in examining and documenting the histories of Latino Americans in their communities, and to foster understanding of local histories in regional, national, and international contexts. A partner to the Libraries on this project were faculty and students from the Hispanic Studies Department. Research in preparation for the grant application revealed that campus demographics do not proportionally reflect those of the community.

The project allowed those of us in the Libraries to better know and appreciate our colleagues across campus, as we arranged for discussants, coordinated events, and mediated panels. The project made an impact in the community, as well. The panel devoted to education was featured in a local news article highlighting the project (Silvy, 2016). The University Libraries have redoubled efforts to collect and preserve the artifacts of students and faculty of color. The Libraries are now collecting the oral histories of first-generation students and preserving those in the digital repository, which provides them with a sense of place within the timeline of the institution (University of Northern Colorado University Libraries, 2017). This work connects the Libraries with the community in a unique way. It is not only a place for high school field trips, but also a potential repository and place of exploration of the multifaceted history of the community and the university.

These examples demonstrate how our contributions as teacher-scholars to engagement at UNC reflect our diverse roles and disciplinary expertise on campus. As faculty who teach and value our students' participation in community, we recognize how CEL and scholarship reinforces the academic content of our classes and encourages students to become more engaged citizens. As researchers, we recognize that these experiences have shaped the way we serve in various administrative and leadership roles, and in essence have provided additional resources to champion engagement activities and policies to larger audiences across campus.

Developing a Common Language for Mutual Understanding

We recognize that our contributions to engagement at UNC reflect our diverse roles and disciplinary expertise, as well as significant ways of referencing engagement work. Without a common language, it is difficult to identify and describe engagement experiences across campus, especially because the units and colleges define what to report and what they value. Since many faculty at our institution consider engagement an inherent and often implicit part of their work, explicitly naming and reporting engagement activities has not always been deemed necessary.

To this end, as part of the initial change years, the Office of Engagement and the assessment subcommittee developed a set of guiding principles and a common language to provide a broad and common framework for referencing engaged student learning outcomes. We began by conducting research on engaged learning and assessment informed by internal and external sources. We consulted the value rubrics produced through Liberal Education and America's Promise (LEAP) from the American Association of Colleges and Universities. We also researched high-impact practices (Kuh, 2008) and scholarly approaches on democratic education (Benson, Harkavy, & Puckett, 2007; Colby, Ehrlich, Beaumont, & Stephens, 2003; Saltmarsh & Hartley, 2011). The guiding principles were developed through faculty open forums and in consultation with engaged faculty experts, instructors, and student affairs professionals. The principles are deliberately broad and focus across the following three areas: academic and professional agency; social and ecological justice; and engaged citizenship and social responsibility. The guidelines are intended to offer direction for faculty and units to develop program- or course-level student learning outcomes, acknowledging that the applied ethics in each field will ultimately determine the relevancy of the principles to the discipline.

As part of this work, we also came to the collective realization that one of the broadest and most useful terms was CEL. The term captured what many people were referring to through myriad other definitions or labels, each with variable connotations, including service learning, experiential learning, practica, internships, and field-based learning. We adopted a term that was not commonly used on our campus and less encumbered than some preexisting terms, and that would embrace the diversity of CEL experiences that exist across our campus and in communities. We defined CEL as indicative of engaged learning activities that connect students with people and/or the environment in community-based contexts as part of the coursework. Students apply, connect, learn, and expand upon course content through these experiences. Engaged learning typically involves mutual benefit and collaboration with peers, community partners, and faculty. The CEL term is the one we most frequently promote, and it is complemented with others such as community-based research, advocacy experience, and indirect experiences as potential other forms of community engagement.

Transforming Challenges into Opportunities

Notwithstanding the progress made on our campus, the process of change remains a path of constant adjustment. We turn here to examine critically how what we learned from our self-assessment process for Carnegie informed subsequent planning and yielded some very concrete action steps and outcomes. Three of the biggest challenges to institutionalizing engagement that we encountered concerned faculty P&T, recognition and identification of engaged learning, and the role of community partners in our work.

Informing the Promotion and Tenure Process. Faculty who are committed and undertake engaged instruction and research do so knowing that individual academic units, which are entrenched in disciplinary traditions that often do not include this work, develop the P&T criteria. We know too that we are not unique in this regard, and that "there is still a long way to go to fully align promotion and tenure policies to encourage and support scholarly outreach and engagement" (Doberneck, 2016, p. 15).

While many administrators and faculty across campus value engaged work and select programs have made advances to acknowledge engagement, revisions to unit criteria are slow to occur. Some units have adopted more inclusive language around engagement, yet frequently this work is viewed as less rigorous and not discipline-specific and, thus, less valuable. The disciplinary peer-review process may not perceive engaged scholarship as relevant due to its collaborative and transdisciplinary nature. Despite support at the highest level, disciplinary resistance, be it toward engaged pedagogies or professional activity (Boyer, 1996), in some instances can be a challenge for new faculty, and ultimately becomes a promotion and retention issue.

The variability in both evaluation criteria and the ways that engagement is interpreted provide an opportunity to inform others, while continuing to build a shared discourse and understanding of engaged pedagogies and scholarship. We sought out engaged faculty and campus leaders who were procuring a web-based portfolio system, Digital Measures®, which would assist faculty and units with documenting and reporting faculty teaching, research, and service activity. Thus far, we have developed two unique codes based on Carnegie Foundation Engagement classification that enable faculty to self-identify professional activity and RSCW as either engaged teaching and learning scholarship or engaged scholarship. Although this may seem like a small step, it will bring added visibility to this work for individuals and for the institution through an increased ability to more readily account for the cumulative volume of engaged activities.

Recognizing Community-Engaged Teaching and Learning. As a result of our identification and classification of community-engaged courses for Carnegie, we found that over 33 percent of faculty reported incorporating some form of community engagement into their instruction. As a collective, we offered over 250 engaged courses, some 60 percent of which were fairly identifiable through course prefixes for practica or internships, yet there were over 100 courses with a CEL experience that was only discernable through the course description or syllabus. Therefore, the Office of Engagement worked in collaboration with the Office of the Registrar and a faculty advisory group to implement a new course designation that identifies courses with a CEL component. This is an elective designation that faculty request be applied to their course if it meets criteria (which include assessment of engaged learning and addressing community impact), with an eventual goal of the notation appearing on future student transcripts. The creation of the CEL course designation provides institutional recognition to both students and faculty who partake in the challenging and rewarding work of engaging with the community. The label will facilitate tracking and assessment of CEL across departments throughout campus, which will help target our efforts more effectively. Finally, the designation will potentially provide access to data on the impact this work has on students and community partners.

Authentically Engaging Community Partners. Although we have solid evidence from both teaching and research that attests to the validity, strength, and mutual benefit of community partnerships and work at the site or project level, we still find that engaging partners and connecting at the administrative level presents challenges. As part of our commitment to change, we reached out to leaders from local organizations and formed a community-based task force composed of representatives from external constituents from across the areas of economics, business, education sectors, city government, health care, nonprofits, energy, and libraries, who worked with support from the Office of Engagement to specifically address issues related to partnership building and collaboration.

As a result, we developed a partnership principles framework that now not only serves as a resource, but also provides a knowledgeable and experienced-based foundation that outlines recommendations for others seeking to partner with UNC. The framework can be used to support new and existing partnerships and address issues of expectations, capacity, impact, communications, and other logistics. Much of this work is ongoing, especially with local school districts, health organizations, and businesses, and we acknowledge that more support is needed, especially to identify main contacts and communication processes. Interestingly, we have seen an increase in organizations appointing community engagement liaisons or specialists, and we hope that these collaborations will be further enhanced by our efforts to launch a community partner portal for building and promoting partnership work.

Sustaining and Advancing Engagement Work

UNC launched its first CCE plan in 2013 and created and distributed a three-year report on accomplishments in 2016. As a regional leader in community engagement, we recently distributed a second plan to advance and sustain engagement efforts at UNC into the year 2020. From its beginnings, UNC has been committed to providing students with a transformational educational experience, and we have been working this past year to revise the institutional student learning outcomes, recommitting to the priority of providing students with learning opportunities that lead to them become engaged citizens. As we advance these strategies, we do so by adhering to the belief that education is a public good and that these academic endeavors are conducive to mutual benefits for faculty, students, campus, and community partners. Before concluding with recommendations, we highlight here some future goals across the following five interrelated areas: institution, office operations, students, faculty, and community.

Institutional Goals and Directions. CCE endeavors at UNC will continue to focus on the following four dimensions of engagement work: engaged teaching and learning; engaged RSCW; community-engaged partnerships; and logistics and operations, and how these are enacted. CCE is as much a part of our institutional identity as it is a part of our everyday educational practices. To this end, we are working continually to promote a culture of engagement through many of the efforts already mentioned and those described below.

Logistics and Operations Related. In the next year, the Office of Engagement will relocate to a new more central location in a university-wide center that will serve as a gateway for campus and community and further enhance community relations and access. Another priority of the Office of Engagement is to improve and expand our ability to make data-driven decisions. With this commitment comes the need to develop a framework that will sustain and advance our engagement efforts. This includes, but is not limited to, how we plan to refine our assessment of the impact and visibility of community-engaged work with faculty, students, and the community, aspects of which are considered here.

Transformative Education for Students. To provide our students with a transformational education, we focus on the engaged teaching and learning priorities. The creation of the CEL designation provides the opportunity for students to search for these courses to meet their learning needs. To encourage students to register for additional CEL courses, we will provide communications to our professional and faculty advisors to inform them of these options and their benefits. CEL courses provide more high-impact practices to students to enhance their educational experiences and have been shown to improve retention of students. These impacts have been especially significant for minority and low-income students (Bringle, Hatcher, & Muthiah, 2010). In order to extend engaged pedagogies more broadly across campus, we will work with faculty and community partners. This includes continuing to monitor student perceptions of community engagement through the college senior survey delivered to graduating seniors and administered by the Higher Education Research Institute.

Fostering Engaged Faculty Success. The faculty contributions to the Office of Engagement have led to extensive professional development opportunities. In addition, the two faculty administrators in the Office of Engagement, working closely with the CCE advisory committee and faculty whose focus is engaged instruction and research, have identified that the P&T processes remains an area of challenge. Therefore, this has become a priority to address, together with the revision of faculty review criteria. We plan to work with individual academic units to review their evaluation criteria and, in particular, to explore the creation of templates and specific language that are more inclusive of engaged work to assist in conducting faculty reviews.

The new plan outlines how the Office of Engagement will assess and support engaged RSCW across campus into the year 2020. This goal will be accomplished by encouraging transdisciplinary work and strengthening existing supports for community-engaged work, while working to develop innovative additions. We also seek to further incentivize engaged work, create and implement new trainings and workshops, and review and improve funding sources for faculty who are considering or who already conduct engaged RSCW projects. This will include the development of an interactive online tool kit with resources from on campus and links to external ones.

Strengthening Community Partnerships. The Office of Engagement is in the process of securing a web-based software program to host our partnership portal. This portal will serve as an online meeting place for community members, faculty, and students alike to partner on projects that benefit both the university community and the community at large. The portal will also allow the Office of Engagement to track and better understand partnerships and their impacts so that we may focus our efforts going forward.

The Office of Engagement will also continue to nurture long-standing campus–community partnerships while seeking new opportunities to extend campus impact into the community. This work includes the recent Civic Health and Equity Initiative, undertaken in collaboration as part of a collective impact project with Campus Compact of the Mountain West and the University of Denver. This initiative engages campus and community partners to assess various aspects of community partnerships and civic health, including perceptions, costs, and benefits, as well as the demographics and diversity of groups served through partnerships both on campus and in the community. The initial survey we designed and delivered will inform future work and shape systematic approaches to create a comprehensive assessment model for CCE. These efforts will complement those mechanisms previously described; the CEL designation, the partner portal, and codes to identity community-engaged faculty work.

Based on our experience and self-study of our process to both institutionalize and sustain engagement, future research could do well to address some of the persistent challenges that both institutions and individuals face concerning community engagement. First, the need remains to further document and analyze matters related to P&T, particularly with regard to the disciplinary differences that shape the perceptions and the value of engaged work among faculty and administrators, especially with a view to supporting new faculty and early adopters (Diener & Liese, 2009; Doberneck & Schweitzer, 2017). Second, additional research would also do well to explore the disciplinary and institutional variation (Vogelgesang, Denson, & Jayakumar, 2010) that exists in support of faculty collaboratively undertaking engagement projects and how this work is both identified and recognized. Finally, additional research could explore the role of community partners, not only in the partnership and planning of engagement, but also in the institutionalization of engagement.

Implications and Recommendations

We close with some implications and recommendations for other institutions that are considering or already undertaking engagement work.

Contextualize and Integrate Your Approach

We learned very early on that if our work was to be successful, it needed to resonate and complement our institutional identity and mission. Accordingly, as academics and professionals, we sought at every step of the way to take a scholarly and evidence-based approach. The approach others take to either institutionalize or further advance engagement should reflect the institutional identity and characteristics as well as the culture and ethos that prevail on campus and within the immediate community. Likewise, efforts and proposals to institutionalize engagement should seek alignment with institutional priorities and strategic planning, wherever possible intersecting with other initiatives, since these processes direct and inform the short- and long-term sustainability of engagement work. Remember, engagement is not an add-on; it is a way of being, a defining characteristic (Holland, 1997), one that ideally should permeate every aspect of the institution. In addition, it is crucial to engage the early adopters, those already doing this work, and key stakeholders from both the faculty and the administration on campus and in the community. These committed individuals are allies and advocates for this work, and their appreciation and understanding can help advance the larger goals and permeate into other areas of engagement.

Foster and Develop Practical Structures and Resources

Because institutionalization is not an end goal, but rather an ongoing process, the work to sustain and advance engagement must benefit from the necessary organizational infrastructure. This should include base funding sufficient to support the oversight and implementation of ongoing and new partnership work, as well as professional development for those involved. We learned that faculty welcome a variety of workshops and hands-on professional development that support aspects of engaged pedagogy, syllabus design, and student engagement projects that can advance faculty, program, and disciplinary goals. This can also be connected to the identification of community-engaged classes by supporting faculty with redesigned syllabi and engaged student learning outcomes that can then result in formal classifications or codes and increased recognition of faculty who undertake this pedagogical approach.

Of equal importance is the need to publicly recognize and reward existing and exemplary engaged teaching and learning, community-engaged scholarship, and professional activity. This should also contemplate and value learning and research that is transdisciplinary in nature, and especially that which promotes high levels of community partner engagement in these aspects. To further advance institutional and program-level support, we encourage support and oversight for the creation of faculty review templates to aide in the advancement of P&T criteria. These templates should acknowledge, although need not require, the disciplinary variety and scope of engagement across teaching and learning, as well as scholarship as a relevant and valuable part of faculty activity.

Nurture and Promote a Culture of Engagement as Process

When engagement exists as a defining characteristic of an institution, this work may be leveraged as a vehicle for further advancement and continued change. Since being an engaged campus is not an end state, but rather a culture embodied in shared knowledge and practices, there will inevitably be a need for continual work across various areas. Our experience indicates that there is an ongoing demand for assessment both on campus and with community partners. This work should aim to evaluate not only the student learning outcomes, but also the community impact in such a way that findings inform next steps, while also encouraging broad representations and participation of internal and external community engagement partners. Assessment of student learning outcomes related to engaged teaching and learning or research is best undertaken as a collaborative effort, working with those preexisting offices or units who bring advanced access to institutional data and analytical techniques, while assessment of community partnerships and the impact on the institution, on partner organizations, and on the community at large should be pursued as a collaborative effort.

Finally, and as we reflect upon how an engagement culture manifests itself at institutions, through our work, we have come to directly appreciate the significance of mentoring and collaboration. Whether it be senior faculty mentoring junior faculty or key stakeholders, administrators, or community partners, the mentoring process provides the support and motivation needed for this oftentimes insulating and complex work. Mentoring and commitment from champions and long-standing supporters also help onboard new faculty and others from across campus, including student affairs professionals and students. In essence, we appreciate that being an engaged campus, across all its multifaceted expressions, is overwhelmingly an ongoing process of relationship building and collaborative work that seeks to educate, inquire, and enrich for the greater public good.

References

Beere, C. A., Votruba, J. C., & Wells, G. W. (2011). *Becoming an engaged campus: A practical guide for institutionalizing public engagement.* San Francisco, CA: Jossey-Bass.

Benson, L., Harkavy, I., & Puckett, J. (2007). *Dewey's dream: Universities and democracies in an age of education reform.* Philadelphia, PA: Temple University Press.

Boyer, E. L. (1996). The scholarship of engagement. *Bulletin of the American Academy of Arts and Sciences, 49*(7), 18–33.

Bringle, R. G., Hatcher, J. A., & Muthiah, R. N. (2010). The role of service-learning on the retention of first-year students to second year. *Michigan Journal of Community Service Learning, 16*(2), 38–49.

Buse, K., & Hawkes, S. (2015). Health in the sustainable development goals: Ready for a paradigm shift? *Globalization and Health, 11*(13), 1–8.

Castillo, R. C. (2014). A paradigm shift to outcomes-based higher education: Policies, principles and preparations. *International Journal of Sciences: Basic and Applied Research, 14*(1), 174–186.

Chambers, T., & Gopaul, B. (2010). Toward a social justice-centered engaged scholarship: A public and a private good. In H. E. Fitzgerald, C. Burack, & S. D. Seifer (Eds.), *Handbook of engaged scholarship: Contemporary landscapes, future directions* (Vol. 1, pp. 55–70). East Lansing, MI: Michigan State University Press.

Charney, M. (2014). Academic librarians and the sustainability curriculum: Building alliances to support a paradigm shift. *Collaborative Librarianship, 6*(1), 20–35.

Colby, A., Ehrlich, T., Beaumont, E., & Stephens, J. (2003). *Educating citizens: Preparing undergraduates for lives of moral and civic responsibility.* San Francisco, CA: Jossey-Bass.

Colorado Department of Education (2017). Culturally and linguistically diverse learners in Colorado: State of the state 2016. Retrieved from www.cde.state.co.us/cde_english/elstateofthestate.

Colorado Department of Labor and Employment (2017). *Labor market information.* Retrieved from www.colmigateway.com/vosnet/analyzer/results.aspx?session=ind202&pu=1&plang=E.

Davidson, C. N. (2014). Why higher education demands a paradigm shift. *Public Culture, 26*(1), 3–11.

Diener, M. L., & Liese, H. (2009). *Finding meaning in civically engaged scholarship: Personal journeys, professional experiences.* Charlotte, NC: Information Age Publishing.

Doberneck, D. M. (2016). Are we there yet?: Outreach and engagement in the Consortium for Institutional Cooperation promotion and tenure policies. *Journal of Community Engagement & Scholarship, 9*(1), 8–18.

Doberneck, D. M., & Schweitzer, J. H. (2017). Disciplinary variations in publicly engaged scholarship: An analysis using the Biglan classification of academic disciplines. *Journal of Higher Education Outreach and Engagement, 21*(1), 78–103.

Dyson, A. H., & Genishi, C. (1994). Introduction: The need for story. In A. H. Dyson & C. Genishi (Eds.), *The need for story: Cultural diversity in classroom and community* (pp. 1–7). Urbana, IL: National Council of Teachers of English.

Enos, S., & Morton, K. (2003). Developing a theory and practice of campus–community partnerships. In B. Jacoby (Ed.), *Building partnerships for service-learning* (pp. 20–41). San Francisco, CA: Jossey-Bass.

Ernst, C., & Chrobot-Mason, D. (2010). *Boundary spanning leadership: Six practices for solving problems, driving innovation, and transforming organizations.* New York: McGraw-Hill Education.

Fitzgerald, H. E., Burack, C., & Seifer, S. D. (Eds.) (2010). *Handbook of engaged scholarship: Contemporary landscapes, future directions* (Vol. 1). East Lansing, MI: Michigan State University Press.

Fraizer, D. (1997). A multicultural reading and writing experience: Read aloud as service learning in English class. *Michigan Journal of Community Service Learning, 4*(1), 98–103.

Freire, P. (1987). *Pedagogy of the oppressed.* New York: Continuum Publishing.

Furco, A. (2010). The engaged campus: Toward a comprehensive approach to public engagement. *British Journal of Educational Studies, 58*(4), 375–390.

Glass, C. R., & Fitzgerald, H. E. (2010). Engaged scholarship: Historical roots, contemporary challenges. In H. E. Fitzgerald, C. Burack, & S. D. Seifer (Eds.), *Handbook of engaged scholarship: Contemporary landscapes, future directions* (Vol. 1, pp. 9–24). East Lansing, MI: Michigan University Press.

Herts, R. D. (2013). From outreach to engaged placemaking: Understanding public land-grant university involvement with tourism planning and development. *Journal of Higher Education Outreach and Engagement, 17*(1), 97–111.

Hodges, R. A., & Dubb, S. (2012). *The road half traveled: University engagement at a crossroads.* East Lansing, MI: Michigan State University Press.

Holland, B. (1997). Analyzing institutional commitment to service: A model of key organizational factors. *Michigan Journal of Community Service Learning, 4*(1), 30–41.

Kania, J., & Kramer, M. (2011). Collective impact. *Stanford Social Innovation Review, 9*(1), 36–41.

Kezar, A. J., Chambers, T. C., & Burkhardt, J. C. (Eds.) (2005). *Higher education for the public good.* San Francisco, CA: Jossey-Bass.

Kuh, G. D. (2008). Why integration and engagement are essential to effective educational practice in the twenty-first century. *Peer Review, 10*(4), 27–28.

Lane, I. F. (2007). Change in higher education: Understanding and responding to individual and organizational resistance. *Journal of Veterinary Medical Education, 34*(2), 85–92.

Larson, R. W. (1989). *Shaping educational change: The first century of the University of Northern Colorado at Greeley.* Boulder, CO: Colorado Associated University Press.

Martínez-Roldán, C. M. (2003). Building worlds and identities: A case study of the role of narratives in bilingual literature discussion. *Research in the Teaching of English, 37* (4), 491–526.

McLeroy, K. R., Bibeau, D., Steckler, A., & Glanz, K. (1988). An ecological perspective on health promotion programs. *Health Education Quarterly, 15*(4), 351–377.

Moore, T. L. (2014). Community–university engagement: A process for building democratic communities. *ASHE Higher Education Report, 40*(2), 1–129.

Mortenson, T. G. (2012). State funding: A race to the bottom. *The Presidency, 15*(1), 26–29.

Office of Engagement, University of Northern Colorado (2017). *Sustaining and Advancing Engagement 2017–2020.* Retrieved from www.unco.edu/provost/pdf/plans/cce-3-year-plan.pdf.

Ramaley, J. A. (2000). Embracing civic responsibility. *Campus Compact Reader, 1*(2), 1–5.

Romero, D. (2013). The power of stories to build partnerships and shape change. *Journal of Community Engagement and Scholarship, 6*(1), 11–18.

Romero, D., & Kimball, M. (2011). *Summary report on National Outreach Scholarship Consortium Conference.* Unpublished manuscript.

Rosaldo, R. (1986). Ilongot hunting as story and experience. In V. W. Turner & E. M. Bruner (Eds.), *The anthropology of experience* (pp. 97–138). Urbana, IL: University of Illinois Press.

Saltmarsh, J., & Hartley, M. (2011). *"To serve a larger purpose": Engagement for democracy and the transformation of higher education*. Philadelphia, PA: Temple University Press.

Schneekloth, L. H., & Shibley, R. G. (1995). *Placemaking: The art and practice of building communities*. New York: Wiley.

Silvy, T. (2016). Panelists at University of Northern Colorado event advocate for solutions for Latino students. *Greeley Tribune*. Retrieved from www.greeleytribune.com/news/local/panelists-at-university-of-northern-colorado-event-advocate-for-solutions-for-latino-students/.

Solinger, R., Fox, M., & Irani, K. (Eds.) (2008). *Telling stories to change the world: Global voices on the power of narrative to build community and make social justice claims*. New York: Routledge.

University of Northern Colorado (2012). *Enhancement of research, scholarship, creative works, and grant activity: 2012–2015*. Retrieved from www.unco.edu/research/pdf/UNCResearchPlan_2012-15.pdf.

University of Northern Colorado (2015). UNC receives "Latino Americans: 500 Years of History" grant [press release]. Retrieved from www.unco.edu/news-archive/releases.aspx?id=8386.

University of Northern Colorado (2017). University District: Inspiring a Sense of Place Retrieved from www.unco.edu/university-district/.

University of Northern Colorado. Institutional Reporting and Analysis Services (2017). *2016 fall final enrollment profile*. Retrieved from www.unco.edu/institutional-reporting-analysis-services/pdf/enrollment-stats/Fall2016Final.pdf.

University of Northern Colorado University Libraries (2015). *Student voices*. Retrieved from http://digscholarship.unco.edu/voices/.

Vogelgesang, L. J., Denson, N., & Jayakumar, U. M. (2010). What determines faculty-engaged scholarship? *The Review of Higher Education*, *33*(4), 437–472.

Wacker, R. (2015). *Taking Stock of Plans and Progress*. Retrieved from www.unco.edu/provost/pdf/Planning-Summary.pdf.

Yin, R. K. (2012). Case study methods. In H. Cooper, P. M. Camic, D. L. Long, A. T. Panter, D. Rindskopf, & K. J. Sher (Eds.), *APA handbook of research methods in psychology* (Vol. 2, pp. 141–155). Washington, DC: American Psychological Association.

21 Building a University Climate to Support Community-Engaged Research

Valerie Holton, Jennifer Early, Meghan Gough, & Tracey Gendron

Animated by the calls from Boyer (1990) and Lynton and Elman (1987) to embrace its public mission, higher education continues a path to enhance its relevance to its students and broader community. Initially, much of this movement focused on curricular innovations, such as service learning, community-based learning, and other high-impact practices that blend classroom and community elements into coursework (Curly & Stanton, 2012; Welch & Saltmarsh, 2013). Today, engagement with the community in knowledge generation is increasingly seen as critical to addressing real-world questions and problems while also providing high-impact learning opportunities for students (Ramaley, 2014). In support of this, academics are calling for and supporting the development of the science of community-engaged research (CEnR), as well as the supports necessary to conduct it. For instance, the Research University Civic Engagement Network was developed by scholars from research universities to explore the opportunities and challenges of civic engagement through research universities (Curly & Stanton, 2012). Similarly, medical academics wrote the Folsom Report that asserts engagement through research is an essential approach to improving community health (Folsom Group, 2012).

Funders are also calling for and providing financial support for the involvement of community members in the research process. For instance, the national Patient-Centered Outcomes Research Institute was established to fund research that has the potential to improve health. They assert that engaging people who live with a chronic condition and their service providers has the potential to increase recruitment and participation in clinical trials, increase community capacity, and improve health outcomes (Patient-Centered Outcome Research Institute, 2017). Similarly, many of the institutes and centers of the National Institutes of Health (NIH) encourage community engagement in research (Ahmed & Palermo, 2010). A large infrastructure grant mechanism funded by NIH, the Clinical and Translational Science Award (CTSA), was launched in 2006 and has since funded approximately 60 academic medical institutions across the country. It requires that the academic medical centers collaborate with community members on medical issues and research questions of highest priority to the community and to generate measurable community benefit (CTSA Community Engagement Key Function Committee, 2011; National Institutes of Health, 2010).

CEnR is an umbrella term that refers to the broad range of approaches and methodologies that involves a process of knowledge creation through collaborative partnership between academic-based researchers, students, and community members that address a knowledge gap in the literature as well as a community-identified need (Holland, 2001). "Community" refers to any group of people who share a common characteristic, whether they live in a common geographic region, experience a similar health condition, belong to a racial, cultural, or ethnic group, commit themselves to a common cause, work in the same profession, or self-identify as part of a community. Benefits of CEnR include the development of research questions relevant to scholarly and public issues, increased recruitment of subjects and response rates, increased capacity building for the community, and long-term sustainability of research efforts (Ahmed & Palermo, 2010; Jagosh et al., 2012; Spector, 2012).

This chapter uses Virginia Commonwealth University (VCU) to illustrate how a large, decentralized institution can develop a strong climate for CEnR. VCU was part of the first cohort recognized by the Carnegie Foundation as "community-engaged" in 2008, and has since established policies and practices intended to create a supportive climate for community-engaged faculty and students. Founded in the professional degree schools of nursing and social work, VCU advances a public mission of teaching and research based in mutually beneficial partnerships and conducted in a manner that positively impacts its students, employees, and community. The powerful combination of a strong research university that is also community engaged led to an effort to create a strong organizational climate for CEnR.

Based on the literatures of organizational climate, innovation adoption, and infrastructure for community engagement within institutions of higher education (IHEs), we offer an initial presentation of the CEnR Climate Framework. The framework includes the components necessary for building a strong climate for CEnR through an infrastructure that (a) ensures faculty have the requisite competencies to conduct CEnR, (b) provides incentives for the conduct of CEnR, and (c) addresses barriers to CEnR through policy and procedures (Kramer, 2000; see Figure 21.1). We describe each component of the CEnR Climate Framework and offer practical examples of how each component can be designed. The chapter then concludes with guidance on evaluating the effectiveness of the efforts to enhance the climate for CEnR, as well as the overall climate of CEnR.

Building a Strong Organizational Climate for CEnR

As IHEs seek to support and encourage engagement of community members in knowledge creation, they must develop and alter their organizational structures, policies, and practices for the purpose of supporting and rewarding CEnR. The concept of organizational climate comes from the field of organization theory. In general, organization scholars define climate as the collective perception of the kinds of events, practices, procedures, and behaviors that are rewarded, supported, and expected within the organization (Klein & Sorra, 1996; Schneider, Ehrhart, & Macey, 2013). Organizational climate can reflect the general environment of an

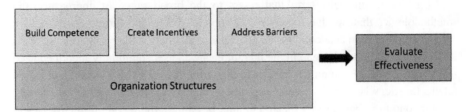

Figure 21.1 *CEnR Climate Framework*

organization or, as we use the term in this chapter, be more focus-specific (Schneider et al., 2013; Zohar & Luria, 2005), such as a climate for diversity and inclusion, or, more relevant to CEnR, a climate for innovation.

In this chapter, we consider CEnR an innovation in higher education. Organizational innovations refer to new products, processes, or systems introduced into the organization (Suranyi-Unger, 1994). Although the concept of CEnR is not new, its institutional use as a university-wide, supported approach to research is new to many universities. Moreover, academic researchers are oftentimes not trained in CEnR as an approach to research. Thus, it is an innovative approach to research at both the institution and individual researcher levels. The more comprehensively and consistently an organization's policies and practices are perceived to encourage, cultivate, and reward the use of an innovation such as CEnR, the stronger the climate for implementation of that innovation (Klein & Sorra, 1996). A climate for CEnR, therefore, refers to the extent to which CEnR is rewarded, supported, and expected. The framework we present here describes the necessary components for building a strong climate for CEnR.

Organization Structure

The first component of the CEnR Climate Framework is organization structure. The organization literature suggests that a primary predictor of an organization's climate for implementation of an innovation such as CEnR is organizational support (Klein & Sorra, 1996; Nutt, 1986). Support for specific innovations can be communicated from leadership across the institution, in large, decentralized organizations such as universities, individual departments and units often retain unique goals and values (Orton & Weick, 1990). Therefore, in order to build a climate across these distinct units, universities must develop and coordinate a structure to align constituents' values, goals, and implementation efforts (Klein & Sorra, 1996; Nutt, 1986; Orton & Weick, 1990). Thus, for complex organizations such as IHEs, the presence of positions and/or units within the organization's hierarchy can be a strong signal of organizational support and capacity to implement the activities and efforts reflected in the remainder of the framework.

There has been limited examination of variation community engagement-related organizational structures, and even less regarding the organizational structures related to CEnR. Evidence suggests that organizational structures supporting community engagement differ across institution types. In a comparative case study of three land-grant and three urban research universities, Weerts and Sandmann (2008) found differences in the organizational structures of the two types of institutions. While the land-grant universities had a separate office dedicated to engagement functions (referred to here as offices of engagement), the urban research universities integrated engagement into their teaching and research such that the responsibility for engagement was more diffuse and not led by one unit.

Welch and Saltmarsh (2013) conducted a review of the infrastructure of over 100 community engagement offices across institutions that received the Carnegie community engagement designation in 2010. They found the majority of offices are housed in academic affairs, led by a full-time administrator (often holding a terminal degree) and supported by budgeted institutional funds. The offices were found to be staffed by people who provide both administrative support and programming. Services tended to center on those that align with the CEnR Climate Framework presented here, albeit with a focus on community engagement broadly rather than CEnR specifically, which is consistent with the organizational location of these offices in academic affairs. For instance, they build competence through providing professional development opportunities, defining and designating courses that involve engagement, and serving as a clearinghouse for information and cross-campus collaboration. They create incentives through engaging in public relations, offering course development grants, and participating in fundraising for engagement-related efforts. They remove barriers by developing relevant policy and guidance, and they evaluate the effectiveness of these efforts through tracking and assessing engagement efforts.

The Division of Community Engagement is VCU's office of engagement, and in 2011 it established the Office of CEnR with the hiring of VCU's inaugural director of community-engaged research. This office was created by the provost with the explicit direction that the Division partner with VCU's Office of Research and the Center for Clinical and Translational Research, a unit at VCU funded by the NIH's Clinical and Translational Science. The major goals of collaboration across these units were to build competency in, remove barriers to, and broadly promote the science of CEnR, while also stimulating collaboration across the university and community. Much of the early efforts to build the climate for CEnR was done in partnership between these two units.

Campus-wide committees are another form of organizational structure that advances the climate of CEnR (Lazarus, Erasmus, Hendricks, Nduna, & Slamat, 2008; Zuiches, 2008). For instance, the University of Colorado Denver has the Partnership of Academicians and Communities for Translation. This governing council incentivizes CEnR through pilot grants and the dissemination of findings from CEnR, builds competencies through training programs, and identifies and removes barriers (Colorado Clinical and Translational Sciences Institute, 2017). In 2012, VCU established such a campus-wide committee: the CEnR Federation. Cochaired by VCU's director of community-engaged research and the codirector of the Center for Clinical Translational Research Community Engagement Core, the Federation was composed of senior researchers and administrators from units with high levels of CEnR, including the schools of Medicine, Nursing, Education, Social Work, and Arts as well as the Office of the Provost (Holton, Early, Resler, Trussell, & Howard, 2016). This group aimed to design and advocate for infrastructure to advance high-quality, high-impact CEnR. However, VCU discovered that campus-wide bodies focused on CEnR can be complicated – while community-engaged researchers were dealing with similar issues across the university, it was difficult to create synergies across diverse research fields. Furthermore, Federation members generally did not have the authority to make decisions related to unit- or university-wide CEnR infrastructure design, such as budgeting and hiring. Therefore, the Federation members did not find the committee instrumental in advancing the agenda of designing and advancing CEnR infrastructure. Harkavey and Hartley (2012) describe similar challenges with an advisory board for the Netter Center at the University of Pennsylvania.

In response to these challenges, VCU's Federation transitioned to operating as a committee of an existing campus-wide council dedicated to advancing community engagement across the university: the Council for Community Engagement. The Council is composed of appointed representatives from all VCU units. Through its committees, the Council "(1) builds and maintains a network of liaisons across units, (2) receives and disseminates information and resources that promotes and supports community engagement, (3) gathers information from the community on critical needs and opportunities, (4) recognizes accomplishments of university–community partnerships, and (5) assists in the coordination of events designed to engage with community partners to address community-identified needs" (Holton et al., 2016). Shifting the Federation to a committee of the Council leveraged the Council's existing network and infrastructure. Its focus no longer centers on designing infrastructure, but rather on embedding CEnR values and resources throughout the council members' home units. Responsibility for infrastructure development was left distributed across multiple university entities and offices.

Additional units within a university structure may be called upon to support CEnR. For example, the Institutional Review Board (IRB) is critical to the advancement of CEnR. To ensure the protection of research participants and the integrity of the research process, there may need to be additional or specialized ethics education and review. The staff must have the knowledge and flexibility to be responsive to the ethical challenges related to partnering with community members (Anderson, 2013; Anderson et al., 2012). For instance, community partners may play multiple roles in a research project, but may have little to no prior research experience. The existing tools for ethics training such as the Collaborative Institutional Training Initiative (CITI) are too complex for use in some contexts, can be difficult and burdensome to translate, and are not written at an appropriate educational level for some community-based researchers (Anderson et al., 2012; Merritt et al., 2010; Shore et al., 2011). Similarly, academic investigators may also need ethics training to appreciate the complexities associated with CEnR (Anderson, 2013; Anderson et al., 2012). The IRB has proved to be a critical organizational partner at VCU.

Building Competency

A strong CEnR climate fosters the institutional integration of CEnR by ensuring that the university's researchers and future scholars are skilled in its use (Kramer, 2000). Thus, the next component of the CEnR model is building competency. At the outset, CEnR's collaborative approach to research is typically new to academics and community members alike, which demands careful preparation and training for faculty on how to build trust with community members, and to develop and sustain partnerships. Yet, traditional doctoral or master's-level curricula, by which university faculty are educated, do not typically include training and instruction on community engagement in research (Ahmed & Palermo, 2010). In response universities are investing in programs to build the competencies of traditionally trained researchers who want to pursue CEnR.

The core competencies for CEnR are the critical skills and knowledge for doing community-engaged scholarship. At its most basic level, CEnR is about the partnerships between researchers and the community members who impact, or are impacted by, the problems under study. Partnerships can be developed and sustained by both the actions aimed at building the partnership (what we do) and the approach to the partnership's work (how we do it) (Mayan & Daum, 2016). Community-engaged partnerships must be built and sustained around principles of mutual respect, shared power, agreed-upon roles, and clear processes for communication and decision-making (Horowitz et al., 2009). In adopting this approach, the partnership operates with the researcher in the role of an "outside expert" and the community member occupying the role of the "inside expert" who understands the needs and experiences related to the problem under investigation.

With partnership as its foundation, VCU identified four core competencies for CEnR: *building knowledge and understanding* of CEnR principles and approaches (the ability to understand the principles of CEnR such as theoretical frameworks, methods of planning, implementation, and evaluation, and clearly communicating this research approach to others); *honing strong interpersonal communication skills* (the ability to work effectively with diverse communities, negotiate across community–academic groups and contexts, and demonstrate skills in conflict resolution and the ability to cope with conflict); *expanding research expertise* to include community-engaged approaches (the ability to write successful grant proposals expressing principles and approaches to community-engaged scholarship, learning to democratize knowledge by validating multiple sources of knowledge, and promoting the use of multiple methods of discovery); and *learning to disseminate research in multiple forms* (the ability to publish peer-reviewed journal articles grounded in the processes and outcomes of community-engaged scholarship and collaborating with community members to generate significant, useful products of community-engaged scholarship that influence practice in the community). These CEnR competencies can be developed through opportunities for individuals to participate in learning networks and mentorship programs, to build knowledge and skills, and to have access to readily available guidance offered directly from the organization (Blanchard et al., 2009; Furco, 2016; Jameson, Clayton, Jaeger, & Brindle, 2012). Below, we showcase skill-building opportunities initiated at VCU to advance CEnR competency for faculty and students. Among these examples are in-person trainings, faculty cohort experiences, readily available guidance documents, and a graduate-level, open-access course on designing and implementing CEnR.

A Common Language. A key starting point for building competency is creating collective knowledge and understanding of what constitutes CEnR through the development of a common language. A common language carries and conveys meaning in ways that allow people to communicate and share ideas, an essential basis for shaping institutional understanding and commitment (Daft & Wiginton, 1979). In order to develop a common language for community engagement broadly and CEnR specifically, various institutions and organizations have established institutional terms and definitions (e.g., Carnegie Foundation for the Advancement of Teaching, 2001; Lynton, 1995).

To develop its common community engagement language, VCU engaged in a yearlong process to define CEnR, among other terms related to community engagement, which resulted in a set of terms and definitions that were introduced into the university's culture. The terms and their definitions were identified through a literature review process and then refined by working groups. VCU defines CEnR as "a collaborative process between the researcher and the community partner that creates and disseminates knowledge and creative expression with the goal of contributing to [an academic or scientific] discipline and strengthening the well-being of the community" (Pelco & Howard, 2016).

Mentorship and Learning Networks. Establishment of strong mentorship structures for faculty is important. However, given the more recent emergence of this research approach, there are limited numbers of tenured faculty to provide CEnR mentorship to junior faculty (Marrero et al., 2013). One approach universities employ is the creation of mentorship programs that draw from the knowledge and skills of experienced community-engaged researchers *as well as* experienced community partners. For example, bidirectional mentoring programs are structured so that faculty and community partners provide mentorship to each other (Carrasquillo et al., 2007). While academics may provide community members with technical or grant-writing assistance, for example, community partners provide important feedback to academics on local needs, as well as the dynamics of particular communities that are important to formulating research agendas and interventions.

In 2013, VCU launched a CEnR Interest Group and listserv to build multiple CEnR core competencies for faculty who needed more flexibility (timing, schedules) than a formal training session. In addition to developing broader knowledge and understanding of CEnR, the Interest Group and listserv helped hone research expertise and create pathways to stronger interpersonal communication strategies through sharing best practices and eliciting suggestions to manage partnership challenges or further develop high-quality CEnR. The listserv functioned as a communication tool for the CEnR Interest Group and attracted over 200 members from across the community and university. In its first two years, the Interest Group met around key issues of interest before deciding to communicate and share information mainly through the listserv. The Office of CEnR was responsible for managing the listserv, and while everyone was welcome to post to it, the information shared was posted mainly by the Office.

Build Knowledge and Skills. In order to build a CEnR foundation, faculty and potential community partners need to understand the core principles of community partnership, as well as demonstrate the skills required. In the context of building knowledge between faculty and community partners, it is important to recognize the role of adult learning theory, known as andragogy. The premise of this theory is that adult learners differ from children because they bring their lived experiences to the process of learning (Knowles, 1984). Research in community engagement suggests that andragogy must inform initiatives to build knowledge and skills in CEnR because adults are motivated to learn when they can find relevance and value in the information to their lives or jobs (Pelco & Early, 2016). Consistent with the assumptions underlying this theory of adult learning, professional development intended to promote core competencies in CEnR must therefore tap the experiences of participants, provide opportunities to learn from each other, and develop new ideas through their own filters of concern and need.

Recognition and demonstration of CEnR methodologies can illuminate approaches for engaging community partners and producing published research findings. One representative example, community-based participatory research (CBPR), assumes a trusting relationship between academic and community partners, who seek shared ownership and decision-making in the research, design the process to encourage co-learning, ensure mutual benefit, and agree to long-term commitment to the research partnership (Israel et al., 2003). Similar to other community-engaged approaches to research, CBPR also recognizes the importance of disseminating research in multiple forms – peer-reviewed outlets that meet academic expectations, as well as accessible formats that support translation into practice (Hicks et al., 2012).

VCU's annual Community Engagement Institute is organized to provide faculty members, community partners, and graduate students with the opportunity to deepen their understanding of community–university engagement. In 2016, the Institute restructured to focus on the previously-described core competencies. This new format combined what were previously offered as separate service-learning and CEnR mini-institutes, affording participants the opportunity to dive deep into the crucial skills needed for successful community–university partnerships. Through highly participatory hands-on workshops, participants were exposed to foundations, ethics, and tools for collaborative work together.

In an effort to learn from experiences of faculty cohorts, the Office of CEnR led the development and facilitation of two faculty learning communities. The Faculty Learning Community on Excellence in CEnR (2012–2013) involved eight faculty members who were active, community-engaged researchers. The members of this community participated in an innovative inquiry process to study the process and practice of doing CEnR. The cornerstone of this program was the development of case studies of exemplary CEnR projects at VCU (George, 2014) that could be used to inform future faculty research. The next faculty learning community was also grounded in CEnR, but focused on the dissemination of research findings using web-based platforms (2015–2016). This community involved 11 members who explored various web-based dissemination methods, then created and implemented their dissemination plans. A guide was developed to reflect on the lessons learned and resources that were accessed to inform their learning and plans. The final product can be found online (http://guides.library.vcu.edu/dissemination).

Additionally, Collaborative Curiosity was an eight-week, open-access, fully online doctoral course. It afforded interested community members and registered, academic credit-seeking university participants an introduction to the purpose, design, and practice of CEnR. Participants engaged with readings and videos about CEnR; participated in synchronous, Twitter-based discussions; prepared and sought feedback on a CEnR grant proposal presented in a series of blog posts; reflected on differences between CEnR and other approaches to research; and created digital "makes" around important questions in CEnR (for more information on the course, see Holton, Gogia, & McKenzie, 2018). As a result of this course, 59 YouTube video shorts were created, organizing the course's hour-long video hangouts into quickly digestible and shareable clips that answer questions about CEnR.

Finally, as noted earlier, IRB is a key partner in this work at VCU. The VCU's directors of the IRB and the Office of CEnR developed training for all IRB reviewers regarding the effective review of all CEnR research protocols. Other resources were codeveloped with the IRB, including a module on ethics in CEnR for a doctoral-level course offered by the university and a series of faculty workshops. Finally, the IRB added two CEnR elective modules to the standard university-wide, online training requirements for research involving human participants.

Readily Available Guidance. A series of guidance documents were prepared and made publically available by VCU Libraries. Among these guidance documents are frequently asked questions related to CEnR and the IRB, compensation of community partners in research, and core competencies for undergraduate community-engaged researchers. Additionally, videos were created that address topics such as the definition of CEnR, benefits to community and academic partnerships, recommendations for successful partnerships, and the roles of trust, respect, conflict, and honesty in CEnR.

Creating Incentives

The third component of the CEnR Climate Framework is creating incentives. Incentives beyond standard compensation may encourage or induce organizational members to engage in activities like CEnR (Orton & Weick, 1990). These incentives may include recognition and awards, funding specifically to support CEnR, and modified institutional policies (Chung et al., 2015; Nyden, 2003).

Recognition. Because CEnR often leads to new discoveries regarding critical public issues, increasing the visibility of CEnR outcomes can gain the attention and support of others (Nyden, 2003). This can include stories that are published across university and community websites, social media, newsletters, and other forms of communication. Recognition can also be in the form of awards for CEnR. VCU's annual "Currents of Change Award" is given annually for outstanding partnerships in CEnR, among others. This award is both a recognition of these efforts, as well as a signal that engaged work is considered important. These internal awards can also be a form of identifying good faculty candidates for national awards.

Funding. Financial support signals the institution's commitment and provides critical resources that encourage and enable the conduct of CEnR (Chadwick & Pawlowski, 2007; Chung et al., 2015). Here, we discuss the role of intramural funding and financial support from donors and foundations. One form of intramural funding – pilot and seed grant programs – is associated with enhanced service delivery, high-quality learning experiences, and published community-engaged scholarship (Leisey, Holton, & Davey, 2012; Zuiches, 2013). Zuiches (2013) found that such grants were effective incentives for faculty to partner with community members and increased the likelihood of faculty being successful in obtaining additional grant funding. To maximize their potential for encouraging and enabling the conduct of high-quality CEnR, funding should be aimed at creating parity in the partnership (Lindau et al., 2011). This can be further supported through academic grant writing training that is offered to both academic and community members that builds the capacity of the partnership (Lewis et al., 2016).

In order to support the conduct of CEnR at VCU, the Council for Community Engagement and the Center for Clinical and Translational Research jointly funded two intramural grant mechanisms. The VCU CEnR Pipeline to Proposal Program supports high-quality, high-impact CEnR from community partnership development to pilot project implementation. Funded projects serve as catalysts for ongoing CEnR sustained by external funding. CEnR Partnership Development Grants, awarding up to $10,000, are intended to support new or potential academic–community research partnerships. Funds from this grant are to be used for building and supporting research partnerships through relationship-building activities, exploring shared research interests, and developing infrastructure and governance for the research partnership.

Successful efforts can then seek funding from the CCE Community Engagement Grants and the Center for Clinical and Translational Research's (CCTR) Endowment Fund. CCE Community Engagement Grants, awarding up to $20,000, aim to advance community-engaged scholarship in any academic or academic support unit and can support a broad array of community-engaged scholarship. Proposals are encouraged from across VCU in partnership with community-based organizations to address community-identified needs. Community-engaged pilot project proposals are welcomed by the CCTR's Endowment Fund, which provides individual research awards of up to $50,000 and multi-school research awards of up to $130,000 for health sciences research. CEnR proposals that meet the CCTR's

Endowment Fund criteria must demonstrate established community–academic partnerships. The funds support a scientifically rigorous research implementation/pilot project to be jointly conducted by academic–community partners.

Although early in its implementation, evidence suggests that the pipeline has the potential to achieve its goal of supporting CEnR from the early stages of partnership development to implementation of a pilot project. For instance, the Partnership for Autism and Aging Research Collaborative was funded during the inaugural year of the CEnR Partnership Development Grants and was funded the following year by the CCE Community Engagement Grants for a CEnR pilot project. At the time of writing this chapter, they are seeking ongoing extramural funding from a variety of sources. A recent evaluation of the CCE Community Engagement Grants demonstrates the impact this kind of funding can have. Over the past ten years (2007–2017), $1,100,600 have been awarded to fund 69 community-engaged projects, which have involved over 219 faculty and 1,350 students and generated 199 community-engaged scholarship products. Grantees have demonstrated success in leveraging $2,706,134 in external funds, which means that for every dollar of seed funding invested, the community engagement grants generated $3.00 from external funding sources to sustain their projects and to support their partnerships.

Another form of intramural funding at VCU explicitly supports undergraduate students interested in CEnR. As part of the larger effort by the Undergraduate Research Opportunity Program (UROP) to support VCU undergraduates to conduct research, the award is offered to undergraduate students and their faculty mentors whose research proposals show the greatest potential for learning and discovery. The fellowship is open to all VCU undergraduates from every academic discipline, and the funded projects represent a wide array of scholarly interests that exemplify the diversity of the academic community. To date, six CEnR awards have been awarded to students who engaged with community partners to explore questions related to community health, education, and the environment.

Addressing Barriers

The fourth component of the CEnR Climate Framework is addressing barriers through university policy and practice. Although the evidence of CEnR as an effective research methodology has raised interest among academicians, barriers at institutional and disciplinary levels have prevented CEnR from becoming a widely-promoted, accepted research model in some IHEs. Furthermore, the inclusion of community members in the research process can challenge existing policies and practices. Here, we discuss the three areas of change triggered by VCU's experiences with involving community partners in knowledge development: memorandums of understanding (MOUs), compensation of community partners, and promotion and tenure.

Memorandums of Understanding

MOUs, sometimes used interchangeably with the term "memorandums of agreement," help to clarify and document roles, expectations, and responsibilities within a partnership. They typically include the principles and procedures of the partnership, the project description, financial and resource responsibilities, obligations to the IRB, data-sharing agreements, authorship agreements, and issues related to risk (Chau et al., 2007; Clinical and Translational Science Awards Consortium, 2011; Gehlert et al., 2014). The process of developing an MOU may reveal issues that the university has not addressed before or may not be adequately covered by existing policy and practice. For instance, universities are only beginning to be equipped with platforms and procedures for data sharing in a way that benefits the community and enables CEnR (Lindau et al., 2011). Furthermore, these MOUs often challenge issues of language and authority. The language of "partnership" is common in collaborative research; however, it has a legal meaning that may have unintended implications. Additionally, as a legally binding document, the signature authority may be those who are not directly involved with the effort. In the university setting, this is likely to mean that the MOU must be reviewed by legal counsel and signed by the dean or another senior-level administrator (Gehlert et al., 2014; Jacobson, Butterill, & Goering, 2004).

Compensation of Community Partners

Because community members can serve as paid consultants, research collaborators, data collectors, students, and study participants, compensation and expense reimbursement may vary by their role and the research protocol (Lindau et al., 2011). There also may be issues that arise when trying to compensate community members. For example, in research on prisoner re-entry, the involvement of ex-felons may be crucial to the project team; however, funder, governmental or university policies may prohibit payment to these individuals. Consequently, the compensation of community members should be explicitly discussed and agreed upon in the beginning of the research endeavor and be reflected in formal documents such as MOUs (Chau et al., 2007; Clinical and Translational Science Awards Consortium, 2011; Lindau et al., 2011), data sharing and authorship agreements (Castleden, Morgan, & Neimanis, 2010; Cochran, et al., 2008), position descriptions, and other formalized agreements (Agency for Healthcare Research and Quality, 2004). Furthermore, the university needs to have clear and transparent processes to make compensation possible without undue burden on community or academic research team members. However, the ability of researchers to consistently ensure reimbursement for community members engaging in research in roles other than traditional research participants has proven challenging. VCU has addressed this through the development of a guidance document on the compensation of community partners.

Promotion and Tenure

Perhaps the most significant barrier to CEnR is the degree to which this research approach is supported in promotion and tenure policies and by the faculty and academic leadership that controls campus-wide narratives about what should be valued – and therefore rewarded – at a particular institution. In Boyer's (1990) landmark report, *Scholarship Reconsidered*, higher education institutions were encouraged to reform policies to emphasize, acknowledge, and support involvement in scholarship that is most appropriate to their institutional missions. Following this advice, academic leaders and scholars have since found increased faculty involvement in diverse forms of scholarship, increased institutional effectiveness and greater faculty retention (Furco, 2016; Weerts & Sandmann, 2008). However, university reward systems such as promotion and tenure policies do not always evolve at the same pace as the evolution of different forms of scholarship (O'Meara, 2005; Saltmarsh et al., 2009). This section examines the challenges and opportunities to reform policies, procedures, and campus norms that better support promotion and tenure outcomes for faculty engaged in CEnR.

One of the ways this value is communicated is through faculty evaluation policies and processes. In many instances, community-engaged scholarship continues to be confused with service, and therefore not "counted" as scholarship in faculty evaluations. For example, community-engaged scholarship often requires a significant amount of time spent immersed within the community of interest, developing relationships, gathering knowledge, and gauging community-identified need. While critical to the development of quality CEnR and scholarship, these activities are often "counted" or understood as service activities. Sobrero and Jayaratne (2014) make the case that this confusion may come from failure to adequately educate administrative leaders and department heads about all realms of scholarship. Given the limited understanding of the metrics and standards for community-engaged scholarship, department heads may be "highly critical of scholarship that does not look like their own" (Sobrero & Jayaratne, 2014, p. 143). While some call for reform by reserving the term "service" only for committee and disciplinary work, the larger reform must involve training, education, and an acceptance of academic culture inclusive of newer methods of research and teaching (Ramaley, 2014).

Addressing this challenge may warrant revision of promotion and tenure policy, but the more effective strategy is to create a shift in the culture of promotion and tenure committees to broaden their assumptions about what constitutes high-quality research. Traditional values influence the senior faculty who make up promotion and tenure committees and are often unfamiliar with newer research methods (Ahmed et al., 2010; Marrero et al., 2013). The approach and research methods used in CEnR necessarily differ from what may be considered more traditional, conventional research. For example, many CEnR projects are unlikely to be anchored by randomized control treatments, and because they integrate community partners in the research, CEnR can take much longer to complete and publish (Marrero et al., 2013). There is evidence that institutions with policy reforms that include regard for CEnR methods have something in common: they are more likely to employ a broader set of criteria to assess scholarship (O'Meara, 2005). For example, some suggest including explicit engagement principles as well as input by community stakeholders into promotion and tenure processes and decisions (Gelmon et al., 2005; Marrero et al., 2013).

In higher education, the promotion and tenure policies effectively clarify the institution's values, which are subsequently reinforced by strategic plans, reward systems, and resulting power structures. As described by O'Meara, Eatman, and Peterson (2015), nearly every change initiated within an institution – be it curriculum reform, recruitment, or retention – has implications for promotion and tenure. However, they find that many faculty struggle with promotion and tenure policies that do not support innovations in scholarship and institutional priorities (O'Meara et al., 2015). As a result, while faculty may be informally recognized for their scholarship innovations affecting new institutional concerns related to community engagement, they are frequently not being validated or rewarded in meaningful ways.

In 2010, VCU initiated a revision of its university promotion and tenure policy to explicitly include CEnR as an acceptable approach to scholarship. As described in detail by Pelco and Howard (2016), the process of policy reform was multifaceted, beginning with building university-wide consensus on community engagement definitions that were informed by peer institutions and national organizations. A revised policy was submitted in 2012, followed by online discussion forums and public comment periods. In 2013, VCU approved the revised promotion and tenure policy, which included the addition of community engagement language into each of the general criteria categories of scholarship, teaching, and service. In conjunction with the policy revision, VCU hired an external consultant to facilitate discussions among campus stakeholders and with deans to build competence around community-engaged scholarship and its relevance to specific disciplines and VCU's mission.

Evaluating Effectiveness

Once an innovation has been implemented, the organization must evaluate its effectiveness in order to determine the benefits that may accrue as a result of its successful implementation (Klein & Sorra, 1996). Thus, the final component of the CEnR Climate Framework is evaluating effectiveness – in other words, examining the extent to which a strong climate for CEnR has been created. Organizational climate can be assessed as both a function of the organization's structure as well as a function of organizational members' perceptions (Ashforth, 1985). The organization structure is seen as the bedrock that shapes the organization environment in such a way that shared perceptions of the climate will form within groups and across the organization (Ashforth, 1985).

Evaluating Organization Structure for CEnR Support

An objective evaluation of organization structure to support CEnR quantitatively and qualitatively accounts for the mere existence of the structural units dedicated to support CEnR and reflects the degree to which the organization structure centralizes and formalizes practices related to building competence, creating incentives, and removing barriers to the conduct of CEnR (Ashforth, 1985). We have outlined in this chapter how VCU has dedicated significant time and resources to its existing structural units, competence-building opportunities, incentive creation, and removal of barriers to the conduct of CEnR. As a rough quantitative measurement of the degree to which organizational structures supporting CEnR exists, VCU has implemented a series of questions within the IRB application process to identify CEnR and gauge the level of involvement of community partners (see Holton, Jettner, Early, & Shaw, 2015, for more information). These data are used in publicly available community engagement dashboards hosted on the university's website. The assumption is that this will support the university's growing focus on CEnR by allowing faculty and administrators to see the scope and trends in their work.

Qualitative evidence for adequate organizational structure to support CEnR can be found in VCU's awards and recognitions. Carnegie has consistently recognized VCU as both a "high-research" and a "community-engaged" institution. The university and its faculty have received other national awards and recognitions for engagement, such as the C. Peter Magrath Community Engagement Scholarship Award in 2016 and the Presidential Honor Roll for student service. While neither require CEnR in order to be awarded, applications reflected the role of CEnR at VCU.

Evaluating Perceptions of CEnR Climate

In the organization literature, perceptions of climate have been measured as employees' collective (Schneider, Bowen, Ehrhart, & Holcombe, 2000) and individual (James & Jones, 1974) perceptions of their work environment. Quantitatively, organization researchers have utilized various climate scales and instruments to measure collective perceptions of an organization's climate for innovation at the team and organization levels. For example, the Support for Innovation scale from the Team Climate Inventory (TCI) developed by Anderson and West (1998) assesses concrete behaviors supportive of innovation within a team. Similarly, Ekvall (1996) developed an instrument for measuring perspectives of organizational structure and climate for creativity and innovation. These scales and instruments can be adapted to assess CEnR climate as a specific type of innovation. Qualitatively, collective perceptions of CEnR climate can be assessed through focus groups, interviews, and other means of understanding the extent to which university employees perceive CEnR as being rewarded, supported, and expected within the organization.

Although VCU has not yet embarked on a formal evaluation of collective perceptions of its CEnR climate, an initial examination of the individual perception of CEnR climate was initiated with two faculty members who have engaged in CEnR and have earned promotion and tenure with an engaged portfolio. Here, they share their reflections and their vision for the future. Faculty reflection regarding the implementation of a CEnR Climate Framework demonstrates how organizational structures and support to build competencies as community-engaged researchers were crucial to faculty success. The infrastructure needed to ensure that faculty have the requisite competency to conduct CEnR was described as an essential component of building the necessary knowledge to become a skilled community-engaged researcher.

> Fortunately, within months of joining the faculty at VCU, I was invited to participate in a service-learning institute. This first point of engagement with community-engaged teaching opened the door to a greater understanding of community-engaged research in general. In fact, my first journal publication described a research project developed around my first service-learning course.

> Efforts to build a climate that valued community-engaged research at VCU informed my progress and my professional identity as a community-engaged scholar, and helped to prepare me for tenure review. Organizational structure and support provided opportunities for me to immerse myself in methods of teaching, research and service that worked in concert to establish myself as a community-engaged faculty member.

Reflections also captured the process by which CEnR was used within the promotion and tenure process at VCU.

> Because of the institutional support, I felt equipped to use community-engaged research as a framework for my promotion and tenure dossier. I had the support needed to effectively present my research and scholarship as critically linked to the overall mission of the university.

> I was successful in receiving tenure at VCU and my experience has set me on a path to ensure that community-engaged researchers proceed with confidence toward their tenure review. As I reflect, while I was offered a series of opportunities to nurture my identity as a community-engaged researcher, my tenure review committees and upper administration did not receive all the resources they needed: none had an operationalization of community-engaged research, nor did they have a metric to determine "excellence" in this method of scholarship.

Faculty members also reflected on the challenges and obstacles to using CEnR as a pathway to recognition and reward in the promotion and tenure process.

> The biggest obstacle to promotion and tenure was due to the limited experience and exposure to CEnR by tenure review committee members. To most members on my committees, the term "community-engaged research" – the foundation of my identity – was absolutely foreign. Thankfully I had the opportunity to formally meet with my review committee to provide a deeper explanation of this term, present its broader recognition by scholars, and remind them that community engagement was recently integrated into the university's promotion and tenure guidelines as a method to count for research, teaching, and service.

Conclusion

As problems facing our communities are increasingly complex, IHEs have the opportunity – and, the authors of this chapter would argue, the obligation – to harness their resources to address real-world issues. In essence, to fulfill its mission of educating the citizenry and generating new knowledge through the principles of engagement. This chapter reviews the components needed to build a climate that supports and advances CEnR in hopes that it enables institutions to achieve this end.

Several lessons learned by those involved in the VCU effort are worth noting here. Because building a climate requires efforts across the campus, collaboration, communication, and transparency are essential. Moreover, institutions have the opportunity to model effective practices and principles of CEnR in the way they approach how they build the climate for CEnR. Furthermore, leveraging existing resources is critical in resource-tight environments. Carnegie's Community Engagement Classification has further motivated colleges and universities to become more focused on building the infrastructure to advance this public mission (Holland, 2001). Applying for recognitions such as these can help to create a sense of urgency that provides additional motivation and can garner additional resources. While this chapter focuses on the climate within an IHE, any effort that involves community–academic partnerships must also address the capacity for public participation within and across communities (Lindau et al., 2011).

References

Agency for Healthcare Research and Quality (2004). *National healthcare disparities report*. Rockville, MD: US Department of Health and Human Services

Ahmed, S. M., & Palermo, A.-G. S. (2010). Community engagement in research: Frameworks for education and peer review. *American Journal of Public Health*, *100*(8), 1380–1387.

Anderson, E. E. (2013). Views of academic and community partners regarding participant protections and research integrity: A pilot focus group study. *Journal of Empirical Research on Human Research Ethics: JERHRE*, *8*(1), 20–31.

Anderson, E. E., Solomon, S., Heitman, E. et al. (2012). Research ethics education for community-engaged research: A review and research agenda. *Journal of Empirical Research on Human Research Ethics: JERHRE*, *7*(2), 3–19.

Anderson, N. R., & West, M. A. (1998). Measuring climate for work group innovation: Development and validation of the team climate inventory. *Journal of Organizational Behavior*, *19*, 235–258.

Ashforth, B. E. (1985). Climate formation: Issues and extensions. *Academy of Management Review*, *10*(4), 837–847.

Blanchard, L. W., Hanssmann, C., Strauss, R. P. et al. (2009). Models for faculty development: What does it take to be a community-engaged scholar. *Metropolitan Universities*, *20*(2), 47–65.

Boyer, E. L. (1990). *Scholarship reconsidered: Priorities of the professoriate*. Princeton, NJ: Princeton University Press.

Carnegie Foundation for the Advancement of Teaching (2001). *A Classification of Institutions of High Education: 2000 Edition*. Carnegie Foundation for the.

Carrasquillo, O., Fleming, C., Ford, M. E. et al. (2007). Mentoring in community-based participatory research: The RCMAR experience. *Ethnicity & Disease*, *17*(1 Suppl. 1), S33–S43.

Castleden, H., Morgan, V. S., & Neimanis, A. (2010). Researchers' perspectives on collective/ community co-authorship in community-based participatory indigenous research. *Journal of Empirical Research on Human Research Ethics: An International Journal*, *5*(4), 23–32.

Chadwick, S. A., & Pawlowski, D. R. (2007). Assessing institutional support for service-learning: A case study of organizational sensemaking. *Michigan Journal of Community Service Learning*, *13*, 31–39.

Chau, T. S., Islam, N., Tandon, S. D. et al. (2007). Using community-based participatory research as a guiding framework for health disparities research centers. *Progress in Community Health Partnerships: Research, Education, and Action*, *1*(2), 195.

Chung, B., Norris, K., Mangione, C. et al. (2015). Faculty participation in and needs around community engagement within a large multiinstitutional clinical and translational science awardee. *Clinical and Translational Science*, *8*(5), 506–512.

Clinical and Translational Science Awards Consortium (2011). *Principles of community engagement*, 2nd edn. Washington, DC: NIH, Community Engagement Task Force on the Principles of Community Engagement.

Cochran, P. A., Marshall, C. A., Garcia-Downing, C. et al. (2008). Indigenous ways of knowing: Implications for participatory research and community. *American Journal of Public Health*, *98*(1), 22–27.

Colorado Clinical and Translational Science Institute (2017). PACT: Partnership of Academicians and Communities for Translation. Retrieved from www.ucdenver .edu/research/CCTSI/community-engagement/pact/Pages/default.aspx.

Curly, M. F., & Stanton, T. K. (2012). The history of TRUCEN. *Journal of Higher Education Outreach and Engagement*, *16*(4), 3–9.

Daft, R. L., & Wiginton, J. C. (1979). Language and organization. *Academy of Management Review*, *4*(2), 179–191.

Early, J. (2017). *CEnR climate framework*. Creative Commons – Attribution – Noncommercial 4.0 International License.

Ekvall, G. (1996). Organizational climate for creativity and innovation. *European Journal of Work and Organizational Psychology*, *5*(1), 105–123.

Folsom Group (2012). Communities of solution: The Folsom report revisited. *Annals of Family Medicine*, *10*(3), 250–260.

Furco, A. (2016). Creating an institutional agenda for community-engaged scholarship faculty development. *Journal of Community Engagement & Higher Education*, *8* (3), 1–5.

Gehlert, S., Fayanju, O. M., Jackson, S. et al. (2014). A method for achieving reciprocity of funding in community-based participatory research. *Progress in Community Health Partnerships: Research, Education, and Action*, *8*(4), 561.

Gelmon, S. B., Seifer, S. D., Kauper-Brown, J., & Mikkelsen, M. (2005). *Building capacity for community engagement: Institutional self-assessment*. Seattle, WA: Community–Campus Partnerships for Health.

In C. George (Ed.), *Excellence in community-engaged research at Virginia Commonwealth University: A compendium of case studies developed through a faculty learning community*. Virginia Commonwealth University. Richmond, VA. http://scholars compass.vcu.edu/cer_resources/5.

Harkavey, I., & Hartley, M. (2012). Integrating a commitment to the public good into the institutional fabric: Further lessons from the field. *Journal of Higher Education Outreach and Engagement*, *16*(4), 17–36.

Hicks, S., Duran, B., Wallerstein, N. et al. (2012). Evaluating community-based participatory research to improve community-partnered science and community health. *Progress in Community Health Partnerships: Research, Education, and Action*, *6*(3), 289–299.

Holland, B. A. (2001). Toward a definition and characterization of the engaged campus: Six cases. *Metropolitan Universities*, *12*(3), 20.

Holton, V., Early, J. L., Resler, M., Trussell, A., & Howard, C. (2016). The university next door: Developing a centralized unit that strategically cultivates community engagement at an urban university. *Metropolitan Universities Journal*, *27*(1), 97–121.

Holton, V., Gogia, L., & McKenzie, T. (2018). Collaborative curiosity: A connected-learning course on community-engaged research. *Public*, *4*(2).

Holton, V., Jettner, J. F., Early, J. L., & Shaw, K. K. (2015). Leveraging existing resources to develop university community engagement data systems. *Metropolitan Universities Journal*, *26*(2), 75–98.

Horowitz, C. R., Robinson, M., & Seifer, S. (2009). Community-based participatory research from the margin to the mainstream: are researchers prepared? *Circulation*, *119*(19), 2633–2642.

Israel, B. A., Schulz, A. J., Parker, E. A., Becker, A. B., Allen, A. J., & Guzman, J. R. (2003). Critical issues in developing and following community-based participatory research principles. In M. Minkler & N. Wallerstein (Eds.), *Community-based participatory research for health* (pp. 56–73). San Francisco, CA: Jossey-Bass.

Jacobson, N., Butterill, D., & Goering, P. (2004). Organizational factors that influence university-based researchers' engagement in knowledge transfer activities. *Science Communication*, *25*(3), 246–259.

James, L. R., & Jones, A. P. (1974). Organizational climate: A review of theory and research. *Psychological Bulletin*, *81*(12), 1096.

Jameson, J. K., Clayton, P. H., Jaeger, A. J., & Bringle, R. G. (2012). Investigating faculty learning in the context of community-engaged scholarship. *Michigan Journal of Community Service Learning*, *18*(2), 40–55.

Jagosh, J., Macaulay, A. C., Pluye, P. et al. (2012). Uncovering the benefits of participatory research: Implications of a realist review for health research and practice. *The Milbank Quarterly*, *90*(2), 311–346.

Klein, K. J., & Sorra, J. S. (1996). The challenge of innovation implementation. *Academy of Management Review*, *21*(4), 1055–1080.

Knowles, M. (1984). *Andragogy in action*. San Francisco, CA: Jossey-Bass.

Kramer, M. (2000). *Make it last forever: The institutionalization of service learning in America*. Washington, DC: Corporation for National Service.

Lazarus, J., Erasmus, M., Hendricks, D., Nduna, J., & Slamat, J. (2008). Embedding community engagement in South African higher education. *Education, Citizenship and Social Justice*, *3*(1), 57–83.

Leisey, M., Holton, V., & Davey, T. (2012). Community engagement grants: Assessing the impact of university funding and engagements. *Journal of Community Engagement and Scholarship*, *5*(2), 41–47.

Lewis, D., Yerby, L., Tucker, M. et al. (2016). Bringing community and academic scholars together to facilitate and conduct authentic community based participatory research: Project UNITED. *International Journal of Environmental Research and Public Health*, *13*(1), 35.

Lindau, S. T., Makelarski, J. A., Chin, M. H. et al. (2011). Building community-engaged health research and discovery infrastructure on the south side of Chicago: Science in service to community priorities. *Preventive Medicine, 52*(3–4), 200–207.

Lynton, E. 1995. Making the case for professional service. Washington, D.C.: American Association for Higher Education.

Lynton, E. A., & Elman, S. E. (1987). *New priorities for the university: Meeting society's needs for applied knowledge and competent individuals. The Jossey-Bass Higher Education Series*. San Francisco, CA: Jossey-Bass.

Marrero, D. G., Hardwick, E. J., Staten, L. K. et al. (2013). Promotion and tenure for community-engaged research: An examination of promotion and tenure support for community-engaged research at three universities collaborating through a clinical and translational science award. *Clinical and Translational Science, 6*(3), 204–208.

Mayan, M. J., & Daum, C. H. (2016). Worth the risk? Muddled relationships in community-based participatory research. *Qualitative Health Research, 26*(1), 69–76.

Merritt, M. W., Labrique, A. B., Katz, J. et al. (2010). A field training guide for human subjects research ethics. *PLoS Medicine, 7*(10), e1000349.

National Institutes of Health (2010). RFA-RM-10-020, Institutional Clinical Translational Science Award. Retrieved from http://grants.nih.gov/grants/guide/rfa-files/RFA-RM-10-020.html.

Nutt, P. C. (1986). Tactics of implementation. *Academy of Management Journal, 29*(2), 230–261.

Nyden, P. (2003). Academic incentives for faculty participation in community-based participatory research. *Journal of General Internal Medicine, 18*, 576–585.

O'Meara, K., Eatman, T., & Petersen, S. (2015). Advancing engaged scholarship in promotion and tenure: A roadmap and call for reform. *Liberal Education, 101*(3), 52–57.

O'Meara, K., Rice, R. E., & Edgerton, R. (2005) *Faculty priorities reconsidered: Rewarding multiple forms of scholarship*. San Francisco, CA: Jossey-Bass.

Orton, J. D., & Weick, D. E. (1990). Loosely coupled systems: A reconceptualization. *The Academy of Management Review, 15*(2), 203–223.

Patient-Centered Outcome Research Institute (2017). What we mean by engagement. Retrieved from www.pcori.org/engagement/what-we-mean-engagement.

Pelco, L. E., & Early, J. (2016). *Professional development for community-engaged research and teaching*. Richmond, VA: Virginia Commonwealth University.

Pelco, L. E., & Howard, C. (2016). Incorporating community engagement language into promotion and tenure policies: One university's journey. *Metropolitan Universities, 27*(2), 87–98.

Ramaley, J. A. (2014). The changing role of higher education: Learning to deal with wicked problems. *Journal of Higher Education Outreach and Engagement, 18*(3), 7–22.

Schneider, B., Bowen, D. E., Ehrhart, M. G., & Holcombe, K. M. (2000). The climate for service: Evolution of a construct. In N. M. Ashkanasy, C. P. M. Wilderom, & M. F. Peterson (Eds.), *Handbook of organizational culture and climate* (pp. 21–36). Thousand Oaks, CA: Sage.

Schneider, B., Ehrhart, M. G., & Macey, W. H. (2013). Organizational climate and culture. *Annual Review of Psychology, 64*, 361–388.

Shore, N., Brazauskas, R., Drew, E. et al. (2011). Understanding community-based processes for research ethics review: A national study. *American Journal of Public Health, 101*(S1), S359–S364.

Sobrero, P., & Jayaratne, K. S. U. (2014). Scholarship perceptions of academic department heads: Implications for promoting faculty community engagement scholarship. *Journal of Higher Education Outreach and Engagement*, *18*(1), 123–153.

Spector, A. (2012). CBPR with service providers: Arguing a case for engaging practitioners in all phases of research. *Health Promotion Practice*, *13*(2), 252–258

Suranyi-Unger, T. (1994). Innovation. In D. Greenwald (Ed.), *Encyclopedia of economics*. New York: McGraw-Hill.

Saltmarsh, J., Giles Jr., D. E., O'Meara, K. et al. (2009). Community engagement and institutional culture in higher education: An investigation of faculty reward policies at engaged campuses. In B. E. Moely, S. H. Billig, & B. A. Holland (Eds.), *Advances in service-learning research. Creating our identities in service-learning and community engagement* (pp. 3–29). Charlotte, NC: IAP Information Age Publishing.

Welch, M., & Saltmarsh, J. (2013). Current practice and infrastructures for campus centers of community engagement. *Journal of Higher Education Outreach and Engagement*, *17*(4), 25–56.

Weerts, D. J., & Sandmann, L. R. (2008). Building a two-way street: Challenges and opportunities for community engagement at research universities. *The Review of Higher Education*, *32*(1), 73–106.

Zohar, D., & Luria, G. (2005). A multilevel model of safety climate: Cross-level relationships between organization and group-level climates. *Journal of Applied Psychology, 90* (4), 616.

Zuiches, J. J. (2008). Attaining Carnegie's: Community-engagement classification. *Change: The Magazine of Higher Learning*, *40*(1), 42–45.

Zuiches, J. J. (2013). The impacts of seed grants as incentives for engagement. *Journal of Higher Education Outreach and Engagement*, *17*(4), 57–73.

22 Putting It All Together

An Interview with Barbara Holland and Final Thoughts

Joseph A. Allen, Roni Reiter-Palmon, Kelly A. Prange, & Barbara A. Holland

As the idea of this handbook emerged, we contemplated how best to bring the many ideas that are contained herein together. Ultimately, we decided to contact a seasoned scholar and advisor to universities concerning community engagement, Barbara A. Holland, PhD, and ask her to participate in a structured interview concerning organizational community engagement and outreach. Before jumping into the interview, where remarkable insights and thoughts concerning community engagement reside, allow us to introduce Dr. Holland.

Across her career, Dr. Holland has not only succeeded in campus administrative and academic roles, but has also had the opportunity to promote a nation of engagement through her leadership of the US Department of Housing and Urban Development Office of University Partnerships and the Learn and Serve America National Service-Learning Clearinghouse. She was at the table for the launch and success of many associations and journals associated with the community engagement field. Her current research and practice interests include the impact of a new generation of faculty on academic culture, leadership of change, and the development of comprehensive data systems for monitoring and measuring engagement's impacts and outcomes. Dr. Holland's bachelor and master's degrees are in Journalism from the University of Missouri and her PhD is in higher education policy from the University of Maryland. She resides in Portland, Oregon. As a complement to the following interview, Dr. Holland prepared a specialized set of readings that may be of interest to readers. This list may be found in Appendix 22.1.

The Interview

INTERVIEWER: Thank you so much for the opportunity to visit with you about organizational community engagement and outreach. What organizational concepts are most needed or underutilized in community engagement efforts? Some of the examples could be: leadership, facilitation, communication, training, selection – organizational concepts that are needed for effective community engagement efforts.

DR. HOLLAND: The primary missing factor in creating successful community engagement initiatives in college universities is the absence of intentionality, goal setting, and strategic planning. This work needs to be integral to every institution's mission and strategy, but "to what end?"

Too often, the work is viewed as a separate stream of activity and is not well integrated into other relevant, corollary, and complimentary objectives of the institution and/or the community. In the few places where it has been more strategically considered, community engagement is integrated and connected to institutional goals regarding progress in teaching, learning, the student experience, and research work.

Where that happens, in whole or in part, we see much more effect in terms of achievement of what we seek, which is, mutually beneficial exchange of knowledge between campus and communities. As long as community engagement is a distinct and separate task, it is held in isolation and, at best, there are coincidental encounters with the core work of the institution: teaching, learning, and research. Across higher education, we need to complete the shift. It's certainly underway. Where it is more integrated, it is more widely appreciated, more effective, and is dramatically improving and contributing to other institutional goals, such as student success, student progress, and student completion, the attraction and retention of faculty, improvements in research productivity, and improvements in philanthropic success and alumni involvement. There's a longer, more detailed list, but this list is pertinent to my contemporary view of the state of engagement. The strength and success of engagement across institutions is very much shaped by the diversity of institutional ability to recognize the power of integrating community engagement into other goals and purposes. An integrated strategy creates the goal that I think everyone wants – improvement in community well-being and improvement in institutional performance. Perhaps, ironically, when advocates pushing so hard for engagement say, "We must be community engaged," they may have unintentionally created an institutional view that engagement is a discrete activity. Thus, it may end up largely sequestered in a single office or center, rather than integrating it into teaching, research, and learning initiatives. The latter approach is proving to be far more successful in terms of beneficial impacts on campus and community.

INTERVIEWER: As a follow-up, what does strategic planning look like in an institution, from an organizational perspective?

DR. HOLLAND: Well, different universities take different approaches to strategic planning, but in general they tend to identify a small set of three to five large, broad goals – growing research, improving the student experience, and so on – and they tend to organize around the same ones and then start breaking them down into more detailed issues. If they mention community engagement, it is too often a separate goal from all the others and it's usually the last. I have seen many campus strategic plans where pillar 5 or goal 5 is community engagement.

The problem is, community engagement doesn't travel well alone because the whole point of engagement involves partnerships, it involves negotiation of approaches and methods and aims, and it produces different potential outcomes and calls on different areas of expertise, or different levels of participation from all the partners that should be at the table. Community engagement strategies are not merely relevant to these other broad strategic goals, but are potentially powerful methods for succeeding on those goals when integrated.

In the USA, we have had – certainly since the 1940s – a stable and common view that we hire faculty to focus on teaching, research, and service. The long commitment to the three bucket model has made the appearance and evolution of community engagement be seen through an overly simplistic lens. For many institutions and academics, community engagement is either a new and additional task or it is seen "just" as a new way to express the service bucket. Each institution, in the context of its mission, has had to negotiate how community engagement fits in the three-bucket framework, but in truth it is an integrating strategy. In many ways, including but not limited to attention to engagement, the three-bucket model is coming to an end as academia recognizes the value of a more integrated approach to scholarly work. This is why I have often said community engagement is a method of teaching, learning, research, and service. It is a way of pursuing those forms of scholarly work in partnership with others through an exchange of knowledge and with the intention of mutually beneficial outcomes.

Please know that this is obviously a lot of generalization – there are certainly exceptional institutions with strong strategies for their engagement agenda – but I'll return to where I began. I am actually very excited about the diversity of views of engagement across institutions and how those that are embracing engagement as an integral strategy are effectively responding to the current public critique of the efficiency and effectiveness of higher education. I think that diversity, as diversity always does, generates new and innovative views. The example of leader institutions will ultimately reach others as their success becomes known more widely.

INTERVIEWER: What research needs to be done to improve the effectiveness and efficiency of community engagement efforts?

DR. HOLLAND: There are at least two broad areas where research on community engagement is really needed: studies of our methods and approaches to engaging in partnerships on specific issues or topics; and studies that measure impacts and outcomes of engagement efforts. Are we contributing productively to improvement and desirable changes or are we just observing and pushing around the edges of community issues? Again, because engagement is treated as an optional activity at most institutions, the lack of a focused agenda within an institution leads to random work that is difficult to measure on both methods and outcomes. So we are back to the problem of: "Is engagement scholarly work?" Or is it a way to shape our image in the public eye?

One of the challenges of introducing community engagement into the mix in higher education going back to the 1970s and 1980s is that it began in a policy and cultural context where higher education was still appreciated and admired, pretty universally, across the United States. As the Cold War ended, there began to be more of a sense of skepticism about higher education's role and benefits. This skepticism emerged in part because national policy shifted federal financial aid from an emphasis on grants to an emphasis on loans. That shifted the cultural, national view of higher education away from being a national benefit to a view that it benefits the individual. In the Jeffersonian model, democracy relies on an educated population. Others have come to the idea that education creates individual opportunity so more of the cost should be covered by the student. In this environment, the political scene, and then therefore ultimately the public scene, shifted to "it's a personal benefit and not a benefit for the rest of us." If you go to college, it's going to help you get a better job, make more money – those are seen as individual benefits. Research continues to show all the other corollary benefits to society and culture and the economy are still present, but they are now no longer regarded that way by the public.

Research efforts in community engagement up until recently have been deeply focused on the design of engagement activities and on the impact on those who are participating. That's been useful because that research informs quality practice and is part of what has especially demonstrated the impact and benefit of effective engagement practices to student success and progress and to faculty performance, including increases in research. The research has largely focused on establishing the benefits of engagement because those who wanted to study it thought it would be helpful in making the case for increasing the relevance of higher education to public concerns and issues, and they may also think the research may help increase internal campus support, involvement, and funding. It's hard to tell if either of those outcomes has been widely achieved, but the weakness in much of the research to date has been the inability to have the resources or the organizational infrastructure across institutions to do large-scale comparative studies that will give us more accurate and detailed information regarding what about community engagement methods creates which outcomes, or not.

There have been some efforts to summarize research around particular themes. For example, Campus Compact created an annotated bibliography of the research that explores the relationship between service learning and student retention. It's been fantastic that there has been so much research establishing that connection. What we have not been able to do is large-scale and more methodical research to discern: Why does service learning improve retention? What about it creates the effect and how is that effect and the method perhaps necessarily different for different types of students for different characteristics, or in different settings? How much is enough? We have research that establishes a connection and an effect, in general, but we know little about what is the actual aspect that makes a difference for which outcomes. Without that detail, we have no way to create new and more intentional designs of service learning, of community partnerships. We don't have any large-scale, cross-cutting research that gives us guidance on – for a partnership on this kind of community topic with these goals for students – what the best methods are. Mostly, we have individual case studies of specific partnerships or specific programs that students participate in or specific things faculty do regarding engagement.

We have, mostly, small or singular samples, and we desperately need larger-scale research. This is why I'm excited by the emergence of a number of attempts to gather data consistently and in similar ways across institutions because that will be, ultimately, like the Carnegie classification. It's a beginning of getting similar data from many institutions, and you can already see some early tapping into that data that is showing us the most significant work. For the most part, this is only been done by Saltmarsh and Welsh (2013) looking at all of the data and developing a comparative portrait of the different forms of infrastructure for community engagement. That is just a hint of what I'm talking about. We need to look at large-scale research that is rigorous and has some controls in it that allows us to start to see patterns and to be more intentional in the design of our work going forward so that the design is more likely to produce the desired effect.

INTERVIEWER: In your opinion, how often and how well is evaluation and assessment used in community engagement efforts?

DR. HOLLAND: Well, it's still wildly uneven. It's just incredibly uneven across the country, and frankly around the world. It covers the whole range. There are institutions that are doing very little except keeping track of how much engagement activity is going on and maybe in what geographic areas and how often. When we position engagement as a separate or discrete activity, it's not strategically integrated into the core business of the institution and seen as a method that contributes to teaching, learning, and research productivity, progress, and success. Then it's traveling in its own path and is not connected to where the core institutional oversight is focused – namely, teaching, research, learning outcomes, and funding. If community engagement is sitting on the side away from those core issues and is not seen as deeply related and integrated with the delivery and the progress of those other core functions, then it's going to be under-resourced, and if it's under-resourced, it's going to be almost impossible to do much in the way of assessment and research.

That's really the dynamic. If we pull back all the way to the moon and look back at the earth and say, "What's the portrait of engagement?" it's still pretty much on the margins in many institutions in terms of integrated attention to it as a core strategy. Every year, more institutions are moving to an intentional strategy and agenda for engaged teaching, learning, and research outcomes and goals regarding the intended effects for the institution and for the communities (as defined by the communities). Then, it all ties together. The Carnegie Classification for Engagement started in 2006, and with each cycle since, it has created greater institutional appreciation for the need for an intentional agenda. Doing so creates a basis for research on what works and why. Eventually, research on engagement can lead to regional and national initiatives around the persistent issues challenging communities. We must study in detail to know what interventions and strategies on common issues leads to positive change and in what contexts. This will help renew public regard and appreciation for higher education's contributions to societal progress and well-being.

I am incredibly optimistic about higher education in general, and about this field. I think, in the end, this field will be seen as part of the transformation and renewal of the public regard of higher education, and I think it's going to happen in the next ten years.

It's clear that institutions are searching for a way to be publicly relevant. In the mid-twentieth century, higher education was a major contributor to national goals and directions – the race to space, the Cold War, civil rights, health, etc. Now we're going to do it again. I see promise in the academic associations that exist around engagement and the ways those are starting to collaborate and connect to the other higher education associations and other networks interested in economic and community development.

Collaboration offers the promise of seeing engagement as one of the tools in our tool kit to restore and renew the contract between higher education and community and public progress, and to be able to do so in a systematic way. For example, the Coalition of Urban and Metropolitan Universities is looking to create a network approach to specific public issues and at how institutional initiatives and engaging with communities and cities on issues of local importance can be compared, contrasted, and connected across many cities that have similar challenges. Everybody is facing similar challenges, and I think the desire to reconnect higher education to public discourse and public progress is probably what's going to refresh higher education's sense of position in society.

Large-scale research is what we've been waiting for, and I think the broad and diverse attention that's being given now to different schemes for collecting and aggregating engagement data will eventually evolve into something that will allow and support that large-scale research, much as general research on higher education did in the 1970s and 1980s.

INTERVIEWER: Yeah. Well, that's a definite hope because it would involve a collaboration across institutions and things of that nature, which can happen, but has not consistently happened in many years.

DR. HOLLAND: Yeah, that's right, because in the 1970s, 1980s, and 1990s, when funding for higher education declined and costs to students grew, the public confidence in higher education waned. Then it was interesting that while "regaining the public confidence" was a frequent conference topic, the institutional responses and strategies were mostly solo efforts. The impact of public criticism seemed to cause each institution to focus on its own response: "We have to get our house in order and think how we're going to respond to this." The immediate response for whatever reason was to atomize, not to collaborate and coalesce with other colleges and universities as a group.

I think now we're entering a period where there is a lot of talk about collaboration across institutions and, certainly, within cities, where there are multiple institutions working together in communities. I'm not saying community engagement is going to be the salvation of higher education, but it will be part of how we restore public interest and appreciation.

Some colleagues are skeptical of my view because they believe the passionate attention to rankings will snuff out any motivation to collaborate. Here are signs I look to as indicators of a more cooperative future in the education industry. We are learning from each other how to improve the teaching and learning environment for all students and how to enhance student success. The emergence of high-impact practices for teaching and learning has been an extensively collaborative process. At the same time, research is becoming more collaborative, internally between disciplines, and externally between institutions with both common and complementary interests and skills. Much of the world's research funding is now going to collaborative, multidimensional research projects. This is the heart of academic culture and will inevitably lead to more shared discussions about academic culture, funding, technology, and engagement!

We've had an individual college reputation focus since the mid-twentieth century, and I think it has run its course. It's time for institutions to collaborate for their own success and improvement and to increase impact on the public good. I'm not saying they're all going to merge, but I think they will learn to work together in their regions, which will make them successful global universities because global cities are globally connected. This growth of collaboration may also increase our attention to engagement in issues beyond our country more than ever. Many of our local public challenges have global dimensions and implications.

INTERVIEWER: What would you say are the top three best practices in community engagement?

DR. HOLLAND: Goal setting, strategic planning, and integrated data collection. I know some people, if they were on this call, they'd say, "Well, that's all just about strategy." Well, we have spent 25 years looking at practice and technique and definitions. It's time to be strategic and outcome oriented. We need to explore community engagement "to what end." "Intentionality" is my new favorite word for engagement. Everywhere I go, we've got to move from a focus on building internal support to being engaged by doing random things to help people see and understand what it is about. It is time to be intentional – build a plan, set goals, and develop a way of measuring our results and assessing them objectively.

That's where we need to go now, and it's time because there's so much good engagement going on that could be more effective and there's so much movement regarding institutional leadership and their understanding of engagement. One thing that hasn't come up yet in this conversation is the emergence of leadership of engagement as a career path. Campus Compact, for example, has recently taken rigorous action toward understanding the professional development needs for people in jobs relating to engagement. That is not unimportant in this dialogue because there are now job opportunities in engagement management and leadership ranging from the entry level to vice presidents for community engagement. The growing professionalization of engagement leadership is part of what makes me optimistic that we are actively moving toward seeing engagement as a normal and necessary institutional function.

INTERVIEWER: What types of organizations should leaders of institutions be trying to engage with?

DR. HOLLAND: Well, if, as an institution, you're developing a more intentional and integrated approach based on the relevance of community engagement to your institutional mission culture and strategic objectives, then it becomes more clear, hopefully, about not just who you partner with, but what types of partners you work with and the specific areas of focus where your institution can make a strong contribution to collaborative partnerships with other sectors.

If we're looking for mutually beneficial outcomes in a context of partnership and reciprocity, then our first responsibility as an entity – a college or university – is we have to be able to express and articulate our goals and objectives to others so that we can inform the public and external entities about our goals so that we can seek partnerships that are going to be contributing to those goals. There has to be a logical fit between the campus and community, as opposed to random self-directed projects.

That's what partnerships and reciprocity is about. We're exchanging knowledge. If we have a clear sense of ourselves as scholars and learners and what we're looking for, then that's going to make it more feasible for those outside higher education to be able to identify and express their goals, interests, and expectations. We are looking for a productive alignment that leads to mutual benefits. That doesn't mean we're in charge; that means we have to be clear about what we're looking for in a partnership, and we have to give our partners enough information so that they can be clear as well about their expectations.

Up to now, engagement has often been dependent on a few interested faculty or staff members, and some institutions have tended to go with community entities that were already familiar to the institution or that were large, highly organized entities that had reach into the community and so were somewhat of a connection that would be a gateway to get to others. There's nothing wrong with that, but it is insufficient in and of itself because without the deeper intentionality of what our goals and intents are for being engaged with community entities, it's difficult for the community to know how to connect to us or how to respond when we approach them.

We need to be able to have a clear story. Mutually beneficial means that each side of the table – campus and community – has to articulate, "The clear goals and objectives for this partnership are X, Y, Z." Too often we connect to community entities with very open-ended ideas. We are hesitant to say, "We also have goals. We have expectations," because there has been such an intense pressure that we should be humble. I think that's not correct. We should be friendly and open to negotiation, but we are looking for a mutually beneficial partnership that involves reciprocity and an exchange of knowledge, and everybody at the table has expertise. To be equal, we have to disclose our goals and our wants, our desires, and our intent, and listen to our partners as they do the same.

We should not pander to communities – they have their own ideas and expectations, and we need to hear them. Dialogue, exchange, and understanding are requirements of collaboration and cooperation. Everybody has to come to the table and speak the plain truth. Sometimes advocates for community engagement go out to communities and appear so incredibly worried about not wanting to overburden the community that they almost don't ask about or observe that the community has its own expertise and ideas, and they can assert these views if we allow them to do so. Listening and reflecting are important skills in engagement.

INTERVIEWER: What other things should community-engaged scholars and administrators keep in mind as they seek to expand their community engagement footprint?

DR. HOLLAND: Well, you expand "to what end?" Again, I have observed and have been troubled by so many people saying to me, "We have to grow service learning." Well, what's the goal or the aims of growth? Service learning's great, and we see that it has good effects on students if it's well designed and well implemented. Then, we want to grow it, and that's great, but you grow things in an organization to an end. It's back to intentionality.

If we see service learning having an effect that is beneficial to students that we can measure in terms of retention progress or other benefits, then we should grow it so that more students get that benefit. If we don't grow, we create inequities by restricting student access to important learning experiences. Perhaps based on misguided belief that bigger student participation will lead to more resources, too many institutions have pursued growth for the sake of growth. The best approach is to be intentional in your design of engagement and rigorous in your examination of the intended impacts on the expected participants, including faculty and partners as well as the student. Then you can grow based on the institution's strategic need to have more students and faculty have those experiences and in the context of the capacity of the community to have larger interaction with the institution.

Growth is conditional based on the identification of mutually beneficial goals between the campus and the community, and the growth is designed and should be assessed by its contribution to the achievement or not of those goals. I would say there are probably a few examples of institutions that have been that intentional. The purpose of research is to show us where and how to get to rigorous and reliable outcomes and impacts through greater intentionality and greater input and specificity regarding community voice and expected outcomes. That's very much the next phase of the work, and for many institutions, I think the Carnegie classification has been very helpful in opening up the conversation.

Going forward, each institution and its communities need to *plan* for engagement – not just what will we do now, but what is the way forward? What are the intended outcomes? What indicates success? How much is enough? How much does it change over time? Is there an end? If we have a partnership, then does it go on forever? Programs and partnerships should change over time. We set clear goals and use integrated assessment to track those goals so that we know if and/or how much progress is being made toward the goals. Goals can be at many levels – institutional, disciplinary, a defined student population, a defined learning experience for all students. At the same time, campus and community benefit when they agree on a few focused topics or issues so that goals can lead to desired changes, and thus can be tracked. Success will inform replication and dissemination.

Again, this is all about getting away from random, self-selected engagement between campus and community, because random is almost impossible to measure or replicate.

INTERVIEWER: I would like to hear your general perspective on community-engaged leadership. What does an administrator or a university need in terms of leadership to be able to do community engagement in the way that you've already talked about so far?

DR. HOLLAND: Well, I think there are some emerging trends that are lighting the way forward. I think it is essential to have at least some administrative infrastructure for engagement. In general, I don't think it should be separate from existing administrative structures. Recently, the leadership of engagement is becoming more frequently knitted into the fabric of academic affairs and/or research support or curricular/experiential learning support units. A few places have created a vice president, vice provost, or vice chancellor for engagement. To put it at that top level and therefore in the president's or provost's cabinet is important at some institutions, but not so important at others. The size and complexity of the campus and the level of ambition regarding the institution's community engagement agenda make a difference to both the size and scale of infrastructure and where it sits in the organizational chart. Again, it helps to have clear goals and an issue-based agenda of engagement areas.

What are the institution's strategic goals and objectives for engagement? What are the outcomes we seek? What are our expected benefits from engagement? What are our goals for involving students or for expanding research? What is the alignment of our disciplinary strengths and the interests, goals, and challenges articulated by communities? There is a lot of internal campus dialogue that is essential to creating a basis for true partnerships with external entities. We have to know and be able to describe our own intentions so communities can understand and share their own perspectives and objectives. Such an exchange of expectations and goals is the basis for developing mutually beneficial partnerships and interactions that lead to desired outcomes and new discoveries. The level of leadership must align with and reflect both campus and community values, culture, and goals. Consistency is a valuable skill as well.

INTERVIEWER: Thank you so much for your time today. Do you have any other thoughts on community engagement you would like to share with us?

DR. HOLLAND: As I reflect on community engagement through the years, I think about the emergence of leadership for engagement. I was around in the 1960s and 1970s when student affairs and fundraising emerged as professional careers with layers from entry level to executive roles. It's pretty clear engagement is going down the same path. Time will tell what that will look like in reality. It's also possible that engagement will become so integrated in some institutions' cultures and strategies that leadership will also be integrated into existing academic structures. I suspect that for some institutions that are deeply identified with their communities, a distinctive and high-profile engagement infrastructure may be a valuable investment toward achieving substantial impacts through complex partnerships.

I think, for many institutions for which engagement is an aspect of what they do and it is largely associated with teaching and learning outcomes for students, that it will probably be managed ultimately by the infrastructure that exists for teaching and learning and will be integrated into that line.

For institutions for whom engagement is largely an activity of service, volunteering, and outreach, it will probably remain governed much as it is today.

Truthfully, community engagement's got enough of a buzz that no institution can afford to ignore it. The growing anecdotal evidence of positive impact from quality engagement is hard to ignore, and it aligns well with the desire for each institution, according to its mission, to improve teaching, learning, and research outcomes and to be a good citizen institution in their local area.

In this context, it seems a good time to press institutions to do more serious research about their engagement. The reality is, some of the colleges and universities that are doing large-scale engagement don't always have access to internal research capacity. If you are leading engagement in a teaching-focused institution, it may be important to develop connections with research-focused universities so as to have access to skilled researchers and evaluators. The continued growth of the database generated from Carnegie Classification applications will also support and inform the growing interest in multi-institutional studies as well. I dream a lot about how we could conduct nationwide research that will, for example, analyze the massive work that colleges and universities across the country are doing by engaging their college students in schools as tutors and mentors. Such a study could reveal what works and what doesn't work well for which children to improve their learning and their progress in school. We need to synthesize large-scale data on other persistent and all-too-common community challenges such as homelessness, drug addiction, hunger, domestic abuse, and so on. Discovery is the heart of academia. Engagement is opening a new way for higher education to use its heart and its skills to identify strategies that work and in what conditions. This vision aligns well with the current growth in attention and support for interdisciplinary and cross-university research.

Conclusion

The chapters in this book provide an overview of significant progress that has occurred in the field of community engagement. These chapters provide us with case studies and reviews, and with work that integrates disciplines, as well as the work of for-profit and nonprofit institutions. Many of these chapters provide work that is anchored in theory – both theory of community engagement and discipline-specific theory such as leadership, management, or industrial/organizational psychology. The interview with Dr. Holland provides us with both a look back and to the road ahead.

An important point made by Dr. Holland is that our efforts at community engagement need to be integrated on a number of fronts. Dr. Holland calls for community engagement to be integrated into the main pillars of academia – teaching, research, and service – as opposed to being stand-alone or limited to service. At that point, community engagement truly becomes part of the strategies of academic institutions. In addition, integration is needed across institutions. Collaboration across academic institutions as well as networks that are interested in economic and community development will allow for further understanding, development of best practices, and more effective community engagement. Finally, integration is needed in data collection – large-scale studies that would provide meaningful information will require collaboration and integration of practices across institutions.

Another important issue raised by Dr. Holland is that of intentionality. She suggests that our approach to community engagement should be intentional and strategic. We need to identify goals, partners in the community, research, and collaboration, all in a strategic manner. In too many cases, the growth and development of community engagement happens without integration with the rest of the institution, and therefore is not strategic. The need for strategy and the need for integration are interrelated. Finally, Dr. Holland raises the need for leadership. She specifically notes the need for engaged leadership to facilitate intentionality and integration. The need to understand community-engaged leadership is also mirrored in our book, with chapters focusing specifically on leadership.

Moving forward, our hope is that Dr. Holland's interview, coupled with the foregoing chapters, will serve as a springboard for action in the domain of organizational community engagement. Specifically, many of the chapters demonstrate successful community engaged efforts that illustrate both intentionality and leadership. Perhaps the patterns set herein, along with deliberate strategies by institutional leadership, will result in the eventual collaboration and goal accomplishment that Dr. Holland and others hope for. In sum, the opportunities for organizational community engagement exist and may serve as the next step in the development of higher education if the strategies, intentionality, and collaboration stated here and shown in this book are carried forward.

Appendix 22.1

Further Readings by Dr. Holland

Furco, A., & Holland, B. A. (2013). Improving research on service learning institutionalization through attention to theories of organizational change. In P. Clayton, R. Bringle,

& J. Hatcher (Eds.), *Research on service learning: Conceptual frameworks and assessment* (pp. 441–470). Herndon, VA: Stylus.

Gelmon, S. B., Holland, B. A., Driscoll, A., Kerrigan, S., & Spring, A. (2001). *Assessing service-learning and civic engagement.* Providence, RI: Campus Compact.

Holland, B. A. (1997). Analyzing institutional commitment to service. *Michigan Journal of Community Service Learning, 4,* 30–41.

Holland, B. A. (1999). Factors and strategies that influence faculty involvement in public service. *Journal of Public Service and Outreach, 4,* 37–43.

Holland, B. A. (2009). Will it last? Evidence of institutionalization at Carnegie classified community engagement institutions. *New Directions for Higher Education, 2009* (147), 85–98.

Holland, B. A. (2016). Factors influencing faculty engagement – Then, now and future. *Journal of Higher Education Outreach and Engagement, 20,* 73.

Holland, B. A. (1999). From murky to meaningful: The role of mission in institutional change. In R. Bringle, R. Games, & E. Malloy (Eds.), *Colleges and universities as citizens* (pp. 48–73). Needham Heights, MA: Allyn and Bacon.

Holland, B. (2005). Real change in higher education: Understanding differences in institutional commitment to engagement. In A. Kezar, T. Chambers, & J. Burkhardt (Eds.), *Higher education for the public good: Emerging voices from a national movement* (pp. 235–259). San Francisco, CA: Jossey-Bass.

Sandy, M., & Holland, B. A. (2006). Different worlds and common ground: Community partner perspectives on campus–community partnerships. *Michigan Journal of Community Service Learning, 13*(1), 30–43.

Ramaley, J. A., & Holland, B. A. (2005). Modeling learning: The role of leaders. *New Directions in Higher Education, 131,* 75–86.

Reference

Welch, M., & Saltmarsh, J. (2013). Current practice and infrastructures for campus centers of community engagement. *Journal of Higher Education Outreach and Engagement, 17*(4), 25–37.

Appendix A: Contributor Biographies

Editors

Joseph A. Allen, PhD, is an associate professor of Industrial and Organizational (I/O) Psychology at the University of Nebraska Omaha. Before he completed his doctorate (PhD) in Organizational Science at the University of North Carolina at Charlotte (UNCC) in 2010, he received his Master of Arts degree in I/O Psychology at UNCC in 2008 and his Bachelor of Science degree in Psychology from the Brigham Young University in 2005. His research focuses on three major areas of inquiry, including the study of workplace meetings, organizational community engagement, and emotional labor in various service-related contexts. He has more than 100 publications in academic outlets, another 20 under review, and many works in progress for a number of journals. He has presented over 150 papers/posters at regional and national conferences and given more than 50 invited presentations on his research. His previous academic outlets include *Human Relations, Human Performance, Journal of Applied Psychology, Journal of Occupational and Organizational Psychology, Journal of Organizational Behavior, Journal of Business Psychology, American Psychologist, Accident Analysis and Prevention*, and *Group and Organization Management*, among others. He serves as a reviewer for various journals including *Journal of Organizational Behavior, Organizational Behavior and Human Decision Processes, Journal of Creative Behavior*, and *Academy of Management Journal*. He is an editorial board member for *Journal of Business and Psychology, Group and Organization Management*, and *European Journal of Work and Organizational Psychology*. He directs the Center for Applied Psychological Services as well as the Volunteer Program Assessment at UNO (VPA-UNO). These activities have led him to consult for more than 350 nonprofit and for-profit organizations. These include animal welfare organizations, human services organizations, large corporations, and government entities, as well as retail conglomerates and external talent management firms. His research has attracted internal and external grant funding of more than $3 million since 2010. Dr. Allen can be reached at josephallen@unomaha.edu.

    Roni Reiter-Palmon is the Varner Professor of Industrial/Organizational (I/O) Psychology and the Director of the I/O Psychology Graduate Program at the University of Nebraska Omaha (UNO). She is also serves as the director for the Center for Collaboration Science. Her research focuses on creativity and innovation in the workplace at the individual and team level, leading creative individuals, and the development and assessment of creativity, teamwork, and leadership skills. She has obtained grants and contracts totaling over $7.5 million from various funding agencies, Fortune 500 companies, the government, and the military. She has over 100 publications in leading journals. She is the editor of *The Psychology of Creativity* and *Aesthetics and the Arts* and an associate editor for *European Journal of Work and Organizational Psychology*. She serves on the editorial boards of a number of top-tier journals in the area of creativity, leadership, and management. She has received the George Mason I/O Psychology distinguished alumni award, UNO's graduate mentor award, and the designation of fellow from the American Psychological Association based on her research. She has received the UNO's College of Arts and Science excellence in research award and the UNO Award for Distinguished Research and Creative Activity. Dr. Reiter-Palmon can be reached at rreiter-palmon@unomaha.edu.

Editorial Board Members and Authors

Alexander Alonso, PhD, SHRM-SCP, is the Society for Human Resource Management's (SHRM) Chief Knowledge Officer leading operations for SHRM's Certified Professional and Senior Certified Professional certifications. During his career, he has worked with numerous subject matter experts worldwide to identify organizational trends, strategies, and performance standards. Alonso has published provocative works in peer-reviewed journals and the popular press, as well as served on the boards of several professional societies.

Thomas Arcaro, PhD, is a professor of sociology at Elon University and founder of Elon's Periclean Scholars program. He has been researching and studying aid and development issues for nearly two decades and most recently published *Aid Worker Voices* (2016) and is now working on a second book, tentatively titled *Local Aid Worker Voices* based on interview and survey data from local aid workers in Zambia, the Philippines, and Jordan. Currently, he is working on implementing a vetting system for community-based learning (both domestic and international) that will ensure the highest ethical pedagogical practices.

Rachael A. Arens is an innovative and energetic Nebraska Teacher of Excellence secondary science teacher and curriculum writer for Omaha Northwest High Magnet School who possesses the ability to bring lessons to life and cultivates hands-on learning experiences for her Advanced Placement Environmental Science, Plants/Propagation, Advanced Horticulture, and Honors Anatomy/Physiology courses. She has a talent for engaging students in service-learning projects that allow them to learn state standards and develop twenty-first century skills while also making a scientific and social difference within their community. She holds a Master of Science degree from the University of Nebraska Omaha (UNO) in Biology, completing her own thesis on the "Morphological and Histological Analyses of the Chronic Effects of Chlorpyrifos on the Development of *Lithobates pipiens*." She also completed the UNO Teacher Academy Project graduate program and received an endorsement in biology. She develops the Anatomy curriculum for the state of Nebraska and serves on the Nebraska Green Ribbons Schools Advisory Board, as well as the Nebraska Association of Teachers of Science Board.

Julie Dierberger is the Paul Sather Distinguished Director of the Service Learning Academy at the University of Nebraska Omaha. She has been developing service-learning experiences in various professional capacities at the University of Nebraska – Lincoln, Midland Lutheran College, and in her current and previous position as the P–16 Coordinator in the Service Learning Academy at the University of Nebraska Omaha. Her research and scholarship focuses around professional development, student learning, and partnership development in experiential contexts. Julie received her MA in Educational Administration and her BA in English from the University of Nebraska – Lincoln and is currently pursuing her PhD in Educational Leadership.

Keristiena S. Dodge is a project specialist at the University of Nebraska Omaha (UNO) Office of Academic Affairs. She leads the community engagement measurement and assessment committee. In addition, Ms. Dodge is responsible for community engagement reporting, data collection and analysis, and award applications. Ms. Dodge is also a member of the UNO Community Engagement Transcript Designation Committee.

Prior to working at UNO, Ms. Dodge worked as a journalist and a community organizer. She has led numerous community projects, including literacy projects for asylum seekers and projects aimed at providing resources to underprivileged communities. As a researcher and a former journalist, Ms. Dodge is particularly interested in how to tell the most powerful data-driven story and how to measure community engagement impacts on students and community partners. She holds a master's degree from the University of London in the United Kingdom and a bachelor's degree from the University College Roosevelt – Utrecht University in the Netherlands.

Alexandra M. Dunn, PhD, is an assistant professor of management at the University of Mary Washington. After receiving her undergraduate degree in psychology and graduating from Elon University as a Periclean Scholar, Alexandra received her PhD from the inter-disciplinary Organizational Science program at the University of North Carolina at Charlotte. Alexandra values service learning, student engagement, and helping her community. Her research interests include employee socialization, the dyadic relationships between newcomers and current employees at work, perceived organizational support, understanding high-reliability organizations (e.g., firefighters and police officers), and insufficient effort responding and its implications for survey research. She has published work in *Journal of Business and Psychology, Human Relations*, and *Journal of Occupational and Organizational Psychology*.

Jennifer Early works in Virginia Commonwealth University's (VCU) Division of Community Engagement as the director of community-engaged research (CEnR) to support and advance CEnR as part of the university's strategic effort to align university-wide community engagement and impact. She oversees the identification, development, and dissemination of CEnR resources for faculty, staff, students, and community partners. She holds a Bachelor of Science in Nursing and a Master of Science in Health Administration. She is a doctoral candidate in VCU's Health Services and Organization Research program. She integrates her community health and organizational development background to support and lead VCU's coordinated efforts to enhance the health and well-being of its community.

Samantha Elliott is a doctoral student in the University of Oklahoma's doctoral program in Industrial and Organizational Psychology. She graduated with her Associate of Arts degree from Dodge City Community College, Dodge City, Kansas. She went on to receive her Bachelor of Science degree in Psychology from Fort Hays State University, Hays, Kansas. While at Fort Hays State University, she received the Outstanding Junior and Senior Student Award for the Department of Psychology as well as the Outstanding Undergraduate Award for the College of Health and Behavioral Sciences. Her current thesis research is investigating how several types and levels of knowledge structures impact leaders' solutions on a creative problem-solving task. She plans to defend her thesis in the fall of 2018. Moreover, Samantha serves as a research assistant on a contract through the US Army Research Institute. The main goal of this project is to develop tools and assessment methods for Army squad leaders to manage negative soldier behavior.

Annie Epperson is Professor of University Libraries liaising with natural sciences disciplines and is tasked with coordinating engagement and academic programming. Holding degrees from Colorado State University in Natural Resource Management (BS) and Environmental Sociology (MA) in addition to her master's in Library and Information Science (University of North Texas), her work spans the natural and social sciences as well as librarianship. She has nearly 15 years of academic library experience. In the Libraries, she facilitates multicultural programming, including hosting traveling exhibits that focus on underrepresented populations. In this work, she also collaborates with public libraries and community colleges in the area to facilitate programming appealing to a diversity of populations. When the University of Northern Colorado launched the strategic plan to institutionalize engagement, she was eager to serve on the planning group. She also serves as Associate Director of Engagement.

Orentheian Everett is a recreation supervisor for the City of Omaha Parks and Recreation, where he has served for 12 years. He is responsible for the administration and management of staff, facilities, and innovative community programming. In this position, he has established numerous partnerships, built community relations, and created awareness about the various programs and activities offered by the City of Omaha Parks and Recreation department. He is a leader and mentor and is well respected in the community. He is an instructor at the University of Nebraska Omaha in the Gerontology Department. He is involved with various local youth associations coaching wrestling, boxing, and football while encouraging youth to explore avenues that lead to success. A native of Miami, FL, he grew up in Dade County. He earned his Bachelor of Science degree in Exercise Physiology and Wellness and his master's degree in Sport Administration and Management from Wayne State College.

Scott T. Fitzgerald is an associate professor, associate chair, and director of graduate studies in the Department of Sociology at the University of North Carolina at Charlotte. He earned a PhD (2003) in Sociology from the University of Iowa, an MA (1997) in Political Science from Iowa State University where he studied homelessness and public policy, and a BA (1994) from Luther College where he majored in philosophy, political science, and sociology. His research and teaching interests include social inequality/stratification, social movements, religion, political sociology, and ethics. His research examines social and economic inequality, religion, and social movements and has appeared in *Social Forces, Mobilization, Sociological Spectrum, The Sociological Quarterly, American Behavioral Scientist*, and *Policy Studies Journal.* He routinely teaches study abroad courses in the United Kingdom, the Netherlands and El Salvador.

Tracey Gendron, PhD, is an associate professor and vice chair of the Department of Gerontology in the School of Allied Health Professions at Virginia Commonwealth University. She has a Master of Science in Gerontology, a Master of Science in Psychology and a PhD in Developmental Psychology. She teaches service-based courses including grant writing, research methods, and the biology of aging. Tracey takes an all-inclusive approach to teaching about aging, particularly highlighting those understudied and underrepresented groups that are at increased risk of negative health outcomes and discrimination. Her research is focused on the language, expression, and perpetuation of ageism, aging, anxiety, and gerontophobia. Her personal and professional goal is to raise awareness of how deeply embedded ageism is within all cultures and settings.

Elizabeth Gilbert is an associate professor of Community Health at the University of Northern Colorado. Her initial work incorporating community and civic engagement into pedagogy and research began more than 20 years ago. Her teaching and research have focused on social determinants that impact the health status of underrepresented and marginalized communities and how to effectively engage with them. She earned her Master's in Health Promotion and Education and her EdD in Higher Education Administration from Peabody College of Vanderbilt University.

Meghan Z. Gough, PhD, is Associate Professor and Chair of Urban and Regional Planning at Virginia Commonwealth University. She teaches community-engaged courses focused on sustainable community development, civic engagement, and plan-making processes. Her scholarly work focuses on the human dimensions of sustainability, particularly creative partnerships that build local capacity to affect positive social change. Her current book project examines partnerships between cultural institutions, municipalities, and local organizations to bring about more livable communities. In collaboration with her community partners, she has led dozens of community planning processes, convening stakeholders and public officials to identify needs and activate local resources.

Jenna Greene is a Weitz Fellow in the Service Learning Academy at the University of Nebraska Omaha. In this position, she assists with service-learning project development and implementation and co-teaches a course on professional development and leadership through the Stephenson–Harrington Internship Program. Previously, she has worked in community programming at the Urban Ecology Center in Milwaukee, Wisconsin, as a youth mentor with the Youth Empowered to Succeed initiative in Milwaukee, and as a research assistant at Marquette University, the Minnesota Center for Environmental Advocacy in St. Paul, and the Fund for Peace in Washington, DC. She is originally from Delafield, Wisconsin. She graduated from Carleton College in Northfield, Minnesota, with a Bachelor of Arts in Environmental Studies. Her senior thesis examined rural Minnesota farmers' views on riparian zone policies. She also studied abroad in Addis Ababa, Ethiopia, where her team conducted research on factors determining the adoption of sustainable energy use practices. While at Carleton, she worked in the Environmental Studies Department and the Sustainability Office. She enjoys hiking, skiing, cooking, and playing violin.

Michael Hein is the director of the Center for Organizational and Human Resource Effectiveness (COHRE) and a Professor of Psychology at Middle Tennessee State University (MTSU). He received his PhD in Industrial/Organizational (I/O) Psychology from the Georgia Institute of Technology in 1990. He has over 30 years of experience consulting with clients in a variety of industries on projects regarding job analysis, employee surveys, training, onboarding, leadership development, and organizational performance measurement. His research interests include leadership, best use of training/practice time, the determinants of skilled task performance, and the development of expertise. He has taught in several areas of I/O psychology, research design, and statistics, such as job performance and appraisal, training, research methodology, and factor analysis. He was awarded the MTSU 2016 Career Achievement Award. He is a member of the Society for Industrial and Organizational Psychology and the American Psychological Society.

Angie Hodge, PhD, is an assistant professor of mathematics education within the department of Mathematics and Statistics at Northern Arizona University. Her research interests include active learning in university classrooms, community outreach, and gender equity in the science, technology, engineering, and mathematics disciplines. She is the co-director of the Academy of Inquiry Based Learning. She may be reached at angie.hodge@nau.edu.

Barbara Holland, PhD, is one of the world's foremost community engagement scholars. Her bachelor's and master's degrees in journalism were earned at the University of Missouri – Columbia and her PhD in higher education policy was awarded by the University of Maryland – College Park. She has held academic appointments at Portland State University, Indiana University–Purdue University Indianapolis, University of North Carolina at Greensboro and the University of Sydney (Australia). In addition to her academic appointments, Holland has served in a number of national leadership roles in the United States, including the directorship of the National Service-Learning Clearinghouse from 2002 to 2009 and an appointment to the US Department of Housing and Urban Development from 2000 to 2002, where she managed large grant programs for university–community partnerships. From 2000 to 2002, she was director of the HUD Office of University Partnerships, and from 2002 to 2007, she was the director of the National Service-Learning Clearinghouse. Throughout her career, she has been an active researcher, author, and consultant on community engagement institutionalization, including community–university partnerships, strategic planning, organizational change, faculty development, and evaluation of engagement's impacts and outcomes. In 2006, she received the Research Achievement Award from the International Association of Research on Service-Learning and Community Engagement (IARSLCE). In 2008, she was one of the first two fellows selected by the Australian Universities Community Engagement Alliance. She was the Editor of *Metropolitan Universities*, the journal of the Coalition of Urban and Metropolitan Universities, and has been on editorial boards for multiple journals related to community engagement.

Valerie Holton, PhD, LCSW, advises higher education institutions in designing the program, policy, and data infrastructure needed to enhance, assess, and demonstrate their impact. Her overarching aim is to identify strategies that support faculty, staff, students, and community partners in developing sustainable and mutually beneficial partnerships. Previously, Valerie served as the inaugural director of community-engaged research at Virginia Commonwealth University. An experienced and committed educator, her focus is on innovative approaches to collaborative learning that foster an organizational climate and methodological preparation that support rigorous community-engaged research. Valerie also serves as the executive editor of the Coalition of Urban and Metropolitan Universities' *Metropolitan Universities*, a quarterly, online journal for scholarship on cutting-edge issues impacting urban and metropolitan universities and colleges. She is currently serving as a senior Fulbright Scholar teaching a course on community-engaged research and researching the role of universities in their communities.

Mathew Johnson is Executive Director of the Howard R. Swearer Center and Associate Dean of Engaged Scholarship at Brown University. He is also a Professor of Practice in Sociology at Brown and leads the College and University Engagement Initiative within the Swearer Center, in which the NASCE is housed in partnership with the Siena College Research Institute.

Rachael Johnson-Murray, MS, is the Manager of Research Translation at the Society for Human Resource Management. She contributes to the creation of research-based content that human resources (HR) professionals can use in an applied setting. She uses the power of data visualization and communication techniques to bridge the gap between HR practices and scientific research. Over the course of her seven-year corporate career, she has applied her knowledge and skills to lead organizational assessments, establish metrics and tracking tools such as HR dashboards, and manage data and systems integrity improvement initiatives.

Joseph Jones, PhD, SHRM-SCP, is the former director of research insights and applications for the Society for Human Resource Management (SHRM), where he oversaw thought leadership, product development, and research for human resources (HR) professional competencies and other HR practices. In this role, he collaborated with members of the HR community to better understand, document, and develop the competencies and other knowledge, skills, abilities, and characteristics necessary to be successful as an HR professional and to lead successful HR programs. He has more than 20 years of HR experience implementing a variety of competency modeling, talent management, HR technology, assessment, and analytics projects for both private- and public-sector organizations.

Simone Kauffeld, PhD, is a full professor of industrial/organizational and social psychology at Technische Universität Braunschweig, Germany. In 1999, she received her PhD from the University of Kassel. She was a visiting scholar at Brooklyn College, New York, and held the chair for Work and Organizational Psychology at the University of Applied Sciences, Northwestern Switzerland. In 2007, she became a full professor at Technische Universität

Braunschweig. Her main research foci are teams, competence management and development, coaching, and leadership. Her various research topics are tied together by interaction analytical research methods. She has published in international, peer-reviewed journals such as *Journal of Occupational and Organizational Psychology, Journal of Vocational Behavior, Small Group Research, Journal of Applied Social Psychology, Journal of Business and Psychology*, and *Journal of Change Management*. In 2012, she joined the board of presidents at Technische Universität Braunschweig as vice president for teaching and diversity.

ReNae S. Kehrberg is a national consultant in instructional leadership and the use of research-based strategies to raise student achievement. She retired in 2017 as the Assistant Superintendent of Curriculum and Instruction Support for the Omaha Public Schools (OPS) for 86 schools. She was an award-winning and nationally recognized Magnet Middle School principal prior to becoming an assistant superintendent. In 2010, she received the Region VII Midwest Principal of the Year Award and her school was cited by the Making Middle Grades Work program as one of the top 15 in the nation. Previously she was Director of Secondary Education, Coordinator of Student Community Services and started her career in art and social studies classrooms as a teacher for the OPS. Her undergraduate degree is from Wayne State College. She received her master's at the University of Nebraska Omaha and her doctorate from the University of Nebraska – Lincoln.

Fabian Klauke is a graduate associate and doctoral candidate at the Department of Industrial/Organizational and Social Psychology at Technische Universität Braunschweig, Germany. He holds a bachelor's degree in Business Psychology from Fresenius University of Applied Sciences in Cologne, Germany, and a master's degree in social psychology from the Vrije Universiteit Amsterdam, the Netherlands. He has been a visiting scholar at BITS Pilani, India, and Purdue University, IN. His research interests focus on social exclusion, group processes, evolutionary psychology, and language psychology. He has published in journals such as *Evolution and Human Behavior* and *PLoS One*.

Shawn D. Long is Associate Dean for Academic Affairs in the College of Liberal Arts and Sciences at the University of North Carolina at Charlotte. He served as department chair (July 2010–July 2015) of the Department of Communication Studies and director of the Communication Graduate Program (2007–2010) at the University of North Carolina at Charlotte. He is a full professor of communication. He also holds an appointment as a full professor in organizational science. He received a Master of Public Administration from Tennessee State University and his PhD from the University of Kentucky.

Christine Marston is Associate Dean of the College of Humanities and Social Sciences, Department Chair and a professor of Economics. She has 20 years of experience at the University of Northern Colorado (UNC). She has been involved with community and civic engagement with her students for the past decade. Her split position provides the opportunity to involve students in engagement while maintaining an active research agenda and an administrative leadership role. She collaborates with a sociologist on campus to research the refugee population in Greeley. The research team works closely with a nonprofit, the Global Refugee Center, to better understand the secondary migration patterns of refugees in our community. Her efforts led to her winning the 2013 UNC Engaged Faculty Scholar Award. She earned her bachelor's in Economics and Spanish from the University of Nevada, Reno, where she also received her master's degree in Economics. Dr. Marston earned her PhD from Colorado State University.

Robert Martin is a doctoral student in the University of Oklahoma's doctoral program in Industrial and Organizational Psychology. His research interests include planning, ethics, creativity, and leadership. He received his Bachelor of Science degree in Psychology from the

University of Georgia in Athens, Georgia. While at the University of Georgia, he worked as a research assistant in social and industrial/organizational psychology labs. Research for his thesis is investigating how identifying, analyzing, and fixing past errors will influence creative problem-solving. He is currently working on a grant funded by the Army. Research for this grant involves running a series of studies to validate collective leadership and collective planning models. Additionally, he is a professional ethics trainer for the Responsible Conduct of Research program at the University of Oklahoma. He plans to defend his thesis in the fall of 2018, and he will then prepare for general exams and begin work on his dissertation.

Annika L. Meinecke is a graduate associate and doctoral candidate at the Department of Industrial/Organizational and Social Psychology at Technische Universität Braunschweig, Germany. She holds bachelor's and master's degrees in psychology from Technische Universität Braunschweig, where she graduated with honors. She has been a visiting scholar at the University of Wisconsin – Milwaukee and Vrije Universiteit Amsterdam. Her research interests include social interaction processes in teams and dyads as well as intercultural differences in team interactions. Her work has been published in academic outlets such as *Group Processes and Intergroup Relations, Small Group Research*, and *Journal of Applied Psychology.*

Richard G. Moffett III is the current Associate Director of the Center for Organizational and Human Resource Effectiveness (COHRE) and Professor of Psychology at Middle Tennessee State University (MTSU). He received his PhD in Industrial/Organizational (I/O) Psychology from Auburn University, Auburn, AL, in 1996. He has over 30 years of experience as a consultant to private- and public-sector organizations and higher education organizations. His areas of consulting expertise include leadership/management training and development, organizational diagnosis and development, survey design and development, group facilitation, and training development and evaluation. During his time at MTSU, he has performed many roles. He has served as the internship coordinator for the I/O psychology graduate program for more than ten years. He helped found COHRE and served as its first director. He is a member of the Society for Industrial and Organizational Psychology and the Society for Human Resource Management.

Joseph E. Mroz is a doctoral student in the industrial/organizational (I/O) psychology program at the University of Nebraska Omaha. He graduated from Rhodes College in Memphis, TN, in 2014 with a bachelor's degree in Psychology. In 2016, he received a master's degree in I/O Psychology from the University of Nebraska. Previous consulting experience includes academic program evaluation based on student satisfaction surveys at Rhodes College and competency modeling, behavioral-based interview development, 360° feedback report development, and assessing adverse impacts of selection tools at ServiceMaster Corporation. He currently serves as the project manager for the Center for Applied Psychological Services at the University of Nebraska Omaha. His research is focused on workplace meetings, attribution theory, and social transgressions.

Lena C. Müller-Frommeyer is a graduate associate and doctoral candidate at the Department of Industrial/Organizational and Social Psychology at Technische Universität Braunschweig, Germany. She holds bachelor's and master's degrees in psychology from Technische Universität Braunschweig, where she graduated with honors. She has been a visiting scholar at Université Nice Sophia Antipolis, France, and BITS Pilani, India. Her research interests include computational linguistics and social interaction processes in dyads and teams, as well as the measurement and development of intercultural competencies.

Michael D. Mumford is the George Lynn Cross Distinguished Research Professor of Psychology at the University of Oklahoma, where he directs the Center for Applied Social

Research. He received his doctoral degree from the University of Georgia in 1983 in the fields of psychometrics and industrial and organizational psychology. Dr. Mumford has published more than 400 peer reviewed articles in the fields of leadership, creativity, planning, ethics, and life history (h-index 81). He is a fellow of the American Psychological Association (Divisions 3, 5, 10, 14), the American Psychological Society, and the Society for Industrial and Organizational Psychology. Dr. Mumford has served as a senior editor of *The Leadership Quarterly*. He sits on the editorial boards of *Group and Organization Management, The Creativity Research Journal, The Journal of Creative Behavior, The Psychology of Aesthetics, Creativity and the Arts, Ethics and Behavior, Accountability in Research*, and *Idea Transactions in Engineering Management*, among other journals. Dr. Mumford has received more than $30 million in grant and contract funding from the National Science Foundation, the National Institutes of Health, the National Aeronautics and Space Administration, the Department of Labor, the Department of Defense, the Department of State, and the Council of Graduate Schools. Dr. Mumford is a recipient of the Society for Industrial and Organizational Psychology's M. Scott Myers Award for Applied Research in the Workplace and the Academy of Management's Eminent Leadership Scholar Award.

Diann Olszowy Jones is a clinical assistant professor at the University of Georgia in the Department of Learning, Leadership, and Organizational Development. She teaches within and manages programs that develop advanced professionals who lead the education and learning of adults and/or developing organizations. She draws on previous professional experience as an insurance executive as well as a managing editor of an academic journal. Her current research interests include the role of leadership in institutionalizing community engagement, managing change and transitions, and strategies for contributing to an organization's long-term sustainable growth. She earned her PhD in Adult Education from the University of Georgia.

April Post is a senior lecturer in Spanish at Elon University, a former mentor of the class of 2016 Periclean Scholars with a focus on Honduras, and current Associate Director of the Periclean Scholars program. Her research interests include effective partnerships, how to avoid toxic charity, and service learning as a pedagogy. She enjoys incorporating the ideals of the Periclean Scholars program into all aspects of her life and learning how to be a more compassionate individual from others.

Kelly A. Prange is a PhD student in Industrial/Organizational Psychology at the University of Nebraska Omaha, where she has completed research on the topics of nonprofit management, collective impact, workplace meetings, and emotional labor. She is also a human resources consultant at Talent Plus, Inc., where she develops, evaluates, and researches employee selection and development practices and tools. She developed a passion for community engagement efforts while working in the Community Engagement Center on the University of Nebraska Omaha's campus.

Janice Rech, PhD, is an associate professor of mathematics education within the Department of Mathematics at the University of Nebraska Omaha. Her research interests include active learning in the university classroom, the study of calculus teaching, and mentoring of pre-service secondary mathematics teachers. She leads AP Calculus workshops across the country. She may be reached at jrech@unomaha.edu.

Doug Reynolds, PhD, is Executive Vice President of Innovations and Technology at Development Dimensions International (DDI), where his departments develop and implement software-based assessment centers, testing, and learning products in Fortune 500 companies. His consulting work has recently focused on the deployment of Internet-based behavioral simulations used for executive and leadership evaluation. He also has served as an expert witness regarding personnel selection practices, and he has published and presented frequently on topics related to the intersection of industrial/organizational psychology and technology. He recently coedited the forthcoming book *Next Generation Technology-Enhanced Assessment* and the *Handbook of Workplace Assessment*, and coauthored *Online Recruiting and Selection*. He is a past president of the Society for Industrial and Organizational Psychology (2012–2013).

Steven G. Rogelberg holds the title of Chancellor's Professor at the University of North Carolina at Charlotte for distinguished national, international, and interdisciplinary contributions. He has over 100 publications addressing issues such as meetings at work, team effectiveness, leadership, employee engagement, and organizational research methods. Other awards and honors include being the inaugural winner of the Society of Industrial and Organizational Psychology (SIOP) Humanitarian Award, receiving the SIOP Distinguished Service Award, the Psi Chi Professor of the Year Award, and the Master Teacher Award. He is the editor of the *Journal of Business and Psychology*.

Deborah Romero is the inaugural faculty director of community and civic engagement at the University of Northern Colorado (UNC) and a professor of Culturally and Linguistically Diverse Education. She has over 25 years of experience across K–12 and higher education in the USA and abroad. Her engaged scholarship agenda focuses on collaborations with local teachers and culturally and linguistically diverse immigrant communities, supporting and understanding multilingualism, literacies and identity development, and the scholarship of engagement. She has published peer-reviewed, scholarly articles and book chapters in both English and Spanish. She earned her bachelor's degree in Applied Language Studies from the University of West London, her master's degree in Educational Psychology from the Autonomous University in Queretaro, Mexico, and a PhD in Education with an emphasis on culturally diverse education and language, interaction, and social organization from the University of California, Santa Barbara. Correspondence concerning her chapter should be addressed to Deborah Romero, Office of Engagement, Campus Box 21, University of Northern Colorado, Greeley, CO, 80639, contact: deborah.romero@unco.edu.

Richard Ronay is an assistant professor of Leadership and Management at the University of Amsterdam Business School, where he teaches courses in leadership and negotiations. His research explores issues related to status and power dynamics in the context of leadership, decision-making, and negotiations.

Enrica N. Ruggs, PhD, is an assistant professor of Psychology and Organizational Science at the University of North Carolina at Charlotte. She received her PhD from Rice University in 2013. Her research examines workplace diversity as well as the manifestation of workplace discrimination, its effects on employees with stigmatized identities, and strategies to reduce discrimination. Her research has appeared in premier academic journals such as *Journal of Applied Psychology* and *Journal of Management*, and her work has been presented in popular media outlets such as *U.S. News & World Report, Business Insider*, and *Fortune*.

Eduardo Salas, PhD, is the Allyn R. & Gladys M. Cline Chair Professor and Chair of the Department of Psychology at Rice University. Previously, he was a trustee chair and Pegasus Professor of Psychology at the University of Central Florida, where he also held an appointment as program director for the Human Systems Integration Research Department at the Institute for Simulation and Training (IST). Before joining IST, he was a senior research psychologist and head of the Training Technology Development Branch of NAWC-TSD for 15 years. During this period, he served as a principal investigator for numerous research and development programs, including TADMUS, which focused on teamwork, team training, decision-making under stress and performance assessment. He has coauthored over 450 journal articles and book chapters and has coedited 27 books. His expertise includes assisting organizations in how to foster teamwork, design and implement team training strategies, facilitate training effectiveness, manage decision-making under stress, and develop performance measurement tools. He is a past president of the Society for Industrial/Organizational Psychology and the Human Factors and Ergonomics Society (HFES), fellow of the American Psychological Association (APA) and HFES, and a recipient of the Meritorious Civil Service Award from the Department of the Navy. He is also the recipient of the 2012 Society for Human Resource Management Losey Lifetime Achievement Award, the 2012 Joseph E. McGrath Award for Lifetime Achievement for his work on teams and team training, and the 2016 APA Award for Outstanding Lifetime Contributions to Psychology.

John Saltmarsh is Professor of Higher Education in the Department of Leadership in Education at the College of Education and Human Development at the University of Massachusetts, Boston. He is also Distinguished Engaged Scholar at the Howard R. Swearer Center for Public Service at Brown University, where he leads the project in which the Swearer Center serves as the administrative partner with the Carnegie Foundation for the Elective Community Engagement Classification.

Lorilee R. Sandmann is a professor emeritus in the Department of Lifelong Education, Administration, and Policy at the College of Education of the University of Georgia. For over 45 years, she held administrative, faculty, extension, and outreach positions at the University of Minnesota, Michigan State University, Cleveland State University, as well as UGA. She is also an editor emeritus of the *Journal of Higher Education Outreach and Engagement*. Her research, teaching, and consulting focuses on leadership and organizational change in higher education with a special emphasis on the institutionalization of community engagement, as well as faculty roles and rewards related to community-engaged scholarship. She received her PhD from the University of Wisconsin – Madison.

Lisa Slattery Walker (formerly Rashotte) is Associate Dean for Advising and Graduation and Professor of Sociology and Organizational Science at the University of North Carolina at Charlotte. She received her PhD in Sociology from the University of Arizona in 1998. Her research focuses on small group interaction, nonverbal behaviors, identity, emotions, gender, and expectations. Her work has appeared in *Social Psychology Quarterly, Social Science Research, Social Forces, Sex Roles*, and numerous other journals. She has been PI or co-PI on six NSF-funded projects. Recently, with Dr. Murray Webster, she has been conducting projects on the effects of behaviors on inequality structures in small groups and how characteristics come to have status value. Current work with Dr. Anita Blanchard examines how groups develop in online environments.

Deborah Smith-Howell, PhD, is Associate Vice Chancellor of Academic Affairs, the Dean of Graduate Studies, and a professor of Communication at the University of Nebraska Omaha (UNO). She is a key member of the UNO community engagement cabinet and has administrative oversight over the Service Learning Academy, the Civic Participation Grants, and community engagement reporting. She has been involved in UNO's strategic planning since it started in the 1990s and she co-led the 2017 strategic plan revision. In addition, she is an executive committee member of the Engaged Scholarship Consortium. She was also the Program Committee Chair of the Coalition of Urban and Metropolitan Universities and the Conference Director of the Engaged Scholarship Consortium conferences held in Omaha, Nebraska, in 2015 and 2016, respectively. Formerly, she was the Department Chair and Founding Director of the UNO School of Communication. Her research interests are in communication education, presidential rhetoric, political communication, and civic participation. She holds a Bachelor of Science from

Northern Michigan University, a Master of Arts from Louisiana State University, and a PhD from the University of Texas.

Sabrina Speights is an Assistant Professor of Business and Management at Wheaton College. She earned her BA at George Mason University in Psychology with a minor in Spanish and her MA and PhD at the University of North Carolina at Charlotte. Her research interests center around the work–nonwork interface, nonstandard work schedules, emotions, and ethics. Sabrina attended the Organizational Science Summer Institute (OSSI) as an undergraduate student and later became a mentor and then the graduate student coordinator. She is committed to diversity in higher education and undergraduate research.

Anthony Starke is a doctoral candidate at the University of Nebraska Omaha (UNO) School of Public Administration. As a doctoral student, he completed coursework in public administration theory, public policy, and black studies. While at UNO, he has worked as the project manager for a research enterprise examining Hispanic/Latino immigrants and access to health care in the Greater Omaha Area and currently serves as the project specialist for UNO's Monitoring, Assessment, Evaluation, and Research for Community Engagement initiative. Prior to beginning his studies at UNO, he was an active leader in the governance and management of service-oriented nonprofits based in Virginia's Greater Fredericksburg and Hampton Roads communities. He holds credentials as a qualified mental health professional and has experience in the field of human development. He is a former Virginia Commonwealth University Wilder Fellow, 2014 ASPA National Founder's Fellow, 2016 ASPA International Young Scholar, 2016 Engagement Scholarship Consortium Emerging Engagement Scholar, 2017 Public Administration Theory Network Fellow, AmeriCorp VISTA Alum, and life member of Kappa Alpha Psi Fraternity, Inc. He holds a Master of Public Administration degree and graduate certificate in Nonprofit Management from VCU and Bachelor of Science degrees from Old Dominion University.

Oscar Jerome Stewart is an assistant professor of management and member of the Sustainable Business Group at San Francisco State University. His main research streams focus on corporate irresponsibility and misconduct, as well as discrimination in higher education and in business organizations. He is also interested in human rights and environmental sustainability. Oscar earned his PhD from the University of North Carolina at Charlotte in Interdisciplinary Studies.

Valerie N. Streets, PhD, is a postdoctoral research fellow at the Society for Human Resource Management (SHRM). She contributes to a number of research initiatives that result in delivering human resources (HR) insights to SHRM members and other HR professionals. She is currently leading research on diversity and talent acquisition. She has ten years of research experience in industrial/organizational psychology and has authored several journal articles, book chapters, and conference presentations on issues such as underrepresented populations at work, workforce readiness, and recruitment.

E. Michelle Todd is a doctoral student in the University of Oklahoma's doctoral program in Industrial and Organizational Psychology. Her research interests include creativity, ethical decision-making, planning, and leadership. She received her Bachelor of Science in Psychology from the University of Georgia and her Master of Science in Psychology from the University of Oklahoma. She has worked on grants and published articles funded by the National Institutes of Health examining the impacts of ethics training and the responsible conduct of research courses. Her current research focuses on collective planning and leadership in military contexts, which is funded by a grant from the Army. She has served as a professional ethics trainer for the Responsible Conduct of Research training program at the University of Oklahoma, and she has taught Elements of Psychology and Intro to I/O

Psychology courses. She has also been a member of the Graduate College Student Senate and continues to serve as a Graduate College Student Ambassador.

Sheridan Trent is a doctoral student in the Industrial/Organizational Psychology program at the University of Nebraska Omaha (UNO). She holds a bachelor's degree in Psychology and a master's degree in Industrial/Organizational Psychology from UNO. Over the past four years, she has worked with dozens of clients through UNO's Volunteer Program Assessment group, where she served as the Assistant Director of Operations for three years and the Assistant Director of Research for one year. She currently serves on the Advisory Council of the Eastern Nebraska Office on Aging's Senior Companion Program. Her research interests include nonprofit organizational effectiveness, incivility in the workplace, volunteerism, and work-life issues.

Dian van Huijstee is a master's student at Vrije Universiteit Amsterdam. After obtaining both her bachelor's (General Psychology) and master's (Applied Social Psychology) diplomas, she is now a research master's student in Social Psychology with the goal of commencing a PhD afterwards. Her research interests include romantic relationships, deception detection, and the psychological processes that motivate revenge.

Shonna D. Waters, PhD, is a senior behavioral scientist at BetterUp, where she partners with organizations to design evidence-based solutions to organizational challenges. She also conducts research to further our understanding of behavior change and embed that knowledge into BetterUp's coaching. Prior to joining BetterUp, she was the Vice President of Research at the Society for Human Resource Management and Technical Director of Human Resource Strategy and Program Design at the National Security Agency. She has spent more than 15 years helping organizations make evidence-based decisions. Waters holds a PhD in industrial/organizational psychology and statistics and a certificate in leadership coaching from Georgetown University's Leadership Coaching Program, and she is an International Coach Federation credential holder. Her work has been published in a variety of peer-reviewed journals, in *HR Magazine*, and in books.

Rasheda L. Weaver, PhD, is an assistant professor of Community Entrepreneurship at the University of Vermont, where she runs the Social Enterprise and Community Development Lab. Her research interests include social enterprise, civic engagement, community development, and applied psychology. She conducted the first large-scale study of US-based social enterprises, which are businesses that strive to combat social problems. In April 2018, she will launch Weaver's Social Enterprise Directory, an online directory that will connect the public to over 1,000 social enterprises in the nation. She has taught and aided in the implementation of various engaged civic learning courses at Rutgers University – Camden, New Jersey and is working to bring such courses to the Iona College, where she currently teaches courses in entrepreneurship and innovation.

Chelsea Willness is a passionate champion of community-engaged scholarship and teaching. She has held two national research grants (SSHRC) for her research on how stakeholders – like job seekers, employees, or consumers – respond to organizations' environmental practices and community involvement (e.g., corporate social responsibility). She has published this work in top journals and book chapters and has presented to academic and professional audiences locally, nationally, and internationally. Chelsea has received university, college, and international teaching awards, including the USSU Teaching Excellence Award (2016), the University of Saskatchewan's Award for Distinction in Community-Engaged Teaching & Scholarship (2014), and the Provost's College Award for Outstanding Teaching (2014). In 2012, she was awarded an Innovation in Teaching Award from the Academy of Management for her design and implementation of human resources courses that integrate community-based experiential learning. Most recently, she was the recipient of her university's highest honor for teaching, the Master Teacher Award (2017), recognizing her educational leadership in creating authentic learning communities. She has a keen interest in governance, sustainability, and social responsibility, and is actively involved in governance initiatives in the not-for-profit sector.

Sara Woods is the Executive Associate to the Senior Vice Chancellor for Community Engagement at the University of Nebraska Omaha (UNO), where she oversees the operation of the university's Barbara Weitz Community Engagement Center. She was heavily involved in the conceptualization, design, and launch of the engagement center. She is also a key member of the UNO community engagement cabinet. In addition, she has been involved in the Strategic Planning Steering Committee since 2000 and has more recently co-led the strategic plan revision. Formerly, she was the Associate Dean of the College of Public Affairs and Community Service (CPACS) at UNO. CPACS was the first college at UNO to incorporate community engagement in its reappointment, promotion, and tenure guidelines. She has both Master of Public Administration and Bachelor of Arts degrees from UNO. She serves on a number of local boards and foundations, including the Nebraska Children and Families Foundation, Phoenix Academy, the Omaha Community Partnership, and the Community Services Fund, and she is the former board chair of the Women's Fund of Omaha and the Nonprofit Association of the Midlands. In 2017, she was recognized as a dedicated public servant in honor of Women's History Month by Congress.

Michael Yoerger is a doctoral student at the University of Nebraska Omaha (UNO). In 2011, he graduated summa cum laude from the University of Northern Iowa with bachelor's degrees in Psychology, Political Science, and Public Administration, as well as certificates in industrial/organizational (I/O) psychology and state/local government. In 2016, he received a master's degree in I/O Psychology. His research interests include teamwork and leadership in the health care context, as well as meeting effectiveness. His previous consulting experience includes serving as a co-director for UNO's Center for Applied Psychological Services (UNO-CAPS), as well as an analyst for UNO's Volunteer Program Assessment (UNO-VPA). He has worked as a UNO teaching assistant, an assistant to the Engagement Scholarship Consortium conference program chair, and as a project associate at the University of Nebraska Medical Center. Ultimately, he plans to work either in health care research or for the government.

Cindy S. York, PhD, is an associate professor of Instructional Technology within the Department of Educational Technology, Research, and Assessment at Northern Illinois University. Her research interests include the examination of practitioners in order to better prepare students in the areas of instructional design and the integration of technology into teacher education. She was the past president of the Division of Distance Learning for AECT. She may be reached at cindy.york@niu.edu.

Stephen J. Zaccaro is a professor of psychology at George Mason University, Fairfax, Virginia. He is also an experienced leadership development consultant. He has written over 125 journal articles, book chapters, and technical reports on leadership, group dynamics, team performance, and work attitudes. He has authored a book titled *The nature of executive leadership: A conceptual and empirical analysis of success*, and has coedited five other books on the topics of organizational leadership, leader development, multi-team systems, cybersecurity, and occupational stress. He has worked with executives and managers from private industry as well as from the public and military sectors. He has served as a principal investigator, co-principal investigator, or consultant on multiple projects in the areas of leadership and executive assessment, leadership and team training, leader adaptability, executive coaching, multi-team systems, and cybersecurity team performance. He serves on the editorial board of *The Leadership Quarterly*, and he is an associate editor for *Journal of Business and Psychology* and for *Military Psychology*. He is a fellow of the Association for Psychological Science and of the American Psychological Association, Divisions 14 (Society for Industrial and Organizational Psychology) and 19 (Military Psychology).

Index